ENCYCLOPEDIA
OF
MARINE
ANIMALS

ENCYCLOPEDIA
OF
MARINE
ANIMALS

NEVILLE COLEMAN

EDITORIAL CONSULTANTS
ISOBEL BENNETT A.O., M.SC (SYDNEY)
DOCTOR ANDREW CAMPBELL, UNIVERSITY OF LONDON
PROFESSOR MICHAEL G. HADFIELD, UNIVERSITY OF HAWAII

Angus&Robertson
An imprint of HarperCollinsPublishers

For the love of my life . . .

Previous pages: Coral reef scene off Barron Island.

AN ANGUS & ROBERTSON BOOK
An imprint of HarperCollinsPublishers

First published in Australia in 1991 by
CollinsAngus&Robertson Publishers Pty Limited (ACN 009 913 517)
A division of HarperCollinsPublishers (Australia) Pty Limited
25-31 Ryde Road, Pymble NSW 2073, Australia

HarperCollinsPublishers (New Zealand) Limited
31 View Road, Glenfield, Auckland 10, New Zealand

HarperCollinsPublishers Limited
77-85 Fulham Palace Road, London W6 8JB, United Kingdom

Distributed in the United States of America by
HarperCollinsPublishers
10 East 53rd Street, New York NY 10022, USA

Copyright © Neville Coleman 1991

National Library of Australia
Cataloguing-in-Publication Data:

Coleman, Neville, 1938-

   Encyclopedia of marine animals.

   Includes index.
   ISBN 0 207 16429 0.

   1. Marine fauna - Encyclopedias. I. Title.

591.92

Cover photography by Neville Coleman
Typeset in Australia by Adtype Graphics Pty Ltd
Separated in Australia by Hartland & Hyde
Printed in Autralia by Griffin Press

5 4 3 2 1
95 94 93 92 91

ACKNOWLEDGMENTS

The photographs in this book are taken from the files of the Australasian Marine Photographic Index (AMPI). The following institutions have helped the AMPI to continue its programme of advancing the knowledge of living marine organisms: Australian Museum, Museum of Victoria, Queensland Museum, Western Australian Museum, CollinsAngus & Robertson, and Sea Australia Resource Centre.

To the trustees of the following institutions and the curators and assistants who have given their time in the identification of specimens and the housing of AMPI collections, I acknowledge my unreserved gratitude: Australian Museum, British Museum (Natural History), National Museum of New Zealand, Museum of Victoria, Smithsonian Institute (USA), Queensland Museum, Western Australian Museum, Northern Territory Museum of Arts and Sciences, Phil Alderslade, Dr Alan Baker, Isobel Bennett, Dr Sandy Bruce, Ailsa M. Clark, Karen Handley, Dr Doug Hoese, Dr John Hooper, Ian Lock, Loisette Marsh, Dr Patricia Mather, Rolly McKay, Dr Gary Morgan, Dr Winston Ponder, Elizabeth Pope, Dr S Prudhoe, Dr Bill Rudman, Dr Frank Rowe, Scoresby Shepherd, Dr Brian Smith, Roger Springthorpe, Helen Tranter, Dr Robin Wass, Dr Barry Wilson, Dr J. Versveldt. My thanks to the consultants on this book: Isobel Bennett, Andrew Campbell and Mike Hadfield.

A special thank you to the editor for this title, Sally Harper, the designer, Linda Maxwell, and to my typists Elaine Leggatt, Mary West and Anne Thomson, and to my collators Karen Handley and Janine Horrocks. Thanks to Marcus Schneck for providing additional species entries.

To my friends Linda and Paul Schutt, Idaz and Jerry Greenberg, Sandi and Don Smith, Jim Tobin, Bob and Dinah Halstead, Walt and Jean Deas, Reg and Kay Lipson, Bill Rossiter and Kathy and Tony Tubberhauer: I thank you one and all.

Neville Coleman

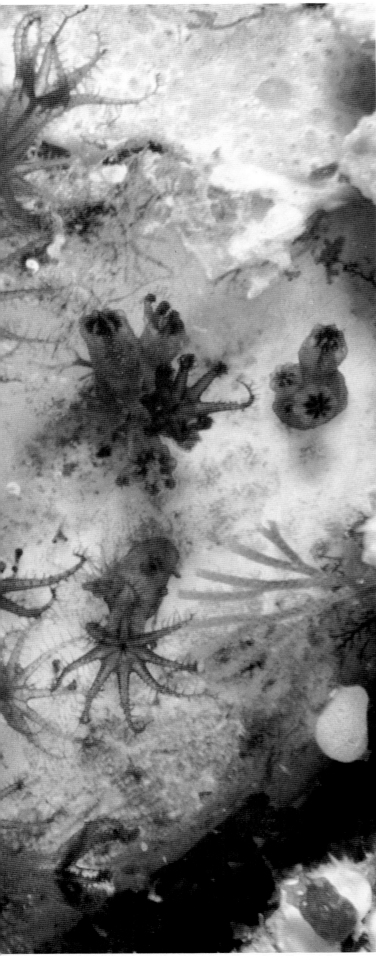

Parerythropodium membranaceum

CONTENTS

An underwater scene near Lord Howe Island.

INTRODUCTION

This book is one of the largest single marine photographic identification guides ever compiled by one person; even so it is but one drop of knowledge into the vast oceans of the unknown. Most people's understanding of the oceans, that immense aquaspheric womb of life which surrounds them, is practically nil. Even those who live within a stone's throw of the sea shore, or visit it on weekends and holidays, only touch it for a moment, and are gone.

Whereas areas of the Northern Hemisphere have been the central focal point of oceanic studies (due to the location of the beginnings of civilization as we know it) the Southern Hemisphere, although explored and mapped, has only been 'discovered' within the last two centuries. It was only in the 1970s that naturalists began photographically recording marine animals underwater in a serious scientific manner. By the mid 1980s scientific institutions were following up that research, and today there are at least 10,000 species of animals and plants which have been photographically recorded from the Australasian area alone (according to the author's personal index).

Any thinking person with a scrap of knowledge and concern about the oceans must surely realise that we cannot continue to exploit the resources of our seas at our present levels. Through over fishing we have already lost scores of fisheries, many before we even knew the biology of the target species. The oceans of the world are as one; all are connected. The billions of tonnes of toxic wastes already dumped have only just begun to affect us, and who knows what catastrophic disasters our misuse may eventually cause?

We see the larger predators at the highest level of marine food chains ailing all over the world. Thousands of seals and dolphins are dying, while massive numbers of fish are killed by unnatural influxes of 'red tide' organisms. We will never know the effects on the smaller and more fragile species because we never understood them to start with. Humans multiplied faster than their understanding of nature. It seems only as yesterday that there was wilderness all around, yet with a minimum of knowledge and maximum technology we slaughtered the oceans' wildlife. There are so few cetaceans and pinnipeds left that even a minor disease could threaten or destroy entire stocks of some species. Interestingly enough, we seem to be more horrified by our unintended destruction than we were by our own merciless deliberate plundering of marine life, for sport, profit, pleasure, or just because it was there.

With the new awareness in the 1990s towards environmental issues (brought about by the greenhouse effect and the decline of many species in the 1980s), this book is most timely. Almost 230,000 ocean species have so far been described, from microscopic plankton to 33-metre (108-foot) Blue Whales. This publication does therefore not pretend completeness. It would take 230 volumes such as this to display that marine fauna, even if the photographs were available.

With a little over 1000 photographs and 100,000 words, this volume is barely an introduction to the extraordinary wealth of life that exists within our world of waters. Yet what an introduction! It is designed to captivate its readers by displaying in intimate visual detail, 1000 life forms shown together in this way for the first time ever.

Simple in construction and terms of reference, this book is an invitation to discovery for all. Its clear format and up-to-date knowledge will help to encourage a greater awareness of marine life, which is ultimately essential for the survival of the human race.

Pixie Pinnacle, Coral Sea.

USING THE BOOK

This book was developed as a general visual identification guide but it displays only a representative selection of known species or genera. Tens of thousands of species still remain undescribed.

The aim is to provide the average person (who is unlikely to ever try to decipher a scientific key or dissect sea creatures) a means by which a basic level of information can be referred to and systematically absorbed.

In most examples, wherever possible, terms of reference are of living organisms, taken in the field. Of course some deep sea organisms living beyond the continental shelf are included and have been photographed from specimens brought up by trawlers and research vessels. These have been photographed to show those features relevant to the specimen's identity, in many cases on the decks of heaving vessels under less than ideal conditions.

Those phyla which do not lend themselves to straight-forward visual identification (for instance, those which are too small) are not included here as the concept is illustrative, rather than textbook biology. This book covers life from sea shores down to deep ocean sea floor, and there are illustrations showing representative external features of each phylum included.

Although visual identification is possible for the majority of the larger groups of marine animals, our knowledge is far from complete. Scientific assistance and preserved specimens must still be studied before accurate identification can be made; for some species this research is likely to extend well into the 21st century. Any system of identification must depend on a reference and the preserved specimen, the first of its kind to be described, is essential. This is the *type specimen*.

Chapters are based on phyla and each has an intro-duction giving a general overview of each phylum, and a basic explanation of its natural history and biology. Next to, above or below the photograph of each species is a list of information with a range of details. The information has been arranged under the following categories:

COMMON NAME

Common names are those which are in general use, have already been published, or are directly based on the original scientific name meanings. Where no such common name is available (for example, for undescribed species), terminology has sometimes been constructed from outstanding features of the species' external anatomy, or failing this, the locality where it was discovered.

SCIENTIFIC NAME

It is important for scientists and others to know what a name refers to. A common name such as the edible sea urchin refers to one animal in the United Kingdom and another in the Caribbean. So a system of scientific names is necessary. In the middle of the 18th century the Swedish botanist, Carolus Linnaeus, published *Systema Natura* and provided the basis of scientific nomenclature which is accepted throughout the world today.

The concept was exceptionally well thought out. The names given to organisms when they are described and published scientifically are written in Latin. In this way it does not matter which language a book is written in, the organism's scientific name will be the same and recognisable throughout the world.

Each scientific name consists of two Latin words and is known as 'binomial nomenclature'. The first name always begins with a capital letter (for example, *Cassis)* and is known as the genus (which might be considered the organism's surname). The second name, which always begins with a lower case letter, (and which might be thought of as the organism's Christian name) is the species name (for example, *pelagicus).*

Generic names are unique within the animal kingdom but species names can be re-used to describe the animal in question. Thus the edible sea-urchin in the United Kingdom is *Echinus esculentus* and in the Caribbean is *Tripneustes esculentus*. It is customary to write the name of the author after the scientific name, for example, *Echinus esculentus* Linnaeus, and to add the date that this name was first published. If the species is transferred to another genus, the author's name is placed in brackets to show it has been re-assigned.

Linnaeus' system was good because it indicated natural relationships. For example, the cats *Pantheria leo* (lion) and *Pantheria pardus* (leopard) are obviously closely related yet they are not the same in appearance and distribution. The cheetah is not very closely related to either and is quite different in appearance and behaviour. It is placed in another genus *Acinonyx* with species name *jubatus*.

Linnaeus also grouped similar genera together into families and similar families into orders. There are several families of two-winged flies: the familiar house flies, the gnats and mosquitos, and the non-biting midges. Each of these three families is distinct and recognisable, but they all fall into the order Diptera— flies with two wings. Likewise orders are grouped into classes and classes into phyla. Thus we end up with an hierarchical system which tells us about the supposed relationships and links between the animals we are dealing with. At the top is the phylum, containing all the animals supposed to have a common evolutionary origin. At the bottom is the species, a unique example of that phylum.

If an animal new to science has not had its name published, or if we are examining an animal for which we know the genus but not the species, we can refer to it by the accepted generic name followed by sp. which is short for species; for example, *Cassis* sp.

If we want to refer to a group of species within a genus we can use spp; for example, *Cassis* spp. *(Cassis* is a genus of large marine predatory snail known as a helmet shell.)

All the names in the hierarchy above the species name are there for the convenience of seeing how the species relate to each other.

We have used family names in this book as well as genera and species because they help us to understand the relationships of closely allied genera. Very often families are recognisable by their special characteristics; for example, the Butterfly Fish family Chaetodentidae.

ACCEPTED CLASSIFICATION SAMPLE

LEVEL	SCIENTIFIC TERM	COMMON TERM
Kingdom	Animalia	Animals
Phylum	Echinodermata	Echinoderms
Class	Asteroidea	Sea Stars (or starfish)
Order	Spinulosida	Spinulosids*
Family	Asterinidae	Asterinids*
Genus	Pateriella	Pateriellids*
Species	nuda	Naked Sea Star*

* Note: Anglicised Latin terms may be used as common terms where no other word is in usage.

MODIFIED MARINE BIOGEOGRAPHIC REGIONS
(from Briggs, 1974, *Marine Zoogeography*)

TROPICAL	WARM TEMPERATE (SOUTHERN)	WARM TEMPERATE (NORTHERN)	COLD TEMPERATE (SOUTHERN)	COLD TEMPERATE (NORTHERN)
Indo-West Pacific	Southern Australia	Mediterranean-Atlantic	Southern South America	Western Atlantic Boreal
Indian Ocean	Northern New Zealand	Carolina	Tasmanian	Eastern Atlantic Boreal
Eastern Pacific	Western South America	California	Southern New Zealand	Western Pacific Boreal
Western Pacific	Eastern South America	Japan	Sub Antarctic	Eastern Atlantic Boreal
Western Atlantic	Southern Africa		Antarctic	Arctic
Eastern Atlantic				

DISTRIBUTION

Distribution has been expressed in marine biogeographic regions as per Briggs, 1974, *Marine Zoogeography*. The map reference on pages 6 and 7 shows a basic understanding of these regions and can be used as a quick reference guide. Abbreviations used throughout the book relate to this reference.

Of course future discoveries may well alter present distribution guidelines.

HABITAT

Where an animal has a specific micro-habitat or obligate association this is given in the remarks.

There are instances of course where a highly mobile animal such as a fish or mammal may range through several major habitats in the space of a day.

Rather than confuse the reader, only one or two of the major habitat types have been provided.

GENERAL WATER DEPTH

Lines on maps and depth indicators mean very little to marine animals. These things can only serve as a point of reference, not as a fixture. Animals go where they please and can survive. Depths have been given in metres and feet; fractions have been taken to the nearest whole figure.

FOOD HABIT

Little is known about the specific food habits of marine animals in general, especially in the Southern Hemisphere. Much of the material in this book is from my own observations and discoveries. Other information has been referenced from the few publications available. With regard to the planktonic food references, the information has been separated into two categories. *Carnivorous: plankton* = animals that have selective devices (such as Nematocysts) which enable them to capture specific prey. *Omnivorous: plankton* = animals which are less selective feeders; for example, suspension feeders, filter feeders, detrital feeders.

Many marine animals are opportunistic carnivorous scavengers; others can actively hunt and catch prey, yet have the ability to survive on plankton if their hunting ability is no longer functional. Some marine animals change their food habits with the seasons, depending on whatever is in good supply.

SIZE

Within the framework of this book, sizes of animals most often refer to the adult size, or individual size which has been recorded in the past. Sizes which refer to colonies are general indications only, as colonial animals such as corals, sponges or investing ascidians may cover quite large areas. Sizes in these cases are those which have generally been observed in regard to the average width or height.

Where metric or imperial figures have been converted, these are only estimates to the nearest millimetre or inch.

DESCRIPTION

Only visual features have been listed, with as few scientific terms as possible being used where the author considered it necessary. In most cases references are made to living colours and forms. In this way people can become familiar with, and more aware of, the ocean as a place of wonderment and consideration.

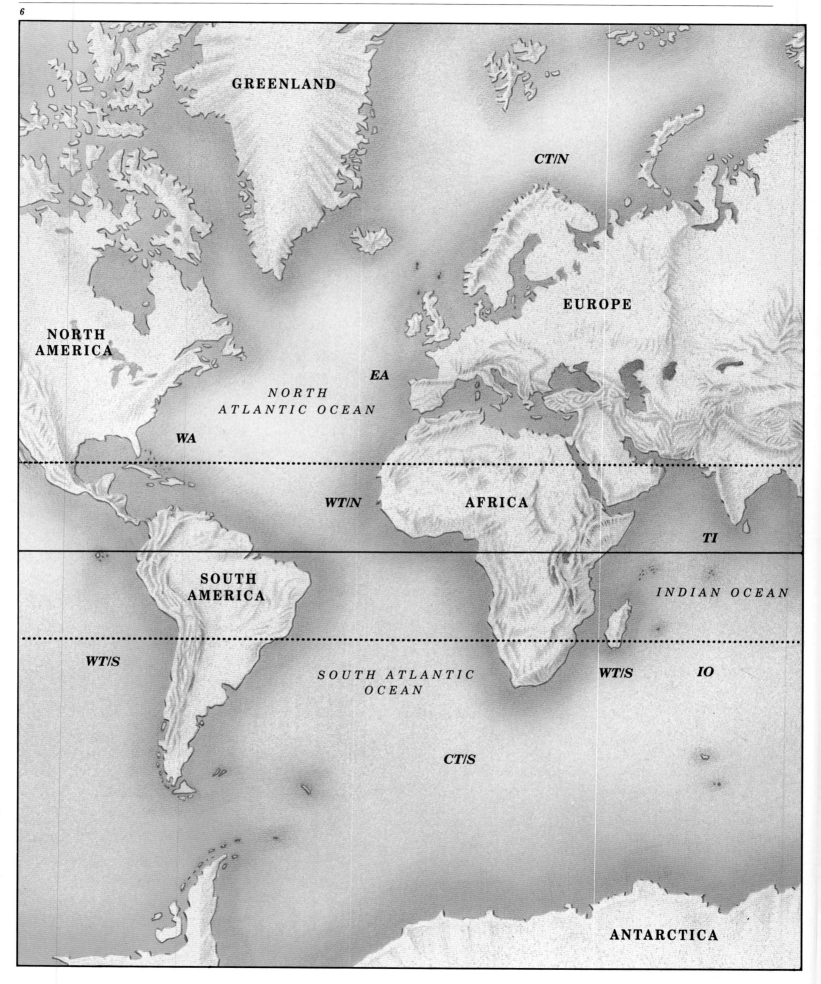

GREENLAND

CT/N

EUROPE

NORTH
AMERICA

EA

*NORTH
ATLANTIC OCEAN*

WA

WT/N

AFRICA

TI

SOUTH
AMERICA

INDIAN OCEAN

WT/S

*SOUTH ATLANTIC
OCEAN*

WT/S

IO

CT/S

ANTARCTICA

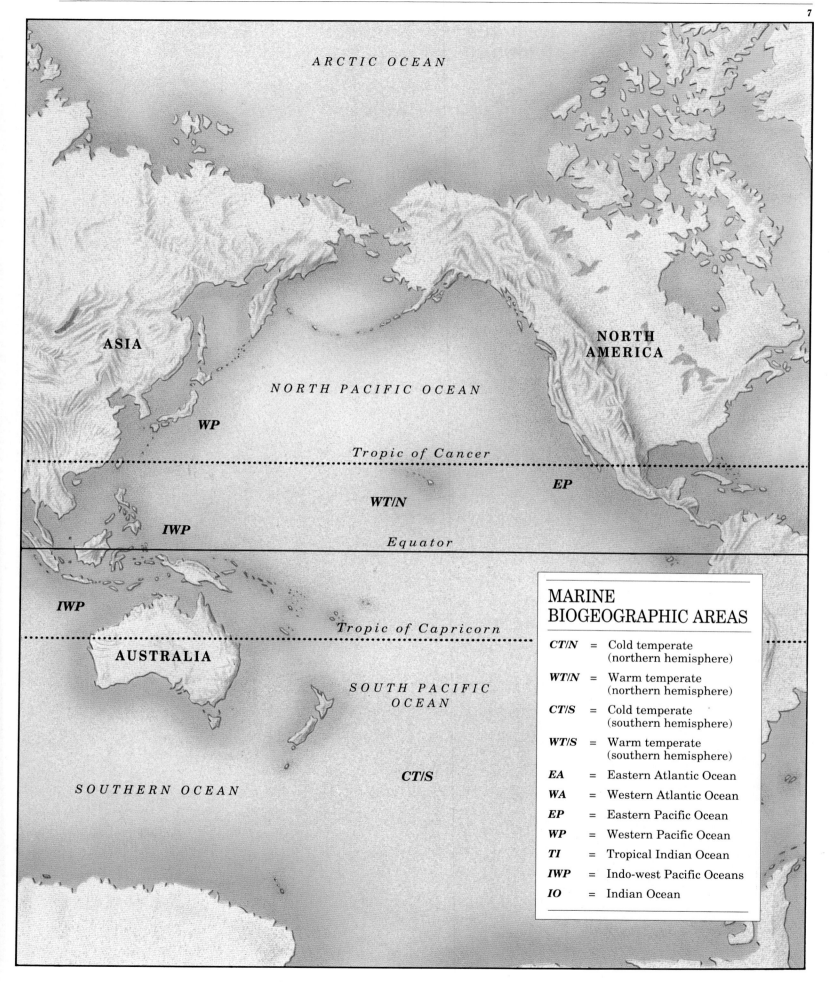

ARCTIC OCEAN

ASIA

NORTH
AMERICA

NORTH PACIFIC OCEAN

WP

Tropic of Cancer

EP

WT/N

IWP

Equator

IWP

Tropic of Capricorn

AUSTRALIA

SOUTH PACIFIC
OCEAN

CT/S

SOUTHERN OCEAN

MARINE
BIOGEOGRAPHIC AREAS

CT/N	=	Cold temperate (northern hemisphere)
WT/N	=	Warm temperate (northern hemisphere)
CT/S	=	Cold temperate (southern hemisphere)
WT/S	=	Warm temperate (southern hemisphere)
EA	=	Eastern Atlantic Ocean
WA	=	Western Atlantic Ocean
EP	=	Eastern Pacific Ocean
WP	=	Western Pacific Ocean
TI	=	Tropical Indian Ocean
IWP	=	Indo-west Pacific Oceans
IO	=	Indian Ocean

Stina's Reef, Providenciales.

Rock garden, South Pacific.

GLOSSARY

Asexual: reproduction by means other than sexual action, for example, by budding or splitting from the parent body.

Autotomy: the spontaneous casting off of part of an animal's body, often to facilitate escape; for example, breaking off a captured limb.

Branchial: respiratory function of an organ (gill) or region of body.

Buccal: relating to the oral cavity.

Byssus: a tuft of strong filaments or thread-like strands with which some bivalves attach themselves to objects, such as rocks.

Calcareous: composed of or containing calcium carbonate, or chalk.

Carapace: chitinous and/or calcareous skin fold enclosing part or whole of the dorsal part of crustaceans and turtles.

Carnivorous: flesh-eating.

Cerata: tentacular processes on the backs of some nudibranch molluscs.

Chela: the prehensile nipper or claw of some arthropods such as crabs; plural chelae.

Chemoreception: sensitivity to water or airborne chemicals, especially developed in marine animals.

Chitin: a horny organic compound forming part of the skin or shell of some marine animals.

Ciliary motion: movement caused by the microscopic threads borne on the outer membranes of cells (cilia) of some marine animals which beat back and forth.

Cirrus: a slender appendage; plural cirri.

Cloaca: common opening for respiratory, reproductive and anal systems in a number of animals.

Colonial: pertaining to communal animals of the same species living together, sometimes with organic attachments to each other, as in corals, or sometimes social links, as bees or wasps.

Colonial organisms: organisms that live together in social or structural colonies.

Commensal: a term applied to two species living in close association with one another, neither one at the expense of the other.

Conspecific: of the same species.

Corallite: skeleton of an individual coral polyp.

Detritus: accumulation of dead animal and plant tissue and fine sediment, usually found on the sea floor.

Dioecious: having separate sexes.

Dorsum: the back or top (dorsal) surface.

Endemic: native to and restricted to a particular locality.

Endoecism: an habitual relationship between two animals where one takes shelter in the tube or burrow of another.

Eversible: capable of being turned inside out.

Fission: reproduction by splitting of a body into two or more parts.

Flange: a lip

Foot: muscular extension of a mollusc's body used for locomotion.

Gastropod: a class of molluscs including snails, having a shell of a singular valve and a muscular foot.

Genus: rank in taxonomic hierarchy: group of animals or plants with common characteristics and orgins, usually containing more than one species.

Gregarious: found together in groups.

Herbivorous: plant-eating.

Hermaphroditic: having both male and female reproductive organs in one animal.

Intertidal: between the extremes of high and low tides.

Invertebrate: animals without backbones.

Magilid: a mollusc belonging to the family Magilidae (coral shells).

Mantle: an outgrowth of the body well which lines the shell in molluscs.

Nematocyst: a coiled thread that can be projected as a sting from the cnidoblast cells that contain it.

Notochord: rudimentary spinal cord found in protochordates.

Nudibranch: a marine gastropod without a shell and true gills, but often with branching external gills on the back or sides of the body.

Obligate: dependent.

Operculum: lid or stopper; for example, a plate on a gastropod that closes the aperture of the shell when the animal is retracted.

Ovulid: a mollusc belonging to the family Ovulidae (allied to cowries).

Papilla: a small projection extending from the body tissue; plural papillae.

Pelagic: inhabiting open waters of oceans or lakes or the water column by swimming or drifting: not living on the sea bottom.

Phylum: a primary taxonomic division of animals and plants.

Pinnate: having branches on either side of an axis.

Plankton: animals or plants, especially minute or microscopic forms, that drift suspended in seas, rivers, lakes and ponds.

Polyp: a sac-like individual within a group of animals such as coral. It can be of solitary or colonial existence.

Proboscis: prehensile snout of a mollusc.

Radiole: respiratory and/or feeding tentacle of some tube worms.

Radula: a ribbon-like tongue bearing rows of teeth with which a mollusc reduces food to digestible particles or drills through other shells.

Rhinophore: sensory tentacle on the head or anterior section of the mantle of opisthobranchs (order Mollusca).

Rhizoids: slender hairlike structures that function as roots in mosses, ferns, fungi and related plants.

Sedentary: immobile; refers to animals that remain attached to a substrate or that are unattached but do not move.

Sessile: attached by the base (generally to a substrate).

Seta: bristle; plural setae.

Siliceous: composed of or resembling silica, a glass-like material.

Species: a group of individuals closely related in structure, capable of breeding within the group, but not normally outside it.

Spicule: a minute, hard, needle-like body found in some invertebrates, such as sponges, soft corals, sea fans, and sea cucumbers.

Subspecies: a geographical or other subdivision of a species that is sufficiently different to be recognised as such; a race.

Substrate: the sea bed on which animals and plants live or are attached; rock, coral, mud or sand.

Subtidal: below low tide level.

Swimmeret: an abdominal limb or appendage adapted for swimming (of a crustacean).

Synonymy: collective names that designate the same species.

Test: the hard covering of some invertebrates such as crustaceans.

Type specimen: the original specimen from which a species was described.

Veliger: the free-swimming larva of many molluscs.

Vertebrate: an animal with a backbone.

Viscera: the intestines.

Water-column: area of water between the sea floor and the surface.

Zooid: an individual forming part of a colony and produced asexually by fission; this term is often used in place of 'polyp'.

SPONGES

PHYLUM: Porifera ('Pore bearers')
CLASS: Calcarea, Demospongiae, Hexactinellida

Divers see sponges every time they venture beneath the sea, yet the frequency with which divers see sponges is not proportionate to the quantity of published information about them. For the purpose of this book only a few of the easily recognised forms have been illustrated.

Identifying living sponges is difficult due to the variation of shape within a single species. Depending on its environment, a single species may develop an encrusting form in areas open to rough seas, or may grow upright and branched in sheltered areas or deeper water. Colour is also variable; sponges that grow in shade may be a different colour from those that grow in the sunlight. All sponges are attached to the substrate. Most prefer hard surfaces, though some live on the soft bottom embedded in the sand or mud. There are commensal sponges that live on the valves of live scallops, or giant sea tulips (see sea squirts) and others that bore holes in shells and rocks, and still others that dissolve living corals. Sponges range from minute encrusting species under rocks to massive structures, one and a half metres (five feet) high, in deep water.

Although more than 5,000 species of marine sponges have been named in scientific papers, most were described last century. Scientists now have difficulty identifying many species because the original nomenclature is confused and entire families need to be revised. Many Southern Hemisphere sponges are endemic to southern waters and cannot be compared with those in other regions. Little work has been carried out on the taxonomy of Indo-West Pacific sponges over the past 50 years, so available information is

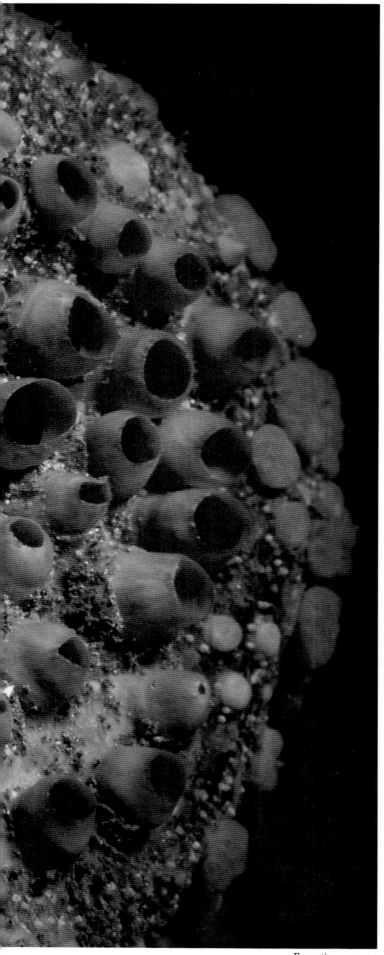

Encrusting sponges

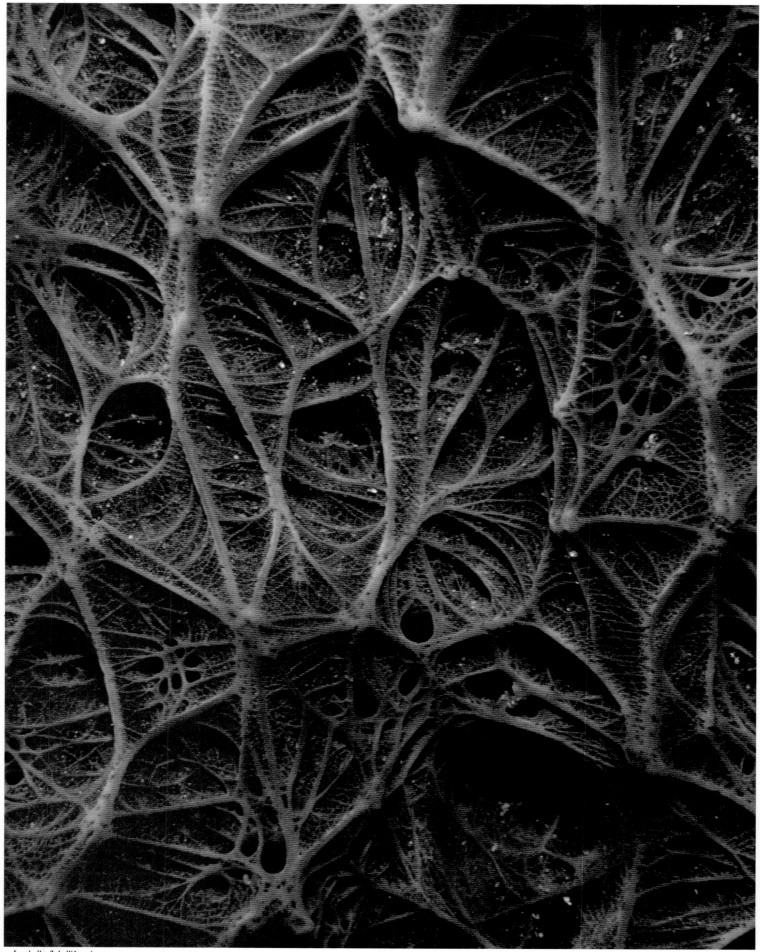

Ianthella flabelliformis

extremely limited. No doubt when the diverse sponge fauna of southern seas is studied in detail, dozens of new species will need to be described and recorded.

Sponges usually have a fibrous skeleton that is made up of a keratin-like material called spongin, only found in sponges. Spongin is very resistant to decomposition, which accounts for the number of sponge skeletons found washed up on beaches, where they often remain for many years before breaking down. Even today, taxonomists rely on spicule or skeleton examination under a microscope to identify sponges. The spicules are small skeletal elements embedded either sporadically or in a definite pattern throughout the body of a sponge, helping to support the structure. These spicules can be either calcareous or siliceous and in most cases are minute. The two classes of sponge are differentiated by their spicules: those of Calcarea are made of lime, while the spicules of Demospongiae are made of silica. Calcarea species also have no spongin fibres.

Sponges are considered by some to be the first multicelluluar animals; their fossil remains have been traced back to the Precambrian era, some 650 million years ago. These simple, primitive life forms are widespread throughout temperate and tropical seas, with around 5000 species recognised worldwide.

Although the tropical seas of the world support a number of specifically shaped and therefore easily recognised sponges, their greatest diversity in shape, colour and species is in temperate waters. Temperate sponges exhibit every colour of the rainbow. To swim into a dark cave at a depth of 25 metres (82 feet), to turn on a torch and to play the beam around the roof and walls, is to be dazzled by an extravaganza of brilliant oranges and reds. And their shapes are as flamboyant as their hues.

The anatomy of a sponge is complex. The body is perforated by many small inhalant pores called ostia and one or a few large exhalant pores called oscula (singular osculum). The ostia lead to the oscula by converging channels passing through the sponge tissue. These channels are wholly or partially lined by special cells called collar cells, thus named because of their shape when seen under the microscope. Each collar cell bears a single filament or flagellum which beats. The combined effect of the beating flagella of the collar cells drives a stream of water through the sponge body from ostia to oscula. Fine protoplasmic extensions on the collar of the collar cells trap suspended fragments of food which are then ingested by the cells. The water stream supplies the sponge with oxygen and removes waste carbon dioxide. One small sponge no bigger than a clenched fist can filter its own body volume of water every four to 20 seconds, which amounts to around 5000 litres (1100 gallons) in one day.

Sponges can reproduce either sexually or asexually, and most are hermaphrodites having both male and female sex cells. Sperm are shed into the water through the exhalant oscula. When sperm are taken in by sponges of the same species through their inhalant ostia, fertilisation occurs inside the parent sponge, where fertilised eggs later develop into small flagellated larvae. The larvae then leave through an exhalant pore to swim in the sea for a time before settling on the bottom and developing into a new sponge colony. Small pieces of broken-off sponge may also form new colonies.

Despite past difficulties with identification of living sponges, today it is relatively simple for the expert to recognise and photograph most sponges that grow below low-tide level on the sea floor. However, precise identification of sponges by amateurs in the field may often be difficult. In many cases an expert will need to look at the skeletal spicules to determine the species.

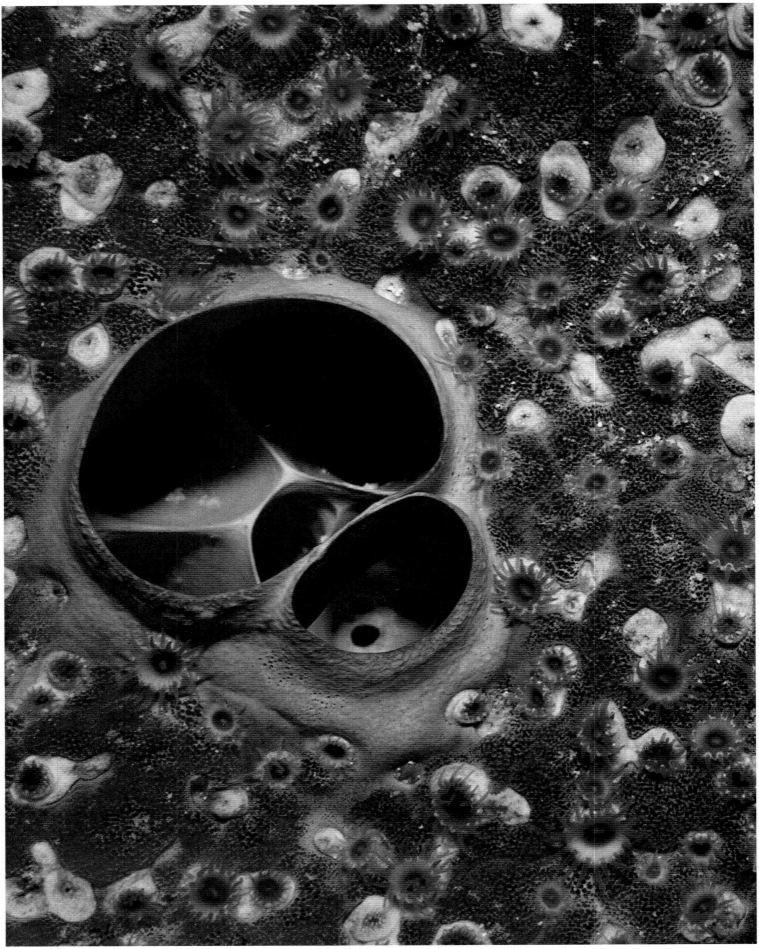

Sponges, Coral Sea

Grantia compressa

■ CLASS: Calcarea

FAMILY: Grantiidae
SCIENTIFIC NAME: *Grantia compressa*
COMMON NAME: Purse sponge
DISTRIBUTION: CT/N;WT/N
HABITAT: Rocky shores; rocky coasts
GENERAL WATER DEPTH: 0–5 m (0–16 ft)
FOOD HABIT: Fine phytoplankton, bacteria
and detritus
SIZE: Growths reaching 50 mm (2 in) long
DESCRIPTION: These sac-like growths with a
large exhalant opening often collapse when
taken out of water to appear like flat purse-
like objects. These are often found in groups
on the lower shore under rocky overhangs.
They may grow amongst red seaweeds. The
colours range from white to yellow, sometimes with a dirty greyish tinge.

Leucosolenia coriacea

FAMILY: Homocoelidae
SCIENTIFIC NAME: *Leucosolenia coriacea*
DISTRIBUTION: CT/N
HABITAT: Rocky shores
GENERAL WATER DEPTH: Low intertidal to
100 m (328 ft)
FOOD HABIT: Omnivorous: plankton

SIZE: Colonies up to 30
mm (1.2 in) in length
DESCRIPTION: The encrust-
ing colonies are formed of
twisted, branching tubes
and are usually found
under stones and boulders,
in colours ranging from
white, grey, or yellow to
pale brown and red. Mem-
bers of this family have
one of the simplest and
most primitive types of
body structure known in
sponges. This genus is a
very large one with over 100
species having been des-
cribed worldwide, occurr-
ing in the Indo-Pacific as well as the Atlantic
Ocean.

Pericharax heteroraphis

FAMILY: Leucettidae
SCIENTIFIC NAME: *Pericharax heteroraphis*
COMMON NAME: Volcano Sponge
DISTRIBUTION: TI–WP
HABITAT: Coral reefs
GENERAL WATER DEPTH: 8–30 m (26–98 ft)
FOOD HABIT: Omnivorous: plankton
SIZE: 300 mm (12 in) (height)
DESCRIPTION: The volcano sponge is a moderately common, easily recognised subtidal
species. Colonies can be seen on reef slopes
and attached to coral heads in offshore
areas. The volcano sponge usually has fluted
sides, two or more large oscula and is often
streaked with yellow. This sponge is relatively brittle to touch and has triradiate spicules
capable of penetrating human skin. The only
predator observed on this sponge is
Gardiner's notodoris nudibranch, *Notodoris
gardineri.*

FAMILY: Sycettidae
SCIENTIFIC NAME: *Sycon* sp.
COMMON NAME: Hairy Tube Sponge

Sycon sp.

DISTRIBUTION: TI–WP; WT/S; CT/S
HABITAT: Rocky reefs
GENERAL WATER DEPTH: Low tide to
30 m (99 ft)
FOOD HABIT: Omnivorous: plankton
SIZE: 100 mm (4 in) (height)
DESCRIPTION: Small, but easily determined
to genus, these characteristic little sponges
are far more common than was once
realised. Due to their whitish colour and
external hair-like spicules (which often have
a lot of detritus clinging to them) they tend
to blend into the background of other sessile
marine growths and usually remain unnoticed. Hairy tube sponges grow along channel slopes and the sides of bommies and can
be found in mainland estuaries and offshore
island reefs.

Dendrilla rosea

■ CLASS: Demospongiae

FAMILY: Aplysillidae
SCIENTIFIC NAME: *Dendrilla rosea*
COMMON NAME: Rose Sponge
DISTRIBUTION: WT/S–CT/S
HABITAT: Rocky reefs
GENERAL WATER DEPTH: Low tide to 32 m
(105 ft)

FOOD HABIT: Omnivorous: plankton
SIZE: 1 m (3 ft) (width)
DESCRIPTION: Shape is not always a good criterion to use when identifying *Dendrilla rosea*, though in upright colonies the tough fibrous skeleton with distinctive basal holdfast is a prominent feature. Colour is fairly constant over its entire range, varying only in shades of pink.

The tissue of the rose sponge is very fragile, and the skeletal material pokes out through the surface, giving it a curious thorny look.

Several species of chromodorid nudibranchs feed exclusively on the rose sponge, including the Tasmanian species, *Chromodoris tasmanensis*.

Microciona prolifera

FAMILY: Clathriidae
SCIENTIFIC NAME: *Microciona prolifera*
COMMON NAME: Red Sponge or Red Beard Sponge
DISTRIBUTION: WA; IO–EP
HABITAT: Rocky shores; calm muddy shores
GENERAL WATER DEPTH: Low tide to at least 26 m (86 ft)
FOOD HABIT: Omnivorous: plankton and dissolved organic matter
SIZE: Usually up to 200 mm (7.9 in) in height
DESCRIPTION: The red sponge is found attached to the shells of bivalve molluscs, and on wharf pilings in calm water. Whilst the young colonies are encrusting, larger colonies may be bush-like, having finger-like, cross branching lobes with colours ranging from red to orange-brown. The species lends itself to experimental work and many studies of its life history and growth have been carried out, especially on the Atlantic coast of the USA.

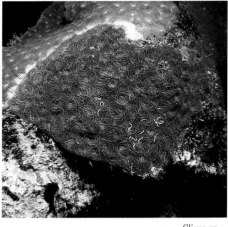

Cliona sp.

FAMILY: Clionidae
SCIENTIFIC NAME: *Cliona* sp.
COMMON NAME: Purple Boring Sponge
DISTRIBUTION: TI–WP
HABITAT: Coral reefs
GENERAL WATER DEPTH: 5–25 m (16–82 ft)
FOOD HABIT: Omnivorous: plankton
SIZE: 300 mm (12 in)
DESCRIPTION: An active destructive agent to living corals, this quick-growing species is easily determined by visual means, as it has a quite readily recognised pattern. Although fragile to touch, the purple boring sponge envelops living corals, dissolving the limestone skeletons with a concentrated acidic substance. It's amazing to think that such a diaphanous creature is capable of causing the downfall of structures that have sunk thousands of ships.

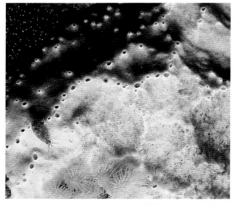

Halichondria panicea

FAMILY: Halichondriidae
SCIENTIFIC NAME: *Halichondria panicea*
COMMON NAME: Breadcrumb or Crumb of Bread Sponge
DISTRIBUTION: Cosmopolitan
HABITAT: Rocky shores
GENERAL WATER DEPTH: Intertidal to about 100 m (328 ft)

FOOD HABIT: Omnivorous: plankton
SIZE: Colonies up to 200 m (7.9 in) in height and 20 mm (0.8 in) thick
DESCRIPTION: This widely distributed and much studied sponge is found on rocks, seaweeds, mussel beds and on wharf pilings. It occurs as encrusting sheets of variable shape. The many oscular openings, sometimes irregularly distributed, are like craters in tiny volcanic cones. Colours range from white, yellow and orange to green and brown. Sea stars and several species of nudibranchs are known to prey on this sponge, which has the ability to repair damage very readily and to produce its own antibiotic materials.

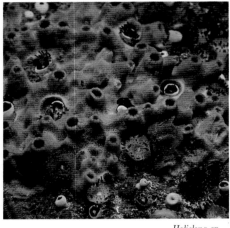

Haliclona sp.

FAMILY: Haliclonidae
SCIENTIFIC NAME: *Haliclona* sp.
DISTRIBUTION: Cosmopolitan
HABITAT: Rocky shores
GENERAL WATER DEPTH: Intertidal to 50 m (164 ft)
FOOD HABIT: Omnivorous: plankton
SIZE: Few centimetres (inches) to over 1 m (3 ft)
DESCRIPTION: A widely distributed genus of more than 200 species, this animal is found on the sides of boulders, in caves and under ledges and in crevices, and occurs as encrusting sheets up to about 40 mm (1.6 in) in thickness. The colours range from violet to rose, or pale orange to yellow. The genus has been widely studied, including the life history of a New Zealand species, but owing to the extreme difficulty of identification, many species may be as yet undescribed. Nudibranches are among the known predators.

FAMILY: Halisarcidae
SCIENTIFIC NAME: *Halisarca magellanica*
COMMON NAME: Magellan Sponge
DISTRIBUTION: WT/S
HABITAT: Rocky reefs
GENERAL WATER DEPTH: 20–40 m (66–131 ft)

Halisarca magellanica

FOOD HABIT: Omnivorous: plankton
SIZE: 76 mm (3 in) (width)
DESCRIPTION: Due to its small colony size and deeper water habitat, magellan sponge is not a well-known species and illustrations are rare. It is an investing species and uses other sessile colonial animals for its support. The specimen shown has almost completely taken over a bryozoan (sea moss) colony so that only the tips of the still living bryozoan can be seen. This sponge lives in caves, under ledges and on the sides of reefs where there is a strong current flow.

Ianthella flabelliformis

FAMILY: Ianthellidae
SCIENTIFIC NAME: *Ianthella flabelliformis*
COMMON NAME: Yellow Dish Sponge
DISTRIBUTION: TI–WP; WT/S
HABITAT: Coral reefs; rocky reefs
GENERAL WATER DEPTH: 20–60 m (66–197 ft)
FOOD HABIT: Omnivorous: plankton
SIZE: 600 mm (2 ft) (width)
DESCRIPTION: Very common on deeper water, hard-bottom areas in channels and beyond coral slopes, this species occurs from the inshore mainland waters of continental

islands to the outer barrier reefs in the South-West Pacific. It appears to be more prevalent in situations of strong current. Although the skeletal fibre is quite resilient, the surface flesh is very soft. Deeper water forms may appear pink or orange around the base and on the underside.

Jaspis stellifera

FAMILY: Jaspidae
SCIENTIFIC NAME: *Jaspis stellifera*
COMMON NAME: Crown Sponge
DISTRIBUTION: TI–WP
HABITAT: Coral reefs
GENERAL WATER DEPTH: 15–25 m (49–82 ft)
FOOD HABIT: Omnivorous: plankton
SIZE: 300 mm (12 in) (height)
DESCRIPTION: These tough textured, dark coloured sponges seem to prefer areas of strong current along channel slopes and reef terraces in offshore locations. Not common to any particular locality, the species does not appear to be gregarious and individuals seem few and far between.

Echinoclathria laminaefarosa

FAMILY: Microcionidae
SCIENTIFIC NAME: *Echinoclathria laminaefarosa*
COMMON NAME: Holey Sponge
DISTRIBUTION: WT/S
HABITAT: Rocky reefs
GENERAL WATER DEPTH: 10–30 m (33–98 ft)
FOOD HABIT: Omnivorous: plankton
SIZE: 450 mm (18 in) (colony height)
DESCRIPTION: Overall size and shape are quite variable in this species, as the colony may have one distinct, long projection, or have a base from which several round-topped projections grow. Sometimes these projections fuse together, forming a solid mass. Colour varies from bluish-white through to grey and ochre. There is some evidence to show that each species of this genus may have characteristic hole shapes, but not enough data on this are available to date.

There are several small crustaceans that inhabit the holey sponge, but it is not known whether the relationships are obligate.

Arenochalina mirabilis

FAMILY: Mycalidae
SCIENTIFIC NAME: *Arenochalina mirabilis*
COMMON NAME: Slimy Lemon Sponge
DISTRIBUTION: WT/S–CT/S
HABITAT: Rocky reefs
GENERAL WATER DEPTH: 8–30 m (26–98 ft)
FOOD HABIT: Omnivorous: plankton
SIZE: 250 mm (10 in) (height)
DESCRIPTION: Very common and easily distinguished (to generic level), this sponge mostly grows in a double-fingered, flat-sided shape and may often be seen growing parallel to current flow. The vernacular name has been given for the most outstanding feature of this species. When a living colony is collected, or brought to the surface, it disintegrates into masses of slimy tissue, leaving a soft pliable skeleton. The internal skeletons of many of these sponges are washed ashore on beaches.

Mycale macilenta

FAMILY: Mycalidae
SCIENTIFIC NAME: *Mycale macilenta*
DISTRIBUTION: CT/N
HABITAT: Rocky shores
GENERAL WATER DEPTH: Intertidal
FOOD HABIT: Omnivorous: plankton
SIZE: Colonies may be 200 mm (7.9 in) or
more across
DESCRIPTION: This sponge occurs as a thin
encrustation on rocks although some tend to
be rounded encrusting massive forms, with
colours ranging from grey to yellow and pale
orange. Members of the family have been
recorded as producing large amounts of
mucus. Species of this genus are also found
in the Pacific Ocean from Japan to southern
Australia, and in the Mediterranean.

Raspailia sp.

FAMILY: Raspailiidae
SCIENTIFIC NAME: *Raspailia* sp.
COMMON NAME: Orange-tufted Sponge
DISTRIBUTION: WT/S
HABITAT: Rocky reefs
GENERAL WATER DEPTH: 18–40 m (59–131 ft)
FOOD HABIT: Omnivorous: plankton
SIZE: 230 mm (9 in) (colony height)
DESCRIPTION: Fairly characteristic in both
its living and its dried state, the orange-

tufted sponge is mostly found on open
coastal and offshore reefs where it grows on
horizontal rock surfaces in isolated positions.
Individual colonies are rarely found in close
proximity to each other, and smaller colonies
(70 mm (3 in)) are more common than the
larger ones. The brittle star, *Ophiothrix
ancestra*, is often observed living amongst
the branches of this sponge.

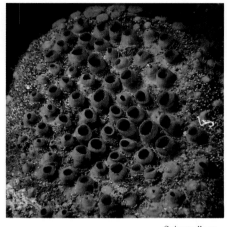

Spirastrella sp.

FAMILY: Spirastrellidae
SCIENTIFIC NAME: *Spirastrella* sp.
COMMON NAME: Vented Sponge
DISTRIBUTION: CT/S
HABITAT: Rocky reefs
GENERAL WATER DEPTH: 20–80 m
(66–262 ft)
FOOD HABIT: Omnivorous: plankton
SIZE: 600 mm (2 ft) height
DESCRIPTION: Moderately common in
deeper waters, this large, solid-bodied
sponge is usually seen on low profile patch
reefs on open areas surrounded by sandy or
muddy plains. It has extremely numerous
and very prominent exhalant openings which
rise above the surrounding surface area.
Most of these openings are at the top. This
species is often inhabited by colonies of commensal snapping shrimps.

FAMILY: Spongiidae
SCIENTIFIC NAME: *Carteriospongia
foliascens*
COMMON NAME: Goblet Sponge
DISTRIBUTION: TI-WP
HABITAT: Coral reefs
GENERAL WATER DEPTH: 2–15 m (6–49 ft)
FOOD HABIT: Omnivorous: plankton
SIZE: 457 mm (18 in) (height)
DESCRIPTION: While on some reefs this
sponge appears to prefer reef tops in shallow
water, in other locations it may be found
along channel slopes and sheltered reef rims.
Its colour is fairly stable, varying from

Carteriospongia foliascens

shades of white to grey. Although most
observed specimens have similar shapes to
that illustrated here, some open cone forms
have been seen, along with colonies that
grow flat-sided. However, all colonies have
the distinct grooving in the sides and are
subject to barnacle infestation.

Caulospongia perfoliata

FAMILY: Suberitidae
SCIENTIFIC NAME: *Caulospongia perfoliata*
COMMON NAME: Staircase Sponge
DISTRIBUTION: TI-WP; WT/S
HABITAT: Coral reefs; rocky reefs
GENERAL WATER DEPTH: 10–25 m (33–82 ft)
FOOD HABIT: Omnivorous: plankton
SIZE: 1 m (3 ft)
DESCRIPTION: Commonly washed up on
Western Australia's northern beaches after
cyclones, the staircase sponge inhabits both

inshore and offshore waters throughout its range. Colours range from orange to red, but the characteristic shape appears constant. Offshore examples (such as those from the Houtman Abrolhos Islands in the southern Indian Ocean) grow larger than coastal forms. This species has an exceptionally strong skeleton and specimens collected hundreds of years ago have shown little deterioration.

Suberites domuncula

FAMILY: Suberitidae
SCIENTIFIC NAME: *Suberites domuncula*
COMMON NAME: Sulphur Sponge or Sea Orange
DISTRIBUTION: CT/N; WT/N
HABITAT: Rocky coasts
GENERAL WATER DEPTH: 1–200 m (3–656 ft)
FOOD HABIT: fine phytoplankton, bacteria and detritus
SIZE: 300 mm (11.8 in) in diameter
DESCRIPTION: The sulphur sponge forms smooth flattened, rounded, or globular growths of fleshy tissue. Orange-yellow in colour, the sulphur sponge may be found on shells occupied by hermit crabs, or as flatter growths on rocks. It has a strong smell of sulphur derived from sulphur compounds secreted in its toxic mucus. This mucus probably defends it against predators such as nudibranchs, but it does not seem to upset the hermit crabs which sometimes carry it on the gastropod shells they use as protective homes. Here the sponge probably serves as camouflage against the crab's predators, such as octopus. After a period of time the gastropod shell may be dissolved by the sponge which then provides full protection for the hermit crab. Similar related species occur in other regions.

Tethya corticata

FAMILY: Tethyidae
SCIENTIFIC NAME: *Tethya corticata*
COMMON NAME: Little Orange Ball Sponge
DISTRIBUTION: WT/S–CT/S
HABITAT: Rocky reefs; rocky shores
GENERAL WATER DEPTH: Low tide to 30 m (98 ft)
FOOD HABIT: Omnivorous: plankton
SIZE: 500 mm (20 in) (width)
DESCRIPTION: The genus *Tethya* is relatively easy to identify visually. However, most identifications to specific level require a specialist taxonomist. The little orange ball sponge is found in many oceans of the world, and is a common resident of shallow subtidal rocky reefs around southern Australia. It is generally found in groups, though some individual specimens may be seen on the undersides of loosely positioned boulders, or beneath ledges in the intertidal zone.

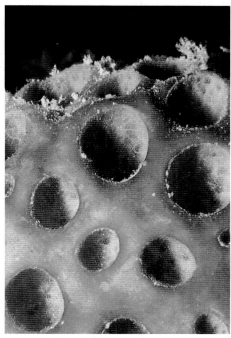

Cinachyra tenuiviolacea

FAMILY: Tetillidae
SCIENTIFIC NAME: *Cinachyra tenuiviolacea*
COMMON NAME: Violet Ball Sponge
DISTRIBUTION: TI–WP
HABITAT: Coral reefs
GENERAL WATER DEPTH: 5–25 m (16–82 ft)
FOOD HABIT: Omnivorous: plankton
SIZE: 20 mm (8 in) (width)
DESCRIPTION: Regularly observed on offshore reefs along the Great Barrier Reef, the violet ball sponge prefers habitats in caves, or under ledges along the sides of bommies, or terraced slopes. It is fairly stable in its growth pattern and colour and although not common, stands out from other sessile life forms and is therefore more regularly noticed. The outside surface is often covered with a residue of white 'coral dust' silt.

Euplectella aspergillum

■ CLASS: Hexactinellida

FAMILY: Euplectellidae
SCIENTIFIC NAME: *Euplectella aspergillum*
COMMON NAME: Venus' Flower Basket
DISTRIBUTION: Cosmopolitan
HABITAT: Rocky reefs
GENERAL WATER DEPTH: Deep water
FOOD HABIT: Omnivorous: plankton
SIZE: Up to 400 mm (15.7 in) in length
DESCRIPTION: This glass sponge is well known throughout the world for its beautiful lattice-like skeleton of spicules which retains its shape after death. It is thus much sought after, being sold in shell and curio shops. Venus' flower basket is only found in deep water, attached to rocks by a tuft of long spicules. When living it is white or pale yellow in colour.

Tubastrea aurea

CNIDARIANS

PHYLUM: Cnidaria (Stingers)
CLASS: Hydrozoa (Hydroids, Hydrocorals, Fire Corals, Portuguese Man-of-War), Ceriantipatharia (Black Corals, Tube Anemones), Alcyonaria (Soft Corals, Gorgonians, Sea-Pens), Scyphozoa (Sea Jellies), Cubozoa (Box Jellies), Zoantharia (Sea-Anemones, Zoanthids, Hard Corals)

At one time all animals with radial symmetry and simple sac-like bodies were placed in the phylum Coelenterata. Instead scientists today recognise two separate phyla at this level: Cnidaria and Ctenophora. All the animals illustrated in this section belong to the larger of the two, the phylum Cnidaria. The term 'Cnidaria' refers to the power to sting, a feature of these animals which have special stinging cells in their bodies. These cells are called cnidoblasts and discharge stinging threads called nematocysts which are used to subdue the prey, to adhere to hard surfaces temporarily, and to ward off predators. In addition to the stinging cells there are other types, including nerve cells, muscle cells, gland cells and reproductive cells. These are all arranged in two layers around the gut, and the inner layer is separated from the outer one by a layer of jelly-like substance called mesogloea. All cnidaria are headless and have a radial symmetry. When viewed from above most are flower-like in shape with a central mouth surrounded by one or more circlets of tentacles, which may be arranged like the petals of a flower. These tentacles are hollow, containing a space which connects with the gut. The nematocysts are usually concentrated in the tentacles.

There are about 9000 species of cnidarians living in the world's oceans. (This number is only an estimate due to continuing changes in taxonomy and new discoveries.)

Cnidarians are separated into the classes Hydrozoa, Scyphozoa, Cubozoa and the subphylum Anthozoa. Within these four groups are two main different body forms—free-swimming medusae (sea jellies) and stationary polyps (hydroids, corals and sea-anemones). Both body forms are radially symmetrical, with the mouth located at the centre. The basic differences between the free-swimming medusa and the stationary polyp are their mode of life and their orientation. The medusa swims with its mouth and tentacles facing downwards, while the stationary polyp is attached to a substrate with its mouth and tentacles facing upwards or outwards.

One important feature of Cnidarians is their ability to form colonies. In the Hydrozoa we find both solitary and colonial forms. Within the colonies there may be several types of individual; for example, defensive, reproductive and feeding. Colonies also occur in the Anthozoa but here all individuals are equivalent.

Cnidarians are widely distributed throughout the world's seas, both in shallow and deep water. However, they are most obvious in the tropics where they form coral reefs. The basic structural unit of a typical cnidarian is the polyp. This polyp has no breathing mechanism, no blood and no excretory system: in short, it is a sac-like organism with an opening at one end surrounded by tentacles. The vital functions of respiration, excretion and food distribution are achieved by simple diffusion. The tentacles bear cnidoblasts which house nematocysts. There are a number of different types of nematocysts; some are barbed, some are sticky, some act as a spring to wrap around and ensnare prey. Basically they are coiled up inside the cnidoblast cell and when given the appropriate stimulus, touch or chemical, they discharge by turning inside out.

Although all cnidarians possess nematocysts, only a few have the capacity to harm humans. Some hydroids, fire corals, sea jellies and sea-anemones can injure humans and a few, including the tropical box jellies, have caused the deaths of some swimmers.

Once the prey is subdued, the tentacles manoeuvre it to the mouth. It then passes to the stomach where it is digested and the useful products are absorbed. The refuse is regurgitated and ejected via the mouth.

The life histories of cnidarians are often varied and complex. The following is only a general account.

Anthozoans and some hydroids spend their entire lives as polyps, for example, as sea-anemones and corals. These colonies may reproduce asexually by budding or splitting, or sexually by producing eggs and sperm. Sperm from one individual may enter the body of another via the mouth and fertilise the eggs inside. A larva will form which may swim out to settle and develop elsewhere; alternatively, the embryo may be 'brooded' inside the body of its parent (or even another adult!) until it is able to lead an independent life.

Most hydroids and scyphozoa have complex life cycles. These involve a fixed polyp phase and a mobile medusa phase. The Medusae reproduce sexually, each organism being male or female and releasing eggs and sperm into the sea. The fertilised eggs develop into polyp forms, and after growth and maturation, these reproduce asexually to give another mobile medusa phase. In the hydrozoa it is the sedentary polyp phase which is dominant and in the scyphozoa it is the medusa phase which is dominant. The polyps in the hydrozoa are often colonial in organisation.

CLASS: Hydrozoa (Sea ferns and hydrocorals)
The order Hydroida (sea ferns) are one of the few cnidarian groups that is more diverse in temperate waters than in tropical seas. Although they flourish in temperate seas, hydroids are certainly not familiar to most divers. The majority are low-profile clusters of fine, fern-like structures that tend to blend in rather than stand out. Many species are very small, and many live on other organisms, such as seaweeds, sponges and shells.

Even though a number of the more prominent forms can be identified by the amateur observer (after some practice), the majority need to be identified by a specialist taxonomist from properly collected and preserved specimens. It will be some time before the full details of life histories of all hydroids are known. Many medusae have different names from the hydroid which constitutes the sessile generation and this complicates matters considerably. Careful breeding work may be necessary to establish which hydroid develops which medusa type. Scientists have recorded many species of hydroids in the world's oceans, though only a few small hydrocorals have been recorded.

The external tubular supporting structure of a hydroid's sedentary colonial stage is composed of flexible chitin. In some cases this merely protects the tubular connexions between polyps in the colony, while in other cases it is extended to form tunnel-like hydranths into which the polyps can withdraw for protection. By contrast, the colonial hydrocorals and fire corals have massive, hard, calcified structures. The fire corals have powerful nematocysts which can inflict severe stings.

CLASS: Scyphozoa (Sea jellies)
Sea jellies belonging to this class are defined as cnidarians where the medusa phase is dominant and there is a subordinate polyp stage. A number of interesting, well-known and easily recognised large species of sea jellies exist in the world's seas, as well as a number of undescribed species. All the larger species can be identified alive, or from

Dendronepthya sp.

Dendronepthya sp.

a good colour transparency. The identification of the sedentary polyp phases is very difficult. The anatomy of the sea jellies is quite complex with the extensive mesogloea (see above) contributing to their gelatinous bulk. Transfer of food from the digestive areas to the tissues is helped by a system of canals; balance organs assist in swimming. Pulses of contraction sweep over the muscles of the bell and cause the tissues to make characteristic beats which enable the animal to swim through the water.

CLASS: Cubozoa (Box jellies)

Members of this class are amongst the most venomous animals in the world. Although box jellies are tropical in their distribution, the largest and most dangerous are in the waters of the southern hemisphere. The common term, 'box jelly', describes this group admirably. The body has a tough gelatinous composition, a box-like, four-sided bell with one or more tentacles attached to each corner. At the underside of the bell the edges curve under, forming a 'skirt' yet not enclosing the body area. Sense organs made up of a balance mechanism and an eye are situated on each of the four sides, usually on the central perpendicular axis towards the base of the bell. Under the bell, hanging from the top, is the stomach and tubular mouth.

This class contains two families: members of Corybdeidae have four single tentacles and are mild stingers, while the Chirodropidae have four clusters of tentacles, with some species being deadly to humans.

SUBPHYLUM: Anthozoa

CLASS: Ceriantipatharia (Black corals, tube anemones)

CLASS: Alcyonaria (Soft corals, blue corals, gorgonians, sea-pens)

CLASS: Zoantharia (Sea-anemones, zoanthids, hard corals)

These animals have no medusa in this life cycle, but many live in colonies of similar sedentary polyps, either with or without hard skeletons. Their radially symmetrical polyps have either six sides (hexacorals) or eight sides (octocorals). In the former case the tentacles are simple and unbranched, while in the latter they are branched or pinnate, making them good at suspension feeding.

Black corals are generally white, pink, yellow, brown or green externally, with tough horny black skeletons that are not easily broken. In many parts of the world these can only be identified to genus level. Examination with a lens will show their polyps to bear six tentacles. Tube anemones have not been well studied and new species are being described from various regions. These animals all live in soft sediments. They secrete a soft mucus protective tube and have two rings of tentacles, the outer ring of tentacles being longer than the inner tentacles. They can be voracious predators and often take small fish, though their major food source is plankton. Soft corals are so called because their skeletal spicules are not rigidly fused together, so their colonies are flexible. They can be identified at genus level *in situ* by an experienced person but identification to species level can only be verified by examining the internal spicules. This requires the expertise of a taxonomist. Soft corals have eight-tentacled pinnate polyps. Gorgonians have similar polyps and may be somewhat easier to identify than soft corals. Their colonies typically make impressive fan-shaped growths. Their bodies are orientated in relation to the prevailing currents to enhance their food collecting ability. Their 'fans' are supported by a special skeletal protein called gorgonin used in conjunction with calcium carbonate spicules.

Sea-pens are quill-shaped colonies of octocorals which live with one special polyp modified to support the whole colony in the sediment. Some are phosphorescent, but the significance of this is not clear. Sea-pens may be identified to species level by a good quality photograph.

The sea-anemones are the most familiar Anthozoa. They are found on rocky shores, reefs and in deeper water, adhering to the substrate by a well-developed sucker. A few are specialised for burrowing in sand and lack a sucker. These solitary organisms are hexacorals with tentacles arranged in multiples of six, often with many whorls. They have no hard skeleton and prey on small animals.

Zoanthids occur in tropical and temperate seas. Some live commensally with other invertebrates such as sponges. They may be solitary or colonial and they are not well studied. Those that have been described to genus or species level may possibly be identified alive.

The hard corals of the world (sometimes referred to as stony or true corals) have been fairly well studied and many species have been photographed in colour. Though some can now be identified alive by visual means, scientists and museums still require a specimen in order to provide an accurate identification to species level. The polyps of living corals have tentacles arranged in multiples of six, and these are not pinnate. An easy means of telling corals from sea-anemones is by touching them: corals have hard skeletons, sea-anemones do not. Hard corals occur in all seas and at most depths, but it is only in warm tropical shallow waters that they are able to secrete calcium carbonate fast enough to be able to form reefs. Reef building corals are physiologically different from non-reef building ones, and they contain minute single-celled plants in their tissues, called zooxanthallae.

Bougainvillia principis

■ CLASS: Hydrozoa

FAMILY: Bougainvilliidae
SCIENTIFIC NAME: *Bougainvillia principis*
DISTRIBUTION: Unknown
HABITAT: Rocky shores
GENERAL WATER DEPTH: Intertidal to
30 m (98.4 ft)
FOOD HABIT: Carnivorous: plankton
SIZE: Unknown
DESCRIPTION: Colonies of this widely distributed hydroid genus consist of whorls of spindle shaped polyps with pale filiform tentacles, attached to rocks and other objects.

Obelia geniculata

FAMILY: Campanulariidae
SCIENTIFIC NAME: *Obelia geniculata*
DISTRIBUTION: Cosmopolitan
HABITAT: Rocky shores; rocky coasts
GENERAL WATER DEPTH: Low intertidal to
50 m (164 ft)
FOOD HABIT: Carnivorous: plankton
SIZE: Colonies up to 250 mm (9.8 in)
DESCRIPTION: A delicate little hydroid, this species is very common and may be found throughout the year in certain places. It

grows on rocks, wharf pilings, seaweeds, shells and other fixed objects from the middle shore downwards. It has been noted that temperature plays a big part in its rate of growth and in the development and release of medusae. The often bushy colonies have creeping stolens and zigzag branching stems on which the bell-shaped cups are borne on alternate sides of the stem, each being supported by a ringed red-brown perisarc. Grazing by nudibranchs can reduce lush colonies to stubby stalks. *Obelia* has been used throughout the world in many different studies and is well-known to zoology students; it contributes to the assessment of water quality.

Clathrozoan wilsoni

FAMILY: Clathrozoanidae
SCIENTIFIC NAME: *Clathrozoan wilsoni*
DISTRIBUTION: WT/S; CT/S
HABITAT: Rocky reefs
GENERAL WATER DEPTH: 25–80 m
(82–263 ft)
FOOD HABIT: Carnivorous: plankton
SIZE: 1 m (3 ft) (colony height)
DESCRIPTION: Wilson's sea fern is the largest hydroid inhabiting this water zone. In some shallow locations only small isolated colonies may be observed, while in deeper waters the growths may well be over 1 m (3 ft) high and 1 m across. Because of its drab appearance this species often goes unnoticed and may easily be mistaken for a dead gorgonian sea fan overgrown with algae. Wilson's sea fern does have a similar growth pattern to the *Mopsella* gorgonians; in poor light at depth, the likeness is even more pronounced. Although the colony structure is basically fan-like, it may often develop into a larger bush-like colony with a poorly defined overall shape.

Sarsia tubulosa

FAMILY: Corynidae
SCIENTIFIC NAME: *Sarsia tubulosa*
DISTRIBUTION: CT/N
HABITAT: Rocky shores
GENERAL WATER DEPTH: General Water
Depth: Lower intertidal
FOOD HABIT: Carnivorous: plankton
SIZE: Colonies up to 50 mm (2 in) in
height
DESCRIPTION: Colonies are commonly found on rocks and wharf pilings in sheltered coastal areas but are also found on harbour floats and on the Eel grass, *Zostera*. The hydroid stage of *Sarsia* forms a branched colony with tentacles which are scattered over the head and club-shaped. Tiny medusae are budded off from the bases of the feeding polyps.

Coryne pusilla

FAMILY: Corynidae
SCIENTIFIC NAME: *Coryne pusilla*
DISTRIBUTION: WT/N–CT/N
HABITAT: Rocky shores
GENERAL WATER DEPTH: Intertidal
FOOD HABIT: Carnivorous: plankton
SIZE: 10 mm (0.4 in) in height
DESCRIPTION: Small colonies have creeping
stolons and stems which are irregularly
branched, with round pink polyps at the end
of each branch. These bear club-shaped tentacles and in the breeding season, round
reproductive bodies may be seen clustered
below them. These hydroids are normally
found growing on seaweeds in rock pools on
the lower shore, though they may also be
found growing on rocks below low tide.

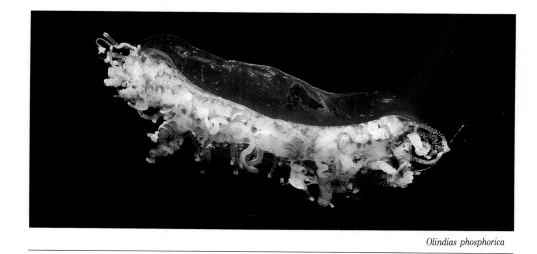

Olindias phosphorica

Hydractinia echinata

FAMILY: Hydractiniidae
SCIENTIFIC NAME: *Hydractinia echinata*
DISTRIBUTION: WT/N; CT/N
HABITAT: Rocky shores; rocky coasts
GENERAL WATER DEPTH: Intertidal
FOOD HABIT: Carnivorous: plankton
SIZE: Polyps up to about 15 mm (0.6 in)
 in height; colonies to 50 mm (2 in) across
DESCRIPTION: Colonies of dense polyps,
white-brown or red in colour and rising from
an encrusting base, are usually found covering the surface of shells inhabited by hermit
crabs. The Japanese *Hydractinia epiconcha* is
found on living shells of molluscs as well as
on those inhabited by hermit crabs. Reproductive bodies develop on the polyps and are
usually released as rounded medusoids
rather than tiny bell-shaped medusae. A lens
will be needed to distinguish the small
flower-like feeding polyps, and the defensive
stinging polyps and spines which grow from
the perisarc.

FAMILY: Milleporidae
SCIENTIFIC NAME: *Millepora tenera*
COMMON NAME: Delicate Fire Coral
DISTRIBUTION: TI–WP
HABITAT: Coral reefs
GENERAL WATER DEPTH: 3–20 m (10–66 ft)
FOOD HABIT: Carnivorous: plankton
SIZE: 3 m (10 ft) (colony width)
DESCRIPTION: The delicate fire coral is one
of the most attractive of the stinging
hydrocorals and grows on the sides and tops
of reefs where maximum water movement
prevails. The hydrocorals are polymorphic
and have several sets of polyps which per-
form different functions, for example feeding
or defence. Some hydrocorals have separate
sets of thread-like tentacles for killing plankton and others for eating the minute animals. The delicate fire coral has stinging
nematocysts which can penetrate human
skin. The sting is moderately painful and
causes a continuous itch. Small fishes of the
genus *Pleurosicya* live in association with this
species but are unaffected by its stinging
polyps.

Millepora tenera

FAMILY: Olindiidae
SCIENTIFIC NAME: *Olindias phosphorica*
COMMON NAME: Iridescent Limnomedusian
DISTRIBUTION: TI–WP; WT/S
HABITAT: Inshore waters; offshore waters
GENERAL WATER DEPTH: Surface to 20 m
 (66 ft)
FOOD HABIT: Carnivorous: plankton
SIZE: 35 mm (1.4 in)
DESCRIPTION: This medusa is the free-
swimming stage of an unknown hydroid. Its
brilliant colours and corkscrew-like tentacles
are good distinguishing features. Many specimens have a brilliant green cross on the
underside of the bell, visually dividing the
medusa into four parts. Another feature of
this species is its ability to alter its body
shape from that of an elongate form when
drifting, to that of a circular bell when swimming. In its elongate shape, the iridescent
limnomedusian settles to the seabed and
moves along by worm-like extensions and
retractions of its body. Despite its small size,
this species is capable of delivering an
uncomfortable sting which may be painful
for two hours.

FAMILY: Physaliidae
SCIENTIFIC NAME: *Physalia physalis*
COMMON NAME: Portuguese Man-of-war
DISTRIBUTION: TI–WP; EP; WT/S;
 WT/N; CT/S
HABITAT: Coastal waters; oceanic waters
GENERAL WATER DEPTH: General Water
 Depth: Surface waters
FOOD HABIT: Carnivorous: plankton; fish
SIZE: 229 mm (9 in)
DESCRIPTION: When washed up on beaches,
the stinging tentacles may get broken off, so
the Portuguese man-of-war seems to have no
tentacles at all. It can still sting, so do not
touch! A Portuguese man-of-war is basically
composed of a float, long fishing tentacles,
feeding polyps, and reproductive zooids.

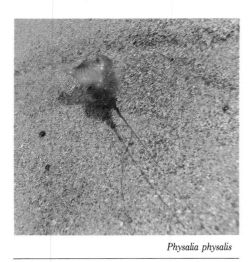

Physalia physalis

Although it is generally thought of as a single animal, it is in fact a colony. Living out their lives on the high seas, these colonies are often swept ashore in vast numbers during strong onshore winds. The fishing tentacles of a Portuguese man-of-war may be as long as 10 m (33 ft) and are studded along their entire length with batteries of powerful stinging cells called nematocysts. These kill small planktonic organisms which stick to the fishing tentacles. They are then retracted so that the feeding polyps can digest the food.

Aglaophenia cupressina

FAMILY: Plumulariidae
SCIENTIFIC NAME: *Aglaophenia cupressina*
COMMON NAME: Cypress Sea Fern
DISTRIBUTION: TI–WP
HABITAT: Coral reefs
GENERAL WATER DEPTH: 1–25 m (3–82 ft)
FOOD HABIT: Carnivorous: plankton
SIZE: 1 m (3 ft) (colony height)
DESCRIPTION: Named for the similarity of its branches to those of the cypress tree, *Aglaophenia cupressina* is the largest stinging hydroid in the tropics and can be seen in

pools on reef flats and in moderately deep water. It generally lives in sheltered areas behind reefs and in lagoons, and at some reefs is extremely common. The sting from its venomous nematocysts is immediate and painful, and the post-sting itching and secondary effects may take up to one month to heal. Bright yellow forms of Dana's brittle star, *Ophiothela danae*, live on some colonies as does the predatory nudibranch, *Doto* sp.

Lytocarpus philippinus

FAMILY: Plumulariidae
SCIENTIFIC NAME: *Lytocarpus philippinus*
COMMON NAME: White-stinging Sea Fern
DISTRIBUTION: TI–WP; WT/S
HABITAT: Coral reefs; rocky reefs; coastal rocks
General Water Depth: 1–25 m (3–82 ft)
FOOD HABIT: Carnivorous: plankton
SIZE: 450 mm (18 in) (colony height)
DESCRIPTION: The fern-like colonies occur in clumps and generally grow in areas of surge, or current, from just below low-tide level down to 30 m (98 ft). The slightest brush of bare flesh against these animals causes immediate pain from hundreds of microscopic stinging cells found in the tentacles of each individual polyp. The affected area will become increasingly itchy and may take up to one month to heal.

FAMILY: Plumulariidae
SCIENTIFIC NAME: *Plumularia setacea*
DISTRIBUTION: WT/N; WT/S
HABITAT: Rocky shores; coasts; in pools; on stones; on algal drift
GENERAL WATER DEPTH: 0–100 m (0–328 ft)
FOOD HABIT: Carnivorous: zooplankton
SIZE: Colonies reaching up to 100 mm (3.9 in) high
DESCRIPTION: The colonies have unbranching vertical stems which carry alternate left and right side branches. The polyps are carried in polyp cups fused to

Plumularia setacea

only one side of the branches. Flask-shaped cups, situated near the junctions of the side branches with the main stem, house the reproductive zooids. Such details are easily made out with the assistance of a hand lens. The feather-like colonies of hydroids rise from creeping stolons. This genus is very widespread and has representatives in many parts of the world.

Solandaria fusca

FAMILY: Solandariidae
SCIENTIFIC NAME: *Solandaria fusca*
COMMON NAME: Dusky Sea Fern
DISTRIBUTION: IWP; WTS
HABITAT: Coral reefs; rocky reefs
GENERAL WATER DEPTH: 3–60 m (9–180 ft)
FOOD HABIT: Carnivorous: plankton
SIZE: Colonies up to 300 mm (11.8 in) across
DESCRIPTION: The colonies of this hydroid have a superficial resemblance to a sea fan. The chitinous skeleton is covered with living tissue and small white polyps with 12 to 15 club-shaped tentacles. These spectacular colonies tend to grow in a uniform fashion throughout its range and are thus fairly easy to recognise, at least to genus.

Distichophora violacea

FAMILY: Stylasteridae
SCIENTIFIC NAME: *Distichophora violacea*
COMMON NAME: Blue Hydrocoral
DISTRIBUTION: TI–WP
HABITAT: Coral reefs
GENERAL WATER DEPTH: 1–30 m (3–98 ft)
FOOD HABIT: Carnivorous: plankton
SIZE: 30 mm (3 in) (colony)
DESCRIPTION: The blue hydrocoral is gener-
ally situated under ledges, along cliff faces,
swim-throughs and in caves, so it is mainly
seen by divers. Most colonies are small and
many are in out of the way nooks and cran-
nies. This stony hydroid colony has its
polyps growing along the peripheral edges of
the branches rather than over the entire surface as its fire coral relatives, *Millepora*, do.
The small blue hydrocoral mollusc,
Pediculariona sp., is a resident predator on
some colonies.

Stylaster elegans

FAMILY: Stylasteridae
SCIENTIFIC NAME: *Stylaster elegans*
COMMON NAME: Elegant Hydrocoral
DISTRIBUTION: TI–WP; WT/S; WT/N
HABITAT: Coral reefs; rocky reefs

GENERAL WATER DEPTH: 3–120 m
(10–394 ft)
FOOD HABIT: Carnivorous: plankton
SIZE: Up to 230 mm (9 in) (colony height)
DESCRIPTION: Like all cnidarians, this
beautiful hydrocoral has nematocysts (stinging cells) to capture its prey, but they are not
as venomous as those of the fire corals and
have no effect on humans. A rather cryptic
species, the elegant hydrocoral lives under
ledges, in caves, and especially in surge or
current pipes and swim-throughs, as it prefers areas of maximum water movement.
Most colonies in shallow waters are relatively small, about 76 mm (3 in), compared
to larger ones in deeper waters. The small
predacious mollusc, *Pediculariona stylasteris*,
allied to the cowries, is often in residence.

Tubularia larynx

FAMILY: Tubulariidae
SCIENTIFIC NAME: *Tubularia larynx*
COMMON NAME: Solitary Hydroid; Oaten
Pipe Polyp
DISTRIBUTION: TI–WP; WT/S; CT/S;
CT/N
HABITAT: Coral reefs; rocky reefs
GENERAL WATER DEPTH: 3–30 m
(10–98 ft)
FOOD HABIT: Carnivorous: plankton
SIZE: 100 mm (4 in)
DESCRIPTION: This hydroid may be found
as a solitary polyp or in a group, in a wide
variety of habitats and micro-habitats. It has
been recorded on rocky reefs, coral reefs, the
backs of dead mollusc shells (*Haliotis*,
Pecten), on soft corals, gorgonians, pylons,
and house bricks. The genus itself is readily
recognisable due to the large naked solitary
polyp. It feeds on plankton and suspended
sediment. There is an association of this
hydroid with small amphipods which not
only live around the upper surface of the
polyp, but often sit in the centre around its
mouth, and in its gonophores.

Porpita porpita

FAMILY: Velellidae
SCIENTIFIC NAME: *Porpita porpita*
DISTRIBUTION: Cosmopolitan
HABITAT: Free floating
GENERAL WATER DEPTH: Surface waters
of the oceans
FOOD HABIT: Carnivorous
SIZE: Float up to about 80 mm
(3 in) in diameter
DESCRIPTION: This beautiful free-floating,
highly modified hydroid is related to *Velella*,
the By-the-wind sailor, and is often washed
ashore with it. The animal has a flat, horny,
cellular disc which supports it on the surface, with numerous short, club-shaped tentacles suspended from it, each with batteries
of powerful stinging cells which are essential
for the capture of its food. *Porpita* is a
member of the floating community of the
'blue layer' — the top few centimetres
(inches) of the ocean's surface; all the animals found there tend to be in tones of blue.
Continuous strong winds will cause these
animals to be washed ashore, along with
other members of this community. On hit-
ting the sand, however, the fragile tentacles
are broken off. Its stinging cells do not
appear to be harmful to humans.

FAMILY: Velellidae
SCIENTIFIC NAME: *Velella velella*
COMMON NAME: By-the-wind Sailor
DISTRIBUTION: Oceanic; TI–WP; WT/N;
WT/S; CT/S
HABITAT: Coastal waters; oceanic surface
waters
GENERAL WATER DEPTH: Surface waters
FOOD HABIT: Carnivorous: plankton
SIZE: 25 mm (1 in)
DESCRIPTION: Cosmopolitan in distribution,
by-the-wind sailors inhabit tropical and tem-
perate regions and those in between. Related
to hydroids, this species is a single animal
living out its entire life cycle on the surface
of the ocean. Very few are ever seen in their

Velella velella

jelly are conflicting with some reports of serious stinging and others of ineffectual contact. The author has been unable to induce stings from this sea jelly during repeated attempts. The occurrence of the mosaic sea jelly is mostly seasonal. It is host to the commensal shrimp, *Latreutes anoplonyx*, and in the southern Indian Ocean it is inhabited by juvenile mosaic leatherjackets, *Eubalichthys mosaicus*.

Cyanea capillata

natural habitat and it is not until they are washed ashore that they are noticed. They are named for their curious sail-like structures mounted diagonally in a wide S-shape across the length of the float. By-the-wind sailors have a very short life span and are not thought to live more than a month.

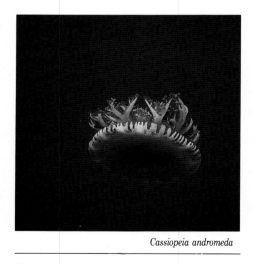

Cassiopeia andromeda

■ CLASS: Scyphozoa

FAMILY: Cassiopeidae
SCIENTIFIC NAME: *Cassiopeia andromeda*
COMMON NAME: Upside-down Sea Jelly
DISTRIBUTION: IWP
HABITAT: Intertidal sandy-mud flats; shallow water
GENERAL WATER DEPTH: Up to 5 m (16.4 ft)
FOOD HABIT: Carnivorous
SIZE: Bell up to 300 mm (11.8 in) in diameter
DESCRIPTION: The bell of this sea jelly tends to be flat on the top with mouth arms below it on which there are protruding bladders. These are filled with tiny symbiotic algae (zooxanthellae) and this probably explains why this animal is usually found lying upside down on the sandy bottom —

this position enabling the algae to photosynthesise much more effectively. Related species are commonly found in Florida and neighbouring seas. They inhabit mangrove areas and sea grass meadows. In Miami, Florida, *Cassiopeia* species may be seen in large numbers, including juveniles and adults, lying in protected inlets amongst the mangroves.

Catostylus mosaicus

FAMILY: Catostylidae
SCIENTIFIC NAME: *Catostylus mosaicus*
COMMON NAME: Mosaic Sea Jelly
DISTRIBUTION: WT/S; TI–WP
HABITAT: Open oceans; estuaries; embayments
GENERAL WATER DEPTH: Surface to 25 m (82 ft)
FOOD HABIT: Carnivorous: plankton
SIZE: 600 mm (2 ft)
DESCRIPTION: Colour is not always a good indication of the identity of this species as it exhibits several different colour forms ranging from brownish to blue or even white. Records of the stinging qualities of this sea

FAMILY: Cyaneidae
SCIENTIFIC NAME: *Cyanea capillata*
COMMON NAME: Lion's Mane Sea Jelly
DISTRIBUTION: TI–WP; WT/S; WT/N; CT/S; CT/N
HABITAT: Ocean waters
GENERAL WATER DEPTH: Surface to 10 m (33 ft)
FOOD HABIT: Carnivorous: plankton; fish
SIZE: 500 mm (19 in) (width)
DESCRIPTION: One of the largest sea jellies, the lion's mane is an open-ocean species which on occasion may reach a length of 2 m (6 ft) (tentacles). Although no fatalities resulting from its stings have been reported, a fully grown specimen of this species could well be capable of injuring an unprotected swimmer to the point of collapse. However, there seems little risk of this happening, as during winter months (when this sea jelly makes its appearance) most swimmers wear wetsuits as protection from the cold. As occurs with many other oceanic sea jellies, numbers of small pelagic fishes are often observed sheltering amongst the tentacles. At least one species of shrimp and an unknown species of angler fish live in association with this sea jelly.

FAMILY: Mastigiidae
SCIENTIFIC NAME: *Phyllorhiza punctata*
COMMON NAME: Spotted Sea Jelly
DISTRIBUTION: WT/S

Phyllorhiza punctata

Pelagia noctiluca

opaque white structures are gonads. These are more visible through the top of the sea jelly. Saucer jellies are either male or female.

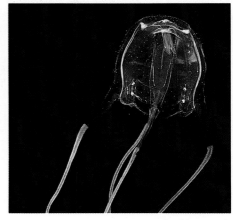

Carybdea rastoni

HABITAT: Estuaries; bays
GENERAL WATER DEPTH: Surface waters to 5 m (16 ft)
FOOD HABIT: Carnivorous: plankton
SIZE: 600 m (2 ft)
DESCRIPTION: Throughout the summer months huge flotillas of this species appear in estuaries, bays, lakes and rivers. The species is easily identified from its size and shape. Swimming close to the surface, the spotted sea jelly is able to support large colonies of zooxanthellae (microscopic algae) in its tissues, and these apparently are responsible for its dark brown colour. This species serves as a protective host for several species of juvenile fishes including jacks and yellowtail scads. Although reputed to sting, repeated attempts by the author to induce any reaction have failed. This sea jelly has oral arms or tentacles (these are distinct from peripheral tentacles).

FAMILY: Pelagiidae
SCIENTIFIC NAME: *Pelagia noctiluca*
COMMON NAME: Purple Stinger
DISTRIBUTION: CT/N; CT/S; WT/S: TI–WP
HABITAT: Open ocean; coastal waters
GENERAL WATER DEPTH: Surface to 10 m (33 ft)
FOOD HABIT: Carnivorous: plankton
SIZE: 100 mm (4 in) (width)
DESCRIPTION: Although small in size, the purple stinger may have tentacles over 1 m (3 ft) in length. These tentacles, as well as the oral lobes and even the bell, are studded with numerous nematocyst batteries. The purple stinger may be dark-brown or red on the top of the bell in some locations, and the oral lobes issuing from beneath the centre of the bell may be long or short depending on their state of contraction. During times of prolonged southerly winds or shore currents, large flotillas often enter estuaries.

FAMILY: Ulmaridae
SCIENTIFIC NAME: *Aurelia aurita*
COMMON NAME: Saucer Jelly, Moon Jelly or Common Sea Jelly
DISTRIBUTION: TI–WP; WT/S; CT/S; CT/N; WT/N
HABITAT: Inshore waters; oceanic waters
GENERAL WATER DEPTH: Surface to 10 m (33 ft)
FOOD HABIT: Carnivorous: plankton
SIZE: 200 mm (8 in) (width)
DESCRIPTION: The saucer jelly resembles a transparent saucer with four U-shaped white structures arranged equidistant from the centre. This jelly is generally around 120–150 mm (5–6 in) across the bell and often occurs in dense clusters close to the surface of the water. This species swims by alternate relaxation and contraction of its bell edges. The contractions force the animal through the water by pushing water away behind it. Beneath the bell is a squarish mouth which has four mouth-arms hanging down, one from each corner. There is also a network of fine canals radiating from the centre which distribute gastric juices and digested food. The four horseshoe–shaped

■ CLASS: Cubozoa

FAMILY: Carybdeidae
SCIENTIFIC NAME: *Carybdea rastoni*
COMMON NAME: Raston's Box-jelly
DISTRIBUTION: WT/S
HABITAT: Coastal waters
GENERAL WATER DEPTH: Surface to 20 m (66 ft)
FOOD HABIT: Carnivorous: plankton
SIZE: 150 mm (6 in)
DESCRIPTION: Very common during the summer months over much of its range, the box-jelly spends a certain amount of the day close to the bottom and is an active swimmer under natural conditions. Some specimens have pink tentacles and these are often seen before the transparent bell becomes apparent. As small as the box-jelly is, its sting can be very painful, raising a large weal which may take several days to subside. In the southern Indian Ocean hundreds of swimmers are stung during a single summer.

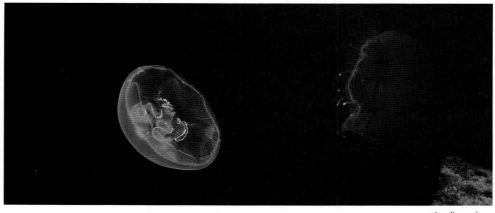

Aurelia aurita

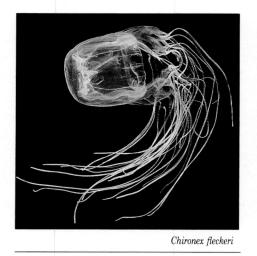

Chironex fleckeri

Antipathes sp.

mud in deeper water. Its food consists of plankton and possibly small fish, and feeding is generally carried out on incoming tides. The mauve-tipped tube anemone lives in a specially constructed slime tube buried deep in the sand or mud. The tube is made from mucus and special nematocysts secreted by the anemone, and can be over 300 mm (12 in) in length. The anemone lives in the tube but is not attached to it, and is able to retract into it rapidly. The nematocysts of this species are very feeble and are not capable of penetrating human skin. Nonetheless, the mauve-tipped tube anemone is highly predatory and will kill fish in an aquarium environment.

FAMILY: Chirodropidae
SCIENTIFIC NAME: *Chironex fleckeri*
COMMON NAME: Flecker's Box-jelly
DISTRIBUTION: TI–WP
HABITAT: Coastal waters
GENERAL WATER DEPTH: Surface to 20 m (66 ft)
FOOD HABIT: Carnivorous: plankton; fish
SIZE: 1 m (3 ft) (length)
DESCRIPTION: The largest and most important of the lethal cubomedusae, *Chironex fleckeri* has been responsible for the deaths of hundreds of people through its range. The majority of people stung have been swimming or wading in creeks, rivers, or shallow waters adjacent to mangrove swamps. Invariably the stings have occurred in the summer months during the equatorial wet season.

The bell of *Chironex fleckeri* is comprised of a smooth, translucent, jelly-like substance which is quite firm and can be lifted from the water without damage to the animal. At each of the four corners at the base of the bell is a protrusion called a pedalium. This species may have up to sixteen tentacles growing from each pedalium.

■ CLASS: Ceriantipatharia

FAMILY: Antipathidae
SCIENTIFIC NAME: *Antipathes* sp.
COMMON NAME: Black Coral
DISTRIBUTION: WT/S; CT/S; WT/N; CT/N
HABITAT: Rocky reefs
GENERAL WATER DEPTH: 15–80 m (49–263 ft)
FOOD HABIT: Carnivorous: plankton
SIZE: 1–2 m (3–6 ft)
DESCRIPTION: To the uninitiated, black coral should, in all situations, be black; and when its dead skeleton is out of the water, or a piece polished and set in a ring, it is. However, living black coral has a fine outer coating of living tissue over the branches and

stock. This may vary in colour depending on the species. Living specimens of southern black coral generally occur in deep water on rock faces, or drop-offs, where there is a good current flow. Southern black coral usually has several differing patterned forms of the clinging snake star, *Astrobrachion adhaerens*, entwined in its branches.

Cerianthus sp.

FAMILY: Cerianthidae
SCIENTIFIC NAME: *Cerianthus* sp.
COMMON NAME: Mauve-tipped Tube Anemone
DISTRIBUTION: WT/S
HABITAT: Sand; mud
GENERAL WATER DEPTH: 3–25 m (10–82 ft)
FOOD HABIT: Carnivorous: plankton
SIZE: 180 mm (7 in)
DESCRIPTION: The mauve-tipped tube anemone is without doubt the most photogenic and easily recognised form of tube anemone. Restricted in range to the waters of the southern Indian Ocean, it lives in clean sand in the shallows, down to soft silty

Parerythropodium membranaceum

■ CLASS: Alcyonaria

FAMILY: Alcyoniidae
SCIENTIFIC NAME: *Parerythropodium membranaceum*
COMMON NAME: Thin-skinned Soft Coral
DISTRIBUTION: WT/S; CT/S
HABITAT: Rocky reefs
GENERAL WATER DEPTH: 15–30 m (49–98 ft)
FOOD HABIT: Carnivorous: plankton
SIZE: 6 mm (0.2 in) (polyp width)
DESCRIPTION: A small, delicate, transparent species found throughout the South Pacific, this soft coral is more common than first realised. Due to its obscure size it is only easily recognised when there are sufficient numbers in one area for it to stand out. It occurs in unconnected groups of individual polyps which bud, forming five to six polyp colonies. Very often the thin-skinned soft coral is seen on the body of the solitary ascidian, *Herdmania momus*.

Sarcophyton glaucum

FAMILY: Alcyoniidae
SCIENTIFIC NAME: *Sarcophyton glaucum*
COMMON NAME: Grey Soft Coral
DISTRIBUTION: TI–WP; WT/S
HABITAT: Coral reefs
GENERAL WATER DEPTH: Low tide to 10 m (33 ft)
FOOD HABIT: Carnivorous: plankton
SIZE: 250 mm (10 in) (colony width)
DESCRIPTION: The genus *Sarcophyton* includes a large group of soft coral species inhabiting all tropical and some subtropical reefs. The grey soft coral is generally positioned on the tops of coral reefs in relatively shallow water. It is firm and leathery to touch and, when the polyps are retracted, has rather large, distinct, equidistant perforations in the upper surface. As in most forms of this genus the polyps are large and fairly distinct, and feed both day and night. While this genus can be identified in the field, species determination needs to be verified by spicule examination.

Sarcophyton trocheliophorum

FAMILY: Alcyoniidae
SCIENTIFIC NAME: *Sarcophyton trocheliophorum*
COMMON NAME: Soft Coral
DISTRIBUTION: TI–WP
HABITAT: Coral reefs
GENERAL WATER DEPTH: Low tide to 25 m (82 ft)
FOOD HABIT: Carnivorous: plankton
SIZE: 1 m (3 ft) (colony width)
DESCRIPTION: With an appearance reminiscent of nothing else on earth, the leather-like exterior of a colony of soft coral at low tide, with all its polyps retracted, is hardly likely to be considered as an animal by the uninitiated reef walker. When submerged by the incoming tide the polyps emerge from within the firm gelatinous tissue and feed on the rich planktonic 'soup' brought in by the rising waters.

Juncella fragilis

FAMILY: Ellisellidae
SCIENTIFIC NAME: *Juncella fragilis*
COMMON NAME: Fragile Sea-whip
DISTRIBUTION: TI–WP
HABITAT: Coral reefs
GENERAL WATER DEPTH: 5–40 m (16–131 ft)
FOOD HABIT: Carnivorous: plankton
SIZE: 1 m (3 ft) (colony)
DESCRIPTION: Found on tropical oceanic reefs, the fragile sea-whip also inhabits waters of shallow or medium depth, especially where tidal races occur close to mainland, island and reefs. At the more temperate extent of its range, colonies seem to prefer deeper water along the slopes of channels and sea floor. Throughout its distribution, the fragile sea-whip may be white, grey, or yellowish in colour, and the polyps are brown. It feeds at night and during the day on incoming tides. The commensal shrimp, *Hamadactylus noumeae*, has been recorded in association with this whip, and the small commensal clingfish, *Tenacigobius yongei*, is commonly encountered on it.

Heliopora coerulea

FAMILY: Helioporidae
SCIENTIFIC NAME: *Heliopora coerulea*
COMMON NAME: Blue Coral
DISTRIBUTION: TI–WP
HABITAT: Coral reefs
GENERAL WATER DEPTH: Low tide to 10 m (33 ft)
FOOD HABIT: Carnivorous: plankton
SIZE: 3 m (10 ft) (colony)
DESCRIPTION: In life, this species may range in external colouration from grey through to dark brown, though the skeleton is bright blue inside. Its form and blue colouration make it relatively easy to identify alive. The cream polyps are very small with eight pinnate tentacles similar to all soft corals. Blue coral is almost always found living in sheltered lagoonal shallows and the polyps may be extended day or night. Small gobiid fishes, *Pleurosicya* sp., live amongst the branches and Gardiner's doridoid nudibranch, *Doridoides gardineri*, is a resident predator.

Isis hippuris

FAMILY: Isididae
SCIENTIFIC NAME: *Isis hippuris*
COMMON NAME: Golden Sea-fan
DISTRIBUTION: TI–WP

HABITAT: Coral reefs
GENERAL WATER DEPTH: 3–25 m
(10–82 ft)
FOOD HABIT: Carnivorous: plankton
SIZE: 500 mm (20 in) (colony height)
DESCRIPTION: Sea-fans are also referred to
as gorgonians, a common name derived from
their scientific order, Gorgonacea. The colour
of this gorgonoid can vary from yellow
through to pink, but invariably the polyps
are golden yellow. The polyps are expanded
both day and night and feed on plankton. A
commensal shrimp and a gobiid fish,
Pleurosicya sp., have been recorded living on
this sea-fan. The fragile internal skeleton is
beautifully fluted and coloured black and
white.

Melitella sp.

FAMILY: Isididae
SCIENTIFIC NAME: *Melitella* sp.
COMMON NAME: Orange Sea-fan
DISTRIBUTION: TI–WP
HABITAT: Coral reefs
GENERAL WATER DEPTH: 5–30 m
(16–98 ft)
FOOD HABIT: Carnivorous: plankton
SIZE: Up to 2 m (6 ft) (colony)
DESCRIPTION: The orange sea-fan is fairly
common and is often observed in areas of
strong tidal influence. The colonies generally
grow on the sides of coral heads and along
channel slopes and bottoms. The orange sea-
fan always faces at right angles to the current flow, allowing the polyps to derive
maximum planktonic food intake from the
water. Feather stars often use this species as
a feeding platform, and the ovulid molluscs,
Pellasimnia semperi and *Phenacovolva* sp.,
are resident predators.

Mopsea australis

FAMILY: Isididae
SCIENTIFIC NAME: *Mopsea australis*
COMMON NAME: Southern Sea-fan
DISTRIBUTION: WT/S; CT/S
HABITAT: Rocky reefs
GENERAL WATER DEPTH: 20–60 m
(66–197 ft)
FOOD HABIT: Carnivorous: plankton
SIZE: 150 mm (6 in) (colony height)
DESCRIPTION: One of the most easily
recognised gorgonians in natural habitat, the
southern sea-fan has only two basic colour
variations—pink and yellow. The shape is a
good distinguishing characteristic as is the
peculiar pointed structure which occurs at
the tip of each frond. For reasons unknown,
the tips are white and without polyps. This
sea-fan generally appears on flat reefs, or on
the terraces below underwater cliffs. Two
unidentified crustacean species have been
recorded on the southern sea-fan, and the
small Rosewater's ovulid mollusc *Crenavolva
rosewateri*, is often observed as a resident
predator.

Mopsea encrinulata

FAMILY: Isididae
SCIENTIFIC NAME: *Mopsea encrinulata*
COMMON NAME: Fishbone Sea-fan
DISTRIBUTION: WT/S
HABITAT: Rocky reefs
GENERAL WATER DEPTH: 18–60 m
(59–197 ft)
FOOD HABIT: Carnivorous: plankton
SIZE: 30 mm (1.2 in) (colony height)
DESCRIPTION: A resident of deeper waters,
the fishbone sea-fan is rarely found above
the 20 m (66 ft) zone, where it lives on relatively low-profile reefs, or on terraces in both
coastal and offshore areas. Colour varies
from pink to yellow, but the shape of the
main stems and of the even, alternately positioned branches allows fairly simple field
identification. The fishbone sea-fan tends to
live at depth in low light conditions and is
rarely observed with its polyps retracted.
Although colonies may be sparsely distributed in the upper reaches of its depth zone,
it can be extremely common below 50–60 m
(165–197 ft).

Melithaea squamata

FAMILY: Melithaeidae
SCIENTIFIC NAME: *Melithaea squamata*
COMMON NAME: Squamose Sea-fan
DISTRIBUTION: TI–WP
HABITAT: Coral reefs
GENERAL WATER DEPTH: 35–80 m
(115–263 ft)
FOOD HABIT: Carnivorous: plankton
SIZE: 1 m (3 ft)
DESCRIPTION: Not often observed in waters
shallower than 20 m (66 ft), the squamose
sea-fan grows as an individual cluster of
branchlets which issue from a single main
stalk. The polyps are arranged in a definite
pattern and occur over the entire area. Like
all alcyonarians, the polyps have eight
pinnate tentacles. The colour is a fairly
stable criterion for identification as the
orange-brown pigmentation does not appear
to occur in other species of *Melithaea* which
overlap in distribution.

Mopsella ellisi

FAMILY: Melithaeidae
SCIENTIFIC NAME: *Mopsella ellisi*
COMMON NAME: Ellis' Sea-fan
DISTRIBUTION: WT/S; CT/S
HABITAT: Rocky coasts
GENERAL WATER DEPTH: 1–60 m
(3–197 ft)
FOOD HABIT: Carnivorous: plankton
SIZE: 1 m (3 ft) (colony height)
DESCRIPTION: Identification to genus level is
as much as can be done in the field of this
species, for it is similar in shape and habitat
to several other related species, and species
determination must be established by spicule
examination. Colour is not a useful identity
guide for Ellis' sea-fan as the author has
recorded some ten different colours and
colour combinations. The polyps of Ellis'
sea-fan may be seen out feeding both day
and night, tending to give the colony an overall furry look; when disturbed they are withdrawn. The predatory ovulid molluscs
Phenacovolva angasi, *Prosimnia semperi
semperi* and *Crenavolva rosewateri* are resident associates.

Dendronephthya mucronata

FAMILY: Nephtheidae
SCIENTIFIC NAME: *Dendronephthya
mucronata*
COMMON NAME: Bladed Soft Coral
DISTRIBUTION: TI–WP; WT/N; WT/S
HABITAT: Coral reefs
GENERAL WATER DEPTH: 5–40 m
(16–131 ft)
FOOD HABIT: Carnivorous: plankton
SIZE: 600 mm (2 ft) (colony)
DESCRIPTION: Soft corals do not have massive fused skeletons as do true corals. Soft
corals generally have skeletal spicules or
crystals of calcium carbonate which are not
fused together as they are in 'hard' corals, so
their colonies are flexible. These spicules are
embedded in their tissues. It is upon these
microscopic spicules that the entire scientific
taxonomy of this group is based. Although
scientific identification of living colonies in
the field is difficult, some genera can be
recognised by those familiar with the group.

Sarcoptylum sp.

FAMILY: Pennatulidae
SCIENTIFIC NAME: *Sarcoptylum* sp.
COMMON NAME: Black Sea-pen
DISTRIBUTION: WT/S
HABITAT: Sand
GENERAL WATER DEPTH: 15–25 m
(49–82 ft)
FOOD HABIT: Carnivorous: plankton
SIZE: 150 mm (6 in)
DESCRIPTION: As yet probably undescribed
(and thus potentially a new species), this
very distinctive sea-pen lives in small colon-
ies in bays and coastal inlets. First discov-

ered by the author in 1969, there appears to
be no colour variation within the colonies.
The polyps are extended in a feeding atti-
tude both day and night, and if unduly disturbed, the black sea-pen is able to retract
into the sand. At the time the black sea-pen
was discovered, the small, sand dwelling,
predatory nudibranch *Armina* sp. was found
feeding on it during rising tides.

Eunicella verrucosa

FAMILY: Plexauridae
SCIENTIFIC NAME: *Eunicella verrucosa*
COMMON NAME: Verrucose Sea-fan
DISTRIBUTION: WT/N
HABITAT: Rocky coasts
GENERAL WATER DEPTH: 10–200 m
(33–656 ft)
FOOD HABIT: Carnivorous: fine
zooplankton
SIZE: Colonies up to 300mm (11.8 in) high
DESCRIPTION: This sea-fan is endangered
by the collecting activities of divers. Its colonies are pale in colour ranging from white
through to pink. The branches occur at all
levels in the colony, which is almost two
dimensional. The small polyps on the ends
of the branches are arranged in two rows
(top and bottom, or left and right). In other
similar related species they may be arranged
all round. Each polyp has eight pinnate tentacles. These colonies grow orientated
towards the prevailing current so as to derive
the maximum benefit from suspended food
material. Similar related species occur in
other regions.

FAMILY: Primnoidae
SCIENTIFIC NAME: *Primnoella australasiae*
COMMON NAME: Southern Sea-whip
DISTRIBUTION: WT/S; CT/S
HABITAT: Rocky reefs
GENERAL WATER DEPTH: 20–270 m
(66–886 ft)
FOOD HABIT: Carnivorous: plankton
SIZE: 1 m (3 ft)

Primnoella australasiae

DESCRIPTION: Restricted to a deep water habitat, the southern sea-whip is generally found in groups. It is easy to identify because it is the only temperate South Pacific sea-whip of orange colouration which enters into areas shallower than 70 m (230 ft). The southern sea-whip has a beautifully sculptured surface made up of necklets of longitudinal beading. Alternate rows of large and small beading run the length of the whip. In deep water, or on overcast days in shallow water, the polyps can be observed extended. No predators are known as yet, but a new species of orange pipe fish has been discovered amongst the whips in South Pacific waters. The deep water anemone *Nemanthus* sp. is often attached to this sea-whip.

Subergorgia suberosa

FAMILY: Subergorgiidae
SCIENTIFIC NAME: *Subergorgia suberosa*
COMMON NAME: Corky Sea-fan
DISTRIBUTION: TI–WP
HABITAT: Coral reefs
GENERAL WATER DEPTH: 8–25 m (26–82 ft)
FOOD HABIT: Carnivorous: plankton
SIZE: 300 mm (12 in) (colony height)

DESCRIPTION: The corky sea-fan is fairly characteristic in shape and relatively easy to recognise to genus level under naturally occurring conditions. The structure is quite thin for a sea-fan, with the branches being very flat-sided. The polyps are white with eight pinnate tentacles and are situated along the inner periphery. There is a distinct central groove aligning the flat sides of the branches. The colour seems stable and in some cases the shrimp, *Hamodactylus noumeae*, is a resident commensal.

Carijoa multiflora

FAMILY: Telestidae
SCIENTIFIC NAME: *Carijoa multiflora*
COMMON NAME: Many-petalled Soft Coral
DISTRIBUTION: TI–WP; WT/S
HABITAT: Coral reefs; rocky coasts
GENERAL WATER DEPTH: 5–30 m (16–98 ft)
FOOD HABIT: Carnivorous: plankton
SIZE: 600 mm (2 ft) (colony height)

DESCRIPTION: The many-petalled soft coral grows in colonies of long stalks in areas of moderate tidal movement and is visually identified to genus by the shape of the stalk and the polyps. The polyps expand from extensions along the outside of the stalk and are always white. The eight pinnate tentacles tipped with trailing 'fishing line' extremities are characteristic of this genus, and being large and numerous contribute to the feeding efficiency of the entire colony, which has a rapid growth rate. The stalks of the many-petalled soft coral are typified by many apparent colour variations. The true colours are light pink, yellow, or white; the blacks, oranges, reds, greys, etc, are due to encrustations of the commensal sponge, *Clathria* sp.

Tubipora musica

FAMILY: Tubiporidae
SCIENTIFIC NAME: *Tubipora musica*
COMMON NAME: Organ Pipe Coral
DISTRIBUTION: TI–WP
HABITAT: Coral reefs
GENERAL WATER DEPTH: Low tide to 25 m (82 ft)
FOOD HABIT: Carnivorous: plankton
SIZE: 300 mm (12 in) (colony)

DESCRIPTION: Many people who visit tropical regions are amazed at bright red pieces of coral which are strewn around on and above the tidelines on beaches, cays and islands. When examined, this coral can be seen to be made up of small tubes held together and strengthened with horizontal plate-like supports. When dead, organ pipe coral is easy to identify, as there is really nothing else like it. However, in its living state, recognition can be a little more difficult unless one is familiar with the species. Organ pipe coral is not a true or hard coral. It belongs to the alcyonarians or soft corals, as indicated by its 8-sided polyp symmetry and pinnate tentacles. Organ pipe coral is one of the few soft corals that have the ability to construct colourful skeletons to house their polyps. All other soft corals have their tiny skeletal spicules of lime embedded free in their bodies and not fused rigidly, as in hard corals. These spicules help support the water-filled columns of their colonies. The polyps and skin of living organ pipe coral are grey or light green and very unobtrusive in comparison to the brilliant red of the skeleton. This species is common on intertidal reef flat areas and can also be found down to 25 m (82 ft).

Cavernularia obesa

FAMILY: Veretillidae
SCIENTIFIC NAME: *Cavernularia obesa*
COMMON NAME: Fat Sea-pen
DISTRIBUTION: WT/S
HABITAT: Sand; mud
GENERAL WATER DEPTH: 5–30 m
(16–98 ft)
FOOD HABIT: Carnivorous: plankton
SIZE: 250 mm (10 in) (colony height)
DESCRIPTION: The fat sea-pen is a soft-bottom dweller living in the protected waters of bays and estuaries. It generally occurs in groups in channels and areas of moderate current. Like other sea-pens, this species has the power to expand during feeding, or retract into the sand if conditions are adverse. Specimens may be seen in expanded positions both day and night, and this generally coincides with the incoming tide. The fat sea-pen is capable of producing light by bioluminescence. When stimulated, it gives off an eerie greenish-blue light which may stimulate colonies nearby to produce light. This may be a form of defence against predators. The sand-dwelling nudibranch, *Armina cyanea*, is a common predator.

Xenia peurtogalarea

FAMILY: Xenidae
SCIENTIFIC NAME: *Xenia peurtogalarea*
COMMON NAME: Small-crested Soft Coral
DISTRIBUTION: TI–WP
HABITAT: Coral reefs
GENERAL WATER DEPTH: Low tide to 20 m
(66 ft)
FOOD HABIT: Carnivorous: plankton
SIZE: 250 mm (10 in) (colony)
DESCRIPTION: *Xenia* as a genus is fairly easy to identify in the field from the characteristic blue-grey colours and the soft, long, waving, pinnately tentacled polyps. However, there are a number of species, and specific determination can only be established by spicule examination. The calcareous spicules of *Xenia* are small, thin, oval-shaped discs, unlike those of other families of alcyonarians which generally have elongated or spindle-shaped rods. Small-crested soft coral generally lives in shallow areas where water movement is maximal, such as the tops of micro-atolls and along sheltered reef crests. Predators are not known, but this genus is inhabited by the soft coral crab, *Caphyra laevis*, and the commensal shrimp, *Hippolyte commensalis*.

Montipora acquituberculata

■ CLASS: Zoantharia

FAMILY: Acroporidae
SCIENTIFIC NAME: *Montipora acquituberculata*
COMMON NAME: Uniform Coral
DISTRIBUTION: WT/S
HABITAT: Coral reefs; rocky reefs
GENERAL WATER DEPTH: 2–10 m (6–33 ft)
FOOD HABIT: Carnivorous: plankton
SIZE: Up to 8 m (26 ft) (colony width)
DESCRIPTION: A very common, often dominant species which prefers sheltered conditions on upper reef slopes and in lagoons. The pictured form is characteristic of the South-West Pacific deeper water form. In shallow or more exposed conditions, the cir-

cular plates are not as well developed. Colours range from brown to purple and, in general, the edges have a lighter margin.

Montipora capricornis

FAMILY: Acroporidae
SCIENTIFIC NAME: *Montipora capricornis*
COMMON NAME: Capricorn Coral
DISTRIBUTION: WT/S
HABITAT: Coral reefs
GENERAL WATER DEPTH: 5–15 m
(16–49 ft)
FOOD HABIT: Carnivorous: plankton
SIZE: 1–2 m (3–6 ft) (colony width)
DESCRIPTION: Undescribed till 1985, this striking species of coral is only known from the southern end of the Great Barrier Reef and around the Houtman Abrolhos Islands in the southern Indian Ocean, off Australia's west coast. Although the genus *Montipora* is very common, living in both sheltered and exposed situations on most tropical reefs, this species is more common in sheltered lagoon areas where it grows in spectacular terraces. Colours range from purple to brown or blue. Upright growth forms also exist.

FAMILY: Actiniidae
SCIENTIFIC NAME: *Actinia tenebrosa*
COMMON NAME: Waratah Sea-anemone
DISTRIBUTION: TI–WP; WTS; WT/N;
CT/S; EP
HABITAT: Coral reefs; rocky reefs
GENERAL WATER DEPTH: Low tide to 2 m
(6 ft)
FOOD HABIT: Carnivorous: plankton,
organic flotsam
SIZE: 70 mm (2.8 in) (width)
DESCRIPTION: The restricted habitat and stable colours of the waratah anemone make it one of the most easily identified intertidal anemones, for the dark red column and bright red tentacles hardly vary over the animal's entire distribution. This gregarious anemone generally inhabits vertical and

Actinia tenebrosa

horizontal cracks and crevices in rocks and tide pools, and is also found beneath stones. When left high and dry by the tide, it retains a certain amount of water within its body. This water helps the anemone to maintain its life functions while exposed to the dehydrating effects of sun and wind. The waratah sea-anemone is a viviparous species; the young are born through the mouth and emerge as minute replicas of the parents. Several other species of *Actinia* are found in different parts of the world; they are often very similar in appearance to the waratah sea-anemone.

Actinodendron plumosum

FAMILY: Actinodendridae
SCIENTIFIC NAME: *Actinodendron plumosum*
COMMON NAME: Stinging Anemone
DISTRIBUTION: TI–WP
HABITAT: Sandy flats
GENERAL WATER DEPTH: Intertidal— adjacent to coral reefs
FOOD HABIT: Carnivorous: invertebrates and small fish; plankton
SIZE: Up to 300 mm (11.8 in)
DESCRIPTION: The spectacular stinging anemone has multibranched tentacles which,

when seen underwater, form a dense mass of tiny branches, resembling a miniature pine tree, with the lower tentacles branching more widely and tapering towards the centre. The colour varies through brown and greyish-blue tones. At low tide it either withdraws completely into the sand, leaving a small hole about 40 mm (1.6 in) in diameter, or else lies flattened on the substrate. This is one anemone which should not on any account be handled, since the stinging cells of the tentacles are extremely toxic to humans.

Anemonia viridis

FAMILY: Actiniidae
SCIENTIFIC NAME: *Anemonia viridis*
COMMON NAME: Snakelocks Anemone
DISTRIBUTION: WT/N
HABITAT: Rocky shores, rocky coasts; seagrass beds
GENERAL WATER DEPTH: 0–20 m (0–66 ft)
FOOD HABIT: Carnivorous: planktonic and larger organisms
SIZE: Base up to 70 mm (2.8 in) in diameter; tentacle span may reach 180 mm (7.1 in)
DESCRIPTION: The base of the snakelocks anemone is not strongly adhesive; the column is very variable in height and may be taller than it is wide. It bears up to 200 flexible and sinuous tentacles which are rarely completely retracted. Green or grey-brown colours are a feature of this species which has two white lines running from opposite sides of the disc to the edges of the mouth. The tentacle tips are purple. This is a common intertidal anemone in warmer regions of the North-East Atlantic where it may be found attached to rocks, algae, or seagrasses. It frequently reproduces by longitudinal splitting; recently divided individuals may often be found crowded together and still showing signs of division in their irregular shapes.

Anthopleura xanthogrammica

FAMILY: Actiniidae
SCIENTIFIC NAME: *Anthopleura xanthogrammica*
DISTRIBUTION: CT/N; WT/N
HABITAT: Rocky shores; open bays; harbours
GENERAL WATER DEPTH: Intertidal
FOOD HABIT: Carnivorous: invertebrates and small fish; plankton
SIZE: Column up to 170 mm (6.7 in) in diameter and 300 mm (11.8 in) in height
DESCRIPTION: Found in rock pools and deep channels on rocky shores and attached to wharf pilings in harbours, the base of this anemone is wider than the column which is covered with irregular adhesive tubercles. The crown of tentacles is wider than the column, which is very firmly attached to the substrate. The tentacles, which are numerous, short and conical, are arranged in circles in a narrow band round the margin of the disc. There is great variation in colour of the different species of *Anthopleura*. In the Pacific species the column is green to brown, with greenish, blue, or white tentacles. Atlantic species have a pink-orange or yellow-green column with translucent tentacles mottled with pink, grey, green, or brown. In the giant green anemone, one of the most spectacular on the US Pacific coast, the brilliant green of animals growing in sunlight is due to green pigments in the skin and symbiotic algae (zooxanthellae) in the inner tissues. Nudibranchs, small snails and sea stars are known to prey on *Anthopleura*.

Dofleina armata

FAMILY: Actiniidae
SCIENTIFIC NAME: *Dofleina armata*
COMMON NAME: Armed Sea-anemone
DISTRIBUTION: TI–WP; WTN
HABITAT: Sand; mud
GENERAL WATER DEPTH: Low tide to 20 m (66 ft)
FOOD HABIT: Carnivorous: plankton, invertebrates, fish
SIZE: 300 mm (12 in)
DESCRIPTION: An extremely virulent species, this sea-anemone is a burrowing form which inhabits sand patches in seagrass meadows and the edges of channel slopes, and is also found living in the oozy black mud of harbour bottoms. Individuals may vary in the colour of their tentacles, but the body, or column, is always vertically striped.

Each tapering tentacle terminates in a slightly bulbous mauve tip. Huge groups of nematocyst batteries stud the soft flabby tentacles, and although it feeds mostly on plankton and suspended detritus, it is capable of killing invertebrates and small fish within seconds of contact. Its venomous nematocysts are harmful to humans.

Epiactis prolifera

FAMILY: Actiniidae
SCIENTIFIC NAME: *Epiactis prolifera*
COMMON NAME: Proliferating Anemone
DISTRIBUTION: CT/N
HABITAT: Rocky shores; open bays
GENERAL WATER DEPTH: Mid-tide to subtidal levels
FOOD HABIT: Carnivorous: zooplankton, small crustaceans
SIZE: Column up to about 50 mm (2 in) in diameter
DESCRIPTION: This anemone is common on and under rocks and on seaweeds and eelgrass. It has a low column which is highly variable in colour, ranging from orange to brown, green, blue, or grey, with brownish-red or dark green stripes. The life history is a unique and particularly interesting one; the tiny juveniles are often found attached round the base of the column, nearly all being females. Mature adults are hermaphrodite, producing both eggs and sperm, the latter fertilising the attached young females. Nudibranch and sea star species are known to prey on this anemone.

Phlyctenanthus australis

FAMILY: Actiniidae
SCIENTIFIC NAME: *Phlyctenanthus australis*
COMMON NAME: Southern Sea-anemone
DISTRIBUTION: WT/S; CT/S
HABITAT: Rocky reefs; high energy coasts
GENERAL WATER DEPTH: 1–35 m (3–115 ft)
FOOD HABIT: Carnivorous: plankton
SIZE: 100 mm (4 in) (width)
DESCRIPTION: The similarity in appearance and name of the southern sea-anemone and the swimming sea-anemone often lead to confusion amongst both professionals and amateurs. However, once the names have been sorted out, the animals themselves can be seen to be only superficially similar. The southern sea-anemone does not have the range of bright colours seen in the swimming sea-anemone, although the column may vary from dark-grey through to brown or orange. The southern sea-anemone is generally attached to a firm substrate rock, or reef, and unlike the swimming sea-anemone, it may be seen in the same position of attachment for months at a time. The Amboin shrimp, *Thor amboinensis*, is often seen as a resident commensal.

Phlyctenactis tuberculosa

FAMILY: Actiniidae
SCIENTIFIC NAME: *Phlyctenactis tuberculosa*
COMMON NAME: Swimming Sea-anemone
DISTRIBUTION: WT/S; CT/S
HABITAT: Rocky coasts; seagrass meadows; algae; rubble
GENERAL WATER DEPTH: 1–35 m (3–115 ft)
FOOD HABIT: Carnivorous: plankton
SIZE: 230 mm (9 in) (length)
DESCRIPTION: Although this species has an exceptional array of colours and colour combinations, it can usually be identified by the longitudinal wavy lines which are often prominent on the closely packed, balloon-like pustules which cover the entire surface of the column. The swimming sea-anemone has been given a rather misleading common name, for it hardly undergoes any motion one could relate to swimming, although it may lash from side to side on infrequent occasions. Like other anemones, it attaches to the substrate by way of an adhesive pad at the base of its column. As this sea-anemone prefers to attach to algae and seagrasses, it often moves from place to place by releasing its adhesive disc and rolling along with the current, or surge, until it finds a more suitable position. This species is apt to be nocturnal, although its brown tentacles may also be seen extended on overcast or dull days.

Urctina felina

FAMILY: Actiniidae
SCIENTIFIC NAME: *Urticina felina* (*Tealia felina*)
COMMON NAME: Dahlia Anemone
DISTRIBUTION: CT/N
HABITAT: Rocky shores
GENERAL WATER DEPTH: 0–100 m (0–328 ft)
FOOD HABIT: Carnivorous: plankton and larger organisms
SIZE: Shore-dwelling examples up to 120 mm (4.7 in) base diameter
DESCRIPTION: This species is frequently found on the lower shore, often in crevices and attached to rocks. Shore-dwelling specimens attach pieces of gravel to the warts on the column, but specimens from deeper water do not seem to exhibit this behaviour. *Urticina felina* has many adhesive warts, and 80–160 stout retractile tentacles. Its colours are variable and often blotchy; the column is frequently reddish with green markings and greyish warts, and the disc bluish grey. Frequently there are red marks around the mouth and among the bases of the tentacles. It should be noted that there is a closely related species, *Urticina eques*; its column is roughly as broad as it is high, and there may be 200 or more tentacles. In this species, the warts are not adhesive and are less conspicuous.

FAMILY: Agariciidae
SCIENTIFIC NAME: *Pachyseris rugosa*
COMMON NAME: Rugose Coral
DISTRIBUTION: TI–WP
HABITAT: Coral reefs
GENERAL WATER DEPTH: 5–10 m (16–33 ft)
FOOD HABIT: Carnivorous: plankton
SIZE: Up to 8 m (26 ft) (colony width)
DESCRIPTION: Owing to its distinctive concentric ridges and thin wavy growth form, rugose coral is one which is easy to identify in the field. It occurs throughout the Indo-Pacific to the Red Sea, where it inhabits reef crests, lagoons and reef slopes. Mostly seen

Pachyseris rugosa

as plate-like aggregations, this species also grows in short, contorted branching forms, but these are usually seen in conjunction with plate formations. Colour seems to be fairly stable and tends to range from grey to cream, and light brown. Despite a fragile look, the thin branches are extremely strong. This coral's polyps do not appear to be expanded during the hours of daylight or evening.

Euphyllia ancora

FAMILY: Caryophylliidae
SCIENTIFIC NAME: *Euphyllia ancora*
COMMON NAME: Anchor Coral

DISTRIBUTION: TI–WP
HABITAT: Coral reefs; rocky reefs
GENERAL WATER DEPTH: 1–30 m (3–98 ft)
FOOD HABIT: Carnivorous: plankton
SIZE: Up to 1 m (3 ft) (colony width)
DESCRIPTION: Although corals of this genus are found on many tropical coral reefs throughout the world, they are uncommon in comparison to other genera such as *Acropora* (staghorn corals) and *Lobophyllia* (brain corals). However, on some of the shallow reefs along the Norfolk Ridge (which stretches from New Caledonia to New Zealand), particularly around Norfolk Island, this coral is by far the most common species. It is one of the few coral species that is taxonomically separated from its nearest relatives by the shape of its tentacles.

Corynactis australis

FAMILY: Corallimorphidae
SCIENTIFIC NAME: *Corynactis australis*
COMMON NAME: Southern Jewel Anemone
DISTRIBUTION: WT/S; CT/S
HABITAT: Rocky reefs; rocky shores
GENERAL WATER DEPTH: Low tide to 60 m (197 ft)
FOOD HABIT: Carnivorous: plankton
SIZE: 20 mm (0.8 in) (single polyp width)
DESCRIPTION: One of the most visually exciting sights underwater is the wall of a drop-off or cave smothered in masses of southern jewel anemones. The brilliant colours, contrasted by the small white club-tipped tentacles, make a spectacular array. Most of those observed tend to be pink, mauve, or red. Intertidally, the southern jewel anemone may be found beneath stones or ledges at the extreme low-tide level, or in pools. Subtidally it prefers shady rocky faces that are away from the sun's rays, the roofs of caves, on wrecks, or beneath ledges. In the turbid water of estuaries it may grow on vertical rock faces, ropes, anchors, or jetty piles. It is able to colonise large areas by asexual division of the polyps.

Balanophyllia bairdiana

FAMILY: Dendrophylliidae
SCIENTIFIC NAME: *Balanophyllia bairdiana*
COMMON NAME: Baird's Solitary Coral
DISTRIBUTION: WT/S
HABITAT: Rocky reefs
GENERAL WATER DEPTH: 10–50 m
(33–164 ft)
FOOD HABIT: Carnivorous: plankton
SIZE: 30 mm (1.2 in)
DESCRIPTION: This is a solitary (non-colonial) coral which may occur in groups in the open, beneath ledges and in caves, especially on cliff faces, or along the edges of drop-offs. The colour of the column is generally white, with a fluorescent tinge of purple, blue, orange, or red around the mouth (caused by bacteria living in the tissues). The tentacles are transparent, and large nematocyst batteries stud each tapering tentacle which terminates in a slightly bulbous tip.

Tubastrea faulkneri

FAMILY: Dendrophylliidae
SCIENTIFIC NAME: *Tubastrea faulkneri*
COMMON NAME: Faulkner's Coral
DISTRIBUTION: TI–WP; WT/S; EP
HABITAT: Coral reefs; rocky coasts

GENERAL WATER DEPTH: 3–30 m
(10–98 ft)
FOOD HABIT: Carnivorous: plankton
SIZE: 12 mm (0.5 in) (polyp width)
DESCRIPTION: Generally found in small, compact clumps of 150 mm (6 in) to 200 mm (8 in), Faulkner's coral lives on the ceilings of caves, overhangs or ledges, on rock faces, on low-profile horizontal reefs, and even on rubble bottom where there is a good current flow. The forms closer to the equator are similar in colour to those pictured, but those in more temperate waters do not always have the intense yellow polyps of their northern relatives. Resident predators on Faulkner's coral are the golden wentletrap shell, *Epitonium billeeanum*, and the golden *Phestilla* nudibranch, *Phestilla melanobranchia*.

Favia favus

FAMILY: Faviidae
SCIENTIFIC NAME: *Favia favus*
COMMON NAME: Honeycomb Coral
DISTRIBUTION: TI–WP
HABITAT: Coral reefs
GENERAL WATER DEPTH: 3–20 m
(10–66 ft)
FOOD HABIT: Carnivorous: plankton
SIZE: 300m (12 in) (colony width)
DESCRIPTION: Almost all the genera and species of corals belonging to the family Faviidae are termed honeycomb corals. However, in *Favia* and other genera of this family (such as Plesiastrea), the individual polyps are separated from their neighbours, so that each coralite has a separate outer wall. In other corals, neighbouring polyps are fused together with a common wall. At the present time identification to species level within this group can only be determined by an expert. This species varies in colour, from red to green.

Plesiastrea versipora

FAMILY: Faviidae
SCIENTIFIC NAME: *Plesiastrea versipora*
COMMON NAME: Versified Coral
DISTRIBUTION: WT/S; CT/S
HABITAT: Rocky reefs; rocky shores
GENERAL WATER DEPTH: Low tide to 60 m
(197 ft)
FOOD HABIT: Carnivorous: plankton
SIZE: Up to 3 m (10 ft) (colony width)
DESCRIPTION: Preferring coastal environments in sheltered conditions, most versified coral colonies in shallow waters are small. However, in deeper waters down to 40 m (131 ft) they grow in sheets over 2 m (6 ft) in width and specimens have been trawled up to 3 m (10 ft) in diameter from deeper waters. Some older colonies have been shown to measure up to 200 mm (8 in) in thickness with generations of living polyps growing on successive older skeletal material. Colours vary from brown to bright green.

Heliofungia actiniformis

FAMILY: Fungiidae
SCIENTIFIC NAME: *Heliofungia actiniformis*
COMMON NAME: Active Mushroom Coral
DISTRIBUTION: TI–WP
HABITAT: Coral reefs

GENERAL WATER DEPTH: 1–20 m (3–66 ft)
FOOD HABIT: Carnivorous: plankton
SIZE: 230 mm (9 in)
DESCRIPTION: All species within this genus are solitary, made up of a single giant polyp. The active mushroom coral has long, waving tentacles reminiscent of some species of sea-anemones. Each tentacle terminates in a yellow or white tip. Colour varies between brown and khaki through to green, with the flesh in the mouth area being striped with yellow. The tentacles are extended both day and night and the shrimp *Periclimenes kororensis* is often resident in some locations. This species is mobile as an adult, moving along by using tentacular movement.

Fungia echinata

FAMILY: Fungiidae
SCIENTIFIC NAME: *Fungia echinata*
COMMON NAME: 'Hedgehog Mushroom Coral
DISTRIBUTION: TI–WP
HABITAT: Coral reefs
GENERAL WATER DEPTH: 1–25 m (3–82 ft)
FOOD HABIT: Carnivorous: plankton
SIZE: 250 mm (10 in)
DESCRIPTION: A distinctive, free-living, solitary coral, the hedgehog mushroom coral is a shallow water dweller. It is not common, nor does it seem to live in groups as other mushroom corals do. Colour appears to be stable throughout its range, varying only in shades of brown. It can be distinguished from other elongated, free-living corals by its round extremities and the serrated edges on the radial plates of its corallite. The polyps of this species are small and rarely expand during the day.

Sandalolitha robusta

FAMILY: Fungiidae
SCIENTIFIC NAME: *Sandalolitha robusta*
COMMON NAME: Robust Basket Coral
DISTRIBUTION: TI–WP
HABITAT: Coral reefs
GENERAL WATER DEPTH: 10–25 m (33–82 ft)
FOOD HABIT: Carnivorous: plankton
SIZE: 750 mm (30 in)
DESCRIPTION: The robust basket coral occurs on reef slopes, terraces and in channels and is readily identified by its distinctive shape and pattern. It lies unattached on the substrate and when inverted, resembles a basket. The structure is comprised of many individuals polyps living in a colony which grows by adding to the outer rim. A number of animals have been discovered living in close association with this coral, including a small undetermined species of shrimp and an unidentified brittle star. Small clingfish often utilise the coral's underside to deposit their eggs.

Adamsia sp.

FAMILY: Hormathiidae
SCIENTIFIC NAME: *Adamsia* sp.
COMMON NAME: Hermit Crab Anemone
DISTRIBUTION: TI–WP

HABITAT: Coral reefs; rocky reefs
GENERAL WATER DEPTH: 2–15 m (6–49 ft)
FOOD HABIT: Carnivorous: plankton
SIZE: 20 mm (0.8 in)
DESCRIPTION: The hermit crab anemone forms symbiotic relationships with either several species or one selected species of hermit crab and its shell (depending on the individual anemone). The anemones on its shell may protect the hermit crab from predators, while the anemones benefit from the rather messy feeding habits of the hermit crab. This hermit crab with its associated anemones lives beneath rocks and coral during the day, coming out to feed during the night. When disturbed, the anemone ejects large amounts of pink nematocyst-laden threads called acontia which protect the anemone and its host.

Calliactis parasitica

FAMILY: Hormathiidae
SCIENTIFIC NAME: *Calliactis parasitica*
COMMON NAME: Parasitic Anemone
DISTRIBUTION: WT/N
HABITAT: Rocky bottoms; sandy bottoms
GENERAL WATER DEPTH: 0–60 m (0–197 ft)
FOOD HABIT: Carnivorous: plankton carrion and larger organisms
SIZE: Base up to 80 mm (3.1 in); height up to 100 mm (3.9 in)
DESCRIPTION: Association with hermit crabs, *Dardanus* spp. and *Pagurus* spp., is typical of this species. The column lacks warts but is tough in texture and has a granular appearance. When the anemone is disturbed, fine defensive threads are emitted from minute holes at the base of the column just above where it attaches to the substrate. It is pale yellow-brown and spotted with darker brown or reddish markings which tend to merge into vertical stripes. There are many cream tentacles—up to 700 in a larger specimen. The anemone helps to defend the crab against predators and probably benefits from food that the crab disperses while feeding.

Aulactis muscosa

FAMILY: Memarthidae
SCIENTIFIC NAME: *Aulactis muscosa*
COMMON NAME: Speckled Sea-anemone
DISTRIBUTION: WT/S; CT/S
HABITAT: Rocky reefs
GENERAL WATER DEPTH: Low tide to 1 m (3 ft)
FOOD HABIT: Carnivorous: plankton and other small animals
SIZE: 120 mm (4.7 in) (width)
DESCRIPTION: The speckled sea-anemone is generally seen at mid-tide level on both sheltered and exposed coasts. It seems to prefer fault lines and cracks in rocks where there is a certain amount of runoff and where accumulations of sand and shell grit occur. This species is also found around the edges of rock pools. The column is a dirty-white colour, with brown, red, green, or black flecks scattered over its surface. These specks are often hidden by the speckled sea-anemone's habit of attaching shell grit and sand to its body, another stable field identification feature. This behaviour, and the presence of opaque white markings along the top edge of the column and the outer tentacles, camouflage the anemone within its chosen habitat.

Metridium senile

FAMILY: Metridiidae
SCIENTIFIC NAME: *Metridium senile*
DISTRIBUTION: G/N–WT/N
HABITAT: Rocky shores
GENERAL WATER DEPTH: Lower intertidal to 3 m (10 ft)
FOOD HABIT: Carnivorous: plankton and small invertebrates
SIZE: Subtidally up to 250 mm (9.8 in) in diameter and 500 mm (19.7 in) in height
DESCRIPTION: This widely distributed anemone is found on wharf pilings, floats, rocks, breakwaters and jetties. It occurs in several colour varieties, from white or cream to orange, tan and brown. It is attached by an adhesive base, and has a smooth column and a crown of very numerous, short, slender tentacles which almost cover the oral disc. Sometimes dense aggregations of small anemones occur in the lower intertidal. Much larger solitary anemones are found subtidally. Long threads (acontia), filled with stinging cells, may be shot out through the mouth and the 'holes' (cinclides) in the body wall if the anemone is roughly handled. It is temperature tolerant and also survives in brackish water. Nudibranches and starfish are known to prey on *Metridium*.

Lobophyllia sp.

FAMILY: Mussidae
SCIENTIFIC NAME: *Lobophyllia* sp.
COMMON NAME: Brain Coral
DISTRIBUTION: TI–WP
HABITAT: Coral reefs
GENERAL WATER DEPTH: Low tide to 25 m (82 ft)
FOOD HABIT: Carnivorous: plankton
SIZE: Up to 3 m (10 ft) (colony width)
DESCRIPTION: Commonly seen on intertidal reef flats and in shallow lagoons, the most impressive brain corals are found along the reef front slopes and in deeper lagoons and channels. Relatively easy to identify to genus in the field, specific identification requires

taxonomic study of the skeleton. Colours of living tissue may be green, yellow, or red. The corallites are large and separated.

Scolymia australis

FAMILY: Mussidae
SCIENTIFIC NAME: *Scolymia australis*
COMMON NAME: Green Solitary Coral
DISTRIBUTION: WT/S; CT/S
HABITAT: Rocky reefs
GENERAL WATER DEPTH: 3–50 m (10–164 ft)
FOOD HABIT: Carnivorous: plankton
SIZE: 30 mm (1.2 in)
DESCRIPTION: Easy recognisable in its natural habitat, the green solitary coral shows little colour variation. Although this species seems to prefer oceanic waters, it is also found in bays and harbours. Observation in shallow waters (5–10 m (16–33 ft)) shows that the green solitary coral settles in widely spaced positions, whereas in deeper waters (30–50 m (98–164 ft)) larvae often settle in close vicinity to one another and may almost be touching. The bright green polyps are not generally extended during daylight hours and, like most other corals, this species feeds mostly on plankton. The only known predator is the admirable coral shell, *Coralliophila mira*.

FAMILY: Nemanthidae
SCIENTIFIC NAME: *Nemanthus* sp.
COMMON NAME: Wandering Sea-anemone
DISTRIBUTION: TI–WP; WT/S
HABITAT: Coral reefs; rocky reefs; coastal waters
GENERAL WATER DEPTH: 5–60 m (16–197 ft)
FOOD HABIT: Carnivorous: plankton
SIZE: 60 mm (2.4 in) (width)
DESCRIPTION: There are a number of colour variations of wandering sea-anemones, which inhabit shallow tropical reefs and the deeper waters of the southern oceans. These sea-anemones attach to sea-whips, hydroids and black corals, often in large numbers. Some are striped, some are spotted and others are

Nemanthus sp.

be more prolific closer to the equator. The colony itself is rather nondescript, contrasting with the delicately structured branches and the unique bristle appearance of the corallite rims. Colours range from green through to brown and grey.

Pocillopora damicornis

Seriatopora hystrix

pure white. Specific colour forms generally congregate together, possibly because of repeated divisions of a single original coloniser. These anemones are of tropical origin, the larvae being brought south by currents. They settle, grow to adult size, and then virtually disappear. Although they may be found in similar places over a period of years, they do not necessarily appear on the same reefs, or territory, over concurrent years.

Acrhelia horresens

FAMILY: Oculinidae
SCIENTIFIC NAME: *Acrhelia horresens*
COMMON NAME: Bristle Coral
DISTRIBUTION: TI–WP
HABITAT: Coral reefs
GENERAL WATER DEPTH: Low tide to
  15 m (49 ft)
FOOD HABIT: Carnivorous: plankton
SIZE: 1 m (3 ft) (colony width)
DESCRIPTION: Preferring sheltered conditions in reef-flat tide pools and slopes, bristle coral is one of the few species of colonial corals which is relatively easy to identify in the field. Although it is found at the temperate limits of coral reefs, it appears to

FAMILY: Pocilloporidae
SCIENTIFIC NAME: *Pocillopora damicornis*
COMMON NAME: Warty Pocillopora Coral
DISTRIBUTION: TI–WP; WT/S
HABITAT: Coral reefs; rocky reefs;
  mangrove swamps
GENERAL WATER DEPTH: Low tide to
  25 m (82 ft)
FOOD HABIT: Carnivorous: plankton
SIZE: 400 mm (16 in) (colony)
DESCRIPTION: Extremely common throughout its range, this species appears to thrive in a range of habitats and temperatures. The polyps themselves are quite small and give the colony a furry look when they are extended. Colours can vary, but most individuals are brown, white, yellow, pink, or deep mauve. Very often the polyp tentacles appear green. When withdrawn, the polyp corallites appear as miniature black circles. Almost every colony is inhabited by commensal crabs or shrimps. The presence of gall crabs is typical in Hawaii.

FAMILY: Pocilloporidae
SCIENTIFIC NAME: *Seriatopora hystrix*
COMMON NAME: Fragile Coral
DISTRIBUTION: TI–WP
HABITAT: Coral reefs
GENERAL WATER DEPTH: 1–20 m (3–66 ft)
FOOD HABIT: Carnivorous: plankton
SIZE: 400 mm (16 in) (colony)
DESCRIPTION: Found in a variety of colours from yellow through to pinks and browns, the fragile coral generally lives in sheltered shallow waters along reef edges to depths of 8 m (26 ft). It grows in small clumps of

250–500 mm (10–20 in) and is fairly easily identified. This species is very common throughout its range and is favoured by the small female gall crab, *Hapalocarcinus marsupialis*. Many galls of this crustacean can be observed within the coral clumps.

Porites lutea

FAMILY: Poritidae
SCIENTIFIC NAME: *Porites lutea*
COMMON NAME: Yellow Porites Coral
DISTRIBUTION: TI–WP
HABITAT: Coral reefs
GENERAL WATER DEPTH: Low tide to 10 m
  (33 ft)
FOOD HABIT: Carnivorous: plankton
SIZE: 2 m (6 ft) (colony width)
DESCRIPTION: *Porites* corals are amongst the longest living life forms on earth; some colonies are estimated to be 1000 years old. Yellow porites coral is a very common species inhabiting shallow lagoons and back reefs throughout many tropical reef systems. In intertidal areas it forms large, round, flat, massive growths in which the outside growing edges are raised higher than the inner dead centre. These are commonly termed micro-atolls. For all their immense size

Porites corals are very porous and light in weight in comparison with their appearance. The corallite has five tall radii, recognisable underwater.

Astrangia woodsi

FAMILY: Rhizangiidae
SCIENTIFIC NAME: *Astrangia woodsi*
COMMON NAME: Wood's Coral
DISTRIBUTION: TI–WP; WT/S
HABITAT: Coastal coral reefs; rocky reefs
GENERAL WATER DEPTH: Low tide to 30 m (98 ft)
FOOD HABIT: Carnivorous: plankton
SIZE: 6 mm (0.2 in) (corallite)
DESCRIPTION: While most true corals have no definite colours in their skeletons, there are some exceptions, and this is one of them. The dark blue-black skeleton of this coral can be seen through the transparent flesh and, as there are no other similar corals, this feature allows easy identification. Wood's coral is a colonial species, generally found growing in small clumps 50–100 mm (2–4 in) in size. It lives in areas of good current flow and seems to be more prolific on horizontal rock-face terraces adjacent to channels, or in deeper water. This species fares exceptionally well in marine aquariums, as do many small temperate water coral colonies. One colony kept alive by the author over a two-year period grew very slowly in comparison with reef-building species.

FAMILY: Rhizangiidae
SCIENTIFIC NAME: *Culicia tenella*
COMMON NAME: Little Coral
DISTRIBUTION: WT/S; CT/S
HABITAT: Rocky reefs
GENERAL WATER DEPTH: Low tide to 60 m (197 ft)
FOOD HABIT: Carnivorous: plankton
SIZE: 7 mm (0.3 in) (corallite)
DESCRIPTION: Although colonial, its polyps

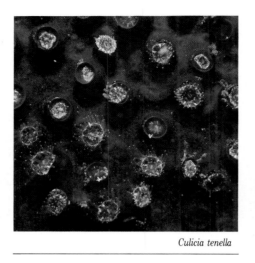

Culicia tenella

are widely separated. It lives on rock faces, the ceilings of caves, under ledges, on low-profile reefs, and even beneath stones. Unlike other corals, the little coral does not always show the partitioning as displayed in this photograph. Colours may be orange, brown, green, mauve, red, or yellow; these are translucent colours rather than opaque ones. Predators in the field include the little southern coral shell, *Liniaxis sertata*, and the strawberry coral shell, *Rhombothais arbutum*.

Anthothoe albocincta

FAMILY: Sagartiidae
SCIENTIFIC NAME: *Anthothoe albocincta*
COMMON NAME: White-striped Sea-anemone
DISTRIBUTION: WT/S; CT/S
HABITAT: Rocky reefs
GENERAL WATER DEPTH: Low tide to 40 m (131 ft)
FOOD HABIT: Carnivorous: plankton
SIZE: 40 mm (1.5 in) (across)
DESCRIPTION: Variable in colour throughout its range, this species is one of the commonest subtidal sea anemones in the South-East Pacific. Although the colours may range from green to orange, the white striping on the

body remains fairly constant. It is generally found in colonies. The white-striped sea-anemone can be harmful to humans. When molested, this sea-anemone shoots out white threads called acontia which are covered with stinging nematocysts. These cause deep-seated blisters which may form small ulcers, especially in sensitive areas such as wrists.

Haliplanella lineata

FAMILY: Sagartiidae
SCIENTIFIC NAME: *Haliplanella lineata*
COMMON NAME: Orange-striped anemone
DISTRIBUTION: Cosmopolitan
HABITAT: Open bays
GENERAL WATER DEPTH: Intertidal
FOOD HABIT: Carnivorous: small crustaceans and annelid worms
SIZE: 20–30 mm (0.8–1.2 in) in diameter.
DESCRIPTION: A common Japanese species, the orange-striped anemone is believed to have been introduced to the Pacific coast of the US on oysters, since it is found at or near places where Japanese oysters have been introduced. However, an anemone thought to be identical with this species is found on the Atlantic coast of the US as well as in the North Sea and Mediterranean. It is dark green in colour with vertical orange stripes on the column and delicate grey-green retractile tentacles.

FAMILY: Siderastreidae
SCIENTIFIC NAME: *Coscinaraea marshae*
COMMON NAME: Marsh's Coral
DISTRIBUTION: WT/S
HABITAT: Rocky reefs
GENERAL WATER DEPTH: 10–40 m (33–131 ft)
FOOD HABIT: Carnivorous: plankton
SIZE: 250 mm (10 in) (colony width)
DESCRIPTION: Endemic to the southern Indian Ocean, Marsh's coral often occurs in aggregations, and it is possible to see up to

Coscinaraea marshae

fifteen colonies within a small area of reef. Named in honour of Loisette Marsh, curator of marine invertebrates at the Western Australian Museum, this species has raised concentric ridges which normally run parallel to the perimeter of the flat plate-like colony. Marsh's coral is usually found in deeper water, and its brown colour varies little over its range. The white, brown, or yellow polyps are not usually seen expanded during the day. No associates or predators have so far been reported.

Radianthus ritteri

FAMILY: Stoichactiidae
SCIENTIFIC NAME: *Radianthus ritteri*
COMMON NAME: Ritter's Sea-anemone
DISTRIBUTION: TI-WP
HABITAT: Coral reefs
GENERAL WATER DEPTH: 5–15 m (16–49 ft)
FOOD HABIT: Carnivorous: plankton
SIZE: 1 m (3 ft) (width)
DESCRIPTION: Ritter's sea-anemone is one of the largest single-structured tropical anemones. It grows to over 1 m (3 ft) in diameter and is generally seen in areas of relatively strong water movement. Usually preferring a subtidal habitat, it lives along the fringes and slopes of coral reefs. The column is mostly a dark orange-brown and the tentacles range from bright green to greenish black. Although records show that Ritter's sea-anemone plays host to several species of anemone fish throughout its range, the Barrier Reef anemone fish, *Amphiprion akindynos*, seems to be the most common associate in the Pacific region. A number of species of commensal shrimps of the genus *Periclimenes* also inhabit its tentacles and column.

Radianthus sp.

FAMILY: Stoichactiidae
SCIENTIFIC NAME: *Radianthus* sp.
COMMON NAME: Radiant Sea-anemone
DISTRIBUTION: TI-WP; WT/S
HABITAT: Coral reefs; rocky reefs
GENERAL WATER DEPTH: 5–40 m (16–131 ft)
FOOD HABIT: Carnivorous: plankton
SIZE: 230 mm (9 in)
DESCRIPTION: Very common in some areas of the South-West Pacific, the radiant sea-anemone is more prevalent in waters around continental islands than on open ocean reefs. Similar to most others within its family, it has a very large disc area in comparison to its short tentacles. It is insensitive to touch and is a plankton and detritus feeder. Within its range the colour is fairly stable and most specimens observed are solitary or in small groups, rarely touching. The green flesh colour is caused by the presence of minute symbiotic algae growing in the tissues. A number of crustaceans have been found in association with this anemone: the shrimps, *Thor amboinensis* and *Periclimenes* sp., and the commensal crabs, *Lissocarcinus* sp. and *Petrolisthes* sp.

Stichodactyla gigantea

FAMILY: Stoichactiidae
SCIENTIFIC NAME: *Stichodactyla gigantea*
COMMON NAME: Giant Anemone
DISTRIBUTION: TI-WP
HABITAT: Seagrass meadows; sandflats; coral reefs
GENERAL WATER DEPTH: Low tide to 10 m (33 ft)
FOOD HABIT: Carnivorous: plankton
SIZE: 500 mm (20 in) (width)
DESCRIPTION: For all its huge size this species has very short tentacles. It is generally found in groups and in some areas may occur over wide expanses. Although this anemone's size is formidable, it is not venomous to humans. It has many associates, and in different locations shrimps, crabs and fish may be found as commensals. In the West Pacific the species appears to be much more common in coastal waters than on outer barrier reefs.

FAMILY: Zoanthidae
SCIENTIFIC NAME: *Palythoa heideri*
COMMON NAME: Heider's Zoanthid
DISTRIBUTION: WT/S; TI-WP
HABITAT: Rocky reefs
GENERAL WATER DEPTH: 5–10 m (16–33 ft)
FOOD HABIT: Carnivorous: plankton
SIZE: 300 mm (1.2 in) (colony)
DESCRIPTION: Zoanthids are mostly colonial and are intermediate in structure between anemones and corals. They feed on plankton and suspended sediment, and the polyps are not always as sensitive to touch as those of anemones or coral polyps. Heider's zoanthid has one of the largest polyps of its family, reaching a size of 45 mm (1.8 in). It ranges in colour from green to brown, and generally

Palythoa heideri

Zoanthus robustus

tinctive red spot at one end and red lines radiate out to the edge of the tentacles. More than eight different species of sponges have been noted as hosts. This zoanthid is an unknown species as are many other subtidal zoanthids which occur quite commonly in the waters of the South Pacific.

occurs in shallow water on reefs where there is continual surge. Although the polyps in this species appear well separated, they are all connected at the base.

Parazoanthus sp.

FAMILY: Zoanthidae
SCIENTIFIC NAME: *Parazoanthus* sp.
COMMON NAME: Yellow Commensal Zoanthid
DISTRIBUTION: WT/S; CT/S
HABITAT: Rocky reefs
GENERAL WATER DEPTH: 10–60 m (33–197 ft)
FOOD HABIT: Carnivorous: plankton
SIZE: 300 mm (12 in)
DESCRIPTION: The yellow commensal zoanthid belongs to a large group of zoanthids which are commensal on various species of sponges. The yellow commensal zoanthid is readily recognised in its natural habitat. The mouth of each polyp has a dis-

FAMILY: Zoanthidae
SCIENTIFIC NAME: *Zoanthus robustus*
COMMON NAME: Robust Zoanthid
DISTRIBUTION: WT/S
HABITAT: Rocky reefs
GENERAL WATER DEPTH: 1–25 m (3–82 ft)
FOOD HABIT: Carnivorous: plankton
SIZE: 50 mm (2 in) (individuals); 1 m (3 ft) (colony)
DESCRIPTION: The robust zoanthid is generally observed in large colonies in areas of low profile rocky reef at the merge between sand and reef edge. It is also seen in sandy hollows, between or amongst reefs. The rock surface the colony is attached to is almost always hidden beneath sand. Preferring exposed situations, these sausage-like zoanthids are not often seen with their tentacles extended during the day. Colour ranges from dark steely grey with small white specks covering the body, to greenish yellow. Minute commensal sea anemones have been photographed living on the surface of the robust zoanthid, but it is likely that no identification of these yet exists. These species is preyed upon by two molluscs: the variegated sundial shell, *Toreina variegeata*, and *Heliacus* sp.

Pseudoceros sp.

FLATWORMS

PHYLUM: Platyhelminthes (Flatworms)
CLASS: Turbellaria, Acoela

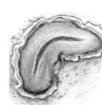

Few divers see flatworms and, if they do, they generally see only the more brightly coloured species. Even then they may confuse them with nudibranchs (shell-less molluscs). Although many tropical species may be seen in the open during the day, temperate species are less obvious, living beneath rocks and stones, or hidden among the hollows or folds of their invertebrate prey, such as Coleman's flatworm *Pseudoceros colemani*. In most cases a closer look will reveal the difference between a flatworm and a nudibranch. The greater number of marine flatworms are grouped in the Order Polycladida. (The term 'flatworm' includes the turbellarians, or free-living flatworms, parasitic flukes and tapeworms, but is used here to refer to the turbellarians.)

Flatworms are for the most part wafer-thin, bilaterally symmetrical creatures that appear to glide over the substrate. There is a head with simple sense organs, including simple tentacles and eye spots, visible under a microscope. The gliding motion is produced by a combination of minute, beating cilia on the underside of the flatworm and muscular contraction. At times some flatworms can also swim by undulating their body margins. Swimming is thought to be an escape response but may also be a means of locomotion. Swimming flatworms have been observed taking off from a high reef and being carried along by the current for up to 20 or 30 metres (65–100 feet).

Flatworms have no external gills (unlike most nudibranchs) but some have marginal tentacles at the 'head' end which may contain eyes, and other species may have dorsal tentacles issuing from the back near the 'head'.

The development of a head and bilateral symmetry is closely related to the evolution of forward locomotion. The body is made up of three layers of cells and contains a gut which opens via the mouth on the underside. The pharynx may be eversible and is sometimes used to engulf whole prey. There is no anus and no circulatory system. Respiration is achieved by the diffusion of oxygen into the body from outside; carbon dioxide escapes by the reverse process. Digested food is also distributed around the body by diffusion.

Flatworms are hermaphrodites, having complex male and female sex organs. Mating and cross fertilisation occur between two individuals. Eggs are laid on the substrate in spirals, similar to an open-ended circle. Remarkably, some flatworm egg ribbon spirals are very similar to those of some nudibranchs.

Most species living in the sea are predatory and carnivorous. In the author's experience many southern temperate and tropical flatworms feed on colonial ascidians. Only a few species show any specific body colour patterns that relate to the markings of the species on which they may prey.

Flatworms are very difficult to identify when preserved. Disposition of the eyes and structures on the head are all-important in laboratory identification using a microscope. It had been thought that variation in the colours and patterns of flatworms prevented their identification with any degree of accuracy, but experience has shown that most patterned species from warmer waters, especially in the genus *Pseudoceros*, can be visually identified.

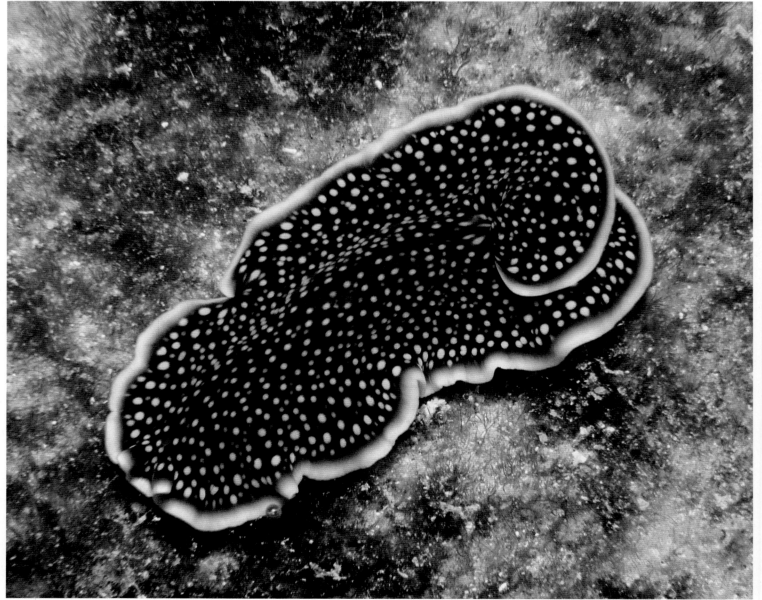

Pseudoceros sp.

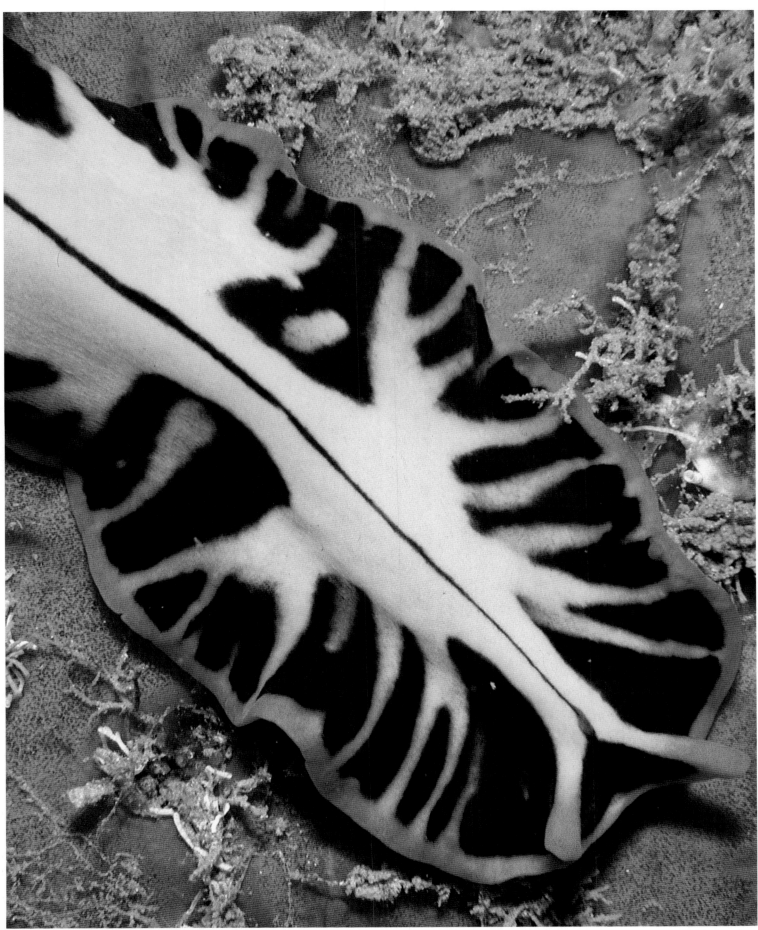

Pseudoceros zebra

Reef wall, Roach Reef

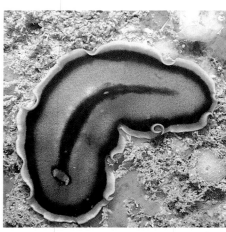

Callioplana marginata

■ CLASS: Turbellaria

FAMILY: Callioplanidae
SCIENTIFIC NAME: *Callioplana marginata*
COMMON NAME: Margined Flatworm
DISTRIBUTION: TI–WP; WT/S; WT/N
HABITAT: Coral reefs; rocky shores
GENERAL WATER DEPTH: Low tide to
  20 m (66 ft)
FOOD HABIT: Carnivorous: bryozoans
SIZE: 50 mm (2 in)
DESCRIPTION: Usually found beneath
stones, the margined flatworm occurs over a
large area of the South Pacific and west
Indo-Pacific. The margined flatworm is readily identifiable by comparing its characteristics with the photograph. Although there is
some colour variation in flatworms the general colours and patterns remain fairly stable
even over a wide distribution. The margined
flatworm is easily distinguished from its
nearest counterpart, Hancock's flatworm
(*Pseudoceros hancockanus*) by the closely
positioned rhinophores at the anterior end.
Many semi-scientific publications have
depicted these two species as the same, causing confusion.

Cycloporus australis

FAMILY: Pseudocerotidae
SCIENTIFIC NAME: *Cycloporus australis*
COMMON NAME: Southern Flatworm
DISTRIBUTION: WT/S
HABITAT: Rocky reefs; rocky shores
GENERAL WATER DEPTH: Low tide to 5 m
  (16 ft)
FOOD HABIT: Carnivorous: ascidians
SIZE: 20 mm (0.8 in)
DESCRIPTION: This little-known flatworm
was discovered by the author in 1978 during
an Australian Museum field trip. It feeds on
colonial ascidians from shallow water and
because its distinctive colouration almost
matches that of its prey it is sometimes difficult to see and is well protected from predators.

Pseudoceros bedfordi

FAMILY: Pseudocerotidae
SCIENTIFIC NAME: *Pseudoceros bedfordi*
COMMON NAME: Bedford's Flatworm
DISTRIBUTION: TI–WP
HABITAT: Coral reefs
GENERAL WATER DEPTH: Low tide to
  20 m (66 ft)
FOOD HABIT: Carnivorous: ascidians;
  amphipods
SIZE: 50 mm (2 in)
DESCRIPTION: As with most flatworms, Bedford's flatworm is
much easier to determine to species level when alive than when
preserved. Its distinctive colours
and pattern vary little over its
wide distribution. Bedford's flatworm is a free-roving predator
and occurs in various habitats,
not being limited to the habitat of
any one type of prey. It is a highly
mobile species and moves with sinuous ease. It can also swim. This
species feeds on compound ascidians and on small invertebrates
such as amphipods captured by
wrapping the victim in mucus.

Pseudoceros colemani

FAMILY: Pseudocerotidae
SCIENTIFIC NAME: *Pseudoceros colemani*
COMMON NAME: Coleman's Flatworm
DISTRIBUTION: WT/S
HABITAT: Rocky reefs
GENERAL WATER DEPTH: 3–10 m
  (10–33 ft)
FOOD HABIT: Carnivorous: brain ascidians
SIZE: 25 mm (1 in)
DESCRIPTION: Discovered by the author in
1972, this small, white-speckled flatworm
was first found when night diving. Since
then, large numbers have been observed in
daylight, especially during summer. These
flatworms were first found as tiny juveniles
on their specific host, the brain ascidian
Sycozoa cerebriformis. Up to 40 flatworms
may infest one colony of ascidians and as
they grow they slowly eat all the living
zooids, reducing the colony to a soft, white
mass of tissue. As the ascidian colony dies,
the flatworms move to another. On reaching
maturity the flatworms mate and lay their
eggs directly on to the ascidian; the adults
then disappear and during winter cannot be
found. Their appearance may be seasonal.

Pseudoceros kentii

FAMILY: Pseudocerotidae
SCIENTIFIC NAME: *Pseudoceros kentii*
COMMON NAME: Kent's Flatworm
DISTRIBUTION: TI–WP; WT/S
HABITAT: Coral reefs; rocky reefs
GENERAL WATER DEPTH: 5–25 m
(16–82 ft)
FOOD HABIT: Carnivorous: ascidians
SIZE: 50 mm (2 in)
DESCRIPTION: A brilliantly coloured, wide-ranging species, this flatworm occurs on rocky reefs, or sandy rubble terrain among coral reefs. It is an activie diurnal predator with an easily recognised colour pattern that can be seen from several metres underwater. As with most animals there is some colour and pattern variation within the species throughout its range.

Pseudoceros mexicanus

FAMILY: Pseudocerotidae
SCIENTIFIC NAME: *Pseudoceros mexicanus*
COMMON NAME: Mexican Flatworm
DISTRIBUTION: EP
HABITAT: Rocks
GENERAL WATER DEPTH: Low intertidal
FOOD HABIT: Carnivorous
SIZE: 100 mm (3.9 in)
DESCRIPTION: Swimming with exaggerated undulations of its brown to dark purple body, this flatworm is abundant throughout its range. White spots are scattered across the central area of the dorsum but do not extend outward as far as the reddish orange margin. Anterior tentacles are formed by folds in the margin.

FAMILY: Pseudocerotidae
SCIENTIFIC NAME: *Pseudoceros* sp.
COMMON NAME: Beautiful Flatworm
DISTRIBUTION: TI–WP
HABITAT: Coral reefs
GENERAL WATER DEPTH: 8–25 m
(26–82 ft)
FOOD HABIT: Carnivorous: ascidians

Pseudoceros sp.

SIZE: 40 mm (1.6 in)
DESCRIPTION: First photographed and recorded by the author over 15 years ago, this spectacularly coloured flatworm has yet to be scientifically described. It is seen regularly in some areas and has been observed both in the open and beneath coral skeletons. Like other flatworm species, the beautiful flatworm feeds on colonial ascidians. Flatworms are separately sexed and are able to regenerate body parts that are injured; for example, a flatworm cut in half will eventually grow into two flatworms. However, quite often the second growth does not match the colouration pattern of the original.

Pseudoceros sp.

FAMILY: Pseudocerotidae
SCIENTIFIC NAME: *Pseudoceros* sp.
COMMON NAME: Norfolk Flatworm
DISTRIBUTION: TI–WP
HABITAT: Rocky reefs
GENERAL WATER DEPTH: 8–25 m
(26–82 ft)
FOOD HABIT: Carnivorous: ascidians
SIZE: 35 mm (1.4 in)
DESCRIPTION: Common on the reefs around Norfolk Island in the South Pacific, this very

attractive flatworm has not been recorded in Australian waters and is assumed to be local to the Norfolk ridge, or part of the New Caledonian fauna. It feeds on colonial ascidians and appears to be fairly stable in colour and pattern. The Norfolk flatworm has yet to be scientifically described.

Thysanozoon sp.

FAMILY: Pseudocerotidae
SCIENTIFIC NAME: *Thysanozoon* sp.
COMMON NAME: Warty Flatworm
DISTRIBUTION: TI–WP; WT/S; CT/S
HABITAT: Rocky reefs; rocky shores
GENERAL WATER DEPTH: Low tide to
10 m (33 ft)
FOOD HABIT: Carnivorous: small
invertebrates
SIZE: 25 mm (1 in)
DESCRIPTION: The genus *Thysanozoon* is widely distributed. Little is recorded or known about the behaviour and natural history of the South Pacific flatworms as only one or two specimens of each described species have ever been collected, and few observations have been made of their behaviour and ecology. As a genus, *Thysanozoon* may be recognised by the presence of papillae, nodules, or rough protuberances on the dorsal surface. Most species are found beneath rocks but others may be seen in the open or around oysters.

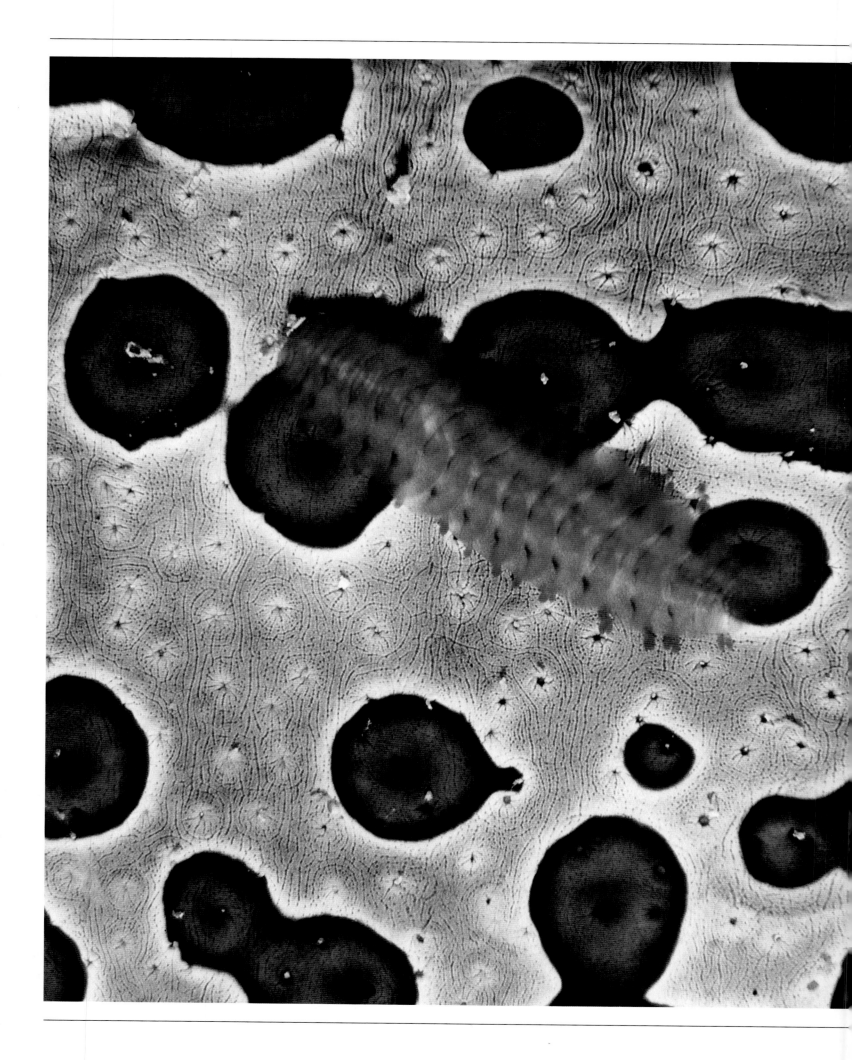

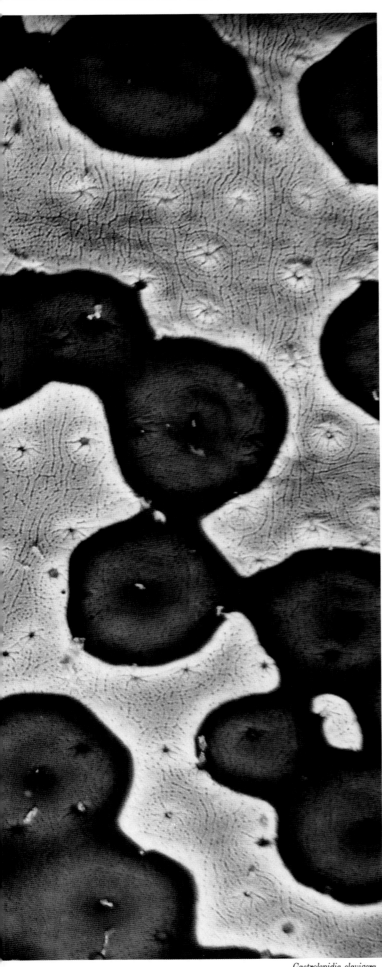

Gastrolepidia clavigera

SEGMENTED WORMS

PHYLUM: Annelida (Segmented worms)
CLASS: Polychaeta

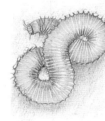

The phylum Annelida, the segmented worms, is one of the major groupings of the animal kingdom. It demonstrates a successful evolutionary pattern of animals constructed from three cell layers. It shows bilateral symmetry, development of a body cavity between the body wall muscles and the gut muscles and, most important, a segmented body. The basic anatomical features of each segment can have different specialised functions. This is best seen in the head segments of some annelids where quite sophisticated organs are borne on different segments for different functions. Of the four or so classes of the Annelida only the Polychaetes are really abundant in the sea.

There are more than 12,000 species and 70 families worldwide and comparatively little is known of the natural history or distribution of this diverse group. Ecologically they are of two types: the active, mobile, foraging Polychaetes, and the sendentary burrowing or tube-dwelling suspension or detrital feeders.

Polychaetes can be found in almost every subtidal habitat. The various forms may be rock boring, tube dwelling, free roving, symbiotic, mud burrowing and even pelagic. They inhabit intertidal areas down to abyssal depths, and in many soft bottom areas are the most common forms of life.

As worms are very vulnerable to predation, many have evolved lifestyles and armour to enhance their chances of survival. Some sedentary species construct tubes of calcium carbonate, sand grains, or mucus in which to live; others bore into coral. The free-living, non-tubiculous worms may live beneath rocks, burrow into mud, be active at night or

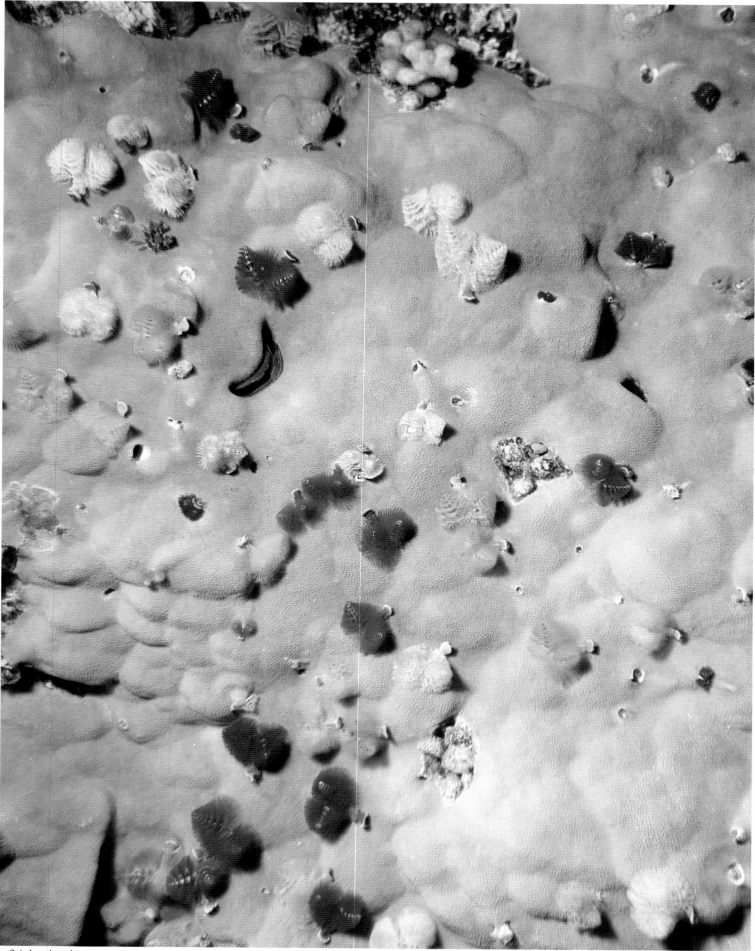

Spirobranchus giganteus

sharp-pointed setae (bristles) for protection. The setae of some species contain venom, and because of this these bristle worms are often referred to as 'fire worms'.

Most of the polychaete worms commonly seen underwater are either the larger, roving bristle worms, scale worms, and 'sea mice', or the stationary deposit-feeding worms, fan worms and tube worms whose brightly coloured feeding tentacles often reveal their presence. Because it is only part of the worm's body that is usually seen, many snorkellers and divers fail to realise that the mystery object is part of a worm.

In fact the people who would have most regular contact with worms (apart from earthworms in the garden) are fishing people who dig or buy worms for bait. It is not yet possible to identify most worms underwater to species level, owing to the lack of available information and the tremendous variation within certain groups. Specimens must usually be collected intact, preserved and delivered to a taxonomist for species identification. However, it is possible to become familiar with characteristics at family level, for example, the chalky tube of the serpulids or the trailing tentacles of the terebellids.

So, with some practice on the more common, well-known forms of sedentary fan worms and tube worms, there are enough recognition features to identify at least to family level and, in some cases, genus and species levels. Basically, bristle worms have bristles and scale worms have scales. Terebellid worms inhabit sand or mud tubes on the bottom or beneath rocks and, as deposit feeders, radiate their many retractable buccal (mouth) tentacles over the substrate to collect food. Serpulid worms build a hard, calcareous tube, either alone or in a colony. Serpulids are filter feeders, using double branchial crown tentacles and, unlike sabellid fan worms, most have a small, stalked operculum that acts as a trapdoor to seal the tube after the worm retracts.

The tubes of sabellid worms are made from sand or mud and in general are built up from the substrate. They may be solitary or in small groups. They are also filter feeders and have two distinct branchial crown tentacles projecting from the tube. They have no operculum to close the tube.

Reproductive techniques of Polychaete worms are as diverse as their lifestyles and vary from shedding eggs and sperm into the sea to incubating their young in brood chambers. Some carry their developing young on their backs and others carry their eggs only until they hatch, releasing the larvae into the sea, where they grow and develop as members of the zooplankton until they are ready to settle and metamorphose.

Protula magnifica

Chloeia flava

■ CLASS: Polychaeta

FAMILY: Amphinomidae
SCIENTIFIC NAME: *Chloeia flava*
COMMON NAME: Golden Bristle Worm
DISTRIBUTION: TI–WP
HABITAT: Mud; sand; rubble shores
GENERAL WATER DEPTH: 0–20 m (66 ft)
FOOD HABIT: Carnivorous
SIZE: 200 mm (8 in)
DESCRIPTION: Many species of bristle worms are called 'fire worms' owing to their needle-sharp, venomous setae or bristles. This species has very characteristic setae and ocelli in the centre of each segment, making it simple to identify in the field. It is generally found among dead coral rubble, or beneath dead coral slabs or sand, in shallow lagoons or sheltered waters. Sometimes at night it can be seen swimming in the water column.

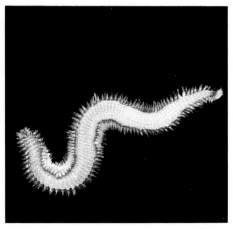

Eurythoe complanata

FAMILY: Amphinomidae
SCIENTIFIC NAME: *Eurythoe complanata*
COMMON NAME: Tropic Bristle Worm
DISTRIBUTION: TI–WP
HABITAT: Sand; mud; rubble shores

GENERAL WATER DEPTH: Low tide to 25 m (82 ft)
FOOD HABIT: Omnivorous: invertebrates; algae
SIZE: 100 mm (4 in)
DESCRIPTION: Extremely common over a wide range of coral reefs and reefs off continental islands as well as on temperate shores (despite the common name), tropic bristle worms are generally found to be gregarious, inhabiting sandy substrate beneath dead coral slabs, or boulders buried in loose rubble. The spines are very sharp and can penetrate some gloves, each bunch of spines being thought to have its own venom gland. The red, tentacle-like structures running in lines down the edge of the segments are the animal's gills.

Aphrodite australis

FAMILY: Aphroditidae
SCIENTIFIC NAME: *Aphrodite australis*
COMMON NAME: Southern Sea Mouse
DISTRIBUTION: WT/S
HABITAT: Sand; mud
GENERAL WATER DEPTH: 2–40 m (6–131 ft)
FOOD HABIT: Carnivorous
SIZE: 180 mm (7 in)
DESCRIPTION: This species is a member of a cosmopolitan genus that inhabits many oceans. Though well known it is not often seen in its natural habitat. Related forms are continually dredged from deep water by research vessels and many of these await description. The southern sea mouse generally lives beneath the surface of sand or mud and comes out from its hide on the turn of the tide, or when the odour of food or prey species is carried to it by the currents. Despite its soft, velvety look, the southern sea mouse has tufted groups of setae set in rows along its back and a golden fringe of these bristles around the entire periphery. These setae are sharp but quite soft and flexible, and although they have been reported to penetrate human skin, injury is unlikely. The species is a food for fish.

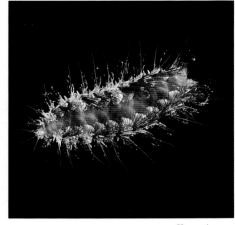

Hermonia sp.

FAMILY: Aphroditidae
SCIENTIFIC NAME: *Hermonia* sp.
COMMON NAME: Bristly Scale Worm
DISTRIBUTION: TI–WP
HABITAT: Rocky reefs
GENERAL WATER DEPTH: Low tide to 10 m (33 ft)
FOOD HABIT: Carnivorous: invertebrates
SIZE: 25 mm (1 in)
DESCRIPTION: Discovered in 1972 and still undescribed, this scale worm lives beneath rocks and dead coral slabs on intertidal continental island rocky reefs in silty situations. Colour and pattern vary little, and the double tufts of well-developed setae are positioned over the yellow dorsal scales. This could be a species that pairs, the female brooding her eggs beneath the scales protected by the setae.

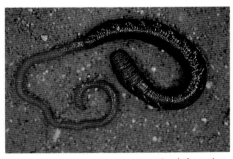

Arenicola marina

FAMILY: Arenicolidae
SCIENTIFIC NAME: *Arenicola marina*
COMMON NAME: Lugworm
DISTRIBUTION: EA; WT/N
HABITAT: Muddy sand
GENERAL WATER DEPTH: Intertidal
FOOD HABIT: Carnivorous
SIZE: Up to 200 mm (7.9 in) or more long
DESCRIPTION: Bushy gills appear on the anterior part of this fleshy worm. Widely used as bait by anglers, the lugworm inhabits U-shaped burrows. The back opening of

these burrows is surrounded with distinctive faeces casts; the other entrance is marked with a shallow depression in the surface of the sand.

Eunice aphroditois

FAMILY: Eunicidae
SCIENTIFIC NAME: *Eunice aphroditois*
COMMON NAME: Aphrodite Worm
DISTRIBUTION: WT/N; WT/S
HABITAT: Sand
GENERAL WATER DEPTH: Shallow
FOOD HABIT: Carnivorous
SIZE: 200 mm (7.9 in)
DESCRIPTION: The body of this species has more than 150 segments. The gills begin at the sixth setiger, becoming comb-shaped with 40 branches each by segment 22. The microscopic acicular and subacicular hooks are black and toothlike. On the back of the head are antennae which are quite short.

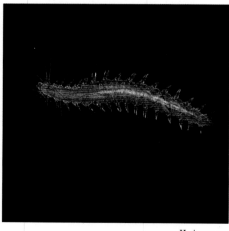

Hesione sp.

FAMILY: Hesionidae
SCIENTIFIC NAME: *Hesione* sp.
COMMON NAME: Dash–dot Hesionid Worm
DISTRIBUTION: TI–WP; WT/S
HABITAT: Rocky reefs
GENERAL WATER DEPTH: 10–25 m
  (33–82 ft)

FOOD HABIT: Carnivorous
SIZE: 40 mm (1.6 in)
DESCRIPTION: Many worm species have excellent individual visual characteristics for identification against scientific description. The dash–dot hesionid worm lives in rocky rubble reef substrate in the southern Indian Ocean and during the day resides beneath stones. At night it ventures out to search for food.

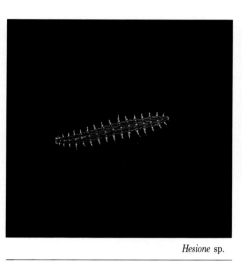

Hesione sp.

FAMILY: Hesionidae
SCIENTIFIC NAME: *Hesione* sp.
COMMON NAME: Long-cirri Hesionid Worm
DISTRIBUTION: TI–WP
HABITAT: Coral reefs
GENERAL WATER DEPTH: 5–20 m
  (16–66 ft)
FOOD HABIT: Carnivorous
SIZE: 35 mm (1.4 in)
DESCRIPTION: Found on tropical coral reefs, this rather spectacular worm lives beneath dead coral slabs that are on hard substrate, generally with a good flow of water beneath. Although long dorsal cirri are characteristic of the family as a whole, in this species they are exceptionally long.

FAMILY: Nereidae
SCIENTIFIC NAME: *Nereis pelagica*
COMMON NAME: Ragworm
DISTRIBUTION: Cosmopolitan
HABITAT: Muddy sand and gravel; among seaweed
GENERAL WATER DEPTH: Intertidal
FOOD HABIT: Omnivorous: detritus
SIZE: Up to or over 100 mm (3.9 in) long
DESCRIPTION: Anglers will be familiar with this species, a popular bait. It may be found under stones or among seaweed undergrowth. On the prostomium can be seen eyes and antennae; feelers are found on the peristonium, while two large palps occur around the mouth.

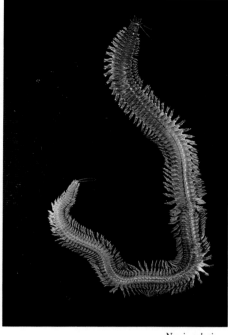

Nereis pelagica

FAMILY: Opheliidae
SCIENTIFIC NAME: *Ophelina acuminata*
DISTRIBUTION: Cosmopolitan
HABITAT: Gravel and muddy sand
GENERAL WATER DEPTH: Subtidal
FOOD HABIT: Omnivorous: organic detritus
SIZE: Up to 50 mm (1.9 in) long
DESCRIPTION: A burrowing worm, this species consumes large amounts of matter from the sea bed from which the organic matter is extracted. It is torpedo shaped, with a pointed head zone. These worms are common but are rarely noticed in their natural habitat due to their subsurface existence.

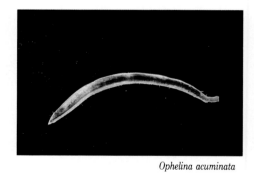

Ophelina acuminata

FAMILY: Pectinariidae
SCIENTIFIC NAME: *Pectinaria* sp.
COMMON NAME: Sand Grain Tube Worm;
  Sand Mason
DISTRIBUTION: TI–WP; WT/S
HABITAT: Sand
GENERAL WATER DEPTH: 5–30 m
  (16–98 ft)
FOOD HABIT: Omnivorous: detritus
SIZE: 60 mm (2.4 in) (tube length)

Pectinaria sp.

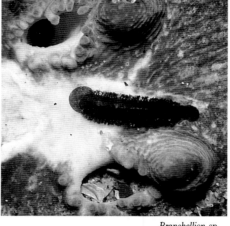

Branchellion sp.

Benhamile pidonotus glaucus

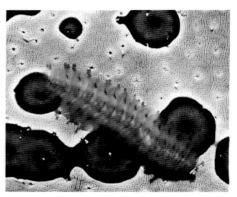

Gastrolepidia clavigera

DESCRIPTION: Looking rather like a sand-struck tusk shell, the sand grain tube worm even lives upside down. Using modified comb-like setae (stiff hairs) on the side of its head the worm can dig its way into the sand in an inverted position with just the tip of the tube's end showing at the surface. Although these worms are quite common, few people have ever seen a live one.

FAMILY: Phyllodocidae
SCIENTIFIC NAME: *Phyllodoce novaehollandiae*
COMMON NAME: Green Paddle Worm
DISTRIBUTION: WT/S
HABITAT: Mud; muddy shores
GENERAL WATER DEPTH: 0–50 m (164 ft)
FOOD HABIT: Scavenger
SIZE: 150 mm (6 in)
DESCRIPTION: Extremely common on intertidal mud flats in estuaries and bays bordering continental islands, the green paddle worm is an active diurnal scavenger that moves at will over the wet mudflats well within the sight and other senses of predators that would normally eat worms. If attacked it can secrete a repellent mucoid substance to defend itself.

FAMILY: Piscicolidae
SCIENTIFIC NAME: *Branchellion* sp.
COMMON NAME: Electric Ray Leech
DISTRIBUTION: TI–WP; WT/S
HABITAT: Rocky reefs; coral reefs
GENERAL WATER DEPTH: 8–25 m (26–82 ft)
FOOD HABIT: Carnivorous: fishes
SIZE: 70 mm (2.8 in)
DESCRIPTION: Inhabiting the spiracles (dorsal vents) and head regions of the short-tailed electric ray (*Hypnos monopterygium*), these large, thick-bodied leeches generally occur in groups. On some electric rays they seem to almost block the entire breathing system of the fish. Leeches that have been in residence for some time remove all the mucus and pigment from the skin. Obviously the electric ray's electric shocks, used when catching prey, do not affect the leeches.

FAMILY: Polynoidae
SCIENTIFIC NAME: *Benhamile pidonotus glaucus*
COMMON NAME: Grey Scale Worm
DISTRIBUTION: TI–WP
HABITAT: Coral reefs
GENERAL WATER DEPTH: 0–10 m (33 ft)
FOOD HABIT: Carnivorous: small invertebrates
SIZE: 20 mm (0.8 in)
DESCRIPTION: Not commonly encountered throughout its range, the grey scale worm inhabits the undersides of dead coral slabs and boulders in shallow tropical lagoons and intertidal continental island reefs. Many scale worms are territorial and will protect their 'home' area from other scale worms. Even females and males may dispute territory. The mating season brings a truce.

FAMILY: Polynoidae
SCIENTIFIC NAME: *Gastrolepidia clavigera*
COMMON NAME: Club-spined Scale Worm
DISTRIBUTION: TI–WP
HABITAT: Coral reefs
GENERAL WATER DEPTH: 0–25 m (82 ft)
FOOD HABIT: Omnivorous
SIZE: 20 mm (0.8 in)
DESCRIPTION: Inhabiting the underside, dorsal, or mouth area of tropical sea cucumbers, this species is thought to be host dependent and has never been recorded in a free-living state. As each resident worm is almost always similar in colour to its host it would appear that they settle from the plankton directly onto the host and assume that colouration as protection from predators.

FAMILY: Polynoidae
SCIENTIFIC NAME: *Heterolepidonotus* sp.
COMMON NAME: Spot-scaled Scale Worm
DISTRIBUTION: TI–WP
HABITAT: Coral reefs
GENERAL WATER DEPTH: 0–20 m (66 ft)
FOOD HABIT: Carnivorous: invertebrates
SIZE: 25 mm (1 in)
DESCRIPTION: Although specimens of this scale worm were discovered by the author in 1971, it awaits scientific description. The species is not rare, however, few people have

Phyllodoce novaehollandiae

Heterolepidonotus sp.

seen it in its natural habitat. It lives beneath dead coral slabs and during the day nestles in a hollow, crack or crevice and is almost impossible to see. This scale worm is very fragile and loses its scales at the slightest disturbance, a characteristic that can complicate identification of species where the number of scales is important.

Laetmonice sp.

FAMILY: Polynoidae
SCIENTIFIC NAME: *Laetmonice* sp.
COMMON NAME: Deep Sea Scale Worm
DISTRIBUTION: WT/S
HABITAT: Mud
GENERAL WATER DEPTH: 400–900 m (1312–2953 ft)
FOOD HABIT: Carnivorous: invertebrates
SIZE: 80 mm (3.2 in)
DESCRIPTION: Still awaiting scientific description (as are many worm species), this animal was brought up by a deep sea research vessel investigating the waters of the continental shelf off the central east coast of Australia. Although most scale worms have two pairs of eyes, the eyes of this species are not visible to the naked eye. Scale worms have an eversible proboscis and well-developed jaws for catching small, mobile invertebrates.

FAMILY: Polynoidae
SCIENTIFIC NAME: *Lepidonotus melanogrammus*
COMMON NAME: Dark-marked Scale Worm
DISTRIBUTION: TI–WP; WT/S

Lepidonotus melanogrammus

HABITAT: Coral reefs; rocky reefs; rocky shores
GENERAL WATER DEPTH: 0–20 m (66 ft)
FOOD HABIT: Carnivorous: invertebrates
SIZE: 50 mm (2 in)
DESCRIPTION: The dark-marked scale worm is one of the most well-known and easily recognised species of South Pacific scale worms. Scale worms of the genus *Lepidonotus* have 12 pairs of overlapping scales with a brown, pigmented, C-shaped pattern around the lower half of the margin. The species lives beneath stones and rubble on intertidal rock platforms and in deeper waters. Its natural history is little known apart from the fact that it is carnivorous and that it tends to shed its scales if handled roughly. Observations by the author suggest that this species is often resident on the underside of the body disc of larger brittle stars.

Sabellaria alveolata

FAMILY: Sabellariidae
SCIENTIFIC NAME: *Sabellaria alveolata*
COMMON NAME: Honeycomb Worm
DISTRIBUTION: CT/N; EA
HABITAT: Rocky reefs and shores
GENERAL WATER DEPTH: Intertidal
FOOD HABIT: Omnivorous: plankton
SIZE: 30–40 mm (1.2–1.6 in) long
DESCRIPTION: So called because of its habit of constructing reefs made of tubes built

with cemented sand grains, the honeycomb worm is easily distinguished by the setae which are modified for this digging function. Colonies will most often be found in intertidal sandy areas of strong wave action, where they will be attached to rocks.

Sabella penicillus

FAMILY: Sabellidae
SCIENTIFIC NAME: *Sabella penicillus*
COMMON NAME: Peacock Fan Worm
DISTRIBUTION: CT/N; EA
HABITAT: Mud; sand
GENERAL WATER DEPTH: Intertidal/ shallow subtidal zone
FOOD HABIT: Omnivorous: plankton
SIZE: 200 mm (7.9 in) or more in length
DESCRIPTION: The distinctive patterning seen in its fan of tentacles gives this species its common name. This gregarious worm is a tube dweller; its membranous tubes may protrude several centimetres above the sea bed. The tentacles reach out into the water to assist with respiration as well as collecting plankton and organic debris.

FAMILY: Sabellidae
SCIENTIFIC NAME: *Sabellastarte indica*
COMMON NAME: Southern Fan Worm
DISTRIBUTION: WT/S; CT/S
HABITAT: Rocky reefs and coasts; jetty piles
GENERAL WATER DEPTH: 2–30 m (6–98 ft)
FOOD HABIT: Omnivorous: plankton; detritus
SIZE: 150 mm (6 in) (length of tube)
DESCRIPTION: A very common resident of southern temperate reefs, the southern fan worm has a wide variety of colour variations. However, its size, general shape and striped or marked radioles distinguish it from its nearest relative, St Joseph's fan worm (*Sabellastarte sanctijosephi*). The spirally arranged pair of head plumes have both respiratory and food gathering functions and are extremely sensitive to fluctuations of

Sabellastarte indica

pressure or light. These fan worms can be seen in large numbers in some areas of enclosed water adjacent to areas of strong tidal influence.

Sabellastarte sanctijosephi

FAMILY: Sabellidae
SCIENTIFIC NAME: *Sabellastarte sanctijosephi*
COMMON NAME: St Joseph's Fan Worm
DISTRIBUTION: TI–WP; WT/S
HABITAT: Mud; sand
GENERAL WATER DEPTH: 2–15 m (6–49 ft)
FOOD HABIT: Omnivorous: plankton; detritus
SIZE: 150 mm (6 in) (length)
DESCRIPTION: St Joseph's fan worm inhabits areas of reef and rubble where there is sufficient sand or mud for it to burrow into and build its tube. This species is usually seen in groups of long, mud-coloured tubes sticking vertically out of the bottom. This worm is a ciliary feeder and close examination of the photograph will reveal plankton and suspended sediment in the water and sticking to the pinnate radioles, where it will soon be transferred down the central food groove to the mouth. Its head radioles are almost always mauve and the collar and mouth parts have distinctive black markings.

Filograna implexa

FAMILY: Serpulidae
SCIENTIFIC NAME: *Filograna implexa*
COMMON NAME: Tangled Tube Worm
DISTRIBUTION: TI–WP; WT/S; WT/N; CT/S
HABITAT: Coral reefs; rocky reefs and shores
GENERAL WATER DEPTH: 0–40 m (131 ft)
FOOD HABIT: Omnivorous: plankton; detritus
SIZE: 4 mm (0.2 in) (tube length); 330 mm (13 in) (colony width)
DESCRIPTION: A common, cosmopolitan species inhabiting many of the world's oceans, the tangled tube worm secretes a thin, calcareous tube from which issues a red, pink, or brown tentacled crown. As a colony it occupies a variety of habitats, but it is intertidal and is very common under boulders or on reefs and rocky shores. Colonies in the open tend to form circular structures, while those in caves, under ledges, wharves, or other dark places grow in an irregular shape and with longer growth extensions.

Galeolaria caespitosa

FAMILY: Serpulidae
SCIENTIFIC NAME: *Galeolaria caespitosa*
COMMON NAME: Intertidal Tube Worm
DISTRIBUTION: WT/S
HABITAT: Rocky reefs
GENERAL WATER DEPTH: Intertidal zone
FOOD HABIT: Omnivorous: plankton; detritus
SIZE: 20 mm (0.8 in) (tube length)
DESCRIPTION: These serpulids prefer a particular level on the shore giving optimum exposure to air and water. Although the larvae settle elsewhere, only those in the most beneficial position in relation to tide levels survive and these form dense and conspicuous aggregations, constituting a clear zone 3–5 m (10–16 ft) wide, on the rocky shore. A small number of individuals will survive above and below this, but they will not flourish. The intertidal tube worm feeds on the incoming tide using special 'head' tentacles. These are feathery and may be black and form a crown characteristic of all serpulid worms. The tentacle crown catches plankton and suspended detritus, which is then conveyed to the mouth by minute cilia. When the tide goes out the worm retracts into its limy tube and blocks its entrance with a calcareous cap or operculum which seals the worm inside and protects it from desiccation by sun and wind.

Hydroides norvegica

FAMILY: Serpulidae
SCIENTIFIC NAME: *Hydroides norvegica*
COMMON NAME: Calcareous Tube-worm
DISTRIBUTION: Cosmopolitan
HABITAT: Attached to any hard object
GENERAL WATER DEPTH: 0–5 m (0–16.4 ft)
FOOD HABIT: Omnivorous: plankton
SIZE: 300 mm (11.8 in) or more long
DESCRIPTION: This tube-worm may attach itself to any hard surface, including the bottom of ships. The entrance to its calcareous tube is guarded with a sophisticated calcareous operculum when the worm withdraws its tentacles.

Protula magnifica

FAMILY: Serpulidae
SCIENTIFIC NAME: *Protula magnifica*
COMMON NAME: Tube Worm
DISTRIBUTION: TI–WP
HABITAT: Coral reefs
GENERAL WATER DEPTH: 2–30 m (6–98 ft)
FOOD HABIT: Omnivorous: plankton;
   detritus
SIZE: 120 mm (4.7 in) (across radioles)
DESCRIPTION: Found from just below low-tide level in the muddy coastal waters of continental islands to the clean clear depths of barrier reefs, the magnificent tube worm is generally observed as a solitary animal. Its calcareous tube may reach a length of 300 mm (12 in) with an aperture of 25 mm (1 in). The tube itself is usually buried in rubble along the slopes of channels or passages where there is good water flow.

Pseudoserpula rugosa

FAMILY: Serpulidae
SCIENTIFIC NAME: *Pseudoserpula rugosa*
COMMON NAME: Rugose Tube Worm
DISTRIBUTION: WT/S
HABITAT: Rocky reefs; rocky coasts
GENERAL WATER DEPTH: 2–10 m (6–33 ft)
FOOD HABIT: Omnivorous: plankton;
   detritus
SIZE: 50 mm (2 in) (across radioles)
DESCRIPTION: This beautiful little tube

worm with its intricate crown of ciliated radioles inhabits subtidal reefs and rubble, where it secretes the limy tube in which it lives. It also inhabits the undersides of rocks. The worms are very sensitive to shadows, movement, noise or pressure changes in the water, and will instantly withdraw for the slightest reason. Unlike other species of tube worms, the serpulids have a stalked operculum which is quite noticeable when the animal extends. When the feeding radioles are retracted into the tube the operculum fits neatly into the opening, sealing the entrance against predators. Nevertheless, the radioles are often eaten by fish. The winged murex shell (*Pterynotus acanthopterus*) and the duffuse murex shell (*P. duffusi*) drill holes in the tubes and feed on the worms.

Serpula vermicularis

FAMILY: Serpulidae
SCIENTIFIC NAME: *Serpula vermicularis*
COMMON NAME: Red Tube Worm
DISTRIBUTION: EP; CT/N; WT/N
HABITAT: Rocks and other structures,
   natural and manmade
GENERAL WATER DEPTH: 0–100 m (328 ft)
FOOD HABIT: Carnivorous: plankton
SIZE: 102 mm (4 in)
DESCRIPTION: Attached to nearly any type of stationary structure, anchored or floating, the funnel of the red tube worm features a cap (operculum) marked by 160 small nicks around its edge. Forty pairs of red to light pink gills form the plume. The species was among those first named by Carolus Linnaeus, the originator of the modern classification system for flora and fauna.

FAMILY: Serpulidae
SCIENTIFIC NAME: *Spirobranchus giganteus*
COMMON NAME: Christmas Tree Worm
DISTRIBUTION: TI–WP
HABITAT: Coral reefs
GENERAL WATER DEPTH: 0–30 m (98 ft)
FOOD HABIT: Omnivorous: plankton;
   detritus
SIZE: 150 mm (6 in) (across radioles)

Spirobranchus giganteus

DESCRIPTION: Exhibiting almost every colour of the rainbow, the Christmas tree worm would pose an identification problem if the species were determined on colour alone. However, for several reasons it is readily identifiable in the field. Christmas tree worms almost always build their calcareous tubes into the living colonies of corals and hydrocorals. They are especially prevalent in large coral 'heads' with small polyps, such as *Porites*. Sometimes as many as 50 worms will be found in one sq. m (11 sq. ft) of coral. The delicate, twin, spiralling radioles are cone-shaped and the operculum has two minor extensions on the lower edge.

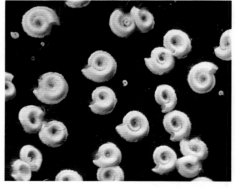

Spirorbis spirorbis

FAMILY: Spirorbidae
SCIENTIFIC NAME: *Spirorbis spirorbis*
COMMON NAME: Spiral Tube Worm
DISTRIBUTION: WT/S–CT/N
HABITAT: Reefs; rubble-kelp beds
GENERAL WATER DEPTH: Intertidal to
   10 m (30 ft)
FOOD HABIT: Omnivorous: plankton
SIZE: 2 mm (0.08 in)
DESCRIPTION: Typically found attached to seaweeds or kelp, this species has a calcareous tube. The tube is smooth and coiled in a clockwise direction. Often a flange appears at the base of the tube to increase the attachment area and give a firmer hold.

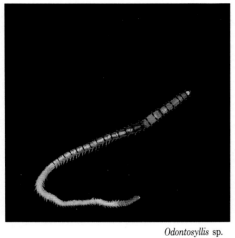

Odontosyllis sp.

FAMILY: Syllidae
SCIENTIFIC NAME: *Odontosyllis* sp.
COMMON NAME: Golden Black-striped Syllid Worm
DISTRIBUTION: TI-WP
HABITAT: Coral reefs
GENERAL WATER DEPTH: 0–8 m (26 ft)
FOOD HABIT: Carnivorous: hydroids and sea mats
SIZE: 35 mm (1.4 in)
DESCRIPTION: A resident of sponges living beneath dead coral slabs, this small but brightly coloured syllid worm has been found inside an encrusting sponge. Many syllid worms are known to feed on hydroids and bryozoans and some females nurse their eggs in tail buds.

Opisthosyllis sp.

FAMILY: Syllidae
SCIENTIFIC NAME: *Opisthosyllis* sp.
COMMON NAME: Soft Coral Syllid Worm
DISTRIBUTION: TI-WP
HABITAT: Coral reefs
GENERAL WATER DEPTH: 1–15 m (3–49 ft)
FOOD HABIT: Carnivorous: hydroids and sea mats
SIZE: 20 mm (0.8 in)

DESCRIPTION: Only found on or near the soft coral genus *Xenia*, this newly discovered syllid worm has yet to be described. Its colours match its host's very well, and when the soft coral polyps are extended for feeding the worm is completely hidden. It has been reported only from Lord Howe Island in the South Pacific.

Amphitrite johnstoni

FAMILY: Terebellidae
SCIENTIFIC NAME: *Amphitrite johnstoni*
COMMON NAME: Johnston's Tube Worm
DISTRIBUTION: CT/N; EA
HABITAT: In sand and gravel
GENERAL WATER DEPTH: 0–5 m (0–16.4 ft)
FOOD HABIT: Omnivorous: plankton, detritus
SIZE: Up to 250 mm (9.8 in) long
DESCRIPTION: A distinctive patch of light-coloured tissue on the underside at the anterior end characterises this animal. A large species, it dwells in a mucous tube; this is normally covered in sand and shell pieces.

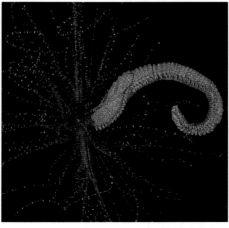

Eupolymnia sp.

FAMILY: Terebellidae
SCIENTIFIC NAME: *Eupolymnia* sp.
COMMON NAME: Medusa Tube Worm
DISTRIBUTION: WT/S

HABITAT: Mud
GENERAL WATER DEPTH: 2–20 m (6–66 ft)
FOOD HABIT: Omnivorous: plankton; detritus
SIZE: 80 mm (3.2 in) (length)
DESCRIPTION: Highly contractile, mobile tentacles radiate from the front of the Medusa tube worm. They are grooved, and food particles are propelled along the grooves towards the mouth by cilia which beat in a co-ordinated fashion. Divers are often puzzled by strange clusters of the tentacles issuing from holes in the sea bottom, out of rubble, or from around or under rocks. When disturbed, the tentacles very quickly withdraw from sight and attempts to find the animal itself are rarely successful. This species, like other terebellid worms, lives in sand or mud tubes manufactured by using bottom detritus glued together with mucus — a fragile covering for their naked bodies. They feed on detrital particles falling to the sea bed or already deposited there.

Reterebella queenslandia

FAMILY: Terebellidae
SCIENTIFIC NAME: *Reterebella queenslandia*
COMMON NAME: Queensland Tube Worm
DISTRIBUTION: TI-WP
HABITAT: Coral reefs
GENERAL WATER DEPTH: 1–20 m (3–66 ft)
FOOD HABIT: Omnivorous: plankton; detritus
SIZE: 1 m (3 ft) (length of tentacle)
DESCRIPTION: With tentacles extending up to 1 m (3 ft), the Queensland tube worm is the largest terebellid worm in the South Pacific. Housed in a parchment tube of its own manufacture and hidden on the undersides of coral boulders and rocks, this worm sends out a number of white, strand-like feeding tentacles which often radiate in a circular fashion. The tentacles are sticky and entrap small organisms and detritus, which are then drawn back to the mouth.

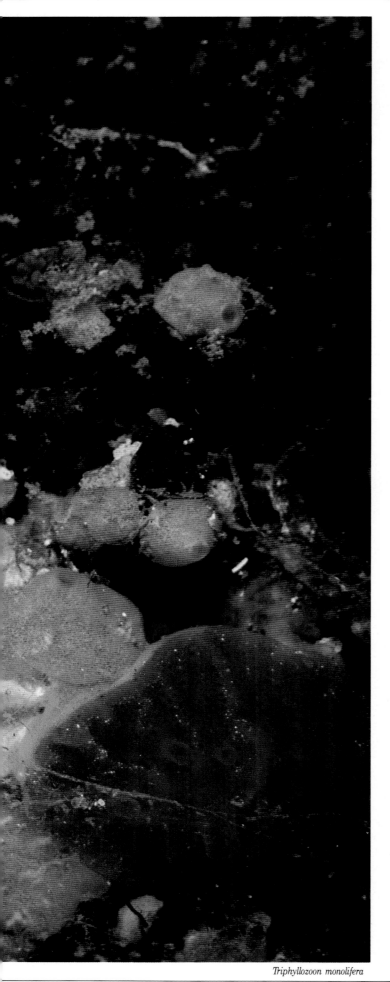

Triphyllozoon monolifera

SEA MOSSES

PHYLUM: Bryozoa
CLASS: Stenolaemata, Gymnolaemata (Sea mosses, bryozoans, polyzoans)

Many species of bryozoans produce character-istic growths (some plant-like) that, together with their living colour, habitat, distribution and shape, can sometimes be recognised in the field to genus level.

The Bryozoa are a fascinating group largely unknown to the layman. Although a microscope is necessary to make out details of individuals, known as zooids, their colonies are easily seen by eye. About 3500 species exist but many more are known from the fossil record; most are marine. The adults live in colonies. They are bilaterally symmetrical but have no head. A protrusile crown of filter-feeding tentacles collects suspended food particles. The body is enclosed in a stiff case, often box-like, which supports and protects the internal organs. The filter-feeding tentacles can be withdrawn inside this for added protection. The case is stiffened by proteins, including a substance resembling insect chitin. In many species this is further reinforced by calcium carbonate which gives the protective cases a distinct greyish-white appearance.

Although a few species have modified stalks and anchor in sand, most bryozoans attach to hard surfaces, from boat bottoms to glass bottles. In fact any smooth surface, provided it is chemically satisfactory, appears to be an ideal settling medium for many bryozoan larvae.

All bryozoans and polyzoans are colonial and grow in an amazing array of shapes, configurations and designs, from small circular encrusting formations, intricate lace-like structures and plant-like tufts, to large clumps of coral-like colonies several metres in circumference.

The individuals in the colony are interconnected. Each

Violet Bryzoan

feeding zooid has a number of ciliated tentacles, grouped into a crown (called a lophophore), that trap plankton and food particles. Not all zooids in the colony catch food; because they are colonial, some zooids can have specialised roles. Some protect the feeding zooids or are cleaners. In some cases zooids may form brood chambers to protect developing embryos.

Some species are known to produce larvae by sexual reproduction. Most are hermaphrodites, some release eggs into the sea, and others pass the fertilised eggs into brood chambers. Whatever the method, after some time as plankton the larvae settle on to surface rock, shell grit, or algae and then attach and change

into a zooid, after which the colony develops from one primordial zooid by asexual budding.

Most marine bryozoa belong to the class Gymnolaemata, which has round or box-like zooids. Polymorphism is common in these colonies. The class Stenolaemata has some living marine examples and many fossil forms. The zooids are cylindrical and polymorphism is less common. A third group is restricted to fresh water.

The term 'sea mosses' relates to the fact that most bryozoan colonies encrust and grow over the surfaces of rocks or other organisms such as algae or shells just as moss may grow on wood or rocks. Bryozoa can be important as fouling organisms because of this habit.

Anderson's Bryozoan

Orange Bryozoan

Adeona grisea

■ CLASS: Gymnolaemata

FAMILY: Adeonidae
SCIENTIFIC NAME: *Adeona grisea*
COMMON NAME: Grey Fan Bryozoan
DISTRIBUTION: WT/S
HABITAT: Rocky reefs
GENERAL WATER DEPTH: 8–25 m
  (26–82 ft)
FOOD HABIT: Omnivorous: plankton
SIZE: 30 mm (1.2 in) (colony height)
DESCRIPTION: The largest of the typical fan bryozoans, this species grows upright from deep reefs, jutting out sideways from drop-offs and upside down from the ceilings of caves in the South Indian Ocean. Colour varies from light fawn through to deep grey, almost to black. It is very thin, especially towards the edges. The grey fan bryozoan attaches to the substrate by a calcareous holdfast shaped somewhat like a tree trunk and roots. Often the branches arc out from the centre of each side towards the colony's edge, giving extra support to the structure. Tube worms are the only observed associate of this species, although the long cirri feather star (*Ptilometra macronema*) often uses this bryozoan as a feeding platform.

Adeonellopsis sulcata

FAMILY: Adeonidae
SCIENTIFIC NAME: *Adeonellopsis sulcata*
COMMON NAME: Cabbage Bryozoan
DISTRIBUTION: WT/S
HABITAT: Rocky reefs
GENERAL WATER DEPTH: 12–40 m
  (39–131 ft)
FOOD HABIT: Omnivorous: plankton
SIZE: 1 m (3 ft) (colony width)
DESCRIPTION: Varying in colour from brown to purple, the cabbage bryozoan is the largest massive bryozoan in the South-West Pacific region. Generally found on coastal and offshore reefs, the species can also occupy positions along channel edges and at the bottom of deep channels, or drop-offs in bays or inlet entrances. Under these conditions large colonies pose few problems in field identification, but smaller colonies of similar shape in sheltered conditions can be determined only by a specialist as there are several other bryozoans that superficially look similar in growth pattern. Predators include the vermilion biscuit star, (*Pentagonaster dubeni*) and the cymbal margin shell (*Microginella cymbalum*), which is a resident predator on cabbage bryozoan in southern waters.

Bugula dentata

FAMILY: Bugulidae
SCIENTIFIC NAME: *Bugula dentata*
COMMON NAME: Blue Polyzoan
DISTRIBUTION: TI–WP; WT/S
HABITAT: Coral reefs; rocky reefs; rocky shores
GENERAL WATER DEPTH: Low tide to 40 m (131 ft)
FOOD HABIT: Omnivorous: plankton
SIZE: 100 mm (4 in) (colony width)
DESCRIPTION: Not all bryozoan colonies secrete rigid calcareous skeletons; some contain calcite in the zooid walls, but the soft pliable tufts can move backwards and forwards in the current or swell. These organisms are commonly known as polyzoans. Looking superficially similar to algae, the blue polyzoan generally occurs in caves and under ledges or on drop-offs or rock faces, and appears to be more common in summer. On tropical reefs, a bright blue pycnogonid sea spider feeds on the blue polyzoan, and in southern Pacific areas it is preyed upon by Verco's nudibranch (*Tambja verconis*). Pycnogonids suck out the soft parts of polyzoans, whereas nudibranchs browse on the entire structure.

Celleporaria sp.

FAMILY: Celleporidae
SCIENTIFIC NAME: *Celleporaria* sp.
COMMON NAME: Nippled Bryozoan
DISTRIBUTION: WT/S
HABITAT: Rocky reefs; rocky coasts
GENERAL WATER DEPTH: 15–25 m
  (49–82 ft)
FOOD HABIT: Omnivorous: plankton
SIZE: 130 mm (5 in) (colony width)
DESCRIPTION: This group of bryozoans can be identified only to genus level as some species appear similar. Found in areas of constant water movement, the white-feeding zooids of the nippled bryozoan contrast with the dark purplish colour of the colony's skeleton. The zooids are expanded during both night and day and there appears to be no adverse reaction or withdrawal on exposure to strong light. Colour is maintained throughout its distribution, and although small colonies may not have the fan shape until adequate base material has been deposited, the nippled bryozoan is readily recognised by a practised observer. No predators or commensal relationships have so far been observed.

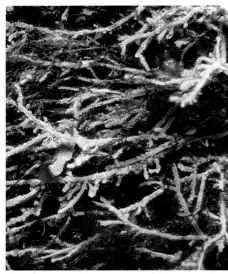

Electra pilosa

FAMILY: Electridae
SCIENTIFIC NAME: *Electra pilosa*
COMMON NAME: Hairy Sea-mat
DISTRIBUTION: CT/N; EA
HABITAT: On shells, stones and seaweeds
GENERAL WATER DEPTH: 0–100 m (328 ft)
FOOD HABIT: Omnivorous: plankton, suspended detritus
SIZE: Colony 30 mm (1.2 in)
DESCRIPTION: The spines and bristles surrounding each zooid give the hairy sea-mat its furred appearance. The outline of the zooids is more rounded than that of *Membranipora mebranacea*, which it superficially resembles. It encrusts shells, seaweeds and stones throughout the distribution area.

Pentapora foliacea

FAMILY: Hippoporinidae
SCIENTIFIC NAME: *Pentapora foliacea*
COMMON NAME: Rose or Ross 'Coral'
DISTRIBUTION: CT/N
HABITAT: Rocky reefs and rocky shores
GENERAL WATER DEPTH: 10–50 m (32.8–164 ft)

FOOD HABIT: Omnivorous: plankton
SIZE: Colonies up to 500 mm (19.7 in) in diameter
DESCRIPTION: Colonies of this species form domed shapes on rocks and are often found where fast currents run. The flattened branches are fused into a network of plates; small crabs shelter in the gaps between these plates. Many bryozoans retain the colour of their skeletal materials long after the animals themselves have perished.

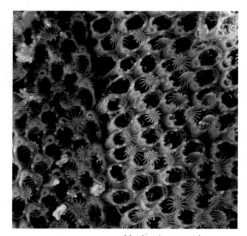

Membranipora membranacea

FAMILY: Membraniporidae
SCIENTIFIC NAME: *Membranipora membranacea*
COMMON NAME: Sea-mat
DISTRIBUTION: Worldwide (temperate)
HABITAT: On kelp
GENERAL WATER DEPTH: Intertidal to 30 m (98 ft)
FOOD HABIT: Omnivorous: plankton
SIZE: Colony 150 mm (6 in)
DESCRIPTION: Sea-mats are likely to be found as an encrustation on kelp plants. The individuals making up the colonies have a rectangular shape. These small fragile colonies are a fascinating study in diversity of shape as no two colonies are the same.

FAMILY: Parmulariidae
SCIENTIFIC NAME: *Lanceopora obliqua*
COMMON NAME: Little Fan Bryozoan
DISTRIBUTION: WT/S
HABITAT: Sand; rubble
GENERAL WATER DEPTH: 15–30 m (49–98 ft)
FOOD HABIT: Omnivorous: plankton
SIZE: 50 mm (2 in) (colony width)
DESCRIPTION: Restricted to areas of good current flow off headlands or in channels, the little fan bryozoan is a rather unusual type of bryozoan colony. Unlike many other sand-inhabiting forms it has an anchoring stalk of soft cellular material upon which the calcareous structure is built. This allows the little fan bryozoan to move in any direction according to the current flow, thus increasing the area and time over which the colony can feed. The species retains its shape and colour throughout its range and can be identified in the field. Damage to colonies seems to be due to intermittent browsing by fish.

FAMILY: Petraliidae
SCIENTIFIC NAME: *Petralia undulata*
COMMON NAME: Wavy Bryozoan
DISTRIBUTION: WT/S
HABITAT: Sand; rubble
GENERAL WATER DEPTH: 10–40 m (33–131 ft)
FOOD HABIT: Omnivorous: plankton
SIZE: 150 mm (6 in) (colony width)
DESCRIPTION: Anchored to the sandy substrate by a bunch of soft rhizoids which are quite often attached to a small shell or stone, the wavy bryozoan is usually found in areas of moderate current off headlands or along the slopes or sea bed adjacent to drop-offs. The wavy bryozoan is a colonial animal that constructs purple limy structures. In some areas the tops of the colonies curl over to form a half tube, and along the growing edge the colour may be yellowish, particularly on smaller colonies. In all colonies the

Lanceopora obliqua

Petralia undulata

holes and the surface patterns on the outside of the calcareous skeleton are retained. The minute zooids feed on plankton both day and night, and as yet no direct predators have been recorded.

Iodictyum phoeniceum

FAMILY: Reteporidae
SCIENTIFIC NAME: *Iodictyum phoeniceum*
COMMON NAME: Purple Bryozoan
DISTRIBUTION: TI–WP; WT/S
HABITAT: Coral reefs; rocky reefs; rocky coasts
GENERAL WATER DEPTH: 15–40 m (49–131 ft)
FOOD HABIT: Omnivorous: plankton
SIZE: Up to 200 mm (8 in) (colony width)
DESCRIPTION: The purple bryozoan is an interesting and fairly easily identified species found on vertical faces as well as the horizontal platforms of coastal and offshore reefs where there is a continual flow of clean oceanic water. Most colonies are small and in the dim light of deeper waters are often overlooked, especially when more dominant

sessile animals are crowded around them. However, at Lord Howe Island in the South-West Pacific, colonies may reach a diameter of over 200 mm (8 in), the largest colonies so far recorded. The purple colour of this species fades very little and some specimens have retained good colour even 15 years after collection. No specific associations have been determined, although some colonies often harbour brittle stars and craylets as do many other discrete bryozoans.

Triphyllozoon monilifera

FAMILY: Reteporidae
SCIENTIFIC NAME: *Triphyllozoon monilifera*
COMMON NAME: Lace Bryozoan
DISTRIBUTION: TI–WP; WT/S
HABITAT: Rocky reefs
GENERAL WATER DEPTH: 5–40 m (16–131 ft)
FOOD HABIT: Omnivorous: plankton
SIZE: 400 mm (16 in) (colony width)
DESCRIPTION: With regard to identification of bryozoans in the field, general opinion has been that shape of the colonies is subject to too much variation to be of worthwhile taxonomic value for, being colonial animals, bryozoans are sensitive to many factors in their environment that influence their growth. However, owing to encouragement by the author, it has been accepted that quite a number of species in the South-West Pacific can be field identified by their living colony structure. Lace bryozoan occurs in clumps on channel bottoms — in some areas carpeting the bottom. Many animals take refuge in its lacy folds and at least two species of the squat lobster (*Munida*) have a commensal relationship.

Schizoporella subsinuata

FAMILY: Schizoporellidae
SCIENTIFIC NAME: *Schizoporella subsinuata*
COMMON NAME: Orange Tube Bryozoan
DISTRIBUTION: WT/S
HABITAT: Rocky reefs; rocky coasts; rubble; seagrass meadows
GENERAL WATER DEPTH: 2–40 m (6–131 ft)
FOOD HABIT: Omnivorous: plankton
DESCRIPTION: There is no doubt that this species is a little difficult to distinguish in its small encrusting stages, but once the colony has begun to branch, the structure becomes fairly typical. The orange tube bryozoan is one of the most common larger bryozoans encountered in the rocky reef zone along the southern Pacific and Indian Ocean shores. It occurs on rocky reefs, rubble and shell grit substrate, especially where there is a good current flow, and also in seagrass meadows. Its tubular protrusions are a haven for a host of marine invertebrates; shrimps, worms, crabs, amphipods, brittle stars, and molluscs can all be found sheltering in and among tubes. Handling of this species, wet or dry, is likely to cause skin irritation. No predators have been identified in the field.

Stenopus hispidus

CRUSTACEANS

PHYLUM: Crustacea (Crustaceans)
CLASS: Cirripedia (Barnacles), Malacostraca (Mantis shrimps, isopods, amphipods, shrimps, prawns, rock lobsters, hermit crabs, crabs), Copepoda, Merostomata (King crabs), Pynogonida (Sea spiders)

For many years crustaceans, together with the land and freshwater insects, spiders, sea spiders, mites, ticks and horseshoe crabs, were included in the phylum Arthropoda. More recent workers have concluded that many of these animals evolved independently.

Crustaceans are by far the most numerous animals in the sea; some types occur in fresh water. Although they vary in superficial structure and habitat, most have a basic design: a jointed, armour-like outer casing (exoskeleton) that protects their soft parts. The underlying parts and the body are divided into segments. The body is bilaterally symmetrical and there is usually a well-developed head and nervous system and sensory organs, many having remarkably acute eyesight. Most crustacean exoskeletons consist of chitin strengthened by calcium salts. Growth is a problem inside a rigid exoskeleton so this is periodically moulted to allow growth. Individuals may eat part of their old outer casing to absorb its calcium, harden their new armour and make use of a resource that would otherwise be wasted.

Many people are familiar with prawns, crabs and lobsters. Divers often recognise other larger crustaceans like rock lobsters, shovelnose lobsters, blue swimmer crabs and prawns. The smaller crustaceans are less known. There are around 30,500 species throughout the world, including many freshwater species, and though much work was done in the nineteenth century, by comparison little has been published in recent times. Species recognition is still based on keys and microscopic studies.

Colour photography of living or recently dead specimens

can aid identification of most of the larger and many of the smaller species.

It is usually possible to identify crustaceans in the field, though colours and patterns vary, external features on juveniles and adults may differ, and sexual dimorphism often occurs.

CLASS: Cirripedia

Most of the intertidal barnacles have been described, along with those washed up on flotsam (which commonly occurs) or dredged; not all are well known, although Charles Darwin realised that barnacles were a very fruitful group to study and made a great contribution to our knowledge of them.

Very few lay people recognise barnacles as crustaceans. After all, who would liken a swift-footed rock crab to a volcano-shaped bunch of shelly plates glued to a rock? Barnacles, in fact, stand on their 'heads' and sweep plankton into their mouths with their feet.

Barnacles are not very prominent subtidally, as most are covered with other forms of encrusting sea life and remain camouflaged. Many species are very small. Some are commensal with other animals, for example, sponges and corals. Some are parasitic and actually live partly inside their host, feeding on its body tissues. *Sacculina* is a parasitic barnacle that castrates its host crab into the bargain! Once a host is known it may be easier to identify the parasite. In most cases smaller barnacles require identification by a specialist. Some are able to bore holes into rock and therefore need less protection from shelly plates.

Almost all species of barnacles are hermaphrodites though cross fertilisation usually occurs, with each barnacle impregnating its neighbour with a penis that can be extended up to 30 times the length of its body. The eggs hatch into planktonic larvae, which unlike their parents are immediately recognisable as crustaceans. After a period of feeding, a non-feeding stage develops that is specially adapted for the critical task of habitat selection. When metamorphosis occurs, this last larval stage must be cemented down, head first, in the correct position, where the adult will spend its entire life. To help in favourable site selection, larvae are often attracted to existing adults of the same species.

In a few species the sexes are separate and in some solitary commensal species self-fertilisation may occur.

CLASS: Malacostraca

This is a very large and varied group of crustaceans. Many species of Malacostraca are popular as food animals and those farmed commercially are fairly well known, so their life histories must have been investigated and understood. In other cases less is known about their development and life histories and the animals themselves are known only by people familiar with the group.

These crustaceans may be found in almost any habitat in the sea. They live in burrows in sand or mud among rubble, on reefs, in caves and under ledges and rocks. Some bury by day and emerge at night. Some carry shells over their heads and others live in them. Some are permanent swimmers in the vast ocean spaces. There are species only millimetres in size that are carried about in the water column as plankton, and giants weighing 15 kilograms (33 pounds) that crawl about on rocky reefs 100 metres (330 feet) below the surface.

They feed on a variety of organisms: bacteria, plankton, sediment, suspended particles, algae, molluscs, fish, worms and other crustaceans and carrion.

Almost all are free living. Some live commensally with other animals such as echinoderms, cnidarians, sponges, bryozoans and ascidians. Some smaller species are obligate commensals and parasites and have highly modified bodies.

The sexes are generally separate and, after mating, the female lays eggs that are carried beneath the abdominal flaps of crabs, on the modified swimmerets (swimming feet) of rock lobsters and shrimps, and on the chests of mantis shrimps. On hatching, the larvae join the plankton and pass through a series of free-swimming stages before settling to the bottom where they metamorphose into juveniles of their particular species.

Spotted Anemone Crab

Ghost Crab

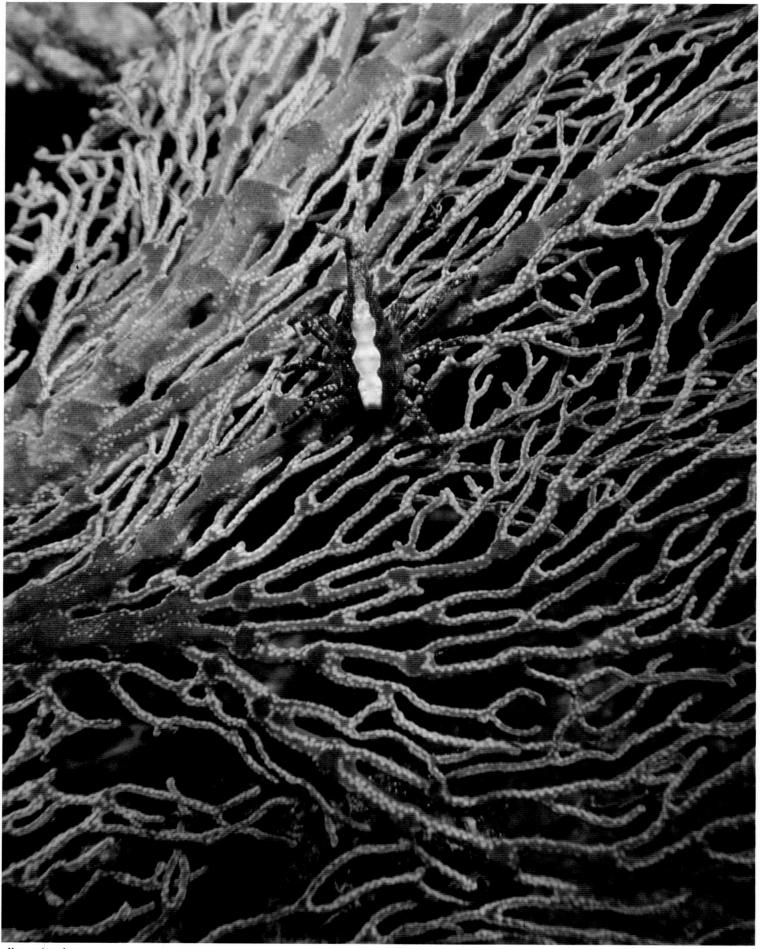

Xenocarcinus depressus

Ghost Crab

Balanus perforatus

■ CLASS: Cirripedia

FAMILY: Balanidae
SCIENTIFIC NAME: *Balanus perforatus*
COMMON NAME: Perforated Barnacle
DISTRIBUTION: CT/N; EA
HABITAT: Rocky shores
GENERAL WATER DEPTH: 0–5 m (0–16.4 ft)
FOOD HABIT: Omnivorous: plankton
SIZE: Up to 20 mm (0.79 in) diameter
DESCRIPTION: Occurring on the lower shore and in shallow water, this barnacle has six strongly built shell plates. These plates are often striated and have a purplish colouration.

Elminius modestus

FAMILY: Balanidae
SCIENTIFIC NAME: *Elminius modestus*
 (*E. convertus*)
COMMON NAME: Modest Barnacle
DISTRIBUTION: CT/S
HABITAT: Rocky reefs; rocky shores
GENERAL WATER DEPTH: 0–5 m (16 ft)
FOOD HABIT: Omnivorous: plankton
SIZE: 12 mm (0.5 in) (width)
DESCRIPTION: The modest barnacle survives better in brackish water than most other species and may be found in the upper limits of the littoral zone, where it attaches

to any suitable substratum. It also occurs on wharf piles, groynes at mid-tide level and sometimes subtidally to 5 m (16 ft). At different places throughout its range there seems to be a variation in selected habitat. This species is a small, very common barnacle often seen in tightly packed communities. It grows to 12 mm (0.5 in) in width, though growth seems to be inhibited in oversettled places. The shell has four main plates, which distinguishes it from many other small barnacles; however, close inspection is necessary. Where there are solitary specimens, two to four attachment holdfasts to each plate may be seen. The shell plates are greyish white and may contribute to the hotch-potch of encrusting organisms that foul the undersides of boats.

Tesseropora rosea

FAMILY: Balanidae
SCIENTIFIC NAME: *Tesseropora rosea*
COMMON NAME: Rose Barnacle
DISTRIBUTION: WT/S; CT/S
HABITAT: Rocky reefs; rocky shores
GENERAL WATER DEPTH: Low tide
FOOD HABIT: Omnivorous: plankton
SIZE: 20 mm (0.7 in) (width)
DESCRIPTION: The rose barnacle is a gregarious, highly populous species that forms dense colonies on exposed rocky reefs and platforms along Australia's south-eastern coasts. It seems to prefer a location in the upper littoral zone where it is exposed to moderate-to-strong wave action. Quite often an area is so densely populated that the shells overgrow each other. The species grows to about 20 mm (0.7 in) in width and may be up to 12 mm (0.5 in) in height. On younger adult shells the orifice is pentagonal; on older shells this feature may not be so apparent, owing to erosion. The species has four shell plates. Adult rose barnacles are pink with a white band around the top of the tall, conical shell. Young rose barnacles are generally white with a band of pink around

their centre. Rose barnacles feed on plankton brought to them by the pounding surf, and in turn are eaten by fish, crabs and carnivorous molluscs. Food is caught by the swift, rhythmic movement of the thoracic appendages, which sweep the water like a net.

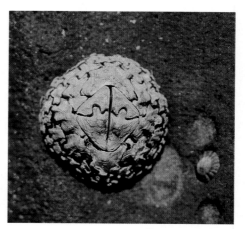

Catomerus polymerus

FAMILY: Chthamalidae
SCIENTIFIC NAME: *Catomerus polymerus*
COMMON NAME: Surf Barnacle
DISTRIBUTION: WT/S; CT/S
HABITAT: Rocky reefs
GENERAL WATER DEPTH: Intertidal
FOOD HABIT: Omnivorous: plankton
SIZE: 25 mm (1 in)
DESCRIPTION: Glued to the rock surface and housed in a shell that looks somewhat like a midget volcano, rock barnacles are among the animals that have successfully colonised the buffer edge of the intertidal zone on exposed coastlines. The surf barnacle is one of the most characteristic barnacles, having eight major shell plates surrounded below by smaller ones, all fitting together like a tiny jigsaw puzzle. This species lives on open coasts and in bays, usually in places exposed to the prevailing weather.

Chthamalus stellatus

FAMILY: Chthamalidae
SCIENTIFIC NAME: *Chthamalus stellatus*
COMMON NAME: Star Barnacle
DISTRIBUTION: CT/N; EA; WA
HABITAT: Rocky reefs and shores
GENERAL WATER DEPTH: Intertidal
FOOD HABIT: Omnivorous: plankton
SIZE: Up to 20 mm (0.79 in) diameter
DESCRIPTION: The star barnacle has six similar-sized shell plates arranged around an oval opening. This common rock-dwelling species has a characteristic arrangement of the joints between the plates: they form a movable lid within the opening.

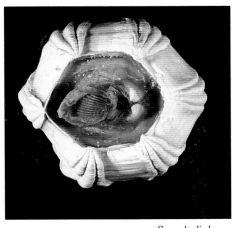

Coronula diadema

FAMILY: Coronulidae
SCIENTIFIC NAME: *Coronula diadema*
COMMON NAME: Diadem Whale Barnacle; Whale Barnacle
DISTRIBUTION: TI–WP; WT/S; WT/N; CT/S
HABITAT: Whales
GENERAL WATER DEPTH: Surface to 4000 m (13,000 ft)
FOOD HABIT: Omnivorous: plankton
SIZE: 65 mm (2.6 in)
DESCRIPTION: Rarely seen as individuals except on beached whales, whale barnacles appear as groups of white encrusting blobs and occur on specific areas on some larger whales such as humpbacks. The diadem whale barnacle has developed a unique habitat, becoming so specialised that it is found nowhere else but on the throat and belly of whales. Similar to all barnacles it is a plankton feeder, though unlike most reef-dwelling barnacles it has a huge orifice which houses the largest and most highly developed gills of any known barnacle. Owing to the host whales visiting both cold southern waters and warm tropical waters, the diadem whale barnacle must maintain its metabolism, which must increase as the temperature gets higher. The shell itself is beautifully sculptured and simple to identify.

Lepas anserifera

FAMILY: Lepadidae
SCIENTIFIC NAME: *Lepas anserifera*
COMMON NAME: Short-stalked Goose Barnacle
DISTRIBUTION: TI–WP; WT/S; CT/S
HABITAT: Oceanic
GENERAL WATER DEPTH: Surface waters
FOOD HABIT: Omnivorous: plankton
SIZE: 50 mm (2 in)
DESCRIPTION: This barnacle is one of several pelagic species that inhabit the oceanic waters. Goose barnacles are sedentary crustaceans that settle from plankton at the larval stage and become fixed for extended periods to almost any object floating in the sea including logs, timber, tins, corks, light bulbs, buoys, bottles, roe, seaweed, pumice and, in some cases, lumps of tar. While the unstalked barnacles are unable to move once their shells are formed, the goose barnacle has a stalk capable of restricted movement. Food is caught by the rhythmical grasping motion of the animal's cirri, which collect plankton and suspended sediment from the water and direct it to the mouth. The short-stalked goose barnacle is hermaphroditic; some barnacles are capable of both self-fertilisation and cross fertilisation, the former being resorted to when no mates are available.

■ CLASS: Malacostraca

FAMILY: Aegidae
SCIENTIFIC NAME: *Aega serripes*
COMMON NAME: Saw-legged Fish Louse
DISTRIBUTION: WT/S
HABITAT: Rocky reefs; coastal waters
GENERAL WATER DEPTH: 5–25 m (16–82 ft)
FOOD HABIT: Carnivorous: fish
SIZE: 50 mm (2 in)
DESCRIPTION: A parasitic crustacean on

Aega serripes

fishes, the saw-legged fish louse is fairly easy to identify because of its shape, segments, and the white streaks running the length of its body. An active swimmer, it attaches to the outside of a fish in the region of its head, central body, or tail using its sharp, hooked feet with which it stretches the flesh of the fish, making a wound with its mandibles. By keeping the wound open the louse can ingest the blood and body juices of the fish. The adult males and females are fairly similar in size, although the male is slimmer and has smaller eyes. Young are carried beneath the female's abdomen, even juveniles up to 7 mm (0.3 in) in size.

Alpheus sp.

FAMILY: Alpheidae
SCIENTIFIC NAME: *Alpheus* sp.
COMMON NAME: Common Snapping Shrimp
DISTRIBUTION: WT/S
HABITAT: Sandy mud; rubble rocky shores
GENERAL WATER DEPTH: 0–20 m (66 ft)
FOOD HABIT: Omnivorous: detrital feeder
SIZE: 25 mm (1 in)
DESCRIPTION: Living at low tide beneath stones and in burrows among rubble and shell grit, the common snapping shrimp is almost always found in pairs. Though to many people snapping shrimps represent only good bait for fish such as bream and

flathead, they have many interesting features. Most species form pair-bond relationships and in many species the females are larger than the males. Common snapping shrimps are often called pistol shrimps owing to their habit of producing loud noises like miniature pistol shots. These noises are made by the large nipper; the hinged top half has a peg and socket system which snaps down when released. The large nipper is also used for defence.

Synalpheus stimpsoni

FAMILY: Alpheidae
SCIENTIFIC NAME: *Synalpheus stimpsoni*
COMMON NAME: Stimpson's Snapping
  Shrimp
DISTRIBUTION: TI–WP
HABITAT: Coral reefs
GENERAL WATER DEPTH: 3–20 m (10–66 ft)
FOOD HABIT: Omnivorous: plankton;
  mucus
SIZE: 20 mm (0.7 in)
DESCRIPTION: Most people are aware of the little snapping shrimps which inhabit the undersides of stones or burrow tunnels in the mud flats where at low tide their sharp staccato sound can be heard echoing out over the tidal flats. The noise comes from their extra large nipper which has a spring-hinged pincer with a nodule that slams into a socket in the lower pincer. This large nipper is used for noise making and also for defence. Stimpson's snapping shrimp is commensal on feather stars where it spends its entire life hidden among the protective arms of its host. Feather stars usually have at least two shrimps present, one male and one female, with colour generally similar to that of the host.

FAMILY: Axiidae
SCIENTIFIC NAME: *Axius plectorhynchus*
COMMON NAME: Slow Yabbie
DISTRIBUTION: TI–WP; WT/S
HABITAT: Coral reefs; rocky reefs

Axius plectorhynchus

GENERAL WATER DEPTH: 0–5 m (16 ft)
FOOD HABIT: Omnivorous: organic detritus
SIZE: 70 mm (2.8 in)
DESCRIPTION: Displaying its brightly coloured, distinctive, red-striped nippers, the slow yabbie is a burrowing species and occurs in many habitats that offer suitable substrate for excavation. The slow yabbie may be seen when decayed coral slabs are overturned or when rocks are moved and the burrows exposed. The eggs are carried by the female beneath the abdomen and attached to the swimmerets. Unlike many other crustacea this species lays relatively few, but very large, eggs. The young hatch out as minute replicas of the parents and are carried around until they grow old enough to fend for themselves. Food includes detritus and suspended matter from which organic materials are separated and digested.

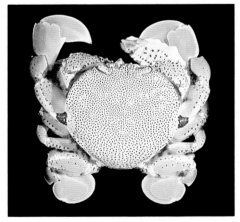

Matuta granulosa

FAMILY: Calappidae
SCIENTIFIC NAME: *Matuta granulosa*
COMMON NAME: Granulated Sand Crab
DISTRIBUTION: TI–WP
HABITAT: Sand shores
GENERAL WATER DEPTH: Low tide to 20 m
  (66 ft)

FOOD HABIT: Carnivorous: invertebrates
SIZE: 100 mm (4 in)
DESCRIPTION: The granulated sand crab occurs both intertidally and subtidally in tropical locations. It has much the same shape as other *Matuta* species and it has similar habits and behaviour. The carapace is dull white and covered with hundreds of minute red specks. There is also a red blotch at the base of each of the large spines located either side and attached to the carapace. The legs are bright yellow with red specks along the tops and sides. The granulated sand crab is far more common than is realised and inhabits some northern Australian beaches in large numbers. However, owing to their habit of staying buried until the rising tide commences to flood, their presence often goes unnoticed. The species is an active carnivore, even attacking and eating members of its own species.

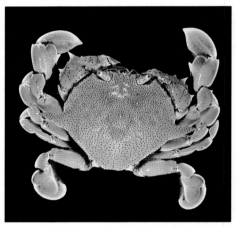

Matuta lunaris

FAMILY: Calappidae
SCIENTIFIC NAME: *Matuta lunaris*
COMMON NAME: Lunar Box Crab
DISTRIBUTION: TWP; WT/S
HABITAT: Sand
GENERAL WATER DEPTH: Low tide to 20 m
  (66 ft)
FOOD HABIT: Carnivorous: invertebrates
SIZE: 76 mm (3 in)
DESCRIPTION: The crabs of this genus are very common residents of shallow, tropical waters. Although they are often very similar in shape, each has a characteristic pattern. Although the lunar box crab looks very similar to the granulated sand crab (*Matuta granulosa*), it has purple flecks on its back and legs. The carapace spines are much larger in comparison and lack the blotches of colour so easily seen in the granulated sand crab. With its specially bladed paddles on all legs except the claws, the lunar box crab is able to swim short distances and, like all other members of its family, buries by a series of backward scuttles. The paddle-like

legs dig the sand away underneath and as the crab goes in backwards the sand settles on top of it, an action that in water-washed sand takes only seconds.

Matuta planipes

FAMILY: Calappidae
SCIENTIFIC NAME: *Matuta planipes*
COMMON NAME: Flat-footed Box Crab
DISTRIBUTION: TI–WP
HABITAT: Sand shores
GENERAL WATER DEPTH: Low tide to 10 m (33 ft)
FOOD HABIT: Carnivorous: invertebrates
SIZE: 125 mm (5 in)
DESCRIPTION: Throughout its range this exquisitely patterned species varies in background colour from white to bright yellow, with a purple, red, or brown design. Depending on the crab's locality, the colour pattern may also be subject to variation. The figured animals are from the Arafura Sea, Indo-Pacific, and crabs from that locality are by far the most colourful. The flat-footed box crab inhabits sandy shores and is most prevalent just below the low-tide level. Although it can swim when disturbed, its main method of protection lies in its ability to disappear beneath the sand in an instant using a backward scuttling movement. It has sharp spines and very strong cutting claws, so that catching one with bare hands is rather hazardous. The crabs prey on most of the animals sharing their sandy retreat and will eat even members of their own species. When this occurs a prey crab is held at the rear or side by one of the attacker's claws, while the other claw is used to tear out the soft parts.

FAMILY: Calappidae
SCIENTIFIC NAME: *Mursia curtispina*
COMMON NAME: Spiny Box Crab
DISTRIBUTION: TI–WP; WT/S
HABITAT: Mud
GENERAL WATER DEPTH: 40–100 m (131–328 ft)

Mursia curtispina

FOOD HABIT: Carnivorous: hermit crabs
SIZE: 100 mm (4 in)
DESCRIPTION: Primarily found in deep water, the spiny box crab is a fairly common inhabitant of the offshore continental shelf and is regularly brought up by trawlers. Its most distinctive features are the strong sharp spines issuing from the lateral edge of the carapace and the strong spiny claws that also bear well-developed spines at the lateral joints. Unlike other box crabs it has no overlapping carapace where the legs can be drawn in and protected. All box crabs are burrowers; lurking beneath the sand with only eyes protruding, they lie in ambush for molluscs and hermit crabs. Many species have modified claws to enable them to break open or chip the shells of their prey into pieces.

Cancer novaezealandie

FAMILY: Cancridae
SCIENTIFIC NAME: *Cancer novaezealandie*
COMMON NAME: New Zealand Stone Crab
DISTRIBUTION: CT/S
HABITAT: Mud; sand; rocky reefs
GENERAL WATER DEPTH: 2–20 m (6–66 ft)
FOOD HABIT: Carnivorous
SIZE: 190 mm (7.5 in)

DESCRIPTION: Living buried beneath the mud around rocks, in sand pockets, or beneath low profile ledges during the day, the New Zealand stone crab is rarely seen by the casual observer. Should the same person visit an area where they abound during the night a much different picture will emerge, with crabs out in the open and foraging for food. If approached too closely they will scuttle backwards into the substrate and hold their large nippers in front as a shield, tucked in under the carapace. As with swimming crabs, no attempt is made to attack; the behaviour is purely defensive. The shape and size of the claws and the shape and pie crust ornamentation of the carapace make identification easier.

FAMILY: Cancridae
SCIENTIFIC NAME: *Cancer pagurus*
COMMON NAME: Edible Crab or Rock Crab
DISTRIBUTION: CT/N; EA
HABITAT: Rocky shores and reefs
GENERAL WATER DEPTH: Subtidal zones
FOOD HABIT: Carnivorous: molluscs
SIZE: 300 mm (11.8 in) or more in width
DESCRIPTION: Highly prized as a food, the edible crab is distinguished by a scalloped edge to its carapace. The massive claws on the first pair of thoracic legs are used to break open mollusc shells. The smaller claw is mainly used for tearing and cutting tissue. Like the lobster, the larger crabs live in a particular crevice; smaller specimens may live under rocks on the shore. This species can reach a weight of 6 kg (13.2 lb).

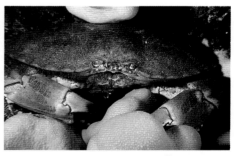

Cancer pagurus

FAMILY: Caprellidae
SCIENTIFIC NAME: *Caprella* sp.
COMMON NAME: Skeleton Shrimp
DISTRIBUTION: WT/S
HABITAT: Rocky reefs; rocky shores
GENERAL WATER DEPTH: Low tide to 60 m (197 ft)
FOOD HABIT: Carnivorous: plankton
SIZE: 12 mm (0.5 in)
DESCRIPTION: The skeleton shrimp is one of the most common macro-shrimps that can be seen. Although small it is by no means

Caprella sp.

out the trauma of being brought to the surface. It might also be expected that some fish may be caught that would have large wounds resulting from attacks by Kapala isopods; however, this does not seem to occur.

Hapalocarcinus marsupialis

difficult to distinguish it underwater once its whereabouts is known. In reality, skeleton shrimps are long, drawn-out, skinny amphipods that cling to underwater growths with their claw-like lower appendages so that they can lean out backwards into the water column and catch plankton. There are many species of skeleton shrimps, and it is known that certain species inhabit particular kinds of host algae and invertebrates. Some appear to mimic their host in behaviour and colouration. Many are so small that a microscope is needed to study them.

FAMILY: Cirolanidae
SCIENTIFIC NAME: *Bathynomus kapala*
COMMON NAME: Kapala Isopod
DISTRIBUTION: WT/S
HABITAT: Mud
GENERAL WATER DEPTH: 500–700 m (1640–2300 ft)
FOOD HABIT: Carnivorous: fish
SIZE: 100 m (4 in)
DESCRIPTION: This species is by far the largest isopod so far discovered in the South-West Pacific. Little is known of its natural history, but it is assumed to have a lifestyle similar to that of other related forms. Even though found in the trawl nets, it has yet to be found attached to a host. This is interesting as a number of other smaller species remain attached to their host fish through-

Gomeza bicornis

FAMILY: Corystidae
SCIENTIFIC NAME: *Gomeza bicornis*
COMMON NAME: Masked Burrowing Crab
DISTRIBUTION: WT/S
HABITAT: Coral reefs; rocky reefs
GENERAL WATER DEPTH: 3–25 m (10–82 ft)
FOOD HABIT: Omnivorous: plankton
SIZE: 45 mm (1.8 in)
DESCRIPTION: The masked burrowing crab featured here was first found by the author during a night dive in 1979. It is unique to southern Australia and only a few specimens have ever been taken alive by hand. This species was thought to burrow into the sand during the day and it had been assumed that its long second antennae (which form a tube when brought together) were used to draw water down to gill cavities. This specimen was found at night clinging to a piece of algae on a reef, intermittently twirling its long, second antennae individually. The latter behaviour suggests that the species also uses its antennae to catch planktonic organisms upon which it feeds, in much the same way that mole crabs do.

FAMILY: Cryptochiridae
SCIENTIFIC NAME: *Hapalocarcinus marsupialis*
COMMON NAME: Gall Crab
DISTRIBUTION: TI-WP; WT/S
HABITAT: Coral reefs; rocky reefs
GENERAL WATER DEPTH: 0–25 m (82 ft)
FOOD HABIT: Omnivorous: plankton

SIZE: 10 mm (0.4 in) (female)
DESCRIPTION: Although the gall crab is a common species it is rarely noticed. When very young, the small female selects a suitable species of coral on which to settle and chooses a site where a new branch is being formed. By intake and expulsion of water it creates currents which, together with its presence, induce the coral to grow around it in a perforated gall of living coral. It is a filter feeder and sexual dimorphism is very marked, the males being so small that they can visit the female through the perforations in the coral gall. Once the gall is formed the female cannot leave the residence.

Dardanus megistos

FAMILY: Diogenidae
SCIENTIFIC NAME: *Dardanus megistos*
COMMON NAME: Red Hermit Crab
DISTRIBUTION: TI-WP
HABITAT: Coral reefs
GENERAL WATER DEPTH: Low tide to 25 m (82 ft)
FOOD HABIT: Carnivorous: scavenger— invertebrates
SIZE: 250 mm (10 in)
DESCRIPTION: The largest of the reef hermit

Bathynomus kapala

crabs, the red hermit crab can be found from low-tide level into deep waters throughout many coral reefs of the world. During the hot sunny days it seeks the shelter of cool recesses beneath coral or under rocks. Mainly predatory, red hermit crabs also scavenge and are able to derive nourishment from detrital feeding. Although many species of hermit crabs are gregarious, the adult red hermit crab lives as a solitary.

Dardanus sp.

FAMILY: Diogenidae
SCIENTIFIC NAME: *Dardanus* sp.
COMMON NAME: Hairy Red Hermit Crab
DISTRIBUTION: WT/S
HABITAT: Rocky reefs; rocky shores
GENERAL WATER DEPTH: Low tide to
   40 m (131 ft)
FOOD HABIT: Carnivorous: invertebrates
SIZE: 150 mm (6 in)
DESCRIPTION: This active predator can be observed both day and night, generally below low-tide level. Not as gregarious as many other species, it is usually encountered singly, but occasionally in pairs. It roams over a fairly wide area, but tends to have a home territory. The hairy red hermit crab is not specific in its food intake and, as an opportunist, will kill and eat fish, molluscs, echinoderms and other hermit crabs; it is also a very efficient scavenger. Most hermit crabs have no hardened cuticle to protect their soft abdomens. After the larvae settle from the plankton on the sea floor and metamorphose, they must find an empty shell of a univalve mollusc with which to protect themselves. During growth hermit crabs periodically leave their old shell for a large one and at these times are very vulnerable. However, it is during this period that they mate. After fertilisation the female produces eggs that are carried attached to abdominal appendages along the body.

Trizopagurus strigatus

FAMILY: Diogenidae
SCIENTIFIC NAME: *Trizopagurus strigatus*
COMMON NAME: Striped Hermit Crab
DISTRIBUTION: TI–WP
HABITAT: Coral reefs; rocky reefs
GENERAL WATER DEPTH: 5–25 m (16–82 ft)
FOOD HABIT: Omnivorous: mobile
   invertebrates
SIZE: 50 mm (2 in)
DESCRIPTION: One of the most striking hermit crabs inhabiting tropical reef waters, this little crustacean is especially adapted to living in cone shells. The striped hermit crab has an extremely flattened body compared to other hermit crabs, enabling it to take advantage of a 'house' that is not available to others. Although the legs, head and claws are brightly coloured, the back is pure white.

FAMILY: Diogenidae
SCIENTIFIC NAME: *Trizopagurus strigimanus*
COMMON NAME: Thin-clawed Hermit Crab
DISTRIBUTION: WT/S; CT/S
HABITAT: Rocky reefs; mud
GENERAL WATER DEPTH: 3–200 m (10–656 ft)
FOOD HABIT: Omnivorous: mobile
   invertebrates
SIZE: 190 mm (7.5 in)

Trizopagurus strigimanus

DESCRIPTION: Mainly encountered during night dives, the thin-clawed hermit crab hides beneath ledges and rocks during the day. Most of the thin-clawed hermit crabs observed inhabited whelk shells much larger than would seem necessary. Two varieties are included in this species. Shallow water forms have very hairy legs and opaque-white spots on bright red bodies. The blue eyes are each bordered by a white circle. There are white spots or broken stripes on the red eye stalks. In contrast, the deepwater forms (pictured) are lighter in colour, less hairy on the legs and have white stripes running the full length of the eye stalks.

Allogalathea elegans

FAMILY: Galatheidae
SCIENTIFIC NAME: *Allogalathea elegans*
COMMON NAME: Elegant Squat Lobster
DISTRIBUTION: TI–WP
HABITAT: Coral reefs
GENERAL WATER DEPTH: 5–25 m (16–82 ft)
FOOD HABIT: Omnivorous: plankton
SIZE: 10 mm (0.4 in)
DESCRIPTION: Found living among the pinnate arms of several species of crinoids (feather stars), the elegant squat lobster has an ideal habitat, safe from most predators. Its colour tends to mimic that of its host. Although most individuals have longitudinal stripes of various thicknesses and colours, those living on red crinoids can be totally red. Specimens are found in pairs, or singly, and the female is larger than the male. Little of the natural history of these animals has been recorded. They may feed on planktonic organisms trapped in the sticky food-collecting system of their host.

Gammarus locusta

FAMILY: Gammaridae
SCIENTIFIC NAME: *Gammarus locusta*
COMMON NAME: Locust Amphipod
DISTRIBUTION: WA; EP
HABITAT: Under stones and seaweeds
GENERAL WATER DEPTH: 0–30 m
(0–98.4 ft)
FOOD HABIT: Omnivorous: plant and
animal debris
SIZE: Up to 20 mm (0.8 in) long
DESCRIPTION: The second antennae of this
species are almost as long as the first, and
small spines are found on the last three
abdominal segments. The females of the spe-
cies are generally smaller than the males.

Cardisoma carnifex

FAMILY: Gecarcinidae
SCIENTIFIC NAME: *Cardisoma carnifex*
COMMON NAME: Giant Land Crab
DISTRIBUTION: TI–WP
HABITAT: Mangroves; wetlands; marshes
GENERAL WATER DEPTH: Low tide
FOOD HABIT: Omnivorous: detritus
SIZE: 150 mm (6 in) (carapace)
DESCRIPTION: With planktonic larvae dispersal it is no wonder that this large land
crab is found in such a wide area of the
Indo-Pacific region. Land crabs live behind
beach dunes where there are areas of low-
lying country offering the cover of grass and
trees. They need a shallow water table near
creeks, swamps and mangroves and soft soil
in which to dig their burrows. Land crabs
feed on vegetable matter and are not often
seen out of their burrows during the day.

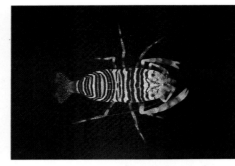

Gnathophyllum americanum

FAMILY: Gnathophyllidae
SCIENTIFIC NAME: *Gnathophyllum
americanum*
COMMON NAME: Zebra Shrimp
DISTRIBUTION: TI–WP; WT/S; WT/N
HABITAT: Coral reefs; rocky reefs; rocky
shores
GENERAL WATER DEPTH: Low tide to 25 m
(82 ft)
FOOD HABIT: Carnivorous
SIZE: 25 mm (1 in)
DESCRIPTION: Although once thought to be
rare, the zebra shrimp is fairly common and
may be found beneath stones, rocks, or dead
coral, in caves, under ledges, and often
beneath sea urchins. It is easily disturbed
and very elusive and unless care is taken it
will very often 'scoot' into hiding once it has
been discovered. The zebra shrimp is cosmopolitan and occurs in many temperate seas
including those of Florida, the United States
and Japan. In the South-West Pacific it has
several colour variations and the banding
may be fine or wide.

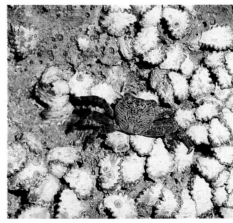

Grapsus albolineatus

FAMILY: Grapsidae
SCIENTIFIC NAME: *Grapsus albolineatus*
COMMON NAME: Swift-footed Rock Crab
DISTRIBUTION: TI–WP
HABITAT: Coral reef rocks; rocky reefs;
rocky shores

GENERAL WATER DEPTH: Intertidal
FOOD HABIT: Omnivorous: algae;
invertebrates
SIZE: 200 mm (8 in)
DESCRIPTION: The swift-footed rock crab
inhabits beach rock along many tropical
reefs. Its body is coloured in a multitude of
greens, blues, oranges and blacks; it is very
beautiful. The males have large claws and
the abdomen is folded under the carapace,
while the females have small claws and carry
their eggs beneath the abdominal flap. It has
been observed feeding on algae and detritus
from the beach rock as well as on small
invertebrates.

Grapsus grapsus

FAMILY: Grapsidae
SCIENTIFIC NAME: *Grapsus grapsus*
COMMON NAME: Mottled Shore Crab
DISTRIBUTION: WA
HABITAT: Rocks; sand; mangroves
GENERAL WATER DEPTH: Above low-tide
line
FOOD HABIT: Herbivore: algae
SIZE: 10 mm (0.4 in)
DESCRIPTION: The mottled shore crab is
most often observed on land, moving swiftly
along the shore or among mangrove roots
and submerging occasionally to feed and
dampen its gills. Its carapace is marked by
many shallow grooves running lengthwise, in
addition to the extensive mottling. The base
colour varies from black to yellow-brown.

FAMILY: Grapsidae
SCIENTIFIC NAME: *Leptograpsus variegatus*
(male)
COMMON NAME: Variegated Shore Crab
DISTRIBUTION: WT/S; CT/S
HABITAT: Rocky reefs
GENERAL WATER DEPTH: Intertidal
FOOD HABIT: Omnivorous: scavenger—
molluscs; algae; crustaceans; flotsam
SIZE: 200 mm (8 in)
DESCRIPTION: A very characteristic, beauti-
fully coloured shore crab, this species occurs
in two colour forms. The commonest (pic-
tured) is usually found beneath rocks, under
ledges, or in cracks and gutters where it

Leptograpsus variegatus (male)

hides from daylight predators. Juveniles and adults may be seen foraging during the day at some locations, although most tend to be more active by night. They are robust and active; the males can give an extremely powerful bite with their large claws which are well-adapted to tearing chitons from rock surfaces, intra-specific fighting, and defending against predators. They eat molluscs, algae and other crabs and also scavenge on fish, sea urchins and sea jellies. The purple-clawed form tends to inhabit the higher reaches of the intertidal zone, while the orange form generally lives at the intertidal fringe and is more likely to be seen in rock pools or among kelp at extreme low water.

Paragrapsus laevis

FAMILY: Grapsidae
SCIENTIFIC NAME: *Paragrapsus laevis* (male)
COMMON NAME: Smooth Shore Crab
DISTRIBUTION: WT/S
HABITAT: Rocky reefs; hard mud; rocky shores; muddy shores
GENERAL WATER DEPTH: Intertidal
FOOD HABIT: Carnivorous
SIZE: 50 mm (2 in)

DESCRIPTION: Generally found in estuaries rather than on the open coast, the smooth shore crab remains somewhat inconspicuous to the average shoregoer as it is rarely seen in the open during the day. It should be seen if rocks are turned over, ledges investigated, holes in the hard mud of river banks dug away, or salt marsh penetrated. The smooth shore crab is easily separated from other shore crabs, and adults (whether male or female) are easily identified as the smooth, shiny-black carapace speckled with yellow and the orange-bronze claws are characteristic and fairly stable features. Juveniles are dark red and not so easy to identify. The species is gregarious and several individuals may be found beneath one rock.

Plagusia chabrus

FAMILY: Grapsidae
SCIENTIFIC NAME: *Plagusia chabrus*
COMMON NAME: Red Bait Crab
DISTRIBUTION: WT/S; CT/S
HABITAT: Rocky reefs; jetties; rocky shores
GENERAL WATER DEPTH: Low tide to 15 m (49 ft)
FOOD HABIT: Carnivorous: scavenger— molluscs; crustaceans; fish
SIZE: 230 mm (9 in)

DESCRIPTION: Visitors to the exposed rocky shore reef of southern Australian waters will often see this crab; fishermen use it as bait for southern blue (groper) wrasse (*Achoerodus gouldi*). It is the largest of the swift-footed shore crabs and is easily recognised by its colour and the deep clefts in the front of its carapace. It lives among rocky reefs and kelp beds subtidally, and when on the shore always seeks the shelter of rock ledges and crevices. Female crabs have much smaller claws than the males but both can deliver a painful nip to a careless hand. The red crab feeds on chitons, limpets and other crabs, as well as being an efficient scavenger. Eggs are red and are carried by

the female beneath the abdominal flap. It appears to be an active daylight predator as it is rarely seen during the night.

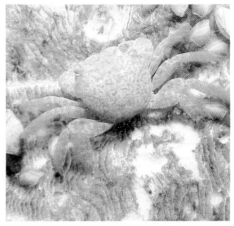

Planes minutus

FAMILY: Grapsidae
SCIENTIFIC NAME: *Planes minutus*
COMMON NAME: Columbus Crab
DISTRIBUTION: TI-WP; WT/S; CT/S
HABITAT: Flotsam
GENERAL WATER DEPTH: Surface waters
FOOD HABIT: Carnivorous
SIZE: 25 mm (1 in)

DESCRIPTION: Found in almost every ocean, the Columbus crab would hardly attract attention or be seen at all, unless some ardent naturalist or beachcomber noticed a likely piece of flotsam or jetsam on the beach and investigated it. Somewhat variable in colour (from blue to brown), it inhabits many objects floating on the ocean, including seaweed and cuttle bones. The wind and tide carry these objects along and the waves and swells crash them on to the shore to be left in the sun. The crabs die along with all the other rafting life. The common name apparently refers to its being found by Columbus during his voyage to the West Indies.

FAMILY: Harposquillidae
SCIENTIFIC NAME: *Harpiosquilla harpax*
COMMON NAME: Javelin Mantis Shrimp
DISTRIBUTION: WT/S
HABITAT: Mud
GENERAL WATER DEPTH: 10–40 m (33–131 ft)
FOOD HABIT: Carnivorous: crustaceans
SIZE: 170 mm (7 in)

DESCRIPTION: Mantis shrimps, or prawn killers as they are known, are some of the most rapacious animals in the sea, and were they of a size that might endanger humans nobody would be safe in the water. Small as they are, ranging from 26 mm to around 300 mm (1–12 in), they can injure an unwary person. The javelin mantis shrimp lives in burrows of its own making in mud or sand

Harpiosquilla harpax

where it shelters during the day. At night it moves out to hunt prey, which generally consists of other crustaceans such as prawns and shrimps. Once a few main features such as colour pattern, shape of the telson (last segment of the body) and claws are known, these types of animals can be identified in the field.

Hippa pacifica

FAMILY: Hippidae
SCIENTIFIC NAME: *Hippa pacifica*
COMMON NAME: Pacific Mole Crab
DISTRIBUTION: TI–WP
HABITAT: Sand; sandy shores
GENERAL WATER DEPTH: Low tide to 10 m (33 ft)
FOOD HABIT: Carnivorous: plankton
SIZE: 40 mm (1.6 in)
DESCRIPTION: This fairly prolific little crab lives in colonies intertidally in coarse sand at

the edge of the surge zone on beaches throughout the Indo-Pacific region. The body shape and smoothness of the Pacific mole crab ideally suit it to its habitat. It swims backward through the loose-moving sand grains in the surf zone and can burrow out of sight in a flash. Trying to catch one can be very frustrating. Like little darts of porcellaneous china they slide between fingers and hands, zipping this way and that. It feeds by using its four hairy antennae which protrude from below its eyes. These antennae are projected from the sand and twirled, creating a current that directs small planktonic creatures towards the hairy mouth parts. The eggs are yellow and carried under the female's abdominal flap which is folded beneath the carapace.

Hippolysmata grabhami

FAMILY: Hippolytidae
SCIENTIFIC NAME: *Hippolysmata grabhami*
COMMON NAME: Grabham's Cleaner Shrimp
DISTRIBUTION: TI–WP; WT/S
HABITAT: Coral reefs; rocky reefs
GENERAL WATER DEPTH: 10–25 m (33–82 ft)
FOOD HABIT: Carnivorous: crustaceans
SIZE: 75 mm (3 in)
DESCRIPTION: Grabham's cleaner shrimp is found in similar habitats to the banded coral shrimp (*Stenopus hispidus*), and both species often share a cleaning station. Although it has the same number of antennae flagella as the banded coral shrimp, its nippers are much smaller. It does not venture far from the protection of the station and seems to attract fish by waving its brilliant white antennae and maxillipeds, which contrast vividly with the dark recesses of the station. Once a fish is attracted and moves into the station, the shrimp's display becomes more vigorous. As the fish hovers, the shrimp reaches out with its maxillipeds and legs, resting the forward half of its body on the fish while removing the parasites and performing other cleaning operations.

Hippolyte inermis

FAMILY: Hipploytidae
SCIENTIFIC NAME: *Hippolyte inermis*
COMMON NAME: Chameleon Prawn
DISTRIBUTION: CT/N; EA
HABITAT: Seagrass meadows
GENERAL WATER DEPTH: Intertidal
FOOD HABIT: Omnivorous
SIZE: 30–40 mm (1.2–1.6 in) long
DESCRIPTION: The common name of this species is derived from the prawn's ability to adapt its colour to that of the substrate on which it lives. It is often found in association with several other closely related species of prawn.

Thor amboinensis

FAMILY: Hippolytidae
SCIENTIFIC NAME: *Thor amboinensis*
COMMON NAME: Amboin Shrimp
DISTRIBUTION: TI–WP; WT/S
HABITAT: Coral reefs; rocky reefs; rocky shores
GENERAL WATER DEPTH: Low tide to 30 m (98 ft)
FOOD HABIT: Omnivorous
SIZE: 12 mm (0.5 in)
DESCRIPTION: This commensal shrimp is common in many areas of coral reef waters and is one of the least specific in its selection of hosts. It inhabits at least seven different species of sea anemones as well as the solitary mushroom coral (*Heliofungia actiniformis*). The Amboin shrimp is usually observed in

pairs on small anemones, but there may be up to six individuals living among the tentacles or beneath the flaps of larger anemones. When frightened or harassed it tends to move beneath the anemone. Females are almost twice the size of males and both have a peculiar behavioural trait that, together with colour pattern, makes them easily identifiable in the field. It holds its abdomen and tail in an almost vertical position and flicks it up and down.

Hymenocera picta

FAMILY: Hymenoceridae
SCIENTIFIC NAME: *Hymenocera picta*
COMMON NAME: Painted Dancing Shrimp
DISTRIBUTION: TI–WP
HABITAT: Coral reefs
GENERAL WATER DEPTH: Low tide to 10 m (33 ft)
FOOD HABIT: Carnivorous: sea stars
SIZE: 60 mm (2.4 in)
DESCRIPTION: The painted dancing shrimp inhabits many tropical coral reefs. It is a very secretive species and few of its habits have been observed under natural conditions. Almost always found in pairs (male and female), the female shrimp is generally the larger. During daylight it keeps to the protection of the reef and ventures forth to feed only during twilight or darkness. Its diet includes the sea stars *Nardoa galathea* and *Fromia elegans*, which are common. Once caught, the sea star is dragged back to the shrimp's lair where the shrimp turns it on its back and feeds at leisure using the short, sharp, strong, feeding nippers. The sea star is eaten from the tip of the arm down to the disc before the shrimp begins on another arm. This method of feeding keeps the sea star alive for several days. The multispotted, flared nippers are used only for display.

Idotea baltica

FAMILY: Idoteidae
SCIENTIFIC NAME: *Idotea baltica*
COMMON NAME: Baltic Sea Centipede
DISTRIBUTION: Cosmopolitan
HABITAT: Amongst seaweed
GENERAL WATER DEPTH: Subtidal
FOOD HABIT: Omnivorous: scavenger
SIZE: 30 mm (1.2 in) long — males; up to 20 mm (0.8 in) long — females
DESCRIPTION: Like most idoteids, this species is very variable in colour, so this criterion should not be used to distinguish between the species. It is characterised by a large central spine and two smaller lateral spines on the rear of the telson. The disparity in size between male and female is a feature of many idoteids.

Ebalia intermedia

FAMILY: Leucosiidae
SCIENTIFIC NAME: *Ebalia intermedia*
COMMON NAME: Smooth Nut Crab
DISTRIBUTION: WT/S
HABITAT: Rocky reefs; rubble; mud
GENERAL WATER DEPTH: Low tide to 15 m (49 ft)
FOOD HABIT: Omnivorous: organic detritus
SIZE: 70 mm (2.8 in)
DESCRIPTION: Smooth nut crabs inhabit sheltered bays and estuaries, as well as exposed coastline, where they live beneath rocks or in the open on a variety of sea floor substrates. Males are larger than females

and generally have longer and better developed claws. During the mating season males have been observed carrying females, holding them firmly in one claw. This practice seems to be widespread in a number of crab families; the author has recorded similar behaviour in other areas with other species. Identification may not be straightforward, especially with juvenile specimens, as the smooth nut crab is a variable species and is often confused with the pebble crab (*Philyra laevis*); they often have somewhat similar habitats. The smooth nut crab has longer claws than its companion and there is a distinct tubercule at the base of the carapace flanked by two phalanges.

Paraleucothoe novaehollandiae

FAMILY: Leucothoidae
SCIENTIFIC NAME: *Paraleucothoe novaehollandiae*
COMMON NAME: New Holland Amphipod
DISTRIBUTION: WT/S
HABITAT: Rocky reefs
GENERAL WATER DEPTH: 5–30 m (16–98 ft)
FOOD HABIT: Omnivorous: plankton; mucus
SIZE: 20 mm (0.8 in)
DESCRIPTION: This little amphipod spends most of its life cycle inside the branchial basket of an ascidian. The photograph depicts the animal in the opened branchial basket of the ascidian *Pyura spinifera*, but it is also found in *P. pachydermatina*. At some time during its larval stage it enters the inhalant siphon of a sea squirt where it becomes established. It feeds on the food particles trapped in the fine network of gill filaments through which the sea squirt draws water for its food and respiration. The relationship of the New Holland amphipod with sea squirts can be both commensalism and endoecism. The females are generally larger than the males and colour tends to vary between blood red and pink.

Ligia exotica

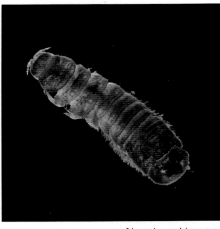

Limnoria quadripunctata

Lysiosquilla tredecimdentata

FAMILY: Ligiidae
SCIENTIFIC NAME: *Ligia exotica*
COMMON NAME: Exotic Shore Slater
DISTRIBUTION: TI–WP; WT/S
HABITAT: Rocky reefs; sand shores; rocky
shores
GENERAL WATER DEPTH: Intertidal
FOOD HABIT: Carnivorous: scavenger
SIZE: 65 mm (2.5 in)
DESCRIPTION: Shore slaters are common
residents of the upper intertidal zone. They
are fast-moving scavengers that can be diurnal and nocturnal, though in some areas one
habit may predominate. In general, the
exotic shore slater seems to prefer rocky
reefs that have sheltered aspects and some
also seem to have an affinity to perpendicular rock faces, underhangs and ledges. This
species grows to around 65 mm (2.5 in). It is
one of the emergent species of marine animals, spending much more time out of water
than in it, although when escaping from
predators such as crabs, rats, or birds it will
drop into the water, swim to the bottom and
crawl out of sight. Like all isopods the shore
slater has twenty fixed body segments. Six
are in the head, eight in the thorax, and six
in the abdomen. Arranged along the body in
pairs are 19 sets of appendages which have
different functions in different regions of the
body; for example, two pairs of sensory
antennae on the head; mandibles; two pairs
of maxillae and maxillipeds also on the head
used for feeding; locomotory poreiopods on
the thorax; and various abdominal appendages used for respiration and copulation and
sensory functions on the abdomen. The movable eye stalks are not counted as appendages.

FAMILY: Limnoriidae
SCIENTIFIC NAME: *Limnoria quadripunctata*
COMMON NAME: Gribble
DISTRIBUTION: Cosmopolitan
HABITAT: Submerged timber

GENERAL WATER DEPTH: Intertidal
FOOD HABIT: Omnivorous
SIZE: Up to 4 mm (0.2 in) long
DESCRIPTION: Before the development of
concrete jetty piles, the gribble was a primary cause for the destruction of timber
piles. This tiny isopod has short antennae
and four small protuberances on the anterior
section of the telson. The species of
Limnoria are difficult to distinguish; all are
wood-borers.

Lomis hirta

FAMILY: Lithodidae
SCIENTIFIC NAME: *Lomis hirta*
COMMON NAME: Hairy Stone Crab
DISTRIBUTION: WT/S; CT/S
HABITAT: Rocky reefs; rocky shores
GENERAL WATER DEPTH: Low tide to
10 m (33 ft)
FOOD HABIT: Omnivorous: plankton
SIZE: 35 mm (1.4 in)
DESCRIPTION: This species is prevalent in
waters along South-Western Pacific coasts
where it can be found living beneath loose
stones and rubble. Specimens also occur at
mid-tide level wherever stones are found in
rock pools or run–offs. Below low-water

mark the crabs tend to become less common
towards the 10 m (33 ft) level. On a sandy
mud bottom the hairy stone crab is almost
impossible to distinguish from its surroundings. Specimens can be found clinging upside
down to the bottom on non-embedded rocks.
The hairy stone crab feeds by filtering planktonic organisms and suspended sediment
from the waters.

FAMILY: Lysiosquillidae
SCIENTIFIC NAME: *Lysiosquilla
tredecimdentata*
COMMON NAME: Thirteen-toothed Mantis
Shrimp
DISTRIBUTION: TI–WP; CT/S
HABITAT: Mud
GENERAL WATER DEPTH: 200–400 m
(656–1312 ft)
FOOD HABIT: Carnivorous: crustaceans
SIZE: 100 mm (4 in)
DESCRIPTION: A deepwater species that is
brought up by trawlers and research vessels,
the thirteen-toothed mantis shrimp's body
pattern doesn't vary much throughout its
range and it is easily identified by the characteristic shape and colour of the telson
(body). Mantis shrimps have remarkably
good eyesight and both the eyes and the
antennules that support them are attached
on movable segments, allowing them full 360
degree vision. This feature is very unusual
for crustaceans. The abdominal swimmerets,
which carry the gills, are used for respiration.

Leptomithrax gaimardi

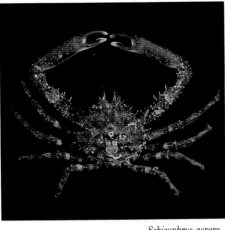

Schizophrys aspera

Mictyris longicarpus

FAMILY: Majidae
SCIENTIFIC NAME: *Leptomithrax gaimardi*
COMMON NAME: Gaimard's Spider Crab
DISTRIBUTION: WT/S; CT/S
HABITAT: Rocky reefs; seagrass meadows;
wharf piles; mud
GENERAL WATER DEPTH: 5–900 m
(16–2953 ft)
FOOD HABIT: Omnivorous: algae
SIZE: 330 mm (13 in)
DESCRIPTION: The largest of the shallow-water spider crabs in the Southern Pacific, Gaimard's spider crab is frequently encountered by skindivers among sponge beds, on sandy bottom areas, algae clumps and rocks on reefs. They are gregarious. Huge aggregations, estimated at around 750,000 specimens, have been seen. One observation showed the crabs, often six deep, in the process of moulting (casting off their old exoskeleton prior to expanding their new one). This spider crab is similar to many other spider crabs in that it uses other marine organisms such as sponges, algae and ascidians as camouflage by attaching them to spines on its carapace and legs. This intentional camouflage (as well as that provided by organisms like barnacles settling naturally on the carapace) makes field determination of species difficult because features may be obscured.

FAMILY: Majidae
SCIENTIFIC NAME: *Schizophrys aspera*
COMMON NAME: Red Spider Crab
DISTRIBUTION: TI-WP; WT/S
HABITAT: Rocky reefs; coral reefs
GENERAL WATER DEPTH: Low tide to
20 m (66 ft)
FOOD HABIT: Omnivorous: algae
SIZE: 50 mm (2 in)
DESCRIPTION: There are a number of different species of spider crabs in southern Pacific waters, most of which have been collected, described and identified by taxon-omists in museums after they have been scrubbed clean of their characteristic marine life growths and keyed out. Even so, they are not always easy to determine. They are also not easy to see in their natural habitat (owing to their camouflage).

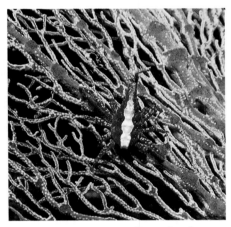

Xenocarcinus depressus

FAMILY: Majidae
SCIENTIFIC NAME: *Xenocarcinus depressus*
COMMON NAME: Depressed Gorgonian
Crab
DISTRIBUTION: TI-WP
HABITAT: Coral reefs
GENERAL WATER DEPTH: 3–20 m (10–66 ft)
FOOD HABIT: Carnivorous
SIZE: 25 mm (1 in)
DESCRIPTION: Restricted to the specific habitat among the fronds and branches of tropical gorgonians, these brightly coloured little crabs are usually found in pairs. Adults seem to differ in size; those from the Pacific Ocean tend to be larger than those from the Indian Ocean. The depressed gorgonia crab is easily identified in the field by its red colour and opaque white stripe, which does not vary throughout its distribution. Some gorgonian fans may have dozens of small juveniles clinging to the fronds. Most either succumb to predators or move on to other gorgonians, as observations of gorgonian clumps generally show no large adult aggregations.

FAMILY: Mictyridae
SCIENTIFIC NAME: *Mictyris longicarpus*
COMMON NAME: Soldier Crab
DISTRIBUTION: TI-WP; WT/S
HABITAT: Sand; mangroves; estuaries;
shores
GENERAL WATER DEPTH: Low tide
FOOD HABIT: Omnivorous: detritus
SIZE: 50 mm (2 in)
DESCRIPTION: Soldier crabs are inhabitants of estuarine shores or those muddy sand areas in bays and inlets that have sheltered, moderately stable conditions. The common name 'soldier crab' stems from their habit of forming large aggregations at certain periods of low tide and 'marching' along in thousands. When feeding they scrape up surface sand with their nippers, and pass it to the mouth parts. These in turn can clean off any residual organic matter and mould the discarded sand grains into small pellets which are deposited back on shore. As the tide comes in the crabs burrow into the sand in a peculiar corkscrew-like motion. The common soldier crab is blue down the centre of the back or carapace, with white or light pink sides. The claws and legs are white with dark red blotches at the joints.

FAMILY: Nephropsidae
SCIENTIFIC NAME: *Homarus gammarus*
COMMON NAME: Common Lobster or
European Lobster
DISTRIBUTION: CT/N; EA
HABITAT: Rocky shores and reefs
GENERAL WATER DEPTH: 20–100 m
FOOD HABIT: Carnivorous: molluscs,
crustaceans
SIZE: Up to 500 mm (19.7 in) long

Homarus gammarus

DESCRIPTION: Much sought after as food, the common lobster boasts large powerful claws which are used to break open mollusc shells. During the day it tends to remain in crevices between rocks rather than foraging in the open, and only its antennae and claws will protrude.

Heloecius cordiformis (male)

FAMILY: Ocypodidae
SCIENTIFIC NAME: *Heloecius cordiformis* (male)
COMMON NAME: Semaphore Crab
DISTRIBUTION: TI–WP; WT/S
HABITAT: Mud flats
GENERAL WATER DEPTH: Intertidal
FOOD HABIT: Omnivorous: organic detritus
SIZE: 35 mm (1.4 in)
DESCRIPTION: Semaphore crabs occur in colonies in estuaries, bays and inlets where there is some soft stable substrate with a high organic content. Females have small claws and large abdominal flaps; males have large claws and small abdominal flaps. Fully adult males have equal-size claws that are purple with white pincers; sub-adult males have pink or orange claws. They live in deep burrows dug in the mud. During high tide they occupy the burrows and rarely move from this protection until the tide recedes. As the water ebbs they come out of their burrows to feed on organic materials on the mud surface. During low tide the males per-

form all the necessary functions of community living; they defend their burrows and surrounding territory from other males, court nearby females, feed, and are continually aware of possible predation from both land and air. At the slightest disturbance they disappear down their burrows.

Macrophthalmus crassipes

FAMILY: Ocypodidae
SCIENTIFIC NAME: *Macrophthalmus crassipes*
COMMON NAME: Sentinel Crab
DISTRIBUTION: TI–WP; WT/S
HABITAT: Mud flats
GENERAL WATER DEPTH: Intertidal to 10 m (33 ft)
FOOD HABIT: Omnivorous: organic detritus
SIZE: 55 mm (2.2 in)
DESCRIPTION: Most crabs in this family are amphibious and spend more time out of the water than in it. The sentinel crab is a little different in that its choice of habitat may vary in specific areas so that in one location it may be living intertidally while in another it may be living totally submerged. The males, at least, are territorial and live in holes burrowed out of the sea floor. During the mating season males engage in ritual territorial display and fights. Unlike other ocypodids the claws of the male sentinel crab are equal in size and both are raised in a threatening stance. The species has a very distinctive shape and is unlikely to be confused with any other shore crab. The carapace is covered with fine granulations.

FAMILY: Ocypodidae
SCIENTIFIC NAME: *Ocypode ceratophthalma*
COMMON NAME: Stalk-eyed Ghost Crab
DISTRIBUTION: TI–WP
HABITAT: Sandy beaches; cays
GENERAL WATER DEPTH: Intertidal
FOOD HABIT: Carnivorous/scavenger: insects; crustaceans; flotsam
SIZE: 200 mm (8 in)

Ocypode ceratophthalma

DESCRIPTION: This crab is the largest of the tropical ghost crabs and can be distinguished by the pointed stalks that protrude above the eyes of adult specimens, the two dark red blotches on its back and the dark red on the underside of the body and legs. Although references maintain that ghost crabs in general are mostly scavengers on the tide lines, observations by the author show the stalk-eyed ghost crab to be a tenacious predator on insects, arachnids, hatching turtles and smaller ghost crabs.

Ocypode cordimana

FAMILY: Ocypodidae
SCIENTIFIC NAME: *Ocypode cordimana*
COMMON NAME: Little Ghost Crab
DISTRIBUTION: TI–WP; WT/S
HABITAT: Sandy beaches
GENERAL WATER DEPTH: Intertidal
FOOD HABIT: Carnivorous: scavenger — flotsam; insects
SIZE: 20 mm (0.8 in) (carapace)
DESCRIPTION: Widespread throughout tropical seas, the little ghost crab has unarmed eyes and tends to be whitish in colour with a few grey blotches. It shows a remarkable turn of speed and can change direction very

quickly. It feeds at the tide line on animal and vegetable flotsam and also devours terrestrial insects. The little ghost crab can change its colour and has been observed to alter from grey to pinkish red during the night-and-day changeover. On some islands in the South-West Pacific, members of this species appear to have darker grey patterning on the carapace with orange marking. Ghost crabs dig burrows above and within the intertidal zone, where they live during the heat of the day.

Scopimera inflata

FAMILY: Ocypodidae
SCIENTIFIC NAME: *Scopimera inflata*
COMMON NAME: Sand Bubbler Crab
DISTRIBUTION: TI–WP
HABITAT: Sand
GENERAL WATER DEPTH: Intertidal
FOOD HABIT: Omnivorous: detritus
SIZE: 20 mm (0.8 in)
DESCRIPTION: The familiar sand ball patterns produced by the sand bubbler crab are a common sight on the low, sloping beaches of tropical and sub-tropical regions and offshore continental islands. During high tide, the sand bubbler crab lives in a burrow it has dug in the firm, hard-packed sand between the high-tide mark and the start of the drainage area. In this area the burrow remains relatively stable and requires only a minimum of sand removal to clear it. As the tide recedes during the night or in the early hours of the morning the sand bubbler digs its way to the surface, clears its burrow and starts to feed by scraping up the surface sand with its larger claws. After eating the organic coverings of the grains it packs the sand into a ball and places the residue in all sorts of designs depending on its feeding pattern for that time. Some patterns are haphazard and others are characteristic. Sand bubblers are the same colour as the sand and grow to 20 mm (0.8 in).

Uca flammula (male)

FAMILY: Ocypodidae
SCIENTIFIC NAME: *Uca flammula* (male)
COMMON NAME: Red Fiddler Crab
DISTRIBUTION: TIO
HABITAT: Mud flats; mangroves
GENERAL WATER DEPTH: Low tide
FOOD HABIT: Omnivorous: detritus
SIZE: 50 mm (2 in)
DESCRIPTION: A brilliantly coloured member of the tropical mangrove fauna, the red fiddler crab is one of the largest fiddler crabs in northern Australia. It is active day and night when the tide is out and can be observed at close range. Like all fiddler crabs this one is gregarious, living in colonies on the mud flats. It digs a vertical burrow into the mud that even during low tide retains some water. The males all have a large claw used to attract females and to repel other males. The colours of the red fiddler crab seem to be more stable than those of other species: the male is bright red with a large black blotch on the carapace that doesn't quite reach the edge; the female has a brown or black carapace with brown legs, brown claws and yellow eye stalks. Females appear to have some colour variation.

Pagurus bernhardus

FAMILY: Paguridae
SCIENTIFIC NAME: *Pagurus bernhardus*
COMMON NAME: Bernhard's Hermit Crab
DISTRIBUTION: CT/N; EA
HABITAT: Gravel and sand substrate
GENERAL WATER DEPTH: Below low tide
FOOD HABIT: Carnivorous
SIZE: Up to 100 mm (3.9 in) long
DESCRIPTION: When adult, this animal is often found dwelling in whelk shells. It is likely to have an association with *Nereis fucata*; this commensal worm lives inside the whelk shell and feeds on scraps left by the crab, putting its head outside the shell to gather them. On the outside of the whelk shell may often be found the commensal anemone *Calliactis parasitica*; up to eight anemones can live on a single crab shell.

Dasycaris zanzibarica

FAMILY: Palaemonidae
SCIENTIFIC NAME: *Dasycaris zanzibarica* (female)
COMMON NAME: Zanzibar Shrimp
DISTRIBUTION: TI–WP
HABITAT: Coral reefs
GENERAL WATER DEPTH: 5–20 m (16–66 ft)
FOOD HABIT: Omnivorous: plankton; mucus
SIZE: 15 mm (0.6 in)
DESCRIPTION: The Zanzibar shrimp inhabits the antipatharian (black coral) *Cirripathes anguinis*. This association seems to be fairly specific and in general both a male and a female live on the one whip. The female is twice the size of the male. In the few specimens observed in the field the male's colour was a dark ochre, very similar to that of the whip, whereas the female (pictured) was much lighter. The species can be readily distinguished from the two other recorded genera of sea-whip shrimps by its unique colour pattern and its larger nipper.

Palaemon serenus

FAMILY: Palaemonidae
SCIENTIFIC NAME: *Palaemon serenus*
COMMON NAME: Serene Shrimp
DISTRIBUTION: WT/S
HABITAT: Rocky reefs; rocky shores
GENERAL WATER DEPTH: 0–10 m (33 ft)
FOOD HABIT: Omnivorous: organic detritus
SIZE: 70 mm (2.8 in)
DESCRIPTION: Many shrimps live in intertidal rock pools, gutters and shallow subtidal reefs around South-West Pacific shores. Many have been recorded, others have not, and certainly very little work has been done to establish new data or update previous work since the early part of this century. As in many other groups of marine animals, small variations once acknowledged as warranting species definition may well turn out to be only variations within one species. The serene shrimp can be distinguished from its companion sea shore shrimp (*Palaemon literus*) by the white and red specks on its body. The latter has red stripes across the body.

Periclimenes colemani

FAMILY: Palaemonidae
SCIENTIFIC NAME: *Periclimenes colemani*
COMMON NAME: Coleman's Shrimp
DISTRIBUTION: TI–WP
HABITAT: Coral reefs

GENERAL WATER DEPTH: 10–30 m (33–98 ft)
FOOD HABIT: Carnivorous
SIZE: 20 mm (0.8 in)
DESCRIPTION: Found only on the dorsal surface of the (venomous) elusive sea urchin (*Asthenosoma intermedium*), Coleman's shrimp was first discovered by the author on the Great Barrier Reef in 1974 and is now known to range as far as the Philippines. Generally observed in pairs (male and female), it adopts a rather unprecedented micro-habitat: all other shrimps known to live in association with sea urchins cling among the urchin's spines; in all observations of this species the shrimps occupied a 'patch' on the urchin's body devoid of spines, pedicellariae, or tube-feet. Elusive sea urchins without shrimps did not have a cleared 'patch'. Females are generally a little larger and more robust than males, and most pairs orientate themselves head to tail in their cleared 'patch' on the urchin.

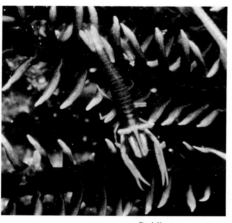

Periclimenes cornutus

FAMILY: Palaemonidae
SCIENTIFIC NAME: *Periclimenes cornutus*
COMMON NAME: Horned Shrimp
DISTRIBUTION: TI–WP
HABITAT: Coral reefs
GENERAL WATER DEPTH: 8–25 m (26–82 ft)
FOOD HABIT: Omnivorous: plankton; mucus
SIZE: 20 mm (0.8 in)
DESCRIPTION: There are quite a number of different species of commensal shrimps living on various echinoderms. Many, including this species, live on feather stars and take on the exact colouration of their host to such a degree that finding them amongst dozens and sometimes hundreds of moving feather star arms is often impossible. In general, a feather star is inhabited by both a male and a female horned shrimp, with the male being the smaller. It is thought that the shrimps feed by gleaning the entrapped plankton from the feather star's pinnules and food grooves.

Periclimenes holthuisi

FAMILY: Palaemonidae
SCIENTIFIC NAME: *Periclimenes holthuisi*
COMMON NAME: Holthuis' Shrimp
DISTRIBUTION: TI–WP; WT/S
HABITAT: Coral reefs; rocky reefs; rocky shores
GENERAL WATER DEPTH: Low tide to 30 m (98 ft)
FOOD HABIT: Omnivorous: plankton; mucus
SIZE: 30 mm (1.2 in)
DESCRIPTION: One of the most widely distributed commensals, Holthuis' shrimp is generally found in pairs or groups. Unlike some other commensal shrimps it is not host specific and can be found on several kinds of sea anemones, soft corals and corals. In some areas it is known as a fish cleaner, and when found inhabiting a sea anemone the shrimps will actively defend the anemone as they would a territory. The distinct patterns and colours of Holthuis' shrimp are fairly easy to recognise in the wild, with both males and females being similarly coloured. Females carrying eggs under the abdomen can be found for most of the year.

FAMILY: Palaemonidae
SCIENTIFIC NAME: *Periclimenes imperator*
COMMON NAME: Imperial Shrimp
DISTRIBUTION: TI–WP
HABITAT: Coral reefs
GENERAL WATER DEPTH: Low tide to 30 m (98 ft)
FOOD HABIT: Omnivorous: plankton; mucus
SIZE: 25 mm (1 in)
DESCRIPTION: During its adult stage the imperial shrimp is found in commensal association with the Spanish dancer nudibranch (*Hexabranchus sanguineus*), and is also known to live on the variegated sea cucumber (*Stichopus variegatus*). The shrimps found on holothurians are generally juveniles, but on some reefs adult imperial

Periclimenes imperator

other marine invertebrates such as echinoderms and cnidarians. Although black coral shrimps may be found living in other associations, the most common place of residence is among the branches of several species of black coral trees. The number of shrimps on each tree varies considerably, and on large trees the population could be several thousand. Juveniles are transparent and adults have a distinct central red stripe on the back. All shrimps have opaque white eyes and are extremely difficult to see amongst the extended polyps of their black coral habitat.

shrimps inhabit other species of sea cucumbers and sea stars. The imperial shrimp is not restricted to two hosts and has been observed living on at least five different kinds of marine animals. Those found on the above-mentioned nudibranch are the only example where the colour pattern is similar to that of the host. Females are generally larger than males in subtropical waters but are of similar size in tropical waters. Most hosts have a mucous covering on their skin and the imperial shrimp may derive nourishment from foraging plankton and detritus trapped in this covering. This shrimp has also been observed to feed on bottom detritus.

Periclimenes psamathe

FAMILY: Palaemonidae
SCIENTIFIC NAME: *Periclimenes psamathe*
COMMON NAME: Black Coral Shrimp
DISTRIBUTION: TI–WP; WT/S
HABITAT: Coral reefs; rocky reefs
GENERAL WATER DEPTH: 15–40 m
 (49–131 ft)
FOOD HABIT: Omnivorous
SIZE: 25 mm (1 in)
DESCRIPTION: Many of the shrimps within the family Palaemonidae are associated with

Pliopontonia furtiva

FAMILY: Palaemonidae
SCIENTIFIC NAME: *Pliopontonia furtiva*
COMMON NAME: Furtive Shrimp
DISTRIBUTION: TI–WP
HABITAT: Coral reefs
GENERAL WATER DEPTH: 10–25 m
 (33–82 ft)
FOOD HABIT: Omnivorous: plankton
SIZE: 20 mm (0.8 in)
DESCRIPTION: Found only in association with an unidentified zoantharian, the furtive shrimp deploys its host's tentacles and outer skin for concealment as it moves over the surface. The author discovered this rather inconspicuous little shrimp in western Pacific waters in 1974. Little is known of its distribution but the species has been observed at depths of around 18 m (59 ft). It is sexually dimorphic, with the larger, dominant female being almost twice the size of the smaller male. Colour patterns are almost identical.

FAMILY: Palinuridae
SCIENTIFIC NAME: *Jasus novaehollandiae*
COMMON NAME: Southern Rock Lobster
DISTRIBUTION: WT/S
HABITAT: Rocky reefs; rocky shores
GENERAL WATER DEPTH: Low tide to 80 m
 (263 ft)

Jasus novaehollandiae

FOOD HABIT: Carnivorous: scavenger —
 molluscs; sea urchins; crustaceans
SIZE: 500 mm (20 in)
DESCRIPTION: The basis of a fairly extensive fishing industry in the South-West Pacific, the southern rock lobster lives on and around both coastal and offshore reefs, generally preferring exposed areas. Like most rock lobsters it is gregarious and lives in caves, beneath ledges, under rocks and seemingly wherever it can shelter. The species has strong, well-developed first legs used to catch and hold prey. Although during the day specimens may be seen out foraging, looking for mates, or migrating, most of these activities are carried out at night. Deepwater forms are generally lighter in colour and are often referred to as 'whites'. Southern rock lobsters are opportunistic feeders, eating sea urchins, abalone, various small molluscs, dead animal tissue and sometimes each other. Males can be distinguished from females by having only one claw on the last pair of legs; females have two.

FAMILY: Palinuridae
SCIENTIFIC NAME: *Panulirus cygnus*
COMMON NAME: Western Rock Lobster
DISTRIBUTION: WT/S
HABITAT: Rocky reefs; coral reefs
GENERAL WATER DEPTH: 5–40 m
 (16–131 ft)
FOOD HABIT: Carnivorous: scavenger —
 molluscs; echinoderms; crustaceans
SIZE: 450 mm (18 in)
DESCRIPTION: During daylight hours the western rock lobster remains in caves or reef cavities and generally ventures forth only if disturbed or attacked. Western rock lobsters are gregarious and often mass together in large numbers amongst shallow water reefs, especially during their juvenile stages. Although it is thought to be primarily a food scavenger, the western rock lobster has been observed to attack and devour live invertebrates, including molluscs, and will also prey

Panulirus cygnus

Panulirus versicolor

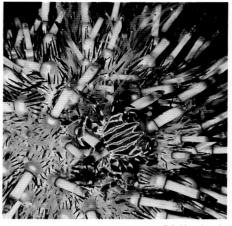

Zebrida adamsi

interesting animals living off continental coasts. The general shape, large head, characteristic rostrum and the spines on its carapace allow fairly accurate identification. They spend their entire adult lives at depth and only migrate vertically to spawn.

on its own kind should one become injured or incapacitated. Mating occurs in the winter months and large males may have a harem of females in the same cave. Eggs usually appear in October or November and are red in colour. The female carries the eggs on modified swimmerets beneath the abdomen. After the eggs hatch, the larvae go through several planktonic stages before settling to the bottom in shallow water and becoming juveniles.

Heterocarpus sibogae

FAMILY: Pandalidae
SCIENTIFIC NAME: *Heterocarpus sibogae*
COMMON NAME: Siboga Prawn
DISTRIBUTION: TI–WP; WT/S
HABITAT: Mud
GENERAL WATER DEPTH: 300–500 m (984–1640 ft)
FOOD HABIT: Omnivorous: detritus
SIZE: 150 mm (6 in)
DESCRIPTION: A strikingly bright red robust species, the Siboga prawn is the same colour alive as shallow-water prawns are when cooked. Caught only by commercial trawlers and research vessels, this deepwater-dwelling prawn is just one of the many thousands of

FAMILY: Panuliridae
SCIENTIFIC NAME: *Panulirus versicolor*
COMMON NAME: Painted Rock Lobster
DISTRIBUTION: TI–WP
HABITAT: Coral reefs
GENERAL WATER DEPTH: Low tide to 40 m (131 ft)
FOOD HABIT: Carnivorous: molluscs
SIZE: 457 mm (18 in)
DESCRIPTION: The largest and most spectacularly coloured tropical species, the painted rock lobster inhabits the more sheltered parts of coral reefs and lagoons. Although specimens have been found in deeper waters beyond 25 m (82 ft), most are observed at depths of 3–10 m (10–33 ft). Young rock lobsters may be seen living in small groups; however, large adults tend to be solitary. Painted rock lobsters do not readily enter traps or pots and this has led fishermen to believe they are vegetarian. However, this species is a carnivorous predator, much the same as others of its family; it will also scavenge dead or dying animals.

FAMILY: Parthenopidae
SCIENTIFIC NAME: *Zebrida adamsi*
COMMON NAME: Adam's Urchin Crab
DISTRIBUTION: TI–WP; WT/S
HABITAT: Coral reefs; rocky reefs; rocky shores
GENERAL WATER DEPTH: Low tide to 40 m (131 ft)
FOOD HABIT: Carnivorous
SIZE: 25 mm (1 in)
DESCRIPTION: This little crab has been found on tropical reefs, but there is very little available information on its habits and

behaviour. In the southern Indian Ocean, Adam's urchin crab can be found inhabiting shallow water in association with the common sea urchin (*Heliocidaris erythrogramma*). It can usually be observed among the dorsal spines of the urchin, or sheltering beneath the body. Only one crab has been seen on any one urchin and those found were on urchins living in colonies. It has modified hooks on the end of each leg which are used to hold on to the urchin's spines. It moves over the urchin by climbing among the primary spines, and rarely seems to rest on the body.

Penaeus plebejus

FAMILY: Penaeidae
SCIENTIFIC NAME: *Penaeus plebejus*
COMMON NAME: Eastern King Prawn
DISTRIBUTION: TI–WP; WT/S

HABITAT: Sand; mud shores
GENERAL WATER DEPTH: Low tide to
220 m (722 ft)
FOOD HABIT: Omnivorous: detrital
organisms
SIZE: 300 mm (12 in)
DESCRIPTION: Eastern king prawns spend
the day buried in the mud or beneath the
sand, hiding from their many predators.
Spawned at sea they enter estuaries and
rivers as juveniles and grow to around
9–90 mm (0.4–3.5 in) in 9–12 months. They
then form dense schools and migrate out to
sea and spawn at a length of 125 mm (5 in).

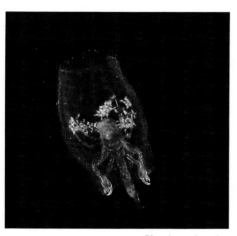

Phronima sedentaria

FAMILY: Phronimidae
SCIENTIFIC NAME: *Phronima sedentaria*
COMMON NAME: Hermit-screw Amphipod
DISTRIBUTION: TI–WP; WT/S; CT/S
HABITAT: Open ocean
GENERAL WATER DEPTH: Surface to 10 m
(33 ft)
FOOD HABIT: Carnivorous: plankton
SIZE: 35 mm (1.4 in)
DESCRIPTION: Propelling its dwelling
through the water column in the most
unfamiliar and seemingly misdirected
manner, the hermit-screw amphipod (often
referred to as the barrel shrimp) is the
oddest of all the planktonic creatures the
author has had the pleasure to observe and
photograph. In their juvenile stages they
occupy the single test of a pelagic tunicate,
or belled sea jelly. While growing they feed
on the soft parts of the host. Mating takes
place inside the empty test and the female
lays her eggs directly on to the inside walls
of the host. Propulsion is by rapid movements of the thorax, which provides a series
of unbalanced, screw-like motions that generally reach a climax as the host vehicle and
its occupant move towards the surface and
then peter out as the arcs get smaller and
the vehicle drifts slowly down.

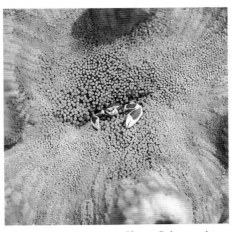

Neopetrolisthes maculatus

FAMILY: Porcellanidae
SCIENTIFIC NAME: *Neopetrolisthes
maculatus*
COMMON NAME: Spotted Porcellanid Crab
DISTRIBUTION: TI–WP
HABITAT: Coral reefs; rocky reefs; rocky
shores
GENERAL WATER DEPTH: Low tide to 25 m
(82 ft)
FOOD HABIT: Omnivorous: plankton
SIZE: 35 mm (1.4 in)
DESCRIPTION: Living in an endoetic relationship (for shelter or protection) with several species of sea anemones, the spotted
porcellanid crab is pictured here on the
anemone *Stoichactis kenti*. When found on
isolated anemones there are often two crabs
in residence, a male and a female. However,
when there are many anemones in close
proximity to one another only one crab may
be present. Although the anemones that
shelter these little crabs can sting, kill and
eat much larger crustaceans, the spotted
porcellanid crab scuttles among the stinging
tentacles and may even enter the mouth and
stomach with impunity. The feeding mechanism is two modified appendages
(maxillipeds), which are among the mouth
parts. These long, arm-like appendages are
thickly fringed with long pinnate hairs. They
are alternately flung out and returned in a
rhythmic procedure, catching plankton and
suspended sediment which are filtered and
transferred to the mouth.

FAMILY: Porcellanidae
SCIENTIFIC NAME: *Petrocheles australiensis*
COMMON NAME: Southern Porcellanid
Crab
DISTRIBUTION: WT/S; CT/S
HABITAT: Rocky reefs; rocky shores
GENERAL WATER DEPTH: Low tide to 20 m
(66 ft)
FOOD HABIT: Carnivorous: plankton
SIZE: 50 mm (2 in)

Petrocheles australiensis

DESCRIPTION: This crab is far more prolific
in Tasman Sea waters than in other areas of
its distribution and is also larger. The species occurs in both exposed and sheltered
waters but more seem to be present in bays,
coves and lower estuaries. Rarely seen in the
open, it hides beneath stones, rocks, debris
and rubble. Its flattened profile enables the
crab to fit into very narrow spaces and its
swift scuttling movement contributes to its
survival. The southern porcellanid crab can
be found intertidally, although its highest
population levels seem to be just below the
low-tide line. Identification is fairly straight-
forward, although there is some colour variation throughout its range.

Caphyra rotundifrons

FAMILY: Portunidae
SCIENTIFIC NAME: *Caphyra rotundifrons*
COMMON NAME: Turtle-weed Crab
DISTRIBUTION: TI–WP
HABITAT: Coral reefs
GENERAL WATER DEPTH: Low tide to 5 m
(16 ft)
FOOD HABIT: Carnivorous
SIZE: 25 mm (1 in)
DESCRIPTION: Found only among the green

silky tresses of the turtle-weed *Chlorodesmis comosa*, this rather ornate little swimming crab seems to be restricted to a reef flat existence. It is sexually dimorphic, the females growing to almost twice the size of the males. It is extremely efficient at climbing among the weed and deploys it with its legs so that it is almost always covered. Wrasses have been observed tearing clumps of turtle-weed to shreds probably while searching for the crabs.

Carcinus maenas

FAMILY: Portunidae
SCIENTIFIC NAME: *Carcinus maenas*
COMMON NAME: Common Shore Crab
DISTRIBUTION: EA; WT/N
HABITAT: Rocky and sandy shores
GENERAL WATER DEPTH: Intertidal
FOOD HABIT: Carnivorous: mobile
  invertebrates
SIZE: Up to 80 mm (3.1 in) diameter
DESCRIPTION: The common shore crab varies in colouration; its body may range from light brown to dark green in colour. Its oval to diamond-shaped carapace bears three blunt protuberances between the eyes and five protuberances on each side.

Lissocarcinus polyboides

FAMILY: Portunidae
SCIENTIFIC NAME: *Lissocarcinus polyboides*
COMMON NAME: Sea Star Crab
DISTRIBUTION: TI–WP; WT/S
HABITAT: Sand; mud
GENERAL WATER DEPTH: 3–25 m
  (10–82 ft)
FOOD HABIT: Carnivorous: scavenger
SIZE: 20 mm (0.8 in)
DESCRIPTION: In the early 1970s, while checking echinoderms in southern Australian waters for commensals, the author found this small crab on many occasions living on or beneath the giant southern sand star (*Luidia australiae*). The sea star crab is generally found near the sand star's mouth; when disturbed, it swims off and burrows into the sand. It has also been found living on or with the sea hare (*Aplysia* sp.), the side-gilled slug (*Pleurobranchus* sp.), and the sea star (*Pentaceraster regulus*).

Ovalipes australiensis

FAMILY: Portunidae
SCIENTIFIC NAME: *Ovalipes australiensis*
COMMON NAME: Surf Crab
DISTRIBUTION: WT/S; CT/S
HABITAT: Sand; mud; muddy shores
GENERAL WATER DEPTH: Low tide to 50 m
  (164 ft)
FOOD HABIT: Carnivorous: crustaceans
SIZE: 150 mm (6 in)
DESCRIPTION: The surf crab is very common in sandy ocean seashores, deeper offshore waters and the sheltered beaches of bays and estuaries. Like most of the larger species of portunid crabs, it has a distinctive colour and pattern making it easy to identify. It is voracious and will attack almost any organic material including all baits, bare feet and fingers. The larger crabs prey heavily on smaller ones. By walking along the bottom a large crab panics smaller ones into revealing their presence beneath the sand, or bluffs them into running for safety. Once one appears, the larger crab rushes in and tears the smaller one to pieces and devours it.

Portunus pelagicus

FAMILY: Portunidae
SCIENTIFIC NAME: *Portunus pelagicus*
COMMON NAME: Blue Swimming Crab
DISTRIBUTION: TI–WP; WT/S
HABITAT: Sand; mud; muddy shores
GENERAL WATER DEPTH: Low tide to 40 m
  (131 ft)
FOOD HABIT: Carnivorous: scavenger —
  invertebrates; fish
SIZE: 300 mm (12 in)
DESCRIPTION: One of the best-known edible crabs, the blue swimmer inhabits the sandy mud bottom of sheltered estuaries and inlets throughout the Indo-Pacific and Indian oceans. Most of the crab's life is spent just below the sand surface where it waits with only its eyes protruding, watching for fish and invertebrates to venture close enough for a successful attack. This burrowing habit is also a protective device as many species of fish are known to prey on it. The male is larger than the female and its colouration is the source of its common name. The female is smaller and tends to be browner with little of the male's bright blue pigmentation. Mating occurs in summer and both sexes enter the shallows in large numbers. The males attach themselves to the females from the rear and spend some time paired, with walking and swimming movements in unison.

FAMILY: Portunidae
SCIENTIFIC NAME: *Portunus sanguinolentus*
COMMON NAME: Blood-spotted Swimming
  Crab
DISTRIBUTION: TI–WP
HABITAT: Sand; mud
GENERAL WATER DEPTH: 5–60 m
  (16–197 ft)
FOOD HABIT: Carnivorous: scavenger —
  invertebrates
SIZE: 300 mm (12 in)
DESCRIPTION: Most commonly seen in trawls, the blood-spotted swimming crab is widely spread throughout the Indo-Pacific and Indian oceans, and though it can be very

Portunus sanguinolentus

extremely characteristic shape and are armed with gigantic, super-strong claws there should be little difficulty in recognising them. Like most portunid crabs the mangrove crab is a carnivore and scavenger and will eat almost anything it can get close to, even one of its own species if injured or casting its shell. It is a very popular food crab, the basis of commercial fisheries in several countries.

variable in colour and patterning throughout its range the three blood red spots on the carapace are a stable identifying feature. In many places where the crab is common it is a commercial species. In the South-West Pacific it is only regarded as an incidental catch, although it is quite good to eat.

FAMILY: Portunidae
SCIENTIFIC NAME: *Scylla serrata*
COMMON NAME: Mangrove Crab/Serrate Swimming Crab
DISTRIBUTION: TI–WP; WT/S
HABITAT: Mud; mangroves; estuaries; muddy shores
GENERAL WATER DEPTH: Low tide to 20 m (66 ft)
FOOD HABIT: Carnivorous: scavenger — crustaceans; fish
SIZE: 300 mm (12 in)
DESCRIPTION: These crabs live in burrows around the roots of mangrove trees and also in the banks of rivers. Intertidal crabs are generally nocturnal and do not venture out to feed during the day. Subtidal crabs come out during the late afternoon, especially on a rising tide. Mangrove crabs may be dark green or brown, and as they have an

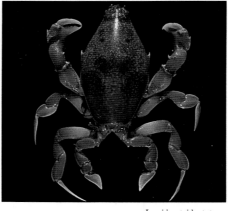

Lyreidus tridentatus

FAMILY: Raninidae
SCIENTIFIC NAME: *Lyreidus tridentatus*
COMMON NAME: Three-toothed Frog Crab
DISTRIBUTION: TI–WP
HABITAT: Mud
GENERAL WATER DEPTH: 40–150 m (131–492 ft)
FOOD HABIT: Omnivorous: plankton
SIZE: 60 mm (2.4 in)
DESCRIPTION: This beautiful little frog crab lives buried in sand and mud and specimens are only encountered in research vessel dredges. The species is widely distributed. Its common name comes from the three spines on the underside of each claw which, together with its shape and colour, make identification very simple. Males and females do not seem to differ markedly in size. The eggs are black and carried on the underside of the female near the very reduced abdominal flap. The egg mass is not as regular as that of other crabs, with more eggs being on one side than the other on observed specimens.

FAMILY: Raninidae
SCIENTIFIC NAME: *Ranina ranina*
COMMON NAME: Spanner Crab
DISTRIBUTION: TI–WP
HABITAT: Sand; mud
GENERAL WATER DEPTH: 5–50 m (16–164 ft)
FOOD HABIT: Omnivorous: plankton; detritus

Scylla serrata

Ranina ranina

SIZE: 200 mm (8 in)
DESCRIPTION: Very common on sandy bottoms adjacent to the mainland and mainland reefs, the spanner crab is trawled and caught with hoop nets over a wide area of the Indo-Pacific region. An important food source in many areas of eastern Australia, heavy exploitation over the last decade has reduced numbers. It prefers the bottom with a strong current flow, and being gregarious, huge catches were made when the resource was first discovered. Although known as the red frog crab in Hawaii, the name spanner crab is Australian, from the unusual claw shape.

Rhynchocinetes australis

FAMILY: Rhynchocinetidae
SCIENTIFIC NAME: *Rhynchocinetes australis*
COMMON NAME: Southern Hinge-beak Shrimp
DISTRIBUTION: WT/S
HABITAT: Rocky reefs; rocky shores
GENERAL WATER DEPTH: Low tide to 20 m (66 ft)
FOOD HABIT: Omnivorous: organic detritus
SIZE: 50 mm (2 in)
DESCRIPTION: Living beneath stones and rubble this distinctively marked species occurs throughout south-western Australian

waters, though it is not common at all localities. It inhabits ledges and some caves in sheltered areas and may be seen alone or in scattered numbers. The southern hinge-beak shrimp appears not to have so well developed a rostrum as its relative, the rugulose hinge-beak shrimp, and it has a smoother shell. Predators are not known, but most specimens observed in situ are very shy and do not venture into the open during the day. A unique feature of the hinge-beak shrimps and one that is restricted to members of its family is the unusually large rostrum which is hinged instead of being rigidly fixed to the carapace as with other shrimps.

Rhynchocinetes hiatti

FAMILY: Rhynchocinetidae
SCIENTIFIC NAME: *Rhynchocinetes hiatti*
COMMON NAME: Hiatt's Hinge-beak Shrimp
DISTRIBUTION: TI–WP; WT/S
HABITAT: Coral reefs
GENERAL WATER DEPTH: Low tide to 20 m (66 ft)
FOOD HABIT: Omnivorous
SIZE: 80 mm (3 in)
DESCRIPTION: Rarely seen out on the reef during the day, Hiatt's hinge-beak shrimp is one of the most spectacular members of the nocturnal fauna. Generally observed in a solitary situation, specimens grow to around 80 mm (3 in) and have the longest rostrum of any hinge-beak shrimps. Although there have been reports of commensal relationships between hinge-beak shrimps and sea urchins, this does not appear to be more than a loose association. The shrimps hide behind the sea urchins during the day when the urchins inhabit the same ledges. Due to their secretive habits these shrimps have been thought of as uncommon, yet they inhabit vast areas of the Indo-Pacific and South-West Pacific reefs.

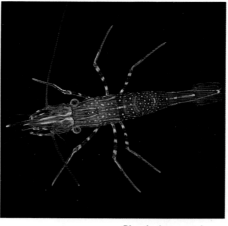

Rhynchocinetes rugulosus

FAMILY: Rhynchocinetidae
SCIENTIFIC NAME: *Rhynchocinetes rugulosus*
COMMON NAME: Hinge-beak Shrimp
DISTRIBUTION: WT/S; CT/S
HABITAT: Rocky reefs; rocky shores
GENERAL WATER DEPTH: Low tide to 80 m (263 ft)
FOOD HABIT: Omnivorous: detritus organisms
SIZE: 60 mm (2.4 in)
DESCRIPTION: To any intertidal fossicker, snorkeler, or skindiver the hinge-beak shrimp is no stranger. Its prevalence, distinctive colour pattern and inquisitive behaviour make it one of the best-known subtidal rock shrimps in South-West Pacific waters. Found beneath rocks and boulders, under ledges, or in caves and crevices, this beautiful little shrimp generally occurs in groups. Although it normally seems slow in movement, it is capable of surprising bursts of speed when eluding predators.

Arctides antipodarum

FAMILY: Scyllaridae
SCIENTIFIC NAME: *Arctides antipodarum*
COMMON NAME: Southern Shovel-nosed Lobster

DISTRIBUTION: WT/S
HABITAT: Rocky reefs
GENERAL WATER DEPTH: 5–40 m (16–131 ft)
FOOD HABIT: Carnivorous: molluscs
SIZE: 300 mm (12 in)
DESCRIPTION: A brilliantly coloured dweller of deepwater rocky reefs, this species is not often seen, even by divers. Of nocturnal habit it hides during the day on the roofs of caves, on ledges and in deep fissures and cracks in underwater cliff faces. Because of its relatively inaccessible habitat and its reluctance to enter rock lobster pots, very little is known of its habits and behaviour. Females tend to be larger than males and carry their red egg mass on modified swimmerets beneath the abdomen. The head of the southern shovel-nosed lobster is somewhat flattened and in place of antennae it has two rounded plates. When threatened it swims backward by rapid movements of its tail flap. It is generally solitary but during the mating season a female may share habitat with several males.

Ibacus alticrenatus

FAMILY: Scyllaridae
SCIENTIFIC NAME: *Ibacus alticrenatus*
COMMON NAME: Deepwater Bug
DISTRIBUTION: WT/S
HABITAT: Sandy mud
GENERAL WATER DEPTH: 20–120 m (66–394 ft)
FOOD HABIT: Omnivorous: detritus organisms
SIZE: 200 mm (8 in)
DESCRIPTION: Commercial quantities of deepwater bugs are still taken by trawlers working off the Australian continental shelf by day and night. This species generally spends some of the time buried in sand with just the tips of its antennae and eyes showing. When swimming it flips its tail vigorously to propel itself backwards for a metre (3 ft) or so at a time. The large head section tends to droop during swimming and may

drag along the bottom. It rarely swims at a height of more than a quarter of a metre (9 in) above the bottom. A related species, the shallow-water Balmain bug (*Ibacus peronii*), inhabits a number of bays and estuaries along the south-eastern Australian coast but it is not prolific as most of the colonies have been fished out during many years of trawling. The deepwater bug may be distinguished from the Balmain bug by its 'furry' exterior and wider gaps in the carapace near the head.

Ibacus brucei

FAMILY: Scyllaridae
SCIENTIFIC NAME: *Ibacus brucei*
COMMON NAME: Bruce's Bug
DISTRIBUTION: WT/S
HABITAT: Mud
GENERAL WATER DEPTH: 350–450 m (1148–1476 ft)
FOOD HABIT: Omnivorous: detrital organisms
SIZE: 170 mm (7 in)
DESCRIPTION: Bruce's bug has a very dark rusty red colouration which is the same in both males and females. The juveniles are light pink in colour with rusty blotches between the ridges on the carapace, and they have a white tail. The specimen in the picture has been damaged at some time during its growth. Note that the left-hand side frontal head flap is not as well developed as the right-hand side. Had this bug not been caught it is very likely that the smaller flap would regrow to match the other in the process of several moultings.

FAMILY: Scyllaridae
SCIENTIFIC NAME: *Scyllarides* sp.
COMMON NAME: Shovel-nose Lobster
DISTRIBUTION: TI–WP; WT/S
HABITAT: Coral reefs; rocky reefs
GENERAL WATER DEPTH: 8–25 m (26–82 ft)
FOOD HABIT: Carnivorous: molluscs
SIZE: 400 mm (16 in)
DESCRIPTION: A large, very attractively coloured lobster, this species inhabits caves, ledges, overhangs and the sides of gullies of subterranean volcanic reefs. During the day

it lives high up towards the backs of caves and is often seen clinging to the roof. Except for some time during the mating season it is solitary and ventures out only at night to

Scyllarides sp.

hunt for food which is thought to consist of molluscs and small invertebrates. Shovel-nosed lobsters can be identified to species level by habitat or by a picture using basic knowledge of colouration, shape of the first and secondary antenna plates and nodules on the carapace.

Squilla empusa

FAMILY: Squillidae
SCIENTIFIC NAME: *Squilla empusa*
COMMON NAME: Common Mantis Shrimp
DISTRIBUTION: WA
HABITAT: Sand; mud
GENERAL WATER DEPTH: Low-tide line to 152 m (500 ft)
FOOD HABIT: Carnivorous: mobile invertebrates, crustaceans
SIZE: 250 mm (10 in)
DESCRIPTION: The common mantis shrimp is regularly dredged up by shrimp trawlers as part of their catch. The fishermen avoid the large appendages of the shrimp's sharp claws, which can easily slash fingers. Many people, however, also relish its meat. The

shrimp-like crustacean has a green to blue-green carapace, darker at the margins. It is distinguished by its large, mantis-like, clawed appendages.

Microprosthema validum

FAMILY: Stenopodidae
SCIENTIFIC NAME: *Microprosthema validum*
COMMON NAME: Robust Shrimp
DISTRIBUTION: TI–WP; WT/S
HABITAT: Coral reefs; rocky reefs; rocky shores
GENERAL WATER DEPTH: Low tide to 20 m (66 ft)
FOOD HABIT: Carnivorous
SIZE: 25 mm (1 in)
DESCRIPTION: Owing to its small size and secretiveness, this shrimp is rarely observed in the field. It lives beneath rocks and coral slabs that allow it free movement. Of nocturnal habit, the robust shrimp is related to cleaner shrimps. When found during daylight it works very slowly over the substrate (rocks, algae, etc.), but when threatened or disturbed it is capable of very swift backward 'flips'. Its creamy buff colour tends to be consistent throughout its range and males appear to be slightly smaller than females. For its size the robust shrimp has extraordinary long antennae.

FAMILY: Stenopodidae
SCIENTIFIC NAME: *Stenopus hispidus*
COMMON NAME: Banded Coral Shrimp
DISTRIBUTION: TI–WP; WT/S
HABITAT: Coral reefs; rocky reefs
GENERAL WATER DEPTH: Low tide to 30 m (98 ft)
FOOD HABIT: Carnivorous: crustaceans
SIZE: 100 mm (4 in)
DESCRIPTION: The banded coral shrimp is a cleaner shrimp. It inhabits the Pacific and Indian oceans and is without doubt the most well-known and thoroughly researched species of all cleaner shrimps. Easily recognised by its long white antennae, red and white

striped body and chelae, the banded coral shrimp generally occurs in pairs or a group of pairs. Cleaning stations are generally in coral or rock crevices or under caves or ledges. Although active during the day, much

Stenopus hispidus

of its cleaning activity is performed on sleeping fish during the night. It uses the pincers of the secondary legs for cutting and picking; the large chelae are used only for display or threat. Adult males and females have similar size and once paired, inhabit the same station for several years. During the breeding season the female carries a clutch of green eggs beneath her abdomen.

Orchestia gammarella

FAMILY: Talitridae
SCIENTIFIC NAME: *Orchestia gammarella*
COMMON NAME: Sand-hopper
DISTRIBUTION: EA; WT/N
HABITAT: Among seaweed and rocks
GENERAL WATER DEPTH: Middle and upper shore
FOOD HABIT: Omnivorous
SIZE: Up to 20 mm (0.8 in) long
DESCRIPTION: Often found amidst decaying seaweed and rocks, the sand-hopper lives up to its common name by jumping vigorously if disturbed, using its strongly developed propulsive limbs. The first antenna is much shorter than the second. In the male, a large pincer terminates the second thoracic leg.

Actaea peronii

FAMILY: Xanthidae
SCIENTIFIC NAME: *Actaea peronii*
COMMON NAME: Thorn-legged Crab
DISTRIBUTION: WT/S
HABITAT: Rocky reefs; rocky shores
GENERAL WATER DEPTH: Low tide to 30 m (98 ft)
FOOD HABIT: Carnivorous
SIZE: 35 mm (1.4 in)
DESCRIPTION: The thorn-legged crab is one of a number of shore and subtidal crabs that are similar at first glance. However, closer examination shows several features that allow it to be distinguished from other species. The thorn-legged crab is always brilliant orange and has two distinct white spots at the base of the carapace. The carapace pattern is fairly stable throughout its range and the tubercules are raised and separate. It is found beneath stones and also in bryozoans and sponges.

Carpilius corallinus

FAMILY: Xanthidae
SCIENTIFIC NAME: *Carpilius corallinus*
COMMON NAME: Coral Crab
DISTRIBUTION: TI–WP
HABITAT: Coral reefs

GENERAL WATER DEPTH: Low tide to 30 m (98 ft)
FOOD HABIT: Omnivorous
SIZE: 20 mm (8 in)
DESCRIPTION: Sometimes seen beneath coral slabs in low-tide areas, the coral crab seems to prefer a deepwater habitat. It can be seen in holes in the reef on overcast days or more often under ledges or in coral at night. It ranges throughout the western Pacific down to Lord Howe Island, where it lives on deep reefs beneath large boulders and in crevices. The southern forms appear to be more rotund than their more tropical relations closer to the equator. When disturbed, the coral crab runs into a depression or hollow where it hangs on tightly, wedging itself into the niche. By presenting its very strong smooth carapace, the coral crab repels any potential predators trying to dislodge it, as they cannot get a grip.

Eriphia sebana

FAMILY: Xanthidae
SCIENTIFIC NAME: *Eriphia sebana*
COMMON NAME: Red-eyed Crab
DISTRIBUTION: TI–WP
HABITAT: Coral reefs
GENERAL WATER DEPTH: Low tide to 5 m (16 ft)
FOOD HABIT: Carnivorous: invertebrates
SIZE: 75 mm (3 in)
DESCRIPTION: A common nocturnal scavenger along the intertidal beach rock, the relatively slow-moving red-eyed crab has thick strong claws that can give a nasty nip. By day it lives beneath ledges and rocks, away from sunlight and predators. It can wedge itself into crevices and hang on so tightly with its strong legs that only partial destruction will allow it to be removed. Colour may vary from pale pink in young specimens to deep dark brown in adults. The bright red eyes are its most distinctive feature.

Etisus splendidus

Lophozozymus pictor

Limulus polyphemus

FAMILY: Xanthidae
SCIENTIFIC NAME: *Etisus splendidus*
COMMON NAME: Splendid Reef Crab
DISTRIBUTION: TI–WP
HABITAT: Coral reefs
GENERAL WATER DEPTH: Low tide to 25 m
(82 ft)
FOOD HABIT: Herbivorous: algae
SIZE: 300 mm (12 in) (carapace)
DESCRIPTION: The splendid reef crab spends the day hidden in the dark labyrinths of coral and rocky reefs. Of solitary habit, it ventures out at dusk to the undersides of ledges and holes in the reef in search of the algae on which it feeds. During twilight the splendid reef crab is never fully exposed and is very sensitive to movement. However on moonless nights it will move into the open to feed. It is fairly slow but extremely powerful and clings to the substrate tenaciously when caught; in fact, removal requires demolition of the substrate first. The splendid reef crab is poisonous and should never be eaten.

FAMILY: Xanthidae
SCIENTIFIC NAME: *Lophozozymus pictor*
COMMON NAME: Red and White Painted
Crab
DISTRIBUTION: TI–WP
HABITAT: Coral reefs
GENERAL WATER DEPTH: Low tide to 20 m
(66 ft)
FOOD HABIT: Omnivorous: algae
SIZE: 200 mm (8 in)
DESCRIPTION: Thick bodied, with strong legs and large claws, the red and white painted crab's deep red colour, white spots and moderate size make it easily recognisable. It spends the day sheltering beneath coral slabs or in holes in the coral. Common on the reef flats, it is usually found in protected coral in pools or lagoons to depths of 10 m (33 ft). During the night, or sometimes on a rising tide in the late afternoon, it may

be seen feeding. Little is known of its habits, but its diet includes algae. It is thought by some to be poisonous.

FAMILY: Xanthidae
SCIENTIFIC NAME: *Pseudocarcinus gigas*
COMMON NAME: Giant Crab
DISTRIBUTION: WT/S; CT/S
HABITAT: Rocky reefs
GENERAL WATER DEPTH: 50–100 m
(164–328 ft)
FOOD HABIT: Carnivorous: scavenger —
invertebrates
SIZE: 400 mm (16 in) (carapace)
DESCRIPTION: Weighing up to 15 kg (33 lb), the giant crab is one of the largest in the world. It is generally found in deep offshore waters in the southern Pacific and most specimens are taken in craypots or brought up in trawls. The giant crab is quite active in the water, but when approached by a diver shows little concern or aggression. Out of the water it can move but the weight of the giant claws is so great that it cannot lift them. Whether in or out of the water, only a small effort is needed to hold the claws apart.

Pseudocarcinus gigas

■ CLASS: Merostomata

FAMILY: Limulidae
SCIENTIFIC NAME: *Limulus polyphemus*
COMMON NAME: King Crab; Horseshoe
Crab
DISTRIBUTION: WA
HABITAT: Muddy and sandy substratum
GENERAL WATER DEPTH: Shallow subtidal
FOOD HABIT: Omnivorous: mainly worms,
molluscs and algae
SIZE: Up to 500 m (19.7 in) long
DESCRIPTION: The king crab has a well-armoured body with few signs of segmentation when seen from above. It picks up food with the chelicerae and passes it to the mouth where it is crushed by the spiny limb bases surrounding the mouth. The king crab's long mobile tail spine is used for forward movement and to right the crab if it is turned over. This order of crabs is a small remnant of a larger group which flourished in the oceans some 200 million years ago.

Chromodoris elisabethina

MOLLUSCS

PHYLUM: Mollusca (Molluscs)
CLASS: Polyplacophora (Chitons), Gastropoda (Univalves), Bivalvia (Bivalves), Cephalopoda (Cuttles, squid, nautilus, octopus)

Besides the four classes described here, there are three other classes of the phylum Mollusca. These are the Scaphopoda, Monaplacophora and Aplacophora, whose representatives are rarely seen. The first class is the tusk shells, while the second includes small, limpet-like animals that live hundreds to thousands of metres down in the deep ocean trenches. The third class consists of small, worm-like molluscs without shells that live in bottom sediments or among algae and sedentary invertebrates.

Like the annelids, the molluscs make up a major part of the world's marine invertebrate faunas. At least 112,000 species of mollusc are known and probably many more remain to be discovered.

Oysters, mussels, scallops and squid are served at restaurants and seafood shops. Besides their importance as a source of food, the shells themselves are highly prized for their beauty, myriad shapes, intricate designs, patterns and colours. As calcium carbonate structures that may exist for hundreds of years after the death of the animal that formed them, they are truly a wonder of nature.

Each class of the phylum Mollusca is relatively easy to distinguish, but no one class shows the overall plan of molluscan architecture well. This is difficult to describe briefly. In essence the basic mollusc consists of a head with sense organs and a mouth, a visceral mass comprising the gut and associated structures, reproductive and excretory organs, and a muscular foot for creeping or digging. The body is formed of three cell layers. There is a small body cavity and the animal is not divided into segments. The visceral hump may be twisted and/

or coiled and covered by a shell. A special area of body wall, the mantle, secretes the shell and this often encloses a mantle cavity which may house the gills, reproductive and excretory openings.

The molluscs may be hermaphroditic or have separate sexes, but cross fertilisation is the rule. In many marine species there is a planktonic larval phase. However, some species release juveniles which have undergone development inside their parents' bodies.

CLASS: Polyplacophora (Chitons)

Chitons are often called 'coat-of-mail' shells because of their resemblance to the armour worn by soldiers in early European history. All chitons are marine and most species exist in the littoral and shallow subtidal zones of the rocky seashore. The majority are slow-moving, active herbivores that feed on minute algae scraped off rocks by the wide, many-toothed, ribbon-like feeding organ called a radula. This works rather like a rasping tongue.

Chitons are born with eight separate valves, held together by a tough, leather-like girdle.

Reproduction occurs in several ways. The males have no penis and simply release sperm into the water, which in turn triggers the female of the species to emit eggs or enables the sperm to be taken into the female's mantle cavity by way of currents in the water set up to bring in oxygen for respiration. Several species of southern chitons are known to brood their young and others lay egg strings attached to the substrate.

Owing to their sometimes cryptic habits, many chitons are not well-known and though most species have been recorded, few have been illustrated in colour. Colour variations within species are far from being recorded photographically and in some regions most identifications rely on fine anatomical features which are best resolved by a specialist.

CLASS: Gastropoda (Univalves)

The class Gastropoda contains more species than any other within the phylum Mollusca and up to 90,000 species are thought to exist worldwide.

Species are fairly well known and numerous colour guides to identification for collectors, naturalists, beachcombers, students and scientists have been published since the eighteenth century. Books with scientific descriptions are also available. This diverse class requires listing to subclass level to simplify description.
SUBCLASS: Prosobranchia (Shells snail-like, generally coiled: cones, cowries, helmets, tritons, murex, winkles, whelks, top shells, etc.)
The molluscs of this subclass have gills and anus in front of their visceral mass, which is sometimes referred to as the visceral hump. In general they have a single shell coiled into a tube, similar to a snail. The tube is open at one end and may be partly sealed by a trapdoor (operculum). The head is well formed, with two eyes, each set at the base of a tentacle and may have a retractable proboscis, or 'trunk', containing a well-developed radula. In most species the sexes are separate, with the male impregnating the female with a penis that issues from the right side of the neck. External fertilisation is also known.

Almost all species are mobile herbivores or carnivores. A few live sedentary lives as filter feeders.
SUBCLASS: Opisthobranchia (Shell reduced, sometimes internal, or absent; nudibranchs, pleurobranchs, sea butterflies, bubble shells, sea hares, etc.)
Entirely marine, this subclass offers the greatest challenge to the naturalist. The opisthobranchs are the 'butterflies' of the sea and are among the most beautiful and spectacular underwater creatures.

These molluscs may have reduced external shells, internal shells, or no shells at all in their adult form. They may have gills behind or beside their visceral mass, or they may have no gills at all, depending on the respiratory functions of the skin, or on the other parts of the body (such as pustules or cerata). Most have a well-defined head, one pair of eyes and at least one pair of tentacles. The eyes are reduced, or non-existent in some species, with most only acting as light receptors.

Almost all species are hermaphrodites with each individual in a mating pair transferring and receiving sperm, though some (such as sea hares) may form groups, or mating chains, each fertilising individual laying its own egg mass or string which is mostly spiral and may contain a million eggs. There are thought to be around 3000 species of opisthobranchs with at least several hundred awaiting discovery.

They are generally active, mobile animals, often with specific plant or animal diets. They may be seasonal in their appearance.
SUBCLASS: Pulmonata (External snail-like shell, generally coiled; land snails and slugs)
This subclass is not described in this book as it comprises mainly air-breathing snails or slugs which are terrestrial, freshwater, or inhabitants of littoral areas on rocky shores or mangrove swamps.

CLASS: Bivalvia (Bivalves)

Bivalves can be easily recognised because they always have two shell valves. Each valve is hinged at the dorsal margin; the animal inside is laterally compressed and can open or close the shell valves by contracting or relaxing

Kaloplocamus yatesi

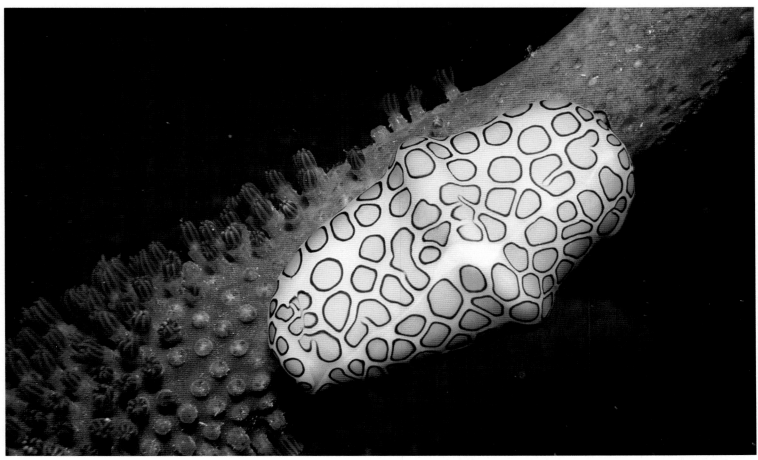

Cyphoma gibbosum

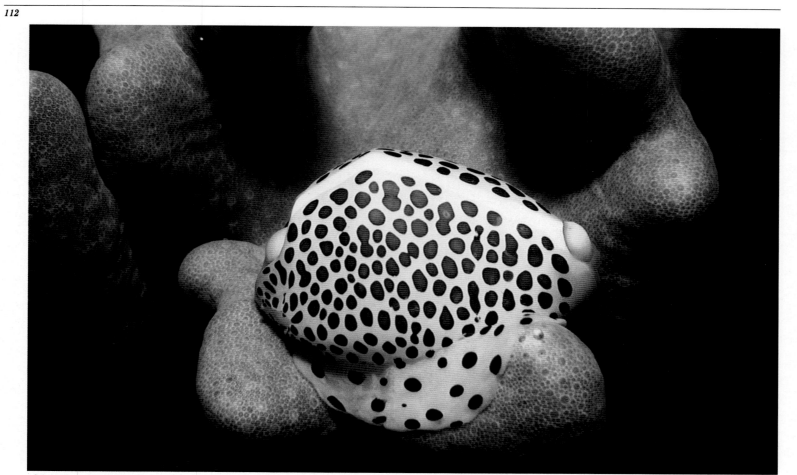

Calpurnus verrucosus

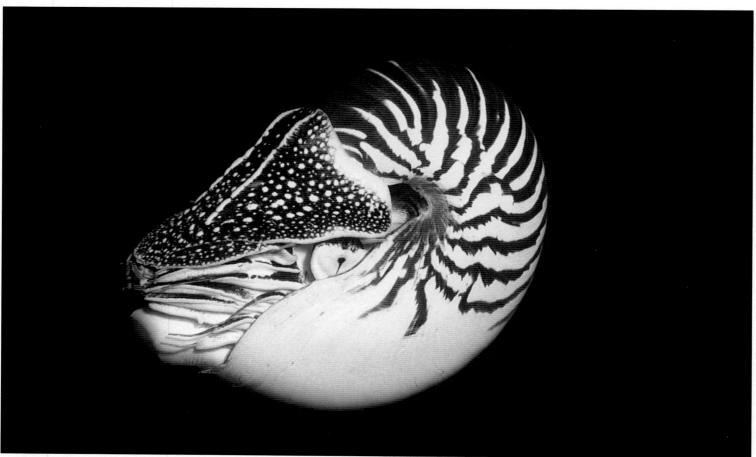

Nautilus pompilius

the adductor muscles attached to the inside of the valves.

Bivalves do not have a head but a well-developed mantle that, as well as lining the shell and building its valves, encloses the gills and the viscera in the mantle cavity. The mantle lobes are often fused and may extend as two siphons through which water is pumped in and out to provide respiration. Plankton and suspended or deposited sediment on which bivalves feed are also pumped in and out of the siphons. These tubes are known as siphons, which may be separate or fused to form one structure.

Many bivalves are attached or fixed to the substrate, either permanently like oysters, or temporarily like mussels; others are free living. Scallops are propelled by water jetted out of the mantle, but this ability to swim is not commonly found. Most burrowers can move and dig by means of a well-developed foot.

Bivalves may not be readily seen. Those that live exposed on reefs or shores are, in many cases, overgrown with other marine life such as barnacles. Free-living forms in sand or mud may be located only by telltale signs made in the substrate by their siphons or shell movements.

Bivalves with colour patterns, designs, or other distinguishing features such as shape, spines, ridges, bumps, or nodules are fairly easy to recognise to species level. Many others require the assistance of an experienced taxonomist for accurate identification.

Most bivalves have separate sexes, though hermaphroditic species do occur. Fertilisation is external and the young hatch as free-swimming larvae.

The harvesting and farming of bivalves is a very important commercial industry throughout the world, worth billions of dollars in domestic consumption and for export. About 15,000 species are known.

CLASS: Cephalopoda (Cuttles, squid, octopus, argonauts, etc)

Animals of this class are the most sophisticated of all the molluscs. They range in size from the 25 millimetre (one inch) long pygmy squids to giant, deepwater squids that may grow to more than 15 metres (50 feet) long. Of all the molluscs that divers find underwater, the cuttles, squids and octopuses appear the most responsive. They have well-developed eyes, complex brain and a highly responsive nervous system.

Cephalopods inhabit shallow reef areas, sand and rubble bottoms and swim freely in the water column. About 750 species are recognised worldwide. Accurate identification of cephalopods to species level is difficult without expert help. Their ability to change colour and blend with the substrate and their highly mobile lifestyle make them difficult to study in the field.

Cephalopods are truly jet-propelled: water enters the mantle cavity in response to the animal's breathing and a funnel leading from the mantle cavity to an opening beneath the head is used to rapidly eject some of this water whenever required. Pigment cells in the skin allow almost instant colour change and, as an added escape response, most produce ink (sepia) that can be jetted causing a 'smoke screen' to cover the animal's escape.

The sexes are separate and males impregnate the females with a modified arm tip that transfers sperm. Eggs are laid by the females, which often die after the eggs hatch. All octopus species lay eggs, brood them until they hatch, and then die. In some species the males die after mating.

Cephalopods are an important food resource.

Ericusa fulgetra

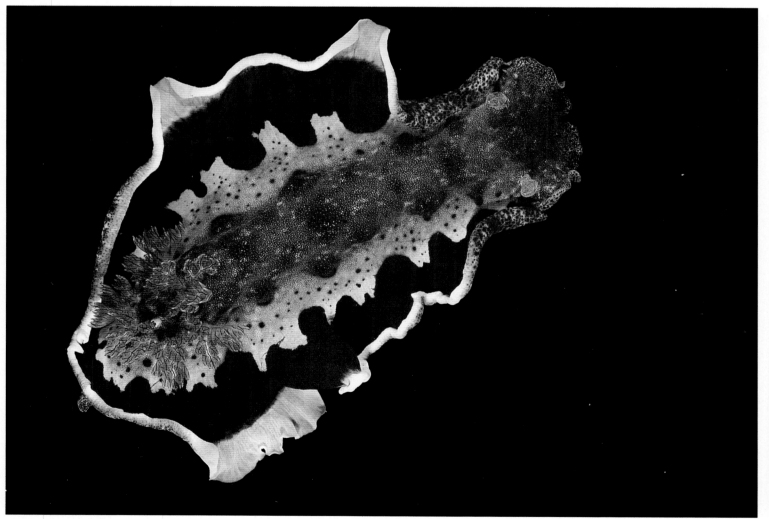

Hexabranchus sanguineus

Acanthochitona communis

■ CLASS: Polyplacophora

FAMILY: Acanthochitonidae
SCIENTIFIC NAME: *Acanthochitona communis*
COMMON NAME: Commune Chiton
DISTRIBUTION: WT/N
HABITAT: Hard substrates
GENERAL WATER DEPTH: Subtidal
FOOD HABIT: Herbivorous: algae
SIZE: Up to 50 mm (2 in) long
DESCRIPTION: Well-developed teeth-like formations are found at the edges of the shell plates in this species. The plates are partly obscured by the girdle, which has tufts of bristles embedded in it between the adjacent plates, towards the rim of the girdle.

FAMILY: Chitonidae
SCIENTIFIC NAME: *Acanthopleura gemmata*
COMMON NAME: Gem Chiton
DISTRIBUTION: TI–WP
HABITAT: Coral reefs; rocky reefs
GENERAL WATER DEPTH: Intertidal
FOOD HABIT: Herbivorous: algae
SIZE: 150 mm (6 in)
DESCRIPTION: Growing to a size of 150 mm (6 in), the gem chiton is one of the larger tropical chitons and inhabits the continental island coasts and barrier reef islands, cays and reefs across the Indo-Pacific region. These molluscs live in crevices, hollows and beneath beach rocks and ledges in the upper littoral zone, just below the high-tide mark. The gem chiton comes out at night during low-tide periods to feed on algae scraped from the beach rock. In general, only large adult chitons are observed, and there seems to be some indication that not all chitons feed at the same time, or even on the same night. Many specimens have special 'homing hollows' in the

rocks where they reside during the day. These hollows have been formed over many generations of chitons; the resident individual always returns to its hollow after foraging. When in its hollow, the chiton's adhesive foot and low profile make it almost impossible for a predator to tear it away from the rock, or storm seas to dislodge it.

Ischnochiton lineolatus

FAMILY: Ischnochitonidae
SCIENTIFIC NAME: *Ischnochiton lineolatus*
COMMON NAME: Lined Ischnochiton
DISTRIBUTION: WT/S; CT/S
HABITAT: Rocky reefs; rocky shores
GENERAL WATER DEPTH: Low tide to 8 m (26 ft)
FOOD HABIT: Herbivorous: algae
SIZE: 50 mm (2 in)
DESCRIPTION: The lined ischnochiton is found beneath stones intertidally and subtidally. This chiton is extremely prevalent in sheltered bays and harbours throughout southern Australia where it has several colour forms. The base colour varies from white to rusty brown overlaid with darker streaks or broken lines along the dorsal surface of the plates. On some specimens these

Acanthopleura gemmata

dark streaks may merge on the lateral areas of the plates to form triangular patches of colour. The girdle is well formed and is marked with dark, irregularly spaced bands of varying widths. The girdle scales are large, round and regularly positioned. Very sensitive to light, the lined ischnochiton stays well hidden during the day. At night it ventures out to feed on micro-algae it scrapes from rocks and reefs with its radula.

Tonicella lineata

FAMILY: Ischnochitonidae
SCIENTIFIC NAME: *Tonicella lineata*
COMMON NAME: Lineate Chiton
DISTRIBUTION: EP
HABITAT: Rocky reefs and shores
GENERAL WATER DEPTH: Intertidal
FOOD HABIT: Herbivorous: algae
SIZE: Up to 50 mm (2 in) long
DESCRIPTION: A pattern of dark brown lines is often found on the plates of this species, as well as white spots on the surrounding smooth girdle. It feeds (mostly at night) by browsing, especially on the coralline algae such as *Lithothamnion*.

■ CLASS: Gastropoda (Prosobranchia)

FAMILY: Buccinidae
SCIENTIFIC NAME: *Buccinum undatum*
COMMON NAME: Common Whelk; Buckie
DISTRIBUTION: CT/N
HABITAT: Mud and sand
GENERAL WATER DEPTH: Intertidal
FOOD HABIT: Carnivorous: worms
SIZE: Up to 100 mm (3.9 in) high
DESCRIPTION: Hermit crabs favour the shells of the common whelk. This edible species is large and heavy shelled, with a short siphonal canal. It feeds extensively on polychaete worms, and is a voracious predator. In particularly muddy areas the common whelk may be found on rocks, though normally it favours sand or mud.

Buccinum undatum

FAMILY: Bursidae
SCIENTIFIC NAME: *Bursa lissostoma*
COMMON NAME: Red-mouthed Frog Shell
DISTRIBUTION: TI–WP; WT/S
HABITAT: Coral reefs; rocky reefs
GENERAL WATER DEPTH: 1–120 m
(3–394 ft)
FOOD HABIT: Carnivorous: ascidians
SIZE: 200 mm (8 in)
DESCRIPTION: Found on the mainland and
offshore reefs in shallow and deep water, the
red-mouthed frog shell was for many years
rarely seen alive, though hundreds of dead
shells inhabited by hermit crabs were
common on tropical reefs and in rock lobster
pots around southern Australia. Females are
often more than twice the size of the males.
The egg capsules, transparent tubes approx-
imately 25 mm (1 in) in height, are secured
to a smooth rock surface in an upright circular mass. The female broods these eggs
until they hatch and will not leave them
except under extreme duress. Left unguard-
ed, the eggs are immediately eaten by any
small fishes close by and also by hermit
crabs.

Bursa lissostoma

Crepidula fornicata

FAMILY: Calyptraeidae
SCIENTIFIC NAME: *Crepidula fornicata*
COMMON NAME: Slipper Limpet
DISTRIBUTION: CT/N
HABITAT: Stones and shells on soft
substrate
GENERAL WATER DEPTH: Intertidal
FOOD HABIT: Omnivorous
SIZE: Up to 50 mm (2 in) long
DESCRIPTION: Often found on oyster beds,
these filter-feeders both compete with the
oysters for food and tend to smother them.
The slipper limpet has a distinctive oval
shape and a ventral partition (characteristic
of all Calyptraeidae species) covering half of
the underside of the shell. Slipper limpets
change from male to female as they get older.
They are usually found as groups in chains
with the oldest animals at the bottom —
hence the animals at the bottom are females
and the younger creatures above are males.

Cassis cornutus

FAMILY: Cassididae
SCIENTIFIC NAME: *Cassis cornutus*
COMMON NAME: Giant Helmet Shell
DISTRIBUTION: TI–WP
HABITAT: Sand

GENERAL WATER DEPTH: 5–30 m
(16–98 ft)
FOOD HABIT: Carnivorous: echinoderms
SIZE: 350mm (14 in)
DESCRIPTION: Ranging from the Red Sea to
southern Japan and across the Indo-Pacific
region to the Tuamotu archipelago, the giant
helmet shell is not only the largest of its
family, but also has the greatest distribution.
They live on sandy sea floors, mostly in
lagoons protected by reefs; they are gregarious. Owing to their size and ease of exploitation, they have been decimated throughout
the world by shell collectors as they provide
excellent materials for the tourist and the
shell markets. Males have smaller shells
than females and have larger knobs. The
species feeds on sand-dwelling heart urchins
and has extraordinary habits which include
social co-operation to save the lives of
endangered relatives.

Phalium bandatum

FAMILY: Cassididae
SCIENTIFIC NAME: *Phalium bandatum*
COMMON NAME: Banded Helmet Shell
DISTRIBUTION: TI–WP
HABITAT: Sand shores
GENERAL WATER DEPTH: Low tide to
40 m (131 ft)
FOOD HABIT: Carnivorous: echinoderms
SIZE: 90 mm (3.5 in)
DESCRIPTION: Very well known throughout
its wide distribution, the banded helmet shell
has been used for centuries as a condiment
container in the shell ornament trade, for
example, salt and pepper shakers. The species is common in shallow water sand banks
where it feeds on sand-dwelling echinoderms
such as sand dollars. Mating takes place in
early summer and eggs are attached to some
solid object, usually a piece of dead coral
rubble or, in one instance, a mangrove leaf.

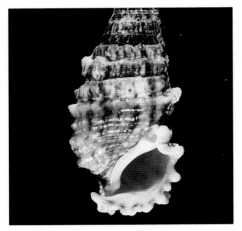

Cerithium echinatum

FAMILY: Cerithiidae
SCIENTIFIC NAME: *Cerithium echinatum*
COMMON NAME: Spiky Creeper
DISTRIBUTION: IWP
HABITAT: Coral reef flats
GENERAL WATER DEPTH: 0–5 m (16 ft)
FOOD HABIT: Herbivorous: algae
SIZE: 60 mm (2.7 in) high
DESCRIPTION: This abundant animal is a grazer, feeding on algae. When found in areas of hard reef its nobbly shell may be covered with algae and small worm tubes, yet when living amongst algae covered sand the shells (although encrusted with detritus) are well preserved.

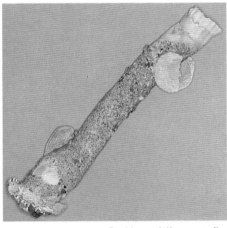

Brechites vaginiferus australis

FAMILY: Clavagellidae
SCIENTIFIC NAME: *Brechites vaginiferus australis*
COMMON NAME: Southern Watering-pot Shell
DISTRIBUTION: TIO
HABITAT: Muddy rubble flats; sandy shores
GENERAL WATER DEPTH: Low tide
FOOD HABIT: Omnivorous: plankton; detritus
SIZE: 200 mm (8 in)

DESCRIPTION: The southern watering-pot shell lives on the north-west coast of Australia in the lower intertidal zone where it can be seen burrowed into the substratum. On the mainland it inhabits muddy sand rubble flats, and on the offshore islands it inhabits coarse sand. Watering-pot shells are bivalve molluscs. Like many bivalves, they begin life as minute planktonic veligers (free-swimming larvae), settle to the bottom as bivalve juveniles, and burrow into the sand; from then on they grow a shell unlike that of any other bivalve. It is a long tube covered with shells and shell grit which sticks up above the sand. At the bottom of the tube is a strange siphonal device shaped like the spout of a watering can and perforated with holes.

Conus ammiralis

FAMILY: Conidae
SCIENTIFIC NAME: *Conus ammiralis*
COMMON NAME: Admiral's Cone
DISTRIBUTION: TI–WP
HABITAT: Sand
GENERAL WATER DEPTH: Low tide to 20 m (66 ft)
FOOD HABIT: Carnivorous: mobile invertebrates
SIZE: 50 mm (2 in)
DESCRIPTION: One of the most attractive of the Indo-Pacific cones, the admiral's cone occurs in some areas of the Indian Ocean, reaching the waters of southern Japan. This species lives in the clear clean waters of off-shore reefs and sand cays where during the day it hides beneath slabs of dead coral and rubble in sandy lagoons. Pattern is variable, but the general solid features and structure of the shell is fairly stable throughout its distribution.

FAMILY: Conidae
SCIENTIFIC NAME: *Conus geographus*
COMMON NAME: Geography Cone
DISTRIBUTION: IWP

Conus geographus

HABITAT: Coral reefs
GENERAL WATER DEPTH: Intertidal
FOOD HABIT: Carnivorous: fish
SIZE: 150 mm (6 in) or more long
DESCRIPTION: This venomous species has a powerful sting which has been known to cause human deaths. Small reef-dwelling fish are its favoured prey. As with other members of this family, *Conus geographus* has no operculum. The shell of this cone is a collector's item.

Conus marmoreus

FAMILY: Conidae
SCIENTIFIC NAME: *Conus marmoreus*
COMMON NAME: Marbled Cone
DISTRIBUTION: TI–WP
HABITAT: Coral reefs
GENERAL WATER DEPTH: 0–20 m (66 ft)
FOOD HABIT: Carnivorous: molluscs
SIZE: 75 mm (3 in)
DESCRIPTION: Inhabiting sandy rubble areas among reefs around continental off-shore islands and outer barrier reefs, the marbled cone is much more common than realised. During the day it lives beneath the sand, or half-buried around coral heads and soft corals. At night it actively hunts other

univalves, attacking them through the aperture of their shell and killing them with a venomous dart. It is venomous to humans.

Conus omaria

FAMILY: Conidae
SCIENTIFIC NAME: *Conus omaria*
COMMON NAME: Omaria Cone
DISTRIBUTION: TI–WP
HABITAT: Coral reefs
GENERAL WATER DEPTH: Low tide to
10 m (33 ft)
FOOD HABIT: Carnivorous
SIZE: 75 mm (3 in)
DESCRIPTION: Although the omaria cone has tent-like markings similar to those of the textile cone, once the two are compared they are easily separated. Similar to other cone species, the omaria cone is nocturnal and during the day dwells buried in sand patches in the reef, usually beneath dead coral and rubble. Not as venomous as some of the fish-eating cones, this species is still regarded as dangerous to humans.

Conus striatus

FAMILY: Conidae
SCIENTIFIC NAME: *Conus striatus*
COMMON NAME: Striated Cone Shell

DISTRIBUTION: TI–WP
HABITAT: Coral reef; sand shores
GENERAL WATER DEPTH: Low tide to
20 m (66 ft)
FOOD HABIT: Carnivorous: fish
SIZE: 100 mm (4 in)
DESCRIPTION: The striated cone, seen most frequently on tropical offshore island reefs, is a medium–large shell of solid construction that inhabits sand and rubble areas where it lives beneath coral and rocks. It also occurs on muddy reefs at some continental island locations. It generally has a white or pink shell with fine brown lines superimposed in characteristic blotches forming a pattern. There is a fine, translucent periostracum covering the shell, as well as a small operculum. The flesh of the animal is white or pink with brown streaks, with a dark red band around the edge of the foot. A nocturnal hunter, it is a fish eater and therefore capable of harming humans. On no account should it be placed anywhere near the body as its sting is venomous.

Conus textile

FAMILY: Conidae
SCIENTIFIC NAME: *Conus textile*
COMMON NAME: Textile Cone
DISTRIBUTION: TI–WP
HABITAT: Coral reefs; rocky reefs
GENERAL WATER DEPTH: Low tide to
30 m (98 ft)
FOOD HABIT: Carnivorous: molluscs
SIZE: 120 mm (5 in)
DESCRIPTION: Easily recognised by its unusual tent-like markings, the textile cone has several different habitats. During the day it seeks hiding places beneath rocks or coral and generally burrows into sand under these objects. Essentially a nocturnal forager, it feeds almost exclusively on other univalve molluscs. By homing in on the scent of its prey, this cone tracks down another gastropod, usually choosing one that has no operculum. When close to the prey, it

expands its long proboscis and tentatively explores the other shell. Having found the aperture the proboscis enters, probing the depths. Upon contact with the flesh a modified radular dart bearing venom is shot into the prey, which succumbs to the cone's venom. Later the dead animal becomes flaccid and is consumed by the cone. Textile cone venom can harm humans and several victims are reported to have died.

Cypraea arabica

FAMILY: Cypraeidae
SCIENTIFIC NAME: *Cypraea arabica*
COMMON NAME: Arabian Cowry
DISTRIBUTION: TI–WP
HABITAT: Coral reefs: rocky reefs
GENERAL WATER DEPTH: Low tide to
10 m (33 ft)
FOOD HABIT: Omnivorous: algae; sponges
SIZE: 50 mm (2 in)
DESCRIPTION: The Arabian cowry is found living beneath large slabs of dead coral, under rocks and in caves where it is protected during the day from diurnal predators (fish) and the sun. Unlike some other cowries they are generally found in pairs and appear to be more abundant just below low-tide level than in deeper waters. There does not appear to be any preference in habitat as they are just as common around continental reefs as they are on barrier reefs and offshore islands.

FAMILY: Cypraeidae
SCIENTIFIC NAME: *Cypraea cribraria*
COMMON NAME: Tan and White Cowry
DISTRIBUTION: TI–WP
HABITAT: Coral reefs; rocky reefs
GENERAL WATER DEPTH: Low tide to
20 m (66 ft)

Cypraea cribraria

FOOD HABIT: Carnivorous: sponges
SIZE: 25 mm (1 in)
DESCRIPTION: Found in all tropical areas, the tan and white cowry is a resident of coral reefs and rocky reefs both on the mainland and on offshore reefs and islands. On offshore tropical reefs it is generally found beneath dead coral slabs at the mid-tide level, while on temperate rocky reefs it tends to be sublittoral. The shell is pure white, overlaid with a very distinctive pattern of light or dark brown which gives the impression of white spots, and the female shells are larger than male shells. The tan and white cowry has a bright red or deep orange animal and the mantle has short papillae covering it. Quite often there may be several papillae which are white. This species can frequently be observed on the underside of rocks covered in red or orange sponges upon which it feeds.

Cypraea mappa

Cypraea marginata

FAMILY: Cypraeidae
SCIENTIFIC NAME: *Cypraea mappa*
COMMON NAME: Map Cowry
DISTRIBUTION: TI–WP
HABITAT: Coral reefs
GENERAL WATER DEPTH: 0–30 m (98 ft)
FOOD HABIT: Carnivorous: sponges
SIZE: 75 mm (3 in)
DESCRIPTION: One of the better-known and characteristically patterned cowries of the Indo-Pacific region, this species occurs over a wide area of tropical reefs. It seems to seek areas of good aeration below the low-tide level, living in caves and holes in the roofs of reef-edge overhangs where there is maximum water movement. Its food consists of sedentary encrusting organisms and it feeds mainly during the night as a protective measure to ensure minimum exposure to predation by fish. Wrasses are particularly fond of cowries; large fish crush the shell to get at the animal and smaller ones bite off chunks from the tentacles, mantle and foot. The translucent, buff-coloured mantle has very few papillae and under natural conditions it is not extended during the day.

FAMILY: Cypraeidae
SCIENTIFIC NAME: *Cypraea marginata*
COMMON NAME: Margin Cowry
DISTRIBUTION: WT/S
HABITAT: Rocky reefs
GENERAL WATER DEPTH: 10–100 m (33–328 ft)
FOOD HABIT: Carnivorous: sponges
SIZE: 70 mm (3 in)
DESCRIPTION: This shell was named from a single specimen and its habitat remained unknown for 100 years after its discovery. Today the margin cowry is found by divers and rock lobster fishermen along the coast of southern Australia. It lives in caves and overhangs on reefs. It inhabits the seaward side of islands and reefs where huge Indian Ocean swells expend their enormous force. Observation of these molluscs can be very hazardous and many specimens have chips and flaws in their delicate shell flanges due to their inclement habitat. Males tend to be smaller and slimmer than females. Eggs are often laid in the valves of dead bivalve shells; the females sit on the eggs, protecting and aerating them until they hatch.

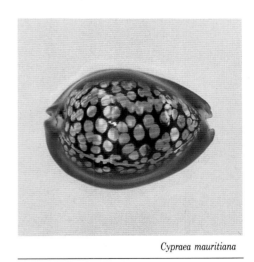

Cypraea mauritiana

FAMILY: Cypraeidae
SCIENTIFIC NAME: *Cypraea mauritiana*
COMMON NAME: Chocolate Cowry Shell
DISTRIBUTION: TI–WP
HABITAT: Coral reefs; rocky reefs
GENERAL WATER DEPTH: 0–5 m (16 ft)
FOOD HABIT: Herbivorous: algae
SIZE: 120 mm (5 in)
DESCRIPTION: Although the chocolate cowry is sometimes found on coral reef edges it is

much more prevalent on and around continental volcanic islands and reefs. It generally lives in exposed situations where there is a good deal of water action (surf zone). Blending in well with its dark habitat, it lives in holes, caves and under ledges during the day, feeding on algae during the night. This cowry shell is extremely well built for its environment, having a thick, solid shell, a wide-based flange and a very powerful foot to anchor it during rough seas and surf. Its distribution covers the Indo-Pacific from Japan to Lord Howe Island in the South-West Pacific.

Cypraea moneta

FAMILY: Cypraeidae
SCIENTIFIC NAME: *Cypraea moneta*
COMMON NAME: Money Cowry
DISTRIBUTION: TI–WP; WT/S
HABITAT: Coral reefs
GENERAL WATER DEPTH: Low tide to 4 m (13 ft)
FOOD HABIT: Herbivorous: algae
SIZE: 30 mm (1 in)
DESCRIPTION: As its common name suggests, this extremely numerous little shell was once used extensively throughout the Indo-Pacific region as trade 'money'. Strings of shells were utilised to buy and trade goods many centuries before metal and paper money came into existence. The molluscs mostly live on intertidal reef flats in lagoon areas, living in run-off habitats under stones and coral as well as under ledges and in holes in the reef. As the tide runs in, they move out of their hideaways to feed on algae. The animal's mantle blends in with this habitat.

FAMILY: Cypraeidae
SCIENTIFIC NAME: *Cypraea nucleus*
COMMON NAME: Nut Cowry
DISTRIBUTION: TI–WP
HABITAT: Coral reefs

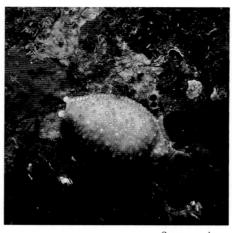

Cypraea nucleus

GENERAL WATER DEPTH: Low tide to 15 m (49 ft)
FOOD HABIT: Omnivorous
SIZE: 25 mm (1 in)
DESCRIPTION: Shells of this species are quite commonly found washed up on beaches across the Indo-Pacific region but the animal is extremely difficult to find alive. It lives beneath coral clumps and on the roofs of caves, and only comes out at night. The transparent mantle is not raised during the day and the animal itself is very sensitive to light. Raised nodules on the shell make it easy to identify.

Cypraea tigris

FAMILY: Cypraeidae
SCIENTIFIC NAME: *Cypraea tigris*
COMMON NAME: Tiger Cowry
DISTRIBUTION: TI–WP
HABITAT: Coral reefs; rocky reefs
GENERAL WATER DEPTH: Low tide to 30 m (98 ft)
FOOD HABIT: Omnivorous: algae
SIZE: 120 mm (5 in)
DESCRIPTION: The tiger cowry is one of the largest cowries in tropical waters. It generally occurs in intertidal lagoons, in caves, on

coral clumps and on underhangs of reef ramparts. Each cowry varies in colour, pattern and size, the largest being those at the extremities of their range. It is basically a nocturnal forager, but specimens are also seen in the late afternoon on a flooding tide, feeding on encrusting algae on the tops of micro-atolls in lagoons. Long tactile papillae stud the cowry's mantle and these usually have an opaque white spot on the tip. The species is often gregarious. Little is known about its breeding habits but egg masses have been observed beneath coral slabs with the female sitting on the eggs. Small crustaceans are sometimes present on the mantle, but no definite association has been noted.

Cypraea vitellus

FAMILY: Cypraeidae
SCIENTIFIC NAME: *Cypraea vitellus*
COMMON NAME: Milk-spot Cowry
DISTRIBUTION: TI–WP; WT/S
HABITAT: Coral reefs; rocky reefs
GENERAL WATER DEPTH: Low tide to 20 m (66 ft)
FOOD HABIT: Carnivorous
SIZE: 50 mm (2 in)
DESCRIPTION: The milk-spot cowry is one of the most well-known, medium-sized tropical cowries. Except for high beach rock areas and sand pockets, they are widely distributed throughout the reef flats in most Indo-Pacific areas. Like most molluscs, this species spurns the harsh sunlight and hides beneath rocks, dead coral and in coral heads during the day. In the spring the females lay white egg masses beneath rocks which turn grey as they develop. Natural predators are mostly octopus and fish and particularly wrasses, which find the molluscs during early morning foragings. Although the milk-spot cowry has a great deal of variation in its shell pattern and the papillae of its mantle, identification is fairly simple.

Epitonium billeeanum

FAMILY: Epitoniidae
SCIENTIFIC NAME: *Epitonium billeeanum*
COMMON NAME: Golden Wentletrap Shell
DISTRIBUTION: TI–WP; WT/S; EP
HABITAT: Coral reefs
GENERAL WATER DEPTH: 5–20 m
  (16–66 ft)
FOOD HABIT: Carnivorous: coral polyps
SIZE: 25 mm (1 in)
DESCRIPTION: Fairly common on many
tropical reefs throughout the Indo-Pacific
Oceans, this species is also found in the
South-West Pacific and all the way across the
Pacific to the Sea of Cortez. It is only present in relation to *Tubastrea* and *Dendro-
phyllia* corals, which it feeds upon. On most
occasions more than one specimen is
observed. The females are larger than the
males and are sexually mature when around
12 mm (0.5 in). The golden-coloured eggs,
held together by extremely sticky gold-
coloured strings, are laid directly on to the
prey corals.

Epitonium scalare

FAMILY: Epitoniidae
SCIENTIFIC NAME: *Epitonium scalare*
COMMON NAME: Precious Wentletrap

DISTRIBUTION: TI–WP
HABITAT: Sand; mud
GENERAL WATER DEPTH: Low tide to
  20 m (66 ft)
FOOD HABIT: Carnivorous: sea anemones
SIZE: 50 mm (2 in)
DESCRIPTION: Known for centuries, the
precious wentletrap is a common, yet very
much sought-after, shell throughout the
world. It occurs in the Indo-Pacific region
and in general seems to prefer the muddy
offshore areas of continental islands rather
than outer barrier reefs. During storms and
cyclones, thousands are washed out of their
sandy-mud retreats and thrown up on
beaches, where they are immediately gathered by beachcombers and seashell enthusi-
asts.

Haliotis asinina

FAMILY: Haliotidae
SCIENTIFIC NAME: *Haliotis asinina*
COMMON NAME: Ass's Ear Shell
DISTRIBUTION: TI–WP
HABITAT: Coral reefs
GENERAL WATER DEPTH: Low tide to 5 m
  (16 ft)
FOOD HABIT: Herbivorous: algae
SIZE: 180 mm (7 in)
DESCRIPTION: Distributed throughout many
areas along continental shores and including
offshore barrier reefs, the ass's ear shell is
the largest *Haliotis* species in the tropics.
The shell is long, ear-shaped and dark green
with light green and brown rays which show
the periods of growth. The animal is much
larger than the shell and the mantle, unlike
that of any other abalone, can completely
cover the shell. This accounts for the outside
of the shell being free from other marine
growths and appearing shiny. Along the outside edge there is a row of distinct holes
through which water leaves the respiratory
system. This water also contains excretory
products, and eggs and sperm of spawning
animals. An extremely active mollusc both

day and night, it can be seen during late
afternoon on incoming tides crawling around
on top of the reefs. The edges of the animal's
mantle are frilled in a similar way to some
opisthobranchs.

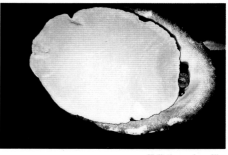

Haliotis cracherodii

FAMILY: Haliotidae
SCIENTIFIC NAME: *Haliotis cracherodii*
COMMON NAME: Abalone
DISTRIBUTION: EP
HABITAT: Rocky shores and reefs
GENERAL WATER DEPTH: Intertidal/
  shallow subtidal
FOOD HABIT: Herbivorous: algae
SIZE: Up to 150 mm (5.9 in) long
DESCRIPTION: The abalone has an ear-
shaped shell with a small spiral at the apex.
Water currents and waste matter pass
through the series of holes around the whorl.
The foot is much sought-after as a food
source. This species is most often found
under stones and in crevices.

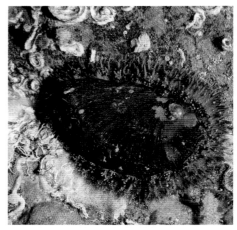

Haliotis tuberculata

FAMILY: Haliotidae
SCIENTIFIC NAME: *Haliotis tuberculata*
COMMON NAME: Green Ormer
DISTRIBUTION: EA
HABITAT: Rocky shores and reefs
GENERAL WATER DEPTH: Subtidal
FOOD HABIT: Herbivorous: algae
SIZE: Up to 80 mm (3.1 in) long
DESCRIPTION: Inside the shell of the green

ormer is a layer of mother-of-pearl, much sought after for buttons and jewellery. The shell is ridged on the upper surface and often coated with calcareous algae.

Harpa amouretta

FAMILY: Harpidae
SCIENTIFIC NAME: *Harpa amouretta*
COMMON NAME: Lesser Harp Shell
DISTRIBUTION: TI–WP
HABITAT: Sand shores
GENERAL WATER DEPTH: Low tide to 25 m (82 ft)
FOOD HABIT: Carnivorous: crustaceans
SIZE: 65 mm (2.5 in)
DESCRIPTION: Covering an area from South Africa through the Red Sea and Indian Ocean to the tropical Pacific from Japan to Western Australia, the lesser harp shell has one of the largest ranges of its family. The species burrows into intertidal sand patches on reefs, and nestles beneath dead coral slabs in lagoon areas during the day. At night it emerges and crawls around on top of the sand, searching for prey such as shrimps and small crabs that are captured by being enveloped in a sticky mucous secretion combined with sand.

Janthina janthina

FAMILY: Janthinidae
SCIENTIFIC NAME: *Janthina janthina*
COMMON NAME: Large Violet Snail
DISTRIBUTION: TI–WP; WT/S; CT/S; WT/N
HABITAT: Open ocean
GENERAL WATER DEPTH: Surface waters
FOOD HABIT: Carnivorous: cnidarians
SIZE: 30 mm (1 in)
DESCRIPTION: Cosmopolitan in distribution, this rather interesting species spends its time upside down, living out its entire life cycle on the undersurface waters of the ocean. The large violet snail is at the mercy of the wind and tides; its presence on beaches is usually a result of strong winds or storms at sea. They can crawl along on the surface tension when small but cannot swim; instead, they secrete mucus that hardens on contact with the water and, aided by trapped air bubbles, acts as a raft. Violet snails feed on other surface-dwelling animals such as by-the-wind sailors.

Littoraria filosa

FAMILY: Littorinidae
SCIENTIFIC NAME: *Littoraria filosa*
COMMON NAME: Mangrove Australwink
DISTRIBUTION: TI–WP; WT/S
HABITAT: Mangroves
GENERAL WATER DEPTH: Generally above high-water mark
FOOD HABIT: Herbivorous
SIZE: 25 mm (1 in)
DESCRIPTION: Very common through the Indo-Pacific region, this species is generally observed on the upper branches and leaves of mangrove trees. Like others of its genus, it seems to prefer a dry habitat rather than a wet one. Scientists have suggested that the species could be evolving into a terrestrial mode of life. The most colourful of australwinks, specimens can be either red, yellow, brown, or various patterned combinations. The female returns to the intertidal

level after mating to release her young. The juvenile snails spend some time in this marine environment before moving up on to tree trunks and branches.

Littorina littorea

FAMILY: Littorinidae
SCIENTIFIC NAME: *Littorina littorea*
COMMON NAME: Common Periwinkle
DISTRIBUTION: EA, WA
HABITAT: Very rocky shorelines
GENERAL WATER DEPTH: Intertidal
FOOD HABIT: Herbivorous: algae
SIZE: 25 mm (1 in)
DESCRIPTION: An abundant species across its entire range, the common periwinkle is always found on rocks. The back of the shell is dull yellowish brown, with the same colour continuing to the aperture side. The lighter, cream-coloured striations are wider and more distinct on the aperture side. The interior of the aperture is dull white. The common periwinkle is sometimes gathered as food; although small, it is excellent to eat.

Mitra mitra

FAMILY: Mitridae
SCIENTIFIC NAME: *Mitra mitra*
COMMON NAME: Giant Mitre Shell

DISTRIBUTION: TI–WP
HABITAT: Sand shores
GENERAL WATER DEPTH: 0–60 m (197 ft)
FOOD HABIT: Carnivorous: worms
SIZE: 150 mm (6 in)
DESCRIPTION: The largest and best-known mitre shell, this species is relatively common on sand-banks and lagoon areas from South Africa to the Red Sea, to southern Japan and across to Hawaii, and down into the South-West Pacific. Like most sand-dwelling molluscs, this species is nocturnal and during the day remains buried and dormant. At night it ploughs along just beneath the surface, forming a raised track in the sand. To probe worm holes it has a proboscis that is almost as long as its body and can emit a dark staining fluid when disturbed.

Chicoreus brunneus

FAMILY: Muricidae
SCIENTIFIC NAME: *Chicoreus brunneus*
COMMON NAME: Burnt Murex Shell
DISTRIBUTION: TI–WP
HABITAT: Muddy reefs; coral reefs
GENERAL WATER DEPTH: Low tide to 20 m (66 ft)
FOOD HABIT: Carnivorous: molluscs (bivalves)
SIZE: 95 mm (4 in)
DESCRIPTION: Very common over much of the Indo-Pacific region this species appears just as much at home on muddy continental reefs as on outer barrier reefs in clean water. Specimens that live in muddy areas develop larger varice extensions than those living on coral reefs which are extremely hard to see because of the marine growths of coralline algae adhering to their varices. The shells are normally black with a distinctive pink aperture. Occasionally in some areas the aperture may be orange or even yellow. Their food consists mainly of bivalves, preference being shown for chama shells. The murex shells have no difficulty in drilling through the thick shells of their prey, but they take

up to three days to consume the animal inside. Eggs are laid in September, usually under ledges and coral rock.

Chicoreus cornucervi

FAMILY: Muricidae
SCIENTIFIC NAME: *Chicoreus cornucervi*
COMMON NAME: Staghorn Murex Shell
DISTRIBUTION: TI–WP
HABITAT: Rocky reefs; mud; sand shores
GENERAL WATER DEPTH: Low tide to 5 m (16 ft)
FOOD HABIT: Carnivorous: bivalves
SIZE: 110 mm (4 in)
DESCRIPTION: The staghorn murex is named for its extravagant varices which resemble the antlers of the old world male deer. It lives on mudflats and rocky rubble tidal flats on both mainland and offshore locations in the Indo-Pacific. There are two main colour forms of this shell: brown with black fronds, and pure white. The white ones are the least common and seem to be restricted to offshore continental islands. At the southern end of the Great Barrier Reef this species seems to be restricted to a subtidal existence, as it is only found by trawling or dredging. Female shells tend to be larger than the males. After mating, egg capsules are laid by the female beneath rocks or ledges and sometimes in dead bivalve shells. They also lay eggs on the sides of rocks. The female generally guards the eggs until they hatch.

FAMILY: Muricidae
SCIENTIFIC NAME: *Murex pecten*
COMMON NAME: Venus Comb Murex Shell
DISTRIBUTION: TI–WP; WT/N
HABITAT: Sand
GENERAL WATER DEPTH: 5–40 m (16–131 ft)
FOOD HABIT: Carnivorous: molluscs
SIZE: 120 mm (5 in)

Murex pecten

DESCRIPTION: An extravagance of molluscan architecture, the venus comb murex shell has a wide distribution through the Indian and Pacific oceans, up to Japan and into the South-West Pacific. It lives mostly in subtidal areas in loose, sandy substrate and is buried for most of the day. At night it comes out of the sand and crawls along the surface in search of prey, which is mostly small bivalves. It detects buried bivalves using chemo-reception, tracking traces of odour released by the bivalve's respiratory system.

Nucella lapillus

FAMILY: Muricidae
SCIENTIFIC NAME: *Nucella lapillus*
COMMON NAME: Atlantic Dogwinkle or Dogwhelk
DISTRIBUTION: CT/N
HABITAT: Rocky shores
GENERAL WATER DEPTH: Intertidal
FOOD HABIT: Carnivorous: barnacles and mussels
SIZE: Up to 50 mm (2 in) long
DESCRIPTION: Formerly harvested for its purple dye in Brittany and Norway (the dye was used to mark laundry), the Atlantic

dogwinkle often occurs in large numbers. It is most frequently found alongside the barnacles and mussels on which it feeds. This whelk has a short siphonal canal and older specimens have eroded shells. Members of this family drill holes into other shells then insert their proboscis. This contains a toothed radula which rasps the prey into pieces to be consumed.

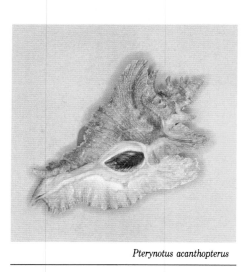

Pterynotus acanthopterus

FAMILY: Muricidae
SCIENTIFIC NAME: *Pterynotus acanthopterus*
COMMON NAME: Spine-winged Murex Shell
DISTRIBUTION: TI–WP; WT/S; WT/N
HABITAT: Rocky reefs; muddy reef shores
GENERAL WATER DEPTH: 0–40 m (131 ft)
FOOD HABIT: Carnivorous: tube worms; bivalves
SIZE: 100 mm (4 in)
DESCRIPTION: Deepwater forms of this species can be found from the Indian Ocean to the Atlantic and South-West Pacific oceans. However, these are quite small (50 mm/2 in) compared to the giants that live intertidally off the north-west coast of Australia. Colour variation ranges from dark brown through to light brown and white. On adult shells the posterior canal is usually filled in by the edge of the apertural lip. It is a transparent white with opaque white or yellow flecks. Males have smaller shells than females. Mating takes place during summer; females lay groups of white egg capsules under rocks and in bivalve shells, then sit on the eggs and protect them until they hatch. Spine-winged murex shells drill holes in bivalves and tube worms and eat their soft parts.

FAMILY: Muricidae
SCIENTIFIC NAME: *Pterynotus tripterus*
COMMON NAME: Lace Murex Shell
DISTRIBUTION: TI–WP

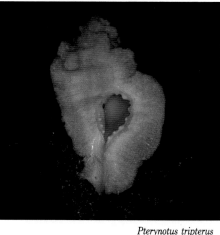

Pterynotus tripterus

HABITAT: Coral reefs
GENERAL WATER DEPTH: 0–30 m (98 ft)
FOOD HABIT: Carnivorous: molluscs
SIZE: 60 mm (2.3 in)
DESCRIPTION: An Indo-Pacific species which ranges from southern Japan to the Great Barrier Reef, the lace murex shell is not an easy species to locate even when its habitat is known. It lives beneath dead coral slabs and is usually very overgrown with coralline algae so that the delicate shell sculpture is not visible. However, the general shape of the shell is easy to recognise, as are the tooth-like nodules around the aperture.

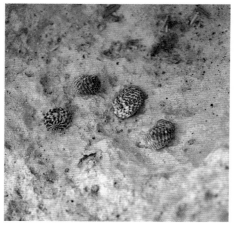

Nerita tessellata

FAMILY: Neritidae
SCIENTIFIC NAME: *Nerita tessellata*
COMMON NAME: Tessellate Nerite
DISTRIBUTION: WA
HABITAT: Rocky shorelines
GENERAL WATER DEPTH: Intertidal to 10 m (32.8 ft)
FOOD HABIT: Herbivorous: algae
SIZE: 1.8 m (0.7 in)
DESCRIPTION: Generally found in areas of many small rocks, the tessellate nerite is an abundant species. It is marked with inter-

mittent bands of dull purple across the otherwise grey to tan exterior of its shell, and has a blue-white operculum with a definite purplish tint.

Amalda elongata

FAMILY: Olividae
SCIENTIFIC NAME: *Amalda elongata*
COMMON NAME: Elongate Ancilla
DISTRIBUTION: TIO
HABITAT: Sand shores
GENERAL WATER DEPTH: 0–10 m (33 ft)
FOOD HABIT: Carnivorous: molluscs
SIZE: 45 mm (2 in)
DESCRIPTION: With its large, characteristically patterned mantle flaps enveloping its shell, the elongate ancilla ploughs its way along the sand or mud surface of its habitat. Cruising with the incoming tide in the late afternoon it must capture its prey and find suitable substrate in which to bury itself before the water becomes deep enough to provide access for predatory fish. By choosing late afternoon or evening to venture out in search of food the elongate ancilla reduces the risk of being eaten by daytime carnivores. Most mollusc-eating fish are diurnal.

FAMILY: Olividae
SCIENTIFIC NAME: *Oliva miniacea*
COMMON NAME: Red-mouthed Olive Shell
DISTRIBUTION: TI–WP
HABITAT: Sand shores
GENERAL WATER DEPTH: 0–5 m (16 ft)
FOOD HABIT: Carnivorous; scavenger
SIZE: 60 mm (2.3 in)
DESCRIPTION: Although individuals may be found on continental island sandflats, the red-mouthed olive shell is more prevalent around offshore sand cays and barrier reef lagoons. The species is both carnivore and scavenger. Lying beneath the sand with just the top of the siphon showing, its response is immediate to any waft of food source that may come by on the current. Some individu-

Oliva miniacea

als may feed on the top of the sand, but most engulf the food and, if it is small, pull it beneath the sand to ingest it. The red-mouthed olive is one of the largest olive shells in the Indo-Pacific region. The shell itself is a creamy white with lightning-like streaks of orange edged with mauve down its length. On the posterior end and at the centre of the shell there is an irregular black band around the circumference.

Calpurnus verrucosus

FAMILY: Ovulidae
SCIENTIFIC NAME: *Calpurnus verrucosus*
COMMON NAME: Toe-nail Cowry
DISTRIBUTION: TI–WP
HABITAT: Coral reefs
GENERAL WATER DEPTH: Low tide to
   8 m (26 ft)
FOOD HABIT: Carnivorous: soft corals
SIZE: 25 mm (1 in)
DESCRIPTION: The toe-nail is easily recognised but is not a true cowry. The peculiar calluses on the anterior and posterior dorsal extremities of this shell are often tinged with mauve, and it is from these unique growths that the mollusc gets its common name. It feeds mostly at night, although it can sometimes be seen walking

on the surface of its soft coral prey during a flooding tide in the late afternoon, or when the skies are overcast. Males are smaller than females and mating takes place in the spring. In early summer the female lays her egg capsules on the soft coral host. The egg capsules are circular and rather flat and contain yellow-green eggs that blend in with the soft coral upon which they are laid. The egg capsules may be laid directly on to the side of an overhanging 'finger' of soft coral, or on the underside of a flap, along the edge of the column. The female usually stays close to the eggs, but does not sit on them as do true cowries.

Globovula cavanaghi

FAMILY: Ovulidae
SCIENTIFIC NAME: *Globovula cavanaghi*
COMMON NAME: Cavanagh's Ovulid
DISTRIBUTION: TI–WP; WT/S
HABITAT: Rocky reefs; mud; sand shores
GENERAL WATER DEPTH: 0–50 m (164 ft)
FOOD HABIT: Carnivorous: soft corals
SIZE: 15 mm (0.5 in)
DESCRIPTION: Cavanagh's ovulid feeds exclusively on the soft corals on which it is normally found. In the north it lives on *Dendronephthya* sp. while in the central and South-West Pacific it lives on the southern soft coral, *D. australis*, and the Gabo Island soft coral, *Capnella gaboensis*. Mating takes place during late winter after which the female deposits egg capsules directly on to the host soft coral. During the day this species has a very interesting habit of wrapping itself up in a soft coral branch where it remains perfectly camouflaged, throughout the day.

FAMILY: Ovulidae
SCIENTIFIC NAME: *Ovula costellata*
COMMON NAME: Costellate Egg Cowry
DISTRIBUTION: TI–WP; WT/S
HABITAT: Coral reefs; rocky reefs
GENERAL WATER DEPTH: 10–30 m
   (33–98 ft)

Ovula costellata

FOOD HABIT: Carnivorous: soft corals
SIZE: 50 mm (2 in)
DESCRIPTION: Not as common as its relative, the larger egg cowry *Ovula ovum*, the costellate egg cowry inhabits the Indo-Pacific region and has been recorded well down into the South-West Pacific, off Lord Howe Island and south-eastern Australia. The mantle colours are fairly stable, the pustules ranging from pink to orange. This species feeds on at least five different kinds of soft corals and is rarely seen away from its prey. Eggs are laid around the sides of the soft coral colony, not directly on the polyp-bearing tissue.

Ovula ovum

FAMILY: Ovulidae
SCIENTIFIC NAME: *Ovula ovum*
COMMON NAME: Egg Cowry
DISTRIBUTION: TI–WP
HABITAT: Coral reefs; rocky reefs
GENERAL WATER DEPTH: 0–30 m (98 ft)
FOOD HABIT: Carnivorous: soft corals
SIZE: 120 mm (5 in)
DESCRIPTION: The egg cowry is a common resident of inshore and offshore coral reefs throughout the Indo-Pacific region, and although it is known to occur in deeper

waters in the South-West Pacific, towards the equator it is found under intertidal conditions. The shell is pure porcellaneous white with a chocolate brown interior. The shape is cowry-like, though the aperture is much wider than that of a true cowry. Egg cowries that belong to the family Ovulidae are often referred to as 'allied cowries' owing to their similarities. On intertidal tropical reefs this species seems to prefer to feed on the green leathery soft coral *Sarcophyton* upon which it is regularly found. The flesh of the egg cowry is a vivid, velvet black with white-yellow or orange-tipped mantle pustules. Sometimes there is an ultra-blue edge to the siphon. Members of this species are unusual ovulids because they are not obligate predators on one colony of soft coral or gorgonian sea fan, but instead move round the sea floor in search of food and mates.

Phenacovolva angasi

FAMILY: Ovulidae
SCIENTIFIC NAME: *Phenacovolva angasi*
COMMON NAME: Angas's Ovulid
DISTRIBUTION: TI–WP; WT/S
HABITAT: Coral reefs; rocky reefs
GENERAL WATER DEPTH: 10–40 m
 (33–131 ft)
FOOD HABIT: Carnivorous: gorgonian sea
 fans
SIZE: 20 mm (1 in)
DESCRIPTION: Found only on their host gorgonian sea fans throughout the Indo- and South-West Pacific waters, these well-camouflaged little shells have mantle patterns and forms which are almost identical in colour and polyp pattern to those of their host. The shell itself is elongate and translucent with colour matching that of the gorgonian it lives on. Females have larger shells than males, mating occurs in summer, and the eggs are laid directly on to the gorgonian sea fan.

Patella aspera

FAMILY: Patellidae
SCIENTIFIC NAME: *Patella aspera*
COMMON NAME: Painted Limpet
DISTRIBUTION: CT/N
HABITAT: Rock pools
GENERAL WATER DEPTH: 0–5 m (16.4 ft)
FOOD HABIT: Herbivorous: algae
SIZE: Up to 70 mm (2.6 in) long
DESCRIPTION: The shell of this limpet is pale in colour both inside and out; there may be a narrow band of chocolate markings around the inner lip of the shell. The foot is yellow or orange. It may often be found quite high up on exposed shores, in rock pools encrusted with calcareous algae.

Patella vulgata

FAMILY: Patellidae
SCIENTIFIC NAME: *Patella vulgata*
COMMON NAME: Common Limpet;
 Common European Limpet
DISTRIBUTION: CT/N; EA
HABITAT: Rocky shores
GENERAL WATER DEPTH: 0–10 m (32.8 ft)
FOOD HABIT: Herbivorous: algae
SIZE: 40 mm (1.6 in) long
DESCRIPTION: By far the most frequently found species of limpet on rocky shores, the

common limpet grazes on young algae. Its shell is light coloured both outside and inside, while the foot is green-grey, yellow or orange. This species generally lives in colonies. Older shells are often eroded at the spire.

Cabestana spengleri

FAMILY: Ranellidae
SCIENTIFIC NAME: *Cabestana spengleri*
COMMON NAME: Spengler's Triton
DISTRIBUTION: WT/S; TWP
HABITAT: Rocky reefs
GENERAL WATER DEPTH: Low tide to
 25 m (82 ft)
FOOD HABIT: Carnivorous: ascidians
SIZE: 200 mm (8 in)
DESCRIPTION: One of the most easily recognised tritons, this species inhabits both intertidal and subtidal rocky reefs along exposed coastlines of eastern Australia. The shell is fawn with a dark brown periostracum which is generally only present on the body whorl. One of its main food sources is cunjevoi, a tunicate which is found at the extreme edge of rocky reefs right in the surge zone. It attaches to the rough exterior of the cunjevoi and forces its proboscis inside the animal through one of the cunjevoi's siphons. The proboscis of Spengler's triton is long enough to eat out the entire soft parts of the cunjevoi. Mating takes place in late winter and early summer, after which the female builds a circular nest which she fills with egg capsules, and broods, protecting the eggs until they hatch. There seems to be a marked size difference, the females being larger than the males. Quite often the spires of old shells are very eroded.

FAMILY: Ranellidae
SCIENTIFIC NAME: *Charonia lampas
 rubicunda*
COMMON NAME: Red Triton
DISTRIBUTION: WT/S; TWP
HABITAT: Rocky reefs; rubble; mud shores

Charonia lampas rubicunda

GENERAL WATER DEPTH: Low tide to
  200 m (656 ft)
FOOD HABIT: Carnivorous: echinoderms
SIZE: 300 mm (12 in)
DESCRIPTION: There are two main colour
forms in the shells of the red triton: one
predominantly brown and the other red. The
flesh of the mollusc is usually pink with
darker pink or brown blotches. Active both
day and night in various localities, the red
triton feeds on sea urchins and sea stars.
Sea urchins are usually penetrated by the
mollusc's proboscis in the vicinity of the anal
or mouth regions, and are held by its foot
until the internal organs are consumed,
which may take several days. Sea stars are
eaten in their entirety and the skeletal plates
stay in the triton's gut until dissolved and
excreted. Female red tritons are larger than
males and egg capsules are deposited under
rocks and ledges in early spring. The eggs
are pink and the female protects the capsules until hatching takes place.

Charonia tritonis

FAMILY: Ranellidae
SCIENTIFIC NAME: *Charonia tritonis*
COMMON NAME: Giant Triton Shell

DISTRIBUTION: TI–WP
HABITAT: Coral reefs
GENERAL WATER DEPTH: Low tide to
  25 m (82 ft)
FOOD HABIT: Carnivorous: echinoderms
SIZE: 455 mm (18 in)
DESCRIPTION: Various species or subspecies
of this shell are found throughout most tropical reefs of the world, and in the more populated areas they have been greatly exploited
by shell collectors to service the huge tourist
and shell ornament trade. The giant triton is
mostly a subtidal dweller found among reefs
in sheltered back waters and also in deeper
barrier reef habitats. It feeds on sea stars
and sea urchins and is known to be one of
the few natural predators of the coral-eating
crown-of-thorns sea star. The giant triton is
no longer a common species. As it takes up
to one week to consume an adult crown-of-
thorns sea star, its role in natural control of
the huge sea star plagues is questionable.

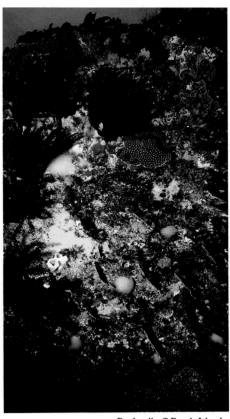

Reef wall off Roach Island

FAMILY: Strombidae
SCIENTIFIC NAME: *Lambis lambis*
COMMON NAME: Common Spider Shell
DISTRIBUTION: TI–WP
HABITAT: Coral and rocky reefs; muddy
  reefs
GENERAL WATER DEPTH: Low tide to
  20 m (66 ft)
FOOD HABIT: Herbivorous: algae

Lambis lambis

SIZE: 230 mm (9 in)
DESCRIPTION: Spider shells are tropical herbivores that inhabit sandy, rubbly and
muddy reef flats where there are sufficient
algae on which they can feed. The common
spider shell is widely found throughout the
tropical Indo-Pacific region, ranging into the
South-West Pacific. Shells observed on
muddy reef flats around continental islands
are generally much smaller and more delicately sculpted than those living on barrier
reefs. The outside of the shell is yellow and
white with brown and black markings, while
the inside is yellow and white with a glossy
orange aperture. Living common spider
shells have a periostracum covering the outside of the shell and the foot has a claw-like
operculum. Shells of females are larger than
those of males, and old shells often have
much shorter varice extensions and a thickly
callused pink underside which can be glazed.
Mating takes place in summer, generally at
night, and can be gregarious. Eggs are laid
soon afterwards, attached to weed and dead
coral.

FAMILY: Strombidae
SCIENTIFIC NAME: *Lambis truncata sebae*
COMMON NAME: Giant Spider Shell
DISTRIBUTION: TI–WP
HABITAT: Coral reefs; rubble; sand
GENERAL WATER DEPTH: 5–15 m
  (16–49 ft)
FOOD HABIT: Herbivorous: algae
SIZE: 300 mm (12 in)
DESCRIPTION: This subspecies is a common
inhabitant of rubble flats and reef slopes and
is usually located subtidally. It is found in
the Red Sea, and also the Indo-Pacific region
from southern Japan to the Tuamotu archipelago. Its subspecific relative, *Lambis
truncata truncata*, inhabits the Indian Ocean.
Giant spider shells are herbivores and feed
on the short, filamentous algae that grows on
dead coral, shell grit and sand. They live in
colonies, have separate sexes and the females

Lambis truncata sebae

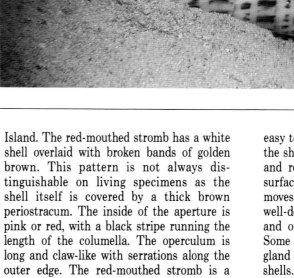

Terebra maculata

grow larger than the males. Molluscs of the stromb family have prehensile, well-developed eyes, are extremely aware of their surroundings and are very sensitive to the approach of possible predators. Although the adult giant spider shell is rather ponderous in size, it is able to move along over rugged terrain by short forward jerks carried out by a strong but agile foot, tipped with a claw-like operculum.

Strombus luhuanus

FAMILY: Strombidae
SCIENTIFIC NAME: *Strombus luhuanus*
COMMON NAME: Red-mouthed Stromb
DISTRIBUTION: TI–WP; WT/S
HABITAT: Coral reefs; rubble; sand shores
GENERAL WATER DEPTH: Low tide to
  10 m (33 ft)
FOOD HABIT: Herbivorous: algae
SIZE: 75 mm (3 in)
DESCRIPTION: Extremely common around continental reef flats, offshore islands and barrier reefs, the red-mouthed stromb's distribution extends into the South-West Pacific. The majority of southern dwelling coastal forms are found subtidally, including those living in the lagoon at Lord Howe

Island. The red-mouthed stromb has a white shell overlaid with broken bands of golden brown. This pattern is not always distinguishable on living specimens as the shell itself is covered by a thick brown periostracum. The inside of the aperture is pink or red, with a black stripe running the length of the columella. The operculum is long and claw-like with serrations along the outer edge. The red-mouthed stromb is a herbivore, feeding on short filamentous algae using a short, thick proboscis. Its main predators are stingrays, ground sharks and wrasses. All strombs are good to eat when prepared properly.

Terebra crenulata

FAMILY: Terebridae
SCIENTIFIC NAME: *Terebra crenulata*
COMMON NAME: Crenulate Auger Shell
DISTRIBUTION: TI–WP
HABITAT: Sand shores
GENERAL WATER DEPTH: Low tide to
  15 m (49 ft)
FOOD HABIT: Carnivorous: worms
SIZE: 150 mm (6 in)
DESCRIPTION: Because of its unusual shell crenulations, this auger shell is relatively

easy to identify. Its body is white. It inhabits the shallow waters of sandy areas in lagoons and reef perimeters. Living just below the surface of the sand, it forms a track as it moves in search of food. Auger shells have a well-developed proboscis to feed on worms and other small invertebrates in the sand. Some species are known to have a poison gland with some similarity to that of cone shells. The crenulate auger moves by extending its foot, anchoring it in the sand, then swelling the end of the foot with fluid to gain a purchase and retracting the muscles behind to drag the shell along.

FAMILY: Terebridae
SCIENTIFIC NAME: *Terebra maculata*
COMMON NAME: Giant Marlin Spike
DISTRIBUTION: TI–WP
HABITAT: Sand shores
GENERAL WATER DEPTH: 0–30 m (98 ft)
FOOD HABIT: Carnivorous: worms
SIZE: 225 mm (9 in)
DESCRIPTION: Favouring sheltered lagoons and back reef sand slopes off offshore cays and barrier reefs, the giant marlin spike lives throughout the Indo-Pacific region and in some localities is quite common. Although members of this family sometimes have a poison apparatus similar to that of cone shells, the poison is not harmful to humans. Occasionally found on intertidal sand banks, they are more plentiful below tide level where they leave distinctive tracks in the sand.

FAMILY: Tonnidae
SCIENTIFIC NAME: *Tonna cepa*
COMMON NAME: Channelled Tun
DISTRIBUTION: TI–WP
HABITAT: Sand; mud shores
GENERAL WATER DEPTH: 0–30 m (90 ft)
FOOD HABIT: Carnivorous: sea cucumbers

Tonna cepa

Gibbula umbilicalis

Syrinx aruanus

SIZE: 100 mm (4 in)
DESCRIPTION: Seen only when foraging at night or on late afternoons on overcast days with an incoming tide, the fleshy part of the channelled tun (when expanded) is larger than its shell. When crawling, the foot of the animal is pumped up with water so that it can expand to its fullest size. When attacked or disturbed it squirts this water out and the body can be withdrawn into the shell. Its prey includes sea cucumbers although it does not seem to attack the larger surface dwellers, preferring smaller burrowing species.

FAMILY: Trochidae
SCIENTIFIC NAME: *Gibbula umbilicalis*
COMMON NAME: Umbilical Trochid
DISTRIBUTION: CT/N
HABITAT: Rocky shores
GENERAL WATER DEPTH: Intertidal
FOOD HABIT: Herbivorous: algae
SIZE: Up to 15 mm (0.6 in) high
DESCRIPTION: A member of the topshell family, this species has a shell which is a compressed cone characterised by purple vertical stripes. Like all topshells, it is a grazer, and is common in the north-east Atlantic. Algae is rasped from rock surfaces using the finely toothed radula.

FAMILY: Trochidae
SCIENTIFIC NAME: *Monodonta lineata*
COMMON NAME: Lined Top Shell; Thick Top Shell
DISTRIBUTION: WA; CT/N–WT/N
HABITAT: Among rocks
GENERAL WATER DEPTH: Intertidal
FOOD HABIT: Herbivorous: algae
SIZE: 2.5 mm (1 in)
DESCRIPTION: The lined top shell is a common species in shallow rocky areas on Europe's Atlantic coast. The exterior of its shell is mottled tan and brown and looks like a woven basket. The interior is a dull grey-brown, much duller than that of most other members of the family. Unlike turban shells which have calcareous operculums for protection, the top shells have more pliable ones.

FAMILY: Turbinellidae
SCIENTIFIC NAME: *Syrinx aruanus*
COMMON NAME: False Trumpet Shell
DISTRIBUTION: TI–WP
HABITAT: Mud; sand; rubble shores
GENERAL WATER DEPTH: 0–60 m (197 ft)
FOOD HABIT: Carnivorous: molluscs
SIZE: 600 mm (24 in)

DESCRIPTION: One of the largest snails in the world, this species inhabits the Indo-Pacific region and is found commonly on seldom-visited mud flats. It is bright yellow and the females lay a white column of egg capsules cemented together and attached to substrate, or any suitable solid object. It is particularly voracious, feeding mostly on other molluscs. The large foot is quite edible, as evidenced by extensive shell remains in Australian Aboriginal middens.

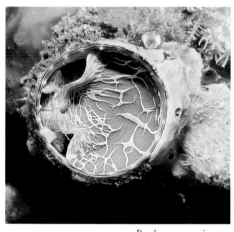

Dendropoma maximum

FAMILY: Vermetidae
SCIENTIFIC NAME: *Dendropoma maximum*
COMMON NAME: Great Coral Worm Shell
DISTRIBUTION: TI–WP
HABITAT: Coral reefs
GENERAL WATER DEPTH: Low tide to 10 m (33 ft)
FOOD HABIT: Carnivorous: plankton
SIZE: 150 mm (6 in)
DESCRIPTION: Although it is the largest shallow-water species of vermetid in the Indo-Pacific region, the great coral worm shell is nevertheless relatively inconspicuous in its natural habitat. The uncoiled calcareous shells of this species are partly buried in

Monodonta lineata

trenches they corrode in beach rock or beneath the growth of living coral. Most worm shells feed by releasing sticky threads of mucus, which are carried by the current and draped over the surrounding terrain. As the water flows over these sticky threads, organic detritus and minute organisms are entrapped in the strands. At intervals the mollusc swallows the threads and digests the adhering organic materials. When the threads are completely reabsorbed, the mollusc releases new ones and the process is repeated.

Amoria maculata

FAMILY: Volutidae
SCIENTIFIC NAME: *Amoria maculata*
COMMON NAME: Spotted Volute
DISTRIBUTION: TWP
HABITAT: Coral reefs; sand; rubble shores
GENERAL WATER DEPTH: Low tide to
  30 m (98 ft)
FOOD HABIT: Carnivorous: molluscs
SIZE: 80 mm (3 in)
DESCRIPTION: Endemic to the waters off north-eastern Australia, this species is reasonably common and ranges the entire length of the Great Barrier Reef. As well as living on and around coral reefs, it is also known to inhabit deeper waters on the continental slope where it is regularly brought up by trawlers. Over its 2000 km (1250 miles) distribution and extremes of depth range there is much natural variation in the shell pattern, but the pattern on the flesh of the live animal varies little, making the species easy to identify.

FAMILY: Volutidae
SCIENTIFIC NAME: *Amoria undulata*
COMMON NAME: Undulate Volute
DISTRIBUTION: WT/S; CT/S; TWP
HABITAT: Sand; mud shores
GENERAL WATER DEPTH: 0–200 m
  (656 ft)
FOOD HABIT: Carnivorous: molluscs

Amoria undulata

SIZE: 100 mm (4 in)
DESCRIPTION: Although the individual designs of the shell and animal patterns of this mollusc are subject to variation throughout its range, the overall pattern is easy to recognise. Far more common in the southern extent of its distribution, this species inhabits sheltered sand banks, estuaries, bays and inlets along southern Australia and is also trawled from the continental shelf. During the day it sleeps beneath the sand, coming out at night to hunt other molluscs on which it feeds. Some specimens found living in muddy areas have a rusty overglaze to the shell.

Cymbiolacca pulchra

FAMILY: Volutidae
SCIENTIFIC NAME: *Cymbiolacca pulchra*
COMMON NAME: Heron Island Volute Shell
DISTRIBUTION: TWP
HABITAT: Coral reefs; rubble; sand shores
GENERAL WATER DEPTH: Low tide to
  10 m (33 ft)
FOOD HABIT: Carnivorous: molluscs
SIZE: 100 mm (4 in)
DESCRIPTION: Locally distinctive colour variations occur throughout the Great Bar-

rier Reef waters and in certain areas some of these forms have been described as subspecies. The Heron Island volute is a carnivorous mollusc and feeds copiously on other snails and bivalves. It usually comes out in search of food during late afternoon, dusk, or at night on the rising tide. Once captured the prey is held within the foot of the animal and taken below the sand to be eaten. Little is known about its breeding or egg laying habits though its predators include baler shells, fish and hermit crabs.

Ericusa fulgetrum

FAMILY: Volutidae
SCIENTIFIC NAME: *Ericusa fulgetrum*
COMMON NAME: Lightning Volute Shell
DISTRIBUTION: WT/S
HABITAT: Sand shores
GENERAL WATER DEPTH: Low tide to
  260 m (853 ft)
FOOD HABIT: Carnivorous: molluscs
SIZE: 160 mm (6 in)
DESCRIPTION: Almost depleted in some southern, shallow water locations by over-zealous divers catering to the lucrative overseas shell markets, the lightning volute is unique to south to south-western Australian waters. The shell pattern is very variable. It lays circular egg capsules up to 25 mm (1 in) in diameter. The capsules are laid singly and are deposited beneath the sand with the foot. The lightning volute feeds specifically on other molluscs, which are usually caught on the surface of the sand and taken below to be eaten.

FAMILY: Volutidae
SCIENTIFIC NAME: *Melo amphora*
COMMON NAME: Baler Shell
DISTRIBUTION: TI–WP
HABITAT: Coral reefs; sand; mud shores
GENERAL WATER DEPTH: Low tide to
  50 m (164 ft)
FOOD HABIT: Carnivorous: molluscs
SIZE: 560 mm (22 in)

Melo amphora

DESCRIPTION: A common inhabitant of continental islands, offshore barrier reefs and deepwater trawling grounds, the baler shell exploits many different niches. It lives on intertidal muddy reefs, mangroves, on sand flats and on rubble. It will also crawl on to rocky reefs and coral reefs in search of food, or when moving from one area to another. The shell is melon-shaped and can be golden brown to dark brown with tent-like markings and wide bands. The shoulder spines may stick straight out, or be recurved towards the spire. Males are smaller than females and it is common for females to eat males. Whether this happens before or after mating is not known. The eggs are laid in summer. The egg mass consists of opaque, white, elastic egg capsules. The female deserts the eggs once laid and they hatch some weeks later as miniature baler shells. Baler shells feed on other molluscs, both bivalves and univalves.

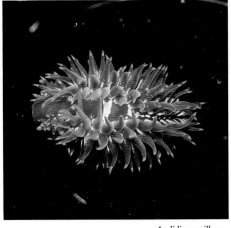

Aeolidia papillosa

■ CLASS: Gastropoda (Opistobranchia)

FAMILY: Aeolidiidae
SCIENTIFIC NAME: *Aeolidia papillosa*
COMMON NAME: Papillose Aeolidia
DISTRIBUTION: CT/N

HABITAT: Rocky reefs and shores
GENERAL WATER DEPTH: Intertidal/ subtidal
FOOD HABIT: Carnivorous: molluscs
SIZE: Up to 100 mm (3.9 in) high
DESCRIPTION: On the back of this animal are numerous unbranched cerata occurring in rows. There are no tentacular sheaths. It feeds on various species of anemone, and is quite common in both the Atlantic and northern Pacific oceans.

Aplysia dactylomela

FAMILY: Aplysiidae
SCIENTIFIC NAME: *Aplysia dactylomela*
COMMON NAME: Black-tailed Sea Hare
DISTRIBUTION: WT/N–WT/S
HABITAT: Among seaweed and seagrass
GENERAL WATER DEPTH: 0–10 m (33 ft)
FOOD HABIT: Herbivorous: algae
SIZE: Up to 300 mm (11.8 in) long
DESCRIPTION: The rings and streaks of dark pigment on the body surface make this species easily distinguishable. These animals often swim by using the muscular flaps of the foot (mantle lobes). When this species is disturbed it exudes copious amounts of purple dye which stains the fingers. Pieces of larger algae are cut off for food, using the strong radula.

FAMILY: Aplysiidae
SCIENTIFIC NAME: *Aplysia parvula*
COMMON NAME: Little Sea Hare
DISTRIBUTION: WT/S; CT/S
HABITAT: Rocky reefs
GENERAL WATER DEPTH: 0–10 m (33 ft)
FOOD HABIT: Herbivorous: algae
SIZE: 30 mm (1 in)
DESCRIPTION: Quite small compared to many of its larger relatives commonly seen washed up on beaches during summer, the little sea hare lives among algae on reefs just below low-tide level throughout the subtropical and tropical Pacific and Indian oceans. Sea hares generally vary little in

Aplysia parvula

colour throughout their distribution but this one ranges from green to brown and pink. The colour often resembles the colour of algae on which they are found. As they cannot alter their colours at will, the colour is mostly determined by pigments from the algae they are eating. Sea hares are hermaphrodites. Many species form mating chains.

Archidoris pseudoargus

FAMILY: Archidorididae
SCIENTIFIC NAME: *Archidoris pseudoargus*
COMMON NAME: Sea-lemon
DISTRIBUTION: EA
HABITAT: Rocky reefs
GENERAL WATER DEPTH: Intertidal/ subtidal
FOOD HABIT: Carnivorous: sponges
SIZE: 50–120 mm (2–4.7 in)
DESCRIPTION: Small protuberances cover the mantle of the sea-lemon. Its favoured prey is the sponge *Halichondria panicea*. When the sea-lemon is alarmed, the external gills are retracted.

Armina variolosa

Cadlinella ornatissima

FAMILY: Arminidae
SCIENTIFIC NAME: *Armina variolosa*
COMMON NAME: Variable Armina
 Nudibranch
DISTRIBUTION: TI–WP
HABITAT: Sand; mud shores
GENERAL WATER DEPTH: Low tide to
 20 m (66 ft)
FOOD HABIT: Carnivorous: sea pens
SIZE: 150 mm (6 in)
DESCRIPTION: One of the largest in its
family, the variable armina nudibranch lives
in subtidal areas on soft bottoms where
there is adequate substrate and moderate
current to support colonies of sea pens, on
which it feeds. Although not a rare species
by any means its attractive colours would
appear to make it stand out yet, like many
ocean dwellers in the Southern Hemisphere,
it is almost unknown and has been illustrated in colour on only a few occasions.

FAMILY: Arminidae
SCIENTIFIC NAME: *Dermatobranchus
 ornatus*
COMMON NAME: Ornate Dermatrobranchus
 Nudibranch

Dermatobranchus ornatus

DISTRIBUTION: TI–WP
HABITAT: Rocky reefs; muddy rubble
 shores
GENERAL WATER DEPTH: Low tide to
 20 m (66 ft)
FOOD HABIT: Carnivorous: gorgonian sea
 fans
SIZE: 70 mm (3 in)
DESCRIPTION: Unlike many of its relations
which feed on sea pens and live in sand, this
species is a reef dweller and specialises in
eating gorgonian sea fans. It is not commonly seen and, though easily identified, few
are seen by divers. The ornate dermatrobranchus nudibranch prefers inshore continental reef habitats and has been recorded
from the Indian Ocean and off Australia in
the Western Pacific.

FAMILY: Chromodorididae
SCIENTIFIC NAME: *Cadlinella ornatissima*
COMMON NAME: Ornate Cadlinella
 Nudibranch
DISTRIBUTION: TI–WP
HABITAT: Coral reefs; rocky reefs
GENERAL WATER DEPTH: Low tide to
 20 m (66 ft)
FOOD HABIT: Carnivorous:
 sponges
SIZE: 20 mm (1 in)
DESCRIPTION: What this beautiful
little nudibranch lacks in size it
certainly makes up for in its
unique form and colouration. Not
often seen by divers, it is most
often encountered intertidally and
prefers areas where there is a good
flow of water such as reef run-offs
and the sides of bommies. It
ranges from southern Japan
through the Indo-Pacific region to
as far as Norfolk Island in the
South-West Pacific Ocean.

FAMILY: Chromodorididae
SCIENTIFIC NAME: *Chromodoris bullocki*
COMMON NAME: Bullock's Chromodoris
 Nudibranch
DISTRIBUTION: TI–WP
HABITAT: Coral and rocky reefs
GENERAL WATER DEPTH: 10–30 m
 (33–98 ft)
FOOD HABIT: Carnivorous: sponges
SIZE: 40 mm (2 in)
DESCRIPTION: Bullock's chromodoris
nudibranch lives subtidally on reefs to
depths of 30 m (98 ft) and is usually found
on the sides of bommies, cave walls, over-
hangs and channels, or on underwater cliff
faces. It is active during the day and, though
not common, is broadly distributed from
Papua New Guinea to the South-West
Pacific. The body composition is soft and
flabby; colours range from pink to light
mauve. There is little colour variation in the
rhinophores and gills.

Chromodoris elisabethina

FAMILY: Chromodorididae
SCIENTIFIC NAME: *Chromodoris elisabethina*
COMMON NAME: Elisabeth's Chromodoris
 Nudibranch

Chromodoris bullocki

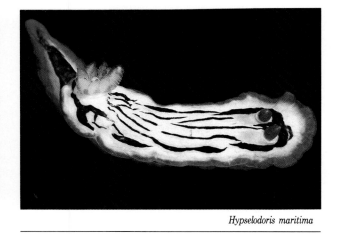

Hypselodoris maritima

DISTRIBUTION: TI–WP
HABITAT: Coral reefs; rocky reefs
GENERAL WATER DEPTH: Low tide to 25 m (82 ft)
FOOD HABIT: Carnivorous: sponges
SIZE: 40–46 mm (1.5–2 in)
DESCRIPTION: Elizabeth's chromodoris nudibranch is a very characteristic nudibranch that ranges throughout the Indo-Pacific region. Although it grows to 46 mm (2 in) and inhabits low-tide areas, most observed specimens appear to be about 40 mm (1.5 in) and are seen subtidally. Like most chromodids it is a sponge feeder, grazing mostly on encrusting sponges. It is a diurnal and open-range nudibranch found on reef walls, in gullies and along the sides of chasms and caves.

FAMILY: Chromodorididae
SCIENTIFIC NAME: *Glossodoris rubroannulata*
COMMON NAME: Red-girdled Glossodoris Nudibranch
DISTRIBUTION: TWP
HABITAT: Coral reefs
GENERAL WATER DEPTH: 6–30 m (20–98 ft)
FOOD HABIT: Carnivorous: sponges

SIZE: 70 mm (3 in)
DESCRIPTION: A very soft, flabby species, the red-girdled glossodoris nudibranch was first discovered by the author in 1974 and eventually described in 1986. An exquisite little creature, it can have variations in its colour pattern like many other marine animals. In some cases the red margin line may be broken in places. Nothing is known of its breeding habits. When disturbed it gives off a white milky substance thought to be a chemical protection against predators. Its range is so far only known to extend from the Great Barrier Reef to the South-West Pacific islands.

FAMILY: Chromodorididae
SCIENTIFIC NAME: *Hypselodoris maritima*
COMMON NAME: Maritime Chromodoris Nudibranch
DISTRIBUTION: TI–WP
HABITAT: Coral reefs; rocky reefs
GENERAL WATER DEPTH: Low tide to 10 m (33 ft)
FOOD HABIT: Carnivorous: sponges
SIZE: 40 mm (1.5 in)
DESCRIPTION: A fairly common, easily recognised species, the maritime chromodoris nudibranch seems more abundant

on inshore continental island reefs than on outer barrier reefs. It is found throughout the Indo-Pacific region. It is very soft and flabby to touch and lives beneath rocks and dead coral slabs intertidally and roams freely over the reef below tide level.

FAMILY: Dorididae
SCIENTIFIC NAME: *Halgerda tessellata*
COMMON NAME: Tessellated Halgerda Nudibranch
DISTRIBUTION: TI–WP
HABITAT: Coral reef
GENERAL WATER DEPTH: Low tide to 15 m (49 ft)
FOOD HABIT: Carnivorous: sponges
SIZE: 30 mm (1 in)
DESCRIPTION: Even though this nudibranch was originally named in 1880 and ranges from the Indian Ocean to the west Pacific, very few people have ever found or seen a live specimen. The adults are remarkable in colour and ornamentation; the juveniles have a yellow raised pattern on the dorsal surface, and in their natural habitat are more difficult to find than the adults. During the day, tessellated halgerdas live beneath dead coral slabs and rocks, browsing on encrusting sponges.

Glossodoris rubroannulata

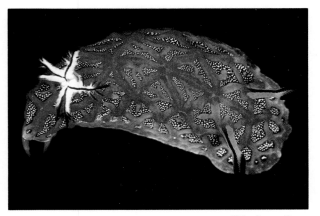

Halgerda tessellata

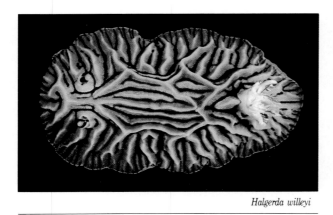

Halgerda willeyi

FAMILY: Dorididae
SCIENTIFIC NAME: *Halgerda willeyi*
COMMON NAME: Willey's Halgerda
  Nudibranch
DISTRIBUTION: TI–WP
HABITAT: Coral reefs; rocky reefs
GENERAL WATER DEPTH: Low tide to
  30 m (98 ft)
FOOD HABIT: Carnivorous: sponges
SIZE: 70 mm (3 in)
DESCRIPTION: Inhabiting caves, ledges and
chasm walls in areas of the Indo-Pacific
region Willey's halgerda appears to be more
prolific around the South-West Pacific
islands of Lord Howe and Norfolk. Over its
range there is a certain amount of variation
in the ridged and the colour patterns. However, the overall visual of the living animals
makes recognition fairly easy. This species is
very firm to touch and can retract its
rhinophores and gills. If removed from the
substrate it will curl up similar to a chiton.
It feeds on red encrusting sponges.

FAMILY: Elysiidae
SCIENTIFIC NAME: *Elysia* sp.
COMMON NAME: Spectrum Sap-sucker
DISTRIBUTION: TI–WP
HABITAT: Coral reefs; rocky reefs/shores
GENERAL WATER DEPTH: 3–10 m
  (10–33 ft)

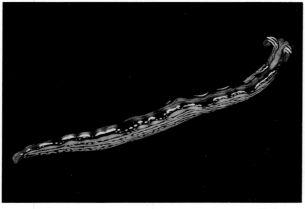

Elysia sp.

FOOD HABIT: Herbivorous: algae
SIZE: 50 mm (2 in)
DESCRIPTION: The spectrum
sap-sucker is a member of a
group known as sacoglossa (sac
tongue) because their used teeth
are stored in a bag in their head.
Each tooth is shaped like a small
scimitar and is used to slice open
the cells of seaweeds from which
the animal sucks out the
protoplasm. However, a few
sacoglossan species eat the eggs
of other sea slugs. Many, but not
all, sacoglossans are green, causing them to blend well with the algae on
which they live. A few species are able to
retain living chloroplasts from the plants
they eat, transporting them into the cells of
their digestive glands where they continue to
function for some time, helping to nourish
the slug. Like all sea slugs, this species is
hermaphroditic. Animals reciprocally copu-
late and then deposit egg strings on rocks or
seaweeds.

Flabellina rubrolineata

FAMILY: Flabellinidae
SCIENTIFIC NAME: *Flabellina rubrolineata*
COMMON NAME: Red-lined Flabellina
  Nudibranch
DISTRIBUTION: TI–WP
HABITAT: Coral reefs
GENERAL WATER DEPTH:
  2–30 m (6–98 ft)
FOOD HABIT: Carnivorous:
  hydroids
SIZE: 40 mm (1.5 in)
DESCRIPTION: The red-lined
flabellina nudibranch is one of
several species of a genus that,
owing to the similarity of their
colour patterns, are not always
easy to identify underwater. The
members of this genus are generally found close to, or on, at least
three species of hydroids, on
which they feed. As its name suggests (regardless of the various colours,
which range from pink to pale blue or
mauve), the red-lined flabellina has a dark
red or purple line along the centre of its
back. Orange-coloured eggs are laid on
hydroids during summer.

FAMILY: Glaucidae
SCIENTIFIC NAME: *Glaucilla marginata*
COMMON NAME: Margined Glaucilla
  Nudibranch
DISTRIBUTION: TI–WP; WT/S; WT/N
HABITAT: Open ocean
GENERAL WATER DEPTH: Surface waters
FOOD HABIT: Carnivorous: siphonophores
  and hydroids (cnidarians)
SIZE: 40 mm (1.5 in)
DESCRIPTION: Cosmopolitan in its distribution, the margined glaucilla nudibranch is a
world traveller on the oceans. Unlike most
nudibranchs, which inhabit the sea floor, it
floats upside down on the surface, among the
colonies of Portuguese-men-of-war (blue bottles) upon which it feeds. When onshore
winds are prevalent, hundreds of these little
molluscs are swept ashore to die
on the beaches.

FAMILY: Hydatinidae
SCIENTIFIC NAME: *Hydatina
  physis*
COMMON NAME: Rose Petal
  Bubble Shell
DISTRIBUTION: TI–WP; WT/S
HABITAT: Coral reefs; rocky reefs
GENERAL WATER DEPTH:
  0–5 m (16 ft)
FOOD HABIT: Carnivorous: worms
SIZE: 50 mm (2 in)
DESCRIPTION: One of the largest

Hydatina physis

Glaucilla marginata

and its colours and patterns are very easy to determine, the species is quite variable across its entire South-West Pacific range. It lives in caves, under ledges and on reefs and is regularly found feeding on sponges. The body is hard and pustulose; when disturbed, it withdraws its rhinophores. More active at night than during the day, this nudibranch grows to 50 mm (2 in) and is quite common in the Indo-Pacific oceans, ranging into the South-West Pacific.

Nembrotha nigerrima

bubble shells, this species is tropical in origin, though it ranges into the South-West Pacific and southern Indian oceans. It can be found on sand, mud and rocky reefs and in sea grass meadows on both sheltered or exposed coasts. Easily identified, the shell is fragile and globose with many fine, crenulated bands with a pearly white lustre inside the aperture. The animal is much larger than the shell, pink to rose red, with beautiful edging to the voluminous folds of its mantle, foot and head. Like other sea slugs, they are hermaphroditic. The rose petal bubble shell is carnivorous and feeds on small invertebrates, including other molluscs.

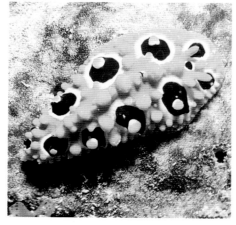

Phyllidia ocellata

FAMILY: Phylidiidae
SCIENTIFIC NAME: *Phyllidia ocellata*
COMMON NAME: Ocellate Phyllidia Nudibranch
DISTRIBUTION: TI–WP
HABITAT: Coral reefs; rocky reefs
GENERAL WATER DEPTH: 5–35 m (16–115 ft)
FOOD HABIT: Carnivorous: sponges
SIZE: 50 mm (2 in)
DESCRIPTION: Even though the ocellate phyllidia has no similarly marked relatives

Kaloplocamus yatesi

FAMILY: Polyceridae
SCIENTIFIC NAME: *Kaloplocamus yatesi*
COMMON NAME: Yate's Kaloplocamus Nudibranch
DISTRIBUTION: TWP; WT/S
HABITAT: Rocky reefs
GENERAL WATER DEPTH: 5–25 m (16–82 ft)
FOOD HABIT: Carnivorous: bryozoans
SIZE: 70 mm (3 in)
DESCRIPTION: Rarely encountered, even with the current encouraging new interest in all things marine, Yate's kaloplocamus nudibranch is a subtidal species that inhabits rocky offshore reefs as well as tidal estuaries. Those found off the Australian mainland have not been as colourful nor as ornate as the specimen pictured here from Lord Howe Island in the South-West Pacific. Most specimens encountered by the author have been crawling in the open near caves and ledges during the day.

FAMILY: Polyceridae
SCIENTIFIC NAME: *Nembrotha nigerrima*
COMMON NAME: Dusky Nembrotha Nudibranch

DISTRIBUTION: TI–WP
HABITAT: Coral reefs
GENERAL WATER DEPTH: 3–8 m (10–26 ft)
FOOD HABIT: Carnivorous: ascidians
SIZE: 100 mm (4 in)
DESCRIPTION: This beautiful nudibranch with its velvet black body, red gills and rhinophores and vivid green spots occurs in shallow lagoon areas. When seen in the open it is easily recognised. It grows to 100 mm (4 in) and is thought to feed on species of colonial ascidians which form encrusting clumps beneath dead coral slabs and boulders. Although widespread throughout the Indo-Pacific region it is considered uncommon. Similar to most nudibranchs, the dusky nembrotha produces a substance that makes it repugnant to most predators.

Tambja sp.

FAMILY: Polyceridae
SCIENTIFIC NAME: *Tambja* sp.
COMMON NAME: Painted Tambja Nudibranch
DISTRIBUTION: TI–WP
HABITAT: Coral reefs
GENERAL WATER DEPTH: Low tide to 30 m (98 ft)

FOOD HABIT: Carnivorous: bryozoans
SIZE: 130 mm (5 in)
DESCRIPTION: An Indo-Pacific species that occurs on offshore barrier reefs and around continental islands from Papua New Guinea to the Great Barrier Reef, this rather large species can be quite common at some localities. Although it varies in colour pattern over its distribution, visual identification is quite easy. The painted tambja nudibranch has not yet been scientifically described and with hundreds of other opistobranchs, has only a common reference.

Pteraeolidia ianthina

FAMILY: Pteraeolidiidae
SCIENTIFIC NAME: *Pteraeolidia ianthina*
COMMON NAME: Violet Pteraeolidia Nudibranch
DISTRIBUTION: TI–WP; WT/S; WT/N
HABITAT: Coral reefs; rocky reefs
GENERAL WATER DEPTH: Low tide to 30 m (98 ft)
FOOD HABIT: Carnivorous: hydroids
SIZE: 100 mm (4 in)
DESCRIPTION: The largest of its type, this species (owing to its size, unusual shape and colour) is one of the most commonly encountered subtidal aeolids. Basic colouration ranges from bright iridescent blue to green, brown and even brilliant white. In all cases, however, the rhinophores, head tentacles, have two pairs of blue bands. Mating and egg laying during winter have been recorded. The egg strings are laid in concertina-like bunches on rock surfaces and the eggs are white. Food species have not yet been isolated though it is known that the species eats hydroids and can store the hydroid's stinging nematocysts in cerata on its back. If handled in this condition the nudibranch itself can use the stored nematocysts and sting a human.

Phestilla melanobrachia

FAMILY: Tergepedidae
SCIENTIFIC NAME: *Phestilla melanobrachia*
DISTRIBUTION: TI–WP; WT/S
HABITAT: Coral reefs
GENERAL WATER DEPTH: 5–20 m (16–66 ft)
FOOD HABIT: Carnivorous: coral polyps
SIZE: 40 mm (1.5 in)
DESCRIPTION: This nudibranch is found only in association with the sunshine corals (*Tubastrea*) on which it feeds. Not easy to see when nestled amongst the polyps of its prey, the cerata on this nudibranch's back are almost a complete replica of the tentacles of half-extended coral polyps. This nudibranch comes in many different colours and takes on the colour of its prey, be it golden, orange, yellow, brown or even — as its scientific name implies — black. Due to their habitat beneath ledges, in caves and darker fissures in the reef, live specimens of this genus have been seen by few divers. It grows to 40 mm (1.5 in) and is soft and fragile to touch.

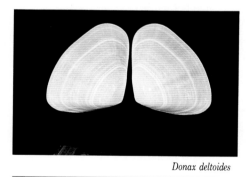

Donax deltoides

■ CLASS: Bivalvia

FAMILY: Donacidae
SCIENTIFIC NAME: *Donax deltoides*
COMMON NAME: Pipi
DISTRIBUTION: TI–WP; WT/S
HABITAT: Surf beaches
GENERAL WATER DEPTH: Low tide to 10 m (33 ft)
FOOD HABIT: Omnivorous: plankton
SIZE: 60 mm (2.4 in)

DESCRIPTION: One of the main commercial clam species used for fish bait throughout eastern and southern Australia, this species inhabits areas of coarse sandy surf beaches where it is abundant along the surf line. Heavily gathered by shell miners with bulldozers, many of its former habitats are now depleted. It is now against Australian law to collect pipis by any mechanical means.

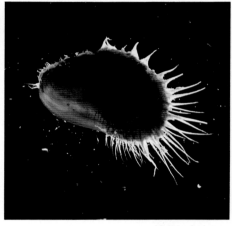

Modiolus barbatus

FAMILY: Mytilidae
SCIENTIFIC NAME: *Modiolus barbatus*
COMMON NAME: Bearded Mussel or Bearded Horse-mussel
DISTRIBUTION: CT/N; EA
HABITAT: Rocky shores; subtidal rocks
GENERAL WATER DEPTH: 0–20 m (65.6 ft)
FOOD HABIT: Omnivorous: plankton; organic particles
SIZE: 50 mm (2 in) long
DESCRIPTION: A valued food source in Mediterranean countries, the bearded mussel is characterised by having many whiskers over its surface. It may be found both on intertidal shores and subtidally under rocks and in crevices, where it often grows in small groups or bunches.

FAMILY: Mytilidae
SCIENTIFIC NAME: *Modiolus modiolus*
COMMON NAME: Northern Horse Mussel
DISTRIBUTION: CT/N; WA; EP; WP
HABITAT: Shallow, rocky areas
GENERAL WATER DEPTH: Low tide to 10 m (32.8 ft)
FOOD HABIT: Omnivorous: plankton
SIZE: 130 mm (5 in)
DESCRIPTION: Generally found attached to rocks by its byssus, the northern horse mussel is an abundant species. Inside the rough sandy frame on the outer shell is a golden brown smooth area. The interior of the shell is coloured bluish white to dull white.

Modiolus modiolus

Ostrea edulis

barrier reef habitats. Young shells are very attractive; older ones are subject to attacks by boring worms. This species is attached by byssal threads while still a juvenile but in time it detaches and becomes free swimming.

Chlamys opercularis

FAMILY: Mytilidae
SCIENTIFIC NAME: *Mytilis edulis*
COMMON NAME: Common Mussel
DISTRIBUTION: Cosmopolitan
HABITAT: Rocky shores; wharf pilings; buoys
GENERAL WATER DEPTH: Intertidal
FOOD HABIT: Omnivorous: plankton
SIZE: 100–150 mm (3.9–5.9 in) long (rarely longer)
DESCRIPTION: Frequently found (as its name implies), the common mussel often occurs in dense clusters, attached by its byssal threads to the rocks or man-made structures. Those in estuarine beds generally grow to a larger size than those individuals on exposed coasts. The common mussel is a popular source of food.

Mytilis edulis

FAMILY: Ostreidae
SCIENTIFIC NAME: *Ostrea edulis*
COMMON NAME: Common European Oyster
DISTRIBUTION: CT/N; EA
HABITAT: Rocks; sand and muddy gravel
GENERAL WATER DEPTH: Low tide downwards

FOOD HABIT: Omnivorous: plankton
SIZE: Up to 100 mm (3.9 in) across
DESCRIPTION: The two valves of the common European oyster have different profiles: the upper is flattened, while the lower is convex. The shell valves often have a rounded outline. This oyster occurs naturally on sand, rocks and firm muddy gravel, as well as being cultivated commercially on man-made hard substrates.

Chlamys leopardus

FAMILY: Pectinidae
SCIENTIFIC NAME: *Chlamys leopardus*
COMMON NAME: Leopard Scallop
DISTRIBUTION: TI–WP
HABITAT: Mud; rubble shores
GENERAL WATER DEPTH: 0–40 m (131 ft)
FOOD HABIT: Omnivorous: plankton; detritus
SIZE: 75 mm (3 in)
DESCRIPTION: An Indo-Pacific dweller, the leopard scallop is trawled in large numbers from mud and coral rubble bottom off continental islands. In many areas it is regarded as a commercial species. However, they are not common throughout their entire range and seem to prefer inshore waters to outer

FAMILY: Pectinidae
SCIENTIFIC NAME: *Chlamys opercularis*
COMMON NAME: Queen Scallop
DISTRIBUTION: CT/N
HABITAT: Subtidal sediments
GENERAL WATER DEPTH: 0–200 m (656 ft)
FOOD HABIT: Omnivorous: plankton
SIZE: Upper shell valve diameter up to 90 mm (3.5 in)
DESCRIPTION: Although this bivalve is capable of swimming, it is usually anchored by byssus threads when young. The upper shell valve is more convex than the lower one, while the pink gonads and numerous well-developed eyes are very distinctive. The queen scallop occurs at greater depths than other scallop species, and swims actively when disturbed by predators such as the sea star *Asterias rubens*. Often the valves have many barnacles and other sedentary invertebrates attached.

FAMILY: Pectinidae
SCIENTIFIC NAME: *Pecten meridionalis*
COMMON NAME: King Scallop
DISTRIBUTION: WT/S; CT/S
HABITAT: Sand; mud
GENERAL WATER DEPTH: 5–70 m (16–230 ft)
FOOD HABIT: Omnivorous: plankton; detritus
SIZE: 150 mm (6 in)
DESCRIPTION: Commercially fished throughout its range, the king scallop lives on the sand, mud and shell grit bottoms of bays, sheltered estuaries and in coastal waters. It is gregarious and generally occurs in large numbers. Like most scallops it is very alert, with a number of well-developed

Pecten meridionalis

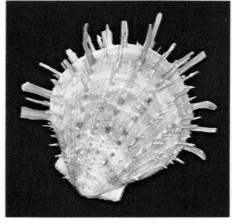

Spondylus tenellus

making, from just below tide level to around 10 m (33 ft) in estuaries around continental islands. In some areas large numbers wash up on beaches after storms and those seeking such interesting gems of nature must compete with the sea birds, who relish the mollusc's flesh but peck the delicate shells to pieces to get at it.

Pteria lata

eyes and chemo-sensory organs that trigger an escape response to attacks by most predators. Natural predators include sea stars, fish, octopuses and volutes. Regardless of its alertness, many are caught and eaten. If alarmed, it can jet up to a metre (3 ft) off the bottom and by continuous flapping movements of its shell valves, controlled by strong adductor muscles, it can force water out of the mantle cavity. This jet-propelled bivalve can cover up to 5 m (16 ft) in a single burst of shell flapping.

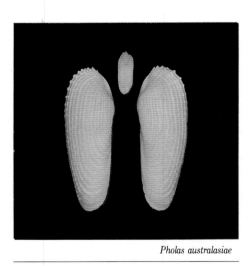

Pholas australasiae

FAMILY: Pholadidae
SCIENTIFIC NAME: *Pholas australasiae*
COMMON NAME: Southern Angel's Wings
DISTRIBUTION: TI–WP; WT/S
HABITAT: Mud flats; estuary river banks
GENERAL WATER DEPTH: 2–10 m (6–33 ft)
FOOD HABIT: Omnivorous: plankton; detritus
SIZE: 100 mm (4 in)
DESCRIPTION: A very common resident of the South-West Pacific, the southern angel's wings is unusual as it has four accessory shell plates. It lives in a burrow of its own

FAMILY: Pteriidae
SCIENTIFIC NAME: *Pteria lata*
COMMON NAME: Red-winged Pearl Shell
DISTRIBUTION: TI–WP; WT/S
HABITAT: Coral reefs; rocky reefs
GENERAL WATER DEPTH: 5–40 m (16–131 ft)
FOOD HABIT: Omnivorous: plankton
SIZE: 150 mm (6 in)
DESCRIPTION: The red-winged pearl shell has a rather delicate shell, made of fragile valves covered with periostracum on the outside and displaying brilliant iridescent nacre on the inside. It is found at depths of 20 m (66 ft) or more, attached by threads to gorgonians, sea whips, sponges, hydroids, sea fans, or soft corals. Found throughout the Indo-Pacific region and into the South-West Pacific, this species is much smaller at its southern range limits and in deeper water. The denuded murex shell is a known predator on the red-winged pearl shell.

FAMILY: Spondylidae
SCIENTIFIC NAME: *Spondylus tenellus*
COMMON NAME: Scarlet Thorny Oyster
DISTRIBUTION: WT/S; CT/S
HABITAT: Rocky reefs; rubble
GENERAL WATER DEPTH: 5–260 m (16–853 ft)
FOOD HABIT: Omnivorous: plankton; detritus
SIZE: 75 mm (3 in)
DESCRIPTION: The scarlet thorny oyster is found on inshore and offshore reefs, flat sea floors, mud and sand. It also inhabits bays

and estuaries. Specimens found in ocean waters have longer spines and less damage from boring organisms such as sponges and worms than those found in estuaries; however, estuarine oysters grow larger. The colour of the scarlet thorny oyster ranges from bright red to pink and white. The reproduction process is similar to that of many other bivalves. The males and females shed eggs and sperm into the water where the eggs are fertilised. Later the larvae hatch and drift as part of the plankton. The larvae then settle to the bottom and attach to a solid object such as a small dead shell or a rock, and grow into small thorny oysters.

Spondylus zonalis

FAMILY: Spondylidae
SCIENTIFIC NAME: *Spondylus zonalis*
COMMON NAME: Ocellate Thorny Oyster
DISTRIBUTION: TI–WP
HABITAT: Coral reefs
GENERAL WATER DEPTH: Low tide to 20 m (66 ft)
FOOD HABIT: Omnivorous: plankton
SIZE: 140 mm (5.5 in)
DESCRIPTION: Many older ocellate thorny oysters are so badly overgrown by coralline

algae and sponges that identification is very difficult. Younger specimens, and those that live beneath dead coral slabs (out of the light), are generally much easier to determine by visual identification as they retain their colour, pattern and shape. The ocellate thorny oyster is often found embedded in the undersides of dead coral boulders or hard reef. Although the species is a well-distributed Indo-Pacific inhabitant, it is not as well known as other thorny oysters.

Hippopus hippopus

FAMILY: Tridacnidae
SCIENTIFIC NAME: *Hippopus hippopus*
COMMON NAME: Horse's Hoof Clam
DISTRIBUTION: TI–WP
HABITAT: Coral reefs; rocky reefs
GENERAL WATER DEPTH: Low tide to 3 m (10 ft)
FOOD HABIT: Omnivorous: plankton
SIZE: 300 mm (12 in)
DESCRIPTION: This relative of the giant clams is more commonly seen on the shallow reefs of offshore tropical islands, cays and reefs than subtidally. Unlike some clams, the horse's hoof clam is not attached but lies in the open as a free-living bivalve. In many places this clam was once common, but owing to its habitat, edibility and attractive shell it is extremely vulnerable to human predation. Although adults have few natural predators, some reefs in the Indian Ocean have been entirely depleted by sustenance collection and exploitation of the clam meat for sale. Thoughtless people have a habit of poking sharp objects and sticks into the clam's open valves to see how quickly they can clamp their valves shut, or to make them squirt out their internal water. This injures the clam's soft parts and as a result, many die or are eaten by predators. This species should be treated with care as its powerful, sharp valves can quite easily chop off an unwary finger.

Tridacna crocea

FAMILY: Tridacnidae
SCIENTIFIC NAME: *Tridacna crocea*
COMMON NAME: Burrowing Clam Shell
DISTRIBUTION: TI–WP
HABITAT: Coral reefs
GENERAL WATER DEPTH: Low tide to 10 m (33 ft)
FOOD HABIT: Omnivorous: plankton; detritus
SIZE: 140 mm (5.5 in)
DESCRIPTION: Seen in a variety of bright colours throughout tropical reefs, the mantle of the burrowing clam shell discloses its position. It buries itself deep within the protection of self-made recesses in coral heads, 'micro-atolls' and reef causeways, but is simple to identify as there are no other clams that have the same habitat. It reaches a size of 140 mm (5.5 in) and is generally observed in groups. Although all members of the family are filter feeders, they also obtain nourishment from a unique symbiotic relationship with microscopic algae technically known as zooxanthellae, living in the tissues of their brightly coloured mantles. In short, the clams actually 'farm' the zooxanthellae and use them as food.

Tridacna gigas

FAMILY: Tridacnidae
SCIENTIFIC NAME: *Tridacna gigas*
COMMON NAME: Giant Clam
DISTRIBUTION: TI–WP
HABITAT: Coral reefs
GENERAL WATER DEPTH: 3–15 m (10–49 ft)
FOOD HABIT: Omnivorous: plankton; algae
SIZE: 1 m (3 ft)
DESCRIPTION: The giant clam is the largest bivalve in the world and Indo-Pacific islanders have used the valves for water storage for centuries. Because of its gourmet qualities the giant clam has been killed in huge numbers by western Pacific fishing crews. They remove the adductor muscles which are then smoked or preserved and shipped to markets for a high profit. The giant clam is now fully protected by law within Australian waters. Because of its food value the giant clam has become almost extinct in some areas of the Pacific. Efforts are now being made to cultivate the species and a pilot experimental project is under way by scientists from James Cook University in northern Queensland. If successful, the scheme will be extended throughout the Pacific Islands. Many stories have been written about this shell's dangerous human-trapping ability, but there is little evidence of this having ever occurred. The valves close in slow, jerking movements, and very rarely completely, under non-fatal duress.

Tridacna squamosa

FAMILY: Tridacnidae
SCIENTIFIC NAME: *Tridacna squamosa*
COMMON NAME: Giant Fluted Clam
DISTRIBUTION: TI–WP
HABITAT: Coral reefs
GENERAL WATER DEPTH: Low tide to 20 m (66 ft)
FOOD HABIT: Omnivorous: plankton; algae
SIZE: 400 mm (16 in)
DESCRIPTION: Easily recognised in the field by its relatively large size and the character-

istic sculpture of its leaf-like flutes, the giant fluted clam has very beautiful mantle lobes. It is a filter feeder and lives below tide level in the shallow waters of coral reefs. Specimens can be found on sand or in coral to depths of 10 m (33 ft). It grows to around 400 mm (16 in) and is fairly common from the Red Sea to South Africa throughout the tropical Indian Ocean, up to southern Japan and through the Indo-Pacific region to Tonga. Several commensal shrimps inhabit it, as does the clam crab (*Xnthasia murigera*).

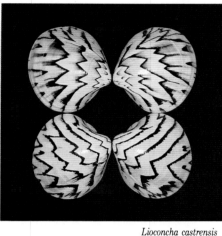

Lioconcha castrensis

FAMILY: Veneridae
SCIENTIFIC NAME: *Lioconcha castrensis*
COMMON NAME: Tent Venus Shell
DISTRIBUTION: TI–WP
HABITAT: Sand
GENERAL WATER DEPTH: 0–20 m (66 ft)
FOOD HABIT: Omnivorous: plankton
SIZE: 50 mm (2 in)
DESCRIPTION: Living in large lagoons within barrier reef complexes, in sand pockets in coral reefs, and on the sandy sea floors off tropical continental islands, the tent venus shell is a fairly common and easily recognised bivalve. When alive, the outsides of the valves are covered by a thin, yellow periostracum. Variation in shell pattern is as common as the shells, no two specimens being exactly alike, though they are simple to identify. They live just below the surface and are not easy to find, with only the tips of their siphons revealing their presence.

■ CLASS: Scaphopoda

FAMILY: Dentaliidae
SCIENTIFIC NAME: *Dentalium elephantinium*
COMMON NAME: Elephant Tusk Shell
DISTRIBUTION: TWP
HABITAT: Sand or mud

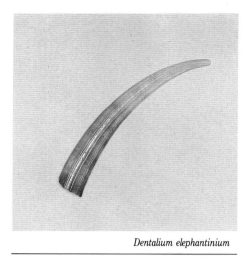

Dentalium elephantinium

GENERAL WATER DEPTH: 25–40 m (82–131 ft)
FOOD HABIT: Omnivorous
SIZE: 100 mm (4 in)
DESCRIPTION: Although tusk shells inhabit many areas of world seas this species is restricted in its range to the waters off the north-east coast of Australia. Similar to all scaphopods, elephant tusk shells live below the surface of the sand where they reside head down at an oblique angle with the posterior end projecting from the sand. They have no eyes, no heart and no gills but are good detectors of vibration. Long, thin tentacles around the mouth capture the shelled protozoans on which they feed.

Argonuta nodosa

■ CLASS: Cephalopoda

FAMILY: Argonautidae
SCIENTIFIC NAME: *Argonauta nodosa*
COMMON NAME: Paper Nautilus
DISTRIBUTION: WT/S; CT/S

HABITAT: Open ocean
GENERAL WATER DEPTH: Surface to 50 m (164 ft)
FOOD HABIT: Carnivorous
SIZE: 500 mm (20 in)
DESCRIPTION: Frequently washed ashore on South-West Pacific beaches, the paper nautilus is not a shell in the strict sense, but an egg case. The argonaut that makes the egg case is a pelagic relation of the octopus and lives in the water column with vast numbers of its fellows. From birth the young female paper nautilus secretes a limy substance from enlarged membranes on its two dorsal arms. This is fashioned into an opalescent shell in which she then resides; the large, shell-secreting membranes cover the exterior surface of the egg case. The male argonaut is very small. Toward the end of their lives the females with their egg cases filled with eggs drift or swim into the shallows. Among the sea grass meadows, reefs and sand flats the females die and the thousands of small argonauts, packed neatly into the protected rear of the egg case, hatch at different intervals.

Nautilus pompilius

FAMILY: Nautilidae
SCIENTIFIC NAME: *Nautilus pompilius*
COMMON NAME: Pearly Nautilus
DISTRIBUTION: TI–WP
HABITAT: Coral reefs
GENERAL WATER DEPTH: 10–200 m (33–656 ft)
FOOD HABIT: Carnivorous: crustaceans; fish
SIZE: 200 mm (8 in)
DESCRIPTION: When alive the pearly nautilus resembles an octopus, but its shell is beautifully striped and has many more arms. Unlike the paper nautilus whose shell is actually the female's egg case the pearly nautilus is attached in its shell and extends a fleshy siphonal tube which passes through a small central canal in the shell's coils. The

chambers in the nautilus shell are filled with gas, and by means of this tube the mollusc can adjust the amount of gas in each chamber, allowing it to rise or sink at will. Mostly a deepwater dweller, the pearly nautilus bumps along the bottom in depths below 200 m (656 ft), yet migrates vertically into shallow waters at night. It feeds on crabs and other invertebrates and is caught and trapped off the barrier reefs throughout the Indo-Pacific region.

Octopus cyaneus

FAMILY: Octopodidae
SCIENTIFIC NAME: *Octopus cyaneus*
COMMON NAME: Blue Octopus
DISTRIBUTION: IWP
HABITAT: Reefs and rocky shores
GENERAL WATER DEPTH: Intertidal and subtidal to 25 m (82 ft)
FOOD HABIT: Carnivorous: molluscs; crustaceans; fish
SIZE: 300 mm (11.8 in)
DESCRIPTION: A common species in shallow waters, this animal has a double row of suckers on the arms, a characteristic shared by other members of this genus. Fins and tentacular cirri are absent. Like other members of its family, the blue octopus lives in a lair. Any crevice, cleft or overhang protected on three sides will suffice.

FAMILY: Sepiidae
SCIENTIFIC NAME: *Sepia apama*
COMMON NAME: Giant Cuttle
DISTRIBUTION: WT/S; TI–WP
HABITAT: Rocky reefs; sand
GENERAL WATER DEPTH: 3–30 m (10–98 ft)
FOOD HABIT: Carnivorous: fish
SIZE: 1 m (3 ft)
DESCRIPTION: The largest cuttlefish in the South-West Pacific and east Indian oceans, this species is found around ledges, caves, reef gutters, underwater cliffs and kelp beds.

Sepia apama

Generally solitary, a pair relationship between males and females is established just before the mating season and courtship behaviour proceeds until mating. Eggs are white and are attached to algae, soft coral, or reefs in protected areas where there is constant water flow. A female may stay near the new-laid eggs for a short time but does not seem to display the same maternal instinct as a female octopus. The giant cuttle usually seeks cover during the middle of the day, emerging to hunt at dawn and dusk. This large cephalopod uses stealth, camouflage and patience to stalk its prey. Once positioned it shoots out two long fishing tentacles from cheek pouches and, on making a strike, jets forward and enmeshes the fish in its tentacles, quickly subduing any resistance. The prey is bitten and held by the powerful, parrot-like beak while the radula rasps it into digestible pieces.

Spirula spirula

FAMILY: Spirulidae
SCIENTIFIC NAME: *Spirula spirula*
COMMON NAME: Ram's Horn Shell
DISTRIBUTION: TI–WP; WT/S; WT/N; CT/S

HABITAT: Oceanic
GENERAL WATER DEPTH: Surface to 300 m (984 ft)
FOOD HABIT: Carnivorous; plankton
SIZE: 25 mm (1 in)
DESCRIPTION: This strange little piece of flotsam that washes up on beaches throughout the world is actually the internal shell of a small, deepwater squid. The living animal has its own light-producing organ at the posterior end of the body. The tail-light squid is known to migrate to shallow waters at night: many deepwater animals swim towards the surface and return to the depths before sunrise. The shell assists in the animal's buoyancy control.

ECHINODERMS

PHYLUM: Echinodermata (Spiny skinned animals)
CLASS: Crinoidea (Sea lilies and feather stars), Asteroidea (Sea stars), Ophiuroidea (Brittle stars), Echinoidea (Sea urchins, heart urchins and sand dollars), Holothuroidea (Sea cucumbers).

Echinoderms, more than any other invertebrates, are perhaps the most often seen. They are large, simple in external design, attractively coloured and in some cases have sharp spines. Rarely would an ocean dive be completed without seeing or touching an echinoderm.

They form one of the most clearly defined groups of sea life, being exclusively marine. Within the five extant classes the adults have penta-radial symmetry (where the body is apparently divided into five similar sections arranged around a central axis). Thus the echinoderm has five sides, five rows of tube feet (ambulacra), or five rays or arms, forming a design unique in the animal kingdom. There is no head and no brain as such. Another unique feature is tentacle-like structures known as tube feet. These tube feet are driven hydraulically by the water vascular system, and when used in conjunction with their suckers they allow many species to move freely on almost any surface. The crinoids and some sea stars, for example *Astropecten*, have no suckers on their tube feet.

Echinoderms live from the intertidal zone to the bottom of the deep-sea trenches and within that range inhabit every type of bottom terrain, from soft mud to rugged coastline pounded by surf. Almost all adults are bottom dwellers, but a few sea cucumbers are pelagic, being swept along by currents.

With so many lifestyles the evolution of feeding mechanisms has played a large part in the success of this phylum. Forms may be carnivorous, omnivorous, herbivorous, or scavengers. There are also detrital foragers and planktonic and suspended sediment feeders. No echinoderm has evolved to live as a true parasite.

Reproduction is by the release of sperm and eggs into the sea. The sexes are generally separate but some species may be hermaphrodites. Most species produce pelagic planktonic larvae which feed on plankton. These larvae are bilaterally symmetrical, unlike their parents. The juveniles develop typical echinoderm features at settlement. Some echinoderms give birth to live young and brood them in special chambers. This is particularly seen in cold water species.

Echinoderms can regenerate missing limbs, arms, spines—even intestines—in response to wounding. Some brittle stars and sea stars can reproduce asexually by breaking a ray or arm which then regenerates a whole new body.

CLASS: Crinoidea (Sea lilies and feather stars)

A few species of sea lily survive in the ocean depths. With their stalked bodies attached to the substrate most crinoids are free and mobile as adults, but the developing larvae pass through a stalked phase.

The arms are arranged in multiples of five, rising from the cup-shaped body. They branch into pinnules. Both arms and pinnules bear suckerless tube feet called tentacles. These are rich in mucus-secreting glands. Crinoids feed by trapping plankton and suspended detritus with a thin 'net' of tentacular tube feet. Food is incorporated into a mucus strand which is passed down a food groove in the pinnule or arm to the mouth, situated on the upper surface of the body. In temperate waters the crinoids are cryptic and live beneath stones, in crevices, or among algae. In tropical waters they may be more conspicuous. The sexes are separate, sperm and ova being released into the sea where fertilisation occurs. A planktonic larval phase follows and at metamorphosis the larvae settle and attach to the substrate. In feather stars the developing individuals break free from their stalked existence, a reminder of their sea lily-like ancestors.

CLASS: Asteroidea (Sea stars)

Many southern Pacific asteroids living in waters from the low-tide level to 70 metres (230 feet) have now been photographed alive, together with a number of their colour forms, which puts them on a similar footing to northern species.

Most large sea stars live in the open, but smaller forms are generally cryptic. There are, of course, exceptions to this rule.

Sea stars live on open coastal reefs or shores in sheltered waters, on rocky sand and in mud. Reef-dwelling species have sucker pads on the end of their tube feet; sand dwelling forms have no suckers, but points for digging. A number of reef-dwelling species may be found feeding on sand, but sand-dwelling forms rarely visit high reefs as they cannot climb very well.

Most sea stars are dioecious (they have separate sexes) and mainly shed sperm and eggs into the sea, where the larvae are dispersed by the currents. Some brood their young within the body, where they eventually emerge as juvenile sea stars. They also lay eggs and/or brood the young beneath the disc.

The natural histories of Southern Hemisphere sea stars have not been studied as well as their northern counterparts. A host of exciting discoveries await anyone interested in examining the southern Pacific sea stars in detail; at least ten new species have been found in the past decade and these were all in water less than 20 metres (66 feet) deep.

CLASS: Ophiuroidea (Brittle stars)

Serpent stars are also known as brittle stars, the more complex armed forms are known as basket stars, and those that wind around black coral 'trees' are known as snake stars.

Ninety-five per cent of brittle stars are cryptic bottom dwellers or are associated with some other invertebrate. They live beneath stones, in holes in reefs, in sponges, bryozoans and algae, on soft coral, in shells, sand and mud and on Echinoderms and Cnidarians. Little is known about any of them.

Some of the larger basket stars are identifiable in the field, as are some of the larger and less variable serpent stars and snake stars. Some of the smaller species, though variable, can be identified by colour pattern and association or relationship, but to identify the majority accurately requires study of specimens by an Echinoderm taxonomist.

Brittle stars can reproduce sexually by shedding sperm and ova into the sea, laying eggs, or brooding young within the body and asexually by self-division (cleaving or autotomy).

CLASS: Echinoidea (Sea urchins)

There are few sea lovers who are not familiar with sea urchins as most have had the unfortunate experience of being 'spined' at some time.

Sea urchins are probably the most readily recognised class of mobile inter- and subtidal invertebrates. Over 800 species of sea urchins have been recorded.

Noble Feather Star

'Regular' sea urchins—those with a rounded skeletal shell, or test—live among reefs and rubble, in algae beds and seagrass meadows and on rocks. The 'irregular' sea urchins, such as heart urchins and sand dollars, live in sand or mud, though a few species of sand dollars inhabit low profile reefs.

Several southern sea urchins have been studied but there is little published information on the life histories of most forms. Some species feed on sponges, some on algae and seagrasses, and others are detrital feeders. In the field, most of the larger species can be identified visually or from a photograph. Most will feed on whatever is locally available, though some species appear to be specialised feeders and are only found in algae beds.

The young are formed indirectly by fusion of sperm and eggs released into the water (generally around dusk) or by direct development (where there is no larval stage). Several direct developing species protect the juveniles by holding them among spines around the mouth, or on the top.

CLASS: Holothuroidea (Sea cucumbers)

The original descriptions of sea cucumbers were based on the spicules contained in the skin; examination requires the preparation of microslides of body wall tissue treated with bleach. However, most larger sea cucumbers, once photographed and cross-referenced against identified spicules from collected specimens, can be identified fairly easily.

Sea cucumbers live on reefs, on rubble or sand, under sand or mud, beneath rocks and on sponges. They use modified tube-feet formed into a fine network of mouth tentacles to catch plankton, use sticky pads to pick up detritus, and pass bottom sediments through their intestines where the organic matter is digested and the 'cleaned' sediment can be voided as faecal matter.

Some species may have separate sexes or be hermaphroditic. Sperm and eggs are released into the sea on a rising tide at dusk and all species have a planktonic larval dispersal.

Conocladus australis

Robust Feather Star

Acanthaster planci

Austrofromia sp.

Antedon bifida

■ CLASS: Crinoidea

FAMILY: Antedonidae
SCIENTIFIC NAME: *Antedon bifida*
COMMON NAME: Feather Star
DISTRIBUTION: CT/N; WT/N
HABITAT: Rocky shores and rocky coasts
GENERAL WATER DEPTH: 0–200 m
FOOD HABIT: Fine detrital particles in
  suspension, phytoplankton and fine
  zooplankton
SIZE: Up to 150 mm in diameter
DESCRIPTION: This delicate crinoid is free-
living as an adult. Its cup-shaped body or
theca supports five, paired, segmented arms
bearing side branches. Short segmented
appendages (cirri) beneath the theca grip the
substrate. The gonads are borne on the
arms. Fertilisation results in a planktonic
larva which settles and attaches to the substrate at metamorphosis. The growing
feather star then breaks free from its attachment (which recalls the sessile mode of life
of its stalked relatives the sea-lilies) so it can
move freely. It may swim by beating its arms
rhythmically. The arms bear suckerless tentacles (homologues of the tube-feet of the
distantly related starfish and sea-urchins).
These are used to sieve the water currents
for food which is collected on the basis of
size, not quality. Hence inorganic particles
like minute sediment grains may be trapped
too. The food is rolled into mucous strands
and passed down the ciliated food grooves of
each arm towards the mouth which is positioned centrally on the disc. On its way to
the mouth the food strands may be stolen by
small ecto-parasites (myzostomes) which live
among the branches of the arms.

FAMILY: Antedonidae
SCIENTIFIC NAME: *Antedon incommoda*
COMMON NAME: Unfortunate Feather Star
DISTRIBUTION: WT/S
HABITAT: Rocky reefs; jetty piles; rocky
  shores
GENERAL WATER DEPTH: Low tide to
  68 m (223 ft)
FOOD HABIT: Omnivorous: fine plankton
SIZE: 100 mm (4 in)

Antedon incommoda

DESCRIPTION: Unlike its relative, Loven's
feather star, the unfortunate feather star is
more likely to be found in sheltered bays,
inlets and estuaries where it lives in, under
and around stones, sea mosses, sponges and
a host of other sedentary objects on the sea
floor. This species does not seem to be as
diurnal in habit as is *Antedon loveni*,
although it may sometimes be seen out in
the open when in the shade of jetties, under
ledges or in caves. The colour is variable but
combinations of orange, brown, white, pink
and grey generally describe most specimens
observed during diving surveys. Preserved
specimens can be determined to species by
comparing the cirri and general size. The
unfortunate feather star has stout cirri with
distal segments that are broader than they
are long while Loven's feather star has slender delicate cirri with distal segments which
are longer than they are broad.

Antedon loveni

FAMILY: Antedonidae
SCIENTIFIC NAME: *Antedon loveni*
COMMON NAME: Loven's Feather Star
DISTRIBUTION: WT/S
HABITAT: Rocky reefs; rocky shores

GENERAL WATER DEPTH: Low tide to
  60 m (197 ft)
FOOD HABIT: Omnivorous: fine plankton
SIZE: 25 mm (1 in)
DESCRIPTION: Found mainly on rocky reefs,
this common, delicate little white feather
star lives in South-West Pacific waters along
the south-eastern coast of Australia. It prefers areas where there is moderate current
flow and, unlike other feather stars in this
class, it does not seek out high places of the
surrounding reef substrate to 'perch' and
catch food. Instead it congregates on rock
faces where there is an up-welling current.
Sometimes it may be found on the sides of
sponges or on algae, but this appears to be
more by accident than by design. In some
areas up to a hundred specimens may be
observed on a single dive. Colour is constant
within the species.

Reometra mariae

FAMILY: Calometridae
SCIENTIFIC NAME: *Reometra mariae*
COMMON NAME: Maria's Feather Star
DISTRIBUTION: TI–WP
HABITAT: Coral reefs
GENERAL WATER DEPTH: 20–60 m
  (66–197 ft)
FOOD HABIT: Omnivorous: plankton
SIZE: 175 mm (7 in)
DESCRIPTION: A spectacular and easily
recognised genus of feather star, this species
lives in the Indo-Pacific region. The colour of
Maria's feather star varies, but the actual
pattern seems to be constant in the few
specimens observed. The spines along the
arms and around the very small disc are firm
and sharp. The species has well-developed
cirri which it uses to cling to gorgonoids in
strong currents. Commensal associations
may occur in this species but this can only
be confirmed by finding and investigating
more specimens. The species maintains its
expanded feeding position during the day.

Comanthina nobilis

FAMILY: Comasteridae
SCIENTIFIC NAME: *Comanthina nobilis*
COMMON NAME: Noble Feather Star
DISTRIBUTION: TI–WP
HABITAT: Coral reefs
GENERAL WATER DEPTH: 5–90 m
(16–295 ft)
FOOD HABIT: Omnivorous: plankton
SIZE: 400 mm (16 in)
DESCRIPTION: Although not common to all areas throughout the Indo-Pacific region the noble feather star has two main colour forms: bright yellow, and black with white, green and yellow colourings. It is found in habitats such as high coral outcrops and ledges directly in the current flow, which favour the catching of planktonic organisms by the sticky tentacles of its pinnate arms. The pinnate arms are also inhabited by commensal shrimps and squat lobsters. Food is transferred down grooves in the arms to the mouth, which unlike other classes of echinoderm is on the upper surface of the disc.

Himerometra robustipinna

FAMILY: Himerometridae
SCIENTIFIC NAME: *Himerometra robustipinna*

COMMON NAME: Robust Feather Star
DISTRIBUTION: TI–WP
HABITAT: Coral reefs
GENERAL WATER DEPTH: 5–30 m
(16–98 ft)
FOOD HABIT: Omnivorous: fine plankton
SIZE: 300 mm (12 in)
DESCRIPTION: Common to the Indo-Pacific region the robust feather star appears to be more prolific on inshore continental island reefs than on the outer barriers. It may be seen feeding during the day on the incoming tide, where its position is on a drop-off or the top of a bommie etc. When so observed, the animal appears red all over but when it is resting with all arms folded in towards the mouth, the underside of the arm's central stem may be bright yellow, white, or grey.

Ptilometra macronema

FAMILY: Ptilometridae
SCIENTIFIC NAME: *Ptilometra macronema*
COMMON NAME: Long-cirried Feather Star
DISTRIBUTION: WT/S
HABITAT: Rocky reefs
GENERAL WATER DEPTH: 25–120 m
(82–394 ft)
FOOD HABIT: Omnivorous: plankton
SIZE: 125 mm (5 in)
DESCRIPTION: An easily recognised species in the field, the long-cirried feather star is found attached to algae, rocky reefs, bryozoans and gorgonians swaying in the current. The species is extremely prevalent in the deeper waters throughout its distribution, and its colour pattern seems to be constant. The animal is firm to the touch with spiny arms and extremely long cirri which it uses to cling to objects on the bottom. The first specimen of this species was studied in Europe over 130 years ago, the type locality being given as King George Sound, Western Australia. It can be distinguished from its eastern counterpart, the southern feather star (*Ptilometra australis*), by the number of arms on adult specimens (25 to 31), and in

most cases *P. australis* is dark purple. Both species are generally fully expanded by night and by day.

Acanthaster planci

■ CLASS: Asteroidea

FAMILY: Acanthasteridae
SCIENTIFIC NAME: *Acanthaster planci*
COMMON NAME: Crown-of-thorns Sea Star
DISTRIBUTION: TI–WP; EP
HABITAT: Coral reefs
GENERAL WATER DEPTH: Low tide to
30 m (98 ft)
FOOD HABIT: Carnivorous: coral polyps
and tissue
SIZE: 400 mm (16 in)
DESCRIPTION: The crown-of-thorns sea star has been responsible for the destruction of living coral reefs over huge areas throughout the tropics in the past 30 years. Many millions of dollars are to be spent on studies, control and eradication programmes. In some respects it is regrettable that this sea star's feeding habits have been responsible for the depletion of many thousands of hectares of living coral. Yet without its threat to the marine environment we would all be much poorer in our understanding of corals and coral reefs throughout the world.

The crown-of-thorns sea star and its close relations should be avoided at all times as their spines can cause severe injury. The small shrimp *Periclimenes soror* has a commensal relationship with the crown-of-thorns sea star. Known predators include the puffer fish (*Arothron* spp.) and the giant triton (*Charonia tritonis*), but there is little evidence that these animals are more than opportunistic predators.

Allostichaster polyplax

FAMILY: Asteriidae
SCIENTIFIC NAME: *Allostichaster polyplax*
COMMON NAME: Many-armed Sea Star
DISTRIBUTION: WT/S; CT/S
HABITAT: Rocky reefs; rocky shores
GENERAL WATER DEPTH: Low tide to 250 m (820 ft)
FOOD HABIT: Carnivorous: molluscs
SIZE: 80 mm (3 in)
DESCRIPTION: The many-armed sea star is generally found beneath rocks and rubble and in crevices. Under subdued light it may be seen in the open during the day. It occurs on exposed coastline and also in sheltered situations. Its variable colour can be orange, brown, grey, black, white, green, or blue; specimens usually have combinations of three colours in a pattern. The many-armed sea star reproduces by both sexual and asexual means. The young hatch with five arms but they rarely stay this way as fission tends to occur annually. Those observed in the field are apt to have from one to six original larger arms and from one to four smaller arms regenerating in place of the larger ones divided off asexually from the body.

Asterias forbesi

FAMILY: Asteriidae
SCIENTIFIC NAME: *Asterias forbesi*
COMMON NAME: Forbes' Sea Star
DISTRIBUTION: WA
HABITAT: All substrates
GENERAL WATER DEPTH: 0–200 m (656 ft)

FOOD HABIT: Carnivorous: molluscs
SIZE: Up to 300 mm (11.8 in) diameter
DESCRIPTION: Bivalve molluscs are the primary food source for this sea star. The upper body surface is warty in appearance, with a conspicuous madreporite (a sieve-like plate connecting the water-vascular system with the exterior). Like many sea stars this species feeds by everting its stomach.

Asterias rubens

FAMILY: Asteriidae
SCIENTIFIC NAME: *Asterias rubens*
COMMON NAME: Common or European Sea Star
DISTRIBUTION: CT/N
HABITAT: Rocks, sand, and mud flats
GENERAL WATER DEPTH: 0–650 m (2132 ft)
FOOD HABIT: Carnivorous: mussels and scallops
SIZE: Up to 260 mm (10.2 in) long; diameter up to 500 mm (19.7 in)
DESCRIPTION: Unlike many other sea stars, the common sea star does not avoid direct sunlight. Its colouration is very varied, though it is chiefly orange, reddish-brown or reddish-violet. The dorsal surface is covered with spiny tubercles. This species is very agile — if turned on its aboral side, it can right itself within 5 seconds. However, it only moves at 50–80 mm (2–3.1 in) per minute, compared to *Luidia sarsi*, which 'runs' at 750 mm (29.5 in) per minute. The common sea star is preyed on by the common sun star *Crossaster papposus* and the purple sun star *Solaster endeca*.

FAMILY: Asteriidae
SCIENTIFIC NAME: *Astrostole insularis*
COMMON NAME: Island Sea Star
DISTRIBUTION: WT/S; TWP
HABITAT: Rocky reefs; rocky shores
GENERAL WATER DEPTH: 0–25 m (82 ft)
FOOD HABIT: Carnivorous: molluscs
SIZE: 220 mm (9 in)
DESCRIPTION: Reaching its largest size at

Astrostole insularis

Lord Howe Island in the South-West Pacific Ocean, where it is reasonably common from the intertidal zone (found beneath rocks) down to at least 25 m (82 ft), the island sea star ranges to the Australian mainland and New Zealand. It is one of the very few blue echinoderms. It can be confused superficially with the eleven-armed sea star when viewed as a preserved specimen. However in life, confusion could only occur in the juvenile stages. Adults generally have seven arms while juveniles may have fewer, as they autotomise. The island sea star is a fast mover and can hunt down the univalve molluscs upon which it feeds.

Astrostole scabra

FAMILY: Asteriidae
SCIENTIFIC NAME: *Astrostole scabra*
COMMON NAME: Rough Sea Star
DISTRIBUTION: WT/S; CT/S
HABITAT: Rocky reefs; rubble
GENERAL WATER DEPTH: 5–40 m (16–131 ft)
FOOD HABIT: Carnivorous: molluscs; echinoderms
SIZE: 400 mm (16 in)
DESCRIPTION: Originally named from the

South-West Pacific, this large voracious sea star ranges from New Zealand to Australia, where it is thought to have been introduced amongst oyster spat brought in from New Zealand. Very large in size and having seven arms, the colour is stable in shades of brown with no distinctive patterns. The rough sea star moves at a fairly rapid rate and is known to feed on both bivalve and univalve molluscs; it is a scourge in oyster and scallop beds.

Coscinasterias calamaria

FAMILY: Asteriidae
SCIENTIFIC NAME: *Coscinasterias calamaria*
COMMON NAME: Eleven-armed Sea Star
DISTRIBUTION: WT/S; CT/S
HABITAT: Rocky reefs; sand; mud; rubble
GENERAL WATER DEPTH: Low tide to
134 m (440 ft)
FOOD HABIT: Carnivorous: molluscs;
echinoderms
SIZE: 400 mm (16 in)
DESCRIPTION: This sea star is one of the two largest predatory, reef-inhabiting asteroids found in the shallow waters of southern Australia. It makes good progress over most types of terrain and has a voracious appetite, feeding on all types of molluscs, echinoderms and other invertebrates. Its common name suggests that it always has eleven arms but, like many other autotomising sea stars, the number can vary from seven to eleven depending on the stage of regeneration. Colour may range from green to brown, and sometimes with blues and orange. The tube feet are very powerful and a clinging sea star torn away may leave dozens of suction pads attached to the substrate. During the breeding season males and females may intertwine and release their reproductive products close to each other.

Marthasterias glacialis

FAMILY: Asteriidae
SCIENTIFIC NAME: *Marthasterias glacialis*
COMMON NAME: Spiny Sea Star
DISTRIBUTION: CT/N; EA
HABITAT: Rocky and sandy shores
GENERAL WATER DEPTH: 0–180 m (590 ft)
FOOD HABIT: Carnivorous: bivalve
molluscs, echinoderms
SIZE: Arms 350 mm (13.8 in) — may
exceptionally reach 500 mm (19.7 in);
diameter up to 800 mm (31.5 in)
DESCRIPTION: This animal has a very variable colouration, though is predominantly grey with greenish, yellowish, reddish or brownish tints. A nocturnal hunter, it is less agile than *Asterias rubens*. It consumes sea urchins but is uninjured by their spines, as it everts its stomach and glides between the spines to digest the echinoderm's soft tissue. The upper surfaces of its long flexible arms are covered by spines surrounded by pedicellariae (minute pincer-like appendages).

Pisaster ochraceus

FAMILY: Asteriidae
SCIENTIFIC NAME: *Pisaster ochraceus*
COMMON NAME: Ochre Sea Star
DISTRIBUTION: EP
HABITAT: Rocky shores with surf
GENERAL WATER DEPTH: Subtidal to
90 m (295 ft)
FOOD HABIT: Carnivorous: molluscs
SIZE: 280 mm (11 in)
DESCRIPTION: A common species, the ochre sea star usually has five arms covered with groups of small white spines; its colour ranges from yellow to brown to purple. The

centre of its disc features a distinct white star shape. Many of the molluscs upon which the ochre sea star feeds have developed a defence/escape mechanism based on detecting the scent of the creature in nearby waters. In turn, the ochre sea star provides food for few predators, notably gulls and otters.

Pycnopodia helianthoides

FAMILY: Asteriidae
SCIENTIFIC NAME: *Pycnopodia helianthoides*
COMMON NAME: Twenty-rayed Star;
Sunflower Star
DISTRIBUTION: EP
HABITAT: Rocks, mud, sand
GENERAL WATER DEPTH: Subtidal to
450 m (1476 ft)
FOOD HABIT: Carnivorous: crustaceans,
fishes
SIZE: 100 cm (39.4 in)
DESCRIPTION: The twenty-rayed star is among the most active, fastest and largest members of its family. These qualities give the star a distinct advantage in competing for food, which includes a large variety of crustacean and fish species. The twenty-rayed star is extremely territorial in dealing with others of its species and other sea star species, engaging in combat whenever encounters occur. Only adults attain the full 24 arms, while juveniles more commonly sport five arms. The colour of the twenty-rayed star ranges from pink to brown.

FAMILY: Asteriidae
SCIENTIFIC NAME: *Smilasterias irregularis*
COMMON NAME: Irregular Sea Star
DISTRIBUTION: WT/S; CT/S
HABITAT: Rocky reefs; rocky shores
GENERAL WATER DEPTH: Low tide to
20 m (66 ft)
FOOD HABIT: Carnivorous: molluscs
SIZE: 50 mm (2 in)
DESCRIPTION: Endemic to southern Australian waters, this unusual little sea star was once thought to be very rare; in fact even up to the early 1960s only a few specimens were held by museums. The irregular sea star is an inhabitant of broken rocky reefs where it lives hidden beneath stones and boulders. Colour varies from red through to brown, or

Smilasterias irregularis

grey. Strangely, though it is rare to find a specimen with equilateral arms, two with recently autotomised arms have been found and photographed living next to the 'parent' sea star. Both were alive and doing well, yet they had autotomised only the lower part of the arm and not at the junction of the arm and body like other sea stars.

Uniophora granifera

FAMILY: Asteriidae
SCIENTIFIC NAME: *Uniophora granifera*
COMMON NAME: Granular Sea Star
DISTRIBUTION: WT/S; CT/S
HABITAT: Rocky reefs; rocky shores; mud; sand; rubble
GENERAL WATER DEPTH: Low tide to 30 m (98 ft)
FOOD HABIT: Omnivorous: molluscs; algae; echinoderms; sponges
SIZE: 135 mm (5 in)
DESCRIPTION: Found throughout the waters bordering southern Australia this species is variable, to say the least, but easy to identify to genus level. The granular sea star can be fat or skinny, have large or small granules covering the surface, and can have long or short arms. It can live intertidally to 30 m

(98 ft) and it can be found in any number of different habitats in the colours pink, purple, orange, yellow, ochre, or brown. Its food intake is just as variable as it consumes algae, molluscs, crustaceans, sponges, ascidians, detritus and echinoderms as well as scavenging dead animal tissue.

Asterina atyphoida

FAMILY: Asterinidae
SCIENTIFIC NAME: *Asterina atyphoida*
COMMON NAME: Modest Sea Star
DISTRIBUTION: WT/S (SA)
HABITAT: Rocky reefs; rocky shores
GENERAL WATER DEPTH: Low tide to 40 m (131 ft)
FOOD HABIT: Omnivorous
SIZE: 22 mm (1 in)
DESCRIPTION: This small secretive species is rarely seen and is not well represented in museum collections. It lives beneath rocks, wood and rubble, in sheltered bays and inlets and also in deeper water off exposed coastlines in the South-West Pacific. Colour is usually pink with an edging of white, and it has a distinct green tip to each of its five arms. This picture was the first colour record of the species.

Asterina gibbosa

FAMILY: Asterinidae
SCIENTIFIC NAME: *Asterina gibbosa*
COMMON NAME: Cushion Star
DISTRIBUTION: EA
HABITAT: Rocky shores
GENERAL WATER DEPTH: Intertidal
FOOD HABIT: Omnivorous: sessile invertebrates and algae
SIZE: Up to 50 mm (2 in) diameter
DESCRIPTION: Two rows of inconspicuous plates border the arms of the cushion star. It is better able to withstand conditions of low salinity than most other sea stars. It is often found under rocky overhangs, under stones and in rock pools.

Nepanthia nigrobrunnea

FAMILY: Asterinidae
SCIENTIFIC NAME: *Nepanthia nigrobrunnea*
COMMON NAME: Black and Brown Sea Star
DISTRIBUTION: TWP
HABITAT: Rocky reefs; rocky shores
GENERAL WATER DEPTH: 10–30 m (33–98 ft)
FOOD HABIT: Omnivorous: algae; ascidians; sponges
SIZE: 90 mm (3.5 in)
DESCRIPTION: Originally discovered by the author in 1975 this recently described species is restricted in range within the Pacific region where it is relatively common around continental islands and offshore island reefs. The black and brown sea star lives exposed on reefs where it feeds on sponges, algae and ascidians. No variation in colour appears to have been observed over its entire distribution and most specimens collected by the author appear to be similar in size. All have five arms and were taken from similar depths.

FAMILY: Asterinidae
SCIENTIFIC NAME: *Nepanthia troughtoni*
COMMON NAME: Troughton's Sea Star
DISTRIBUTION: WT/S
HABITAT: Rocky reefs; rocky shores

Nepanthia troughtoni

GENERAL WATER DEPTH: Low tide to
73 m (240 ft)
FOOD HABIT: Omnivorous: sponges; algae
SIZE: 100 mm (4 in)
DESCRIPTION: The original description of
this sea star was made from a specimen
taken intertidally. Troughton's sea star is not
a commonly encountered species anywhere
throughout its range. Subtidally it lives in
fairly high energy coastal areas in south-
western Australia at depths of 5–10 m
(16–33 ft). It appears on the walls of overhangs and beneath kelp canopy on boulders.
Food consists of algae and encrusting
sponges, of which several different species
have been noted. Identification is relatively
simple, as no other *Nepanthia* is within its
range, its colour shows no variation overall
and its pattern is quite discernible.

Paranepanthia grandis

FAMILY: Asterinidae
SCIENTIFIC NAME: *Paranepanthia grandis*
COMMON NAME: Grand Sea Star
DISTRIBUTION: WT/S; CT/S
HABITAT: Rocky reefs; rocky shores
GENERAL WATER DEPTH: Low tide to
40 m (131 ft)

FOOD HABIT: Carnivorous: molluscs; sea
stars; ascidians
SIZE: 70 mm (3 in)
DESCRIPTION: A secretive nocturnal species
inhabiting southern Australian seas, the
grand sea star is rarely seen in the open
during the day. It hides beneath rocks in
crevices and under ledges and prefers areas
with piles of boulders and stones among
broken reef. It is a voracious predator of
other sea stars, especially those in its own
family and related families (owing to their
small size). It also eats molluscs and
ascidians.

Patiria miniata

FAMILY: Asterinidae
SCIENTIFIC NAME: *Patiria miniata*
COMMON NAME: Bat Star
DISTRIBUTION: EP
HABITAT: Rocks, sand, gravel, algae
GENERAL WATER DEPTH: Subtidal to
300 m (984 ft)
FOOD HABIT: Omnivorous: scavenger
SIZE: 200 mm (7.9 in)
DESCRIPTION: Common within its range,
the bat star varies from red to orange in
colour, and may be monocoloured or mottled.
Its arms are short and triangular and
usually number five. Aboral plates have concave margins that face the centre. To feed,
the bat star extends its stomach over many
species of animals and plants, both living
and dead, occasionally including those in
suspension. It is sometimes cannibalistic.
The Pugett annelid *Ophiodromus pugettensis*
commonly lives about the oral surface of the
bat star.

FAMILY: Astropectinidae
SCIENTIFIC NAME: *Astropecten polyacanthus*
COMMON NAME: Comb Sea Star
DISTRIBUTION: TI–WP; WT/S
HABITAT: Sand; mud
GENERAL WATER DEPTH: Low tide to
40 m (131 ft)
FOOD HABIT: Carnivorous: molluscs
SIZE: 170 mm (7 in)
DESCRIPTION: This is a very widespread

Astropecten polyacanthus

cosmopolitan species that ranges from the
Red Sea and Zanzibar across to Hawaii,
north to Japan and throughout the Indo-
Pacific region and the South-West Pacific to
New Zealand. The comb sea star lives on
sand or sandy mud bottoms, and spends
most of the time beneath the substrate. On
the turn of the tide it breaks cover and glides
on pointed tube feet. The colour range
includes brown with dark brown spines and
pink with white spines. It feeds on small
bivalves, ingesting up to five whole at once.
When a bivalve opens its shell to respire, the
strong stomach juices of the star enter the
shell and kill the mollusc. Once the valves
relax the sea star feeds and when finished
drops the empty shell out through the
mouth. This procedure may take several
days.

Astropecten preissi

FAMILY: Astropectinidae
SCIENTIFIC NAME: *Astropecten preissi*
COMMON NAME: Preiss's Sand Star
DISTRIBUTION: WT/S
HABITAT: Sand; sandy shores
GENERAL WATER DEPTH: Low tide to
140 m (459 ft)

FOOD HABIT: Carnivorous: molluscs
SIZE: 220 mm (9 in)
DESCRIPTION: Endemic to the waters of south-western Australia, this very conspicuous sand dweller has two separate colour forms. One, as pictured, is violet and the other is yellowish brown, though the latter seem to be rarer. Most of the daylight hours they spend buried (as do all sand stars in shallow waters) and they can only be found by their outline in the sand. They surface on the rising tide or around dusk, and crawl around seeking prey which they detect by scent. Their food consists of small bivalve molluscs which they ingest whole, sometimes several at a time.

Astropecten vappa

FAMILY: Astropectinidae
SCIENTIFIC NAME: *Astropecten vappa*
COMMON NAME: Spoilt Sand Star
DISTRIBUTION: TI–WP; WT/S
HABITAT: Sand; mud; sandy shores; muddy shores
GENERAL WATER DEPTH: Low tide to 100 m (328 ft)
FOOD HABIT: Carnivorous: molluscs
SIZE: 125 mm (5 in)
DESCRIPTION: Due to our inadequate knowledge and record of living underwater animals it is not always possible to state the key characters of a species when there is so wide a distribution around the entire Australian continent. There are at least five easily identifiable colour morphs and forms of the spoilt sand star so far recorded. No doubt others will be discovered in the future.

FAMILY: Echinasteridae
SCIENTIFIC NAME: *Echinaster colemani*
COMMON NAME: Coleman's Sea Star
DISTRIBUTION: TWP; WT/S
HABITAT: Rocky reefs
GENERAL WATER DEPTH: 10–120 m (33–394 ft)
FOOD HABIT: Omnivorous: algae; sponges

Echinaster colemani

SIZE: 137 mm (5 in)
DESCRIPTION: When first discovered in 1968 this species was only known from a few locations off the east coast of Australia, and due to its very restricted range it was not studied in detail at the time. Recent investigations have shown it to occur over a much greater area of the South-West Pacific (with an epicentre around Norfolk Island) and consequently it has been described. It is unlike any other *Echinaster* in colour and does not appear to overlap any of the Indo-Pacific species that might be confused with it, for example, the luzon sea star (*E. luzonicus*).

Echinaster glomeratus

FAMILY: Echinasteridae
SCIENTIFIC NAME: *Echinaster glomeratus*
COMMON NAME: Round-armed Sea Star
DISTRIBUTION: WT/S
HABITAT: Rocky reefs; rocky shores
GENERAL WATER DEPTH: Low tide to 40 m (131 ft)
FOOD HABIT: Carnivorous: sponges; ascidians
SIZE: 150 mm (6 in)
DESCRIPTION: Endemic to the south-western coastline of Australia, this sea star

is easily distinguished from others of its genus either in the field or in a preserved state. It lives in the open on both exposed and sheltered reefs and feeds on encrusting sponges and ascidians. Live specimens are like soft velvet to the touch but they have closely grouped sets of short spines beneath the skin. Three main colour variations have been recorded, with yellow and wine red being the most prevalent and orange being seen only occasionally.

Henricia leviuscula

FAMILY: Echinasteridae
SCIENTIFIC NAME: *Henricia leviuscula*
COMMON NAME: Small-mouthed Sea Star
DISTRIBUTION: EP
HABITAT: Rocks, in pools and in caves
GENERAL WATER DEPTH: Subtidal to 450 m (1476 ft)
FOOD HABIT: Carnivorous: sessile invertebrates
SIZE: 160 mm (6.3 in)
DESCRIPTION: This creature is commonly found where rock surfaces are covered with sponges and bryozoans, which form part of the sea star's diet. Bacteria are caught in mucus and moved to the mouth by rows of cilia. There are usually five long, tapering arms. Many subspecies of the sea star have been described because of the great variation in colour, form and size. The colour varies from tan to purple, sometimes banded with darker shades of the same colour.

FAMILY: Goniasteridae
SCIENTIFIC NAME: *Iconaster longimanus*
COMMON NAME: Icon Sea Star
DISTRIBUTION: TI–WP
HABITAT: Coral reefs; rubble
GENERAL WATER DEPTH: 10–46 m (33–151 ft)
FOOD HABIT: Omnivorous
SIZE: 100 mm (4 in)
DESCRIPTION: Rarely seen in its natural habitat, this delicate little star with its well-

Iconaster longimanus

Tosia australis

varied than they are on the magnificent sea star and there are less distinct morphological variants. The most commonly observed foods for the southern biscuit star are compound ascidians of at least five species, although sponges, algae and bryozoans have also been noted. The author made the first discovery of this species brooding its young; since then several other southern Australian species in the genus have been observed to do this as well.

Tosia magnifica

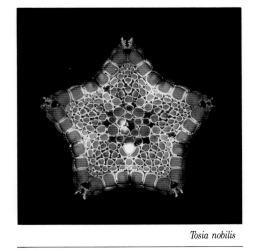

Tosia nobilis

defined shape and colour pattern offers no identification problems. It ranges throughout the Indo-Pacific region at least to the Philippines. It is known to live on rubble bottoms, in channels between reefs, on reef slopes and under coral slabs around continental islands as well as barrier reefs.

FAMILY: Goniasteridae
SCIENTIFIC NAME: *Tosia australis*
COMMON NAME: Southern Biscuit Star
DISTRIBUTION: WT/S; CT/S
HABITAT: Rocky reefs; jetty piles
GENERAL WATER DEPTH: Low tide to
  20 m (66 ft)
FOOD HABIT: Carnivorous: ascidians;
  bryozoans; sponges
SIZE: 70 mm (3 in)
DESCRIPTION: The southern biscuit star is an inhabitant of both open coast and sheltered inlets, although its numbers are greater in the latter areas. This species is smaller than the magnificent sea star (*Tosia magnifica*) and has fewer supra-marginal plates, which may vary from six to eight on each side. Colours and patterns are far more

FAMILY: Goniasteridae
SCIENTIFIC NAME: *Tosia magnifica*
COMMON NAME: Magnificent Sea Star
DISTRIBUTION: WT/S; CT/S
HABITAT: Rocky reefs; mud
GENERAL WATER DEPTH: Low tide to
  200 m (656 ft)
FOOD HABIT: Omnivorous: sponges;
  ascidians; algae
SIZE: 85 mm (3.5 in)
DESCRIPTION: Very common on the rocky shallows of inlets and bays around southeastern Australia, this species has a very hard texture almost like plastic. At the southern extent of its range it is found in large numbers on a soft, mud-bottom habitat. At maturity, the magnificent sea star is larger than its relative *Tosia australis* and has around 10 to 16 supra-marginal plates on each of its symmetrical sides. Most specimens of the magnificent sea star have five arms, although four or six are not unknown. The colours vary though there is some basic design in the patterns of living specimens, and sometimes stars can be found with similar colours and patterns.

FAMILY: Goniasteridae
SCIENTIFIC NAME: *Tosia nobilis*
COMMON NAME: Noble Sea Star
DISTRIBUTION: WT/S
HABITAT: Rocky reefs
GENERAL WATER DEPTH: Low tide to
  15 m (49 ft)

FOOD HABIT: Omnivorous: sponges; algae
SIZE: 40 mm (1.5 in)
DESCRIPTION: This species may or may not be valid, but it exists in the literature as do many records and described species which in their day were based on the knowledge of their day. Of course, over 160 years later we still don't know very much about our oceans and their living inhabitants; we especially lack knowledge in natural history and behaviour. This rather exquisite little sea star inhabits the Indian Ocean off the southwestern coast of Australia. It is moderately common and exists in a range of colour combinations. The noble sea star may one day prove to be just a local variety morph of *Tosia australis*, but that will hardly detract from its beauty.

Luidia australiae

FAMILY: Luidiidae
SCIENTIFIC NAME: *Luidia australiae*
COMMON NAME: Southern Sand Star
DISTRIBUTION: WT/S
HABITAT: Sand; mud; sandy shores;
  muddy shores; seagrass meadows
GENERAL WATER DEPTH: Low tide to
  110 m (361 ft)

FOOD HABIT: Carnivorous: molluscs; echinoderms

SIZE: 1 m (3 ft)

DESCRIPTION: The southern sand star is an extremely common resident of soft-bottom communities in sheltered bays, inlets, harbours and estuaries in southern Australian seas. Most of the time it buries itself under the sand to shelter from the light and from predators. Sand stars differ from reef stars in the shape of their tube feet (sand stars have pointed tube feet). The southern sand star is generally found in groups. Little is known of its natural history, although a large number are observed with damaged or newly regenerated arm tips, perhaps caused by some as yet unknown predator. It feeds on bivalves, heart urchins, sea stars and brittle stars, and in some areas has a commensal crab, *Lissocarcinus polyboides*, living on or beneath it.

Austrofromia polypora

FAMILY: Ophidiasteridae

SCIENTIFIC NAME: *Austrofromia polypora*

COMMON NAME: Many-pored Sea Star

DISTRIBUTION: WT/S; CT/S

HABITAT: Rocky reefs; mud

GENERAL WATER DEPTH: 5–160 m (16–525 ft)

FOOD HABIT: Omnivorous: algae; sponges; bryozoans

SIZE: 140 mm (5.5 in)

DESCRIPTION: A common inhabitant of both inshore and offshore rocky reefs, the many-pored sea star is a diurnally conspicuous resident of the entire southern Australian coastline. It has little colour variation. This species is regularly observed in depths to 22 m (72 ft) and it has been trawled on mud bottom in deeper waters. Large specimens have distinctly fattened arms close to the central disc, giving them a somewhat flat appearance. Observations have shown that the food taken is mostly sedentary sponges, algae and bryozoans, although it might be

expected that they would feed on other bottom-dwelling invertebrates as well. Only two records of predation have been noted, in one instance by fish and the other by a triton shell.

Fromia monilis

FAMILY: Ophidiasteridae

SCIENTIFIC NAME: *Fromia monilis*

COMMON NAME: Necklace Sea Star

DISTRIBUTION: TI–WP

HABITAT: Coral reefs

GENERAL WATER DEPTH: Low tide to 25 m (82 ft)

FOOD HABIT: Omnivorous: algae; detritus

SIZE: 70 mm (3 in)

DESCRIPTION: This species occurs off the northern coast of Western Australia throughout the Indo-Pacific region. The pictured specimen is fairly typical of the colour form found in the Indian Ocean although some specimens may have solid red patches on the disc and arms similar to those found in the Papua New Guinea area and the Coral Sea. It occurs in shallow water lagoon areas among living coral reefs, and on channel slopes between reefs and on drop offs in moderately deep water. This star is quite hard to the touch and its rigid skeleton does not allow it to be bent without breaking. Its feeding habits include algae and detritus and predators seem restricted to the dancing shrimp (*Hymenocera picta*).

FAMILY: Ophidiasteridae

SCIENTIFIC NAME: *Leiaster leachi*

COMMON NAME: Leach's Sea Star

DISTRIBUTION: TI–WP

HABITAT: Coral reefs; rocky reefs

GENERAL WATER DEPTH: 1–180 m (3–591 ft)

FOOD HABIT: Omnivorous

SIZE: 450 mm (18 in)

DESCRIPTION: With a range extending from Mauritius in the west Indian Ocean to Lord Howe and Norfolk Island in the South-West

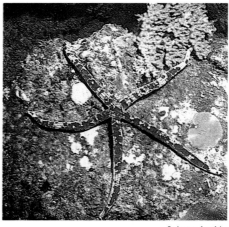

Leiaster leachi

Pacific, this large sea star inhabits a wide area although it is not regarded as common. Those first found by the author were entwined deep in shallow crevices on the top of a reef that was being pounded incessantly by the huge breakers of the Indian Ocean. On the top of the reef one arm could be seen but it was enough to recognise a species not recorded from the area and it took an hour to extricate it. Leach's sea star is a nocturnal forager. It uses its long arms to anchor itself against the surge of the waves, and actually hangs on with its arms. The tube feet seem small and inadequate for the size of the star and their suction powers are fairly weak. It cannot walk very fast but if danger looms it can disappear into the reef with surprising agility.

Linckia laevigata

FAMILY: Ophidiasteridae

SCIENTIFIC NAME: *Linckia laevigata*

COMMON NAME: Blue Sea Star

DISTRIBUTION: TI–WP

HABITAT: Coral reefs; rocky reefs; rocky shores

GENERAL WATER DEPTH: Low tide to 30 m (98 ft)

FOOD HABIT: Omnivorous: algae
SIZE: 400 mm (16 in)
DESCRIPTION: Commonly encountered intertidally throughout the Indo-Pacific Ocean coral reefs, this well-known sea star is generally only recognised in its blue form (its commonest colour). However, on some reefs colour forms exist and may be grey, pink, or yellow. The species also inhabits continental island rocky reefs in deeper water, where the colour is generally khaki. The shallow water form has a stark blue colouring that is rarely found in other sea stars. The species inhabits pools or shallow submerged reef flats near lagoons and sheltered reef ramparts.

Linckia multifora

FAMILY: Ophidiasteridae
SCIENTIFIC NAME: *Linckia multifora*
COMMON NAME: Multi-pore Sea Star
DISTRIBUTION: TI–WP
HABITAT: Coral reefs; rocky shores
GENERAL WATER DEPTH: Low tide to 46 m (151 ft)
FOOD HABIT: Omnivorous: algae; detritus
SIZE: 100 mm (4 in)
DESCRIPTION: Occurring on Indo-Pacific reefs, this species appears to be more prevalent in the West Pacific. A relative of the blue sea star, the multi-pore sea star is much smaller and rarely occurs in the open on intertidal reef flats. It is a very common species and is abundant at depths of 5–30 m (16–98 ft) and is generally observed on bommies and underhangs. It feeds both night and day on a diet of filamentous algae and detritus. Occasionally small parasitic snails may be seen on the undersides of the tube feet, feeding on the star's body fluids.

FAMILY: Ophidiasteridae
SCIENTIFIC NAME: *Nardoa novaecaledoniae*
COMMON NAME: New Caledonian Sea Star
DISTRIBUTION: TI–WP
HABITAT: Coral reefs
GENERAL WATER DEPTH: Low tide to 5 m (16 ft)

Nardoa novaecaledoniae

FOOD HABIT: Herbivorous: algae
SIZE: 200 mm (8 in)
DESCRIPTION: With a range from the Philippines to New Caledonia, this common reef flat species is not known from some areas of the southern Pacific. A resident of the lagoon shallows, it is usually found in quiet waters. Colour and design seem to be fairly constant and almost all specimens found are complete and free from damage. No predators of fully grown adults have yet been observed. A small commensal worm can often be found on the underside of this sea star near the tube feet furrows.

Nardoa rosea

FAMILY: Ophidiasteridae
SCIENTIFIC NAME: *Nardoa rosea*
COMMON NAME: Rose Sea Star
DISTRIBUTION: TWP
HABITAT: Coral reefs; rubble
GENERAL WATER DEPTH: 8–25 m (26–82 ft)
FOOD HABIT: Omnivorous: algae; detritus
SIZE: 80 mm (3 in)
DESCRIPTION: A resident of offshore barrier reefs of the Pacific from the Coral Sea to Papua New Guinea, this very attractive sea

star is not common anywhere within its range. Although originally described in 1921, it wasn't until some 50 years later that it was rediscovered and photographed by underwater naturalists. So distinctive were its visual features that for some years afterwards it was thought by scientists to be a new species. It lives on reef slopes and rubble in channels.

Ophidiaster confertus

FAMILY: Ophidiasteridae
SCIENTIFIC NAME: *Ophidiaster confertus*
COMMON NAME: Orange Sea Star
DISTRIBUTION: TWP; WT/S
HABITAT: Rocky reefs; rocky shores; coral reefs
GENERAL WATER DEPTH: Low tide to 25 m (82 ft)
FOOD HABIT: Omnivorous: sessile invertebrates; algae
SIZE: 250 mm (10 in)
DESCRIPTION: Not as common on continental island reefs as it is around the volcanic outer islands of the Norfolk Ridge in the South-West Pacific, this species has its highest density at Lord Howe Island, where it is very common on reefs below 15 m (49 ft). It lives in the open both day and night and is slow moving. Colour variation is minimal throughout its range and no distinct predators have been recorded. An unidentified species of brittle star has a commensal relationship with the orange sea star on some Australian mainland reefs.

FAMILY: Oreasteridae
SCIENTIFIC NAME: *Anthaster valvulatus*
COMMON NAME: Valvulate Sea Star
DISTRIBUTION: WT/S
HABITAT: Rocky reefs; rocky shores; rubble; sand
GENERAL WATER DEPTH: Low tide to 50 m (164 ft)
FOOD HABIT: Omnivorous: algae; sponges
SIZE: 250 mm (10 in)

Anthaster valvulatus

DESCRIPTION: As this is the only known sea star species in this particular genus, and as it only occurs in south-western Australian seas, there is little likelihood of confusing it with other sea stars. The valvulate sea star sits out on the open bottom during the day, and with its bright red or red and pink colouration is quite conspicuous. In the eastern shallow coastal waters all specimens observed by the author were bright red with small purple beads running out along short, stubby arms. Those specimens taken in deep water around offshore islands at the eastern edge of the Great Australian Bight were all similar to the specimen pictured: pink and red colouration with much longer arms. This sea star feeds on algae and sponges.

Anthenea edmondi

FAMILY: Oreasteridae
SCIENTIFIC NAME: *Anthenea edmondi*
COMMON NAME: Edmond's Sea Star
DISTRIBUTION: WT/S
HABITAT: Sand; mud; rubble
GENERAL WATER DEPTH: 8–80 m
 (26–263 ft)
FOOD HABIT: Omnivorous: detritus
SIZE: 150 mm (6 in)

DESCRIPTION: Like most sea stars this species has rarely been reproduced in colour. Edmond's sea star is a soft-bottom dweller and is mostly seen on the sandy-mud floor of harbours and bays from where it often enters rivers and estuaries. It is brought up in trawls fairly regularly. Large with hard texture, the species has five symmetrical arms and does not bury itself in the substrate.

Asterodiscides truncatus

FAMILY: Oreasteridae
SCIENTIFIC NAME: *Asterodiscides truncatus*
COMMON NAME: Firebrick Sea Star
DISTRIBUTION: WT/S
HABITAT: Rocky reefs
GENERAL WATER DEPTH: 20–400 m
 (66–1312 ft)
FOOD HABIT: Omnivorous: sponges; algae
SIZE: 200 mm (8 in)

DESCRIPTION: This brilliantly coloured species is extremely simple to identify in its live state. Its large size, prominent tubercles, five symmetrical arms and colour pattern make it like no other temperate Australian water species. The firebrick sea star is a member of continental island and offshore reef fauna where it lives on rocky reefs down to the surrounding sand level of some 60 m (197 ft). In deeper waters it lives on the mud bottom and is only obtainable by trawling. Strangely, very few juvenile specimens have been collected from reefs. This may be due to the species having the same juvenile behaviour as its tropical relative the pin-cushion sea star (*Culcita*), whose juveniles remain hidden during the day. The commensal shrimp *Periclimenes soror* lives on this species in some locations.

FAMILY: Oreasteridae
SCIENTIFIC NAME: *Culcita novaeguineae*
COMMON NAME: Pin-cushion Sea Star
DISTRIBUTION: TI–WP
HABITAT: Coral reefs
GENERAL WATER DEPTH: Low tide to
 30 m (98 ft)
FOOD HABIT: Omnivorous: algae; detritus;
 corals

Culcita novaeguineae

SIZE: 250 mm (10 in)
DESCRIPTION: The pin-cushion sea star is moderately common on reef flats at low tide and also inhabits deeper waters to 30 m (98 ft) from Mauritius in the Indian Ocean to Samoa in the Pacific. It is more recognisable as a sea star in the juvenile stage when the arms are quite distinct. When held out of the water it is quite heavy owing to the large amount of seawater contained within the body and the massive skeleton. The pin-cushion sea star feeds on a variety of organisms including algae, bottom detritus and the polyps and flesh of some corals. It grows larger in deeper water and can be found in a variety of colours and colour combinations. Occasionally the small commensal shrimp *Periclimenes soror* may be seen living on the underside of the sea star.

Nectria macrobrachia

FAMILY: Oreasteridae
SCIENTIFIC NAME: *Nectria macrobrachia*
COMMON NAME: Large-plated Sea Star
DISTRIBUTION: WT/S
HABITAT: Rocky reefs; rocky shores
GENERAL WATER DEPTH: Low tide to
 180 m (591 ft)

FOOD HABIT: Omnivorous: sponges; bryozoans; algae; ascidians

SIZE: 100 mm (4 in)

DESCRIPTION: Found only in the waters surrounding southern Australia, this sea star is fairly uniform in colour and is the easiest of all of this genus to identify in the field. It lives on inshore and offshore rocky reefs and, like all species of this endemic genus, is diurnally and nocturnally conspicuous. Sometimes specimens may be seen in caves, but this is due more to the animal's feeding habits than any protective behaviour. It often occurs in areas of shallow-water turbulence where it appears to be well adapted, wedging itself among growths on rock walls and on the sea floor and even feeding while being swept by a strong surge. Its food consists mainly of sponges, bryozoans, algae and compound ascidians. There are no records of predation or any associates.

Nectria multispina

FAMILY: Oreasteridae

SCIENTIFIC NAME: *Nectria multispina*

COMMON NAME: Multi-spined Sea Star

DISTRIBUTION: WT/S

HABITAT: Rocky reefs; rocky shores

GENERAL WATER DEPTH: Low tide to 20 m (66 ft)

FOOD HABIT: Carnivorous: sponges; bryozoans

SIZE: 150 mm (6 in)

DESCRIPTION: This genus of sea star is endemic to the waters of southern Australia. It has very large, fairly smooth dorsal tabulae at the centre of the disc and very underdeveloped platelets. The tabulae extend to the ends of the arms. The multi-spined sea star inhabits both inshore and offshore rocky reefs, where it is generally seen at depths below 10 m (33 ft). Its colour pattern is variable, although the majority have a predominance of red. The multi-spined sea star feeds on sponges, bryozoans and algae and has no known predators or associates in its adult form.

Nectria ocellata

FAMILY: Oreasteridae

SCIENTIFIC NAME: *Nectria ocellata*

COMMON NAME: Ocellate Sea Star

DISTRIBUTION: WT/S; CT/S

HABITAT: Rocky reefs; seagrass meadows

GENERAL WATER DEPTH: Low tide to 230 m (755 ft)

FOOD HABIT: Omnivorous: sponges; algae; bryozoans

SIZE: 150 mm (6 in)

DESCRIPTION: A dominant shallow water asteroid in the waters below Bass Strait off Tasmania, its depth range increases towards the northern extent of its distribution. The ocellate sea star is fairly variable in colour, but throughout its geographical range tends to be dominated by reds and pinks. No commensal have been observed, nor have any predators been recorded. This species is an opportunist feeder and will consume sponges, algae, bryozoa, encrusting ascidians and detritus.

Nectria saoria

FAMILY: Oreasteridae

SCIENTIFIC NAME: *Nectria saoria*

COMMON NAME: Saori Sea Star

DISTRIBUTION: WT/S

HABITAT: Rocky reefs

GENERAL WATER DEPTH: Low tide to 25 m (82 ft)

FOOD HABIT: Omnivorous: sponges; ascidians; red algae

SIZE: 125 mm (5 in)

DESCRIPTION: The Saori sea star was discovered by scuba divers in the early 1960s, its name being taken from the research vessel *Saori* used in many expeditions in southern Australia. Easily identified in the field due to its very different visual characteristics, the Saori sea star has intermediate dorsal tabulae spinelets that are not fused together and these, together with the major tabulae, extend right to the ends of the arms. It lives on high energy coastline at depths of around 10 m (33 ft) on reefs where it is mostly observed beneath kelp canopy, under ledges and in caves. The bright red colour is stable throughout its range and it feeds on sponges and ascidians.

Nectria wilsoni

FAMILY: Oreasteridae

SCIENTIFIC NAME: *Nectria wilsoni*

COMMON NAME: Wilson's Sea Star

DISTRIBUTION: WT/S

HABITAT: Rocky reefs; rocky shores; seagrass meadows

GENERAL WATER DEPTH: Low tide to 44 m (144 ft)

FOOD HABIT: Omnivorous: algae; seagrass; sponges

SIZE: 170 mm (7 in)

DESCRIPTION: Wilson's sea star is more common in shallow water than it is in deep water. Certainly, throughout its known range in south-western Australia its visual characteristics are stable, with well-developed, widely spaced, irregular dorsal tabulae bordered by well-developed marginal plates. The larger tabulae phase out just beyond the junction of the arms and disc and are replaced by small granules. There are two main colour forms and these are without design or dorsal patterns; the illustrated colour form (orange) is uncommon, the red form is the most prevalent. Wilson's sea star feeds on red algae, green algae, the seagrass *Halophyllia* and encrusting sponges.

Crossaster papposus

FAMILY: Solasteridae
SCIENTIFIC NAME: *Crossaster papposus*
COMMON NAME: Common Sun Star
DISTRIBUTION: CT/N
HABITAT: On rock and sand
GENERAL WATER DEPTH: 0–1200 m (3937 ft)
FOOD HABIT: Carnivorous: molluscs; echinoderms
SIZE: Up to 340 mm (13.4 in) diameter
DESCRIPTION: During its first year of life, the common sun star can grow from 40 to 90 mm (1.6–3.5 in). It has 8–13 short arms on the large central disc, and is tolerant of strong sunlight. Amongst its prey are *Asterias rubens* and *Mytilis* spp. The latter are swallowed whole; the soft tissues are digested within 24 hours, and the empty shells voided by stomach eversion.

Solaster endeca

FAMILY: Solasteridae
SCIENTIFIC NAME: *Solaster endeca*
COMMON NAME: Purple Sun Star
DISTRIBUTION: CT/N

HABITAT: Rocky substrate
GENERAL WATER DEPTH: Intertidal
FOOD HABIT: Carnivorous: molluscs and echinoderms
SIZE: Up to 300 mm (11.8 in) diameter
DESCRIPTION: The purple sun star has 7–13 arms with suckered tube feet. Its upper surface is less spiny than that of *Crossaster papposus* and the body is soft and flabby.

Amphiodia occidentalis

■ CLASS: Ophiuroidea

FAMILY: Amphiuridae
SCIENTIFIC NAME: *Amphiodia occidentalis*
COMMON NAME: Occidental Brittle Star
DISTRIBUTION: EP
HABITAT: Rocks; sand; mud; algae
GENERAL WATER DEPTH: Subtidal to 375 m (1230 ft)
FOOD HABIT: Carnivorous: plankton
SIZE: 165 mm (6.5 in)
DESCRIPTION: The undulating, tentacle-like arms of this species range in length from nine to 15 times the diameter of the disc. It is coloured varying shades of grey. The upper side of the disc lacks spines but has three flattened arm spines on each side of each segment. It generally burrows into the soft bottom, moving sand and mud from beneath its arms and piling them on top. When this activity is observed in its entirety, the creature appears to sink into the sand. Just the tips of its arms are exposed during daylight hours, with more being exposed at night. Arms are shed easily and regenerated.

FAMILY: Asteroschematidae
SCIENTIFIC NAME: *Astrobrachion adhaerens*
COMMON NAME: Clinging Snake Star
DISTRIBUTION: TI–WP; WT/S; CT/S
HABITAT: Rocky reefs
GENERAL WATER DEPTH: 6–180 m (20–591 ft)
FOOD HABIT: Omnivorous: protein enriched mucus
SIZE: 300 mm (12 in)
DESCRIPTION: Only found on black coral 'trees', this interesting and unusual brittle

Astrobrachion adhaerens

star generally has two main colour patterns, both of which are illustrated. Thought to be a tropical species, as there are some records from tropical Indo-Pacific regions, the original types were dredged up from the Indian Ocean off north-west Australia. Although the author has not observed this species in tropical waters (probably due to its habitat being at extreme depths), the clinging snake star is certainly well established in the South-West Pacific as far south as New Zealand. Some black coral trees may have as many as 40 of these nocturnal mucus feeders clinging to the branches. The snake stars are found in no other micro-habitat and are totally dependent on the black coral colony for food.

Astrobrachion constrictum

FAMILY: Asteroschematidae
SCIENTIFIC NAME: *Astrobrachion constrictum*
COMMON NAME: Grasping Snake Star
DISTRIBUTION: TI–WP; WT/S
HABITAT: Rocky reefs; coral reefs
GENERAL WATER DEPTH: 18–180 m (59–591 ft)
FOOD HABIT: Omnivorous: protein enriched mucus

SIZE: 150 mm (6 in)

DESCRIPTION: Generally confined to moderately deep water in the Indo-Pacific region, this species lives exclusively among the fronds and branches of black coral trees (antipatharians). During the day it clings tightly to its perch, coiling long, serpent-like arms around the branches in such a way that nothing short of total destruction would enable them to be moved. Unlike the basket stars, which use sponges as feeding platforms, the grasping snake star is totally dependent on the protein-enriched mucus produced by the black coral polyps, further fortified by entrapped settling plankton. Large, black coral trees 1–2 m (3–6 ft) high may have as many as 50 specimens wrapped around their branches. The colours vary and include reds, oranges, blacks, whites, golds and yellows.

Astroboa ernae

FAMILY: Gorgonocephalidae
SCIENTIFIC NAME: *Astroboa ernae*
COMMON NAME: Erna's Basket Star
DISTRIBUTION: WT/S
HABITAT: Rocky reefs
GENERAL WATER DEPTH: 0–60 m (197 ft)
FOOD HABIT: Omnivorous: plankton
SIZE: 300 mm (12 in)

DESCRIPTION: Although not common all over the southern Indian Ocean, in some specific localities off Australia Erna's basket star may occur in numbers. The largest of the temperate, shallow-water basket stars, it spends the daylight hours curled up in a circular 'pad' on sponges, bryozoans or cave ceilings. Almost always pink in colour, Erna's basket star is readily identified in the field either in juvenile or adult form. At night it moves around to a high spot in the current and spreads its arms out in a feeding position. Small planktonic organisms and suspended sediment become entrapped in the fine branches and are transferred along food grooves under the arms to the mouth.

Astroboa globiferum

FAMILY: Gorgonocephalidae
SCIENTIFIC NAME: *Astroboa globiferum*
COMMON NAME: Globular Basket Star
DISTRIBUTION: TWP
HABITAT: Rocky reefs
GENERAL WATER DEPTH: 20–50 m (66–164 ft)
FOOD HABIT: Omnivorous: coarse plankton
SIZE: 1 m (3 ft) (expanded)

DESCRIPTION: It's no wonder the early naturalists and collectors, who relied on dredges and traps and tangle nets to collect specimens, missed the globular basket star. Even when their habitat is known they are difficult to find. Living as they do during the day wrapped up in a resting 'pad' under caves, ledges and undercuts in volcanic reefs, they blend into their surroundings admirably. Like most basket stars this species is extremely sensitive to light, and even when it is expanded during night feeding the mere flash of a torch will send it scurrying into the dark recesses of the reef. It is known to live in the one place for up to three years, always returning to the same hideaway after its nightly feeding.

Astrosierra amblyconus

FAMILY: Gorgonocephalidae
SCIENTIFIC NAME: *Astrosierra amblyconus*
COMMON NAME: Domed Basket Star
DISTRIBUTION: WT/S
HABITAT: Rocky reefs; continental shelf
GENERAL WATER DEPTH: 20–135 m (66–443 ft)
FOOD HABIT: Carnivorous: coarse plankton
SIZE: 150 mm (6 in)

DESCRIPTION: Originally described from dredged specimens brought up by the research vessel *Thetis*, until recently this species was known under the genus *Conocladus*. It lives at moderate depths in bays and inlets off south-east Australia but is much more prevalent in the deeper offshore areas. The species does not seem to vary much in colour throughout its distribution. Those observed or collected have a pinkish, off-white base, with darker tubercles. The domed basket star does not have associations with any specific sedentary animal. The sponges, sea whips, sea fans, soft corals and hydroids to which it is found clinging are only used as feeding platforms by which the basket star can move further up into the water column, thereby gaining access to richer planktonic food sources. It feeds at night.

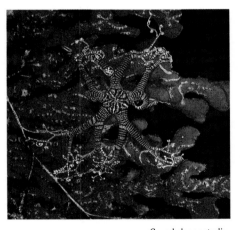

Conocladus australis

FAMILY: Gorgonocephalidae
SCIENTIFIC NAME: *Conocladus australis*
COMMON NAME: Southern Basket Star
DISTRIBUTION: WT/S; CT/S
HABITAT: Rocky reefs
GENERAL WATER DEPTH: 6–500 m (20–1640 ft)
FOOD HABIT: Omnivorous: coarse plankton
SIZE: 200 mm (8 in)

DESCRIPTION: Found in rocky reef waters in the South Pacific, the southern basket star is associated with many species of sponges and gorgonians, seemingly because the animal uses these sedentary invertebrates as feeding platforms, enabling it to obtain greater food intake by being higher in the water column. During darkness it unfolds its many arms and spreads them to enmesh the plankton and detritus on which it feeds. Colour patterns within the species are extremely varied but usually the base colours are brown or grey splashed with assorted blotches, rings and spots of black or dark red. The juveniles often show little similarity to the adult owing to the extreme variation of the disc growth and patterns of the young.

Ophiactis savignyi

FAMILY: Ophiactidae
SCIENTIFIC NAME: *Ophiactis savignyi*
COMMON NAME: Savigny's Brittle Star
DISTRIBUTION: TI–WP; EP; WT/S; WT/N
HABITAT: Rocky reefs; coral reefs; rocky shores
GENERAL WATER DEPTH: Low tide to 500 m (1640 ft)
FOOD HABIT: Omnivorous
SIZE: 50 mm (2 in)
DESCRIPTION: Savigny's brittle star is widely distributed in the west Indo-Pacific region. The photograph shows the most common colour combination of greens, blacks and white found in the Indian Ocean and Pacific forms. This species is often gregarious and may inhabit sponges or encrusting ascidians in dozens, particularly when juvenile. Although it breeds in a normal way from sperm and eggs, this species often reproduces asexually by splitting. The missing parts then regenerate to form two normal adults but the regenerated parts may not be recognisable until maturity.

FAMILY: Ophiodermatidae
SCIENTIFIC NAME: *Ophiarachna incrassata*
COMMON NAME: Green Serpent Star
DISTRIBUTION: TI–WP
HABITAT: Coral reefs
GENERAL WATER DEPTH: Low tide to 10 m (33 ft)

Ophiarachna incrassata

FOOD HABIT: Omnivorous: detritus
SIZE: 200 mm (8 in)
DESCRIPTION: A large ophiuroid inhabiting many coral reefs, the green serpent star avoids light and during the day hides beneath coral slabs or in crevices and crannies in shallow water. The colour-oriented common name is warranted as its colour varies little over its entire range. The species is well distributed and has been recorded from many areas in the Indian and Pacific oceans, from Zanzibar to the Fiji Islands. When disturbed it moves quickly towards cover. Even at night when foraging on the reef it will scurry into the coral from one flash of torchlight. The species tends to be solitary.

Ophiarachnella ramsayi

FAMILY: Ophiodermatidae
SCIENTIFIC NAME: *Ophiarachnella ramsayi*
COMMON NAME: Ramsay's Serpent Star
DISTRIBUTION: WT/S
HABITAT: Rocky reefs; rocky shores
GENERAL WATER DEPTH: 0–20 m (66 ft)
FOOD HABIT: Omnivorous: detritus
SIZE: 120 mm (5 in)

DESCRIPTION: Sometimes difficult to identify by colour or pattern alone, Ramsay's serpent star occurs along the southern coasts of Australia in shallow waters and could almost be termed an intertidal species. It does not live in the open, but hides beneath rocks and stones. Localised forms tend to be colour specific, however, each area seems to produce its own variation, though the overall pattern can be recognised with a little practice. Colour variations include browns, reds, ochres and greys. It moves swiftly to cover when disturbed and is eaten by several species of wrasses and boar fish.

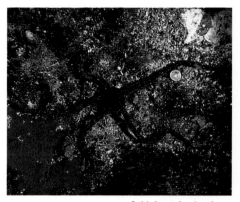

Ophioderma longicaudum

FAMILY: Ophiodermatidae
SCIENTIFIC NAME: *Ophioderma longicaudum*
DISTRIBUTION: EA
HABITAT: Rocks and sand
GENERAL WATER DEPTH: Intertidal/ subtidal
FOOD HABIT: Omnivorous
SIZE: Up to 300 mm (11.8 in) diameter
DESCRIPTION: A common species in the Mediterranean, this animal has a leathery central disc from which radiate long arms with short lateral spines. It is able to make lateral movements and limited vertical movements with its arms, but cannot coil the arms around objects. This species is generally found sheltering beneath rocks and ledges during the day.

FAMILY: Ophiodermatidae
SCIENTIFIC NAME: *Ophiopeza assimilis*
COMMON NAME: Similar Brittle Star
DISTRIBUTION: WT/S
HABITAT: Rocky reefs; rocky shores; rubble; sand
GENERAL WATER DEPTH: 0–146 m (479 ft)
FOOD HABIT: Omnivorous
SIZE: 175 mm (7 in)
DESCRIPTION: A very active species, the similar brittle star lives beneath rocks and rubble on sand or mud. When disturbed it shows amazing speed, always heading for the

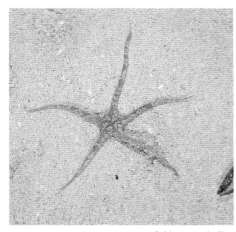

Ophiopeza assimilis

Ophiothela danae

and daubs. It is secretive, and during the day hides beneath rocks, dead coral slabs, among rubble banks and under ledges. Like most serpent stars it can move quickly when disturbed and is not easily deterred from seeking shelter. Known predators are mostly fish.

Ophionereis schayeri

closest concealment: shadow, crevice, or rock where it immediately takes refuge. Over its distribution its basic pattern remains fairly similar although the colour may range from orange to brick red. It is more robust in the arms than previously illustrated species and doesn't shed them as readily when held. In the Indian Ocean it has a star-shaped pattern on the disc, but this may not be present on the Pacific forms.

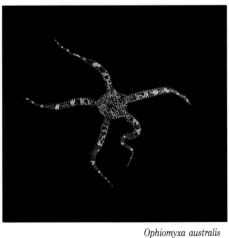

Ophiomyxa australis

FAMILY: Ophiomyxidae
SCIENTIFIC NAME: *Ophiomyxa australis*
COMMON NAME: Southern Serpent Star
DISTRIBUTION: TI–WP; WT/S
HABITAT: Coral reefs; rocky reefs; rocky shores; rubble
GENERAL WATER DEPTH: Low tide to 300 m (984 ft)
FOOD HABIT: Omnivorous
SIZE: 240 mm (9 in)
DESCRIPTION: Found throughout the Indian and Pacific oceans from Mauritius to Fiji and north to Japan, this species is widely distributed. Its colour is remarkably diverse, appearing in browns, yellows, reds and olives with large, small and erratic spots, dashes

FAMILY: Ophionereidae
SCIENTIFIC NAME: *Ophionereis schayeri*
COMMON NAME: Schayer's Brittle Star
DISTRIBUTION: WT/S; CT/S
HABITAT: Rocky reefs; rocky shores; rubble
GENERAL WATER DEPTH: Low tide to 183 m (600 ft)
FOOD HABIT: Omnivorous
SIZE: 260 mm (10 in)
DESCRIPTION: A common intertidal species, Schayer's brittle star is even more common below tide level. It lives on and around rocky reefs or rubble flats, where it hides beneath rocks and stones to avoid sunlight and diurnal predators. At night it moves about in search of food. Because it has such a wide distribution there is some variation within the species, but with a little practice and the advantage of knowing most of the colour forms, one finds that field identification is not difficult. Juvenile specimens have very pale discs and much darker arm bands than the adults observed by the author. The disc on adults is usually speckled with white or grey. Most have five to ten lines on the disc radiating out to each arm, or between each arm from the centrally positioned anus. All forms have tricolour arm bands. The species is eaten by fish and is often host to the scale worm (*Lepidonotus melanogrammus*), which lives beneath its disc.

FAMILY: Ophiotrichidae
SCIENTIFIC NAME: *Ophiothela danae*
COMMON NAME: Dana's Brittle Star
DISTRIBUTION: TI–WP; WT/S
HABITAT: Coral reefs; rocky reefs

GENERAL WATER DEPTH: 5–60 m (16–197 ft)
FOOD HABIT: Omnivorous
SIZE: 10 mm (0.5 in)
DESCRIPTION: Very common through the Indo-Pacific region, Dana's brittle star is a small, beautifully patterned, colourful commensal that is only found attached to or on other invertebrates. Large specimens have six arms and small ones generally have three. It therefore seems probable that Dana's brittle star reproduces by fission. Over six years the author photographed and collected over 35 hosts of small, multi-coloured brittle stars to determine on which host each species lived. Years later after taxonomic identification of all specimens it was discovered that they were all Dana's brittle star. Its hosts include sea urchins, sponges, sea whips and bryozoans.

Ophiothrix caespitosa

FAMILY: Ophiotrichidae
SCIENTIFIC NAME: *Ophiothrix caespitosa*
COMMON NAME: Spiny-armed Brittle Star
DISTRIBUTION: TI–WP; WT/S
HABITAT: Rocky reefs; rocky shores; rubble; seagrass; sand

GENERAL WATER DEPTH: Low tide to 183 m (600 ft)

FOOD HABIT: Omnivorous: plankton

SIZE: 50 mm (2 in)

DESCRIPTION: Common across the southern half of the Indian and Pacific oceans, the spiny-armed brittle star lives in a variety of niches; it is found beneath rocks and stones and also inhabits holes and spaces in many other animal colonies. It has been found living with tube worms, bryozoans, ascidians, sponges and corals as well as in the holdfasts of kelp and beneath algae. It is usually found in communities of individuals of all sizes. The colour and shape of the soft disc is often quite variable. In the hundreds of specimens observed by the author all have had the prominent red stripes on the arms; even the tiny juveniles. In this genus there are five or six closely related species, and only a trained taxonomist can tell them apart when they are preserved.

Ophiothrix ciliaris

FAMILY: Ophiotrichidae

SCIENTIFIC NAME: *Ophiothrix ciliaris*

COMMON NAME: Hairy Brittle Star

DISTRIBUTION: TI–WP; WT/S

HABITAT: Rocky reefs; coral reefs

GENERAL WATER DEPTH: Low tide to 80 m (263 ft)

FOOD HABIT: Omnivorous: plankton

SIZE: 30 mm (1.5 in)

DESCRIPTION: Although the hairy brittle star is commonly found inhabiting sponges, it may also live beneath rocks and rubble. Gregarious by nature, it is not uncommon to find dozens of specimens all living in the same sponge. This species is extremely diverse in colouration and in numbers and sizes of spines on the dorsal surface, and it is these extremes that make it necessary to have specimens checked by a taxonomist for accurate identification. Sponge-dwelling brittle stars take advantage of the current activated by the sponge, drawing water into

itself for oxygen and food. By stealing from the sponge's efforts the brittle stars obtain plankton for food without having to find it themselves. They also use the sponge for protection from predators. Most sponge-dwelling brittle stars have very spiny arms.

Ophiothrix fragilis

FAMILY: Ophiotrichidae

SCIENTIFIC NAME: *Ophiothrix fragilis*

COMMON NAME: Common Brittle Star

DISTRIBUTION: CT/N; EA

HABITAT: Hard and muddy substrate

GENERAL WATER DEPTH: 0–475 m (1558 ft)

FOOD HABIT: Omnivorous: algae; small invertebrates; plankton

SIZE: Disc up to 20 mm (0.8 in); arms up to 100 mm (3.9 in) long

DESCRIPTION: Often found in large aggregations, the common brittle star usually dwells under stones or in plant growth. The central disc is generally very colourful and the arms have contrasting light and dark bands, as well as prominent spines. At deeper habitats the central disc is more intensely coloured and the spines longer and more fragile. The disc is most often pentagonal. This brittle star has very diverse feeding methods: it may graze on algae, feed on carrion, capture small prey using its coiling arms or by suspending mucous nets, or rake the water's surface film. The slightest touch to the common brittle star may in some cases induce self-mutilation (autotomy), although it is possible to take whole specimens with care.

FAMILY: Ophiotrihidae

SCIENTIFIC NAME: *Ophiothrix spiculata*

COMMON NAME: Spiculate Brittle Star

DISTRIBUTION: EP

HABITAT: Rocks; algae

GENERAL WATER DEPTH: Subtidal to 2000 m (6562 ft)

FOOD HABIT: Carnivorous: plankton

SIZE: 140 mm (5.5 in)

DESCRIPTION: The arm length is five to eight times the diameter of the disc.

Ophiothrix spiculata

Colouration is extremely variable. Prominent spines appear on the arms and disc. This occasionally abundant species is generally found with one or more of its arms anchored in rock crevices. All free arms extend into the water to coil around small organisms or to trap them in sticky mucus.

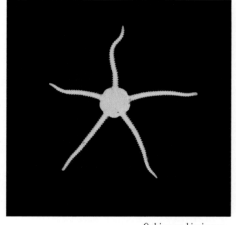

Ophioceres bispinosus

FAMILY: Ophiuridae

SCIENTIFIC NAME: *Ophioceres bispinosus*

COMMON NAME: Two-spine Brittle Star

DISTRIBUTION: WT/S; CT/S

HABITAT: Rocky reefs; rocky shores

GENERAL WATER DEPTH: Low tide to 20 m (66 ft)

FOOD HABIT: Omnivorous: detritus

SIZE: 50 mm (2 in)

DESCRIPTION: A rare species for about 60 years after its discovery, the two-spine brittle star is still relatively difficult to find. It lives beneath rocks, stones and rubble on sheltered and exposed coasts in south-western Australia and seems to be at its highest abundance in 3–5 m (10–16 ft) of water. Failure to find it was due to the collection methods of some of the early collectors and recorders of our subtidal fauna. As this species is a reef-dweller, dredging was unsuccessful. Because of its small size, insignificant colour and plain design, observers usually regard it as a juvenile of some other species. It is not uncommon to find several under one rock. Like most brittle stars it is sensitive to light and, when exposed, speedily retreats to concealment. Colour varies little, although some specimens have grey stripes on their arms.

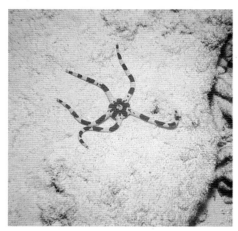

Ophiolepis superba

FAMILY: Ophiuridae
SCIENTIFIC NAME: *Ophiolepis superba*
COMMON NAME: Superb Brittle Star
DISTRIBUTION: TI–WP; WT/S
HABITAT: Coral reefs
GENERAL WATER DEPTH: Low tide to 20 m (66 ft)
FOOD HABIT: Omnivorous
SIZE: 100 mm (4 in)
DESCRIPTION: The superb brittle star has very distinct markings so it is relatively easy to identify in the field. The disc is a basic white, ochre or yellowish colour; the pattern on the disc and the stripes on the legs can be chocolate, green or red. This species lives beneath dead coral slabs that are on or close to sand. Like most of its relatives it is nocturnal. Its structure is quite robust; it is not fragile like the brittle stars with long spines on their arms. Generally considered a tropical species, the superb brittle star is nevertheless found in southern waters though it is strictly a resident of subtidal waters there and hardly as common as it is in the tropics. Although some brittle stars are gregarious, the species is generally found to be either solitary or, at most, in pairs.

FAMILY: Ophiuridae
SCIENTIFIC NAME: *Ophiura texturata*
COMMON NAME: Textured Brittle Star
DISTRIBUTION: CT/N; EA
HABITAT: Sandy or muddy substrates
GENERAL WATER DEPTH: 0–300 m (984 ft)
FOOD HABIT: Carnivorous: small molluscs and crustaceans
SIZE: Diameter up to 200 mm (7.9 in)
DESCRIPTION: This common species is red-

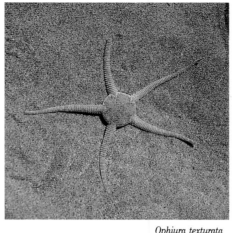

Ophiura texturata

dish or greyish-brown with a yellowish oral surface. The stout tapering arms are edged with short spines, and small combs of spines are found at the base of the arms. It can move 1.8 m (5.9 ft) in one minute by moving its arms in an action resembling butterfly stroke. Due to predation by fish and sea stars very few species of shallow-water brittle stars are found in the open during the day.

Arbacia punctulata

■ CLASS: Echinoidea

FAMILY: Arbaciidae
SCIENTIFIC NAME: *Arbacia punctulata*
COMMON NAME: Purple Sea Urchin
DISTRIBUTION: WA
HABITAT: Rocks
GENERAL WATER DEPTH: Shore to 213 m (700 ft)
FOOD HABIT: Omnivorous: algae
SIZE: 44 mm (1.75 in)
DESCRIPTION: Various parts of this abundant species — particularly the eggs — are used by humans as food. The body is encircled by cactus-style spines which are pink to purple with darker, unprotected areas between them. Ten rows of feet, each foot equipped with suckers, hold the sea urchin in place. The mouth, with its five grinding

teeth, is also on the underside. As its spines are venomous, this species is considered dangerous to humans and should never be touched with bare hands.

Eucidaris metularia

FAMILY: Cidaridae
SCIENTIFIC NAME: *Eucidaris metularia*
COMMON NAME: Measured Sea Urchin
DISTRIBUTION: IWP
HABITAT: Rocks and reefs
GENERAL WATER DEPTH: Intertidal
FOOD HABIT: Omnivorous: sessile invertebrates
SIZE: 30 mm (1.2 in) diameter
DESCRIPTION: The rigid test of this species is marked with a striking pattern; this is bare, in contrast with the spines which are often encrusted with a variety of organisms. The plates between the rows of tube-feet bear a massive primary spine surrounded by small spines.

Eucidaris tribuloides

FAMILY: Cidaridae
SCIENTIFIC NAME: *Eucidaris tribuloides*
DISTRIBUTION: EA
HABITAT: Rocky reefs and shores
GENERAL WATER DEPTH: Low-tide zone
FOOD HABIT: Omnivorous
SIZE: Up to 50 mm (2 in)

DESCRIPTION: The spines of this animal are large and blunt-tipped. Normally they are covered with organisms; only if they have recently been regenerated will the spines be clean. It favours rock crevices around the low-tide zone.

Goniocidaris tubaria

FAMILY: Cidaridae
SCIENTIFIC NAME: *Goniocidaris tubaria*
COMMON NAME: Thorny Sea Urchin
DISTRIBUTION: WT/S; CT/S
HABITAT: Rocky reefs; sand; rubble
GENERAL WATER DEPTH: 5–300 m
(16–984 ft)
FOOD HABIT: Omnivorous: algae; sponges
SIZE: 100 mm (4 in)
DESCRIPTION: Unique to the waters around southern Australia from the Indian Ocean to the South-West Pacific, this attractive little urchin is more common in the southern extent of its range. Although it tends to be extremely variable throughout its range, the thorny sea urchin is nevertheless easy to identify in the field. Older specimens tend to have stunted spines covered by all kinds of marine growths, while the younger ones have clean, tapering spines with alternating rows of sharp thorns. Colour varies from light pink to dark brown. Little has been recorded of its behaviour but food intake seems to be detritus, algae and some sponges.

FAMILY: Clypeastridae
SCIENTIFIC NAME: *Clypeaster tumidus*
COMMON NAME: Tumid Sand Dollar
DISTRIBUTION: WT/S
HABITAT: Sand; rubble; rocky reefs
GENERAL WATER DEPTH: 10–30 m
(33–98 ft)
FOOD HABIT: Omnivorous: organic debris
SIZE: 140 mm (6 in)
DESCRIPTION: Known only from the central coast of Australia, this high-domed, irregular urchin has been found only twice since its

Clypeaster tumidus

original description. The type was located hanging upside down in a garden house where it was being used as a flower basket. It had a number of holes reputedly made by a fishing spear. This seems unlikely as irregular urchins are very brittle and punching holes would almost certainly shatter part of the skeleton. Also it would be difficult to spear only the underneath side and not puncture the shell entirely. The holes had the appearance of having been drilled. The illustrated specimen, found by the author, was the first one known to science to be taken live. Inhabiting flat rocky reefs around offshore islands, the tumid sand dollar is not likely to be collected by dredging and will probably remain restricted to discovery by divers.

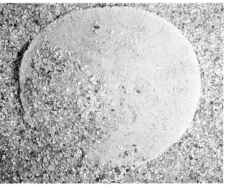

Dendraster excentricus

FAMILY: Dendrasteridae
SCIENTIFIC NAME: *Dendraster excentricus*
COMMON NAME: Excentric Sand Dollar
DISTRIBUTION: EP
HABITAT: Sand; mud
GENERAL WATER DEPTH: Subtidal to 80 m
(262 ft)
FOOD HABIT: Omnivorous: detritus; living organisms
SIZE: 75 mm (3 in)
DESCRIPTION: The abundant excentric sand dollar, which occurs in heavy localised popu-

lations, ranges from pink-grey to red to black in colour. The underside of the sand dollar is marked by a central mouth hole and an anal hole near the posterior edge. The upper surface of the test displays a central flower-like pattern, with five evenly developed petals. Populations vary significantly in colour and in the structure of their tests from one environment to another. Some populations tend to bury their posterior third or half in the sand. The excentric sand dollar moves about using a system of small spines on its underside. Feeding is accomplished by drawing in water over grooves that lead to the mouth, entrapping prey in spines on the underside of the body and grasping these with the sucker-tipped podia.

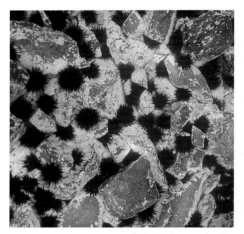

Centrostephanus rodgersii

FAMILY: Diadematidae
SCIENTIFIC NAME: *Centrostephanus rodgersii*
COMMON NAME: Rodger's Sea Urchin
DISTRIBUTION: WT/S; CT/S
HABITAT: Rocky reefs; rocky shores
GENERAL WATER DEPTH: 0–110 m (361 ft)
FOOD HABIT: Herbivorous: algae
SIZE: 230 mm (9 in)
DESCRIPTION: Ranging throughout the South-West Pacific, Rodger's sea urchin is extremely abundant and lives in both exposed and sheltered waters in coastal and offshore locations. It inhabits caves, ledges and crevices as well as the edges of rocks and hollows. Although it may be seen feeding during the day, it is much more active by night. In rough seas, strands of algae that brush past in the tide, swell, or current are caught among its spines. The tube-feet immediately grasp them and transfer them to the mouth, where they are eaten. At other times it leaves shelter and scrapes encrusting algal turf from the surrounding rocks with its strong, sharp teeth. This urchin is fished commercially for its roe.

Centrostephanus tenuispinus

Diadema palmeri

Echinothrix calamaris

FAMILY: Diadematidae
SCIENTIFIC NAME: *Centrostephanus tenuispinus*
COMMON NAME: Western Thin-spined Sea Urchin
DISTRIBUTION: WT/S
HABITAT: Rocky reefs; rocky shores
GENERAL WATER DEPTH: 0–200 m (656 ft)
FOOD HABIT: Herbivorous: algae
SIZE: 170 mm (7 in)
DESCRIPTION: Confined to reefs off the south-western area of Australia, this species is far more easily identified alive than it is when dead. Whereas preserved specimens of the western thin-spined sea urchin and Rodger's sea urchin could possibly be confused, in the field the comparison speaks for itself. The living mauve colouration of the western thin-spined sea urchin is in vivid contrast to the deep velvet, green-sheened black spines of its relation. Nowhere is this species as prevalent as Rodger's sea urchin, neither is it as gregarious, although in some areas they share a similar habitat. It feeds on red algae, moving out after dark from its shelter, hollow or ledge to browse. The spines are not venomous, but they will give some initial pain and may cause local swelling.

FAMILY: Diadematidae
SCIENTIFIC NAME: *Diadema palmeri*
COMMON NAME: Palmer's Sea Urchin
DISTRIBUTION: WT/S; CT/S
HABITAT: Coral reefs; rocky reefs
GENERAL WATER DEPTH: 20–60 m (66–197 ft)
FOOD HABIT: Herbivorous: algae
SIZE: 200 mm (8 in)
DESCRIPTION: Originally described from specimens collected in the 1960s by divers in deep water off New Zealand, this species is now known on reefs along the east coast of Australia where it is considered rare. The few specimens seen have a brilliant red body with the blue and white markings seen in all species of *Diadema*. The spines are brown, and juvenile urchins have striped spines similar to those of the spiny sea urchin (*D. setosum*). The anal cone of Palmer's sea urchin is light brown with an intense black patch at the top. This species should not be handled as its spines are venomous.

Diadema savignyi

FAMILY: Diadematidae
SCIENTIFIC NAME: *Diadema savignyi*
COMMON NAME: Savigny's Sea Urchin
DISTRIBUTION: TI–WP; WT/S
HABITAT: Coral reefs; rocky reefs; sea shores
GENERAL WATER DEPTH: 0–25 m (82 ft)
FOOD HABIT: Herbivorous: algae
SIZE: 230 mm (9 in)
DESCRIPTION: The spiny sea urchin *Diadema setosum*, which is venomous, has an orange anal ring with white and blue markings on the test; Savigny's sea urchin has a black anal cone and no white on the body. However all specimens photographed by the author (identified from collected specimens by trained taxonomists) have white spots on the body and the one illustrated confuses the issue even more. Found in small pockets in reefs or around rocks, Savigny's sea urchin has a wide range throughout the Indo-Pacific region. At least one species of commensal shrimp lives among the spines. Creeping ctenophores are also present on some, wrapped around the spines.

FAMILY: Diadematidae
SCIENTIFIC NAME: *Echinothrix calamaris*
COMMON NAME: Banded Sea Urchin
DISTRIBUTION: TI–WP; WT/S
HABITAT: Coral reefs; rocky reefs; rocky shores
GENERAL WATER DEPTH: 0–15 m (49 ft)
FOOD HABIT: Herbivorous: algae
SIZE: 250 mm (10 in)
DESCRIPTION: From the Indian Ocean to the Red Sea, and from Hawaii to Tahiti, this species is one of the most striking tropical sea urchins. Confined to shadowy recesses within the reef during the day, it moves out of hiding at night to feed on algae and detritus deposits. Juvenile specimens live beneath coral slabs and often have pure white primary spines. The banded sea urchin should be avoided and certainly not touched as its secondary spines are extremely fine and sharp and capable of penetrating most gloves. These spines are highly venomous and cause painful wounds. Owing to its secretive habits little of its behaviour has been recorded. Undetermined species of commensal shrimps live among its spines, as well as the small cardinal fish (*Apogon* sp.).

FAMILY: Diadematidae
SCIENTIFIC NAME: *Echinothrix diadema*
COMMON NAME: Diadem Sea Urchin
DISTRIBUTION: TI–WP
HABITAT: Coral reefs; rocky reefs and shores
GENERAL WATER DEPTH: 0–25 m (82 ft)
FOOD HABIT: Herbivorous: algae
SIZE: 230 mm (9 in)
DESCRIPTION: Not commonly seen on reefs during daylight hours, these relatively large

Echinothrix diadema

velvet-black (or dark crimson in the Red Sea) urchins hide under ledges and in caves along the reef edges. They are conspicuous during the day in shallow protected areas where they feed on algae scraped from dead coral surfaces in the shallows. Specimens 230 mm (9 in) across the larger spines have been observed. The finer intermediate spines are capable of a very painful sting. This species appears to be more prevalent in the Indian Ocean than it is on the Pacific reefs.

Echinus esculentus

FAMILY: Echinidae
SCIENTIFIC NAME: *Echinus esculentus*
COMMON NAME: Edible Sea Urchin
DISTRIBUTION: CT/N
HABITAT: Rocky reefs and shores
GENERAL WATER DEPTH: 0–50 m (0–164 ft)
FOOD HABIT: Herbivorous: algae and encrusting animals
SIZE: Test diameter up to 200 mm (7.9 in)
DESCRIPTION: One of the sea urchins most frequently found on European coasts, the edible sea urchin is generally flesh coloured. Numerous small spines cover the test; this is slightly flattened in juveniles but high-domed in adult specimens. The ventral mouth has five prominent jaws. Extensible suckered tube-feet are used for propulsion. In spring, the edible sea urchin migrates

from deeper zones to coastal regions. Spawning usually occurs in spring and summer in the Northern Hemisphere, and is dependent on temperature.

Echinometra mathaei

FAMILY: Echinometridae
SCIENTIFIC NAME: *Echinometra mathaei*
COMMON NAME: Mathae's Sea Urchin
DISTRIBUTION: TI–WP
HABITAT: Coral reefs; rocky reefs; rocky shores; tide pools
GENERAL WATER DEPTH: 0–5 m (16 ft)
FOOD HABIT: Herbivorous: algae
SIZE: 85 mm (3 in)
DESCRIPTION: Ranging from the Red Sea to the South-West Pacific, Mathae's sea urchin is a cosmopolitan rock-boring species that thrives in the rugged conditions of exposed intertidal situations. Occupying reef and lagoon areas, it inhabits burrowed out grooves in reef causeways, coral boulders, the edges and sides of inner reef pool rims and beneath dead coral slabs. The grooves are formed for protection but it is not known how long they take to produce. In most cases the grooves are old, having been occupied by many generations. This urchin is a herbivore, scraping algae from boulders and rubble close to its hollow at night and catching drifting algae. Juveniles live on the underside of coral rocks and in crevices. It can be brown, pink, green, or purple, but the spines usually have a white circle around the base.

FAMILY: Echinometridae
SCIENTIFIC NAME: *Heliocidaris erythrogramma*
COMMON NAME: Purple Sea Urchin
DISTRIBUTION: WT/S; CT/S
HABITAT: Rocky reefs; rubble; seagrass meadows
GENERAL WATER DEPTH: 0–20 m (66 ft)
FOOD HABIT: Herbivorous: algae; seagrass
SIZE: 100 mm (4 in)
DESCRIPTION: Any animal that ranges over

Heliocidaris erythrogramma

several thousand kilometres of coastline and in any number of habitats and micro-habitats is naturally subject to variation. In the purple sea urchin, variation is so significant that on first sight a South-West Pacific specimen and an Indian Ocean specimen could appear to be different species when placed side by side. There are only five major colour forms and three spine forms. Colours range from white to mauve and brown. The animal often has some form of bottom debris held on its back by tube feet. It forms homing hollows in soft rocky shores and mud, where it resides during the day. In the South-West Pacific in protected areas the spines may be long and in exposed situations they may be short. In the Indian Ocean the species has thicker spines which are often striped.

Heliocidaris tuberculata

FAMILY: Echinometridae
SCIENTIFIC NAME: *Heliocidaris tuberculata*
COMMON NAME: Tuberculate Sea Urchin
DISTRIBUTION: TWP; WT/S; CT/S
HABITAT: Rocky and coral reefs; sea shores
GENERAL WATER DEPTH: 0–20 m (66 ft)
FOOD HABIT: Herbivorous: algae

SIZE: 100 mm (4 in)

DESCRIPTION: A large, easily recognised urchin, the tuberculate sea urchin ranges out into the South-West Pacific waters as far as Norfolk Island, where it lives at various depths on exposed or sheltered coastline and around offshore reefs and islands. The species is well entrenched on the central eastern Australian mainland reefs and offshore continental islands. However, nowhere is it as abundant as it is at Lord Howe Island, where it is certainly the most common regular echinoid. This urchin feeds on algae, and in some areas the commensal shrimp *Athanas dorsalis* may be found on the underside. The spines may be long or short, depending on habitat.

Pachycentrotus bajulus

FAMILY: Echinometridae
SCIENTIFIC NAME: *Pachycentrotus bajulus*
COMMON NAME: Brooding Sea Urchin
DISTRIBUTION: WT/S (SA)
HABITAT: Rocky reefs; rubble; sea shores
GENERAL WATER DEPTH: 0–25 m (82 ft)
FOOD HABIT: Herbivorous: algae
SIZE: 35 mm (1.5 in)
DESCRIPTION: Only recently added to the South-West Pacific marine faunal lists, this small, secretive sea urchin is by no means easy to find. It lives among algae, and at first glance looks similar to juveniles of more common species. It has a dark ring at the base of the spines (unlike juveniles of non-specific relations), but it is not yet known if this a good field identification characteristic. Until more specimens are found it will be necessary to have the animal classified by a taxonomist for accurate identification.

FAMILY: Echinothuriidae
SCIENTIFIC NAME: *Asthenosoma ijimai*
COMMON NAME: Ijima's Sea Urchin
DISTRIBUTION: TI–WP
HABITAT: Coral reefs; rocky reefs
GENERAL WATER DEPTH: 10–140 m (33–459 ft)
FOOD HABIT: Herbivorous: algae
SIZE: 200 mm (8 in)
DESCRIPTION: The ijima's sea urchin is not

Asthenosoma ijimai

a well-known species even though it occurs throughout the Indo-Pacific region. It is a large sea urchin that inhabits coral and rocky reef slopes and isolated coral outcrops in channels and between patch reefs. It blends with its habitat so well that it is usually hard to distinguish. Its spines, with venom glands on the tips, produce an extremely painful sting, which may be another reason why it has been collected on only a few occasions. Two main colour forms have been observed, one predominantly red and the other yellow. Its food is algae and detritus scraped from the surface of dead coral. It is the only known host to Coleman's shrimp (*Periclimenes colemani*). Its close relative, the variable sea urchin (*Asthenosoma varia*), occurs in the Indian Ocean and as far as the Philippines.

Breynia australasiae

FAMILY: Loveniidae
SCIENTIFIC NAME: *Breynia australasiae*
COMMON NAME: Southern Heart Urchin
DISTRIBUTION: TI–WP; WT/S
HABITAT: Sand; mud; rubble
GENERAL WATER DEPTH: 0–30 m (98 ft)
FOOD HABIT: Omnivorous: detritus

SIZE: 120 mm (5 in)

DESCRIPTION: A common species throughout the South-West Pacific, the southern heart urchin is most prevalent in the lagoon at Lord Howe Island. It lives beneath the sand with only a raised bump in the substrate to show its whereabouts, and is brown throughout its range. It doesn't grow as big in the tropics as in southern waters. It spawns just on dusk in the late summer with the release of white spurts of sperm into the water; this induces the females to release eggs. The flower-like patterns of respiratory pores that decorate the dorsal surface of the skeleton make it attractive to beachcombers. An unidentified commensal worm is often found on the underside.

Lovenia elongata

FAMILY: Loveniidae
SCIENTIFIC NAME: *Lovenia elongata*
COMMON NAME: Elongate Heart Urchin
DISTRIBUTION: TI–WP
HABITAT: Sand
GENERAL WATER DEPTH: 0–88 m (289 ft)
FOOD HABIT: Omnivorous: detritus
SIZE: 90 mm (3.5 in)
DESCRIPTION: Because the elongate sea urchin spends most of its life beneath the sand it is not often seen live. However its white empty test is very common in the debris on tropical sandy bottoms. It is a far-ranging species found throughout the Indo-Pacific region. Gregarious in its behaviour, it lives in colonies and feeds on organic matter from minute animals, sand and detritus passed through its internal organs. When on the surface of the sand it erects long, sharp dorsal spines for defence. When it burrows they lie along the back. Predators include Cassidae molluscs and some sea stars.

FAMILY: Temnopleuridae
SCIENTIFIC NAME: *Holopneustes inflatus*
COMMON NAME: Inflated Sea Urchin
DISTRIBUTION: WT/S
HABITAT: Rocky reefs; rocky shores; rubble; seagrass meadows
GENERAL WATER DEPTH: 0–30 m (98 ft)
FOOD HABIT: Herbivorous: algae
SIZE: 65 mm (2.5 in)

Holopneustes inflatus

DESCRIPTION: One of three species of this endemic Australian genus found on the southern coasts, this species can be identified in the field by its colours which are fairly constant over its distribution. It feeds on algae and is quite commonly seen wrapped in the leaves of kelp, or on rocky reefs with pieces of algae attached. The algae are kept in place by the many suckers of its tube feet. The inflated sea urchin inhabits both exposed coastline and sheltered bays and inlets and is prolific at depths of 3–6 m (10–20 ft). It can be distinguished from its closest relative *Holopneustes porosissimus* by the latter's red spines.

Holopneustes porosissimus

FAMILY: Temnopleuridae
SCIENTIFIC NAME: *Holopneustes porosissimus*
COMMON NAME: Red-spined Sea Urchin
DISTRIBUTION: WT/S
HABITAT: Rocky reefs
GENERAL WATER DEPTH: 0–15 m (49 ft)
FOOD HABIT: Omnivorous: algae; sponges
SIZE: 60 mm (2 in)
DESCRIPTION: Almost always found wrapped up in algae while it is feeding, the red-

spined sea urchin eats both free-standing algae and filamentous turfs. In one observation it had been eating a sponge. The red spines on this species are a stable identifying feature over its distribution, though some specimens may be red all over. There is a certain amount of variation in the shape of the test (thick body wall), with some being higher and more narrow than others that are lower and wider.

Toxopneustes pileolus

FAMILY: Toxopneustidae
SCIENTIFIC NAME: *Toxopneustes pileolus*
COMMON NAME: Flower Urchin
DISTRIBUTION: TI–WP; WT/N; WT/S
HABITAT: Coral reefs; rocky reefs
GENERAL WATER DEPTH: 0–30 m (98 ft)
FOOD HABIT: Herbivorous: algae
SIZE: 120 mm (5 in)
DESCRIPTION: Although known to have caused the death of three divers in Japan there are no records of other injuries to divers in the South-West Pacific since specimens were discovered there in 1965. Normal handling to collect specimens (before identity was known) brought no adverse results. However as the specimens were small and only picked up on the dorsal surface there was little time for the pedicillariae to bite. Very large specimens occur at Lord Howe Island and in the South-West Pacific; these urchins have very large venomous pedicillariae that are presumed to be dangerous to touch. It is a very distinctive species and easily recognised in the field by its beautiful flower-like pedicillariae. Like many other short-spined urchins it often carries seaweed or shell valves on its back to shade it from the light. It should never be touched with bare hands.

FAMILY: Toxopneustidae
SCIENTIFIC NAME: *Tripneustes gratilla*
COMMON NAME: Cake Urchin
DISTRIBUTION: TI–WP; WT/S; WT/N
HABITAT: Rocky reefs; coral reefs; rocky shores; rubble; seagrass meadows
GENERAL WATER DEPTH: 0–25 m (82 ft)
FOOD HABIT: Herbivorous: algae; seagrass
SIZE: 150 mm (6 in)

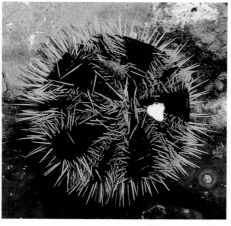

Tripneustes gratilla

DESCRIPTION: This species is widespread throughout the Indo-Pacific region and has a number of colour variations throughout its distribution. The pattern of body spaces between the spines is a reliable visual feature. Colour of the tube feet of the large, star-shaped, five body spaces and the five smaller ones may be purple, black, brown or red, and even green. The cake urchin feeds on algae and seagrass and often carries around pieces of weed and shells held on its back by tube-feet. In some areas it is sold.

Heterocentrotus mammillatus

■ CLASS: Echinoidea (Euechinoidea)

FAMILY: Echinometridae
SCIENTIFIC NAME: *Heterocentrotus mammillatus*
COMMON NAME: Slate Pencil Urchin
DISTRIBUTION: IWP
HABITAT: Coral reefs (surf zone)
GENERAL WATER DEPTH: Intertidal to 10 m (33 ft)
FOOD HABIT: Herbivorous: algae
SIZE: Diameter up to 250 mm (9.8 in)
DESCRIPTION: A distinctive feature of this species is the large, stout spines which are long and tapering; shorter secondary spines form a mosaic over the test. This animal is

able to dig and bury itself in the substratum. It is very agile; rarely seen by day, it emerges at night from very narrow crevices to move about on the reef. In the past the large spines were used to write on slates; they are now sought after to make wind chimes and jewellery.

Echinocardium cordatum

FAMILY: Loveniidae
SCIENTIFIC NAME: *Echinocardium cordatum*
COMMON NAME: Heart Urchin; Sea Potato
DISTRIBUTION: Cosmopolitan
HABITAT: Sandy or muddy substratum
GENERAL WATER DEPTH: 0–230 m (754.6 ft)
FOOD HABIT: Carnivorous: molluscs, crustaceans, worms and small echinoderms
SIZE: Test up to 100 mm (3.9 in)
DESCRIPTION: The only echinoid found worldwide, the heart urchin is so called because of its heart-shaped test which is anteriorly grooved, with four petals. This species is greyish to yellowish-grey. The test is covered with a fur of backward-pointing short spines of varying shape and functions. A burrowing species, the heart urchin is often found in high concentrations, and may be buried in sand up to 200 mm (7.9 in) in depth. The lateral spines are primarily used for digging.

FAMILY: Mellitidae
SCIENTIFIC NAME: *Mellita sexiesperforata*
COMMON NAME: Sand Dollar
DISTRIBUTION: EA
HABITAT: Coral sands and mud
GENERAL WATER DEPTH: Subtidal to 30 m (98.4 ft)
FOOD HABIT: Omnivorous: detritus
SIZE: Up to 100 mm (3.9 in) diameter
DESCRIPTION: Most often buried in sand and mud, the sand dollar is able to bury itself in two or three minutes if exposed. The

Mellita sexiesperforata

rigid test is shaped like a flattened disc, and is perforated by six slits. Almost all sand dollars live in large colonies and bury in the sand or mud.

Actinopyga agassizi

■ CLASS: Holothuroidea

FAMILY: Holothuriidae
SCIENTIFIC NAME: *Actinopyga agassizi*
COMMON NAME: Agassize Sea Cucumber
DISTRIBUTION: EA
HABITAT: Reefs and eelgrass beds
GENERAL WATER DEPTH: 0–20 m (66 ft)
FOOD HABIT: Omnivorous: detritus
SIZE: Up to 300 mm (11.8 in) long
DESCRIPTION: In this common species, the warty dorsal surface is clearly distinct from the creeping sole with many tube-feet. The commensal pearlfish *Carapus* may often be seen protruding from its anus.

Bohadschia argus

FAMILY: Holothuriidae
SCIENTIFIC NAME: *Bohadschia argus*
COMMON NAME: Eyed Sea Cucumber
DISTRIBUTION: TI–WP
HABITAT: Sand; rubble
GENERAL WATER DEPTH: 0–20 m (66 ft)
FOOD HABIT: Omnivorous: detritus
SIZE: 450 mm (18 in)
DESCRIPTION: A well-known, easily recognised, tropical holothurian, the eyed sea cucumber is found throughout the Indo-Pacific region. Although its colour may vary over its range, the pattern remains fairly constant. It is a suctorial feeder (specialised for suction). When disturbed the eyed sea cucumber may eject sticky, white threads from its cloaca. These are produced by the cuvierian organs and snare or deter aggressors. Some specimens are inhabited by small, commensal scale worms (*Lepidonotus*). Mucus from the skin of this species is reported to cause damage to the eyes. It is collected for the bêche-de-mer industry.

Bohadschia graeffei

FAMILY: Holothuriidae
SCIENTIFIC NAME: *Bohadschia graeffei*
COMMON NAME: Graeffe's Sea Cucumber
DISTRIBUTION: TI–WP
HABITAT: Coral reefs; sand; rubble
GENERAL WATER DEPTH: 5–20 m (16–66 ft)
FOOD HABIT: Omnivorous: detritus
SIZE: 250 mm (10 in)
DESCRIPTION: Found on offshore reefs and cays along barrier reefs, Graeffe's sea cucumber varies in colour from a basic light green to a light brown. Its feeding behaviour involves the intake of sediments and small animals caught up in the soft, sticky 'catching pads' of its feeding tentacles. However, in some areas this species has adopted an unusual method of obtaining its detrital food intake by 'cleaning' the settled sediment from the fronds of living algae. The holothurian's body is moderately firm to the touch, but it must be treated carefully or it will eviscerate, that is, throw out its gut and

associated organs (which may afterwards be regenerated) as a vigorous defensive action.

Holothuria hartmeyeri

FAMILY: Holothuriidae
SCIENTIFIC NAME: *Holothuria hartmeyeri*
COMMON NAME: Hartmeyer's Sea Cucumber
DISTRIBUTION: WT/S
HABITAT: Sand; rubble
GENERAL WATER DEPTH: 0–40 m (131 ft)
FOOD HABIT: Omnivorous: detritus
SIZE: 250 mm (10 in)
DESCRIPTION: Hartmeyer's sea cucumber is endemic to southern Australian waters and occurs in small, widely separated groups in areas of still water on sand or sandy patches between reefs. It feeds by taking in large quantities of sand and detritus from which it obtains organic material; the 'cleaned' sand grains and shell grit are then defecated by the cloaca. Earlier observers noted that the species showed little colour diversity.

Holothuria leucospilota

FAMILY: Holothuriidae
SCIENTIFIC NAME: *Holothuria leucospilota*
COMMON NAME: Black-fringed Sea Cucumber
DISTRIBUTION: TI–WP
HABITAT: Sand; rubble
GENERAL WATER DEPTH: 0–10 m (33 ft)
FOOD HABIT: Omnivorous: detritus feeder
SIZE: 600 mm (2 ft)
DESCRIPTION: Very common on many coral reefs throughout the tropics, this conspicuous member of the shallow lagoon reef flats and tide pools varies from deep chocolate to

black. Its body is very soft and fringed all over with very small papillae-like tube-feet. The black-fringed sea cucumber is a detritus feeder that uses extendible oral tube-feet tipped with sticky membranous pads to gather sand and minute surface debris from which it extracts organic materials. The undigested sand and solids are defecated. When threatened by contact it can eject toxic threads from its cloaca. These are extremely tough and sticky and are produced in the cuvierian organs.

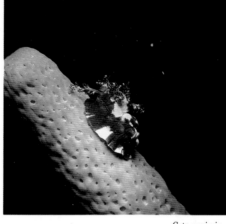

Ceto cuvieria

FAMILY: Psolidae
SCIENTIFIC NAME: *Ceto cuvieria*
COMMON NAME: Cuvier's Sea Cucumber
DISTRIBUTION: WT/S
HABITAT: Rocky reefs
GENERAL WATER DEPTH: 15–70 m (49–230 ft)
FOOD HABIT: Carnivorous: plankton
SIZE: 70 mm (3 in)
DESCRIPTION: This beautiful little Indian Ocean sea cucumber resembles a miniature boot. It has a firm external surface and throughout its range the only substrate on which it has been observed is sponges. The tube-feet on the underside are very well developed and have strong suction. Cuvier's sea cucumber feeds during the night and also on overcast days. By protruding branched, sticky tentacles from its mouth it snares plankton and suspended sediment which are then transferred into the mouth. Its association with sponges allows it to climb and feed at higher levels in the water column to take advantage of suspended food that other bottom-dwelling species cannot reach.

FAMILY: Stichopodidae
SCIENTIFIC NAME: *Stichopus chloronotus*
COMMON NAME: Dark Green Sea Cucumber

Stichopus chloronotus

DISTRIBUTION: TI–WP
HABITAT: Sand; rubble
GENERAL WATER DEPTH: 0–10 m (33 ft)
FOOD HABIT: Omnivorous: detritus feeder
SIZE: 300 mm (12 in)
DESCRIPTION: A distinctive, shallow water species inhabiting the Indo-Pacific region, this species can be seen on almost any reef flat or lagoon during the day. Although firm to the touch it is very soft and will eviscerate if handled for too long. Like most holothurians this species has amazing regenerative power. It can not only replace its internal organs but also repair major structural damage to its body walls. Colour varies little over its entire range though occasionally the orange tips on the four-corner positioned papulae may be missing. It feeds with extensible mouth tentacles tipped with soft, sticky pads which collect bottom detritus; this in turn is transferred to the mouth. The commensal scale worm *Lepidonotus* is often found on the sea cucumber's underside, as well as a curious small commensal fish of the genus *Carapus* which is known to shelter within the body.

Stichopus mollis

FAMILY: Stichopodidae
SCIENTIFIC NAME: *Stichopus mollis*
COMMON NAME: Soft Sea Cucumber
DISTRIBUTION: WT/S; CT/S
HABITAT: Rocky reefs; rocky shores; rubble; sand; mud

GENERAL WATER DEPTH: 0–25 m (82 ft)
FOOD HABIT: Omnivorous: plankton
SIZE: 175 mm (7 in)
DESCRIPTION: Quite common in the South-West Pacific ranging to New Zealand, the soft sea cucumber is generally a nocturnal plankton feeder and hides from the light during the day beneath rocks and ledges and in caves. However, like many other nocturnal foraging animals it may continue to feed into daylight hours on overcast days or if it is in deep water. Not very appealing in form or colour, this species is subject to considerable variation in pigmentation over its wide range. In general, it is dark brown in colour with black specks along the body. The craylet *Munida* sp. has been observed to have a loose association with the soft sea cucumber in the southern Indian Ocean.

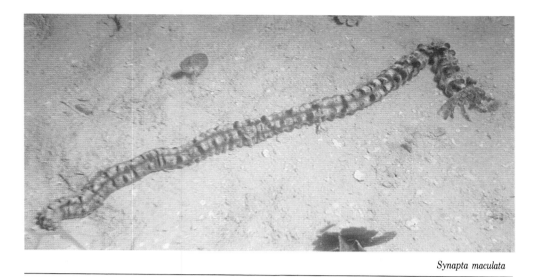

Synapta maculata

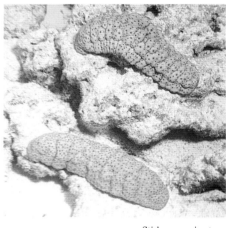

Stichopus variegatus

FAMILY: Stichopodidae
SCIENTIFIC NAME: *Stichopus variegatus*
COMMON NAME: Variegated Sea Cucumber
DISTRIBUTION: TI–WP
HABITAT: Sand; rubble
GENERAL WATER DEPTH: 0–30 m (98 ft)
FOOD HABIT: Omnivorous: detritus
SIZE: 900 mm (35 in)
DESCRIPTION: Its wide distribution, ranging from Zanzibar and the Red Sea north to southern Japan and into the South-West Pacific, allows considerable variation within the species, but this very common, large inhabitant of coral reefs is nevertheless reasonably easy to recognise throughout the entire Indo-Pacific region. The species lives on a sand or rubble bottom and feeds by passing sand and coral detritus through its intestines to extract nourishment from the organic material it contains. It often hosts the slim-bodied pearl fish (*Carapus* sp.), which takes refuge in the sea cucumber's body during the day. (It actually enters through the cloaca.) The imperial shrimp

(*Periclimenes imperator*) may also reside on its body surface.

Thelenota ananas

FAMILY: Stichopodidae
SCIENTIFIC NAME: *Thelenota ananas*
COMMON NAME: Pineapple Sea Cucumber
DISTRIBUTION: TI–WP
HABITAT: Coral reefs
GENERAL WATER DEPTH: 5–40 m (16–131 ft)
FOOD HABIT: Omnivorous: detritus
SIZE: 750 mm (30 in)
DESCRIPTION: Living in a variety of habitats, this giant-sized holothurian is without doubt the most easily recognised sea cucumber. The firm, pointed, dorsal papillae are unique to the species and give it its common name. Colour varies from brilliant orange in southern deep waters to pink, red, or brown in more tropical waters. It is a detrital feeder and generally occurs in isolated groups dispersed over a wide area. Natural predators are unknown but at least one species of scale worm, *Lepidonotus*, is commensally associated. Several scale worms may be present on the one animal and are generally situated on

the underside. This species of sea cucumber was almost fished out in north Australian waters at the height of the bêche-de-mer fishery industry at the turn of the century.

FAMILY: Synaptidae
SCIENTIFIC NAME: *Synapta maculata*
COMMON NAME: Spotted Sea Cucumber
DISTRIBUTION: TI–WP
HABITAT: Coral reefs; sand; rubble; seagrass/algae meadows
GENERAL WATER DEPTH: 0–30 m (98 ft)
FOOD HABIT: Omnivorous: detritus
SIZE: 1 m (3 ft)
DESCRIPTION: This sea cucumber is common in shallow water lagoons and on continental reefs and grass flats. Unlike other species described in this book, but in common with a number of related species, the animal is extremely soft and flabby and tends to adhere when touched. This 'sticky' feeling is due to minute hook or anchor-shaped calcium carbonate spicules embedded in the body walls. Each holothurian has spicules of various shapes, sizes and designs, and it is by classifying these spicules that taxonomists separate the species. The spotted sea cucumber has no locomotory tube-feet and it moves along by extending and contracting its body. It feeds almost continuously night and day using its branched mouth tentacles (oral tube-feet), picking up detritus and transferring food-bearing tentacles alternately into the mouth. This holothurian has recently been observed as host to the beautifully coloured little imperial shrimp (*Periclimenes imperator*).

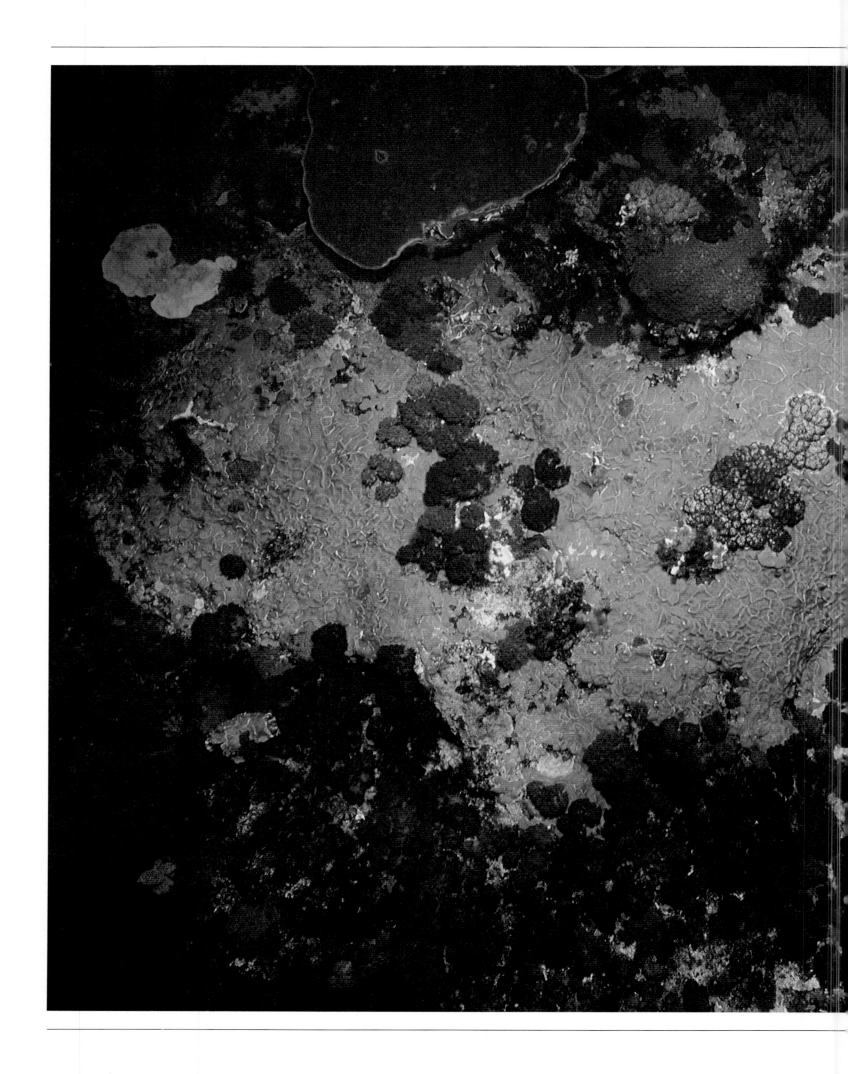

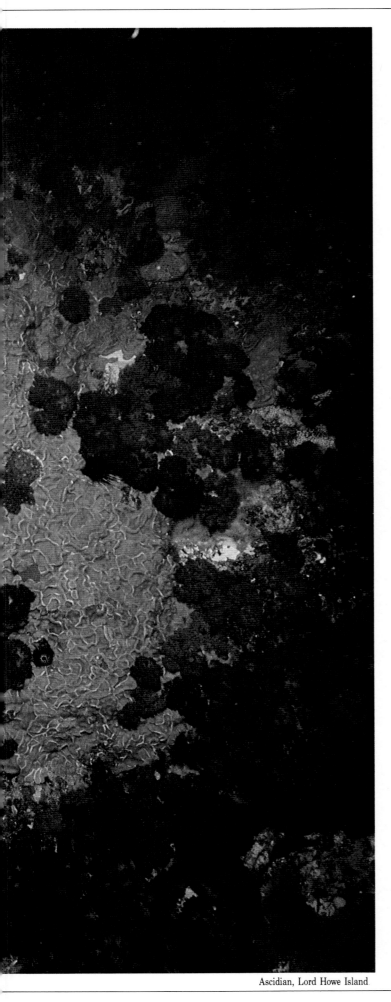

Ascidian, Lord Howe Island

SEA SQUIRTS

PHYLUM: Chordata

CLASS: Ascidiacea (Sea squirts, colonial ascidians and compound ascidians)

Sea squirts, or ascidians, may not be the best-known underwater creatures but they are the most advanced of invertebrates. Adults are strangely shaped, sac-like creatures that often eject jets of water when touched—hence the name sea squirt. On the other hand the larvae are distinctly tadpole-like and have a notochord or rudimentary backbone. It is the presence of the notochord in the larvae that shows sea squirts to be related to animals with backbones (vertebrates).

The group is entirely marine with representatives on the sea shore and in subtidal waters. They are extremely common members of the subtidal fauna and some are among the most attractive life forms in the seas.

The name sea squirt generally refers to solitary ascidians but some are colonial with many individuals either connected by a stalk to a common base or with the zooids embedded in a firm, jelly-like matrix-investing sheet of tissue. Some are beautifully coloured.

There are a number of colour variations within certain species and, until all have been recorded, identification of genera to species is best done by a specialist using a properly preserved specimen.

There are about 1350 types of ascidians in the world's oceans. Ascidians live wherever they can find their preferred settlement area; some species are specific in their choice of substrate, others are not. They can be found on reefs, rubble, algae, seagrasses, shells or rocks, in caves and under ledges and in sand and mud. There are even pelagic ascidians that drift in ocean currents and have complex life histories.

The basic tunicate or sea squirt is round or sac-like and is permanently anchored to the substrate. The body is enclosed in a tunic of cellulose (a rare substance in the animal kingdom) which is the source of its name. Each individual has two body openings: one is an inlet for water which brings oxygen for respiration and suspended plankton and detritus for food; the other is an exhalant siphon through which water bearing carbon dioxide and waste is pumped out of the body. The inhalant siphon is generally larger and nearer the top of the body. The large internal gills are ciliated and act as the pump.

In some investing compound ascidians each zooid may have a separate intake siphon but waste products are channelled into communal exhalent siphons.

Most species of ascidians are hermaphrodites. Eggs are released from the exhalant siphon and fertilised by free-swimming sperm in open water, or are held in the exhalant siphon and fertilised by sperm taken in through the inhalant siphon. The embryos in many species develop quickly, often in a few hours. This may be important in enabling them to settle and develop in suitable situations near their parents. They have also been of great value to embryologists and because of their rapid development have been very useful in experimental studies.

Pyctnoclavella detorta

Didemnum moseleyi

Polycarpa aurata

Polycitor giganteum

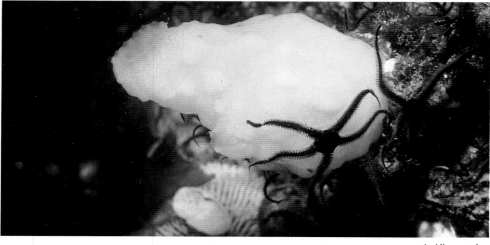

Ascidia mentula

■ CLASS: Ascidiacea

FAMILY: Ascidiidae
SCIENTIFIC NAME: *Ascidia mentula*
COMMON NAME: Sea Squirt
DISTRIBUTION: CT/N; WT/N
HABITAT: Rocky shores and rocky coasts
GENERAL WATER DEPTH: 0–200 m
FOOD HABIT: Fine detrital particles and phytoplankton
SIZE: Up to 100 mm high or more
DESCRIPTION: Each solitary individual has a smooth body, and an exhalent siphon about two thirds of the way between the terminal inhalent siphon and the base. It has a thick, greyish or pinkish body wall with rounded swellings on the surface and cartilaginous texture. This species is not colonial and is attached directly to rocks.

Phallusia julinea

FAMILY: Ascidiidae
SCIENTIFIC NAME: *Phallusia julinea*
COMMON NAME: Juline's Ascidian
DISTRIBUTION: TI-P
HABITAT: Coral reefs; rocky reefs; rocky coasts

GENERAL WATER DEPTH: 2–25 m (6–82 ft)
FOOD HABIT: Omnivorous; plankton
SIZE: 175 mm (7 in) (length)
DESCRIPTION: Reasonably common throughout the Indo-Pacific region, the species is found living on the undersides of rocks or coral slabs as well as growing from crevices and holes in corals and coral 'heads'. Living specimens have a clear translucent body with myriad small yellow spots on the outside. The intake siphon is ribbed with bright red and yellow stripes and the translucent entrance flange has bright yellow spots between the spines. The species has been reported in the literature without yellow spots; this may have been a local colour variation.

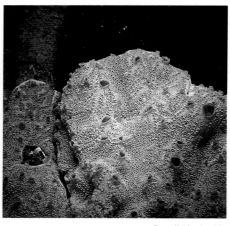

Botrylloides leachi

FAMILY: Botryllidae
SCIENTIFIC NAME: *Botrylloides leachi*
COMMON NAME: Leach's Ascidian, Star Ascidian
DISTRIBUTION: TI-WP; WT/S; EP; WA; EA; WT/N
HABITAT: Rocky reefs; rocky coasts; rubble; seagrass meadows
GENERAL WATER DEPTH: 1–25 m (3–82 ft)

FOOD HABIT: Omnivorous: plankton
SIZE: 350 mm (14 in) (colony)
DESCRIPTION: Often forming large colonies of up to 1 m (3 ft) in diameter, Leach's ascidian tends to accelerate its growth during the summer. Colour is not a good criterion for species identification as it can vary within a locality and over its range. Yellow, purple, white, brown, orange and various combinations are all common. Size and shape of the colony depend on maturity and the nature of the substrate on which the colony is growing. However it can be identified to genus level in the field wherever sufficient colony growth is present. It is a cosmopolitan species and has been recorded from the Red Sea, East Africa, the northwest Atlantic, the Mediterranean and the Caribbean.

Botryloides magnicoecum

FAMILY: Botryllidae
SCIENTIFIC NAME: *Botryloides magnicoecum*
COMMON NAME: Magnificent Ascidian
DISTRIBUTION: TI-WP; WT/S
HABITAT: Rocky reefs; rocky coasts; seagrass meadows
GENERAL WATER DEPTH: 5–20 m (16–66 ft)
FOOD HABIT: Omnivorous: plankton
SIZE: 300 mm (12 in) (colony)
DESCRIPTION: Although this ascidian is beautiful when growing as a single lobe, it is truly magnificent when many lobes grow together and sometimes cover up to a quarter of a square metre (2.7 sq ft), hence its common name. Although the base colour may range from blue to purple, the gold patterning seems to be a stable feature. In some colonies the lobes may appear to be solitary but the species is colonial and closer investigation will reveal a common base. It grows on continental inshore reefs and in bays and estuaries and appears to prefer sheltered conditions with a good current flow.

Ciona intestinalis

FAMILY: Cionidae
SCIENTIFIC NAME: *Ciona intestinalis*
COMMON NAME: Transparent Sea Squirt
DISTRIBUTION: CT/N; WT/N; CT/S; WT/S
HABITAT: Rocky shores, estuaries, rocky coasts, often in silty conditions
GENERAL WATER DEPTH: 0–500 m (1640 ft)
FOOD HABIT: Fine detrital particles and phytoplankton
SIZE: Up to 120 mm (5 in) high
DESCRIPTION: This species is solitary and non-colonial. It is a greenish translucent tubular shaped animal, bearing terminal inhalent and sub-terminal exhalent siphons. The soft and retractile body, encased in a test of cellulose, is attached to a substrate. The inhalent siphon is guarded by eight distinct lobes interposed with red or orange pigment spots. The exhalent siphon has six lobes and is similarly adorned. The retractor muscles, gut, gonads and large filter-feeding and respiratory pharynx may be visible through the body wall. This species is often found growing in great numbers on man-made structures such as piers and pilings and even in marine aquaria. It sometimes uses seaweeds as a substrate. The animal is hermaphrodite like all sea squirts. Sperm and eggs are discharged into the atrial space leading to the exhalent siphon. Fertilisation occurs in the sea and a tadpole larva is formed after about 25 hours. This has a short life span, usually around 36 hours, but is dependent on the temperature, after which it settles and metamorphoses. This tadpole larva has certain chordate characters includ-

Clavelina australis

FAMILY: Clavelinidae
SCIENTIFIC NAME: *Clavelina australis*
COMMON NAME: Blue-throated Ascidian
DISTRIBUTION: TI–WP; WT/S
HABITAT: Rocky reefs; rocky coasts
GENERAL WATER DEPTH: 5–20 m (16–66 ft)
FOOD HABIT: Omnivorous: plankton
SIZE: 175 mm (7 in) (colony)
DESCRIPTION: Colour is one of the most attractive features of ascidians, and this one adequately displays it with its incredibly intense blue colouration. The blue-throated ascidian has individual lobes joined to a common base. It occurs in areas of tidal movement along ledges and bottoms of channels. Small clumps may be found at various times of the year but during the summer there is a marked upsurge in the number of colonies and their growth. The eggs of this species are produced and fertilised within the parental oviduct and are released into the plankton as swimming larvae.

Clavelina huntsmani

FAMILY: Clavelinidae
SCIENTIFIC NAME: *Clavelina huntsmani*
COMMON NAME: Light-bulb Tunicate
DISTRIBUTION: EP
HABITAT: Rocky shorelines
GENERAL WATER DEPTH: Subtidal to 40 m (131.2 ft)
FOOD HABIT: Herbivorous: plankton
SIZE: 50 mm (2 in)
DESCRIPTION: Colonies of the light-bulb tunicate have been measured at more than 50 cm (19.7 in) across, with the individual zooids resting in dense clusters. Members of the colony occur in separate transparent tunics, each with a pair of orange bands along the distal end. They appear much smaller during the winter months, regressing into the tips of the stolons in response to lower temperatures.

Pycnoclavella diminuta

FAMILY: Clavelinidae
SCIENTIFIC NAME: *Pycnoclavella diminuta*
COMMON NAME: Diminutive Ascidian
DISTRIBUTION: WT/S
HABITAT: Rocky reefs; rocky coasts
GENERAL WATER DEPTH: 3–30 m (10–98 ft)
FOOD HABIT: Omnivorous: plankton
SIZE: 230 mm (9 in) (colony)
DESCRIPTION: The diminutive ascidian is a small, stalked colonial species that lives in groups attached to a common base. Each individual animal has two openings like the larger, more obvious, simple ascidians. Colonies vary in size depending on the season; those seen by the author have been from 30 mm (1 in) in diameter to 230 mm (9 in) in diameter (illustrated). Colonies grow continually throughout their life by budding off new individuals asexually. This is very common among most colonial ascidians. Colour does not seem to vary much within the species and is mostly white or blue. Predators or associates are not known.

Didemnum molle

FAMILY: Didemnidae
SCIENTIFIC NAME: *Didemnum molle*
COMMON NAME: Soft Didemnum Ascidian
DISTRIBUTION: TI–WP
HABITAT: Coral reefs
GENERAL WATER DEPTH: Low tide to 20 m
(66 ft)
FOOD HABIT: Omnivorous: plankton
SIZE: 250 mm (10 in) (colony)
DESCRIPTION: A common tropical species
found in the Indian and Pacific regions, the
soft didemnum ascidian is found mostly in
shallow, sheltered waters growing on dead
coral slabs from the Philippines to the
South-West Pacific. During the early years of
underwater exploration many people thought
these attractive, very common little communal ascidians were sponges because they had
only one exhalent siphon. Its secret is now
known and has often been published. These
delicate little colonies grow to around 25 mm
(1 in) and are generally grouped. The green
colour within is due to the animals being
inhabited by masses of minute blue-green
algae, which grow as symbionts in the
ascidians' cloacal cavities. The outer colour
can be white, brown, or greenish.

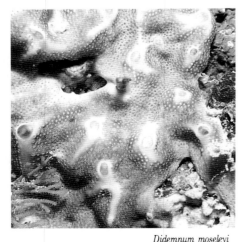

Didemnum moseleyi

FAMILY: Didemnidae
SCIENTIFIC NAME: *Didemnum moseleyi*
COMMON NAME: Moseley's Ascidian
DISTRIBUTION: TI–WP; WT/S
HABITAT: Coral reefs; rocky reefs; rocky
coasts; rubble
GENERAL WATER DEPTH: 10–20 m
(33–98 ft)
FOOD HABIT: Omnivorous: plankton
SIZE: 250 mm (10 in) (colony)
DESCRIPTION: Moseley's ascidian is an
interesting species of colonial, encrusting
ascidian which grows in investing sheets over
many surfaces. It is not confined to South-
West Pacific waters, but ranges into many
Indo-Pacific areas. The colour is variable and
can be yellow with white cloacal openings or
orange with dark rims around the openings.
The colour form illustrated is from the Great
Barrier Reef and in this area it ranges from
deep purple to light mauve with white rims
around the openings. Fairly firm to the
touch, Moseley's ascidian has a beautiful,
lattice-like outer skin. The only purple-blue
colour forms of the sea star, *Bunaster
uniserialis*, have been taken from beneath or
around encrustations of this ascidian. Normally *B. uniserialis* is brown.

Diplosoma macdonaldi

FAMILY: Didemnidae
SCIENTIFIC NAME: *Diplosoma macdonaldi*
COMMON NAME: Macdonald's Ascidian
DISTRIBUTION: EA/WA; EP/WP
HABITAT: Rocks, man-made pilings
GENERAL WATER DEPTH: Low intertidal to
50 m (164 ft)
FOOD HABIT: Omnivorous: plankton
SIZE: 20 mm (7.9 in) colony
DESCRIPTION: Small colonies of *Diplosoma
macdonaldi* commonly occur in sheltered,
quiet waters through the species' range. The
tunic of the colony is transparent, revealing
the individual zooids inside. The colony is
arranged in a sheet less than 2 mm (0.08 in)
thick and as much as 20 cm (7.9 in) across.

There are no spicules. Because of its transparent quality, this species provided some of
the first glimpses into the feeding mechanisms of the tunicates.

Sycozoa cerebriformis

FAMILY: Holozoidae
SCIENTIFIC NAME: *Sycozoa cerebriformis*
COMMON NAME: Brain Ascidian
DISTRIBUTION: WT/S
HABITAT: Rocky reefs; rocky coasts
GENERAL WATER DEPTH: 5–25 m
(16–82 ft)
FOOD HABIT: Omnivorous: plankton
SIZE: 200 mm (8 in) (colony)
DESCRIPTION: A wide-ranging species
around Australia, the brain ascidian inhabits
many lower estuaries of southern Australia,
particularly where tidal movement is great.
It lives on vertical rock faces and ledges
facing tidal channels. Most of its habitats,
though open to strong tidal influence, are
silty and at times even turbid. Colours range
from orange to grey. The species is colonial,
composed of many individual zooids interconnected with a firm jelly matrix of distinguishable shape. Coleman's flatworm
(*Pseudoceros colemani*) has been found only
in this ascidian. Parkinson's triton shell
(*Sassia parkinsoniana*) is another predator.

FAMILY: Molgulidae
SCIENTIFIC NAME: *Molgula manhattensis*
COMMON NAME: Manhatten Ascidian
DISTRIBUTION: CT/N; WT/N
HABITAT: Rocky shores and rocky coasts,
in estuaries and on man-made structures
including ships' bottoms
GENERAL WATER DEPTH: 0–90 m (295 ft)
FOOD HABIT: Fine detrital particles and
phytoplankton
SIZE: Up to 30 mm (1.2 in) in diameter
DESCRIPTION: These animals are solitary
individuals with spherical bodies and
inhalent and exhalent siphons close together.
The individual's rounded, soft body is cov-

Molgula manhattensis

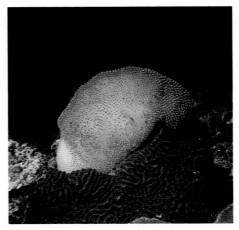

Polycitor giganteum

ered with small fibrils which sometimes adhere to particles of sand and broken shell. The body wall is grey to bluish green in colour. It may live in clusters.

Perophora annectens

FAMILY: Perophoridae
SCIENTIFIC NAME: *Perophora annectens*
COMMON NAME: Adhering Ascidian
DISTRIBUTION: WT/N
HABITAT: Rocky shores and coasts; weedbeds etc
GENERAL WATER DEPTH: 0–30 m (0-98 ft)
FOOD HABIT: Fine detrital particles and phytoplankton
SIZE: Individuals up to 1.5 mm (0.06 in) long
DESCRIPTION: These animals are colonial, but have flask-shaped individuals recognisable (with the help of a lens). These individuals are connected by or embedded in a sheet-like ground matrix which may break up as the colony ages. Individuals are transparent, bright greenish-orange and highly retractile, being able to withdraw into the dull green ground matrix when disturbed. These colonies may grow on stones, sticks and weeds, and are well-known from the lower shore rocks of California.

FAMILY: Polycitoridae
SCIENTIFIC NAME: *Polycitor giganteum*
COMMON NAME: Giant Jelly Ascidian
DISTRIBUTION: TI–WP; WT/S
HABITAT: Coral reefs; rocky reefs; rocky coasts
GENERAL WATER DEPTH: 10–40 m (33–131 ft)
FOOD HABIT: Omnivorous: plankton
SIZE: 300 mm (12 in) (colony)
DESCRIPTION: One of the most noticeable types of colonial ascidian found in coral reef shallows and the deeper coastal waters of the South-West Pacific, the giant jelly ascidian has two distinct colour forms. In one the zooids are pure white and in the other (as pictured) they are bright orange. These zooids are communal and interconnected throughout the thick, jelly-like matrix housing the colony. The mass is firm but little pressure is needed to squash it. When the colony is feeding the zooids protrude a little from their matrix; when disturbed they retract deep into the protective tissues. Like all ascidians the giant jelly ascidian is a filter feeder consuming both plankton and suspended sediment.

Aplidium sp.

FAMILY: Polyclinidae
SCIENTIFIC NAME: *Aplidium* sp.
DISTRIBUTION: CT/N; WT/N; CT/S; WT/S
HABITAT: Rocky shores; rocky coasts; sea-grass meadows; algal beds etc
GENERAL WATER DEPTH: Species of this genus are found between 0 and 800 m (2624 ft) deep
FOOD HABIT: Fine detrital particles and phytoplankton
SIZE: Dependent on the species and growth form, but occasionally colonies reach 200 mm (8 in) long or wide
DESCRIPTION: These animals are colonial ascidians with up to 50 individuals embedded in a common fleshy matrix and their exhalent siphons grouped around a common opening serving the whole colony. The grouping may be star-shaped or irregular. The individuals are narrow and elongated with their inhalent siphons guarded by six lobes. The colonies may be variously shaped.

Individuals are not easily distinguished within the colonies with the anterior two thirds or so of their body being taken up by the pharynx and gut. They are hermaphrodite and viviparous, the embryos developing while still in the oviduct of the parents. The presence of embryos may affect the colour of the colony which, like the growth pattern, varies according to species. The colonies may be encrusting, with a broad base, sessile or even club-shaped with 'stalks' of degenerating older individuals. They may be attached to rocks, stones, shells, algae or seagrasses and are sometimes found in crevices and even as pendants under overhanging rocks.

Polyclinum sp.

FAMILY: Polyclinidae
SCIENTIFIC NAME: *Polyclinum* sp.
COMMON NAME: Small-celled Ascidian
DISTRIBUTION: CT/S
HABITAT: Rocky reefs

GENERAL WATER DEPTH: 20–63 m
(66–207 ft)
FOOD HABIT: Omnivorous: plankton
SIZE: 1 m (3 ft) (colony height)
DESCRIPTION: The small-celled ascidian is a giant in actual colony height and there are few species that can match its proportions. Although much smaller examples are seen in shallower water the one pictured was photographed and a piece collected in 63 m (207 ft) of water in Bass Strait, southern Australia. It is soft to the touch (as are most colonial ascidians), yet quite firm. The few specimens observed do not seem to vary much in colour but this could be due to the small number seen and the narrow area surveyed. Growing patterns appear to be similar and once a sizable colony has been memorised by pattern, others can be recognised.

Halocynthia papillosa

FAMILY: Pyuridae
SCIENTIFIC NAME: *Halocynthia papillosa*
COMMON NAME: Red Sea Squirt
DISTRIBUTION: Medit
HABITAT: Sandy or rocky substrate
GENERAL WATER DEPTH: Subtidal
FOOD HABIT: Omnivorous: plankton
SIZE: Up to 100 mm (3.9 in) high
DESCRIPTION: Because of its vivid red colouration, the red sea squirt is most conspicuous. Its coarse leathery tunic bears many papillae; bristle-like structures surround the siphonal openings. It is a solitary ascidian found on open rocks and in caves. Red sea squirts are also known to live on silty reefs in estuaries and embayments.

FAMILY: Pyuridae
SCIENTIFIC NAME: *Herdmania momus*
COMMON NAME: Red-throated Ascidian
DISTRIBUTION: TI–WP; WT/S; CT/S
HABITAT: Rocky reefs; rocky coasts
GENERAL WATER DEPTH: 3–50 m
(10–164 ft)

Herdmania momus

FOOD HABIT: Omnivorous: plankton
SIZE: 200 mm (8 in) (height)
DESCRIPTION: A solitary species, the red-throated ascidian is by far the most commonly encountered subtidal species. It lives in almost every type of niche that a reef or rubble bottom has to offer. In clean rubble areas in deep water the white semi-transparent skin may be covered in a fine coating of hydroids, or red algae. In shallow water areas the tests are usually heavily overgrown with brown algae, so much so that often only the inhalent and exhalent siphons are distinguishable. The rims of the siphons are usually edged in red and in some areas this colouration may extend into the animal's throat. Field investigations by the author have shown the pearl fish (*Carapus* sp.) to be established living commensally in the tests of the red-throated ascidian in the South-West Pacific. This fish is normally found living inside tropical sea cucumbers (holothurians) and in pearl shells. Do not handle the species with bare hands.

FAMILY: Pyuridae
SCIENTIFIC NAME: *Pyura gibbosa*
COMMON NAME: Gibbose Sea Tulip
DISTRIBUTION: WT/S; CT/S
HABITAT: Rocky reefs
GENERAL WATER DEPTH: Low tide to 25 m (82 ft)
FOOD HABIT: Omnivorous: plankton
SIZE: 300 mm (12 in) (length)
DESCRIPTION: Very common at the lower edge of the intertidal zone, the gibbose sea tulip grows in clumps with the long stalk of each animal attached to a common base or holdfast. It seems to prefer locations exposed to moderate or rough ocean conditions and may be found on coastal and offshore reefs. It also occurs in bays and estuaries in situations adjacent to harbour entrances where there is maximum water movement. Like all ascidians, the sea tulip is a filter feeder. Each

Pyura gibbosa

animal has two openings through which a current flows, set up by internal cilia. Water is sucked through the basal inlet siphon into the body where the oxygen, edible plankton and suspended organic matter are extracted and the water is expelled through the dorsal siphon. Sea tulips are covered by an epidermis and when this skin becomes old and overgrown with encrusting organisms the animal can shed it.

Pyura spinifera

FAMILY: Pyuridae
SCIENTIFIC NAME: *Pyura spinifera*
COMMON NAME: Giant Sea Squirt
DISTRIBUTION: WT/S
HABITAT: Rocky reefs; rocky coasts
GENERAL WATER DEPTH: 5–60 m
(16–197 ft)
FOOD HABIT: Omnivorous: plankton
SIZE: 600 mm (2 ft) (length)
DESCRIPTION: The giant sea squirt inhabits coastal and offshore reefs in southern Australia. Its long, tough stalk is firmly fixed to the reef by a holdfast and allows the animal to reach up into the water column for maximum food intake. It takes a battering in rough seas and often the water movement is

so great in shallow water that the squirt hits the bottom. In various areas throughout its distribution it appears to vary in colour from bright yellow (natural colour) to pink. These are not the colours of the tunicate, but of commensal encrusting sponges that grow on the outside of the body and stalk. The small bright red commensal amphipod *Paraleucothoe novaehollandiae* lives within the yellow branchial basket of the giant sea squirt.

Pyura stolonifera

FAMILY: Pyuridae
SCIENTIFIC NAME: *Pyura stolonifera*
COMMON NAME: Cunjevoi
DISTRIBUTION: WT/S
HABITAT: Rocky reefs; rocky shores
GENERAL WATER DEPTH: Intertidal
FOOD HABIT: Omnivorous: plankton
SIZE: 150 mm (6 in) (height)
DESCRIPTION: Cunjevoi, the intertidal sea squirt, lives in large colonies at the lower reaches of the rocky reef intertidal zone in the South Pacific and is common on South African rocky shores. The area is very well defined and is often referred to by zoologists as the cunjevoi band. During low tides, when the cunjevoi is exposed to air and desiccation by the hot sun, it can avoid being dehydrated by retaining water within its body cavity. This is often squirted out intermittently, especially if the animal is stimulated. This behaviour gives cunjevoi and other ascidians the name sea squirt. The cunjevoi belongs to the simple ascidians; in some books it is called a tunicate. In past years the simple ascidians were likened to leather bottles then used to carry liquids; the Greek for leather bottle is *askidion*, from which the name derives.

FAMILY: Styelidae
SCIENTIFIC NAME: *Metandrocarpa taylori*
COMMON NAME: Taylor's Ascidian
DISTRIBUTION: EP

Metandrocarpa taylori

HABITAT: Rocky shorelines
GENERAL WATER DEPTH: Low intertidal to 25 m (82 ft)
FOOD HABIT: Herbivorous: plankton
SIZE: Colony up to 200 mm (7.9 in)
DESCRIPTION: The colony is bright red to orange, made up of round zooids that are usually less than 5 mm (0.2 in) each. The zooids appear to be tiny simple ascidians, but are in fact joined by a thin tunic encrusted on the substratum. The older a colony grows the more densely packed it appears, as newly budded zooids fill in open areas among older zooids. These types of investing ascidians are generally termed colonial ascidians.

Polycarpa clavata

FAMILY: Styelidae
SCIENTIFIC NAME: *Polycarpa clavata*
COMMON NAME: Club Ascidian
DISTRIBUTION: WT/S
HABITAT: Rocky reefs
GENERAL WATER DEPTH: 8–25 m (26–82 ft)
FOOD HABIT: Omnivorous: plankton
SIZE: 230 mm (9 in) (height)
DESCRIPTION: A solitary species found in

south-western Australian seas, the club ascidian can sometimes be seen in small groups of well-separated individuals in depths of around 10 m (33 ft) on flat reefs. Club ascidian is a good common description of the animal. It is attached to the substrate by a thick, strong, flexible stalk which allows the animal to be turned by the current or by any water movement. As a filter feeder it has two siphons, one at the top and one at the base of the club-shaped head. The basal lower inhalent acts as a siphon mouth through which water is continuously drawn into the animal to supply oxygen and food. Excess water and wastes are expelled through the upper exhalent siphon.

Styela sp.

FAMILY: Styelidae
SCIENTIFIC NAME: *Styela* sp.
COMMON NAME: Sea Squirt
DISTRIBUTION: CT/N; WT/N; T; CT/S; WT/S
HABITAT: Rocky shores, rocky coasts, estuaries and harbours
GENERAL WATER DEPTH: 0–600 m (1968 ft)
FOOD HABIT: Omnivorous: fine detrital particles and phytoplankton
SIZE: Height up to 120 mm (4.7 in)
DESCRIPTION: These animals are solitary individuals, with bodies either squat and low with a broad base, or tall and carried on a tapering stalk. Inhalent and exhalent openings are quite close together and nearly on the same level. The body is generally leathery in texture and the siphons are guarded by four lobes each. Many species shed their sperm and eggs into the sea directly where fertilisation takes place. Members of this genus are widely distributed round the world and some have been immigrants into new areas, carried on ships' hulls etc.

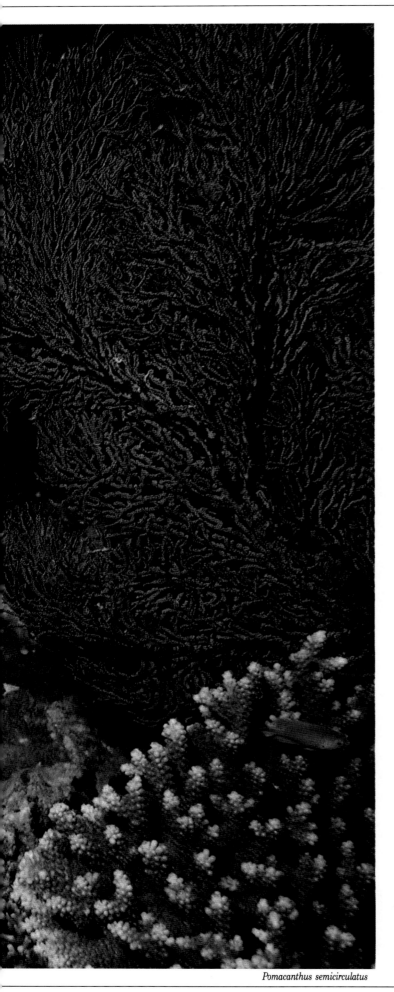

Pomacanthus semicirculatus

FISHES

PHYLUM: CHORDATA

CLASS: Actinopterygii (Bony fishes), Elasmobranchii (Cartilaginous fish — sharks and rays), Holocephali (Chimaeras), Myxini (Hagfishes), Cephalaspidomorphi (Lampreys), Sarcopterygii (Coelacanths)

Almost everyone has seen a fish, if not alive in an aquarium at least in the fishmonger's shop, kitchen or restaurant. Fish are familiar in shape and design. They are superb swimming machines, with well developed heads, sense organs, fins and a powerful muscled body for swift propulsion.

Fish are the oldest vertebrates, very distant relatives of ourselves. They are abundant in almost all aquatic habitats and they have diversified to occupy almost all available niches. About 20–25,000 species are known today.

The basic anatomy of a fish is quite well known and needs little elaboration here. The body is supported by a cartilaginous skeleton in the sharks, skates and rays, and by a hard bony skeleton in the bony fish such as salmon, cod and groper. All fish are active and tend to search out their food. This food may be vegetable in the case of some mullets and surgeonfish; plankton in the case of basking sharks, whale sharks, manta rays and herrings; and other animals (including other fish) in the case of other sharks and countless other fish species. To find food requires good sense organs and the ability to swim and catch it. Many fish respond to smell and vibrations in the water. In some species eyesight is important too.

All fish have well developed jaws and teeth to deal with the food. In the voracious the teeth may be large and of use in identification. It is possible to tell quite a lot about a fish's feeding habits by looking at its teeth. This is especially true in reef fishes where such a wide variety of food sources is available.

Most sharks and their allies need to swim to keep afloat.

They have a number of gill slits on the side of the head and their tail fin is asymmetrical. The males have modified pelvic fins, known as claspers, which enable transfer of sperm to the female. In some sharks the embryos are then laid in a horny sac (or egg case) which is usually attached to weeds or rocks, and from it a juvenile fish hatches. In other sharks the females keep the embryos in their body until they give birth. Most fish are single sexed, males or females, but many reef fishes are hermaphroditic, spending time first as one sex and then the other.

The bony fish have a swim bladder which acts as a buoyancy medium. The amount of gas it contains can be adjusted, so keeping the fish at a particular depth in the water, even if it is stationary. The gills open to the outside, as in sharks, but they are all covered in one body flap, the operculum, situated behind the mouth. there is no real 'mating' here, although males and females liberate their eggs into the sea synchronously. Some eggs drift into the plankton after fertilisation. In other cases the eggs are attached to the sea bed. A fish lava may spend some time in the plankton before developing into an adult and adopting adult ways.

Photographs of the fish are very useful aids to fish identification, particularly where shape and disposition of fins are concerned. Many fish are able to change colour rapidly and the photograph available may not match all the varieties of colouration. Fish colours respond to moods, reproductive and courtship cycles, hunting, camouflage, etc. In some cases fish need to be examined for the numbers of finrays or fins, teeth on the gill covers (opercula), and teeth in the jaws for precise identification to be possible. Most of the fish species in this book were 'shot' under natural conditions. Some were photographed against neutral backgrounds. In this encyclopedia, bony fishes are listed first, followed by shark and rays, then chimaeras.

Schooling is a phenomenon widely distributed amongst different groups of fish, and confers 'safety in numbers' from predators. Coral reef fish perhaps show the zenith of interesting underwater associations, e.g. those between clown fish and sea anemones, and those between cleaner fish and their 'patients'. The mimicry of the cleaner fish by the opportunistic sabretoothed blenny adds a further episode to this fascinating story.

Thalassoma lutescens

Agrioposphyraena barracuda

Valencienna immaculatus

Premnas biaculentus

Neosebastes pandus

Caranx latus

Lepadichthys caritus

Chaetodon plebeius

Callanthus allporti

Acanthurus dussumieri

■ CLASS: Acturopterygii

FAMILY: Acanthuridae
SCIENTIFIC NAME: *Acanthurus dussumieri*
COMMON NAME: Dussumier's Surgeonfish
DISTRIBUTION: TI–WP
HABITAT: Coral and rocky reefs; rubble
GENERAL WATER DEPTH: 5–20 m
(16–66 ft)
FOOD HABIT: Herbivorous: algae
SIZE: 400 mm (16 in)
DESCRIPTION: Dussumier's surgeonfish inhabits shallow coral reef areas down to around 20 m (66 ft) where it feeds on filamentous algae cropped from dead coral rubble and at times even from sand surfaces. Preferring lagoons and back reefs in quieter water, it is quite commonly seen on barrier reefs where it generally swims in pairs or schools, often in the company of feeding parrotfish. Like all surgeonfish this species has a razor-sharp retractable scalpel in each side of the tail junction capable of inflicting a nasty wound to those who mistakenly handle it during a night dive.

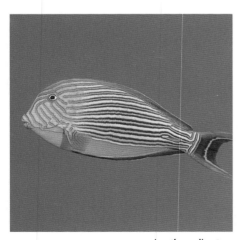

Acanthurus lineatus

FAMILY: Acanthuridae
SCIENTIFIC NAME: *Acanthurus lineatus*
COMMON NAME: Blue-lined Surgeonfish
DISTRIBUTION: TI–WP
HABITAT: Coral and rocky reefs
GENERAL WATER DEPTH: 1–8 m (3–26 ft)
FOOD HABIT: Herbivorous: algae
SIZE: 270 mm (11 in)
DESCRIPTION: The most beautiful of all the surgeonfish and one of the most common, the species lives on and around the tops of reefs where it maintains a small area of algae-covered reef surrounded by territories of its own kind. The blue-lined surgeonfish is a fast swimming fish that can be seen on reefs where there is moderate current or water movement on headlands and on the seaward platforms, and reef rims of reef fronts. Although attractively coloured it must not be handled alive with bare hands as it has razor-sharp extendible blades on the caudal peduncle.

Acanthurus pyroferus

FAMILY: Acanthuridae
SCIENTIFIC NAME: *Acanthurus pyroferus*
COMMON NAME: Orange-gilled Surgeonfish
DISTRIBUTION: TI–WP
HABITAT: Coral reefs
GENERAL WATER DEPTH: 3–25 m
(10–82 ft)
FOOD HABIT: Herbivorous: algae
SIZE: 250 mm (10 in)
DESCRIPTION: A few surgeonfish, especially the very dark coloured ones without distinguishing patterns or markings, are difficult to identify underwater. The orange-gilled surgeonfish can be almost black all over but has an orange patch near the gill, a white line around its nose, and a bright orange or yellow-edged lunate tail. It inhabits terraces and channel slopes below the reef rim, in lagoons and along back reefs. It is a fast, elusive swimmer that has a pair of sharp caudal blades.

Acanthurus thompsoni

FAMILY: Acanthuridae
SCIENTIFIC NAME: *Acanthurus thompsoni*
COMMON NAME: Thompson's Surgeonfish
DISTRIBUTION: TI–WP
HABITAT: Coral reef
GENERAL WATER DEPTH: 8–25 m
(26–82 ft)
FOOD HABIT: Carnivorous: zooplankton
SIZE: 200 mm (8 in)
DESCRIPTION: A relatively small member of the family, Thompson's surgeonfish is known to occur in schools in some Pacific areas, but so far has been observed only on offshore barrier reefs. Colour does not vary greatly; the body is bluish grey to black and the tail is lunate and a startling white. It has a distinct black spot just below the posterior end of the dorsal fin above the tail junction. The species may be seen on reef fronts and also behind back reefs, close to deep channels, where it feeds on plankton.

Naso lituratus

FAMILY: Acanthuridae
SCIENTIFIC NAME: *Naso lituratus*
COMMON NAME: Clown Unicornfish
DISTRIBUTION: TI–WP
HABITAT: Coral and rocky reefs

GENERAL WATER DEPTH: 2–25 m (6–82 ft)
FOOD HABIT: Herbivorous: algae
SIZE: 500 mm (20 in)
DESCRIPTION: Difficult to get close to underwater, the clown unicornfish is generally a solitary species that lives around continental island reefs and is frequently sighted on barrier reefs. Very easy to identify, it has a pair of thorn-like projections on the caudal peduncle and, like other members of the family, can cause injury if held in the hand. The male clown unicornfish has a long filament at the top and bottom of the tail. It inhabits reef front and lagoon areas, and is territorial, using a special crevice in the reef it occupies to escape from predators.

Naso tuberosus

FAMILY: Acanthuridae
SCIENTIFIC NAME: *Naso tuberosus*
COMMON NAME: Humphead Unicornfish
DISTRIBUTION: TI–WP
HABITAT: Coral reefs
GENERAL WATER DEPTH: 8–30 m (26–98 ft)
FOOD HABIT: Omnivorous
SIZE: 600 mm (2 ft)
DESCRIPTION: Usually sighted at a distance, swimming very fast in the opposite direction, humphead unicornfish are very difficult to approach underwater and most swim high off the bottom. The species occurs on reef fronts and in deepwater channels leading through the seaward platforms of the outer and inner reefs. It may be observed alone, in small groups, or more rarely, in huge schools. There are two immobile, recurved eels on the caudal peduncle but they are not as sharp as in the genus *Acanthurus*.

FAMILY: Acanthuridae
SCIENTIFIC NAME: *Naso unicornis*
COMMON NAME: Long-nosed Unicornfish
DISTRIBUTION: TI–WP
HABITAT: Coral reefs
GENERAL WATER DEPTH: 10–30 m
  (33–98 ft)

Naso unicornis

FOOD HABIT: Herbivorous: algae
SIZE: 550 mm (22 in)
DESCRIPTION: The long-nosed unicornfish is very easy to identify as an adult, owing to its colour, shape of its horn and the two bright blue fixed keels on the caudal peduncle. Sometimes seen alone and at other times in small groups, the long-nosed unicornfish is difficult to get close to underwater, though it is often speared. The species feeds primarily on algae which it takes from around bommies and dead reef surfaces. Juveniles do not begin to form a horn until they are about 120 mm (5 in) in size, when there is a small bump present on the forehead near the eye. Rarely line caught, it is quite edible. The blue keels may inflict wounds if the fish is held alive with bare hands.

Zebrasoma scopas

FAMILY: Acanthuridae
SCIENTIFIC NAME: *Zebrasoma scopas*
COMMON NAME: Brown Tang
DISTRIBUTION: TI–WP
HABITAT: Coral and rocky reefs
GENERAL WATER DEPTH: 2–10 m (6–33 ft)
FOOD HABIT: Herbivorous: algae
SIZE: 200 mm (8 in)

DESCRIPTION: One of the smaller surgeonfish, with a characteristic shape, the brown tang is found on mainland reefs and offshore reefs. It 'flits' above the coral, staying close to the bottom in lagoons, and along sheltered back reefs. This little fish is very popular with marine aquarists and is quite hardy. The juveniles occupy small territories and are exquisite in form and colouration.

Zebrasoma veliferum

FAMILY: Acanthuridae
SCIENTIFIC NAME: *Zebrasoma veliferum*
COMMON NAME: Sailfin Tang
DISTRIBUTION: TI–WP; IWP
HABITAT: Coral and rocky reefs
GENERAL WATER DEPTH: 2–20 m (6–66 ft)
FOOD HABIT: Herbivorous: algae
SIZE: 400 mm (16 in)
DESCRIPTION: Distinctively marked and shaped, the sailfin tang can be seen alone, in pairs, or in a school. Like most acanthurids it ranges over a large area feeding on filamentous algae. It lives in sheltered lagoons and along the edges of terraced back reefs and is sometimes seen feeding in shallow reef flats as the tide runs in. Sailfin tang range from mainland reefs to outer barrier reefs and pairs often spend much time chasing each other and displaying their 'sails'. At night it sleeps in caves and crevices with 'sails' erect.

FAMILY: Anguillidae
SCIENTIFIC NAME: *Anguilla reinhardti*
COMMON NAME: Long-finned Eel
DISTRIBUTION: WT/S
HABITAT: Estuaries; rivers; mud
GENERAL WATER DEPTH: 1–20 m (3–66 ft)
FOOD HABIT: Carnivorous
SIZE: 1.3 m (4 ft)
DESCRIPTION: Generally fished in coastal streams, rivers, ponds, dams and lakes, including those containing fresh water, the long-finned eel is becoming increasingly important as a food fish. However it is of

Anguilla reinhardti

divers have ever seen more than one or two species. The spot-tailed anglerfish is one of the largest shallow water anglerfish and despite its size, is difficult to locate as it has an amazing resemblance to the bottom growths. Like most anglerfish, it has a gross appetite and attracts its prey towards its mouth by means of a 'fishing rod' and an energetically wriggled 'lure'.

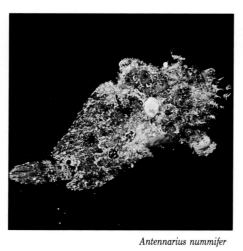

Antennarius nummifer

Antennarius striatus

lesser importance than the short-finned eel which is widely preferred for taste. European migration has influenced eating habits to a point where there now seems to be a substantial market for it. The long-finned eel is caught in nets, traps, and on hand lines and is fairly good to eat, but I believe it tastes better when jellied or pickled, rather than when fresh. The dorsal fin reaches a point on the body about double the distance from the nose to the pectoral fin.

Antennarius commerssoni

FAMILY: Antennariidae
SCIENTIFIC NAME: *Antennarius commerssoni*
COMMON NAME: Spot-tailed Anglerfish
DISTRIBUTION: TI-WP
HABITAT: Rocky reefs; mud; coral reefs
GENERAL WATER DEPTH: 1–20 m (3–66 ft)
FOOD HABIT: Carnivorous: fishes; crustaceans
SIZE: 220 mm (9 in)
DESCRIPTION: Anglerfish are often far more prevalent than the records show for unless collected by fish poison, or trawled, very few are found without some knowledge of their habitats. Underwater, only a few experienced

FAMILY: Antennariidae
SCIENTIFIC NAME: *Antennarius nummifer*
COMMON NAME: Coin-bearing Anglerfish
DISTRIBUTION: TI-WP
HABITAT: Coral and rocky reefs; rubble
GENERAL WATER DEPTH: 5–25 m (16–82 ft)
FOOD HABIT: Carnivorous: fishes; crustaceans
SIZE: 160 mm (6 in)
DESCRIPTION: A very curious little anglerfish, this species resides on mainland reefs and offshore islands and cays where it lives among rubble reefs on channel slopes and near dead coral patches behind the reefs. It has a rough-textured skin with small filaments. There are extensive filaments around the lower mouth area and the short 'fishing rod' resembles a small bunch of weed rather than the normal modified dorsal spine of other anglerfish. The coin-bearing anglerfish has rarely been illustrated in colour and although there is some variation within the species, all specimens have an ocellus at the base of the dorsal fin between the seventh and ninth ray.

FAMILY: Antennariidae
SCIENTIFIC NAME: *Antennarius striatus*
COMMON NAME: Striated Anglerfish
DISTRIBUTION: TI-WP; WT/S
HABITAT: Rubble; spongebeds; mud; seagrass
GENERAL WATER DEPTH: 3–25 m (10–82 ft)

FOOD HABIT: Carnivorous: fishes; crustaceans
SIZE: 150 mm (6 in)
DESCRIPTION: This bottom dwelling species is a problem to underwater naturalists as it can be found in a large variety of colours (black, white, orange, brick red, brown and grey); it can be patterned or unpatterned. When a pattern is present, identification is simple, but if there is no pattern, one must look harder. Each species of anglerfish has its own type of movable bait on its 'fishing rod'; the striated anglerfish has two worm-like baits, unlike any other anglerfish.

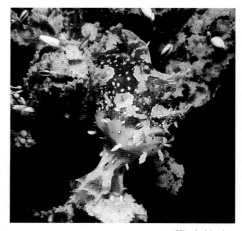

Histrio histrio

FAMILY: Antennariidae
SCIENTIFIC NAME: *Histrio histrio*
COMMON NAME: Sargassum Anglerfish
DISTRIBUTION: TI-WP; WT/N
HABITAT: Open sea
GENERAL WATER DEPTH: Surface to 20 m (66 ft)
FOOD HABIT: Carnivorous: fishes; crustaceans
SIZE: 125 mm (5 in)
DESCRIPTION: A master of camouflage, the sargassum anglerfish uses colouration,

stealth, skin appendages and its speed, to hunt, lure and eventually engulf its prey. The species lives on rafts of drifting algae borne across the sea by wind and tides and inhabits other floating debris on the surface. Specimens have been found living on partly submerged trees; even waterlogged coconuts serve as temporary residences. Although a number of anglerfish occur throughout the world, none has such patterns or colours as this species.

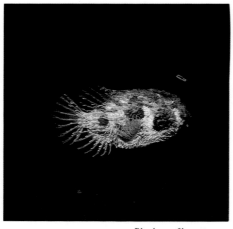

Rhycherus filamentosus

FAMILY: Antennariidae
SCIENTIFIC NAME: Rhycherus filamentosus
COMMON NAME: Tasselled Anglerfish
DISTRIBUTION: WT/S; CT/S
HABITAT: Rocky reefs; algae; wharf piles
GENERAL WATER DEPTH: 5–20 m
  (16–66 ft)
FOOD HABIT: Carnivorous: fishes;
  crustaceans
SIZE: 230 mm (9 in)
DESCRIPTION: A distinctly different species, the tasselled anglerfish can be identified in most circumstances. An inhabitant of algae-covered reefs it is extremely difficult to find. Unlike some other anglerfish, it is a strong swimmer over a short distance but only resorts to swimming when its location has been discovered and its critical distance zone penetrated. Its 'fishing rod' is extremely well developed and tipped with a double lure.

FAMILY: Aploactinidae
SCIENTIFIC NAME: Aploactisoma milesii
COMMON NAME: Velvetfish
DISTRIBUTION: WT/S; CT/S
HABITAT: Rocky reefs
GENERAL WATER DEPTH: Intertidal to
  25 m (82 ft)
FOOD HABIT: Carnivorous: crabs; molluscs
SIZE: 230 mm (9 in)
DESCRIPTION: This little fish is unlikely to be caught by line, or to be observed by most

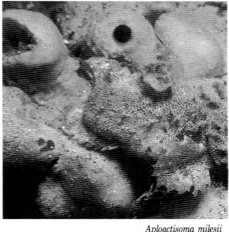

Aploactisoma milesii

divers. It lives in shallow waters in and among reefs, algae and sponges, where it remains motionless in ambush, waiting for prey to come within range. Sometimes the velvetfish will lie on its side, looking almost like a piece of dead weed.

FAMILY: Aplodactylidae
SCIENTIFIC NAME: Aplodactylus etheridgi
COMMON NAME: Etheridge's Sea Carp
DISTRIBUTION: TWP
HABITAT: Rocky and coral reefs
GENERAL WATER DEPTH: 2–25 m (6–82 ft)
FOOD HABIT: Herbivorous
SIZE: 400 mm (16 in)
DESCRIPTION: With a distinctive pattern and colours, Etheridge's sea carp is easy to identify. Endemic to the South-West Pacific, it occurs at Lord Howe Island and Norfolk Island. Seen in most areas of shallow water and algae-covered reef, the species also inhabits deeper water caves offshore. Like all members of its family, Etheridge's sea carp is diurnal. The flesh is edible, though apt to have a weedy taste.

Crinodus lophodon

FAMILY: Aplodactylidae
SCIENTIFIC NAME: Crinodus lophodon
COMMON NAME: Sea Carp
DISTRIBUTION: WT/S
HABITAT: Rocky reefs
GENERAL WATER DEPTH: 1–20 m (3–66 ft)
FOOD HABIT: Herbivorous: algae
SIZE: 450 mm (18 in)
DESCRIPTION: Considerable sexual dimorphism exists between male and female in this species; males grow larger with a much blunter snout and grey-black colouration; females are yellow-black. The sea carp feed mostly on algae but it is often hooked on a variety of baits. Usually chased and killed by most beginners with spear guns, the sea carp is still extremely common in some areas of shallow, wave-washed rocks, though it is not always easy to approach. The flesh is edible but the strong weed-like taste needs to be concealed.

FAMILY: Apogonidae
SCIENTIFIC NAME: Apogon doederleini
COMMON NAME: Doederlein's Cardinalfish

Aplodactylus etheridgi

Apogon doederleini

DISTRIBUTION: TI–WP
HABITAT: Coral and rocky reefs
GENERAL WATER DEPTH: 3–10 m
(10–33 ft)
FOOD HABIT: Carnivorous: crustaceans
SIZE: 120 mm (5 in)
DESCRIPTION: This species lives beneath
shallow ledges that have a sandy floor, is
mostly solitary and is easily approached. It
is a nocturnal forager feeding on small
shrimps and other crustaceans. Most adults
are pink but semi-adults may be silver. The
four black lines that run from the front of
the fish down the back are characteristic of
daytime colouration. At night they fade to a
blur. There is a black spot without a halo
near the tail.

Apogon kallopterus

FAMILY: Apogonidae
SCIENTIFIC NAME: *Apogon kallopterus*
COMMON NAME: Kallopterus Cardinalfish
DISTRIBUTION: TI–WP
HABITAT: Coral reefs
GENERAL WATER DEPTH: 8–20 m
(26–66 ft)
FOOD HABIT: Carnivorous: crustaceans
SIZE: 100 mm (4 in)

DESCRIPTION: This species can be found
around bommies and coral heads in lagoons
and the lee sides of barrier reef islands and
cays. Generally solitary, it can be recognised
by its very coarse scale pattern, yellow dorsal
fin, and the wide black stripe from the snout
through the eye and down to the tail. There
is a large black spot on the caudal peduncle
(tail junction). Depending on the time of day
or night, and the mood of the fish, the heavy
body stripes may be shorter and narrower
towards the tail.

Apogon ruppelli

FAMILY: Apogonidae
SCIENTIFIC NAME: *Apogon ruppelli*
COMMON NAME: Ruppell's Cardinalfish
DISTRIBUTION: TI–WP; WT/S
HABITAT: Rocky reefs
GENERAL WATER DEPTH: 1–20 m (3–66 ft)
FOOD HABIT: Carnivorous: crustaceans
SIZE: 120 mm (5 in)
DESCRIPTION: A distinctive black-spotted
species that forms small schools and lives
under ledges, overhangs, holes in pylons and
caves on both inshore reefs and offshore
islands, Ruppell's cardinalfish is often
observed during the day. It also occurs in
coastal rivers where it may be abundant in

Apogon victoriae

brackish or estuarine waters, and rather surprisingly, can be found in places where the
salinity is twice that of sea water.

FAMILY: Apogonidae
SCIENTIFIC NAME: *Apogon victoriae*
COMMON NAME: Victoria's Cardinalfish
DISTRIBUTION: WT/S
HABITAT: Rocky reefs
GENERAL WATER DEPTH: 3–15 m
(10–49 ft)
FOOD HABIT: Carnivorous: crustaceans
SIZE: 100 mm (4 in)
DESCRIPTION: Like most cardinalfish, this
species lives beneath ledges and in caves
during the day. In the breeding season the
eggs are laid by the female and immediately
fertilised by the male which swims above,
releasing milt. The male then collects the
eggs in its mouth where they stay until
hatched. This behaviour occurs in many species of cardinalfish and in summer, mature
males are easily recognised by their dis-
tended throat and gill covers. The scientific
name was for a Western Australian area
known in the 1850s as the Victoria District.
The species is confined to Western Australia
and does not occur in the State of Victoria.

Archamia fucata

FAMILY: Apogonidae
SCIENTIFIC NAME: *Archamia fucata*
COMMON NAME: Red-barred
Cardinalfish
DISTRIBUTION: TI–WP
HABITAT: Coral and rocky reefs
GENERAL WATER DEPTH: 4–20 m
(13–66 ft)
FOOD HABIT: Carnivorous:
crustaceans
SIZE: 70 mm (3 in)
DESCRIPTION: A beautifully mark-
ed species, the red-barred cardinal-
fish is found in colonies living
among corals in sheltered condi-

Cheilodipterus macrodon

tions. During the day it hovers in the coral complex of fissures and branches in the reef. Occasionally, solitary or paired specimens may reside in caves. At dusk it commences to move from the depths or the coral clumps to the outer periphery, retreating into the coral at the slightest hint of danger. At night it can be found in the open, above the coral, or on the bottom, feeding on small crustaceans.

FAMILY: Apogonidae
SCIENTIFIC NAME: *Cheilodipterus macrodon*
COMMON NAME: Big-toothed Cardinalfish
DISTRIBUTION: TI-WP
HABITAT: Coral and rocky reefs
GENERAL WATER DEPTH: 8–25 m
  (26–82 ft)
FOOD HABIT: Carnivorous: crustaceans
SIZE: 200 mm (8 in)
DESCRIPTION: One of the largest cardinalfish, this species inhabits both inshore and offshore reefs and during the day can be seen under ledges, in caves, and on the floor of deeper reef fissures, in subdued light. A solitary species, in many areas it is relatively shy, facing head first into a ledge or crevice whenever it is approached too closely. However, during the breeding season pairs are observed at which time the male may be seen to have an enlarged mouth and throat owing to the presence of eggs incubating in its mouth.

FAMILY: Apogonidae
SCIENTIFIC NAME: *Cheilodipterus quinquelineatus*
COMMON NAME: Five-lined Cardinalfish
DISTRIBUTION: TI-WP
HABITAT: Coral and rocky reefs
GENERAL WATER DEPTH: 2–20 m (6–66 ft)
FOOD HABIT: Carnivorous: crustaceans
SIZE: 100 mm (4 in)
DESCRIPTION: To the novice, cardinalfish with stripes may all look identical; however, with a good colour reference they are fairly

Cheilodipterus quinquelineatus

simple to identify. Each one has a feature by which it can be recognised. The five-lined cardinalfish has five lines from the snout to the base of the tail where a black spot is surrounded by a bright yellow patch on the caudal peduncle. Five-lined cardinalfish are seen during the day sheltering under ledges and in caves with sand bottoms; they feed at night and are generally observed alone.

Vincentia conspersa

FAMILY: Apogonidae
SCIENTIFIC NAME: *Vincentia conspersa*
COMMON NAME: Southern Gobbleguts
DISTRIBUTION: WT/S; CT/S
HABITAT: Rocky reefs
GENERAL WATER DEPTH: 3–10 m
  (10–33 ft)
FOOD HABIT: Carnivorous: crustaceans
SIZE: 40 mm (1.5 in)
DESCRIPTION: Rarely seen in the open during the day except on overcast days near dusk, the southern gobbleguts resides under ledges and in caves and is difficult to photograph. At night it drifts over the sandy bottom looking for shrimps which it seems able to detect by moonlight and starlight.

Arripis truttaceus

FAMILY: Arripidae
SCIENTIFIC NAME: *Arripis truttaceus*
COMMON NAME: West Australian Salmon
DISTRIBUTION: WT/S
HABITAT: Rocky reefs; open water; beaches; jetty piles
GENERAL WATER DEPTH: Surface to 25 m
  (82 ft)
FOOD HABIT: Carnivorous: fishes
SIZE: 910 mm (3 ft)
DESCRIPTION: Forming huge schools that migrate along the coast from the southern Indian Ocean to the southern Pacific, the West Australian salmon is completely separate from the eastern salmon, *A. trutta*, which occurs only in the South-West Pacific. West Australian salmon are caught in large quantities by both professional and amateur fishermen. In several places their flesh is canned and sold.

FAMILY: Atherinidae
SCIENTIFIC NAME: *Atherinomorus ogilbyi*
COMMON NAME: Ogilby's Hardyhead
DISTRIBUTION: TI-WP; WT/S
HABITAT: Surface waters
GENERAL WATER DEPTH: Surface to 10 m
  (33 ft)

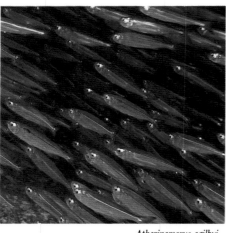

Atherinomorus ogilbyi

FOOD HABIT: Carnivorous: zooplankton
SIZE: 170 mm (7 in)
DESCRIPTION: A small, extremely common schooling species, Ogilby's hardyhead inhabits both inshore waters and the waters of offshore islands. It has a very small first dorsal fin and a black patch on the end of the pectorals. This species is netted in very large numbers for use as bait.

Aulopus purpurissatus

FAMILY: Aulopidae
SCIENTIFIC NAME: *Aulopus purpurissatus*
COMMON NAME: Sergeant Baker
DISTRIBUTION: TI–WP; WT/S
HABITAT: Rocky and coral reefs
GENERAL WATER DEPTH: 2–100 m
  (6–328 ft)
FOOD HABIT: Carnivorous: fishes;
  crustaceans
SIZE: 600 mm (2 ft)
DESCRIPTION: Commonly observed by divers along coastal inshore and offshore reefs sergeant baker is a territorial demersal that sits in the open during the day. It seems to choose lofty positions that provide good visual coverage of its immediate area. Males can be distinguished from females by the

long anterior fin ray on the first dorsal. The sergeant baker is regularly caught by fishing parties and though very bony, is good to eat.

Aulostoma chinensis

FAMILY: Aulostomidae
SCIENTIFIC NAME: *Aulostoma chinensis*
COMMON NAME: Painted Flutemouth
DISTRIBUTION: TI–WP
HABITAT: Coral and rocky reefs
GENERAL WATER DEPTH: 3–20 m
  (10–66 ft)
FOOD HABIT: Carnivorous: fishes
SIZE: 750 mm (30 in)
DESCRIPTION: Unlikely to be mistaken for any other species, the painted flutemouth has three main colour phases: bright yellow, grey with white markings, and red with white and black markings. It inhabits shallow waters around inshore and offshore reefs where it is an active, diurnal predator. Very often the painted flutemouth chooses another fish as a cover to approach schools of small damselfish, or others on which it preys. The cover fish are either herbivores or large carnivores that only hunt at dawn or dusk. By choosing this type of cover species, it can get within striking distance of an unsuspecting prey. Yellow phase forms normally choose yellow cover fish, while grey phase forms choose dark cover fish.

FAMILY: Balistidae
SCIENTIFIC NAME: *Balistapus undulatus*
COMMON NAME: Vermiculated Triggerfish
DISTRIBUTION: TI–WP
HABITAT: Coral reefs
GENERAL WATER DEPTH: 5–25 m
  (16–82 ft)
FOOD HABIT: Omnivorous: sessile
  invertebrates; algae
SIZE: 350 mm (14 in)
DESCRIPTION: A fast swimming, very distinctive species, the vermiculated triggerfish inhabits back reefs, channel slopes, bommies and reef-front terraces adjacent to drop-offs.

Balistapus undulatus

It is most difficult to get close to underwater, and takes refuge in the nearest hole or under coral at the slightest hint of danger. It is territorial and usually seen alone. Small specimens make good aquarium pets. Larger fish should not be eaten as they are believed to be poisonous.

Balistoides conspicillus

FAMILY: Balistidae
SCIENTIFIC NAME: *Balistoides conspicillus*
COMMON NAME: Clown Triggerfish
DISTRIBUTION: TI–WP; IWP
HABITAT: Coral reefs
GENERAL WATER DEPTH: 3–30 m
  (10–98 ft)
FOOD HABIT: Carnivorous: invertebrates
SIZE: 350 mm (14 in)
DESCRIPTION: This brilliantly coloured species is much sought after as an aquarium fish. It can be seen in the shallows of lagoons or at depth around terraced reef fronts on outer barrier reefs. It is generally territorial and almost always seen alone. It is not easy to get close to and when pursued, holes up or flees out of sight. The triggerfish needs careful handling as it has strong sharp teeth and will bite anything within reach. It is believed to be poisonous to eat.

Sufflamen chrysopterus

FAMILY: Balistidae
SCIENTIFIC NAME: *Sufflamen chrysopterus*
COMMON NAME: Eye-stripe Triggerfish
DISTRIBUTION: TI–WP
HABITAT: Coral reefs; rubble
GENERAL WATER DEPTH: 3–20 m
  (10–66 ft)
FOOD HABIT: Carnivorous: molluscs;
  worms; echinoderms
SIZE: 220 mm (9 in)
DESCRIPTION: Though the eye-stripe triggerfish varies in colour throughout its distribution from light brown to dark brown, the stripe below its eye is always present. It is a territorial triggerfish that inhabits sheltered back reefs and lagoons on the mainland and around continental islands and barrier reefs. Within its territory there are generally one or two coral clumps that have escape holes. When approached closely, the eye-stripe triggerfish dives into the closest hole, bites into a piece of coral and locks its dorsal spine into place. Short of demolishing the coral clump, nothing will remove the fish.

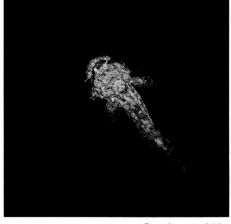

Batrachomoeus dahli

FAMILY: Batrachoididae
SCIENTIFIC NAME: *Batrachomoeus dahli*
COMMON NAME: Dahl's Frogfish

DISTRIBUTION: TIO
HABITAT: Rocky reefs
GENERAL WATER DEPTH: 1–20 m
  (3–66 ft)
FOOD HABIT: Carnivorous:
  invertebrates; fishes
SIZE: 150 mm (6 in)
DESCRIPTION: Dahl's frogfish is very localised in distribution and is only known from Shark Bay to Broome, Western Australia, occurring along the mainland and on offshore islands adjacent to the coast. This fish inhabits intertidal pools and has also been taken by trawlers from soft bottom, coral rubble sea floor. Like other frogfish it engulfs its food whole and has an extremely large appetite, often attacking prey it cannot completely swallow.

Batrachomoeus dubius

FAMILY: Batrachoididae
SCIENTIFIC NAME: *Batrachomoeus dubius*
COMMON NAME: Dubious Frogfish
DISTRIBUTION: WT/S
HABITAT: Rocky reefs
GENERAL WATER DEPTH: 3–140 m
  (10–459 ft)
FOOD HABIT: Carnivorous: fishes;
  crustaceans
SIZE: 250 mm (10 in)
DESCRIPTION: Sheltering beneath a layer of muddy sand under a ledge, the dubious frogfish is hard to see at any time, but when the ledge is underwater where visibility is poor the observer may be dubious. It lives in the central reaches of harbours and bays and prefers a silty or sandy mud habitat around or among rocky reefs. For all its muddy appearance, when viewed in the open at dusk with all its fins up it has quite a distinctive colour pattern. It is sometimes caught by hand line.

Batrachomoeus rubricephalus

FAMILY: Batrachoididae
SCIENTIFIC NAME: *Batrachomoeus rubricephalus*
COMMON NAME: Pink-headed Frogfish
DISTRIBUTION: WT/S
HABITAT: Rocky reefs
GENERAL WATER DEPTH: 10–30 m (33–98 ft)
FOOD HABIT: Carnivorous: crustaceans;
  molluscs; fishes
SIZE: 260 mm (10 in)
DESCRIPTION: The pink-headed frogfish is a shallow water coastal species that lives on and around rocky reefs in South-West Australia, where it may be found beneath ledges and under large stones. Like most frogfish it hides during the day and moves around after dusk and just before dawn in search of food. It has non-venomous spines. Specimens have been caught by line and also landed in rock lobster pots.

Halophryne diemensis

FAMILY: Batrachoididae
SCIENTIFIC NAME: *Halophryne diemensis*
COMMON NAME: Banded Frogfish
DISTRIBUTION: TI–WP
HABITAT: Coral and rocky reefs; mud
GENERAL WATER DEPTH: Intertidal to
  20 m (66 ft)

FOOD HABIT: Carnivorous: crustaceans; molluscs
SIZE: 190 mm (7 in)
DESCRIPTION: Quite a common species, the banded frogfish is rarely seen in the open during the day and is found only by searching in caves or beneath slabs of dead coral in sheltered protected shallows, or deeper sandy reef slopes. When exposed it makes little or no effort to move away until the diver moves; then it speeds off. Little is known of its breeding habits, though specimens are often brought up by trawlers from silty bottom habitats. The gill slit of the banded frogfish extends along only half to two-thirds of the pectoral fin base.

Platybelone argalus

FAMILY: Belonidae
SCIENTIFIC NAME: *Platybelone argalus*
COMMON NAME: Needlefish
DISTRIBUTION: TI–WP
HABITAT: Surface waters
GENERAL WATER DEPTH: Surface to 5 m (16 ft)
FOOD HABIT: Carnivorous: fishes
SIZE: 500 mm (20 in)
DESCRIPTION: The needlefish is an offshore species found around islands and cays of the barrier reefs. Like all belonids, it is gregarious and forms schools patrolling the surface waters of lagoons and semi-sheltered waters, feeding on small sprats. Underwater the needlefish is very shy and on the approach of a diver melts into the distance. It must move very fast when feeding or being chased by larger carnivores as I once found a skull and beak imbedded in a floating coconut.

FAMILY: Berycidae
SCIENTIFIC NAME: *Centroberyx affinis*
COMMON NAME: Nannygai
DISTRIBUTION: WT/S
HABITAT: Rocky reefs; mud
GENERAL WATER DEPTH: 8–130 m (26–427 ft)

Centroberyx affinis

FOOD HABIT: Carnivorous: fishes
SIZE: 460 mm (18 in)
DESCRIPTION: The brilliant red hues of the nannygai which is caught by line on and around reefs are well-known to most fishermen. It is a skill in itself to get the bait past the schooling 'nannies', swimming above good ground, to reach snapper and flathead on the bottom. Nannygai is commercially trawled in deeper waters where it appears in moderate quantities and is quite acceptable to eat.

Centroberyx gerrardi

FAMILY: Berycidae
SCIENTIFIC NAME: *Centroberyx gerrardi*
COMMON NAME: Red Snapper
DISTRIBUTION: WT/S
HABITAT: Rocky reefs; mud
GENERAL WATER DEPTH: 8–260 m (26–853 ft)
FOOD HABIT: Carnivorous: fishes
SIZE: 460 mm (18 in)
DESCRIPTION: In some areas, especially in shallow water, the red snapper leads a solitary life and is regularly seen in the open during the day. This seems to be in contrast with the nannygai and the swallotail nannygai which are almost always seen in

schools. The red snapper's deeper body, white-trimmed fins and coarser striping allow it to be distinguished from the nannygai. Often caught by hand line, red snapper is also trawled and is very good eating.

Centroberyx lineatus

FAMILY: Berycidae
SCIENTIFIC NAME: *Centroberyx lineatus*
COMMON NAME: Swallowtail Nannygai
DISTRIBUTION: WT/S
HABITAT: Rocky reefs
GENERAL WATER DEPTH: 15–260 m (49–853 ft)
FOOD HABIT: Carnivorous: fishes
SIZE: 360 mm (14 in)
DESCRIPTION: Easily recognised by its slender shape and characteristic tail, the swallowtail nannygai was considered until recently to be a deepwater species confined to the continental shelf. However, in some areas of southern Australia swallowtails may be seen around reefs in relatively shallow water.

Blennius sp.

FAMILY: Blenniidae
SCIENTIFIC NAME: *Blennius* sp.
COMMON NAME: Blenny

DISTRIBUTION: CT/N; WT/N; T; CT/S; WT/S
HABITAT: Rocky shores, rocky coasts, coral reefs, algal beds, sands and muds
GENERAL WATER DEPTH: 0–30 m (0–100 ft)
FOOD HABIT: Carnivorous: small invertebrates and fish
SIZE: Up to 300 mm
DESCRIPTION: There are no scales on the skins of the blenny and the jaws carry many small closely set teeth. The pelvic fins are set well forward near the gill slits and have two long rays. The head is large with large eyes and often with ornamental skin flaps. The dorsal fin is sometimes divided into two lobes by a dip or near central notch. It has worldwide distribution and can be found in rock pools and shallow water. It often shelters among rocks and weeds where its protective colouration renders it hard to see until it moves.

Escenius australianus

FAMILY: Blenniidae
SCIENTIFIC NAME: *Escenius australianus*
COMMON NAME: Pale-spotted Coral Blenny
DISTRIBUTION: TI–WP
HABITAT: Coral reefs
GENERAL WATER DEPTH: 8–20 m (26–66 ft)
FOOD HABIT: Omnivorous: algae
SIZE: 50 mm (2 in)
DESCRIPTION: Being small, blennies remain unseen by most divers and as they do not appear in nets and are of insufficient size for food, very little is known about them. However, as herbivores they have an important role maintaining the balance within the coral reef ecosystem. With well over 70 species already discovered and many new ones awaiting description, blennies constitute one of the largest families of marine fish. The pale-spotted coral blenny lives throughout barrier reef areas and is quite commonly

seen in the open, scooting about the sides of bommies and slopes, feeding on algae which it tears off with its thick lips.

Escenius stictus

FAMILY: Blenniidae
SCIENTIFIC NAME: *Escenius stictus*
COMMON NAME: Japanese Coral Blenny
DISTRIBUTION: TI–WP
HABITAT: Coral reefs
GENERAL WATER DEPTH: 1–8 m (3–26 ft)
FOOD HABIT: Herbivorous: algae
SIZE: 40 mm (2 in)
DESCRIPTION: Blennies are rather comical little fish to observe. With their large heads and big eyes they forever seem to be 'sitting up'. When feeding, the Japanese coral blenny is similar to other algae-eating blennies. It makes short, sharp, biting movements, cropping algae from the substrate, then sits back for a time to swallow before repeating the process. This bottom-dwelling species appears to be selective and has been observed to feed on filamentous algae attached to the bodies of ascidians, scooting around its territory taking a few mouthfuls at a time from each ascidian.

Exallias brevis

FAMILY: Blenniidae
SCIENTIFIC NAME: *Exallias brevis*
COMMON NAME: Leopard Blenny
DISTRIBUTION: TI–WP
HABITAT: Coral reefs
GENERAL WATER DEPTH: 5–20 m (16–66 ft)
FOOD HABIT: Omnivorous: coral tissue and mucus
SIZE: 90 mm (4 in)
DESCRIPTION: The leopard blenny has the peculiar habit of sitting in clumps of staghorn coral (*Acropora*) in a semi-vertical position, lying along the coral with its head elevated. Whereas other species of blennies are seen in the open during the day actively feeding on algae, the leopard blenny rarely leaves its coral habitat. The species is one of the few blennies that are not entirely herbivorous.

Meiacanthus atrodorsalis atrodorsalis

FAMILY: Blenniidae
SCIENTIFIC NAME: *Meiacanthus atrodorsalis atrodorsalis*
COMMON NAME: Lyretail Blenny
DISTRIBUTION: TI–WP; WT/S
HABITAT: Rocky and coral reefs
GENERAL WATER DEPTH: 5–25 m (16–82 ft)
FOOD HABIT: Carnivorous
SIZE: 80 mm (3 in)
DESCRIPTION: Known to inhabit inshore reef areas, this attractive little free-swimming blenny is generally seen around small grottoes, caves and broken bottom areas. It is somewhat similar to the false lyretail blenny *Plagiotremus laudandus* which mimics it so as to come within attacking range of a prey species. The lyretail blenny can be distinguished by a black line through the eye and the separated lobes of the main upper and lower caudal fins.

FAMILY: Blenniidae
SCIENTIFIC NAME: *Parablennius laticlavius*
COMMON NAME: Crested Blenny

Parablennius laticlavius

DISTRIBUTION: WT/S
HABITAT: Rocky reefs
GENERAL WATER DEPTH: 5–25 m
(16–82 ft)
FOOD HABIT: Omnivorous
SIZE: 50 mm (2 in)
DESCRIPTION: Identity of the Australian species has not been determined; a related species is found near Norfolk Island. Specimens can be identified by two brown bands running from behind the eyes to the tail, which is bordered on the lower side by a thin white line.

Parablennius tasmanianus

FAMILY: Blenniidae
SCIENTIFIC NAME: *Parablennius tasmanianus*
COMMON NAME: Tasmanian Blenny
DISTRIBUTION: WT/S; CT/S
HABITAT: Rocky reefs
GENERAL WATER DEPTH: 1–20 m (3–66 ft)
FOOD HABIT: Omnivorous: algae
SIZE: 130 mm (5 in)
DESCRIPTION: Active during the day, the species seems at home in exposed areas of coastline where it frequents rock pools and tidal gutters, as well as in sheltered estuaries where it may live among mussels or other sessile growths. At night the Tasmanian blenny sleeps among ascidians and soft corals and in hole or crevices. It is distinguished by its grey and white bands and striking head ornamentation.

Petroscirtes lupus

FAMILY: Blenniidae
SCIENTIFIC NAME: *Petroscirtes lupus*
COMMON NAME: Brown Sabretoothed Blenny
DISTRIBUTION: TI–WP; WT/S
HABITAT: Sand; rubble; seagrass; mud
GENERAL WATER DEPTH: 1–25 m (3–82 ft)
FOOD HABIT: Carnivorous
SIZE: 120 mm (5 in)
DESCRIPTION: This aggressive, bottom-dwelling territorial fish grows to a large size for a blenny and even though it may well originate in the tropics, it is a firmly entrenched common resident of several large estuaries in southern Australia. Not inconvenienced by the irresponsible human practice of dumping disposable objects into the sea, the brown sabretoothed blenny uses any suitable container for its residence; bottles and cans now take the place of empty sea urchin tests and shells.

Plagiotremus rhinorhynchos

FAMILY: Blenniidae
SCIENTIFIC NAME: *Plagiotremus rhinorhynchos*
COMMON NAME: Blue-lined Blenny
DISTRIBUTION: TI–WP; WT/S; IWP
HABITAT: Rocky and coral reefs
GENERAL WATER DEPTH: 5–25 m (16–82 ft)
FOOD HABIT: Carnivorous: mucus and dermal tissue of fish
SIZE: 70 mm (3 in)
DESCRIPTION: The blue-lined blenny is one of the sabretoothed blennies, having large, venomous fangs in the lower jaw. The species lives within a well-defended territory and generally resides in the apertures of dead worm shells, worm tubes or the holes of long-dead, boring molluscs or crustaceans. It moves in a snake-like fashion and often swims with other similarly-shaped fish until close enough to a prey species, when it flashes out and bites off a piece of fin. When chased it goes tail first down its hole.

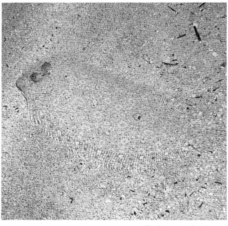

Bothus pantherinus

FAMILY: Bothidae
SCIENTIFIC NAME: *Bothus pantherinus*
COMMON NAME: Leopard Flounder
DISTRIBUTION: TI–WP
HABITAT: Sand
GENERAL WATER DEPTH: 1–30 m (3–98 ft)
FOOD HABIT: Carnivorous: crustaceans
SIZE: 230 mm (9 in)
DESCRIPTION: The leopard flounder can be caught by hand line, trawled, or seined on mainland and offshore sandy or mud bottom. Like other members of the family the species can alter its colouration to match its surroundings; however, its body pattern can be detected whether on dark or light substrate. It is a diurnal predator that hides under sand with only its telescopic eyes showing above the surface. These eyes can see in all directions and pick up any disturbance in the sand caused by buried prey. A very attractive species, it is covered with blue-edged ocelli and has a large black crest on the lateral line towards the tail.

Engyprosodon grandisquamma

FAMILY: Bothidae
SCIENTIFIC NAME: *Engyprosodon grandisquamma*
COMMON NAME: Spiny-headed Flounder
DISTRIBUTION: TI–WP
HABITAT: Sand
GENERAL WATER DEPTH: 6–35 m
 (20–115 ft)
FOOD HABIT: Carnivorous: crustaceans
SIZE: 200 mm (8 in)
DESCRIPTION: Commonly trawled on coarse sand and gravel bottom and with a colour pattern almost identical to the substrate, the little spiny-headed flounder is almost impossible to see. It can be readily identified by the black spot on either side of its tail and the prominent ocelli along the junction of the dorsal and anal fins. Though small, it is an excellent food fish.

Pseudorhombus arsius

FAMILY: Bothidae
SCIENTIFIC NAME: *Pseudorhombus arsius*
COMMON NAME: Large-toothed Flounder
DISTRIBUTION: WT/S
HABITAT: Sand; mud
GENERAL WATER DEPTH: 8–70 m
 (26–230 ft)
FOOD HABIT: Carnivorous: crustaceans
SIZE: 320 mm (12.5 in)
DESCRIPTION: Superficially similar to the small-toothed flounder, *P. jenynsii*, the large-toothed flounder can be distinguished by the

long canine teeth in the front of the upper jaw (but which may also occur in the lower jaw). It is slimmer than the small-toothed flounder and although its dorsal surface is covered with medium-size circles and brown spots it lacks the prominent ocelli of the small-toothed species. A good fish to eat, it is caught by hand line and trawled in moderate quantities.

FAMILY: Bothidae
SCIENTIFIC NAME: *Pseudorhombus jenynsii*
COMMON NAME: Small-toothed Flounder
DISTRIBUTION: WT/S
HABITAT: Sand; mud
GENERAL WATER DEPTH: 1–60 m
 (3–197 ft)
FOOD HABIT: Carnivorous: crustaceans
SIZE: 340 mm (13 in)
DESCRIPTION: A medium-size flounder inhabiting sand and mud bottom, at offshore, inshore and estuarine locations, the small-toothed flounder is commonly caught by hand line, trawled, hand seined and speared in the shallows at night. A superb table fish it can usually be distinguished by the five very prominent ocelli on the dorsal surface that do not seem to vary in position or intensity over the entire geographical distribution of the species.

FAMILY: Bovichtidae
SCIENTIFIC NAME: *Bovichtus augustifrons*
COMMON NAME: Variegated Marblefish
DISTRIBUTION: WT/S
HABITAT: Rocky reefs; jetties
GENERAL WATER DEPTH: 1–15 m (3–49 ft)
FOOD HABIT: Carnivorous: crustaceans
SIZE: 280 mm (11 in)
DESCRIPTION: For many years this species was called *Bovichtus variegatus* which is now known to occur in New Zealand and subantarctic islands. There is little possibility of confusing it with any other southern

Pseudorhombus jenynsii

Bovichtus augustifrons

ocean-dwelling species, as the colour, shape and long, non-venomous, opercular spines all aid identification. Variegated marblefish are diurnal sea-floor-inhabiting fish that can be caught by line. The male is larger than the female and they have distinct territories. Courting is a lengthy process and males are very attentive in July and August. The male in the photograph is in full courting regalia and was seen to use its pelvic fins to 'embrace' the female.

FAMILY: Brachionichthyidae
SCIENTIFIC NAME: *Brachionichthys hirsutus*
COMMON NAME: Prickly-skinned Handfish
DISTRIBUTION: WT/S; CT/S
HABITAT: Sand; mud
GENERAL WATER DEPTH: 20–200 m
 (66–656 ft)
FOOD HABIT: Carnivorous: crustaceans
SIZE: 140 mm (6 in)
DESCRIPTION: Handfish are rarely seen by divers, are unlikely to be caught on hand lines and only occasionally appear in trawls. A photograph of one in its natural habitat is rare, yet for all that this unique fish is of profound interest. The prickly-skinned handfish lives on sand or mud bottoms in and around some bottom growths. It rarely swims; instead it 'walks' along the bottom on its modified pectoral fins, aided by its forward positioned pelvics. Owing to its colouration and pattern the species is unlikely to be confused with any other handfish.

Brachionichthys hirsutus

Callionymus calauropomus

Synchiropus splendidus

FAMILY: Caesionidae
SCIENTIFIC NAME: *Caesio caerulaurea*
COMMON NAME: Scissor-tail Fusilier
DISTRIBUTION: TI–WP
HABITAT: Coral reefs
GENERAL WATER DEPTH: 2–10 m (6–33 ft)
FOOD HABIT: Carnivorous: zooplankton
SIZE: 270 mm (11 in)
DESCRIPTION: The scissor-tail fusilier is a gregarious schooling species that inhabits outer areas of barrier reefs. It can be identified by a single, broad yellow stripe that runs along the lateral line, and a greenish upper body area that runs into the caudal. Each lobe of the tail has a black or dark red streak.

Caesio caerulaurea

FAMILY: Callionymidae
SCIENTIFIC NAME: *Callionymus calauropomus*
COMMON NAME: Common Stinkfish
DISTRIBUTION: WT/S
HABITAT: Rocky reefs; rubble; seagrass; mud
GENERAL WATER DEPTH: 3–60 m (10–197 ft)
FOOD HABIT: Carnivorous
SIZE: 300 mm (12 in)

DESCRIPTION: One of the larger southern stinkfish, the species is caught by line and also trawled. It can be displayed in a large aquarium but it should on no account be eaten as its flesh contains poisonous alkaloids. It has a very prominent spine on the preoperculum with two sharp upward-pointing spikes, the front one often recurved towards the head.

Dactylopus dactylopus

FAMILY: Callionymidae
SCIENTIFIC NAME: *Dactylopus dactylopus*
COMMON NAME: Dragonet
DISTRIBUTION: TI–WP
HABITAT: Seagrass; sand; mud
GENERAL WATER DEPTH: 1–20 m (3–66 ft)
FOOD HABIT: Carnivorous: crustaceans
SIZE: 170 mm (7 in)
DESCRIPTION: Dragonets, like most other specifically coloured and patterned fish are fairly simple to identify in the field. Once seen, its colours and patterns and high positioned dorsal fin can hardly be confused with those of any other species. It has finger-like extensions on the pelvic fin that assist it to 'walk' along the bottom. The species should not be eaten.

FAMILY: Callionymidae
SCIENTIFIC NAME: *Synchiropus splendidus*
COMMON NAME: Splendid Mandarinfish
DISTRIBUTION: TI–WP
HABITAT: Coral reefs
GENERAL WATER DEPTH: 10–20 m (33–66 ft)
FOOD HABIT: Carnivorous
SIZE: 100 mm (4 in)
DESCRIPTION: Many callionymids are brilliantly coloured but none can match the mandarinfish. It is rarely seen, but occurs on fringing reefs around northern continental islands and adjacent offshore barrier reefs in both the Indian Ocean and Pacific waters. The species lives in sheltered lagoons and generally occurs in pairs, with the male a little larger than the female. The splendid mandarinfish inhabits broken coral bottom under cover. It is a very commercial fish in the aquarium trade.

Carangoides fulvoguttatus

FAMILY: Carangidae
SCIENTIFIC NAME: *Carangoides fulvoguttatus*
COMMON NAME: Gold-spotted Trevally
DISTRIBUTION: TI–WP

HABITAT: Coral reefs
GENERAL WATER DEPTH: 5–40 m
(16–131 ft)
FOOD HABIT: Carnivorous: fishes;
crustaceans
SIZE: 1 m (3 ft)
DESCRIPTION: The offshore waters of barrier reefs and continental islands are the favourite habitat of this fish. Juveniles may school, though adult gold-spotted trevally are mostly seen in pairs or small groups. It is a fast swimming, cautious species and once seen will rarely return to view. It can be caught on cut fish bait in shallow lagoons and also by trolling around coral heads or the edges of back reefs. It is an excellent fighting fish and good to eat.

Caranx ignobilis

FAMILY: Carangidae
SCIENTIFIC NAME: *Caranx ignobilis*
COMMON NAME: Giant Trevally
DISTRIBUTION: TI–WP
HABITAT: Coral reefs
GENERAL WATER DEPTH: 1–30 m (3–98 ft)
FOOD HABIT: Carnivorous: fishes;
crustaceans
SIZE: 1.4 m (5 ft)
DESCRIPTION: The trevally often swims alone or in pairs and inhabits offshore reefs and cays. In many localities it is commonly caught by bottom fishing and at times by trolling with lures. The species occurs in shallow or deep water either on the reef front or behind. It also enters lagoons and when excited by bait is extremely pugnacious, even taking food from feeding sharks. The fins are dark, there is no black spot on the operculum, and the caudal peduncle (tail junction) scutes have a number of black bands; the ventral fin has a white edge.

FAMILY: Carangidae
SCIENTIFIC NAME: *Caranx melampygus*
COMMON NAME: Blue-fin Trevally
DISTRIBUTION: TI–WP

Caranx melampygus

HABITAT: Coral and rocky reefs
GENERAL WATER DEPTH: 5–40 m
(16–131 ft)
FOOD HABIT: Carnivorous: fishes;
crustaceans
SIZE: 680 mm (27 in)
DESCRIPTION: Usually swimming in pairs, (though groups of four to six are not uncommon), the blue-fin trevally inhabits both open reef fronts and sheltered lagoons. When encountered underwater it will approach a diver at close quarters, make one or two passes and move on. In the adult, the second dorsal fin, caudal and anal fins are bright blue, with a scattering of darker blue or black spots over the head and upper half of the body. It can be caught by bottom fishing with fish bait or by trolling with lures.

Caranx sexfasciatus

FAMILY: Carangidae
SCIENTIFIC NAME: *Caranx sexfasciatus*
COMMON NAME: Bigeye Trevally
DISTRIBUTION: TI–WP
HABITAT: Coral and rocky reefs
GENERAL WATER DEPTH: 5–60 m
(16–197 ft)
FOOD HABIT: Carnivorous: fishes;
crustaceans

SIZE: 1.4 m (5 ft)
DESCRIPTION: Big, exciting fish, hundreds all around a diver in a huge school; fish in every direction, milling, swimming, banking; wall-to-wall fish; a thrilling scene, and then nothing — just empty blue. It is unbelievable: and then you remember your camera. Such is a diver's experience of bigeye trevally and sometimes I am asked why I gave up fishing with a line! It is an inshore and offshore species, common in more equatorial areas. Occasionally confused with turrum, bigeye trevally are slimmer with 19 to 21 rays in the soft dorsal fin and a very distinctive black blotch on the top of the gill cover; the soft dorsal fin is black with a white tip.

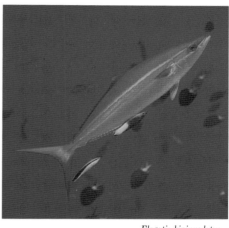

Elagatis bipinnulatus

FAMILY: Carangidae
SCIENTIFIC NAME: *Elagatis bipinnulatus*
COMMON NAME: Rainbow Runner
DISTRIBUTION: TI–WP
HABITAT: Open ocean; coral and rocky reefs
GENERAL WATER DEPTH: Surface to 50 m (164 ft)
FOOD HABIT: Carnivorous: fishes
SIZE: 1.2 m (4 ft)
DESCRIPTION: Usually caught near coral reefs, rocky reefs and in open ocean around the peaks of sea mounts, the rainbow runner inhabits both inshore and offshore areas. Like other carangids (*Seriola*), schools of these fish often follow larger fish, and vice versa, and will at times herald the presence of sharks, giant stingrays and tuna. Its shoaling behaviour is not one of tight formation; most individuals seem to maintain a wider spatial zoning than other carangids. When near offshore reefs, individuals often leave the school and swim to a cleaner-fish station. It is very nervous and erratic when being cleaned. The rainbow runner bites hard and fights well on light gear. It is frequently taken when trolling for Spanish mackerel.

Gnathanodon speciosus

FAMILY: Carangidae
SCIENTIFIC NAME: *Gnathanodon speciosus*
COMMON NAME: Golden Trevally
DISTRIBUTION: TI–WP
HABITAT: Coral and rocky reefs; sand;
 rubble
GENERAL WATER DEPTH: 5–40 m (16–131 ft)
FOOD HABIT: Carnivorous: fishes; molluscs;
 crustaceans
SIZE: 1.2 m (4 ft)
DESCRIPTION: Commonly seen in schools,
the golden trevally also swims in pairs or
small groups, especially when feeding on the
bottom. As it is feeding, its colour intensifies
and resembles the deep gold of dead fish;
normally it is silvery with yellowish head and
fins and darker cross bars on the back. The
minute teeth of the juvenile fish are entirely
lost with age. The golden trevally can be
caught on cut fish bait and is fairly good to
eat. It occurs on inshore and offshore reefs
throughout its range.

Pseudocaranx dentex

FAMILY: Carangidae
SCIENTIFIC NAME: *Pseudocaranx dentex*
COMMON NAME: Silver Trevally
DISTRIBUTION: TWP; WT/S

HABITAT: Coral reefs; sand; rocky reefs
GENERAL WATER DEPTH: 1–30 m (3–98 ft)
FOOD HABIT: Carnivorous: fishes;
 crustaceans
SIZE: 1.2 m (4 ft)
DESCRIPTION: While most silver trevally are
seen swimming in mid-water around reefs,
or picking over sandy bottom just on dusk,
some have been observed following schools of
goatfish around. As it feeds, the goatfish dis-
turbs the bottom and scares, or grubs out,
small animals which the trevally seizes. The
species grows much larger than its western
counterpart, the skipjack. Big fish have a
slightly concave forehead and a prominent
snout. The fins are pale yellow, a black spot
appears on the operculum and definite
yellow stripes occur from the caudal
peduncle (tail junction) to midway along the
body.

Seriola dumerili

FAMILY: Carangidae
SCIENTIFIC NAME: *Seriola dumerili*
COMMON NAME: Amberjack
DISTRIBUTION: TI–WP
HABITAT: Coral and rocky reefs
GENERAL WATER DEPTH: 10–50 m
 (33–164 ft)
FOOD HABIT: Carnivorous: fishes
SIZE: 1.5 m (5 ft)
DESCRIPTION: Amberjack is not
as common as the yellowtail kingfish to which it is closely related,
nor does it appear to school in
large numbers as does the kingfish.
It can be caught by trolling on the
surface and also on fish bait while
bottom fishing. Besides being
mauve coloured on the back, the
amberjack has a yellow median
stripe from the gill cover through
to the tail and a black stripe from
the nose, through the eye, to the
top of the head. It often swims
around divers on the bottom.

Seriola hippos

FAMILY: Carangidae
SCIENTIFIC NAME: *Seriola hippos*
COMMON NAME: Samson Fish
DISTRIBUTION: WT/S
HABITAT: Rocky reefs; open sea
GENERAL WATER DEPTH: 10–30 m
 (33–98 ft)
DESCRIPTION: The samson fish is a swift-
swimming species that differs from other
kingfish by tending to swim singly as well as
in pairs or in small schools. I have never
seen it in the huge aggregations often formed
by other kingfish. However, underwater its
approach is similar to that of its relatives as
it races in, circles a diver several times at a
very close range, then loses interest. It
approaches very rapidly and is usually difficult to photograph.

FAMILY: Carangidae
SCIENTIFIC NAME: *Seriola lalandi*
COMMON NAME: Yellowtail Kingfish
DISTRIBUTION: TI–WP; WT/S
HABITAT: Coral reefs; open sea; rocky
 reefs
GENERAL WATER DEPTH: 10–30 m
 (33–98 ft)
FOOD HABIT: Carnivorous: fishes
SIZE: 2.5 m (8 ft)
DESCRIPTION: A far more attractive species
than its stouter, blunt-headed relative the
samson fish, the yellowtail kingfish is elon-
gated, has a yellow tail and fins and a nar-
rower head. It is a beautiful fish, a great
fighter and excellent to eat. Those taken in

Seriola lalandi

southern Queensland inshore (South-West Pacific) waters may have unpalatable flesh due to infection with a minute sporozoan parasite.

Trachinotus botla

FAMILY: Carangidae
SCIENTIFIC NAME: *Trachinotus botla* (*T. coppingari*)
COMMON NAME: Snub-nosed Dart
DISTRIBUTION: TI–WP
HABITAT: Open surface waters; surf
GENERAL WATER DEPTH: 0–10 m (33 ft)
FOOD HABIT: Carnivorous: zooplankton; crustaceans; fishes
SIZE: 600 mm (24 in)
DESCRIPTION: Inhabiting surface waters off coastal beaches, this fish also occurs around offshore islands. It can be distinguished by the four to seven large fingerprint smudges above or on the lateral line and the very dark edges to its caudal, dorsal and ventral fins. It usually hunts its prey in or just behind the surf zone and is a fighter when hooked on light gear. Sometimes it may be seen in schools, but these are spread over some distance, giving an impression of small numbers.

FAMILY: Carangidae
SCIENTIFIC NAME: *Trachurus novaezelandiae*
COMMON NAME: Yellowtail
DISTRIBUTION: WT/S
HABITAT: Rocky reefs; jetties
GENERAL WATER DEPTH: Surface to 20 m (66 ft)
FOOD HABIT: Carnivorous: fishes; crustaceans
SIZE: 300 mm (12 in)
DESCRIPTION: Of all the various species of fish with which I have come in contact, yellowtails are the ones I associate most readily with childhood. We pulled in these little fish hand-over-fist from jetties and dock wharves. Using fly hooks and split shot,

Trachurus novaezelandiae

we filled our berley tin and raced home to have them cooked, small as they were. Now, as then, yellowtails are mainly used as bait for more sought-after species.

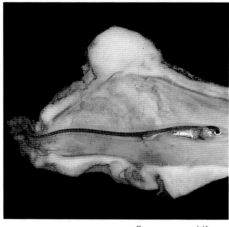

Carapus margaritiferae

FAMILY: Carapidae
SCIENTIFIC NAME: *Carapus margaritiferae*
COMMON NAME: Pearlfish; Cucumberfish

DISTRIBUTION: WT/S; TI–WP
HABITAT: Rocky reefs
GENERAL WATER DEPTH: 20–50 m (66–164 ft)
FOOD HABIT: Carnivorous
SIZE: 120 mm (5 in)
DESCRIPTION: Initially known to occur in the vents of certain sea cucumbers (holothurians) in the tropics, the red-throated ascidian *Herdmania momus* is another known host of this commensal fish. Sometimes two fish will live in one ascidian. The pearlfish stays within the body of its host during the day and comes out at night to feed on minute organisms. Related species inhabit some species of bivalve molluscs including pearl shells and winged pearl shells of the family Pteridae.

FAMILY: Centropomidae
SCIENTIFIC NAME: *Psammoperca waigiensis*
COMMON NAME: Pink-eyed Bass
DISTRIBUTION: TI–WP
HABITAT: Rocky and coral reefs; seagrass meadows
GENERAL WATER DEPTH: 1–25 m (3–82 ft)
FOOD HABIT: Carnivorous: fishes
SIZE: 380 mm (15 in)
DESCRIPTION: Found throughout many tropical seas, this species inhabits mainland reefs and some closely situated mainland islands where it congregates in small groups. It comes into shallow water during high tide and is often seen in the deep intertidal pools or reefs; in these situations it is speared by Aborigines in Northern Australia who, for some reason, are not very interested in diving for it. The flesh is white and firm and when fresh is as good as its relative the barramundi. Pink-eyed bass can be distinguished from barramundi by its colouration which is bronze brown, compared to the barramundi's green or grey.

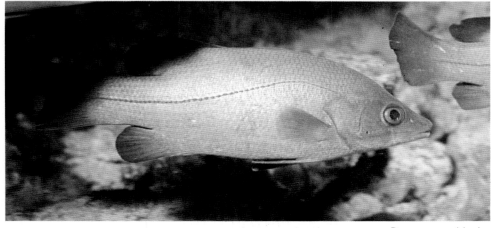

Psammoperca waigiensis

Chaetodon aureofasciatus

FAMILY: Chaetodontidae
SCIENTIFIC NAME: *Chaetodon aureofasciatus*
COMMON NAME: Golden-striped
  Butterflyfish
DISTRIBUTION: TI–WP
HABITAT: Coral and rocky reefs
GENERAL WATER DEPTH: 5–15 m
  (16–49 ft)
FOOD HABIT: Carnivorous: coral polyps
SIZE: 120 mm (5 in)
DESCRIPTION: The golden-striped butterfly-fish was the first species of butterflyfish to be photographed in its natural habitat, feeding on living coral polyps. Since the 1970s many species have been shown to feed on coral polyps and coral mucus. The species is common in some areas and may be seen alone, in pairs, or foraging in small schools, or groups (usually a number of juveniles following several adults).

Chaetodon auriga

FAMILY: Chaetodontidae
SCIENTIFIC NAME: *Chaetodon auriga*
COMMON NAME: Threadfin Butterflyfish
DISTRIBUTION: TI–WP
HABITAT: Coral and rocky reefs
GENERAL WATER DEPTH: 1–20 m (3–66 ft)

FOOD HABIT: Carnivorous: worms;
  crustaceans
SIZE: 220 mm (9 in)
DESCRIPTION: Sometimes observed swimming in pairs, the threadfin butterflyfish inhabits coral reef areas and is usually seen in relatively shallow depths with most specimens found in the 5–20 m (16–66 ft) range. Adults are readily distinguished by the thin, black, cross-directional lines, black eye bar and characteristic black ocellus below the thread-like filament on the golden soft dorsal fin. The body stripes, sloped towards the ventral fin, may be disrupted in some specimens. It is easily approached underwater and will accept captivity well if kept in a large tank. Specific food preferences of the species have so far been difficult to establish, though it is often seen picking among living coral polyps. Coral mucus may form part of its diet.

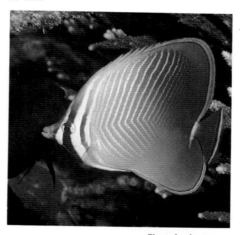

Chaetodon baronessa

FAMILY: Chaetodontidae
SCIENTIFIC NAME: *Chaetodon baronessa*
COMMON NAME: Triangular Butterflyfish
DISTRIBUTION: TI–WP
HABITAT: Coral and rocky reefs
GENERAL WATER DEPTH: 3–10 m
  (10–33 ft)
FOOD HABIT: Carnivorous: coral polyps
SIZE: 150 mm (6 in)
DESCRIPTION: An easily identified species, triangular butterflyfish adults are usually seen in pairs around back reefs, bommies, on reef flats and slopes and in sheltered lagoons. They appear to be very selective in choice of polyps and are continually on the move, rarely showing interest in anything but staghorn corals. It is very shy and elusive so it is not easy to keep in an aquarium.

FAMILY: Chaetodontidae
SCIENTIFIC NAME: *Chaetodon citrinellus*
COMMON NAME: Speckled Butterflyfish
DISTRIBUTION: TI–WP
HABITAT: Coral and rocky reefs

Chaetodon citrinellus

GENERAL WATER DEPTH: 1–10 m (3–33 ft)
FOOD HABIT: Carnivorous: benthic
  invertebrates
SIZE: 120 mm (5 in)
DESCRIPTION: The speckled butterflyfish is a common species found in sheltered lagoon habitats. Sometimes solitary, but usually seen in pairs, it frequents inshore and offshore reefs and occurs around continental islands. It can be approached easily underwater, shows little fear of divers or other butterflyfish and is more intolerant of other species when two are together. Body colouration appears to intensify with maturity; the smaller fish has a much lighter body colour than the larger one which can be almost gold.

Chaetodon ephippium

FAMILY: Chaetodontidae
SCIENTIFIC NAME: *Chaetodon ephippium*
COMMON NAME: Saddled Butterflyfish
DISTRIBUTION: TI–WP
HABITAT: Coral and rocky reefs
GENERAL WATER DEPTH: 5–15 m
  (16–49 ft)
FOOD HABIT: Omnivorous: algae; worms;
  coral polyps
SIZE: 250 mm (10 in)

DESCRIPTION: Inhabiting lagoons and inner reef areas bordering reef slopes and channels, the saddled butterflyfish is usually seen in pairs when it is often wary of divers. Unlike many other species of butterflyfish the colour pattern of the juvenile is very similar to that of the adult. Owing to its specialised feeding habits it requires extra care when in aquaria.

Chaetodon lineolatus

FAMILY: Chaetodontidae
SCIENTIFIC NAME: *Chaetodon lineolatus*
COMMON NAME: Lined Butterflyfish
DISTRIBUTION: TI-WP; WT/S
HABITAT: Coral reefs
GENERAL WATER DEPTH: 5–25 m
 (16–82 ft)
FOOD HABIT: Omnivorous: coral polyps;
 algae
SIZE: 310 mm (12 in)
DESCRIPTION: The largest of the butterflyfish, this species is moderately common in lagoon areas and shallow, protected reef slopes throughout the tropical Pacific and Indian oceans. In some areas the lined butterflyfish is solitary and difficult to approach; elsewhere, at certain times of the year a number will congregate and swim as a school. During this stage they are not so shy towards divers.

FAMILY: Chaetodontidae
SCIENTIFIC NAME: *Chaetodon melannotus*
COMMON NAME: Black-backed Butterflyfish
DISTRIBUTION: TI-WP
HABITAT: Coral and rocky reefs
GENERAL WATER DEPTH: 1–25 m (3–82 ft)
FOOD HABIT: Carnivorous: sessile
 invertebrates
SIZE: 170 mm (7 in)
DESCRIPTION: A common fish on inshore and offshore coral reefs, the black-backed butterflyfish may be seen living in lagoons and sheltered waters, usually among lush

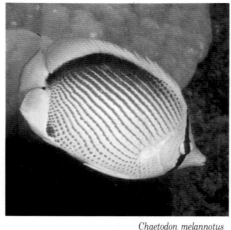

Chaetodon melannotus

coral growth. Like many of the smaller butterflyfish, it is easily approached underwater and has little fear of divers. Active during the day, it feeds over a wide area of reef and is observed to be solitary more commonly than in pairs. It is easily maintained in aquaria and will accept a variety of natural foods as well as commercial packet or frozen food.

Chaetodon ornatissimus

FAMILY: Chaetodontidae
SCIENTIFIC NAME: *Chaetodon ornatissimus*
COMMON NAME: Ornate Butterflyfish
DISTRIBUTION: TI-WP
HABITAT: Coral and rocky reefs
GENERAL WATER DEPTH: 8–25 m
 (26–82 ft)
FOOD HABIT: Carnivorous: coral polyps;
 coral mucus
SIZE: 170 mm (7 in)
DESCRIPTION: Occurring in many tropical seas, the ornate butterflyfish may be seen on continental island reefs as well as offshore island reefs and cays. It is not common over any of its range and although much admired by aquarists is not easily kept, owing to its specialised feeding habits.

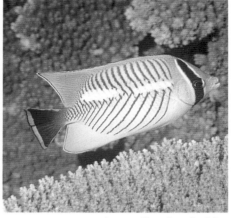

Chaetodon trifascialis

FAMILY: Chaetodontidae
SCIENTIFIC NAME: *Chaetodon trifascialis*
COMMON NAME: Chevroned Butterflyfish
DISTRIBUTION: TI-WP
HABITAT: Coral reefs
GENERAL WATER DEPTH: 2–10 m (6–33 ft)
FOOD HABIT: Carnivorous: coral polyps
SIZE: 180 mm (7 in)
DESCRIPTION: This highly territorial species is found only on or around tabular colonies of staghorn corals in shallow water. In some very rich coral areas where several formations of tabular coral overlap or terrace, the chevroned butterflyfish may allow a few butterflyfish into its territory but otherwise it will chase away all other coral-eating butterflyfish. Owing to its territorial behaviour it is easy to photograph. It is unlikely to do well in aquaria.

Chaetodon trifasciatus

FAMILY: Chaetodontidae
SCIENTIFIC NAME: *Chaetodon trifasciatus*
COMMON NAME: Striped Butterflyfish
DISTRIBUTION: TI-WP
HABITAT: Coral and rocky reefs
GENERAL WATER DEPTH: 1–15 m (3–49 ft)
FOOD HABIT: Carnivorous: coral polyps

SIZE: 120 mm (5 in)
DESCRIPTION: The striped butterflyfish is common in rich coral areas around back reefs, bommies, reef flats and in sheltered lagoons. It is always seen in pairs and is more common in shallow than deep water. It is non-territorial and browses on coral polyps so it is best to introduce juveniles to a tank and train them to take other food.

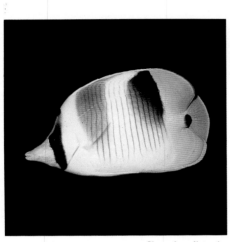

Chaetodon ulietensis

FAMILY: Chaetodontidae
SCIENTIFIC NAME: *Chaetodon ulietensis*
COMMON NAME: Double-saddled Butterflyfish
DISTRIBUTION: TI–WP
HABITAT: Coral reef
GENERAL WATER DEPTH: 5–10 m (16–33 ft)
FOOD HABIT: Carnivorous: benthic invertebrates
SIZE: 150 mm (6 in)
DESCRIPTION: Preferring a habitat of coral slopes, edges of channels within reefs and around bommies beyond back reefs, this species has a very smooth, streamlined appearance. Though much smaller in size, it is somewhat similar at first glance to the larger, lined butterflyfish (*C. lineatus*). Underwater the double-saddled butterflyfish is more easily approached than its relative and can be distinguished by the bright yellow posterior third of its body, the black spot on the caudal peduncle (tail junction), the black edge of the tail, and the two dark saddles, as the common name indicates. Whereas the lined butterflyfish is almost always seen in pairs, the double-saddled butterflyfish is regularly seen to be solitary.

FAMILY: Chaetodontidae
SCIENTIFIC NAME: *Chaetodon unimaculatus*
COMMON NAME: Teardrop Butterflyfish
DISTRIBUTION: TI–WP
HABITAT: Coral reefs

Chaetodon unimaculatus

GENERAL WATER DEPTH: 1–15 m (3–49 ft)
FOOD HABIT: Omnivorous: stony and soft corals; sponges; algae; worms
SIZE: 230 mm (9 in)
DESCRIPTION: Although the teardrop butterflyfish is found from the Indian Ocean to the central Pacific, it is not common and does not seem to be prolific at any one location. Like other butterflyfish it pairs during spring and summer for a short period and sometimes the pair will be joined by a third one. Whether seen on sheltered reef slopes or outer barrier reefs it remains shy and elusive and difficult to approach.

Chelmon rostratus

FAMILY: Chaetodontidae
SCIENTIFIC NAME: *Chelmon rostratus*
COMMON NAME: Beaked Coralfish
DISTRIBUTION: TI–WP
HABITAT: Coral and rocky reefs
GENERAL WATER DEPTH: 1–25 m (3–82 ft)
FOOD HABIT: Carnivorous: invertebrates
SIZE: 160 mm (6 in)
DESCRIPTION: Almost the type fish of the Great Barrier Reef waters, the beaked coralfish warrants every bit of public admiration. Certainly one of the most attractive reef fish, it usually lives in pairs that 'flit'

around reefs, gutters and coral heads picking small organisms from the sides and roofs of coral overhangs and caves. Active during the day it sleeps in holes and crevices at night. Usually a shallow water species, it has been recorded to 30 m (98 ft) depth and in some areas grows to 200 mm (4 in).

Chelmonops truncatus

FAMILY: Chaetodontidae
SCIENTIFIC NAME: *Chelmonops truncatus*
COMMON NAME: Southern Coralfish
DISTRIBUTION: WT/S
HABITAT: Rocky reefs
GENERAL WATER DEPTH: 5–40 m (16–131 ft)
FOOD HABIT: Carnivorous: worms; crustaceans; sessile invertebrates
SIZE: 200 mm (8 in)
DESCRIPTION: A very beautiful fish that could hardly be mistaken for any other species, the southern coralfish inhabits algae-covered reefs in areas of protected bays or sheltered waters. It can be seen on coastal reefs but is more common in sheltered places. Adults pair for some time and may mate for life. Juveniles have a spot or ocellus on the soft dorsal fin, like many other juvenile coralfish.

FAMILY: Chaetodontidae
SCIENTIFIC NAME: *Coradion altivelis*
COMMON NAME: Highfin Coralfish
DISTRIBUTION: TI–WP
HABITAT: Coral and rocky reefs
GENERAL WATER DEPTH: 8–25 m (26–82 ft)
FOOD HABIT: Carnivorous
SIZE: 150 mm (6 in)
DESCRIPTION: Not so commonly encountered as some species of butterflyfish, the highfin coralfish is mostly observed in pairs on broken bottom, or around the bases of bommies on continental and offshore barrier reefs. The highfin coralfish is similar to the

Coradion altivelis

orange-banded coralfish, but is easily distinguished by its high dorsal fin and the lack of a black ocellus on the rear of the dorsal fin of adults; the juveniles have a large ocellus on the soft dorsal fin that is lost at maturity. It is easy to keep in aquaria.

Coradion chrysozonus

FAMILY: Chaetodontidae
SCIENTIFIC NAME: *Coradion chrysozonus*
COMMON NAME: Orange-banded Coralfish
DISTRIBUTION: TI–WP
HABITAT: Coral and rocky reefs
GENERAL WATER DEPTH: 10–35 m (33–115 ft)
FOOD HABIT: Carnivorous: invertebrates
SIZE: 150 mm (6 in)
DESCRIPTION: This little fish seems to prefer deeper waters around back reefs and coral bommies where it spends the day picking at invertebrates in the marine growth on cave walls and around the bases of coral clumps. On occasion, pairs have been seen to range over an area of 30–40 m (98–131 ft). It is also seen on broken bottom in moderately deep water. At night, orange-banded coralfish sleep in crevices in coral caves. It is fairly easy to approach underwater and is easily kept in aquaria.

Heniochus varius

FAMILY: Chaetodontidae
SCIENTIFIC NAME: *Heniochus varius*
COMMON NAME: Humphead Bannerfish
DISTRIBUTION: TI–WP
HABITAT: Coral reefs
GENERAL WATER DEPTH: 2–15 m (6–49 ft)
FOOD HABIT: Omnivorous
SIZE: 180 mm (7 in)
DESCRIPTION: A rather pronounced hump above its eyes (even when juvenile) grows into pronounced horns when the humphead bannerfish fully matures. Many observations show it to be more secretive than other bannerfish and although some often swim in pairs, it generally stays close to caves and underhangs in the reef. Obviously this is its food source. Humphead bannerfish inhabit the Indian and Indo-Pacific oceans and are not common in the western Pacific.

Cheilodactylus ephippium

FAMILY: Cheilodactylidae
SCIENTIFIC NAME: *Cheilodactylus ephippium*
COMMON NAME: Painted Morwong
DISTRIBUTION: WT/S
HABITAT: Rocky and coral reefs
GENERAL WATER DEPTH: 2–25 m (6–82 ft)

FOOD HABIT: Carnivorous: molluscs; crustaceans
SIZE: 350 mm (14 in)
DESCRIPTION: Generally found in the South-West Pacific island reefs, this species is unlikely to be confused with any other. The painted morwong seems to spend most of the day visiting cleaner stations or just lying on the bottom. At night it hides in holes and crevices in the reef. It feeds during early morning. Although it congregates in assemblies during the day, feeding appears to be a solitary activity.

Cheilodactylus fuscus

FAMILY: Cheilodactylidae
SCIENTIFIC NAME: *Cheilodactylus fuscus*
COMMON NAME: Red Morwong
DISTRIBUTION: WT/S
HABITAT: Rocky reefs; seagrass; sand
GENERAL WATER DEPTH: 3–40 m (10–131 ft)
FOOD HABIT: Carnivorous: molluscs; crustaceans
SIZE: 500 mm (20 in)
DESCRIPTION: The morwong is mainly gregarious, forming large aggregations that mill around in gutters or at the base of drop-offs. Towards late afternoon they tend to lie on the bottom, especially in areas of low sloping rockfalls, where they sleep in crevices. They feed during early morning and some continue throughout the day. A percentage of their food consists of molluscs sucked off the rocks with rubbery lips. The red morwong can be hooked but most are taken by spear or gill net.

FAMILY: Cheilodactylidae
SCIENTIFIC NAME: *Cheilodactylus gibbosus*
COMMON NAME: Western Morwong
DISTRIBUTION: WT/S
HABITAT: Rocky reefs
GENERAL WATER DEPTH: 3–25 m (10–82 ft)
FOOD HABIT: Carnivorous: molluscs

Cheilodactylus gibbosus

caught in gill nets. It is mainly taken by spearing and its distinctive pattern makes it readily identifiable. It feeds on molluscs, worms and algae that it catches by taking indiscriminate mouthfuls of bottom sediments and ejecting the residue in typical morwong fashion — from the back of the gills.

Cheilodactylus spectabilis

Cheilodactylus vestitus

SIZE: 350 mm (14 in)
DESCRIPTION: Found only in the Indian Ocean waters off Western Australia, the western morwong occurs around inshore reefs and offshore islands and is not often caught. It is superficially similar to the eastern morwong *C. vestitus*, but the two can be distinguished by checking the position of the black longitudinal dorsal stripe. On *C. vestitus* the line crosses the caudal peduncle (tail junction), and completely blacks out the lower caudal fin; on *C. gibbosus* the line terminates at the top of the caudal peduncle.

FAMILY: Cheilodactylidae
SCIENTIFIC NAME: *Cheilodactylus nigripes*
COMMON NAME: Magpie Morwong
DISTRIBUTION: WT/S
HABITAT: Rocky reefs
GENERAL WATER DEPTH: 5–30 m
 (16–98 ft)
FOOD HABIT: Carnivorous: molluscs;
 worms; crustaceans
SIZE: 410 mm (16 in)
DESCRIPTION: Generally restricted to shallow water reefs, this species is rarely encountered by line fishermen or trawlers but is

FAMILY: Cheilodactylidae
SCIENTIFIC NAME: *Cheilodactylus spectabilis*
COMMON NAME: Banded Morwong
DISTRIBUTION: WT/S; CT/S
HABITAT: Rocky reefs
GENERAL WATER DEPTH: 5–30 m
 (16–98 ft)
FOOD HABIT: Carnivorous: molluscs;
 crustaceans
SIZE: 700 mm (28 in)
DESCRIPTION: Most morwong are considered to be good eating fish and the banded morwong is no exception. Owing to its feeding habits, not many are caught on lines. It is usually seen in small groups of several individuals and tends to inhabit areas under ledges or in caves. Solitary fish have been seen feeding over flat reef during the day, removing molluscs from rocks.

FAMILY: Cheilodactylidae
SCIENTIFIC NAME: *Cheilodactylus vestitus*
COMMON NAME: Eastern Morwong
DISTRIBUTION: TWP
HABITAT: Rocky and coral reefs
GENERAL WATER DEPTH: 5–30 m
 (16–98 ft)
FOOD HABIT: Carnivorous: molluscs
SIZE: 300 mm (12 in)
DESCRIPTION: One of the smallest of the morwong family, the eastern morwong is found around offshore islands, inshore reefs, and in bays and inlets and is frequently observed in estuaries. It has long been confused with the western morwong, *C. gibbosus* (Indian Ocean); both may have a similar common name because of their likeness. The eastern morwong is not often taken by line, but it is speared. Despite its small size its flesh is well worth eating.

FAMILY: Cheilodactylidae
SCIENTIFIC NAME: *Dactylophora nigricans*
COMMON NAME: Dusky Morwong
DISTRIBUTION: WT/S
HABITAT: Rocky reefs; seagrass meadows
GENERAL WATER DEPTH: 1–25 m (3–82 ft)

Cheilodactylus nigripes

Dactylophora nigricans

FOOD HABIT: Omnivorous: algae; worms; crustaceans

SIZE: 1.2 m (4 ft)

DESCRIPTION: The dusky morwong grows much larger than any other morwong species. The juvenile differs markedly from the adult in colour. Easily approached underwater, it falls prey to eager spearfishermen who cannot resist a sitting target whether or not they intend to use the fish. The dusky morwong generally does not take a hook. It can be gill netted and caught in baitless traps but mainly becomes rock lobster bait. Juveniles make reasonably palatable eating.

Nemadactylus douglasii

FAMILY: Cheilodactylidae
SCIENTIFIC NAME: *Nemadactylus douglasii*
COMMON NAME: Douglas's Morwong
DISTRIBUTION: Rocky reefs; sand; mud
HABITAT: WT/S
GENERAL WATER DEPTH: 15–100 m (49–328 ft)
FOOD HABIT: Carnivorous: molluscs; crustaceans; worms
SIZE: 600 mm (2 ft)

DESCRIPTION: A well-known commercial species, Douglas's morwong is hooked near inshore and offshore reefs and is regularly trawled in deeper waters. It feeds by taking

in mouthfuls of sand or detritus, swallowing the organic matter, and ejecting the residue through the gills. Of beautiful appearance with succulent flesh it is superficially similar to the jackass morwong, *Nemadactylus macropterus*, which has a distinctive black band behind the head. Douglas's morwong is regularly seen by divers, seeming to be most prolific at 30 m (98 ft) depth.

FAMILY: Cheilodactylidae
SCIENTIFIC NAME: *Nemadactylus valenciennesi*
COMMON NAME: Blue Morwong
DISTRIBUTION: WT/S
HABITAT: Rocky reefs; sand
GENERAL WATER DEPTH: 10–100 m (33–328 ft)
FOOD HABIT: Carnivorous: invertebrates
SIZE: 760 mm (30 in)

DESCRIPTION: A high-quality food fish, not easily lured on to the hook, the blue morwong is taken regularly by spearfishermen and also in trawls and gill nets. The second largest of the morwong family, it has bright yellow scroll-like markings across the head near the eyes. It does not seem to rest on the bottom as much as other species do. The juvenile is similar in shape to the adult, with a light brown to buff base colour and blue stripes running the length of the body. Molluscs may be ingested whole and can be removed from the gut contents in perfect condition. Some rare shells have been collected in this manner.

FAMILY: Cirrhitidae
SCIENTIFIC NAME: *Cirrhitichthys aprinus*
COMMON NAME: Blotched Hawkfish
DISTRIBUTION: TI-WP; WT/S
HABITAT: Rocky reefs
GENERAL WATER DEPTH: 6–30 m (20–98 ft)
FOOD HABIT: Carnivorous: fish; crustaceans
SIZE: 100 mm (4 in)

DESCRIPTION: The blotched hawkfish is readily seen resting in the open and makes full use of rocks, underhangs and small ledges to mask its position. It also inhabits black coral 'trees', soft corals and sponges. The papillae on the dorsal fin are very similar to the soft coral polyps that the fish often inhabits, and, together with its disruptive camouflage, make it a very effective predator.

Nemadactylus valenciennesi

Cirrhitichthys aprinus

FAMILY: Cirrhitidae
SCIENTIFIC NAME: *Cirrhitichthys falco*
COMMON NAME: Falcon Hawkfish
DISTRIBUTION: TI-WP; WT/S
HABITAT: Rocky and coral reefs
GENERAL WATER DEPTH: 10–20 m (33–66 ft)
FOOD HABIT: Carnivorous: crustaceans
SIZE: 80 mm (3 in)

DESCRIPTION: A small unobtrusive yet colourful and interesting fish, the falcon hawkfish is not often seen as most divers swim too fast and too far off the bottom, thereby missing many less prominent species. It is a diurnal carnivore that rests in the open and has a 'wait and watch' style of hunting, allowing smaller marine life to approach closely before pouncing down to devour them.

Cirrhitichthys falco

Cirrhitichthys oxycephalus

FAMILY: Cirrhitidae
SCIENTIFIC NAME: *Cirrhitichthys oxycephalus*
COMMON NAME: Spotted Hawkfish
DISTRIBUTION: TI-WP
HABITAT: Coral and rocky reefs
GENERAL WATER DEPTH: 10–25 m (33–82 ft)
FOOD HABIT: Carnivorous: crustaceans
SIZE: 80 mm (3 in)
DESCRIPTION: The spotted hawkfish is one of the smaller hawkfishes inhabiting the fringing reefs of offshore barrier reefs. Owing to its size and its habit of utilising the lower areas of the reef among coral, it escapes the notice of most divers. When in the undergrowth, it tends to select places of medium height on which to rest on the lookout for prey.

Cirrhitus splendens

FAMILY: Cirrhitidae
SCIENTIFIC NAME: *Cirrhitus splendens*
COMMON NAME: Splendid Hawkfish
DISTRIBUTION: TWP; WT/S
HABITAT: Rocky and coral reefs
GENERAL WATER DEPTH: 5–30 m (16–98 ft)

FOOD HABIT: Carnivorous: crustaceans
SIZE: 200 mm (8 in)
DESCRIPTION: The largest and most beautiful of the South-West Pacific hawkfishes, the splendid hawkfish was first recorded from Lord Howe Island where it was thought to be endemic. Although it is by no means as common on continental reefs and around other islands as it is at Lord Howe, more intensive observation is likely to discover it in other locations. Although active during the day, individuals may on occasion hunt right through dusk until after dark.

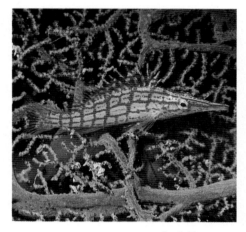

Oxycirrhites typus

FAMILY: Cirrhitidae
SCIENTIFIC NAME: *Oxycirrhites typus*
COMMON NAME: Long-nosed Hawkfish
DISTRIBUTION: TI-WP
HABITAT: Coral and rocky reefs
GENERAL WATER DEPTH: 20–30 m (66–98 ft)
FOOD HABIT: Carnivorous: crustaceans
SIZE: 140 mm (6 in)
DESCRIPTION: A beautiful and unique species found in the South-West Pacific, this territorial hawkfish lives among the branches of black coral 'trees' and giant sea fans that are attached to cliff faces and drop-offs. Very often there is a pair of fish on one sea fan. However, in the Sea of Cortez they have territories on rocky reef slopes. Easily approached underwater, this species has a wide range over tropical reef areas and makes an ideal aquarium fish.

FAMILY: Cirrhitidae
SCIENTIFIC NAME: *Paracirrhites arcatus*
COMMON NAME: Ring-eyed Hawkfish
DISTRIBUTION: TI-WP
HABITAT: Coral reefs
GENERAL WATER DEPTH: 2–20 m (6–66 ft)
FOOD HABIT: Carnivorous: crustaceans; fishes
SIZE: 150 mm (6 in)
DESCRIPTION: Quite common, and easily

Paracirrhites arcatus

approached underwater, the ring-eyed hawkfish is an attractive fish found around fringing continental island reefs as well as throughout outer barrier reefs. It is probably the most conspicuous of all the hawkfish, for it nests in the open on the tops of corals and hydrocorals and would appear to have little chance of ambushing prey. It possibly feeds direct from the surrounding water.

Paracirrhites forsteri

FAMILY: Cirrhitidae
SCIENTIFIC NAME: *Paracirrhites forsteri*
COMMON NAME: Forster's Hawkfish
DISTRIBUTION: TI-WP
HABITAT: Coral reefs
GENERAL WATER DEPTH: 2–10 m (6–33 ft)
FOOD HABIT: Carnivorous: crustaceans
SIZE: 250 mm (10 in)
DESCRIPTION: One of the largest of the tropical hawkfish, Forster's hawkfish has several different colour phases, including black. It lives around fringing reefs of continental islands and outer barrier reefs. During the day it rests among the branches of staghorn corals (*Acropora*) where it also sleeps at night. It is territorial but is easily approached by divers.

Heteroclinus johnstoni

Heteroclinus perspicillatus

FAMILY: Clinidae
SCIENTIFIC NAME: *Heteroclinus johnstoni*
COMMON NAME: Johnston's Weedfish
DISTRIBUTION: WT/S
HABITAT: Rocky reefs
GENERAL WATER DEPTH: 2–25 m (6–82 ft)
FOOD HABIT: Carnivorous: crustaceans
SIZE: 300 mm (12 in)
DESCRIPTION: Johnston's weedfish is one of
the largest inhabiting the rocky foreshores of
the South-West Pacific and its colours are
apt to vary slightly, depending on geographical location. Young specimens may be found
around rocky or stony reefs where loose
rocks abound; older fish seem to spend their
time moving around in dense algae-covered
terrain. It has about seven darker bars
across the body, each terminating in a dorsal
ocellus. It has a white patch under the eye
and the dorsal fin is lower at the head in this
species than in other weedfish.

FAMILY: Clinidae
SCIENTIFIC NAME: *Heteroclinus
    perspicillatus*
COMMON NAME: Robust Weedfish
DISTRIBUTION: WT/S
HABITAT: Rocky reefs; seagrass meadows
GENERAL WATER DEPTH: 2–20 m (6–66 ft)
FOOD HABIT: Carnivorous: crustaceans
SIZE: 90 mm (4 in)
DESCRIPTION: Many weedfish are known to
produce living young, some bearing up to
four hundred. The robust weedfish is
encountered in relatively shallow weed beds,
rocky or rubble reef and in seagrass meadows. The colour is almost always a shade of
green with specific patterning. It has a characteristic dark patch with a bright yellow
surround at the base of the first dorsal on
top of the head.

FAMILY: Clinidae
SCIENTIFIC NAME: *Heteroclinus tristis*
COMMON NAME: Forster's Weedfish

DISTRIBUTION: WT/S
HABITAT: Rocky reefs
GENERAL WATER DEPTH: 3–10 m
    (10–33 ft)
FOOD HABIT: Carnivorous: crustaceans
SIZE: 120 mm (5 in)
DESCRIPTION: A Forster's weedfish crawling
among red algae, or winding its sinewy body
through clumps of bottom debris, resembles
a reptile rather than a fish. Even when
observed at close range it is easy to lose
sight of as its highly adaptive camouflage
and deceptive resemblance to weed make it
seem to disappear into its natural habitat. It
has a well-developed crest that projects well
over its eyes.

Heteroclinus tristis

FAMILY: Clupeidae
SCIENTIFIC NAME: *Clupea harengus*
COMMON NAME: Herring
DISTRIBUTION: CT/N; WT/N
HABITAT: Coastal surface waters
GENERAL WATER DEPTH: 0–200 m
    (656 ft)
FOOD HABIT: Carnivorous: zooplankton,
    especially crustaceans such as copepods,
    other small pelagic invertebrates and
    small fishes

Clupea harengus

SIZE: Up to 430 mm (16.9 in)
DESCRIPTION: The herring is still an abundant fish in North Atlantic coastal waters,
but it has been overfished for food, especially
in the North Sea. The eggs are laid on
gravels and shells on the sea bed. It is flat
sided and its scales are easily rubbed off.
Young herrings have a keel-like ridge on
the belly with a sharp edge, but this gets
more rounded with age. The dorsal fin is in
the middle of the back and the pelvic fins
start just behind the beginning of the dorsal
fin. The tail is well forked. Off-shore aggre-
gate extraction has harmed some breeding
grounds. Several races are recognised, mainly according to their breeding seasons.

FAMILY: Congridae
SCIENTIFIC NAME: *Conger wilsoni*
COMMON NAME: Wilson's Conger Eel
DISTRIBUTION: WT/S
HABITAT: Rocky reefs
GENERAL WATER DEPTH: 5–25 m
    (16–82 ft)
FOOD HABIT: Carnivorous: fishes;
    crustaceans
SIZE: 2 m (6 ft)

Conger wilsoni

DESCRIPTION: Like the moray, the conger eel has a reputation for being a strong, aggressive fighter, but unlike the moray, it is good to eat. It can be hand fed underwater and some enterprising divers have been known to put a gaff, or large hook in with the bait; when hooked, the eel is skull-dragged in by a companion on shore with a heavy line. (Certainly, dragging in a big conger can be exciting, but after having skinned half a dozen the initial excitement tends to decrease.)

Paraplagusia unicolor

FAMILY: Cynoglossidae
SCIENTIFIC NAME: *Paraplagusia unicolor*
COMMON NAME: Lemon Tongue Sole
DISTRIBUTION: WT/S
HABITAT: Sand; mud
GENERAL WATER DEPTH: 2–36 m
  (6–118 ft)
FOOD HABIT: Carnivorous
SIZE: 300 mm (12 in)
DESCRIPTION: The lemon tongue sole is rarely seen by divers as it spends most of its time well hidden under a layer of sand. It occurs in open sandy areas, and along the fringe edges close to reefs. Sometimes caught on lines, most are trawled. The lemon tongue

sole is a commercial species, eagerly sought by seafood restaurants because it is a fine-textured, pleasant-tasting fish. Colour varies from shades of lemon yellow to light brown. Some specimens have spots or a marble pattern.

Dactyloptaena orientalis

FAMILY: Dactylopteridae
SCIENTIFIC NAME: *Dactyloptaena orientalis*
COMMON NAME: Oriental Sea Robin
DISTRIBUTION: TI–WP
HABITAT: Sand; mud; rubble
GENERAL WATER DEPTH: 3–40 m
  (10–131 ft)
FOOD HABIT: Carnivorous: crustaceans;
  worms; molluscs
SIZE: 400 mm (16 in)
DESCRIPTION: The oriental sea robin is a bottom-dwelling fish that inhabits inshore and offshore localities near sandy rubble terraces, reef slopes or muddy sea floor. When searching for food it crawls along the sandy bottom on its modified pelvic fins (used as ventral feelers) with its wings folded along its sides using the mobile, finger-like extensions of its huge pectoral fins to disturb prey from the sand. It is caught in trawls and also by line. When disturbed, powerful thrusts of the body and tail launch the fish to heights or 1–2 m (3–6 ft) off the bottom. Then the pectorals are expanded and it glides back to the bottom some distance away.

FAMILY: Dasyatidae
SCIENTIFIC NAME: *Amphotistius kuhlii*
COMMON NAME: Blue-spotted Stingray
DISTRIBUTION: TI–WP; WT/S
HABITAT: Coral and rocky reefs; sand;
  rubble
GENERAL WATER DEPTH: 8–50 m
  (26–164 ft)
FOOD HABIT: Carnivorous: fishes; molluscs;
  crustaceans
SIZE: 380 mm (15 in)
DESCRIPTION: Not as common as the blue-

Amphotistius kuhlii

spotted fantail ray, the blue-spotted stingray generally inhabits deeper waters in lagoons and along the bases of underwater cliffs and the slopes of estuarine channels. It is easily distinguished from the blue-spotted fantail ray by its triangular disc. The blue spots on the stingray are not as bright as those on the fantail ray and are apt to fade once the fish is dead. There are, however, a number of smaller black spots on the back which are very prominent and stable. A venomous spine is found on the tail. When swimming it holds its tail high; it is a very nervous little ray and not easy to approach. Specimens are caught by line and some also in trawls.

Dinolestes lewini

FAMILY: Dinolestidae
SCIENTIFIC NAME: *Dinolestes lewini*
COMMON NAME: Long-finned Pike
DISTRIBUTION: WT/S
HABITAT: Rocky reefs; seagrass; sheltered
  and open water
GENERAL WATER DEPTH: 5–40 m
  (16–131 ft)
FOOD HABIT: Carnivorous: fish
SIZE: 510 mm (20 in)
DESCRIPTION: One might expect a fish of

this shape to be a member of the barracuda family, as it seems to have some of the features of the Sphyraenidae. However, the long-finned pike is an enigma. Taxonomically it has a close affinity to the cardinalfish but with different behaviour. It is a diurnal species that often hangs mid-water in large schools, drifting back and forth in the swell and always alert for prey or predator.

Diodon holocanthus

FAMILY: Diodontidae
SCIENTIFIC NAME: *Diodon holocanthus*
COMMON NAME: Freckled Porcupinefish
DISTRIBUTION: TI–WP
HABITAT: Coral and rocky reefs
GENERAL WATER DEPTH: 1–25 m (3–82 ft)
FOOD HABIT: Carnivorous: molluscs; crustaceans
SIZE: 500 mm (20 in)
DESCRIPTION: This fish may be found during the day sleeping in a curve-tailed position among bottom growths, under ledges, or in rock fissures. It hardly moves when touched but becomes active at night when it feeds. When asleep its colours are unchanged which is unusual, as most fish have different day and night colour patterns. If caught on a line it is best to cut it off as the teeth can cause injury.

FAMILY: Diodontidae
SCIENTIFIC NAME: *Diodon nichthemerus*
COMMON NAME: Globefish
DISTRIBUTION: WT/S
HABITAT: Rocky reefs; seagrass; jetties
GENERAL WATER DEPTH: 1–25 m (3–82 ft)
FOOD HABIT: Carnivorous: molluscs; echinoderms
SIZE: 280 mm (11 in)
DESCRIPTION: The long, sharp-pointed spines extending well over the head when erected, as well as the fairly distinctive colouration and the three black body bars, allow the globefish to be easily recognised.

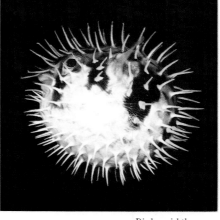

Diodon nichthemerus

When threatened it swallows water (or air when out of water), which fills the body and causes the spines to be locked into a rigid defensive position. It is often line caught, netted and trawled.

Echeneis naucrates

FAMILY: Echeneidae
SCIENTIFIC NAME: *Echeneis naucrates*
COMMON NAME: Slender Suckerfish
DISTRIBUTION: TI–WP
HABITAT: Open sea; coral reefs
GENERAL WATER DEPTH: 1–40 m (3–131 ft)
FOOD HABIT: Carnivorous: zooplankton; fishes
SIZE: 1 m (3 ft)
DESCRIPTION: Seen with, or attached to, a variety of fish and marine mammals, the slender suckerfish has been regarded as fully reliant on food scraps from its host's meals. However, this is not entirely true as the slender suckerfish is quite able to forage for itself and in some cases may 'clean' its host, though this seems doubtful in many cases. Small juveniles may be seen on rock cod, turtles and even snapper.

Remora remora

FAMILY: Echeneidae
SCIENTIFIC NAME: *Remora remora*
COMMON NAME: Remora or Shark Sucker
DISTRIBUTION: WT/N; T; WT/S
HABITAT: Ocean and coastal waters
GENERAL WATER DEPTH: 0–300 m (985 ft)
FOOD HABIT: Carnivorous: small fish; crustaceans
SIZE: Up to 460 mm (18.1 in)
DESCRIPTION: The remora is easily recognised by its streamlined appearance, protruding lower jaw and strangely modified first dorsal fin which serves as a sucker. This enables it to attach to its host. The sucker extends back only as far as the tips of the pelvic fins. It is coloured an even dark grey-brown. It may be seen free, or attached by its powerful sucker to the undersides of larger fish, rays, sharks, whales and turtles. It has been thought to clean these larger animals of their external parasites; however, it is the author's opinion that the association is based on transport and opportunistic feeding rather than any cleaning function.

FAMILY: Enoplosidae
SCIENTIFIC NAME: *Enoplosus armatus*
COMMON NAME: Old Wife
DISTRIBUTION: WT/S
HABITAT: Rocky reefs; rubble; jetties; seagrass
GENERAL WATER DEPTH: 5–40 m (16–131 ft)
FOOD HABIT: Carnivorous: crustaceans; worms
SIZE: 250 mm (10 in)
DESCRIPTION: A fish as distinctively shaped as old wife hardly requires description. Old wife is the only representative of this family. At different times it can be seen to be solitary, in pairs, or part of a large school. Sometimes during the day a school will remain in the shade of a jetty, high overhang

Enoplosus armatus

Platax pinnnatus

GENERAL WATER DEPTH: 3–20 m
(10–66 ft)
FOOD HABIT: Omnivorous: algae; salps; sea
jellies; zooplankton
SIZE: 500 mm (20 in)
DESCRIPTION: This large batfish swims in
groups, occupying selected areas of reef for a
long period. It feeds during the early morning on filamentous algae. In summer when
sea jellies and salps (pelagic ascidians) are
abundant the species has been seen to prey
on them. The round-faced batfish has yellow
pelvic fins, in contrast to the black pelvics of
the pinnate batfish, *P. pinnatus*. It is easily
approached underwater and, though edible,
is extremely tough and flavourless.

of rock, or a ledge. It is an easily approachable species that almost always swims with
fins erect. At night individuals separate from
the school and sleep in crevices and seagrass
meadows.

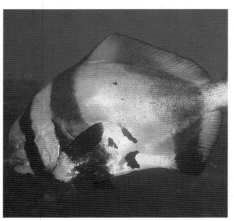

Platax batavianus

FAMILY: Ephippidae
SCIENTIFIC NAME: *Platax batavianus*
COMMON NAME: Humphead Batfish
DISTRIBUTION: TI–WP
HABITAT: Coral and rocky reefs
GENERAL WATER DEPTH: 8–40 m
(26–131 ft)
FOOD HABIT: Omnivorous: algae;
zooplankton
SIZE: 500 mm (20 in)
DESCRIPTION: During early morning the
humphead batfish moves out over the sandy
coral rubble bottom and feeds on algae. A
school later reforms to rest for the day facing
into the current in the lee of a reef. Adoles-
cents are found in lagoons and around back
reefs, while adults may sometimes be seen
swimming alone or in pairs in surge channels and over exposed reefs. The species
inhabits both mainland and offshore reefs
and has little fear of divers. It has coarse,
tough flesh and is rarely eaten.

FAMILY: Ephippidae
SCIENTIFIC NAME: *Platax pinnnatus*
COMMON NAME: Pinnate Batfish
DISTRIBUTION: TI–WP
HABITAT: Coral and rocky reefs
GENERAL WATER DEPTH: 8–20 m
(26–66 ft)
FOOD HABIT: Omnivorous: algae
SIZE: 500 mm (20 in)
DESCRIPTION: The young pinnate batfish
lives in coral reef areas on continental
islands and along barrier reefs, usually
inhabiting caves, or living beneath close-
lying ledges. Very small ones actually swim
on their sides and it has been suggested that
they mimic inedible flatworms. It is
extremely popular as aquarium fish and
grows to up to 300 mm (12 in) before beginning to lose its juvenile colour. The batfish
undergoes very remarkable changes in shape
with growth.

Platax teira

FAMILY: Ephippidae
SCIENTIFIC NAME: *Platax teira*
COMMON NAME: Round-faced Batfish
DISTRIBUTION: TI–WP
HABITAT: Coral and rocky reefs

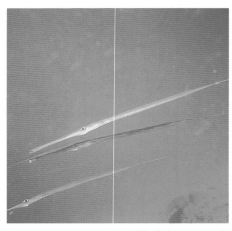

Fistularia commersonii

FAMILY: Fistulariidae
SCIENTIFIC NAME: *Fistularia commersonii*
COMMON NAME: Smooth Cornetfish
DISTRIBUTION: TI–WP; WT/S
HABITAT: Sand; rubble; seagrass
GENERAL WATER DEPTH: 5–30 m
(16–98 ft)
FOOD HABIT: Carnivorous: fish
SIZE: 1.5 m (5 ft)
DESCRIPTION: The smooth cornetfish may
occur in small schools but it seems to lead a
mainly solitary life especially when full-
grown. It feeds both in the water column and
among reefs where it hunts by stealthily
positioning itself near small schooling fish.
Despite its ability to strike swiftly it often
misses its target.

FAMILY: Gerridae
SCIENTIFIC NAME: *Gerres ovatus*
COMMON NAME: Ovate Silverbiddy
DISTRIBUTION: WT/S
HABITAT: Sand; mud; seagrass
GENERAL WATER DEPTH: 1–25 m (3–82 ft)
FOOD HABIT: Carnivorous: crustaceans;
worms
SIZE: 200 mm (8 in)
DESCRIPTION: The ovate silverbiddy is a

Gerres ovatus

Girella zebra

and is a favourite bait species. It feeds during the day over sandy bottom or on sandy mud substrate on, or near, reefs.

Girella elevata

diurnal species, feeding over soft bottom. Individuals have been observed in the same local area over several weeks. They feed by sifting out small organisms from mouthfuls of sand and detritus and are not always easy to approach. Good photographs are difficult to obtain owing to its shining, highly-polished scales and its habit of living in turbid estuaries.

Parequula melbournensis

FAMILY: Gerridae
SCIENTIFIC NAME: *Parequula melbournensis*
COMMON NAME: Melbourne Silverbelly
DISTRIBUTION: WT/S
HABITAT: Sand; seagrass; jetties; rocky reefs
GENERAL WATER DEPTH: 3–20 m (10–66 ft)
FOOD HABIT: Carnivorous
SIZE: 180 mm (7 in)
DESCRIPTION: To the casual observer the silverbelly resembles a small bream but on closer inspection it can be seen that the larger eye, low-slung operculum (gill cover) and pointed nose have little in common with the bream. It is generally caught in bait seines and sometimes in dip nets at night

FAMILY: Girellidae
SCIENTIFIC NAME: *Girella elevata*
COMMON NAME: Black Rockfish
DISTRIBUTION: WT/S
HABITAT: Rocky reefs
GENERAL WATER DEPTH: 1–25 m (3–82 ft)
FOOD HABIT: Herbivorous:
SIZE: 560 mm (22 in)
DESCRIPTION: There are times in the life of an underwater naturalist or photographer when one wonders whether it is worth the strain to get a photograph of an elusive species. The black rockfish is an example as it lives in the white water of swell-pounded coastal reefs during the day and sleeps in black caverns at night. After two hours a photographer could have twelve pictures: six of foam, four showing the rock where the fish had been and two actually with the fish in the frame, one of which, with luck, can be used.

FAMILY: Girellidae
SCIENTIFIC NAME: *Girella zebra*
COMMON NAME: Zebrafish
DISTRIBUTION: WT/S
HABITAT: Rocky reefs; seagrass
GENERAL WATER DEPTH: 3–15 m (10–49 ft)
FOOD HABIT: Herbivorous: algae
SIZE: 330 mm (13 in)
DESCRIPTION: The zebra-fish is a shallow water

herbivore that swims in both large and small schools near algae-covered reef where there is good water movement. It occurs near mainland reefs as well as around offshore islands and reefs. More often gill-netted than line caught it has flesh that is quite good to eat if the fish is cleaned soon after capture.

FAMILY: Glaucosomidae
SCIENTIFIC NAME: *Glaucosoma hebraicum*
COMMON NAME: West Australian 'Jewfish'
DISTRIBUTION: TIO; WT/S
HABITAT: Rocky reefs
GENERAL WATER DEPTH: 10–40 m (33–131 ft)
FOOD HABIT: Carnivorous: fish; crustaceans; molluscs
SIZE: 1 m (3 ft)
DESCRIPTION: Very good to eat, this species enters shallow waters during the breeding season and may often be found in huge schools in areas around shallow water reefs where it is caught by hand line on a variety of baits. The West Australian 'jewfish' may be found on both coastal and offshore reefs and is very easily speared as it often 'holes up' under ledges and reef overhangs.

Glaucosoma hebraicum

Glaucosoma scapulare

FAMILY: Glaucosomidae
SCIENTIFIC NAME: *Glaucosoma scapulare*
COMMON NAME: Pearl Perch
DISTRIBUTION: WT/S; TIO
HABITAT: Rocky and coral reefs
GENERAL WATER DEPTH: 10–60 m
(33–197 ft)
FOOD HABIT: Carnivorous: fishes;
crustaceans; molluscs
SIZE: 660 mm (26 in)
DESCRIPTION: Generally hand lined on deep reefs, the pearl perch comes into shallow offshore waters during the day, usually adjacent to rock faces, gutters and terraces of bomboras and islands. It seems to prefer places of high water movement in shallow water, yet seeks the protection of isolated reefs in gutters and channels when in deeper water. It tends to stay in one area for up to six months and although solitary fish have been observed, most are seen in small groups or schools. Like others in the family it is a very good table fish with clear white flesh of good flavour and texture.

FAMILY: Gobiesocidae
SCIENTIFIC NAME: *Aspasmogaster tasmaniensis*
COMMON NAME: Tasmanian Clingfish
DISTRIBUTION: WT/S; CT/S

Aspasmogaster tasmaniensis

HABITAT: Rocky reefs
GENERAL WATER DEPTH: Intertidal to
10 m (33 ft)
FOOD HABIT: Carnivorous: crustaceans
SIZE: 64 mm (2.5 in)
DESCRIPTION: A curious and interesting species, the Tasmanian clingfish lives under rocks and stones in tidal pools and is extremely common just below tide level to 5 m (16 ft). Mating occurs in early summer and eggs are laid on the undersurface of rocks from October until February. The female deposits eggs in a single layer in close formation; they are then fertilised and tended by the male. There may at one time be as many as three lots at various stages of development. Although the male may be a good protector he loses quite a number of young embryos to an unidentified species of fish-egg-eating nudibranch.

Amblygobius decussatus

FAMILY: Gobiidae
SCIENTIFIC NAME: *Amblygobius decussatus*
COMMON NAME: Crossed Goby
DISTRIBUTION: TI–WP
HABITAT: Sand; coral reef; rubble
GENERAL WATER DEPTH: 5–15 m
(16–49 ft)
FOOD HABIT: Probably omnivorous:
invertebrates, algae
SIZE: 150 mm (6 in)
DESCRIPTION: Because many sand gobies feed by taking in mouthfuls of sand, ingesting the organic matter and letting the rest pass out through their gills, it is necessary to have sand in an aquarium set-up. Even when they take food dropped into the tank, their habit is still to take in sand. The crossed goby lives in sheltered lagoon waters on continental mainland reefs and offshore barrier reefs. It generally prefers a broken rubble bottom.

Amblygobius phalaena

FAMILY: Gobiidae
SCIENTIFIC NAME: *Amblygobius phalaena*
COMMON NAME: Barred Goby
DISTRIBUTION: TI–WP; WT/S
HABITAT: Sand; rubble; seagrass meadows
GENERAL WATER DEPTH: 3–25 m (10–82 ft)
FOOD HABIT: Omnivorus: invertebrates;
mainly algae and diatoms
SIZE: 200 mm (8 in)
DESCRIPTION: Very distinctive in colour and pattern the barred goby is territorial and bottom-dwelling, of tropical descent and lives beneath hollows under stones, in burrows under rocky rubble, and sometimes in algae carpets. Like some gobies it is generally observed in a pair-bond relationship, though individual fish, usually young, are not rare.

Bryaninops yongei

FAMILY: Gobiidae
SCIENTIFIC NAME: *Bryaninops yongei*
COMMON NAME: Yonge's Seawhip Goby
DISTRIBUTION: TI–WP
HABITAT: Coral reefs
GENERAL WATER DEPTH: 8–30 m (26–98 ft)
FOOD HABIT: Carnivorous: planktonic
organisms
SIZE: 250 mm (10 in)
DESCRIPTION: This small fish has a close association with black coral and gorgonian seawhips growing on channel slopes and bot-

toms where there is good current flow. It feeds mainly during incoming tides when the seawhip polyps are also expanded. It feeds in the water column, making short darts away from the host whip to catch drifting planktonic organisms. Depending on the locality, the species can be seen at depths of 8–30 m (26–98 ft) in Indo-Pacific areas.

Fusigobius signipinnis

FAMILY: Gobiidae
SCIENTIFIC NAME: *Fusigobius signipinnis*
COMMON NAME: Flasher Goby
DISTRIBUTION: TI–WP
HABITAT: Sand
GENERAL WATER DEPTH: 5–20 m (16–66 ft)
FOOD HABIT: Carnivorous
SIZE: 100 mm (4 in)
DESCRIPTION: First photographed alive off the northern coast of Western Australia in 1971, the flasher goby is now known to occur in lagoons and sheltered back reefs along many barrier and continental reefs. During the day it does not venture out from its territorial cave or ledge. It selects caves with sandy floors and at night occupies an excavated burrow at the rear, well away from the entrance. The fish has a black spot on its dorsal fin that is often erected and retracted very quickly, hence the name, flasher goby.

FAMILY: Gobiidae
SCIENTIFIC NAME: *Nemateleotris magnifica*
COMMON NAME: Fire Goby
DISTRIBUTION: TI–WP
HABITAT: Coral reefs
GENERAL WATER DEPTH: 2–25 m (6–82 ft)
FOOD HABIT: Carnivorous
SIZE: 50 mm (2 in)
DESCRIPTION: Always in a pair, the fire goby is a delicate little fish that maintains a head-high stance and rarely rests on the bottom. Instead it maintains a position close to its burrow, a few centimetres to half a metre (18 in) off the bottom, and appears to feed on plankton. With a little care it can be observed at close range. It tends to live on

Nemateleotris magnifica

hard bottom and may be seen around the terraces of large bommies in open water and midway along surge gutters in reef fronts.

Pomatoschistus minutus

FAMILY: Gobiidae
SCIENTIFIC NAME: *Pomatoschistus minutus*
COMMON NAME: Sand Goby
DISTRIBUTION: CT/N; W/N
HABITAT: Sandy shores; sandy coasts and estuaries
GENERAL WATER DEPTH: 0–10 m (33 ft)
FOOD HABIT: Carnivorous: small crustaceans
SIZE: Up to 95 mm (4 in) long, often less
DESCRIPTION: The sand goby is coloured sandy brown with a lattice of fine dots and a saddle pattern across its back. The male has a white-edged spot on the trailing edge of the first dorsal fin and four cross bars. It is slender with rounded pectoral fins and a sucker-like arrangement of pelvic fins. The first dorsal fin has six rays and the second between 58 and 70. The species is very common on the lower part of the sandy shore and in shallow water in north-west Europe. The female deposits eggs in empty shells; they are guarded by the male until they hatch.

FAMILY: Gobiidae
SCIENTIFIC NAME: *Signigobius biocellatus*
COMMON NAME: Four-eyed Goby

Signigobius biocellatus

DISTRIBUTION: TI–WP
HABITAT: Sand; coral reefs
GENERAL WATER DEPTH: 3–25 m (10–82 ft)
FOOD HABIT: Carnivorous
SIZE: 50 mm (2 in)
DESCRIPTION: Only recently described, the four-eyed goby, though small, is one of the most interesting of all gobies. It lives around continental islands and barrier reefs where it excavates burrows in the sand or on occasion takes over unoccupied burrows of other species. Habitat is on open sand among broken reef, or on sandy terraces and even in the sandy floors of caves. A male and female are always together and they may mate for life. It spends much of the day excavating its burrow, bringing out mouthfuls of sand and ejecting it to one side. Each goby takes a turn to go below while the other, perched on its large pelvic fins, watches at the entrance.

Valenciennea immaculata

FAMILY: Gobiidae
SCIENTIFIC NAME: *Valenciennea immaculata*
COMMON NAME: Immaculate Goby
DISTRIBUTION: TI–WP; WT/S
HABITAT: Sand; mud
GENERAL WATER DEPTH: 5–20 m (16–66 ft)
FOOD HABIT: Carnivorous: worms; crustaceans
SIZE: 120 mm (5 in)
DESCRIPTION: Quite a common species in tropical and some temperate areas the immaculate goby is a bottom-dwelling species with strong pair-bonding behaviour.

Pairing fish excavate holes in sand or mud, usually under dead coral slabs on rocks lying on the surface of the substrate. In one case even a living sea star provided shelter for an enterprising pair. It is very territorial and individuals have been seen to bite and drive away other gobies.

Valenciennea longipinnis

FAMILY: Gobiidae
SCIENTIFIC NAME: *Valenciennea longipinnis*
COMMON NAME: Ocellated Goby
DISTRIBUTION: TI-WP
HABITAT: Sand; sandy rubble
GENERAL WATER DEPTH: 1–10 m (3–33 ft)
FOOD HABIT: Carnivorous: worms; crustaceans
SIZE: 200 mm (8 in)
DESCRIPTION: One of the larger gobies, the ocellated goby has a very beautiful colour pattern and lives in lagoons on broken rubble bottoms dotted by sand patches. It usually occurs in pairs and may be found on mainland reefs, continental reefs and on off-shore reefs. Each pair excavates a hole under a buried piece of dead coral slab, or a clump of dead coral. During the day each takes turns at house cleaning, bringing out pieces of dead coral and mouthfuls of sand and depositing it near the entrance.

Valenciennea muralis

FAMILY: Gobiidae
SCIENTIFIC NAME: *Valenciennea muralis*
COMMON NAME: Mural Goby
DISTRIBUTION: TI-WP

HABITAT: Sand
GENERAL WATER DEPTH: 1–15 m (3–49 ft)
FOOD HABIT: Carnivorous: invertebrates
SIZE: 100 mm (4 in)
DESCRIPTION: Mural gobies are almost always seen in pairs, living around mainland reefs, continental island reefs and along outer barrier reefs and selecting areas of fine sand in lagoons and along the fringes of back reefs. The burrow is generally in the open and territorial holes have a wide rim of sand. When feeding, it rarely ventures very far from the burrow and at the first sign of danger (or an over-anxious underwater photographer), the pair will dive into the burrow.

Gonorhynchus greyi

FAMILY: Gonorhynchidae
SCIENTIFIC NAME: *Gonorhynchus greyi*
COMMON NAME: Beaked Salmon
DISTRIBUTION: WT/S; CT/S
HABITAT: Sand; mud
GENERAL WATER DEPTH: 5–100 m (16–328 ft)
FOOD HABIT: Carnivorous: worms
SIZE: 380 mm (15 in)
DESCRIPTION: Not often encountered by line fishermen, this rather strange and some-what primitive fish lives on soft bottoms where it grubs around in the sediment searching for the small invertebrates on which it feeds. Identification is very simple; no other fish resembles it. The fins have dark blotches, the scales are quite small and there are small sensory papillae under the nose. The flesh is firm, white and good to eat. Most specimens are taken by trawling.

FAMILY: Grammistidae
SCIENTIFIC NAME: *Diploprion bifasciatum*
COMMON NAME: Yellow Soapfish
DISTRIBUTION: TI-WP
HABITAT: Coral and rocky reefs
GENERAL WATER DEPTH: 5–50 m (16–164 ft)
FOOD HABIT: Carnivorous: fishes; invertebrates
SIZE: 380 mm (15 in)
DESCRIPTION: A very easily recognised species from juvenile through to adult, the yellow soapfish is more likely to be seen at scuba diving depths than in lagoon shallows. Almost always seen as a solitary species, it has a fairly wide range from the Indian

Diploprion bifasciatum

Ocean up to Japan and down into the Western Pacific Ocean. The fish has in the past been called yellow emperor, or two-banded perch, neither name being correct.

Grammistes sexlineatus

FAMILY: Grammistidae
SCIENTIFIC NAME: *Grammistes sexlineatus*
COMMON NAME: Six-lined Soapfish
DISTRIBUTION: TI-WP
HABITAT: Coral reefs
GENERAL WATER DEPTH: 10–25 m (33–82 ft)
FOOD HABIT: Carnivorous: fishes; crustaceans
SIZE: 270 mm (11 in)
DESCRIPTION: Rarely seen in the open, the six-lined soapfish inhabits crevices, caves and holes in cliff faces and drop-offs and is difficult to find. Solitary by habit, the sub-adult fish has dramatic bold stripes, but as it gets older and mature the stripes often break up into spots. With a range from Africa to Japan and down through the Indo-Pacific region, this little soapfish (like others of its kind) has a particularly noxious mucous coating on its skin. This is produced by the fish as a predator-inhibiting agent.

FAMILY: Synodontidae
SCIENTIFIC NAME: *Saurida gracilis*
COMMON NAME: Slender Saury; Saury
DISTRIBUTION: TI-WP; WT/S

Saurida gracilis

HABITAT: Sand; mud; seagrass; rubble
GENERAL WATER DEPTH: 1–20 m (3–66 ft)
FOOD HABIT: Carnivorous: fishes;
crustaceans
SIZE: 270 mm (11 in)
DESCRIPTION: Most likely to be seen or caught in sheltered bays, estuaries or lagoons, the slender saury is far more deceptive in its hunting behaviour than is the related variegated lizardfish (*Synodus variegatus*), and it seldom perches on high places in full view. Instead, it tends to be found among algae-covered rubble or sandy mud around reefs. The slender saury is sometimes caught on a hand line or in trawls. In tropical waters it may be used as bait for larger species.

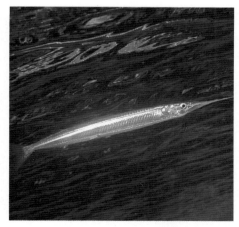

Hyporhampus australis

FAMILY: Hemiramphidae
SCIENTIFIC NAME: *Hyporhampus australis*
COMMON NAME: Eastern Sea Garfish
DISTRIBUTION: TWP; WT/S
HABITAT: Surface; water column
GENERAL WATER DEPTH: Surface to 10 m
(33 ft)
FOOD HABIT: Carnivorous: plankton;
crustaceans

SIZE: 450 mm (18 in)
DESCRIPTION: An important angling species that is very good to eat, the sea garfish is one of the largest garfishes found in southern waters. For most of the year it lives in open surface waters, only venturing into estuaries, bays and inlets during spring and early summer to spawn. Large schools congregate in the shallows near seagrass and algae beds where they lay their eggs. It is difficult to approach underwater and shies away from divers as it would from any other predators.

Hyporhampus melanochir

FAMILY: Hemiramphidae
SCIENTIFIC NAME: *Hyporhampus
melanochir*
COMMON NAME: Dusky Sea Garfish
DISTRIBUTION: WT/S
HABITAT: Surface waters
GENERAL WATER DEPTH: Surface to 5 m
(16 ft)
FOOD HABIT: Carnivorous
SIZE: 510 mm (20 in)
DESCRIPTION: Because it lives along the inshore coastal fringes, the dusky sea garfish is accessible to both commercial and amateur fishermen the year round. This fact is well-supported by the catch rates which for this species alone often make up 75 per cent of the total Australian garfish tonnage. Garfish are naturally school fish and have many predators, including seabirds and other fish. They make excellent bait; at night many species form densely-packed aggregations in the shallows.

FAMILY: Holocentridae
SCIENTIFIC NAME: *Myripristis adustus*
COMMON NAME: Blackfin Squirrelfish
DISTRIBUTION: TI–WP
HABITAT: Coral reefs
GENERAL WATER DEPTH: 10–25 m
(33–82 ft)
FOOD HABIT: Carnivorous: fishes;
crustaceans
SIZE: 150 mm (6 in)
DESCRIPTION: Rather than live in the upper parts of the reef crest corals as do other species of squirrelfish, the blackfin squirrel-

Myripristis adustus

fish tends to live along the drop-offs and reef slopes that border deeper channels. It is not always easy to approach and will invariably turn away from the camera, with the result that the photograph shows an underexposed dark head. This species is common in some localities close to the equator. It is distinguished by its black tipped fins, black gill spot and nocturnal habit.

Myripristis murdjan

FAMILY: Holocentridae
SCIENTIFIC NAME: *Myripristis murdjan*
COMMON NAME: Crimson Squirrelfish
DISTRIBUTION: TI–WP
HABITAT: Rocky and coral reefs
GENERAL WATER DEPTH: 5–20 m
(16–66 ft)
FOOD HABIT: Carnivorous: fishes;
crustaceans
SIZE: 300 mm (12 in)
DESCRIPTION: Easily distinguished from other squirrelfish, the crimson squirrelfish has no spine at the base of the preopercular (gill cover) and the leading edges of all fins are tipped with white. During the day it congregates in groups beneath ledges and in caves, often where there is a cleaner shrimp station. At night it ventures out to feed on nocturnal crustaceans and small fish.

Myripristis vittatus

FAMILY: Holocentridae
SCIENTIFIC NAME: *Myripristis vittatus*
COMMON NAME: Red-orange Squirrelfish
DISTRIBUTION: TI–WP
HABITAT: Coral reefs
GENERAL WATER DEPTH: 10–30 m
(33–98 ft)
FOOD HABIT: Carnivorous: fishes
SIZE: 140 mm (6 in)
DESCRIPTION: A rather beautiful species, the red-orange squirrelfish lives in groups along the cliff faces and channel slopes of outer reefs in the Indian and Pacific Oceans. Rather than inhabiting coral, it tends to inhabit holes and caves lower down the reef slope. The red-orange squirrelfish is easily identifiable as all its fins, with the exception of the pectorals, are bright red with white edges or tips.

Sargocentron cornutus

FAMILY: Holocentridae
SCIENTIFIC NAME: *Sargocentron cornutus*
COMMON NAME: Horned Squirrelfish
DISTRIBUTION: TI–WP
HABITAT: Coral reefs
GENERAL WATER DEPTH: 10–20 m
(33–66 ft)

FOOD HABIT: Carnivorous: fishes;
crustaceans
SIZE: 200 mm (8 in)
DESCRIPTION: The horned squirrelfish is nocturnal and even on late afternoons rarely comes out in the open. When it does dart from one hole to another to snatch an inquisitive look at an underwater photographer it wastes no time. It has a characteristic colour pattern and a large preopercular (first gill cover) spine, and is encountered over a wide expanse of tropical reefs.

Sargocentron ruber

FAMILY: Holocentridae
SCIENTIFIC NAME: *Sargocentron ruber*
COMMON NAME: Red Squirrelfish
DISTRIBUTION: TI–WP
HABITAT: Rocky and coral reefs
GENERAL WATER DEPTH: 3–20 m
(10–66 ft)
FOOD HABIT: Carnivorous: fishes;
crustaceans
SIZE: 220 mm (9 in)
DESCRIPTION: Found along inshore and off-shore barrier reefs, the red squirrelfish is probably the best known of the entire squirrelfish family. This is not very surprising as although all species are basically nocturnal hunters and spend the day in the dark places of the reef, a few, including the red squirrelfish, may be seen out of their coral fortresses during overcast days or during late afternoon when the sun is low. They also often congregate in small groups beneath tabular staghorn corals, though never foraging far from their protective holes or ledges. Sometimes a school will congregate near a cleaner wrasse station and line up to take their turns at being cleaned. The species has a very long preopercular (first gill cover) spine and serrated scales. It feeds on smaller fish and crustaceans and is sometimes caught on hand lines.

Sargocentron spinifer

FAMILY: Holocentridae
SCIENTIFIC NAME: *Sargocentron spinifer*
COMMON NAME: Spiny Squirrelfish
DISTRIBUTION: TI–WP
HABITAT: Coral and rocky reefs
GENERAL WATER DEPTH: 10–25 m
(33–82 ft)
FOOD HABIT: Carnivorous: fishes
SIZE: 260 mm (10 in)
DESCRIPTION: Like all squirrelfishes, the spiny squirrelfish is nocturnal and lives in caves and beneath high ledges during the day. Even at night it rarely goes far from its hole in the reef, retreating as soon as a light beam is shone in its direction. The largest of the squirrelfishes, it is easily identified by its longer snout, yellow fins, dark red spot behind the eye and the red edging on its dorsal fin.

Sargocentron violaceus

FAMILY: Holocentridae
SCIENTIFIC NAME: *Sargocentron violaceus*
COMMON NAME: Violet Squirrelfish
DISTRIBUTION: TI–WP
HABITAT: Coral reefs
GENERAL WATER DEPTH: 5–10 m
(16–33 ft)

FOOD HABIT: Carnivorous: fishes; crustaceans

SIZE: 220 mm (9 in)

DESCRIPTION: The violet squirrelfish has been observed to live in gutters behind the outer reef ramparts where it inhabits holes and ledges along the sides and lower areas of the gutters. Of nocturnal habit, it is very shy during the day and although its inquisitive nature often gets the better of it, it is not easily photographed in the surging waters breaking over the reef. It is found on Pacific and Indian Ocean reefs. Distinguishing features are a red head, violet-barred scales, a red spot on the upper caudal peduncle (tail junction) and a black mark on the upper operculum (gill cover). Like all other members of this genus it has a very sharp prominent preopercular spine.

Istiophorus platypterus

FAMILY: Istiophoridae
SCIENTIFIC NAME: *Istiophorus platypterus*
COMMON NAME: Sailfish
DISTRIBUTION: Worldwide (warm seas)
HABITAT: Open ocean
GENERAL WATER DEPTH: Near surface
FOOD HABIT: Carnivorous
SIZE: Up to 328 cm (10.76 ft)

DESCRIPTION: The sailfish is dark blue on the upper half of its sides, changing to a silvery cast on the lower half. The namesake dorsal fin is dark blue with even darker spots. Its longest rays are near the middle. The long bill of the sailfish is used in slashing through schools of prey, injured individuals of which are captured by mouth after the attack. There have been documented cases of 'attacks' on small boats.

FAMILY: Kyphosidae
SCIENTIFIC NAME: *Kyphosus cornelii*
COMMON NAME: Cornel's Drummer
DISTRIBUTION: TIO
HABITAT: Rocky and coral reefs
GENERAL WATER DEPTH: 2–20 m (6–66 ft)

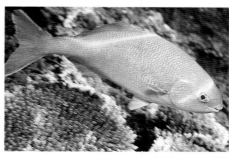

Kyphosus cornelii

FOOD HABIT: Herbivorous: algae
SIZE: 600 mm (2 ft) (adult)

DESCRIPTION: Cornel's drummer is smaller and slimmer in body shape than the silver drummer. It lives around coastal and offshore reefs and islands off Western Australia and is often difficult to approach underwater. When alive it has a distinct white trim on the upper and lower edges of the caudal fin, bordering on a light brown stripe, which then fades into its general body colour. As with its relative the silver drummer, it is often shot, disembowelled and hung on floats to attract larger and more commercial species such as kingfish.

Kyphosus sydneyanus

FAMILY: Kyphosidae
SCIENTIFIC NAME: *Kyphosus sydneyanus*
COMMON NAME: Silver Drummer
DISTRIBUTION: TI–WP; WT/S
HABITAT: Rocky reefs
GENERAL WATER DEPTH: 2–35 m (6–115 ft)
FOOD HABIT: Herbivorus: algae
SIZE: 760 mm (30 in)

DESCRIPTION: A powerful, schooling and excitable fish, the drummer lives around inshore and offshore reefs, will take a bait, and on light gear in the swell surge makes good sport. The flesh can be eaten if the fish is cleaned on capture, though it may taste weedy. In some parts of southern Western

Australia it is common to be besieged by hundreds of these bounding weed eaters milling around at speed, filling the once clear water of a chosen photographic site with swirling clouds of faeces.

Achoerodus gouldii (male)

FAMILY: Labridae
SCIENTIFIC NAME: *Achoerodus gouldii* (male)
COMMON NAME: Western Blue (Groper) Wrasse
DISTRIBUTION: WT/S
HABITAT: Rocky reefs
GENERAL WATER DEPTH: 5–40 m (16–131 ft)
FOOD HABIT: Carnivorous: invertebrates
SIZE: 2 m (6 ft)

DESCRIPTION: The colours of the western blue (groper) wrasse may vary, as do those of most animal species. Depending on locality and age, the male may vary from dark blue, in hump-headed giants, to green in younger ones. The female also varies but tends to be in shades of grey through to red. Heavily fished by line, gill net and spear, it is partially protected from spearing in Western Australia and South Australia. At all growth stages the species is very fond of red bait crabs and abalone and is good to eat.

FAMILY: Labridae
SCIENTIFIC NAME: *Achoerodus viridis* (female)
COMMON NAME: Eastern Blue (Groper) Wrasse
DISTRIBUTION: WT/S
HABITAT: Rocky reefs
GENERAL WATER DEPTH: 5–40 m (16–131 ft)
FOOD HABIT: Carnivorous: crustaceans; molluscs
SIZE: 1 m (3 ft)

DESCRIPTION: There has been some confusion as to the colours and geographical forms of both the eastern blue and the western

Achoerodus viridis (female)

blue wrasse and it is still not common knowledge that there are two species and both vary in colour. The male of the eastern blue (groper) wrasse may be blue or green; the mature female is red or brown and juveniles are grey with a few yellow spots. The species feeds on molluscs, echinoderms and crustaceans and in some areas is protected.

Bodianus axillaris

FAMILY: Labridae
SCIENTIFIC NAME: *Bodianus axillaris*
COMMON NAME: Axil Pigfish or Coral Pigfish
DISTRIBUTION: TI–WP
HABITAT: Coral reefs
GENERAL WATER DEPTH: 2–20 m (6–66 ft)
FOOD HABIT: Carnivorous: crustaceans
SIZE: 200 mm (8 in)
DESCRIPTION: The axil pigfish is territorial and may be seen to swim in patterns in and around its territory; these patterns may often be repetitive. The juvenile is totally dissimilar in colour and pattern to the adult, being black with white spots, and in the middle 1960s was thought to be new to science. Whereas the adult may be seen in the open, 'flitting' around ledges and over reefs close to the bottom, the juvenile is mostly found in caves.

Bodianus diana

FAMILY: Labridae
SCIENTIFIC NAME: *Bodianus diana*
COMMON NAME: Diana's Pigfish
DISTRIBUTION: TI–WP
HABITAT: Coral reefs
GENERAL WATER DEPTH: 10–30 m (33–98 ft)
FOOD HABIT: Carnivorous: crustaceans
SIZE: 250 mm (10 in)
DESCRIPTION: Unlike many other pigfish commonly seen in the open reef and among lagoonal coral growths, Diana's pigfish is rather shy and secretive, living on cliff faces and drop-offs in deeper waters. During the day it can be seen swimming up and down the reef faces on front or back reefs, searching the ledges, caves, gutters and crevices for food. Like the adult, the juvenile is territorial and may be found living in caves.

Bodianus frenchii

FAMILY: Labridae
SCIENTIFIC NAME: *Bodianus frenchii*
COMMON NAME: Fox Wrasse
DISTRIBUTION: WT/S
HABITAT: Rocky reefs
GENERAL WATER DEPTH: 10–40 m (33–131 ft)
FOOD HABIT: Carnivorous: molluscs; crustaceans
SIZE: 450 mm (18 in)
DESCRIPTION: All observations point to

there being little sexual dimorphism between the male and female of this species. It is also possible that it is not polygamous like other wrasses, and forms pair relationships during the breeding season. The sub-adult fish has a black spot at the base of the pectoral fin; it was once thought to be a separate species. For many years this fish was known as *Bodianus vulpinus*.

Bodianus loxozonus

FAMILY: Labridae
SCIENTIFIC NAME: *Bodianus loxozonus*
COMMON NAME: Reef Pigfish
DISTRIBUTION: TI–WP
HABITAT: Coral reefs
GENERAL WATER DEPTH: 3–40 m (10–131 ft)
FOOD HABIT: Carnivorous: molluscs; crustaceans
SIZE: 400 mm (16 in)
DESCRIPTION: The reef pigfish is a spectacular species that inhabits both shallow lagoons and the deep waters of reef front drop-offs. It is territorial, and shallow water males may have several females within their territory. Not always easy to approach underwater, the male and female have identical colour. Its absence from territory during night dives may be due to a habit of sleeping under sand, as do other members of their genus.

FAMILY: Labridae
SCIENTIFIC NAME: *Bodianus unimaculatus* (male)
COMMON NAME: Red Pigfish
DISTRIBUTION: WT/S
HABITAT: Rocky reefs
GENERAL WATER DEPTH: 10–40 m (33–131 ft)
FOOD HABIT: Carnivorous: molluscs; crustaceans
SIZE: 600 mm (2 ft)
DESCRIPTION: Until recently, the male and female red pigfish were thought to be different species. Like most wrasses, the male and female have a high degree of sexual

Bodianus unimaculatus (male)

Cheilinus undulatus

FAMILY: Labridae
SCIENTIFIC NAME: *Cheilinus trilobatus* (male)
COMMON NAME: Triple-tail Maori Wrasse
DISTRIBUTION: TI–WP
HABITAT: Coral reefs
GENERAL WATER DEPTH: 2–10m (6–33 ft)
FOOD HABIT: Carnivorous: crustaceans
SIZE: 660 mm (26 in)
DESCRIPTION: The triple-tail Maori wrasse is a shallow water, territorial species with the male maintaining a territory along the edges of back reefs, fringing reefs and lagoons. The territory may be marked by a high piece of coral or some other significant object and may extend over 20 m² (215 sq ft). Within the territory there may be up to six females, usually swimming as a group. The male continually patrols the perimeter, occasionally rounding up females that stray too close to the edges and chasing off other males as far as 15 m (49 ft) away from the territory.

dimorphism in body shape and colour. This species is regularly caught off deep coastal and offshore reefs in the South-West Pacific, as far as New Zealand. Strangely, only females seem to be caught by line.

Cheilinus diagrammus

FAMILY: Labridae
SCIENTIFIC NAME: *Cheilinus diagrammus*
COMMON NAME: Violet-lined Maori Wrasse
DISTRIBUTION: TI–WP
HABITAT: Coral and rocky reefs
GENERAL WATER DEPTH: 2–25 m (6–82 ft)
FOOD HABIT: Carnivorous: crustaceans; molluscs
SIZE: 380 mm (15 in)
DESCRIPTION: As well as in barrier reef areas, the violet-lined Maori wrasse can also be seen around the fringing reefs of continental islands and some mainland reefs. Like the scarlet-breasted Maori wrasse *C. fasciatus* this species hovers, using hard corals, soft corals and sea fans as camouflage while hunting. It is easy to get close to underwater and at night sleeps deep in coral grottoes. Unlike some wrasses it does not go to sleep at sunset; individuals may be seen in midwater, or in caves, as late as 8 pm.

Cheilinus trilobatus (male)

FAMILY: Labridae
SCIENTIFIC NAME: *Cheilinus undulatus*
COMMON NAME: Giant Maori Wrasse
DISTRIBUTION: TI–WP
HABITAT: Coral reefs
GENERAL WATER DEPTH: 10–40 m (33–131 ft)
FOOD HABIT: Carnivorous: molluscs; crustaceans
SIZE: 2.3 m (7 ft)
DESCRIPTION: The giant Maori wrasse is mostly seen along the deeper parts of reef fronts that have sandy, rubble terraces where deep gaps lead into the reef, along the slopes of channels and in deeper places in lagoons. Very often several fish may swim together headstanding among the dead coral and

rubble to tear up the bottom in their search for molluscs and crabs. Although large specimens have been caught by line, it is more susceptible to spearfishing, for, when chased, it holes up and is often speared within its 'safe' retreat. Medium size fish are good eating, but large ones are somewhat tough. The extended forehead is characteristic of this species.

Cheilo inermis

FAMILY: Labridae
SCIENTIFIC NAME: *Cheilo inermis*
COMMON NAME: Sharp-nosed Wrasse
DISTRIBUTION: TWP; WT/S
HABITAT: Rocky reefs; seagrass; loose algal mats
GENERAL WATER DEPTH: 2–20 m (6–66 ft)
FOOD HABIT: Carnivorous
SIZE: 400 mm (16 in)
DESCRIPTION: A slim, elusive species living among weed, the sharp-nosed wrasse is rarely seen by most divers. Owing to its small size and specific habitat, the chance of it taking a hook is remote, and as it is not a commercial species, few people have heard of it. Difficult to find, though easy to approach, the sharp-nosed wrasse can usually elude a photographer by keeping beneath the algae strands, tendrils, or fronds.

Choerodon albigena

FAMILY: Labridae
SCIENTIFIC NAME: *Choerodon albigena*
COMMON NAME: Blue Tuskfish
DISTRIBUTION: TI–WP
HABITAT: Carnivorous: molluscs
GENERAL WATER DEPTH: 1–25 m (3–82 ft)
FOOD HABIT: Carnivorous: molluscs
SIZE: 710 mm (28 in)
DESCRIPTION: A good size food fish, normally feeding on molluscs, the blue tuskfish is easily caught with hand lines, or cut fish baits. It tends to enter very shallow waters on the top of the reef flats and during low water is often caught in tide pools. Some specimens have been found in a few centimetres of water lying on their sides under dead coral slabs where they have taken shelter to await the returning tide. When cleaned, it has green or bluish bones but this should not be a deterrent to eating the flesh as it is excellent.

Choerodon fasciatus

FAMILY: Labridae
SCIENTIFIC NAME: *Choerodon fasciatus*
COMMON NAME: Harlequin Tuskfish
DISTRIBUTION: TI–WP
HABITAT: Coral reefs

GENERAL WATER DEPTH: 5–30 m (16–98 ft)
FOOD HABIT: Carnivorous: invertebrates
SIZE: 300 mm (12 in)
DESCRIPTION: The harlequin wrasse is a fairly common territorial species that is very active during the day and easily approachable for photographs. With its unique colour pattern of bright red stripes and prominent blue teeth there is no mistaking this fish, and owing to its boldness it is not difficult to get close to underwater. It soon learns that divers inadvertently provide access to food by stirring up the bottom and dislodging small creatures and it will often swim close by, sometimes becoming a nuisance. Owing to similar colour, male and female are difficult to tell apart, unlike most other wrasses.

Choerodon graphicus

FAMILY: Labridae
SCIENTIFIC NAME: *Choerodon graphicus*
COMMON NAME: Graphic Tuskfish
DISTRIBUTION: TI–WP
HABITAT: Coral reefs
GENERAL WATER DEPTH: 5–30 m (16–98 ft)
FOOD HABIT: Carnivorous: molluscs; crustaceans
SIZE: 450 mm (18 in)
DESCRIPTION: Easily recognised and approached underwater, the graphic tuskfish is a very adept hunter and has a number of tactics to obtain its prey. On coral rubble, it will dig a hole by removing coral piece by piece with its protruding teeth and placing it aside. It then gets into the hole and by vigorous fanning with fins and tail stirs up the bottom in a flurry of coral dust. It will then back off and watch for any movement; if not successful, it repeats the process until it finds its prey.

Choerodon rubescens

FAMILY: Labridae
SCIENTIFIC NAME: *Choerodon rubescens*
COMMON NAME: Baldchin Tuskfish
DISTRIBUTION: TIO
HABITAT: Rocky and coral reefs
GENERAL WATER DEPTH: 1–40 m (3–131 ft)
FOOD HABIT: Carnivorous: molluscs
SIZE: 750 mm (30 in)
DESCRIPTION: Endemic to the waters of the Indian Ocean, the baldchin tuskfish ranges along the Western Australian coast. The common name refers to the well-developed, light-coloured chin of the adult fish; in the juvenile, this feature is less prominent. A popular food fish, well-known to all fishermen, the species is fished commercially by hand lining on deep reefs and is easily speared in the shallows.

Choerodon schoenleinii

FAMILY: Labridae
SCIENTIFIC NAME: *Choerodon schoenleinii*
COMMON NAME: Black-spot Tuskfish
DISTRIBUTION: TI–WP
HABITAT: Coral and rocky reefs
GENERAL WATER DEPTH: 4–30 m (13–98 ft)
FOOD HABIT: Carnivorous: molluscs; crustaceans

SIZE: 1 m (3 ft)

DESCRIPTION: The black-spot tuskfish is found in lagoons and the deeper waters along the terraces and fringes of back reefs. During the day it can be seen foraging among dead coral rubble and around the edges of coral slabs lying on sand. It uses its large tusk-like teeth to pick up and turn over quite large pieces of coral and shingle. It drags them to one side, then lies on its side in the hole and fans the sand away with its pectoral fins, exposing molluscs and crabs which are immediately seized, crushed and swallowed. It readily accepts cut fish baits and is very good eating.

Coris bulbifrons

the male in colour and pattern. The brilliant white body, dark lateral comb-like body stripe, yellow-centred tail and bright red head cap of the female make recognition simple. The juvenile and adult female will often clean schools of other fish. A male may be close by, keeping the females within the territory but no male actively engaged in cleaning has been observed.

Cirrhilabrus temmincki (male)

FAMILY: Labridae
SCIENTIFIC NAME: *Cirrhilabrus temmincki* (male)
COMMON NAME: Japanese Rainbow Wrasse
DISTRIBUTION: TI–WP
HABITAT: Coral reefs
GENERAL WATER DEPTH: 1–20 m (3–66 ft)
FOOD HABIT: Carnivorous: crustaceans
SIZE: 200 mm (8 in)

DESCRIPTION: The Japanese rainbow wrasse frequents lagoons and sheltered back reefs as well as terraces and slopes of reef fronts. It is absent from some reefs, while at others it is most abundant. The females swim in a group about 2 m (6 ft) off the substrate, and several males may swim around and through the group, displaying their colourful dorsal and ventral fins. This genus is recognised by its exceptionally long pelvic fins which are lowered when the male displays.

FAMILY: Labridae
SCIENTIFIC NAME: *Coris bulbifrons*
COMMON NAME: Doubleheader
DISTRIBUTION: TWP
HABITAT: Rocky and coral reefs
GENERAL WATER DEPTH: 1–25 m (3–82 ft)
FOOD HABIT: Carnivorous: molluscs; echinoderms; fishes

SIZE: 600 mm (2 ft)

DESCRIPTION: Only recently described (because its identify was mistaken nearly a century ago), the doubleheader is very common at Lord Howe Island in the South-West Pacific, where for at least 10 years it has been protected from spearing, although islanders and visitors catch it by line and relish the flesh. Although once the El Dorado of big-time spearfishermen, Lord Howe Island is now a haven, and all spear-fishing is discouraged. It is a fish watcher's paradise.

Coris picta (female)

FAMILY: Labridae
SCIENTIFIC NAME: *Coris picta* (female)
COMMON NAME: Comb Wrasse
DISTRIBUTION: TWP; WT/S
HABITAT: Rocky and coral reefs; hard sea floor
GENERAL WATER DEPTH: 1–150 m (3–492 ft)
FOOD HABIT: Carnivorous: crustaceans; echinoderms
SIZE: 220 mm (9 in)

DESCRIPTION: The comb wrasse is one species of wrasse where the female outclasses

Coris sandageri (female)

FAMILY: Labridae
SCIENTIFIC NAME: *Coris sandageri* (male)
COMMON NAME: Sandager's Wrasse
DISTRIBUTION: WT/S; TWP
HABITAT: Rocky reefs
GENERAL WATER DEPTH: 10–40 m (33–131 ft)
FOOD HABIT: Carnivorous: molluscs; crustaceans; echinoderms
SIZE: 500 mm (20 in)

DESCRIPTION: Though Sandager's wrasse is not uncommon in its juvenile and female growth stages, the male is often hard to find, especially in areas where spearfishermen abound. The male is very distinctive in colour pattern and easy to recognise underwater but is not easily approached; most photographs have been obtained from depths of 20–30 m (66–98 ft). At night it sleeps under the sand.

FAMILY: Labridae
SCIENTIFIC NAME: *Epibulus insidiator* (male)
COMMON NAME: Sling-jaw Wrasse
DISTRIBUTION: TI–WP
HABITAT: Coral reefs
GENERAL WATER DEPTH: 3–25 m (10–82 ft)

Epibulus insidiator (male)

FOOD HABIT: Carnivorous: crustaceans
SIZE: 330 mm (13 in)
DESCRIPTION: Although the male sling-jaw wrasse is quite conspicuous in coral gardens, the female, owing to her drab black or brown colouration, is generally overlooked. The species has unique extendible jaws that can telescope out and catch prey in a flash. The sling-jaw wrasse is territorial but I have never seen more than one female at a time within the male's territory. It prefers rich coral cover in shallow water and may be seen in sheltered lagoons or on reef fronts, though it is rather timid.

Gomphosus varius (female)

FAMILY: Labridae
SCIENTIFIC NAME: *Gomphosus varius* (female)
COMMON NAME: Bird Wrasse
DISTRIBUTION: TI–WP
HABITAT: Coral reefs
GENERAL WATER DEPTH: 5–20 m (16–66 ft)
FOOD HABIT: Carnivorous: crustaceans
SIZE: 250 mm (10 in)
DESCRIPTION: The bird wrasse is easily identified by its protruding 'beak'. A swimming behaviour of sculling with its pectorals

in typical wrasse-like fashion, gives it an even more bird-like image as it flits around in shallow coral areas. The female bird wrasse is much more commonly encountered and several may be seen swimming together. Fish of this species will also swim with groups of other wrasses as they feed. The male has similar shape to the female; though larger, it has a blue beak and head with a yellow-green blotch above the pectoral fins. The central part of the body is green, blending into a blue tail.

Hemigymnus melapterus

FAMILY: Labridae
SCIENTIFIC NAME: *Hemigymnus melapterus*
COMMON NAME: Thick-lipped Wrasse
DISTRIBUTION: TI–WP
HABITAT: Rocky and coral reefs
GENERAL WATER DEPTH: 3–25 m (10–82 ft)
FOOD HABIT: Carnivorous: invertebrates
SIZE: 1 m (3 ft)
DESCRIPTION: The thick-lipped wrasse is more familiar to snorkelers, divers and spearfishermen than it is to line fishermen because owing to its diet and feeding behaviour, few are caught on hand lines. It inhabits lagoons and during the day swims around areas of broken bottom and sandy rubble. When feeding it sucks in a mouthful of detritus from the bottom, sorts out the edible portion inside the mouth, swallows the food and allows the residue to trickle out through the gill covers. It is fairly easy to approach underwater and is good eating.

FAMILY: Labridae
SCIENTIFIC NAME: *Labroides bicolor*
COMMON NAME: Bicolor Cleaner Wrasse
DISTRIBUTION: TI–WP
HABITAT: Coral reefs
GENERAL WATER DEPTH: 1–20 m (3–66 ft)
FOOD HABIT: Carnivorous: crustaceans
SIZE: 120 mm (5 in)
DESCRIPTION: Certainly not so prevalent as

Labroides bicolor

the common cleaner wrasse *Labroides dimidiatus*, the bicolor cleaner wrasse inhabits lagoons near back reefs and also on terraces and in deeper surge channels on some reef fronts. Whereas other cleaner wrasses have definite territorial stations where fish come to be cleaned, the bicolor cleaner wrasse, though territorial, ranges more widely in its search for host fishes and is far more aggressive in its approach, often chasing a prospective 'client' high above the sea floor.

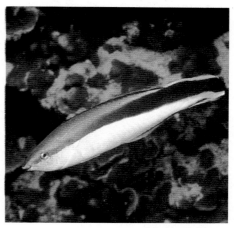

Labroides dimidiatus

FAMILY: Labridae
SCIENTIFIC NAME: *Labroides dimidiatus*
COMMON NAME: Common Cleaner Wrasse
DISTRIBUTION: TI–WP; WT/S
HABITAT: Rocky and coral reefs
GENERAL WATER DEPTH: 3–30 m (10–98 ft)
FOOD HABIT: Carnivorous: crustaceans (ectoparasites)
SIZE: 100 mm (4 in)
DESCRIPTION: Without doubt the best-known cleaner fish, the common cleaner wrasse has entertained and educated thousands of divers, naturalists, photographers and aquarists for many years. These little

fish set up a cleaning station. Each cleaner station supports a male and female pair of cleaner wrasses and fish in the immediate area know and regularly visit the station to be cleaned; some go every day. The cleaners not only investigate and remove parasites from the outside of the fish's body and fins but also go right inside the mouth. Fish require the services of cleaners to maintain their health.

Notolabrus fucicola (male)

FAMILY: Labridae
SCIENTIFIC NAME: *Notolabrus fucicola* (male)
COMMON NAME: Southern Wrasse
DISTRIBUTION: WT/S; CT/S
HABITAT: Rocky reefs
GENERAL WATER DEPTH: 2–90 m (6–295 ft)
FOOD HABIT: Carnivorous: crustaceans; molluscs
SIZE: 380 mm (15 in)
DESCRIPTION: Because of its speed, dark colour and habit of living in exposed kelp-covered reef, the southern wrasse appears less common that it really is. To the average diver these drab-coloured wrasses hardly rate a second glance, the spearfisherman would not bother with them and the line fisherman would only encounter one by accident. The female has light-coloured indistinct blotches, or bars, but lacks the bright yellow dorsal spots of the male.

FAMILY: Labridae
SCIENTIFIC NAME: *Notolabrus inscriptus* (female)
COMMON NAME: Inscribed Wrasse
DISTRIBUTION: WT/S
HABITAT: Rocky and coral reefs
GENERAL WATER DEPTH: 1–30 m (3–98 ft)
FOOD HABIT: Carnivorous: crustaceans; echinoderms
SIZE: 400 mm (16 in)
DESCRIPTION: Endemic to the South-West

Notolabrus inscriptus (female)

Pacific islands of Lord Howe and Norfolk as well as a few coastal reefs off southern Australia, the inscribed wrasse is an inquisitive, medium size species very quick to recognise that divers (clumsy as they are) often provide food, and so follow them. The male grows larger than the female and is a dark greenish-blue with a mesh of fine speckles.

Ophthalmolepis lineolatus

FAMILY: Labridae
SCIENTIFIC NAME: *Ophthalmolepis lineolatus*
COMMON NAME: Maori Wrasse
DISTRIBUTION: WT/S
HABITAT: Rocky reefs
GENERAL WATER DEPTH: 2–40 m (6–131 ft)
FOOD HABIT: Carnivorous: invertebrates
SIZE: 410 mm (16 in)
DESCRIPTION: The Maori wrasse is far more common over its range than the number caught on lines might suggest. A cheeky, territorial species, it soon learns that divers hand out free meals by disturbing the bottom, breaking open sea urchins and turning rocks. Sometimes when it comes up to a diver's mask and expectantly looks inside, it almost seems that it is using 'behavioural language' to suggest that it be fed.

Pictilabrus laticlavius (male)

FAMILY: Labridae
SCIENTIFIC NAME: *Pictilabrus laticlavius* (male)
COMMON NAME: Senator Fish
DISTRIBUTION: WT/S; CT/S
HABITAT: Rocky reefs
GENERAL WATER DEPTH: 3–25 m (10–82 ft)
FOOD HABIT: Carnivorous: crustaceans; worms
SIZE: 220 mm (9 in)
DESCRIPTION: The male senator fish is an attractive, easily recognised species; the female is not so distinguished, having only the fine iridescent blue lines and specks of the male superimposed on a drab brown body. It inhabits coastal and offshore islands and reefs in exposed and sheltered conditions where it swims close to dense seaweed growth. Senator fish are caught in gill nets and sometimes speared for rock lobster bait.

Pseudolabrus luculentus (male)

FAMILY: Labridae
SCIENTIFIC NAME: *Pseudolabrus luculentus* (male)
COMMON NAME: Luculentus Wrasse
DISTRIBUTION: WT/S
HABITAT: Rocky reefs; seagrass
GENERAL WATER DEPTH: 2–20 m (6–66 ft)
FOOD HABIT: Carnivorous: crustaceans

SIZE: 250 mm (10 in)

DESCRIPTION: An attractive and somewhat inquisitive little wrasse, the luculentus wrasse is seen by divers around mainland and offshore islands and reefs. Like all wrasses, the species varies in colour. The male can be brick-red through to grey-green, the female brown-shaded with white spots on the belly. At Lord Howe Island in the South-West Pacific the male is bright green and very territorial. In some locations its territory is in seagrass meadows which is unusual, though it allows easy observation; it mainly likes the edges of rocky reefs.

Pseudolabrus tetricus (male)

FAMILY: Labridae
SCIENTIFIC NAME: *Pseudolabrus tetricus* (male)
COMMON NAME: Blue-throated Wrasse
DISTRIBUTION: WT/S
HABITAT: Rocky reefs
GENERAL WATER DEPTH: 3–30 m (10–98 ft)
FOOD HABIT: Carnivorous: invertebrates
SIZE: 460 mm (18 in)
DESCRIPTION: Often incorrectly termed the blue-throated parrotfish, this species is a wrasse, contrary to some published information. Parroftfish have fused teeth and wrasses have separate teeth. The female is mottled with a large black patch on the side. The blue-throated wrasse is line caught, gill netted and speared.

FAMILY: Labridae
SCIENTIFIC NAME: *Stethojulius bandanensis* (male)
COMMON NAME: Banda Wrasse
DISTRIBUTION: TI–WP
HABITAT: Coral reefs
GENERAL WATER DEPTH: 1–10 m (3–33 ft)
FOOD HABIT: Carnivorous: crustaceans
SIZE: 120 mm (5 in)
DESCRIPTION: The banda wrasse is a small,

Stethojulius bandanensis (male)

very fast swimming shallow water fish that inhabits rich coral areas, or reef tops and slopes, in lagoons. The male is territorial and at times may have small groups of females (up to four or five) within a territory. It has very distinctive male and female forms and this rather incredible example of sexual dichromatism has in the past led many people, including ichthyologists, to regard each as separate species. The female is smaller than the male, of dark colour with myriad white specks on its back. It has a small light blue bar and red spot at the topside of the pectoral fin junction and a yellow patch below the eye towards the nose.

Thalassoma amblycephala (male)

FAMILY: Labridae
SCIENTIFIC NAME: *Thalassoma amblycephala* (male)
COMMON NAME: Blue-headed Wrasse
DISTRIBUTION: TI–WP
HABITAT: Rocky and coral reefs
GENERAL WATER DEPTH: 1–10 m (3–33 ft)
FOOD HABIT: Carnivorous: crustaceans
SIZE: 150 mm (6 in)
DESCRIPTION: The blue-headed wrasse lives in shallow water lagoons and protected reefs

where it spends a great deal of its time swimming 1–2 m (3–6 ft) above the substrate. It moves very fast and although it can be readily approached, is always a challenge to the photographer. Constantly attended by one or more males, the females swim in groups of up to 15 and are dark blue on the top half of the body with dozens of thin black bands on the upper sides. The lower half of the body is white.

Thalassoma lunare (male)

FAMILY: Labridae
SCIENTIFIC NAME: *Thalassoma lunare* (male)
COMMON NAME: Moon Wrasse
DISTRIBUTION: TI–WP
HABITAT: Rocky and coral reefs
GENERAL WATER DEPTH: 1–20 m (3–66 ft)
FOOD HABIT: Carnivorous: molluscs; crustaceans
SIZE: 300 mm (12 in)
DESCRIPTION: The gaudy male moon wrasse is one of the most easily noticed on the reef, flitting in groups around sheltered lagoons and back reef areas. The female can be distinguished from the male by the absence of the crescent-shaped blue tail with its yellow centre. The tail of the female is generally transparent with a hint of blue and red at the leading edges. Younger ones have a black blotch on the caudal peduncle (tail junction) and a small black spot halfway along the soft dorsal fin. The female also lacks the strongly coloured pectoral of the male.

FAMILY: Labridae
SCIENTIFIC NAME: *Thalassoma lutescens* (male)
COMMON NAME: Yellow-green Wrasse
DISTRIBUTION: TI–WP
HABITAT: Rocky and coral reefs
GENERAL WATER DEPTH: 3–25 m (10–82 ft)
FOOD HABIT: Carnivorous: molluscs; crustaceans

Thalassoma lutescens (male)

SIZE: 300 mm (12 in)
DESCRIPTION: There is little doubt that wrasses are among the most beautiful of fish. They also form one of the largest families, are the most difficult to identify (because of their many colour phases) and are very difficult to photograph. The yellow-green wrasse inhabits inshore and offshore reefs and islands in the South-West Pacific and Indian oceans. The female is yellow and lacks the sickle-shaped tail of the male.

Thalassoma purpureum (male)

FAMILY: Labridae
SCIENTIFIC NAME: *Thalassoma purpureum* (male)
COMMON NAME: Green-blocked Wrasse
DISTRIBUTION: WT/S
HABITAT: Rocky and coral reefs; rubble
GENERAL WATER DEPTH: 1–10 m (3–33 ft)
FOOD HABIT: Carnivorous: crustaceans
SIZE: 300 mm (12 in)
DESCRIPTION: Blue is not a common colour in mobile marine invertebrates, yet fish have a bold assortment of blue colours. However, very few can compare with the brilliance of the male green-blocked wrasse. In fact it has to be seen to be believed. It could probably

be hooked on a line and could certainly be speared, but killing such a rare and beautiful animal is hardly excusable.

Xyrichthys taeniouris (juvenile)

FAMILY: Labridae
SCIENTIFIC NAME: *Xyrichthys taeniouris* (juvenile)
COMMON NAME: Olive-scribbled Wrasse
DISTRIBUTION: TI–WP
HABITAT: Coral reefs
GENERAL WATER DEPTH: 2–15 m (6–49 ft)
FOOD HABIT: Carnivorous: crustaceans
SIZE: 300 mm (12 in)
DESCRIPTION: The young juvenile of the olive-scribbled wrasse is exquisite, being beautifully marked, and with such a long head adornment that it might be expected that it would be easy to see. Strangely this is not so underwater as it swims in a very peculiar way close to the bottom and sometimes on its sides. When side swimming it alternates from side to side and looks remarkably like a piece of loose bottom debris being wafted to and fro by the water. The adults generally swim together in pairs and sometimes in threes or fours. They are very determined in searching for food and stir up clouds of silt, particularly on coral rubble bottom.

FAMILY: Latridae
SCIENTIFIC NAME: *Latridopsis aerosa*
COMMON NAME: Bastard Trumpeter
DISTRIBUTION: WT/S; CT/S
HABITAT: Rocky reefs; sand
GENERAL WATER DEPTH: 5–40 m (16–131 ft)
FOOD HABIT: Carnivorous: molluscs; crustaceans
SIZE: 610 mm (2 ft)
DESCRIPTION: The bastard trumpeter is more often seen in the deeper waters of South-West Pacific mainland areas than in

Latridopsis aerosa

oceanic locations. Most sightings have been of small groups of individuals occupying various locations for short periods before moving on. It is speared, gill netted and caught by line and is exceptionally good to eat.

Gymnocranius audleyi

FAMILY: Lethrinidae
SCIENTIFIC NAME: *Gymnocranius audleyi*
COMMON NAME: Collared Sea Bream
DISTRIBUTION: TI–WP
HABITAT: Coral reef; sand
GENERAL WATER DEPTH: 5–30 m (16–98 ft)
FOOD HABIT: Carnivorous: invertebrates
SIZE: 400 mm (16 in)
DESCRIPTION: This very distinctive species is prominently marked by a white band formed into a circle, or collar, behind the eye. The collared sea bream is a diurnal species feeding on areas of broken coral, rubble and sand. It is a solitary species, appears to be territorial, is commonly hand lined, and is easy to approach underwater. The flesh is white and palatable, occasionally having an iodine flavour.

Gymnocranius enanus

FAMILY: Lethrinidae
SCIENTIFIC NAME: *Gymnocranius enanus*
COMMON NAME: Japanese Sea Bream
DISTRIBUTION: TI-WP
HABITAT: Coral reef; sand
GENERAL WATER DEPTH: 10–30 m (33–98 ft)
FOOD HABIT: Carnivorous: crustaceans;
molluscs
SIZE: 500 mm (20 in)
DESCRIPTION: This species may vary in
colour from pink to bronze, the body is dappled with dark smudges, most of which occur
below the lateral line, and all fins are edged
with white. During the day the Japanese sea
bream hovers several metres above the inter-
face between the reef and the sand in sheltered lagoons. It is good eating.

Gymnocranius griseus

FAMILY: Lethrinidae
SCIENTIFIC NAME: *Gymnocranius griseus*
COMMON NAME: Naked-headed Sea Bream
DISTRIBUTION: TI-WP; IWP
HABITAT: Coral reef; sand
GENERAL WATER DEPTH: 5–20 m (16–66 ft)
FOOD HABIT: Carnivorous: molluscs;
crustaceans

SIZE: 500 mm (20 in)
DESCRIPTION: Encountered around sandy
lagoons along outer barrier reef islands and
cays, the naked-headed sea bream is usually
solitary. It swims a few metres from the
bottom, making short forays to the sandy sea
floor to investigate any movement that might
indicate the presence of prey. It may vary in
colour from silvery-white to silvery-pink, has
several black streaks on its pectoral and a
very distinct black eyebrow. It will take a fish
bait and is good eating.

Lethrinus miniatus

FAMILY: Lethrinidae
SCIENTIFIC NAME: *Lethrinus miniatus*
COMMON NAME: Red-throated Emperor
DISTRIBUTION: TI-WP
HABITAT: Coral reefs
GENERAL WATER DEPTH: 5–30 m
(16–98 ft)
FOOD HABIT: Carnivorous: fishes;
crustaceans; molluscs
SIZE: 1 m (3 ft)
DESCRIPTION: The red-throated emperor
forms schools during the day and hovers over
coral or coral heads sometimes in mid-water
and sometimes close to the bottom. However
it forages as an individual and may be seen
picking over the substrate around sand and
rubble areas, pressing under the edges of
rocks and in the sand in search of crabs and
other prey. It feeds mostly from dusk to
dawn. Identifying features include a bright
red dorsal fin, a red blotch at the base of the
pectoral fin and the inside of the mouth is
orange or red. It is a popular angling and
commercial food fish, most of the catch
being 2–3 kg (4.5–6.5 lb).

FAMILY: Lethrinidae
SCIENTIFIC NAME: *Lethrinus nebulosus*
COMMON NAME: Spangled Emperor
DISTRIBUTION: TI-WP
HABITAT: Coral and rocky reefs; sand

Lethrinus nebulosus

GENERAL WATER DEPTH: 1–160 m
(3–525 ft)
FOOD HABIT: Carnivorous: fishes;
invertebrates
SIZE: 800 mm (31.5 in)
DESCRIPTION: The spangled emperor occurs
in small schools around mainland and offshore reefs and islands. With each school
there is one really big fish, and these 'old
men' seem to have a certain aloofness, often
separating themselves from the rest of the
school. Some may even become solitary residents of specific reefs and can be hand fed
by divers. Majestic and exciting to watch, it
is a powerful adversary on a line and is
excellent to eat. Juveniles, or sub-adults,
form large schools in the sheltered waters of
sandy lagoons during the day; at night they
scatter and feed. The spangled emperor is
caught by hand line and also trawled.

Lethrinus reticulatus

FAMILY: Lethrinidae
SCIENTIFIC NAME: *Lethrinus reticulatus*
COMMON NAME: Reticulated Emperor
DISTRIBUTION: TI-WP
HABITAT: Coral and rocky reefs
GENERAL WATER DEPTH: 1–25 m (3–82 ft)

FOOD HABIT: Carnivorous: fishes; crustaceans, molluscs
SIZE: 400 mm (16 in)
DESCRIPTION: Not so common or as large as the red-throated emperor, the reticulated emperor has a much wider distribution and is recorded from inshore and offshore localities. In some areas it does not school during the day and sightings are mainly of individuals. It is caught by line on fish bait, often in association with the red-throated emperor. When excited by bait or berley, both species go into a feeding frenzy and will bite at anything resembling bait. It has red inside the mouth, a pink upper lip, red on the upper pectoral fin and a yellow patch on top of its eye. It is good eating.

Monotaxis grandoculis

FAMILY: Lethrinidae
SCIENTIFIC NAME: *Monotaxis grandoculis*
COMMON NAME: Large-eyed Sea Bream
DISTRIBUTION: TI–WP
HABITAT: Coral reefs; sand
GENERAL WATER DEPTH: 10–20 m (33–66 ft)
FOOD HABIT: Carnivorous: crustaceans; molluscs
SIZE: 760 mm (30 in)
DESCRIPTION: Occurring around continental islands, the large-eyed sea bream is very common in the reef complexes of the outer barrier reefs. Although only a small sea bream, its large eyes, short snout and three white body bars are diagnostic. Swimming as individuals or in groups, the large-eyed sea bream feeds over sandy coral rubble and broken reef.

FAMILY: Lutjanidae
SCIENTIFIC NAME: *Lutjanus adetti*
COMMON NAME: Hussar
DISTRIBUTION: TI–WP
HABITAT: Coral reefs
GENERAL WATER DEPTH: 8–30 m (26–98 ft)

Lutjanus adetti

FOOD HABIT: Carnivorous: fishes; crustaceans
SIZE: 450 mm (18 in)
DESCRIPTION: The hussar frequents inshore and offshore reefs, sometimes congregating during the day into schools, resting in large caves, or beneath ledges, often near a cleaner fish station. The hussar is a very attractive little snapper, with its bright pink colouration and yellow median stripe, making it easy to identify. It is caught by hand line during the day and also at dusk. Owing to its small size, it is often used for bait by some fishermen, though it is quite good eating. With the protection offered by marine park policy and the encouragement given by divers and tourists hand feeding them, the species is very prolific at many dive sites on barrier reefs.

Lutjanus argentimaculatus

FAMILY: Lutjanidae
SCIENTIFIC NAME: *Lutjanus argentimaculatus*
COMMON NAME: Mangrove Jack
DISTRIBUTION: TI–WP
HABITAT: Coral and rocky reefs; mangroves

GENERAL WATER DEPTH: 1–80 m (3–263 ft)
FOOD HABIT: Carnivorous: fishes; crustaceans
SIZE: 1 m (3 ft)
DESCRIPTION: This species is landed in large quantities by amateur anglers throughout its range, though far more are taken around the mainland reefs and estuaries than from the offshore reefs. The mangrove jack is excellent sport on light gear and superb eating. When juvenile, it tends to school up, but as a large adult it is mostly solitary.

Lutjanus bohar

FAMILY: Lutjanidae
SCIENTIFIC NAME: *Lutjanus bohar*
COMMON NAME: Bohar Snapper
DISTRIBUTION: TI–WP
HABITAT: Coral reefs
GENERAL WATER DEPTH: 3–70 m (10–230 ft)
FOOD HABIT: Carnivorous: fishes; crustaceans
SIZE: 910 mm (3 ft)
DESCRIPTION: Recorded from coastal reefs, continental islands and offshore reefs, this snapper is common over its entire range. In the Coral Sea it is very abundant and a nuisance to line fishermen. The snapper is territorial and very curious, even to mouthing cameras left on the bottom. Underwater it is bronze-grey; when caught, angry, or speared, it turns dark red. It is known to cause ciguatera fish poisoning and therefore should not be eaten. It has a deep groove in front of each eye.

FAMILY: Lutjanidae
SCIENTIFIC NAME: *Lutjanus carponotatus*
COMMON NAME: Stripey snapper
DISTRIBUTION: TI–WP
HABITAT: Coral and rocky reefs
GENERAL WATER DEPTH: 4–20 m (13–66 ft)

Lutjanus carponotatus

FOOD HABIT: Carnivorous: fishes; crustaceans
SIZE: 380 mm (15 in)
DESCRIPTION: In some areas this species schools during the day behind large reefs, or hangs in midwater over corals. Sometimes it will take up positions in a coral-covered surge channel, but mostly is seen in the open. In other areas, schooling does not occur and only ones and twos are observed in caves during the day. Its colour varies very little throughout the range but the number of stripes varies between six and twelve. An excellent food fish, the stripey snapper can be caught by line and taken by trolling over shallow reef areas.

Lutjanus fulvus

FAMILY: Lutjanidae
SCIENTIFIC NAME: *Lutjanus fulvus*
COMMON NAME: Blacktail Snapper
DISTRIBUTION: TI–WP
HABITAT: Coral and rocky reefs
GENERAL WATER DEPTH: 8–20 m (26–66 ft)
FOOD HABIT: Carnivorous: fishes
SIZE: 430 mm (17 in)
DESCRIPTION: Occurring in both mainland

and continental islands, the blacktail snapper is not a well-known species. It may be seen in pairs or as individuals around deep gutters and surge channels where, during the day, it is often found under ledges and in open caves close to the bottom. In shape and size it is very similar to the Moses snapper *Lutjanus russelli* but its bronze colouration, black tail, white-edged caudal, soft dorsal, ventral and pelvic fins are distinctive.

Lutjanus gibbus

FAMILY: Lutjanidae
SCIENTIFIC NAME: *Lutjanus gibbus*
COMMON NAME: Paddletail
DISTRIBUTION: TI–WP
HABITAT: Coral reefs
GENERAL WATER DEPTH: 5–15 m (16–49 ft)
FOOD HABIT: Carnivorous: fishes
SIZE: 600 mm (2 ft)
DESCRIPTION: The paddletail is one of the most frustrating species to get close to underwater. One can be in an area where there are hundreds, all milling around in a large school, and the closest you can get to it is 10 m (33 ft). Even solitary fish are very shy and flighty. Some are seen on the edge of the seaward outer barrier reefs but most are seen behind the reef in semi-lagoon situations. Its main distinguishing features are the all-black fins trimmed with white, a yellow upper lip, a bright yellow patch at the base of the dorsal fin and some yellow on the gill cover. The tail is very characteristic, being broad and paddle-like, recurving at the tips. The paddletail should not be eaten as in some areas it is responsible for ciguatera poisoning.

FAMILY: Lutjanidae
SCIENTIFIC NAME: *Lutjanus kasmira*
COMMON NAME: Four-lined Snapper
DISTRIBUTION: TI–WP; WT/S
HABITAT: Coral and rocky reefs
GENERAL WATER DEPTH: 10–30 m (33–98 ft)

Lutjanus kasmira

FOOD HABIT: Carnivorous: fishes; crustaceans
SIZE: 380 mm (15 in)
DESCRIPTION: Exquisitely coloured, the four-lined snapper inhabits inshore reefs, continental islands, and barrier reefs. It is commonly seen in the open around coral heads where there are large caves and fissures. It is sometimes difficult to approach underwater and although it schools, most swim in small groups, rarely alone. This little snapper is very good eating and may be caught on a variety of fish or shrimp bait during the day or night.

Lutjanus russelli

FAMILY: Lutjanidae
SCIENTIFIC NAME: *Lutjanus russelli*
COMMON NAME: Moses Snapper
DISTRIBUTION: TI–WP
HABITAT: Coral and rocky reefs
GENERAL WATER DEPTH: 5–35 m (16–115 ft)
FOOD HABIT: Carnivorous: fishes; crustaceans
SIZE: 500 mm (20 in)
DESCRIPTION: Relatively abundant over its entire distribution, the Moses snapper

ranges from mainland estuaries to continental island reefs as well as to outer barrier reefs. Although it has been observed in large schools it is more likely to be seen in pairs or small groups. During the day it 'holes up' under ledges or gutters with overhangs but sometimes remains almost motionless in the current behind a coral head or reef. Distinguishing features are the black patch at the base of the pectoral, with yellow pectorals, pelvics and white-edged yellow ventral fins. The black spot on or above the lateral line may be well defined, or just a smudge.

Lutjanus sebae (sub-adult)

FAMILY: Lutjanidae
SCIENTIFIC NAME: *Lutjanus sebae* (sub-adult)
COMMON NAME: Red Emperor
DISTRIBUTION: TI–WP
HABITAT: Coral reefs
GENERAL WATER DEPTH: 15–100 m (49–328 ft)
FOOD HABIT: Carnivorous: fishes
SIZE: 1.1 m (3.5 ft)
DESCRIPTION: Far more prevalent in offshore waters than it is on the mainland or continental island reefs, the red emperor occurs around coral heads in deeper water where it spends the day hovering close to the bottom. Because of its excellent eating quality the red emperor is a well-known reef fish with adults reaching a weight of a little over 20 kg (44 lb). Pictured here in its easily recognised form, the juvenile tends to inhabit shallower reef areas than the adult. It generally feeds during twilight, consuming molluscs, crustaceans and fish. Sometimes juveniles accompany small schools of other bottom-feeding fish. The adult is bronze red with the characteristic darker patches seen on the sub-adult still apparent on the top of the soft dorsal fin, top and bottom of the caudal area, and the bottom of the ventral area. All fins are white edged except the caudal which has a white stripe.

Macolor niger

FAMILY: Lutjanidae
SCIENTIFIC NAME: *Macolor niger*
COMMON NAME: Black and White Snapper
DISTRIBUTION: TI–WP
HABITAT: Coral reefs
GENERAL WATER DEPTH: 3–25 m (10–82 ft)
FOOD HABIT: Carnivorous: small fishes; crustaceans
SIZE: 600 mm (2 ft)
DESCRIPTION: With its rounded forehead, solitary habits and outer reef-edge habitat, the black and white snapper is a rather unusual member of its family. In many localities it can be seen hovering over the edge of drop-offs. Sometimes pairs are observed and then seem bolder than solitary fish. The common name only applies to the juvenile and sub-adult, as the mature fish is dark blue with white speckles on the tail and soft dorsal fin; the other fins are black.

Paracaesio xanthurus

FAMILY: Lutjanidae
SCIENTIFIC NAME: *Paracaesio xanthurus*
COMMON NAME: Southern Fusilier; Gold-backed Fusilier
DISTRIBUTION: TI–WP; WT/S

HABITAT: Coral and rocky reefs
GENERAL WATER DEPTH: 10–30 m (33–98 ft)
FOOD HABIT: Carnivorous: zooplankton
SIZE: 380 mm (15 in)
DESCRIPTION: Distinctively coloured, the gold-backed fusilier is a schooling species that inhabits areas around offshore islands and reefs. During the late afternoon it feeds by picking small animals out of the water mass. At night the school breaks up as each fish seeks out its own resting place. At daybreak the school slowly re-forms and often at this time visits a cleaner station to have parasites removed by cleaner fish. The southern fusilier can sometimes be caught by line and is very good eating.

Symphorus nematophorus

FAMILY: Lutjanidae
SCIENTIFIC NAME: *Symphorus nematophorus*
COMMON NAME: Chinamanfish
DISTRIBUTION: TI–WP
HABITAT: Coral and rocky reefs
GENERAL WATER DEPTH: 8–80 m (26–263 ft)
FOOD HABIT: Carnivorous: fishes; crustaceans
SIZE: 1 m (3 ft)
DESCRIPTION: A large snapper with a round forehead, this species is recognised by its colour and conspicuous groove before the eye. Over sand the background colour may change to pink with numerous blue lines running the length of the body. Younger fish have long filaments on the soft dorsal fin. The chinamanfish is often seen in groups of four to six individuals. It will bite aggressively on fish bait and although eaten in some areas it has caused ciguatera poisoning so is generally avoided.

Macrorhamphosus elevatus

FAMILY: Macrorhamphosidae
SCIENTIFIC NAME: *Macrorhamphosus elevatus*
COMMON NAME: Common Bellowsfish
DISTRIBUTION: WT/S
HABITAT: Mud; sand
GENERAL WATER DEPTH: 25–160 m (82–525 ft)
FOOD HABIT: Carnivorous
SIZE: 150 mm (6 in)
DESCRIPTION: There are five species of bellowsfish in South-West Pacific waters, each fairly characteristic in body shape and colouring. Of the three species with elongated bodies, the common bellowsfish is the stoutest and has the largest second dorsal spine; by comparison its other dorsal fin rays are very small. Colour ranges from red to pink on the top part of the body and silvery bronze on the belly. It schools in large numbers and at times a single trawl may bring up several hundred. Curiously, some survive after being brought up from deep water and can be kept alive in aquaria. However, feeding presents problems and the fish generally die after a few days.

Coelorhinchus innotabilis

FAMILY: Macrouridae
SCIENTIFIC NAME: *Coelorhinchus innotabilis*
COMMON NAME: Notable Rattail
DISTRIBUTION: WT/S
HABITAT: Mud
GENERAL WATER DEPTH: 450–900 m (1476–2953 ft)
FOOD HABIT: Carnivorous
SIZE: 240 mm (9.5 in)
DESCRIPTION: Strange dwellers of the deep, representatives of this genus are found living off the coast of South America and South Africa in both the Pacific and Atlantic oceans as well as the South-West Pacific. It has a pointed snout ending in a spine; the other three species inhabiting its area have no spine on the nose. Like many other deep-water species it has a light organ on its abdomen which houses symbiotic luminescent bacteria.

Mola mola

FAMILY: Molidae
SCIENTIFIC NAME: *Mola mola*
COMMON NAME: Sun Fish
DISTRIBUTION: WT/N; T; WT/S
HABITAT: Open ocean
GENERAL WATER DEPTH: 150–350 m (490–1150 ft)
FOOD HABIT: Carnivorous: large planktonic organisms especially sea jellies, salps, comb jellies, fish larvae and crustaceans
SIZE: Up to 4 m (13 ft) long
DESCRIPTION: This is a true oceanic fish, widely distributed in the warmer waters of the world. Despite its size it has no commercial value. It is an unmistakable huge circular-bodied fish with dorsal and anal fins balancing each other either side of the lobed tail, and a small mouth with fused teeth resembling the bill of a parrot (compare the puffer fish, to which it is distantly related). Often mistaken for a shark when feeding close to the surface, the sunfish is a gentle creature and is easily approached by divers. The external body casing is quite hard to touch.

Alutera scripta

FAMILY: Monacanthidae
SCIENTIFIC NAME: *Alutera scripta*
COMMON NAME: Scribbled Leatherjacket
DISTRIBUTION: TI–WP
HABITAT: Coral and rocky reefs
GENERAL WATER DEPTH: 2–25 m (6–82 ft)
FOOD HABIT: Omnivorous
SIZE: 1.2 m (4 ft)
DESCRIPTION: The scribbled leatherjacket is the largest of its family and one of the most ornamental. With such a distinct shape and colour pattern it is easy to identify and even when dead retains some of its colours. This solitary species inhabits shallow water lagoons and the rich coral slopes of back reefs, usually in sheltered water. It ranges over a wide area of reef and is rather shy. It is reported in some areas as being poisonous to eat.

Anacanthus barbatus

FAMILY: Monacanthidae
SCIENTIFIC NAME: *Anacanthus barbatus*
COMMON NAME: Ribbon Leatherjacket
DISTRIBUTION: TI–WP
HABITAT: Coral and rocky reefs; sand; rubble
GENERAL WATER DEPTH: Surface to 20 m (66 ft)

FOOD HABIT: Carnivorous
SIZE: 250 mm (10 in)
DESCRIPTION: This very distinctive species occupies a wider range of habitats than any other leatherjacket and when young, swims alongside floating objects on the surface. Unless one is very observant, its rather unusual behaviour and cryptic colour pattern makes the ribbon leatherjacket very difficult to find. It has a tail one-third as long as its body, with a long chin barbel, and is often associated with bottom growths where it adopts a head-down position. It is very frequently caught by trawlers.

Brachaluteres jacksonianus

FAMILY: Monacanthidae
SCIENTIFIC NAME: *Brachaluteres jacksonianus*
COMMON NAME: Pygmy Leatherjacket
DISTRIBUTION: WT/S
HABITAT: Rocky reefs; jetties; seagrass meadows
GENERAL WATER DEPTH: 1–30 m (3–98 ft)
FOOD HABIT: Carnivorous: crustaceans
SIZE: 80 mm (3 in)
DESCRIPTION: About 54 leatherjacket species are known to occur in Australasian waters, almost twice the number found in any other area of the world. The pygmy leatherjacket is the second smallest representative and although it has been seen around offshore islands and coastal reefs, it is more common in bays, estuaries and inlets. The species is variable in colour and intensity of pattern, but easily recognised.

FAMILY: Monacanthidae
SCIENTIFIC NAME: *Meuschenia trachylepis*
COMMON NAME: Yellow-finned Leatherjacket
DISTRIBUTION: WT/S
HABITAT: Rocky reefs
GENERAL WATER DEPTH: 5–30 m (16–98 ft)

Meuschenia trachylepis

FOOD HABIT: Carnivorous: sponges; crustaceans; molluscs
SIZE: 400 mm (16 in)
DESCRIPTION: The yellow-finned leatherjacket inhabits coastal and offshore areas around islands and reefs. It seems to be far more common in sheltered bays and estuaries than on the exposed coast. The male, at least, is territorial in feeding behaviour and will threaten other males by a bluffing 'dance' procedure that includes head-to-tail pivoting and the repeated opening and closing of the tail flag. This species can be caught by hand, gill netted and hand lined, and is good to eat.

Meuschenia venusta (female)

FAMILY: Monacanthidae
SCIENTIFIC NAME: *Meuschenia venusta* (female)
COMMON NAME: Beautiful Leatherjacket
DISTRIBUTION: WT/S
HABITAT: Rocky reefs
GENERAL WATER DEPTH: 15–30 m (49–98 ft)
FOOD HABIT: Carnivorous
SIZE: 110 mm (4 in)
DESCRIPTION: Ranging from the South-West Pacific to the Southern Indian Ocean,

this species generally swims over and among algae beds where it seems to prefer the leafy branches at the tops of kelp forests. Owing to its small size it is unlikely to be caught by line. The male is larger than the female and has a blue-mesh pattern behind the eye.

Monacanthus chinensis

FAMILY: Monacanthidae
SCIENTIFIC NAME: *Monacanthus chinensis*
COMMON NAME: Fantail Leatherjacket
DISTRIBUTION: TWP; WT/S
HABITAT: Rocky reefs; jetty piles; mud; seagrass
GENERAL WATER DEPTH: 2–25 m (6–82 ft)
FOOD HABIT: Omnivorous: invertebrates; seagrass
SIZE: 380 mm (15 in)
DESCRIPTION: The fantail leatherjacket is a large, extremely abundant, delicious eating, hard-fighting and easily approachable species that occurs in harbours, bays and estuaries. It may even be found high upstream in polluted waters. It is easily caught in traps, by line and in trawls. The flesh is white, firm and keeps well.

FAMILY: Monacanthidae
SCIENTIFIC NAME: *Nelusetta ayraudi*
COMMON NAME: Chinaman Leatherjacket
DISTRIBUTION: WT/S
HABITAT: Rocky reefs; seagrass; jetties; mud
GENERAL WATER DEPTH: 2–160 m (6–525 ft)
FOOD HABIT: Carnivorous: crustaceans; worms

Nelusetta ayraudi

SIZE: 500 mm (20 in)
DESCRIPTION: One of the larger and more common commercial leatherjackets, the Chinaman leatherjacket is brought up in large numbers by trawlers, fish traps and hand lines on and around coastal and offshore reefs. Juveniles swarm in harbours, bays and estuaries and when biting will consume virtually any bait. This species is caught in drop nets and crab snares and can make fishing for other species virtually impossible. But as it is good to eat, only very fussy cooks throw it back.

Cleidopus gloriamaris

FAMILY: Monocentridae
SCIENTIFIC NAME: *Cleidopus gloriamaris*
COMMON NAME: Knightfish; Pineapplefish
DISTRIBUTION: WT/S; TI–WP
HABITAT: Rocky reefs; mud
GENERAL WATER DEPTH: 5–200 m
  (16–656 ft)
FOOD HABIT: Carnivorous: crustaceans
SIZE: 220 mm (9 in)
DESCRIPTION: Before the introduction of scuba diving, the knightfish or pineapplefish was thought to occur on the continental shelves in very deep water as it was only

known from trawls. The knightfish generally lives in small schools, hiding in caves and under ledges during the day and moving into the open at night when it hunts shrimps by means of small light organs on its lower lips.

Lotella rhacinus

FAMILY: Moridae
SCIENTIFIC NAME: *Lotella rhacinus*
COMMON NAME: Beardie
DISTRIBUTION: WT/S
HABITAT: Rocky reefs
GENERAL WATER DEPTH: 8–90 m
  (26–295 ft)
FOOD HABIT: Carnivorous: fishes; crustaceans
SIZE: 510 mm (20 in)
DESCRIPTION: The beardie is probably the most common member of the family Moridae regularly observed by divers. It lives among rocky reefs and generally resides in a cave, ledge or crevice during the day so it is often too shy and elusive to photograph. Superficially similar to the bearded cod, *Pseudophycis barbata* (which has wide black edging on its dorsal, anal and caudal fins), the beardie has fins edged with a thin white trim. It is caught mainly by line on mainland and offshore reefs during the day or night.

Pseudophycis barbata

FAMILY: Moridae
SCIENTIFIC NAME: *Pseudophycis barbata*
COMMON NAME: Bearded Codfish
DISTRIBUTION: WT/S; CT/S
HABITAT: Rocky reefs; mud
GENERAL WATER DEPTH: Intertidal to
  40 m (131 ft)
FOOD HABIT: Carnivorous: fishes; crustaceans
SIZE: 440 mm (17 in)
DESCRIPTION: Sometimes seen in the open during the day, the bearded codfish can be caught quite readily on a hand line and is also trawled in quantity. It has been the subject of intensive research in southern oceans where it has commercial status. Some individuals have been found to live up to 11 years. Its black-trimmed fins are distinctive.

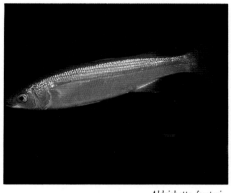

Aldrichetta forsteri

FAMILY: Mugilidae
SCIENTIFIC NAME: *Aldrichetta forsteri*
COMMON NAME: Yelloweye Mullet
DISTRIBUTION: TWP; WT/S
HABITAT: Sand; mud; seagrass; surface waters
GENERAL WATER DEPTH: Surface to 10 m
  (33 ft)
FOOD HABIT: Omnivorous: algae; detritus; worms
SIZE: 400 mm (16 in)
DESCRIPTION: One of the main commercial species in southern Australian waters, the yelloweye mullet inhabits bays, estuaries, lakes and rivers, even moving up into fresh water. Like all mullet, this species schools and feeds mostly by foraging in soft bottom sediments. It is easy to identify as its eyes are yellow, and it is very conspicuous underwater.

FAMILY: Mugilidae
SCIENTIFIC NAME: *Mugil cephalus*
COMMON NAME: Sea Mullet
DISTRIBUTION: TI–WP
HABITAT: Estuaries; open ocean
GENERAL WATER DEPTH: Surface to 20 m
  (66 ft)

Mugil cephalus

FOOD HABIT: Omnivorous: algae; detritus; crustaceans

SIZE: 760 mm (30 in)

DESCRIPTION: The sea mullet is found in coastal waters, though stragglers do make their way out to barrier reefs. The young fish spends its life in the estuaries and enters fresh water. The sea mullet migrates annually to spawn and during this time it is netted commercially. After spawning, large adults may penetrate well into estuaries where they are shot, speared, jagged, as well as being caught by line, rod and net. Some estuarine specimens may have lesions. It is a popular food fish and is at its best when grilled over an open fire.

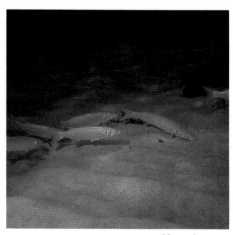

Myxus elongatus

FAMILY: Mugilidae

SCIENTIFIC NAME: *Myxus elongatus*

COMMON NAME: Sand Mullet

DISTRIBUTION: WT/S

HABITAT: Sand; seagrass

GENERAL WATER DEPTH: 1–10 m (3–33 ft)

FOOD HABIT: Omnivorous

SIZE: 380 mm (15 in)

DESCRIPTION: The sand mullet seems to prefer cleaner conditions than do some of the

estuarine mullet species. It inhabits shallow water sand bars, river mouths, ocean inlets and offshore island lagoons where it feeds during the day by taking in mouthfuls of sand and sifting out the edible matter. It is elusive and can be extremely difficult to photograph. This species is taken on lines and netted. It can be distinguished by its very flat head, lack of teeth on the tongue, the black spot at the base of the pectoral fin and the gold blotch on the gill cover.

Mulloidichthys flavolineatus

FAMILY: Mullidae

SCIENTIFIC NAME: *Mulloidichthys flavolineatus*

COMMON NAME: Yellow-lined Goatfish

DISTRIBUTION: TI–WP

HABITAT: Coral reefs; sand; rocky reefs

GENERAL WATER DEPTH: 1–20 m (3–66 ft)

FOOD HABIT: Carnivorous: crustaceans; worms

SIZE: 400 mm (16 in)

DESCRIPTION: The yellow-lined goatfish swims in schools near coral and rocky reefs, mostly in offshore waters. During the day it searches for invertebrates in the sand, using long chin barbels to sense prey. When feeding on sand the large adult turns white and the yellow body stripe may be subdued; the black spot on the centre of the body on the lateral line is always a good distinguishing feature.

FAMILY: Mullidae

SCIENTIFIC NAME: *Mulloidichthys vanicolensis*

COMMON NAME: Gold-striped Goatfish

DISTRIBUTION: TI–WP

HABITAT: Coral reefs

GENERAL WATER DEPTH: 3–20 m (10–66 ft)

FOOD HABIT: Carnivorous: crustaceans; worms

SIZE: 200 mm (8 in)

DESCRIPTION: One of the smaller goatfish, this attractive species is observed in small

Mulloidichthys vanicolensis

groups of up to 10 fish. Specimens seen on the reef during the day are either resting or being attended by cleaner fish. Unlike the yellow-lined goatfish *M. flavolineatus* the gold-striped goatfish has no black spot on the body. It is very easily approached underwater.

Parupeneus barberinus

FAMILY: Mullidae

SCIENTIFIC NAME: *Parupeneus barberinus*

COMMON NAME: Dash-and-dot Goatfish

DISTRIBUTION: TI–WP

HABITAT: Coral reefs; sand

GENERAL WATER DEPTH: 5–20 m (16–66 ft)

FOOD HABIT: Carnivorous: worms; molluscs; crustaceans

SIZE: 500 mm (20 in)

DESCRIPTION: A large, active diurnal goatfish that swims in small groups of four or five, or as individuals, this species is found in sandy lagoons on offshore islands and cays. Goatfish are the chameleons of the fish world and can change colour and pattern rapidly, depending on mood, time, or when feeding. It should be stressed that these patterns are never haphazard; each acts as a signal and can be photographically recorded. The dash-and-dot goatfish is fairly easy to identify; the large black dot right on the caudal peduncle (tail junction), and the high back stripe remain stable. It is extremely good to eat.

Parupeneus bifasciatus

FAMILY: Mullidae
SCIENTIFIC NAME: *Parupeneus bifasciatus*
COMMON NAME: Double-bar Goatfish
DISTRIBUTION: TI–WP
HABITAT: Coral reefs
GENERAL WATER DEPTH: 2–60 m (6–197 ft)
FOOD HABIT: Carnivorous: crustaceans; worms
SIZE: 260 mm (10 in)
DESCRIPTION: Like many goatfish this species spends the daylight hours resting on the bottom in hollows among coral reefs. On some occasions a school may rest, all lying down and facing the same direction. When feeding, the double-bar goatfish is usually solitary and in the early mornings forages in sand pockets inside lagoons. It has a very characteristic colour pattern and good tasting flesh.

Parupeneus porphyreus

FAMILY: Mullidae
SCIENTIFIC NAME: *Parupeneus porphyreus*
COMMON NAME: Red Goatfish

DISTRIBUTION: TI–WP
HABITAT: Coral reefs
GENERAL WATER DEPTH: 3–20 m (10–66 ft)
FOOD HABIT: Carnivorous: crustaceans; worms
SIZE: 300 mm (12 in)
DESCRIPTION: The large adult red goatfish is generally solitary and has been observed over a three-year period to return to the same resting place after early morning feeding. The juvenile is brown on the upper half and orange below, with two prominent white bars running from the snout through the eye to the centre of the back. There is a white spot at the base of the soft dorsal fin, which is prominent on the juvenile and the adult. Red goatfish juveniles frequently swim in large schools. Individuals, pairs and even groups of a dozen or more, will sometimes mill around cleaner-fish stations, intermixed with other goatfish.

Parupeneus signatus

FAMILY: Mullidae
SCIENTIFIC NAME: *Parupeneus signatus*
COMMON NAME: Black-spot Goatfish
DISTRIBUTION: TWP; WT/S
HABITAT: Rocky reefs; sand
GENERAL WATER DEPTH: 5–80 m (16–263 ft)
FOOD HABIT: Carnivorous: invertebrates
SIZE: 450 mm (18 in)
DESCRIPTION: The black-spot goatfish can be caught by line near sandy areas around inshore or offshore reefs. During most of the day individual fish may sleep in the open or under growths close to their foraging area. Towards late afternoon, loose aggregations are formed as one fish awakens and excites others by its feeding activity. Goatfish have sensory barbels under their lower jaws that enable them to feel out edible material from sand, algae or rubble.

Upeneichthys lineatus

FAMILY: Mullidae
SCIENTIFIC NAME: *Upeneichthys lineatus*
COMMON NAME: Black-striped Goatfish
DISTRIBUTION: WT/S; CT/S
HABITAT: Rocky reefs; sand; seagrass
GENERAL WATER DEPTH: 3–20 m (10–66 ft)
FOOD HABIT: Carnivorous: invertebrates
SIZE: 220 mm (9 in)
DESCRIPTION: A very common, widespread species, the black-striped goatfish may be observed in many different colours from white to bright red, depending on its surroundings, its mood, or whether it is being observed during day or night. In all its colour forms, the dark brown stripe and the iridescent blue spots remain constant. It ranges over the bottom in small schools, searching in the soft sediments for food located with barbels under its chin. Although small, it is a very good food fish.

Enchelycore ramosa

FAMILY: Muraenidae
SCIENTIFIC NAME: *Enchelycore ramosa*
COMMON NAME: Mosaic Moray
DISTRIBUTION: WT/S
HABITAT: Rocky and coral reefs

GENERAL WATER DEPTH: 20–40 m
  (66–131 ft)
FOOD HABIT: Carnivorous: cephalopods
SIZE: 1.5 m (5 ft)
DESCRIPTION: Of all the eels I have photographed, from three-metre (10 ft) giants to pencil-thin snake eels, the mosaic moray is by far the most dramatic. Its characteristic mosaic pattern and curved open jaws lined with long, needle-sharp teeth give it a nightmarish appearance. Despite this it is a shy creature and when confronted by a diver generally withdraws into a crevice. At Lord Howe Island in the South-West Pacific it has been observed eating cuttles and it may also prey on octopus.

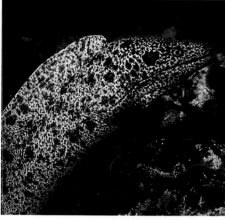

Gymnothorax annasona

FAMILY: Muraenidae
SCIENTIFIC NAME: *Gymnothorax annasona*
COMMON NAME: Lord Howe Island Moray
DISTRIBUTION: WT/S
HABITAT: Coral reefs
GENERAL WATER DEPTH: 2–10 m (6–33 ft)
FOOD HABIT: Carnivorous
SIZE: 1.5 m (5 ft)
DESCRIPTION: A moray eel commonly found in the waters of Lord Howe Island and Norfolk Island in the South-West Pacific, this species tends to be restricted to shallow areas among coral reefs rather than in deeper volcanic terrain. Although most often seen with its head issuing from protective coral lairs during the day, it is more active at dusk and at night, when individuals have occasionally been seen in the open. It is not aggressive.

FAMILY: Muraenidae
SCIENTIFIC NAME: *Gymnothorax eurostus*
COMMON NAME: Abbott's Moray
DISTRIBUTION: TI–WP
HABITAT: Coral and rocky reefs
GENERAL WATER DEPTH: 5–10 m (16–33 ft)
FOOD HABIT: Carnivorous: fishes;
  crustaceans

Gymnothorax eurostus

SIZE: 1 m (3 ft)
DESCRIPTION: Rarely seen in the open, this moray eel is generally found in holes or beneath coral ledges around offshore islands and reefs. Very few specimens have been collected. The black tail with its bright yellow spots is in direct contrast with the front half of the body which has much more prominent yellow markings. As with other moray eels, the flesh should never be eaten as it could well be poisonous. Divers will find it to be rather shy.

Gymnothorax favagineus

FAMILY: Muraenidae
SCIENTIFIC NAME: *Gymnothorax favagineus*
COMMON NAME: Tessellated Moray
DISTRIBUTION: TI–WP
HABITAT: Rocky and coral reefs
GENERAL WATER DEPTH: 2–25 m (6–82 ft)
FOOD HABIT: Carnivorous: fishes;
  crustaceans; molluscs
SIZE: 1 m (3 ft)
DESCRIPTION: The tessellated moray is an easily identified tropical moray eel more frequently seen on offshore islands and reefs than around continental islands. It is often seen by coral reef fossickers wading back

through shallow lagoons after a day on the reef flats. It will not attack waders because the moray is not as aggressive as some people suggest. However, each one should be treated with respect, even when hand feeding, as its sense of smell is very acute and when the smell of food permeates the water it cannot distinguish fish from fingers by sight, especially when the fingers have been doing the feeding.

Gymnothorax flavimarginatus

FAMILY: Muraenidae
SCIENTIFIC NAME: *Gymnothorax*
  flavimarginatus
COMMON NAME: Leopard Moray
DISTRIBUTION: TI–WP
HABITAT: Coral reef crevices
GENERAL WATER DEPTH: 2–15 m (6–49 ft)
FOOD HABIT: Carnivorous: fishes
SIZE: 2 m (6 ft)
DESCRIPTION: Named for its yellow body markings which show through its overlay of brown, the leopard moray always has a spot or patch at the gill opening. Commonly hand-fed by divers throughout tropical oceans, this species can be gentle but has been responsible for many accidental injuries to humans. Moray eels have a very well-developed sense of smell and will try to eat what they smell as fish. Even though a diver has fed the eel fish and there is no food left, it can still smell it in the water and if the strongest scent comes from the hand that held the fish, it cannot tell the difference.

FAMILY: Muraenidae
SCIENTIFIC NAME: *Gymnothorax meleagris*
COMMON NAME: Spotted Moray
DISTRIBUTION: TI–WP
HABITAT: Coral reefs
GENERAL WATER DEPTH: 2–25 m (6–82 ft)
FOOD HABIT: Carnivorous
SIZE: 1 m (3 ft)
DESCRIPTION: The characteristic white opaque spots on a brown background appear

Gymnothorax meleagris

to be more defined in the head region of the species than on the body. Not as common as some of the other tropical moray eels, it is shy and retiring during the day. It inhabits holes in reefs, or crevices, rather than ledges, and like most morays, hunts at night. A small black smudge appears at the gill opening. Although the species occurs in parts of the Indo-Pacific it seems to be more prolific in the western Pacific.

Gymnothorax prasinus

FAMILY: Muraenidae
SCIENTIFIC NAME: *Gymnothorax prasinus*
COMMON NAME: Green Moray
DISTRIBUTION: WT/S
HABITAT: Rocky reefs
GENERAL WATER DEPTH: 1–30 m (3–98 ft)
FOOD HABIT: Carnivorous: crustaceans; cephalopods; fishes
SIZE: 1.5 m (5 ft)
DESCRIPTION: Living in rocky reef habitats, the green moray seems to be more prolific in shallow than in deep waters. Shy and elusive in intertidal rock pools, it is certainly more confident when approached underwater and will slide part way out of its hole with jaws agape and nostrils aflare. Moray eels can be

aggressive and their teeth can certainly cause painful wounds, but if handled correctly some are docile enough to be hand fed. However, if one of these line-tanglers that ties knots in its own body is caught, it is best to cut if off and let it go.

Gymnothorax prionodon

FAMILY: Muraenidae
SCIENTIFIC NAME: *Gymnothorax prionodon*
COMMON NAME: Sawtoothed Moray
DISTRIBUTION: WT/S; TWP
HABITAT: Rocky reefs
GENERAL WATER DEPTH: 15–60 m (49–197 ft)
FOOD HABIT: Carnivorous: cephalopods; crustaceans
SIZE: 1 m (3 ft)
DESCRIPTION: Little is known about this moray eel as it is not seen or caught very often and appears to be one of the rarer species. Some moray eels hunt at night but most feed during the day or at dusk. This species shows little colour variation throughout its range.

School of Four-lined Snapper, *Lutjanus kasmira*

FAMILY: Myctophidae
SCIENTIFIC NAME: *Myctophum punctatum*
COMMON NAME: Lantern Fish
DISTRIBUTION: CT/N; WT/N; WT/S
HABITAT: Open sea especially at the edge of the continental shelf
GENERAL WATER DEPTH: 0–500 m (1650 ft)
FOOD HABIT: Carnivorous
SIZE: Up to 150 mm long
DESCRIPTION: The lantern fish spends the day at depth but may come to the surface at night, sometimes in great numbers. In the Mediterranean Sea lantern fish may be cast up on beaches following stormy weather. As it lives in more or less permanent darkness, the display of lights in the particularly characteristic pattern set by the anatomical position of the light-producing organs serves in species identification and mate recognition. It has a large head with large eyes, tapering body, small dorsal fin and adipose fin. Small pearl-like light-producing organs are arranged in a horizontal row below the mouth and along the belly. Several short rows of light-producing organs branch from the horizontal row, including one between the pectoral and anal fins.

Gnathodentex aureolineatus

FAMILY: Nemipteridae
SCIENTIFIC NAME: *Gnathodentex aureolineatus*
COMMON NAME: Gold-spot Bream
DISTRIBUTION: TI–WP; WT/S
HABITAT: 5–25 m (16–82 ft)
GENERAL WATER DEPTH: Carnivorous
FOOD HABIT: 250 mm (10 in)
DESCRIPTION: Found around offshore islands and reefs, the gold-spot bream is a densely-schooling diurnal species with very distinctive colouration and a characteristic gold spot on the back. Although a school will mill around in one area for quite some time it is not known whether it is restricted to one location or is migratory. Although specimens are line caught it is not generally considered a commercial species.

Pentapodus vitta

FAMILY: Nemipteridae
SCIENTIFIC NAME: *Pentapodus vitta*
COMMON NAME: Threadfin Bream
DISTRIBUTION: TWP; WT/S
HABITAT: Sand; seagrass
GENERAL WATER DEPTH: 3–20 m
  (10–66 ft)
FOOD HABIT: Carnivorous: molluscs;
  crustaceans
SIZE: 220 mm (9 in)
DESCRIPTION: A delightful little fish, the threadfin bream occurs in sheltered bays, inlets and estuaries where it obtains its food in a similar way to related bream. It takes a mouthful of sand, then like many other sand-feeding fish it stops, remains stationary in the water and sifts out the food, the debris passing out through the gills. It can be caught by line and though small, the skinned fillets are reasonably good to eat.

Scolopsis bilineatus

FAMILY: Nemipteridae
SCIENTIFIC NAME: *Scolopsis bilineatus*
COMMON NAME: Bridled Monocle Bream
DISTRIBUTION: TI–WP
HABITAT: Coral and rocky reefs
GENERAL WATER DEPTH: 3–25 m (10–82 ft)

FOOD HABIT: Carnivorous: crustaceans
SIZE: 220 mm (9 in)
DESCRIPTION: The fish of this family use a 'start-stop' movement when swimming that is much more apparent when feeding. The bridled monocle bream is a common little fish found on reefs around continental islands and offshore coral reefs and cays. It prefers sheltered waters and is prolific in lagoons and behind the reef proper in the shallow backwaters. It is very distinctly marked and coloured, and is quite easy to recognise in the field. The juvenile has black and yellow stripes. It does well in aquaria.

Scolopsis lineatus

FAMILY: Nemipteridae
SCIENTIFIC NAME: *Scolopsis lineatus*
COMMON NAME: Lined Monocle Bream
DISTRIBUTION: TI–WP
HABITAT: Coral reefs
GENERAL WATER DEPTH: 2–10 m (6–33 ft)
FOOD HABIT: Carnivorous: crustaceans
SIZE: 250 mm (10 in)
DESCRIPTION: The lined monocle bream often swims in groups of up to a dozen or so above the reef flats whereas most other monocle bream are solitary. It inhabits areas within lagoons, along the reef flats and back edges of reefs, and continental islands. Colours seems to be stable throughout its distribution. Schools are not easily approached underwater, though solitary fish appear less cautious.

FAMILY: Nemipteridae
SCIENTIFIC NAME: *Scolopsis margaritifer*
COMMON NAME: Pearly Monocle Bream
DISTRIBUTION: TI–WP
HABITAT: Coral reefs
GENERAL WATER DEPTH: 2–15 m (6–49 ft)
FOOD HABIT: Carnivorous: crustaceans;
  molluscs
SIZE: 250 mm (10 in)
DESCRIPTION: A solitary, coral-associated monocle bream, this species is generally ter-

Scolopsis margaritifer

ritorial and occupies areas in reefs where there are one or two sand patches. It can be identified by the presence of pearly spots of blue, silver or yellow on the scales, often forming stripes on the body. Light blue spots occur on the cheeks and a light blue stripe runs from the nose up over the eye. The fins are translucent blue. The pearly monocle bream is not commonly caught by line.

Scolopsis monogramma

FAMILY: Nemipteridae
SCIENTIFIC NAME: *Scolopsis monogramma*
COMMON NAME: Monogrammed Monocle
  Bream
DISTRIBUTION: TI–WP
HABITAT: Coral and rocky reefs; sand;
  rubble
GENERAL WATER DEPTH: 15–30 m
  (49–98 ft)
FOOD HABIT: Carnivorous: invertebrates
SIZE: 430 mm (17 in)
DESCRIPTION: The monogrammed monocle bream occurs throughout barrier, mainland, and continental island reefs, and inhabits areas of sand and sandy rubble along the sheltered drop-offs of back reefs. It is an active diurnal feeder taking in mouthfuls of

sand, extracting the food items and allowing the refuse to filter through the back of the gill plates. The flesh is firm and white but without flavour.

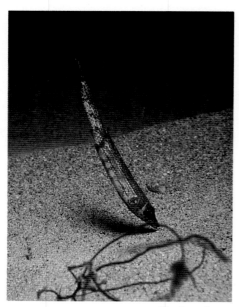

Neoodax radiatus

FAMILY: Odacidae
SCIENTIFIC NAME: *Neoodax radiatus*
COMMON NAME: Weed Whiting
DISTRIBUTION: WT/S
HABITAT: Seagrass; sand; rocky reefs
GENERAL WATER DEPTH: 3–10 m (10–33 ft)
FOOD HABIT: Carnivorous: crustaceans
SIZE: 180 mm (7 in)
DESCRIPTION: Owing to its small size and close association with algae and seagrass, the weed whiting generally remains unnoticed by most divers. It often lies on the bottom among dead seagrass fronds and at other times stands on its head imitating its surroundings. It is quite unrelated to Australian whiting which in turn bear no resemblance to the true whiting of the Northern Hemisphere.

FAMILY: Ogcocephalidae
SCIENTIFIC NAME: *Halieutaea brevicauda*
COMMON NAME: Short-finned Batfish
DISTRIBUTION: WT/S
HABITAT: Mud
GENERAL WATER DEPTH: 40–200 m (131–656 ft)
FOOD HABIT: Carnivorous
SIZE: 200 mm (8 in)
DESCRIPTION: The short-finned batfish varies in colour from grey, green and brown through to bright pink. The skin is covered in short prickles that become sharp when the fish is dried. Completely adapted to a life on the soft ooze of deep ocean floors, it has a

Halieutaea brevicauda

very flat dorsal profile and its modified pectoral fins are used to push itself along the bottom. The batfish is related to the anglerfish and has a similar short fishing tentacle on its head used to attract prey.

Leiuranus semicinctus

FAMILY: Ophichthyidae
SCIENTIFIC NAME: *Leiuranus semicinctus*
COMMON NAME: Banded Snake Eel
DISTRIBUTION: TI-WP
HABITAT: Sand and seagrass meadows
GENERAL WATER DEPTH: 1–10 m (3–33 ft)
FOOD HABIT: Carnivorous
SIZE: 500 mm (20 in)
DESCRIPTION: The snake eel is a delightfully interesting fish that inhabits sandy lagoons and harbours in both inshore and offshore areas. Although most are nocturnal, some individuals may be seen on overcast days, or around dusk, foraging in the open for food. The banded snake eel has an extremely good sense of smell and when searching for food, slides slowly along the bottom, inserting its nose into the sand as it goes, apparently picking up the scent of prey. Rarely caught on lines and unlikely to be trawled, it is impossible to catch and hold by

hand. Invariably it slips away and burrows tail first into the sand, to be gone in an instant.

Muraenichthys ogilbyi

FAMILY: Ophichtidae
SCIENTIFIC NAME: *Muraenichthys ogilbyi*
COMMON NAME: Ogilby's Worm Eel
DISTRIBUTION: WT/S
HABITAT: Sand; seagrass
GENERAL WATER DEPTH: 3–8 m (10–26 ft)
FOOD HABIT: Carnivorous: date mussels
SIZE: 450 mm (18 in)
DESCRIPTION: The photograph was taken using a snorkel as the eel would not emerge from its hole in the sand when scuba diving was attempted, owing to the noise of the exhaust bubbles escaping from the regulator. Ogilby's worm eel is a shy nocturnal forager, preying exclusively on date mussels which it swallows whole. The shells are regurgitated once the mussel has been digested.

Ostorhinchus conwaii

FAMILY: Oplegnathidae
SCIENTIFIC NAME: *Ostorhinchus conwaii*
COMMON NAME: Knifejaw
DISTRIBUTION: WT/S
HABITAT: Mud
GENERAL WATER DEPTH: 60–255 m (197–837 ft)
FOOD HABIT: Carnivorous
SIZE: 410 mm (16 in)

DESCRIPTION: The knifejaw is the only representative of its family occurring in Southern Hemisphere waters and it is found in deeper offshore areas where trawlers bring up small numbers. Its common name is derived from the unusual fusing of the teeth in each jaw, like toadfish and parrotfish. Although the flesh is very good to eat, the knifejaw is not generally seen in fish-shop windows because of its unusual appearance. Cooks usually buy only what they are familiar with so most knifejaws are used by fish-and-chip shops, where they are filleted and sold under another name.

Neocyttus rhomboidalis

FAMILY: Oreosomatidae
SCIENTIFIC NAME: *Neocyttus rhomboidalis*
COMMON NAME: Spiky Dory
DISTRIBUTION: WT/S
HABITAT: Water column; over mud
GENERAL WATER DEPTH: 640–820 m
(2100–2690 ft)
FOOD HABIT: Carnivorous: fishes
SIZE: 280 mm (11 in)
DESCRIPTION: Very few of these little fish are ever seen, even by commercial trawl fishermen. They were first discovered off South Africa and, like so many other inter-ocean deepwater fish, those in South-West Pacific seas have few differences from those originally described. Owing to its size and deepwater habitat there is little likelihood that the species will become commercially important. It remains an interesting oddity in museums and on fish species lists, occasionally being found in the nets of research vessels.

FAMILY: Ostraciidae
SCIENTIFIC NAME: *Aracana aurita* (female)
COMMON NAME: Shaw's Cowfish
DISTRIBUTION: WT/S; CT/S
HABITAT: Rocky reefs; seagrass; jetties
GENERAL WATER DEPTH: 5–20 m (16–66 ft)

Aracana aurita (female)

FOOD HABIT: Omnivorous: algae; sessile invertebrates
SIZE: 220 mm (9 in)
DESCRIPTION: At first glance, the female Shaw's cowfish may look similar to the female ornate cowfish, but they differ. The latter has a blunt forehead while the former has a sloping forehead and a pointed snout. The male is easily distinguished but, like the male of the ornate cowfish, it has a blue tail flag. It seems more approachable than the ornate cowfish even though it has similar habitat and behaviour. It is poisonous if eaten.

Aracana ornata

FAMILY: Ostraciidae
SCIENTIFIC NAME: *Aracana ornata*
COMMON NAME: Orange Boxfish
DISTRIBUTION: WT/S
HABITAT: Rocky reefs; seagrass; jetties
GENERAL WATER DEPTH: 3–20 m
(10–66 ft)
FOOD HABIT: Omnivorous: molluscs; algae
SIZE: 150 mm (6 in)
DESCRIPTION: An absolutely exquisite fish, the orange boxfish is one of the most colourful and easily recognised species. It

usually lives in the shallow, sheltered waters of bays and estuaries and is not always easy to approach underwater. Rarely caught on a line, it gets into beach seines and is sometimes washed up after storms. The female is more robust than the male and her body is striped. Lacking the male's bright blue tail ornamentation. The orange boxfish is poisonous if eaten.

Ostracion cubicus

FAMILY: Ostraciidae
SCIENTIFIC NAME: *Ostracion cubicus*
COMMON NAME: Cubed Boxfish; Blue Spotted Boxfish
DISTRIBUTION: WT/S
HABITAT: Rocky and coral reefs
GENERAL WATER DEPTH: 10–40 m
(33–131 ft)
FOOD HABIT: Omnivorous: molluscs; algae
SIZE: 450 mm (18 in)
DESCRIPTION: Like many other boxfish, the cubed boxfish has startling colours and though not a fast swimmer, it is not always easy to approach closely. It makes an interesting aquarium specimen; larger ones must be kept separate from other fish, especially in small tanks, as they exude a toxic substance that may kill other species. Like all boxfish, this species is poisonous if eaten.

FAMILY: Ostraciidae
SCIENTIFIC NAME: *Ostracion meleagris*
(male)
COMMON NAME: Spotted Boxfish
DISTRIBUTION: TI-WP
HABITAT: Coral and rocky reefs
GENERAL WATER DEPTH: 3–20 m (10–66 ft)
FOOD HABIT: Omnivorous: sessile invertebrates; sponges; algae
SIZE: 220 mm (9 in)
DESCRIPTION: Some boxfish are extraordinarily beautiful and this species is no exception; the female is blue with bright yellow spots and markings. Sometimes seen in shel-

Ostracion meleagris (male)

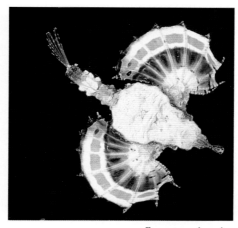

Eurypegasus draconis

FOOD HABIT: Carnivorous: crustaceans
SIZE: 120 mm (5 in)
DESCRIPTION: A small, elongate, schooling species that inhabits coral reefs in the tropics, this little fish is found during the day under ledges, in caves and under overhangs. A school consists of some 30 to 40 closely packed individuals. The colouration during the day is translucent yellowish at the front, with a bronze tail region. The vertebrae can be seen through the posterior part of the body. It hunts small crustaceans at night.

tered lagoons and back reefs along barrier reefs, the spotted boxfish is more numerous on the inshore lagoon reefs. It feeds on a variety of organisms and is always easy to approach. The spotted boxfish is poisonous and when threatened, releases a highly toxic substance. It is a popular aquarium fish but may need a separate tank.

FAMILY: Pegasidae
SCIENTIFIC NAME: *Eurypegasus draconis*
COMMON NAME: Short Dragonfish
DISTRIBUTION: TI–WP; WT/S
HABITAT: Sand; rubble
GENERAL WATER DEPTH: 3–50 m
 (10–164 ft)
FOOD HABIT: Carnivorous: crustaceans
SIZE: 70 mm (2.5 in)
DESCRIPTION: The short dragonfish lives on sandy weed bottom around reefs, or among sandy rubble, and is resident in inshore as well as offshore waters. There may be sexual dimorphism within the species. It crawls around the bottom with its large pectorals extended, but doesn't seem to swim very frequently. Few have ever been seen in that natural habitat, owing to their small size.

Pempheris analis

FAMILY: Pempheridae
SCIENTIFIC NAME: *Pempheris analis*
COMMON NAME: Bronze Bullseye
DISTRIBUTION: TI–WP; WT/S
HABITAT: Coral and rocky reefs
GENERAL WATER DEPTH: 5–40 m
 (16–131 ft)
FOOD HABIT: Carnivorous: crustaceans
SIZE: 170 mm (7 in)
DESCRIPTION: The bronze bullseye is a nocturnal species that during the day lives under caves and ledges in small groups. If approached too closely it will swim deep into the shelter of the reef. It inhabits inshore mainland reefs and offshore reefs, emerging from their caverns some time after dusk to feed on small crustaceans. Dorsal, ventral and caudal fins have black tips.

Rhynchostracion nasus

FAMILY: Ostraciidae
SCIENTIFIC NAME: *Rhynchostracion nasus*
COMMON NAME: Long-nosed Boxfish
DISTRIBUTION: TI–WP
HABITAT: Rocky and coral reefs
GENERAL WATER DEPTH: 2–20 m (6–66 ft)
FOOD HABIT: Omnivorous
SIZE: 200 mm (8 in)
DESCRIPTION: The long-nosed boxfish is far more common on continental reefs and islands than on coral cays and reefs. It is generally solitary and quite active during the day. Its white body colour can sometimes be yellow with the black spots varying in size. Owing to its poor swimming capability, it is very frequently washed up on shore during storms. It is regularly trawled and taken in seine nets and is poisonous.

Parapriacanthus ransonneti

FAMILY: Pempheridae
SCIENTIFIC NAME: *Parapriacanthus ransonneti*
COMMON NAME: Ransonnet's Bullseye
DISTRIBUTION: TI–WP
HABITAT: Coral reefs
GENERAL WATER DEPTH: 3–15 m
 (10–49 ft)

FAMILY: Pempheridae
SCIENTIFIC NAME: *Pempheris klunzingeri*
COMMON NAME: Klunzinger's Bullseye
DISTRIBUTION: WT/S
HABITAT: Rocky and coral reefs
GENERAL WATER DEPTH: 5–25 m
 (16–82 ft)
FOOD HABIT: Carnivorous: crustaceans
SIZE: 180 mm (7 in)
DESCRIPTION: The large eye of this fish gives a clue to its nocturnal habits and though it can be seen in the open on overcast days, it is mainly seen under ledges or in

Pempheris klunzingeri

Evistias acutirostris

Parapercis haackei

caves during the day. A schooling species, Klunzinger's bullseye inhabits inshore and offshore reefs with relatively sheltered aspects. At night it ventures into the open water column where it is thought to feed on planktonic crustaceans. This species is often caught by night fishermen.

Pempheris oualensis

FAMILY: Pempheridae
SCIENTIFIC NAME: *Pempheris oualensis*
COMMON NAME: Copper Bullseye
DISTRIBUTION: WT/S; WT/N
HABITAT: Rocky and coral reefs
GENERAL WATER DEPTH: 3–25 m (10–82 ft)
FOOD HABIT: Carnivorous: crustaceans
SIZE: 200 mm (8 in)
DESCRIPTION: A shallow water, schooling species, the copper bullseye can be distinguished from the rough bullseye by its untapered dorsal fin, large scales and the eight or nine longitudinal stripes that run along the alternate rows of scales. It is very well known to divers as it inhabits caves, ledges and rock crevices during the day. Many caves have resident cleaner shrimps, or fish that provide the school with a parasite removal service during their daytime rest periods.

FAMILY: Pentacerotidae
SCIENTIFIC NAME: *Evistias acutirostris*
COMMON NAME: Japanese Boarfish
DISTRIBUTION: WT/S
HABITAT: Rocky and coral reefs
GENERAL WATER DEPTH: 15–40 m (49–131 ft)
FOOD HABIT: Carnivorous: echinoderms
SIZE: 550 mm (22 in)
DESCRIPTION: Seen in pairs or in small groups close to the bottom, this large, deep-bodied species occurs in Indo-Pacific waters from Japan to Lord Howe Island and Norfolk Island in the South-West Pacific. Most observations show it to inhabit areas of sandy sea floor between reefs at depths of around 30 m (98 ft). Occasionally pairs are seen in caves.

Pentaceropsis recurvirostris

FAMILY: Pentacerotidae
SCIENTIFIC NAME: *Pentaceropsis recurvirostris*
COMMON NAME: Long-snouted Boarfish
DISTRIBUTION: WT/S
HABITAT: Rocky reefs; mud
GENERAL WATER DEPTH: 10–260 m (33–853 ft)
FOOD HABIT: Omnivorous: invertebrates; algae

SIZE: 510 mm (20 in)
DESCRIPTION: Remarkable in appearance, the long-snouted boarfish is unique to the South-West Pacific, good to eat and naturally photogenic. It occurs in waters around reefs below 10 m (33 ft) and though not commonly encountered by line fishermen it is regularly speared, gill netted and trawled. The boarfish is usually solitary and in areas not heavily speared is easy to approach.

FAMILY: Pinguipedidae
SCIENTIFIC NAME: *Parapercis haackei*
COMMON NAME: Wavy Grubfish
DISTRIBUTION: WT/S
HABITAT: Sand; seagrass; low profile rocky reefs
GENERAL WATER DEPTH: 1–35 m (3–115 ft)
FOOD HABIT: Carnivorous: crustaceans
SIZE: 90 mm (3.5 in)
DESCRIPTION: The wavy grubfish is a small, easily identified fish that occupies well-defended territories on open areas where it rests during the day, ever alert to the appearance of prey or trespassing members of its own species. The prominent dark lateral line may differ in thickness and be either straight or wavy, depending on locality. The black spot on the separate first dorsal fin seems to be a stable feature over its range in the South-West Pacific.

FAMILY: Pinguipedidae
SCIENTIFIC NAME: *Parapercis hexophtalma*
COMMON NAME: Speckled Grubfish
DISTRIBUTION: TI–WP
HABITAT: Sand; rubble
GENERAL WATER DEPTH: 5–25 m (16–82 ft)
FOOD HABIT: Carnivorous: crustaceans
SIZE: 200 mm (8 in)
DESCRIPTION: The speckled black-spot grubfish is a moderately common species

Parapercis hexophtalma

found on sandy lagoon floors, reef slopes, and sand and rubble terraces among coral reefs. A rather curious and somewhat 'comical' fish, it is territorial and feeds on sand-dwelling invertebrates. Able to look in two directions at once, the independently controlled eyes often make it appear cross-eyed. Like many fish it is very inquisitive.

Neoplatycephalus richardsoni

FAMILY: Platycephalidae
SCIENTIFIC NAME: *Neoplatycephalus richardsoni*
COMMON NAME: Tiger Flathead
DISTRIBUTION: WT/S
HABITAT: Sand; mud; rubble
GENERAL WATER DEPTH: 1–40 m (3–131 ft)
FOOD HABIT: Carnivorous: fishes; crustaceans
SIZE: 410 mm (16 in)
DESCRIPTION: Caught on lines and by seining in sheltered bays, inlets and estuaries, the tiger flathead often occurs in large numbers in some areas and may have a density of one to two per square metre. It is easily approached on the bottom, has little reaction to a diver and seems to maintain a very small critical distance zone. It has a prominent lower preopercular (gill cover) spine and the tail is spotted on the upper part, with a dark blotch on the lower half.

Platycephalus caeruleopunctatus

FAMILY: Platycephalidae
SCIENTIFIC NAME: *Platycephalus caeruleopunctatus*
COMMON NAME: Eastern Blue-spotted Flathead
DISTRIBUTION: TWP; WT/S
HABITAT: Sand; mud
GENERAL WATER DEPTH: 3–50 m (10–164 ft)
FOOD HABIT: Carnivorous: fish; crustaceans
SIZE: 760 mm (30 in)
DESCRIPTION: The eastern blue-spotted flathead is generally line caught in mainland estuaries, bays and inlets on prawn bait and has a very characteristic colour pattern on the tail. It is very easy to approach under water and even when disturbed, only moves a small distance away. It is an excellent food fish.

Platycephalus laevigatus

FAMILY: Platycephalidae
SCIENTIFIC NAME: *Platycephalus laevigatus*
COMMON NAME: Rock Flathead
DISTRIBUTION: WT/S
HABITAT: Rocky reefs; seagrass; sand
GENERAL WATER DEPTH: 3–40 m (10–131 ft)

FOOD HABIT: Carnivorous: fishes; crustaceans
SIZE: 510 mm (20 in)
DESCRIPTION: These flathead are not usually seen in the open during the day. They lie buried in sand under algae stands, or shelter under the all-protecting cover of seagrass. They become active in the late afternoon just before dusk, some moving out towards the edges of the seagrass and others taking up positions on low reefs and in sand patches between reefs with algae cover. In one small area alone I have counted over 20 fish waiting to ambush prey.

Platycephalus longispinus

FAMILY: Platycephalidae
SCIENTIFIC NAME: *Platycephalus longispinus*
COMMON NAME: Long-spined Flathead
DISTRIBUTION: WT/S
HABITAT: Sand; mud
GENERAL WATER DEPTH: 40–100 m (131–328 ft)
FOOD HABIT: Carnivorous: fishes
SIZE: 380 mm (15 in)
DESCRIPTION: It is unusual to catch the long-spined flathead in water shallower than 40 m (131 ft), and though well-known to commercial fishermen, it would rarely be encountered by the average amateur. It has very long preopercular spines and red-spotted pectoral and pelvic fins. Almost all specimens are taken by trawlers, but owing to its small size it is not always kept.

FAMILY: Platycephalidae
SCIENTIFIC NAME: *Platycephalus marmoratus*
COMMON NAME: Marbled Flathead
DISTRIBUTION: WT/S
HABITAT: Mud; sand
GENERAL WATER DEPTH: 40–100 m (131–328 ft)
FOOD HABIT: Carnivorous: fishes
SIZE: 550 mm (22 in)

Platycephalus marmoratus

DESCRIPTION: The depth range of the marbled flathead is too great for the average fisherman; some are caught by line around offshore reefs but most are brought up from commercial trawling grounds. It has a very distinctive pattern with white edges on the large pelvic and pectoral fins and a white edging on the otherwise dark tail. Like most flathead it is an excellent food fish.

Platycephalus speculator

FAMILY: Platycephalidae
SCIENTIFIC NAME: *Platycephalus speculator*
COMMON NAME: Castelnau's Flathead
DISTRIBUTION: WT/S
HABITAT: Sand; mud
GENERAL WATER DEPTH: 8–30 m
  (26–98 ft)
FOOD HABIT: Carnivorous: fishes;
  crustaceans
SIZE: 500 mm (20 in)
DESCRIPTION: Inhabiting the shallow water sandy sea floor, both on the coast and around offshore islands, Castelnau's flathead is often seen in the open during the day. Rarely bothering to hide under sand, it makes full use of its chromatophores (pigment cells) to take on the colour of its sur-

roundings and, like all flathead, employs a patient ambush-like style of hunting its food. The characteristic tail 'flag' is easy to see in the photograph.

Thysanophrys cirronasus

FAMILY: Platycephalidae
SCIENTIFIC NAME: *Thysanophrys cirronasus*
COMMON NAME: Tassel-snouted Flathead
DISTRIBUTION: WT/S
HABITAT: Rocky reefs; rubble
GENERAL WATER DEPTH: 5–30 m
  (16–98 ft)
FOOD HABIT: Carnivorous: fishes
SIZE: 380 mm (15 in)
DESCRIPTION: The tassel-snouted flathead is far more familiar to the line fisherman and to a few spearfishermen than to any underwater fish watcher. Its colouration is so similar to its surroundings that to find it, one has virtually to stumble on it. It has two small tassels on its snout and very well-developed cranial spines. Although small, it is good to eat.

Assessor flavissimus

FAMILY: Plesiopidae
SCIENTIFIC NAME: *Assessor flavissimus*
COMMON NAME: Yellow Assessor
DISTRIBUTION: TI–WP
HABITAT: Coral reefs
GENERAL WATER DEPTH: 5–20 m (16–66 ft)
FOOD HABIT: Carnivorous: crustaceans
SIZE: 40 mm (1.6 in)
DESCRIPTION: The yellow assessor is found in the same type of territory as Macneill's assessor, preferring low caves and ledges with sandy bottoms. In many instances both species can be seen in the same cave, while at other locations they may be separate. It is far more common in the Indo-Pacific than in the South-West Pacific.

Assessor macneilli

FAMILY: Plesiopidae
SCIENTIFIC NAME: *Assessor macneilli*
COMMON NAME: Macneill's Assessor
DISTRIBUTION: TI–WP
HABITAT: Coral reefs
GENERAL WATER DEPTH: 5–20 m
  (16–66 ft)
FOOD HABIT: Carnivorous: crustaceans
SIZE: 40 mm (1.5 in)
DESCRIPTION: Macneill's assessor is a very common and easily overlooked species that lives on offshore reefs and cays. It is rarely noticed by divers owing to its dark blue colour and the fact that it inhabits crevices and ledges where it swims upside down, often in a vertical position. Much patience and determination is required to photograph this elusive little fish for they are rarely still and swim in a way that makes focusing difficult. It spawns in summer, the male incubating the eggs in its mouth; incubation takes 15 to 16 days, during which time the male does not feed.

FAMILY: Plesiopidae
SCIENTIFIC NAME: *Paraplesiops bleekeri*
COMMON NAME: Bleeker's Devilfish
DISTRIBUTION: WT/S

Paraplesiops bleekeri

HABITAT: Rocky reefs
GENERAL WATER DEPTH: 8–40 m
(26–131 ft)
FOOD HABIT: Carnivorous: molluscs;
crustaceans
SIZE: 300 mm (12 in)
DESCRIPTION: The shape of its head, the distinctive bars on the body and the yellow fins all make Bleeker's devilfish easy to identify. Like its relative the blue devilfish it spends most of the day under deep ledges and caves. It is a little shyer than the blue devilfish and though not impossible to catch on a line, most specimens are taken by spearfishermen. It is a protected species.

Ammotretis rostratus

FAMILY: Pleuronectidae
SCIENTIFIC NAME: *Ammotretis rostratus*
COMMON NAME: Long-snouted Flounder
DISTRIBUTION: WT/S
HABITAT: Sand; mud
GENERAL WATER DEPTH: 1–40 m
(3–131 ft)
FOOD HABIT: Carnivorous: crustaceans
SIZE: 250 mm (10 in)
DESCRIPTION: Very common in shallow water inlets, bays and estuaries, the long-

snouted flounder also inhabits coastal and offshore areas. It is taken by hand line, seine net and trawl. It is delicious to eat despite its small size. It has a straight lateral line and the back of the gill cover ends in a distinct point. Previous descriptions state that the colour varies from dark to light brown and spots may or may not be present. All the fish I have seen alive are similar to the one pictured here.

Ammotretis tudori

FAMILY: Pleuronectidae
SCIENTIFIC NAME: *Ammotretis tudori*
COMMON NAME: Spotted Flounder; Tudor's
Flounder
DISTRIBUTION: WT/S; CT/S
HABITAT: Sand; mud
GENERAL WATER DEPTH: 5–70 m
(16–230 ft)
FOOD HABIT: Carnivorous: crustaceans;
fishes
SIZE: 230 mm (9 in)
DESCRIPTION: All the flounders belonging to the family Pleuronectidae are known as right-handed flounders as the eyes and mouth are on the right hand side of the fish, unlike those of the family Bothidae which are on the left hand side. Like most flat fishes, the spotted flounder can assume the colouration of the substrate directly under it. Although described as light grey to brown with small evenly-distributed black spots over the dorsal surface, in life the colours and pattern are as shown here.

FAMILY: Pleuronectidae
SCIENTIFIC NAME: *Limanda limanda*
COMMON NAME: Dab
DISTRIBUTION: CT/N
HABITAT: Sandy bottoms
GENERAL WATER DEPTH: 20–40 m
(65.6–131.2 ft)
FOOD HABIT: Carnivorous: bottom-living
invertebrates, crustaceans, worms and
molluscs
SIZE: Up to 420 mm (16.5 in)

Limanda limanda

DESCRIPTION: This small oval flat fish lies on its left side and has both eyes on the right side of its body. The anal fin has 50 to 64 rays. The lateral line is distinctly curved over the pectoral fin. The dab is usually sandy coloured above but may vary from pale brown to grey-brown. This colouration is overlain by small darker spots as well. The 'blind' side is white. The left eye moves across the head after metamorphosis of the free-swimming larva into a bottom-dwelling fish. It is abundant in shallow waters like the North Sea where it is an important commercial fish.

Rhombosolea tapirina

FAMILY: Pleuronectidae
SCIENTIFIC NAME: *Rhombosolea tapirina*
COMMON NAME: Greenback Flounder
DISTRIBUTION: WT/S
HABITAT: Sand; rubble; mud
GENERAL WATER DEPTH: 1–40 m
(3–131 ft)
FOOD HABIT: Carnivorous: crustaceans
SIZE: 360 mm (14 in)
DESCRIPTION: Larger specimens of the greenback flounder may vary from dark greenish to brown, or grey, with or without blotches. Smaller specimens usually have blotches on the back as well as a white blotch at the centre of the dorsal surface on

the lateral line and the characteristic white spot at the base of the pectoral fin. It is trawled, seined and line caught and is very good to eat.

Cnidoglanis macrocephalus

FAMILY: Plotosidae
SCIENTIFIC NAME: *Cnidoglanis macrocephalus*
COMMON NAME: Estuary Catfish
DISTRIBUTION: TI–WP; WT/S
HABITAT: Rocky and coral reefs; sand; mud; seagrass
GENERAL WATER DEPTH: 1–40 m (3–131 ft)
FOOD HABIT: Carnivorous: crustaceans; worms; molluscs
SIZE: 1 m (3 ft)
DESCRIPTION: Mainly a coastal species living in shallow water bays and estuaries, the estuary catfish is a nocturnal forager, coming out at night from the holes, caves and ledges in which it seeks protection during the day. Its colour tends to be of various mixtures of brown, yellow and black, giving it a dappled appearance. It is a commercially important species with soft, white good-tasting flesh, but it has venomous dorsal and pectoral spines.

Plotosus lineatus

FAMILY: Plotosidae
SCIENTIFIC NAME: *Plotosus lineatus*
COMMON NAME: Lined Catfish
DISTRIBUTION: WT/S
HABITAT: Rocky reef; mud; sand; seagrass
GENERAL WATER DEPTH: 1–30 m (3–98 ft)
FOOD HABIT: Carnivorous: invertebrates; organic detritus
SIZE: 1 m (3 ft)
DESCRIPTION: As it is the only catfish with such well-defined stripes along the body, the lined catfish presents little difficulty in identification. It lives mostly in sheltered bays and estuaries where large schools may be seen foraging during daylight hours. It has sometimes been observed around offshore islands. It is a nuisance to night fishermen as it often takes bait meant for a more desirable fish. Despite a repulsive appearance and its three venomous dorsal and pectoral spines, good-size specimens produce fillets of firm, boneless flesh.

Apolemichthys trimaculatus

FAMILY: Pomacanthidae
SCIENTIFIC NAME: *Apolemichthys trimaculatus*
COMMON NAME: Three-spot Angelfish
DISTRIBUTION: TI–WP
HABITAT: Coral reefs
GENERAL WATER DEPTH: 15–35 m (49–115 ft)
FOOD HABIT: Omnivorous: algae; benthic invertebrates
SIZE: 150 mm (6 in)
DESCRIPTION: Preferring the deeper waters of drop-offs and submerged terraces around offshore continental islands and reefs, the three-spot angelfish is mostly solitary, spending the day actively moving around its territory picking among corals and encrusting marine growths on cliff faces. It is easily recognised owing to its bright yellow body, blue mouth and gill spine, three darker head spots and rounded dorsal and anal fins. No significant external difference between the male and female appears to exist. Its range is from Africa across the Indo-Pacific.

Centropyge bicolor

FAMILY: Pomacanthidae
SCIENTIFIC NAME: *Centropyge bicolor*
COMMON NAME: Bicolor Angelfish
DISTRIBUTION: TI–WP
HABITAT: Coral and rocky reefs
GENERAL WATER DEPTH: 1–10 m (3–33 ft)
FOOD HABIT: Omnivorous: encrusting organisms; algae
SIZE: 150 mm (6 in)
DESCRIPTION: The bicolor angelfish inhabits reef and broken bottoms in lagoons, and the slopes of back reefs in sheltered shallow water, remaining within a defined territory that is often shared by several adults and juveniles. More open-ranging than *C. bispinosus*, it swims very rapidly when moving from one coral patch to another. It occurs throughout outer reef areas and occupies fringing reefs around continental islands. It is fairly easy to maintain in an aquarium.

Centropyge bispinosus

FAMILY: Pomacanthidae
SCIENTIFIC NAME: *Centropyge bispinosus*
COMMON NAME: Two-spined Angelfish
DISTRIBUTION: TI–WP
HABITAT: Coral and rocky reefs
GENERAL WATER DEPTH: 5–10 m (16–33 ft)

Food Habit: Omnivorous: encrusting
organisms; algae
Size: 120 mm (5 in)
Description: In areas of broken, dead coral
reef surrounded by stands of staghorn coral,
the two-spined angelfish inhabits a territory
that contains a number of escape holes. It is
often seen in pairs and sometimes singly but
in every case it stays close to the reef. This
shy behaviour makes it extremely difficult to
get close to and in many cases any photographs are hardly worthwhile. It does well in
aquaria.

Centropyge flavicauda

Family: Pomacanthidae
Scientific Name: *Centropyge flavicauda*
Common Name: White-tail Angelfish
Distribution: TI–WP
Habitat: Coral reefs
General Water Depth: 10–20 m
(33–66 ft)
Food Habit: Omnivorous: algae
Size: 60 mm (2.4 in)
Description: One of the smallest of its
family, the white-tail angelfish inhabits lush,
living reef areas on coral slopes and terraces.
Owing to its small size, secretive habits and
resemblance to damselfish, the species is
very rarely noticed. It can be easily distinguished from damselfish by the spine on its
gill cover which all angelfish have. Very shy
and difficult to get close to, it ranges from
the Indian Ocean to the Western Pacific and
is common along the Great Barrier Reef.

Family: Pomacanthidae
Scientific Name: *Centropyge heraldi*
Common Name: Herald's Angelfish
Distribution: TI–WP
Habitat: Coral reefs
General Water Depth: 5–30 m
(16–98 ft)
Food Habit: Omnivorous: algae;
crustaceans; worms

Centropyge heraldi

Size: 100 mm (4 in)
Description: Bright golden yellow all over,
with only a hint of dark smudging behind
the eyes in some specimens, herald's angelfish has a range that covers much of the
Pacific area. Its habitat appears to be
restricted to outer barrier reef slopes and it
is certainly not common in Western Pacific
waters. Superficially similar in shape, size
and colour to the lemonpeel angelfish *C.
flavissimus*, it lacks the blue markings
around the eyes and gill covers and on the
gill spike.

Centropyge tibicen

Family: Pomacanthidae
Scientific Name: *Centropyge tibicen*
Common Name: Keyhole Angelfish
Distribution: TI–WP
Habitat: Coral reefs
General Water Depth: 5–25 m
(16–82 ft)
Food Habit: Omnivorous
Size: 180 mm (7 in)
Description: With its characteristic verti-
cally elongated white blotch and yellow-
edged lower fins, the keyhole angelfish is not
difficult to identify, especially as the juvenile

also has a white blotch. It is generally found
in protected waters on offshore reefs from
the Indian Ocean through the Pacific to
Japan, and down to the South-West Pacific
where it inhabits deeper water than in the
tropics. It grows larger than any other fish of
its genus and is mostly seen close to the
undersides of caves and ledges.

Chaetodontoplus mesoleucus

Family: Pomacanthidae
Scientific Name: *Chaetodontoplus
mesoleucus*
Common Name: Vermiculated Angelfish
Distribution: TI–WP
Habitat: Coral reefs
General Water Depth: 2–20 m (6–66 ft)
Food Habit: Omnivorous: algae; benthic
invertebrates
Size: 180 mm (7 in)
Description: A moderately common
Indian Ocean and Pacific species, the
vermiculated angelfish is usually seen as a
solitary fish that inhabits continental
inshore reefs in relatively shallow depths.
There is little significant colour variation
throughout its range and it is easy to identify and easy to approach underwater. The
male and female are little different in shape
or colour.

Family: Pomacanthidae
Scientific Name: *Pomacanthus imperator*
Common Name: Emperor Angelfish
Distribution: TI–WP; IWP
Habitat: Coral and rocky reefs
General Water Depth: 10–25 m
(33–82 ft)
Food Habit: Carnivorous: encrusting
sessile organisms
Size: 380 mm (15 in)
Description: Living on both mainland,
island and barrier reefs, the emperor angelfish is territorial and often seen in caves and
grotto complexes on the edges of reef slopes,
gutters and surge channel overhangs. In
common with many of the larger angelfish,
the juvenile is dark blue, with white mark-

Pomacanthus imperator

can be kept in community aquaria but the adult is very territorial and will continually harass other angelfish or fish with similar feeding habits. The adult is solitary for most of the year, except in the mating season. The juvenile is black with blue and white semicircular markings covering the body and it is this spectacular pattern on the young fish that accounts for its scientific name.

Abudefduf sexfasciatus

Pomacanthus semicirculatus

ings forming a ring on the back of the body. The fish makes an exquisite pet, but care must be taken to ensure that it is not placed with conspecifics, or other large angelfish, as they are territorial and will fight.

FAMILY: Pomacanthidae
SCIENTIFIC NAME: *Pomacanthus semicirculatus*
COMMON NAME: Semicircle Angelfish; Blue Angelfish
DISTRIBUTION: TI–WP; IWP
HABITAT: Coral and rocky reefs
GENERAL WATER DEPTH: 5–25 m (16–82 ft)
FOOD HABIT: Carnivorous: encrusting sessile organisms
SIZE: 380 mm (15 in)
DESCRIPTION: By far the most photographed tropical angelfish, the semicircle angelfish lives below the reef edge in sheltered lagoons and back reefs and also inhabits continental reefs which are open to surge. During the day it roams its territory feeding on sponges, ascidians and algae that it scrapes from the walls of caves and overhangs with its brush-like teeth. A juvenile

Pygoplites diacanthus

FAMILY: Pomacanthidae
SCIENTIFIC NAME: *Pygoplites diacanthus*
COMMON NAME: Regal Angelfish
DISTRIBUTION: TI–WP
HABITAT: Coral and rocky reefs
GENERAL WATER DEPTH: 10–25 m (33–82 ft)
FOOD HABIT: Carnivorous: encrusting sessile organisms
SIZE: 220 mm (9 in)
DESCRIPTION: This fish is exceptionally beautiful and is a favourite of underwater photographers. Found on reef slopes adjacent to channels, on reef drop-offs, and among coral heads in the deeper parts of some lagoons, the regal angelfish feeds during the day and has been observed biting pieces from encrusting sessile organisms attached to cave walls and underhangs. Although pairing occurs during the mating season, most are solitary. Like many of the larger angelfish it swims constantly (usually along a particular route) and is territorial.

FAMILY: Pomacentridae
SCIENTIFIC NAME: *Abudefduf sexfasciatus*
COMMON NAME: Scissor-tail Sergeant
DISTRIBUTION: TI–WP; IWP
HABITAT: Coral reefs
GENERAL WATER DEPTH: 1–8 m (3–26 ft)
FOOD HABIT: Omnivorous: zooplankton; algae
SIZE: 150 mm (6 in)
DESCRIPTION: Very common in sheltered

lagoon shallows and back reefs from Japan to the South-West Pacific, it has four to six characteristic blackish-blue vertical stripes and two black tail bars from which it gets its common name. It is usually found in colonies which, on the run-in of the tide or towards dusk, will often form feeding aggregations as they pick plankton from the water column. The scissor-tail sergeant mates during summer, the female laying many thousands of eggs on specially prepared substrate. Both male and female may at times protect the eggs from predators.

Amblyglyphidodon aureus

FAMILY: Pomacentridae
SCIENTIFIC NAME: *Amblyglyphidodon aureus*
COMMON NAME: Golden Damsel
DISTRIBUTION: TI–WP
HABITAT: Coral reef
GENERAL WATER DEPTH: 10–20 m (33–66 ft)
FOOD HABIT: Omnivorous: zooplankton; algae
SIZE: 100 mm (4 in)
DESCRIPTION: The brightly coloured golden damsel prefers a deeper habitat than many

other damsels and is usually found several metres down the fronts of cliff faces, or drop-offs on front and back reefs. It is also seen on the edges and pinnacles of bommies and coral heads. In every instance it seems to select a territory with some high object in it, either a sea fan, soft coral, black coral, or a small coral outcrop. During the day it stays around or above this object, swimming up high then racing down in typical damsel fashion. The golden damsel is solitary and reasonably easy to get close to.

Amblyglyphidodon curacao

FAMILY: Pomacentridae
SCIENTIFIC NAME: *Amblyglyphidodon curacao*
COMMON NAME: Staghorn Damsel
DISTRIBUTION: TI–WP
HABITAT: Coral reefs
GENERAL WATER DEPTH: 3–15 m (10–49 ft)
FOOD HABIT: Omnivorous: zooplankton; crustaceans; algae
SIZE: 90 mm (3.5 in)
DESCRIPTION: Large groups of the little staghorn damsel shelter among the spike-like branches of staghorn coral in calm areas of lagoons, or along the edges of reef slopes and back reef drop-offs; the species may also live under ledges formed by other living corals where it may be seen singly. It is cheeky and easily approached underwater. Colour varies over its range, some having green-grey backs with white undersides and four darker green bands down the body.

FAMILY: Pomacentridae
SCIENTIFIC NAME: *Amphiprion akindynos*
COMMON NAME: Barrier Reef Anemonefish; White-tailed Clown Fish
DISTRIBUTION: TI–WP
HABITAT: Coral reefs
GENERAL WATER DEPTH: 1–20 m (3–66 ft)
FOOD HABIT: Omnivorous: algae
SIZE: 80 mm (3 in)

Amphiprion akindynos

DESCRIPTION: Often found inhabiting the noxious sea anemone *Radianthus malu*, the Barrier Reef anemonefish is generally seen in pairs, or as several adults with a number of juveniles living in the same anemone. It is usually found in anemones within lagoonal or sheltered reefs along the reef fringe or slopes. Not so widely distributed as other species, the Barrier Reef anemonefish ranges from Australia to New Caledonia and the Loyalty Islands. Anemonefish are unusual in being able to change sex from male to female. Many other reef fish can change sex from female to male.

Amphiprion latezonatus

FAMILY: Pomacentridae
SCIENTIFIC NAME: *Amphiprion latezonatus*
COMMON NAME: Wide-striped Anemonefish
DISTRIBUTION: TI–WP
HABITAT: Rocky and coral reefs
GENERAL WATER DEPTH: 20–45 m (66–148 ft)
FOOD HABIT: Omnivorous
SIZE: 100 mm (4 in)
DESCRIPTION: The wide-striped anemone-fish lives in small and large anemones and during the summer months the female lays a

series of yellow eggs on a patch of cleared rock under the 'skirt' of the host anemone. Both male and female tend the eggs until they hatch, chasing away other fish and potential predators.

Amphiprion ocellaris

FAMILY: Pomacentridae
SCIENTIFIC NAME: *Amphiprion ocellaris*
COMMON NAME: Clown Anemonefish
DISTRIBUTION: TI–WP
HABITAT: Coral reefs
GENERAL WATER DEPTH: 2–20 m (6–66 ft)
FOOD HABIT: Omnivorous: algae; zooplankton
SIZE: 70 mm (3 in)
DESCRIPTION: The clown anemonefish is popular in aquaria and is probably everyone's idea of a typical anemonefish. It usually lives in large sea anemones such as *Radianthus ritteri* and *Stoichactis giganteum*, but specimens can be mainted in aquaria witthout an anemone host. It is found on inshore and offshore reefs. In some northern areas the bright orange colouration may take on a black shade. Normally a pair of adult fish and several juveniles occupy the same anemone.

FAMILY: Pomacentridae
SCIENTIFIC NAME: *Amphiprion perideraion*
COMMON NAME: Pink Anemonefish
DISTRIBUTION: TI–WP
HABITAT: Coral and rocky reefs
GENERAL WATER DEPTH: 3–20 m (10–66 ft)
FOOD HABIT: Omnivorous: zooplankton; algae
SIZE: 70 mm (3 in)
DESCRIPTION: The pink anemonefish is one of the most attractive and easily idenfitied of the anemonefish. Its most common host is the giant Ritter's sea anemone, *Radianthus ritteri*, which is generally found in depths below 5 m (16 ft) attached to the reef by its adhesive foot. Most anemones have two

Amphiprion perideraion

Chromis hypselepsis

HABITAT: Coral reefs
GENERAL WATER DEPTH: 1–20 m (3–66 ft)
FOOD HABIT: Omnivorous: zooplankton
SIZE: 60 mm (2 in)
DESCRIPTION: The reticulated dascyllus is a small, easily identified pomacentrid that inhabits lagoons and back reefs and usually occurs in shallow waters. It does not vary much in colour and is often seen in the company of *Dasycllus aruanus*. Its habitat is in, or around, isolated patch reefs of staghorn corals on sandy bottom, reef slopes, or growing adjacent to larger patches of reef. Although some specimens may be seen singly, most live in groups using the staghorn coral as a fortress, rising above to feed in the water column and quickly taking over when threatened.

adults and up to five juvenile fish living among the tentacles. On some reefs they live in 20 m (66 ft) of water at the base of exposed reef fronts in rather turbulent conditions. The species breeds in summer, the female laying eggs on the substrate beneath the side of the anemone. Both adults mind and protect the eggs.

Chromis atripectonalis

FAMILY: Pomacentridae
SCIENTIFIC NAME: *Chromis atripectonalis*
COMMON NAME: Black-axil Chromis
DISTRIBUTION: TI–WP
HABITAT: Rocky and coral reefs
GENERAL WATER DEPTH: 1–12 m (3–39 ft)
FOOD HABIT: Omnivorous: zooplankton
SIZE: 60 mm (2 in)
DESCRIPTION: The experience of watching hundreds of these emerald coloured fish swim out of their coral abodes and rise up with the sun at daybreak in a mass underwater ballet, is unforgettable. However the colour of the black-axil chromis is rather variable and ranges from iridescent green to iridescent blue. Its habitat is largely among, or above, staghorn corals in sheltered lagoons and along the edges and terraces of back reefs.

FAMILY: Pomacentridae
SCIENTIFIC NAME: *Chromis hypselepsis*
COMMON NAME: One-spot Chromis
DISTRIBUTION: WT/S
HABITAT: Rocky reefs
GENERAL WATER DEPTH: 3–45 m
  (10–148 ft)
FOOD HABIT: Omnivorous: algae;
  zooplankton
SIZE: 170 mm (7 in)
DESCRIPTION: During late afternoon these schooling plankton feeders form dense aggregations above rocky reef cliff faces, submerged headlands and isolated reef outcrops. Steadily climbing up into the water column, the one-spot chromis faces into the current to feed, then as dusk descends, it also descends. At night the schools disband and each fish lies in the rocks. During the breeding season, the male has a small territory into which females go to lay their eggs. The male fertilises the eggs and then guards them until they hatch.

Dascyllus reticulatus

FAMILY: Pomacentridae
SCIENTIFIC NAME: *Dascyllus reticulatus*
COMMON NAME: Reticulated Dascyllus
DISTRIBUTION: TI–WP

Dischistodus prosopotaenia

FAMILY: Pomacentridae
SCIENTIFIC NAME: *Dischistodus prosopotaenia*
COMMON NAME: Honeyhead Damsel
DISTRIBUTION: TI–WP
HABITAT: Coral reefs; silty areas
GENERAL WATER DEPTH: 1–12 m (3–39 ft)
FOOD HABIT: Omnivorous: algae
SIZE: 130 mm (5 in)
DESCRIPTION: Mostly inhabiting lagoon drop-offs and reef slopes across the Indo-Pacific, the honeyhead damsel is territorial and generally seen as a solitary species. It has a well-defined territory and owing to its home-ranging habits is easy to observe and photograph. Fairly common on some reefs, it is not restricted to offshore locations and may be seen on continental island reefs.

FAMILY: Pomacentridae
SCIENTIFIC NAME: *Parma victoriae*
COMMON NAME: Victoria's Scalyfin
DISTRIBUTION: WT/S
HABITAT: Rocky reefs
GENERAL WATER DEPTH: 1–25 m (3–82 ft)
FOOD HABIT: Omnivorous: algae

Parma victoriae

SIZE: 200 mm (8 in)
DESCRIPTION: Growing much larger than the white–ear, Victoria's scalyfin seems to prefer a more algae-covered habitat, and as an adult can be readily distinguished from any other species of southern pomacentrid by its colouration. It is occasionally landed by line and is often attacked by the hand spears of raw beginners anxious to demonstrate their prowess as spearfishermen. (This is unfortunate, as they rarely eat the fish after they have killed it.)

Pomacentrus coelestis

FAMILY: Pomacentridae
SCIENTIFIC NAME: *Pomacentrus coelestis*
COMMON NAME: Neon Damsel
DISTRIBUTION: TI–WP; WT/S
HABITAT: Coral and rocky reefs; rubble
GENERAL WATER DEPTH: 1–12 m (3–39 ft)
FOOD HABIT: Omnivorous: zooplankton; algae
SIZE: 80 mm (3 in)
DESCRIPTION: More common within its northern range limits than its southern ones, the neon damsel is a wide-ranging species that lives from southern Japan through the Indo-Pacific into the South-West Pacific. Its colours vary, with some fish having more or less blue or gold in some locations. It is very popular with aquarium keepers owing to its attractive hues, small size and hardy adaptability. Neon damsels often form groups and are found around dead coral patches, clumps on channel slopes, or reef rims.

Plectorhinchus chaetodontoides

FAMILY: Pomadasyidae
SCIENTIFIC NAME: *Plectorhinchus chaetodontoides*
COMMON NAME: Many-spotted Sweetlips
DISTRIBUTION: TI–WP
HABITAT: Coral and rocky reefs
GENERAL WATER DEPTH: 4–25 m (13–82 ft)
FOOD HABIT: Carnivorous: crustaceans; molluscs; fishes
SIZE: 600 mm (2 ft)
DESCRIPTION: A very conspicuous species, the many-spotted sweetlips is an inhabitant of mainland reefs, continental island reefs, offshore cays, and true coral island reefs. By day it hangs in the current in the lee of coral bommies, visits cleaner-fish stations on reef surrounds, or groups up with a few others of its kind in a cave, or beneath an overhang. It is a rather tame fish, easily speared. The flesh is of fair quality but large fish are dry and quite tasteless.

Plectorhinchus chrysotaenia

FAMILY: Pomadasyidae
SCIENTIFIC NAME: *Plectorhinchus chrysotaenia*
COMMON NAME: Many-lined Sweetlips
DISTRIBUTION: TI–WP
HABITAT: Coral and rocky reefs
GENERAL WATER DEPTH: 8–25 m (26–82 ft)
FOOD HABIT: Carnivorous: molluscs
SIZE: 400 mm (16 in)
DESCRIPTION: At first glance this rather elegant species resembles some snappers which have a similar colour pattern. However, the rounded profile of the head and the thick lips are unlike those of a snapper. The many-lined sweetlips appears to be solitary and despite its wide distribution is not commonly observed. It is found near reef clumps and coral heads during the day, usually on the lee side of an island or reef. There is little apparent variation in colour.

Plectorhinchus flavomaculatus

FAMILY: Pomadasyidae
SCIENTIFIC NAME: *Plectorhinchus flavomaculatus*
COMMON NAME: Gold-spotted Sweetlips
DISTRIBUTION: TI–WP; WT/S
HABITAT: Coral and rocky reefs
GENERAL WATER DEPTH: 8–160 m (26-525 ft)
FOOD HABIT: Carnivorous: fishes, crustaceans
SIZE: 400 mm (16 in)
DESCRIPTION: A tropical species ranging into temperate waters, the gold-spotted sweetlips is taken by line, net and spear on both coastal and offshore reefs. It has coarse flesh. The quality of most fish seems to improve with cleaning, bleeding and gutting as soon as possible after capture; the gold-spotted sweetlips is no exception. It is easily approached underwater and may be over-fished by spearfishermen in some areas.

Pomatomus saltatrix

FAMILY: Pomatomidae
SCIENTIFIC NAME: *Pomatomus saltatrix*
COMMON NAME: Tailor
DISTRIBUTION: TI–WP; WT/S
HABITAT: Surface waters
GENERAL WATER DEPTH: 1–10 m (3–33 ft)
FOOD HABIT: Carnivorous: Fishes
SIZE: 1.2 m (4 ft)
DESCRIPTION: The tailor has powerful jaws full of sharp teeth and is a voracious feeder. It generally swims in schools and is a free-roving fish that migrates to spawn in the open ocean. Tailor may be found over off-shore and inshore reefs, along surf beaches and in harbours, bays and estuaries. Most are caught by netting, spinning, trolling and lining, and it is a strong fighter on light gear. The flesh is of good quality, but at times, especially with larger specimens, can be rather dry. Tailor resembles the Bluefish found in waters off the USA.

Priacanthus hamrur

FAMILY: Priacanthidae
SCIENTIFIC NAME: *Priacanthus hamrur*
COMMON NAME: Lunar-tailed Glasseye
DISTRIBUTION: TI–WP
HABITAT: Coral reefs

GENERAL WATER DEPTH: 5–25 m (16–82 ft)
FOOD HABIT: Carnivorous: free-swimming crustaceans; cephalopods
SIZE: 400 mm (16 in)
DESCRIPTION: The lunar-tailed glasseye is generally a nocturnal species often seen during night-diving excursions over reefs, sand and rubble. The daytime colour pattern (see photograph) differs from the night-time colouration of pinkish mottled spots. During the day it shelters under ledges, or behind coral cover and is rarely seen in the open, towards the late afternoon some individuals may emerge but they tend to keep very close the the protection of the coral. The lunar tailed glasseye has black fins and can be caught on hand lines.

Congrogadus subducens

FAMILY: Pseudochromidae
SCIENTIFIC NAME: *Congrogadus subducens*
COMMON NAME: Ocellated Eel Blenny
DISTRIBUTION: TI–WP
HABITAT: Coral reefs
GENERAL WATER DEPTH: 1–5 m (3–16 ft)
FOOD HABIT: Carnivorous
SIZE: 500 mm (20 in)
DESCRIPTION: The largest of the eel blennies, this species is a territorial carni-vore that lives in lagoons in sheltered waters, and occurs on mainland and offshore reefs. With its long body and eel-like movements the ocellated eel blenny glides among the corals in search of prey. Eel blennies can be distinguished from true blennies by their confluent dorsal, caudal and anal fins, and by the absence of pelvic fins. The peculiar shape of the head, size, the dark ocellus on the gill plate, and the rather distinct pattern are also characteristic. It is not well-known in the South-West Pacific and very few occurrences have been recorded.

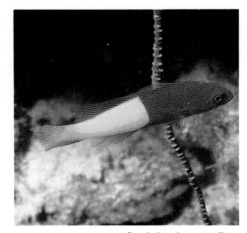

Pseudochromis paccagnellae

FAMILY: Pseudochromidae
SCIENTIFIC NAME: *Pseudochromis paccagnellae*
COMMON NAME: Bicolor Dottyback
DISTRIBUTION: TI–WP
HABITAT: Coral reefs
GENERAL WATER DEPTH: 10–35 m (33–115 ft)
FOOD HABIT: Carnivorous: crustaceans
SIZE: 70 mm (3 in)
DESCRIPTION: A shy and rather timid spe-cies, the bicolor dottyback is often seen in fissures in bommies or in areas where one coral head is undercut and flanked by another. Territorial by nature, it patrols along several metres of vertical reef face searching for food. It occurs in greater num-bers in deeper water and swims in a head-high position. A favourite with marine aquarists, it is fairly easily maintained in an aquarium and is captured in increasing num-bers for the trade throughout its distribution. It is much more widespread than formerly belived.

FAMILY: Salmonidae
SCIENTIFIC NAME: *Oncorhynchus nerka*
COMMON NAME: Sockeye Salmon; Blueback Salmon; Red Salmon
DISTRIBUTION: IWP
HABITAT: Anadromous (migrating up rivers)
GENERAL WATER DEPTH: Open ocean to coastal streams
FOOD HABIT: Carnivorous
SIZE: Up to 84 cm (33 in)
DESCRIPTION: In the ocean the sockeye salmon is metallic blue-green above and silver below. At spawning, the fish has a green head with a white lower jaw, a red body and a green caudal fin. Very small black specks appear across the back and caudal fin; there are 28 to 38 gill rakers. Naturally occurring and man-made land-locked populations are found in various loca-

Oncorhynchus nerka

Scarus ghobban (male)

tions. Spawning occurs in summer, with the fry emerging in spring. The young psend their first one or two years in fresh water before moving to the ocean. Spawning maturity is reached after two to four years in salt water.

FAMILY: Scaridae
SCIENTIFIC NAME: *Scarus frenatus* (male)
COMMON NAME: Bridled Parrotfish
DISTRIBUTION: TI–WP
HABITAT: Coral reefs
GENERAL WATER DEPTH: 5–20 m
  (16–66 ft)
FOOD HABIT: Herbivorous: algae
SIZE: 350 mm (14 in)
DESCRIPTION: Like the wrasses, the sexual dichromatism within the family Scaridae has led to much taxonomic confusion. The male and female differ in colouration and sometimes even in general body shape. This problem, coupled with the marked differences in many juveniles, has made the parrotfish family one of the most difficult to identify underwater. The female bridled parrotfish has an orange-red head and fins, with large distinct yellow scales covering the stomach

area, over a dark brown body. Parrotfish feed on algae scraped from living coral tissues and also on algae growing on dead coral rubble. The bridled parrotfish is not easily approached underwater and few are caught on lines, though they are quite good eating.

FAMILY: Scaridae
SCIENTIFIC NAME: *Scarus ghobban* (male)
COMMON NAME: Blue-barred Parrotfish
DISTRIBUTION: TI–WP
HABITAT: Coral reefs
GENERAL WATER DEPTH: 1–30 m (3–98 ft)
FOOD HABIT: Herbivorous: algae
SIZE: 1.1 m (40 in)
DESCRIPTION: The adult blue-barred parrotfish is usually seen in deeper water than is the juvenile. It feeds on algae living in coral tissue; the flesh is either scraped off coral surfaces, or pieces of coral are bitten off, crunched up by pharyngeal teeth in the throat and conveyed to the stomach. The organic material is digested and the coral particles are excreted as coral dust. The species may also feed on algae growing on dead coral.

FAMILY: Scaridae
SCIENTIFIC NAME: *Scarus microrhinos*
  (male)
COMMON NAME: Steep-head Parrotfish
DISTRIBUTION: TI–WP; IWP
HABITAT: Coral reefs
GENERAL WATER DEPTH: 2–30 m (6–98 ft)
FOOD HABIT: Herbivorous: algae
SIZE: 500 mm (20 in)
DESCRIPTION: The steep-head parrotfish inhabits the slopes and terraces of back reefs, channel entrances, and bommies. The male is usually alone, although male and female pairs are likely to be seen during summer. At some localities it seems to be unafraid of divers and at others it is quite shy. It also appears to prefer algae taken from dead coral surfaces rather than live coral but this may change with location. Although very few are caught on lines, some are taken by spearing. The flesh has excellent quality.

FAMILY: Scaridae
SCIENTIFIC NAME: *Scarus niger* (male)
COMMON NAME: Dusky Parrotfish
DISTRIBUTION: TI–WP

Scarus frenatus (male)

Scarus microrhinos (male)

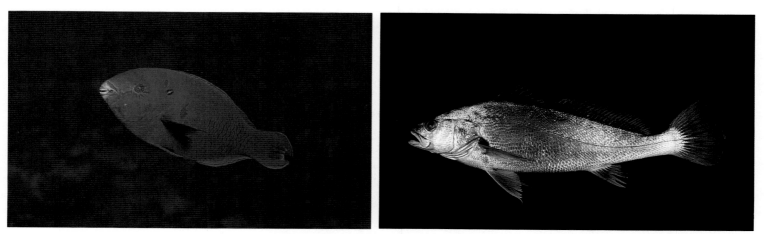

Scarus niger (male)　　　　　　　　　　　　　　*Argyrosomus hololepidotus*

HABITAT: Coral reefs
GENERAL WATER DEPTH: 2–25 m (6–82 ft)
FOOD HABIT: Herbivorous: algae
SIZE: 400 mm (16 in)
DESCRIPTION: The dusky parrotfish is probably the most simple of all the parrotfish to identify as it varies little in colour throughout its distribution. The tail colours and the black-edged green spot behind the eye are characteristic. The dusky parrotfish is usually solitary but females are apt to forage together as a small group. It feeds on algae by scraping and biting off live and dead coral with its fused, parrot-like scalloped teeth. It is found in lagoons or around sloping back reefs in sheltered water; at night it sleeps in caves in the reef.

FAMILY: Sciaenidae
SCIENTIFIC NAME: *Argyrosomus hololepidotus*
COMMON NAME: Jewfish; Mulloway
DISTRIBUTION: WT/S
HABITAT: Sand; mud; rocky reefs
GENERAL WATER DEPTH: 5–100 m (16–328 ft)
FOOD HABIT: Carnivorous: fishes; crustaceans; molluscs; worms
SIZE: 2 m (6 ft)
DESCRIPTION: The jewfish is one of the largest commercially important species in the South-West Pacific and is landed in large quantities by trawling, netting, and spearfishing, as well as by set line, rods and hand line. A big jewfish has great prestige value among fishermen and in season, many fish for nothing else. It inhabits both inshore and offshore areas, often penetrating far into the estuaries. It eats a wide range of food, including surface-swimming garfish and sand crabs, and is active both day and night. It was known for many years by the scientific name *Johnius antarctica*.

FAMILY: Scombridae
SCIENTIFIC NAME: *Grammatorcynus bicarinatus*
COMMON NAME: Shark Mackerel
DISTRIBUTION: TI–WP
HABITAT: Open water; coral and rocky reefs
GENERAL WATER DEPTH: 8–30 m (26–98 ft)
FOOD HABIT: Carnivorous: fishes
SIZE: 1 m (3 ft)
DESCRIPTION: Common in both inshore and offshore areas, the shark mackerel may be seen in schools but most observations are made on larger lone fish that patrol the reef edges at around 5–10 m (16–33 ft). It is caught on outriggers, rods and trolled hand lines using small surface fish and spoon lures. The double lateral line makes this fish easy to recognise. Its common name is derived from its shark-like smell when cleaned. It is good eating, provided it is bled on capture and cleaned as soon as possible.

Grammatorcynus bicarinatus

FAMILY: Scombridae
SCIENTIFIC NAME: *Gymnosarda unicolor*
COMMON NAME: Dogtooth Tuna

Gymnosarda unicolor

DISTRIBUTION: TI–WP
HABITAT: Open sea; coral reefs
GENERAL WATER DEPTH: 10–45 m (33–148 ft)
FOOD HABIT: Carnivorous: fishes; squid
SIZE: 1.5 m (5 ft)
DESCRIPTION: Regularly seen by divers on outer barrier reefs, the dogtooth tuna is a powerful predator, swimming in small groups. It tends to be wary, yet very inquisitive as it will swim around a diver at a distance of several metres. It has quite large, dog-style protruding teeth which can be seen in the jaws even at a distance underwater. It can be caught by line and is sometimes trolled by marlin fishermen. The flesh is white and quite palatable.

FAMILY: Scombridae
SCIENTIFIC NAME: *Scomberomorus commerson*
COMMON NAME: Narrow-barred Spanish Mackerel
DISTRIBUTION: TI–WP
HABITAT: Open sea; coral and rocky reefs
GENERAL WATER DEPTH: Surface to 30 m (98 ft)

Scomberomorus commerson

FOOD HABIT: Carnivorous: fishes
SIZE: 2.5 m (8 ft)
DESCRIPTION: A well-known commercial fish, the narrow-barred Spanish mackerel is trolled around mainland and barrier islands and associated cays and bommies. Although seen underwater, this fast swimming species remains near the surface in open water around the edges of reefs. The narrow-barred Spanish mackerel feeds voraciously on surface-schooling fish. It is caught by trolling outriggers, hand lines and rods using fish bait or spoon lures and is very good to eat; however, in some areas it has been responsible for ciguatera poisoning.

Centropogon australis

FAMILY: Scorpaenidae
SCIENTIFIC NAME: *Centropogon australis*
COMMON NAME: Southern Fortesque
DISTRIBUTION: WT/S; TWP
HABITAT: Rocky reefs; mud; rubble; seagrass; jetty piles
GENERAL WATER DEPTH: Intertidal to 30 m (98 ft)
FOOD HABIT: Carnivorous: fishes; crustaceans
SIZE: 100 mm (4 in)

DESCRIPTION: In some estuaries, this little scorpaenid is so common that it is difficult to put one's hand on the bottom without having to move several fish. Surprisingly, few divers are ever stung underwater. Most stings occur when the fish is line caught by children, or when searching beneath rocks in muddy water for bait. My encounter with a southern fortesque took place many years ago when collecting clump mussels for trap bait; the effect of its venomous dorsal spines was so memorable that I have since taken care to avoid being stung.

Dampierosa daruma

FAMILY: Scorpaenidae
SCIENTIFIC NAME: *Dampierosa daruma*
COMMON NAME: Northwest Stonefish
DISTRIBUTION: TI–WP
HABITAT: Rocky reefs; mud; sand
GENERAL WATER DEPTH: Intertidal to 30 m (98 ft)
FOOD HABIT: Carnivorous: fishes; crustaceans
SIZE: 200 mm (8 in)
DESCRIPTION: Recorded from the Indian Ocean (Arafura Sea area) on offshore reefs, this little stonefish prefers a sandy mud and

Dendrochirus brachypterus

rubble rock habitat. Since discovery of the northwest stonefish, few have ever seen it alive. Recognition is straightforward as there are no other fish of similar appearance. It has been taken in seine nets and also comes up in the cod ends of trawlers. It can inflict a most agonising sting with its dorsal spines.

FAMILY: Scorpaenidae
SCIENTIFIC NAME: *Dendrochirus brachypterus*
COMMON NAME: Short-finned Scorpionfish
DISTRIBUTION: TI–WP; WT/S
HABITAT: Coral and rocky reefs
GENERAL WATER DEPTH: 5–40 m (16–131 ft)
FOOD HABIT: Carnivorous: fishes; crustaceans
SIZE: 200 mm (8 in)
DESCRIPTION: Generally inhabiting inshore reefs, the short-finned scorpionfish is not so commonly encountered as the zebra scorpionfish *D. zebra*, but it has the same basic habits and is rarely observed swimming in the open. It often lies about in soft corals waiting for small fish to swim past. It makes a good aquarium pet and can be weaned off live food, although natural feeding is much more desirable. The body pattern and the shape of the large pectoral fins are somewhat similar to those of *D. zebra* but it can be distinguished by the broad dark bars on the pectoral fin.

FAMILY: Scorpaenidae
SCIENTIFIC NAME: *Dendrochirus zebra*
COMMON NAME: Zebra Scorpionfish
DISTRIBUTION: TI–WP; WT/S
HABITAT: Coral and rocky reefs; rubble
GENERAL WATER DEPTH: 8–45 m (26–148 ft)
FOOD HABIT: Carnivorous: fishes; crustaceans
SIZE: 300 mm (12 in)
DESCRIPTION: Although the zebra scorpionfish resembles other scorpionfish of the genus *Pterois* it can be easily identified by its colour pattern and the shape of its butterfly-like pectoral fins. It also differs from the *Pterois* group in its behaviour. Whereas *P. volitans* is mostly seen with its pectorals extended (even when on the bottom), quite often the zebra scorpionfish is observed hiding among bottom growths with its pectoral fins folded, lying in ambush for unsuspecting prey. In contrast to its slow swimming behaviour, it has

Dendrochirus zebra

Pterois volitans

an extremely swift hunting strike. Despite its venomous dorsal spines the flesh is edible.

Neosebastes pandus

FAMILY: Scorpaenidae
SCIENTIFIC NAME: *Neosebastes pandus*
COMMON NAME: Gurnard Scorpionfish
DISTRIBUTION: WT/S
HABITAT: Rocky reefs; seagrass meadows
GENERAL WATER DEPTH: 5–50 m
(16–164 ft)
FOOD HABIT: Carnivorous: fishes;
crustaceans
SIZE: 330 mm (13 in)
DESCRIPTION: An absolutely magnificent fish in its natural habitat, the gurnard scorpionfish is a master at camouflage. It sits almost immobile, with just a hint of life from the barely perceptible movement of its gill covers. It frequents shallow waters on inshore reefs and although very common, is not often caught on a line. It lives mainly among algae-covered reef and normally strikes only at moving prey. The long dorsal spines inflict extremely painful wounds, but the flesh is delicious.

FAMILY: Scorpaenidae
SCIENTIFIC NAME: *Pterois volitans*
COMMON NAME: Fire Fish
DISTRIBUTION: TI–WP; WT/S
HABITAT: Coral and rocky reefs
GENERAL WATER DEPTH: 8–40 m (26–131 ft)
FOOD HABIT: Carnivorous: fishes;
crustaceans
SIZE: 380 mm (15 in)
DESCRIPTION: Common on lagoon reefs and around deepwater coral heads, the fire fish is usually in a pair or a group. It inhabits the same cave, ledge or underhang for a number of years. Observations have shown that it hunts day or night, although there seems to be higher activity towards twilight and darkness. It is venomous and painful stings can be inflicted by the dorsal spines. Superficially similar to the butterfly scorpionfish, the fire fish can be distinguished by its separated pectoral fin rays. Colour ranges from pink to black, the body being crossed with thin pairs of white bands. An easy way to separate the species of the genus *Pterois* is to look closely at the pectoral fins; each species has characteristic pectoral fins, regardless of colour or geographical location.

Synanceia horrida

FAMILY: Scorpaenidae
SCIENTIFIC NAME: *Synanceia horrida*
COMMON NAME: Horrid Stonefish
DISTRIBUTION: TI–WP
HABITAT: Mud; coral and rocky reefs;
rubble
GENERAL WATER DEPTH: 1–40 m
(3–131 ft)
FOOD HABIT: Carnivorous: fishes;
crustaceans
SIZE: 330 mm (13 in)
DESCRIPTION: Found on continental island reefs, embayments, muddy estuaries, lagoons and offshore coral reefs, it is the most commonly encountered species of stonefish distinguished by a deep groove behind the eyes. The horrid stonefish is one of the most venomous fish in tropical waters; concealed in dorsal sheaths along the back are 13 of the most efficient natural injection systems to be found in any marine animal. Needle-sharp dorsal spines, each with a twin venom sac, produce wounds of unbearable pain, and the victim must receive medical attention as soon as possible.

Atypichthys latus

FAMILY: Scorpididae
SCIENTIFIC NAME: *Atypichthys latus*
COMMON NAME: Eastern Footballer
DISTRIBUTION: TWP
HABITAT: Rocky and coral reefs
GENERAL WATER DEPTH: 3–40 m
(10–131 ft)
FOOD HABIT: Carnivorous: benthic
invertebrates
SIZE: 150 mm (6 in)
DESCRIPTION: As far as it is known, this species occurs only near Lord Howe, the Kermedec and Norfolk Islands in the South-West Pacific where it is similar to the more common mado on the mainland. The eastern footballer swims in schools, and as it seems to prefer the area above reefs rather than the places within the reef itself, it was once thought to feed on plankton. However gut contents do not support this theory as their stomachs often contain bottom-living invertebrates and algae.

Atypichthys strigatus

FAMILY: Scorpididae
SCIENTIFIC NAME: *Atypichthys strigatus*
COMMON NAME: Mado
DISTRIBUTION: WT/S
HABITAT: Rocky reefs; jetties; groynes
GENERAL WATER DEPTH: 1–25 m (3–82 ft)
FOOD HABIT: Carnivorous
SIZE: 250 mm (10 in)
DESCRIPTION: The common name mado is the Australian Aboriginal name for the species which has been retained unmodified, as have so many others. The mado is typical of a number of smaller fish caught by children off wharves and jetties. It is generally used for bait, tossed back, or taken home for the cat; some fishermen use it for fish soup. It is an excellent aquarium fish.

Microcanthus strigatus

FAMILY: Scorpididae
SCIENTIFIC NAME: *Microcanthus strigatus*
COMMON NAME: Stripey
DISTRIBUTION: TWP; WT/S
HABITAT: Rocky reefs; coral reefs
GENERAL WATER DEPTH: 10–30 m (33–98 ft)
FOOD HABIT: Carnivorous: crustaceans
SIZE: 150 mm (6 in)

DESCRIPTION: The stripey swims in small, closely compacted schools, and unlike most of the other sweeps, rarely swims up in the open water column during the day, preferring the dark side of ledges, caves or gutters. Although it usually swims fairly close to the reef, it may be taken in open spaces by trawl net. It is easy to keep in aquaria and will survive on a varied diet of both natural and packaged fish foods. The stripey has a most unusual distribution, being found in the South-West Pacific, near Hawaii and Japan.

Acanthistius ocellatus

FAMILY: Serranidae
SCIENTIFIC NAME: *Acanthistius ocellatus*
COMMON NAME: Eastern Wirrah
DISTRIBUTION: WT/S
HABITAT: Rocky reefs
GENERAL WATER DEPTH: 5–30 m (16–98 ft)
FOOD HABIT: Carnivorus: fishes
SIZE: 450 mm (18 in)
DESCRIPTION: The eastern wirrah inhabits inshore and offshore island reefs and is often taken in shallow waters by rock fishermen both in estuaries and on open coast. Divers do not often see this species as it usually lives in caves, beneath rocks and under ledges. It will often take a bait and lie on it, putting little effort into resisting the hook, or line drag. It is known in Australia as the 'boot'. Characteristic features are the dark-edged blue spots on the body and the blue-edged fins.

FAMILY: Serranidae
SCIENTIFIC NAME: *Acanthistius serratus*
COMMON NAME: Western Wirrah
DISTRIBUTION: WT/S
HABITAT: Rocky reefs
GENERAL WATER DEPTH: 5–30 m (16–98 ft)
FOOD HABIT: Carnivorous: fishes
SIZE: 500 mm (20 in)
DESCRIPTION: The western wirrah is found around coastal and offshore island reefs in

Acanthistius serratus

the Indian Ocean off south-western Australia where during the day it lives under ledges and in caves. An inquisitive species that can be encouraged a short distance from its residence by wiggling a finger, the western wirrah is caught by rock fishermen who generally put a knife through its head and throw it back, or take it home for the cat. The flesh is very tough, without much flavour.

Aethaloperca rogaa

FAMILY: Serranidae
SCIENTIFIC NAME: *Aethaloperca rogaa*
COMMON NAME: Red-mouthed Rock Cod
DISTRIBUTION: TI–WP
HABITAT: Coral reefs
GENERAL WATER DEPTH: 10–40 m (33–131 ft)
FOOD HABIT: Carnivorous: fishes
SIZE: 600 mm (2 ft)
DESCRIPTION: The red-mouthed rock cod is a very distinctive fish, having an all-over black colour trimmed with a tinge of white on the edge of the caudal, anal and pelvic fins. An interesting feature is the bright orange colour inside the mouth. It is not a very well-known fish, although it is caught quite regularly in some reef areas. It lives in caves and gutters in the reef and is difficult to find and photograph.

Cephalopholis cyanostigma

FAMILY: Serranidae
SCIENTIFIC NAME: *Cephalopholis cyanostigma*
COMMON NAME: Blue-spotted Rock Cod
DISTRIBUTION: TI–WP
HABITAT: Coral and rocky reefs
GENERAL WATER DEPTH: 5–25 m (16–82 ft)
FOOD HABIT: Carnivorous: fishes; crustaceans
SIZE: 350 mm (14 in)
DESCRIPTION: The blue-spotted rock cod inhabits offshore islands and cays. It is often seen behind a screen of staghorn coral in the shallows where it lies in wait for prey; in deeper water it sits in the open among broken coral rubble and scattered coral clumps; in rocky reef areas it inhabits caves and ledges. Distinguishing features are six obscure vertical bars (these are not always discernible on living fish) which are broken up by a patchwork of paler markings. Bright blue spots surrounded by darker ocelli cover the body, head and fins, and the tips of the spines on the dorsal fin are red. On living specimens there is also a very black patch at the rear top of the gill cover.

Cephalopholis miniata

FAMILY: Serranidae
SCIENTIFIC NAME: *Cephalopholis miniata*
COMMON NAME: Coral Rock Cod
DISTRIBUTION: TI–WP
HABITAT: Coral and rocky reefs
GENERAL WATER DEPTH: 10–40 m (33–131 ft)
FOOD HABIT: Carnivorous: fishes; crustaceans
SIZE: 450 mm (18 in)
DESCRIPTION: Sometimes mistaken for one of the coral trouts, the coral rock cod can be distinguished by its larger blue spots, blue-edged fins, brighter red colour, deeper body, nine dorsal spines and the rounded margin of the tail. The coral rock cod is common in some areas but it does not come out into the open as much as coral trout, preferring to stay within caves, ledges and coral labyrinths. It is caught on inshore and offshores reefs with fish bait.

Cromileptes altivelis

FAMILY: Serranidae
SCIENTIFIC NAME: *Cromileptes altivelis*
COMMON NAME: Barramundi Rock Cod
DISTRIBUTION: TI–WP
HABITAT: Coral and rocky reefs
GENERAL WATER DEPTH: 5–20 m (16–66 ft)
FOOD HABIT: Carnivorous: fishes
SIZE: 660 mm (26 in)
DESCRIPTION: The barramundi rock cod was once a common species on most reefs throughout the Indo-Pacific area but fishing pressure and its negligible fear of underwater hunters has significantly reduced its numbers. It is a pity that such commercial fish are not more adequately known, or managed in some way, as they are fast becoming rare. The barramundi rock cod lives in gutters or beneath overhangs and caves, and is mostly observed singly.

Plectropomus leopardus

FAMILY: Serranidae
SCIENTIFIC NAME: *Plectropomus leopardus*
COMMON NAME: Common Coral Trout
DISTRIBUTION: TI–WP
HABITAT: Coral reefs
GENERAL WATER DEPTH: 3–50 m (10–164 ft)
FOOD HABIT: Carnivorous: fishes; crustaceans
SIZE: 700 mm (27.5 in)
DESCRIPTION: The common coral trout is the 'real' coral trout, fished commercially throughout tropical reef waters as an important food fish. It is a relatively shallow water species and its most preferred depth during the day seems to be 5–10 m (16–33 ft). The tail margin is concave. This species can be red, brown or dark grey and is covered with small blue dots. It is easily approached underwater and is very commonly speared. At night it sleeps under ledges and overhangs where it takes on a dappled shade of brown and pink. The common coral trout is hand lined on cut fish and is also taken on lures by trolling.

FAMILY: Serranidae
SCIENTIFIC NAME: *Pseudanthias huchtii* (male)
COMMON NAME: Hucht's Fairy Vasslet
DISTRIBUTION: TI–WP
HABITAT: Coral reefs
GENERAL WATER DEPTH: 5–10 m (16–33 ft)
FOOD HABIT: Carnivorous: zooplankton
SIZE: 110 mm (4 in)
DESCRIPTION: An exquisite, easily recognised species, Hucht's fairy vasslet is a shallow water anthiad that occurs on the tops of reefs and bommies along the northern outer areas of barrier reefs. Not so common as some other species of anthiads, it generally has a ratio of six to eight females to one male. It is a plankton feeder and spends much time in the water column above the reef, feeding on small drifting micro-organisms.

Pseudanthias huchtii (male)

Siganus lineatus

FAMILY: Serranidae
SCIENTIFIC NAME: *Pseudanthias pleurotaenia* (male)
COMMON NAME: Blotched Fairy Basslet
DISTRIBUTION: TI–WP
HABITAT: Coral reefs
GENERAL WATER DEPTH: 10–30 m (33–98 ft)
FOOD HABIT: Carnivorous: zooplankton
SIZE: 110 mm (4 in)
DESCRIPTION: An absolutely exquisite, highly coloured and easily identified species, the blotched fairy basslet must capture the imagination of every fish enthusiast. It may be seen feeding in the water column several metres above the bottom close to cliff faces, or on the slopes of underwater reefs. During the breeding season the male is territorial and selects special areas such as a specific gorgonian sea fan or a ledge of dead reef. In regions where this fish abounds there may be a male every few metres. They seem to congregate in a specific place and compete for females which usually swim around in groups.

FAMILY: Siganidae
SCIENTIFIC NAME: *Siganus lineatus*
COMMON NAME: Golden-lined Rabbitfish
DISTRIBUTION: TI–WP
HABITAT: Coral and rocky reefs
GENERAL WATER DEPTH: 2–20 m (6–66 ft)
FOOD HABIT: Herbivorous: algae
SIZE: 350 mm (14 in)
DESCRIPTION: Sometimes occurring in large schools which enter the surge channels of open water reefs around continental islands, the golden-lined rabbitfish also inhabits sheltered mainland reefs and lagoons along barrier reefs. It is one of the largest and most gaily coloured of the rabbitfish and can be readily identified by the bright golden lines and the yellow spot at the rear of the dorsal fin. It is a diurnal herbivore that varies little in its colour pattern. The flesh is edible, though requiring some preparation and added condiments. It should be handled carefully as it has venomous spines.

HABITAT: Coral and rocky reefs
GENERAL WATER DEPTH: 5–20 m (16–66 ft)
FOOD HABIT: Herbivorous: algae
SIZE: 300 mm (12 in)
DESCRIPTION: Rabbitfish are rarely caught by line, though many are netted. Their flesh, though edible, has a definite weedy taste and the fish should be cleaned and skinned immediately on capture. The blue-lined rabbitfish inhabits lagoons and also lives around mainland reefs and continental islands. Like other rabbitfish, the blue-lined rabbitfish is often sighted in pairs and is not always easy to approach underwater. It should never be touched with bare hands as it has venomous spines.

Siganus punctatus

FAMILY: Siganidae
SCIENTIFIC NAME: *Siganus punctatus*
COMMON NAME: Gold-spotted Rabbitfish
DISTRIBUTION: TI–WP
HABITAT: Coral reefs
GENERAL WATER DEPTH: 5–20 m (16–66 ft)
FOOD HABIT: Herbivorous: algae
SIZE: 380 mm (15 in)
DESCRIPTION: The gold-spotted rabbitfish is almost always observed in pairs swimming close together. It ranges over hundreds of metres of reef feeding exclusively on algae from dead coral surfaces and the walls of cliff faces. It is most abundant around the offshore reefs and cays. The flesh has a weedy taste but is not poisonous; the spines are sharp and painfully venomous.

Pseudanthias pleurotaenia (male)

Siganus puellus

FAMILY: Siganidae
SCIENTIFIC NAME: *Siganus puellus*
COMMON NAME: Blue-lined Rabbitfish
DISTRIBUTION: TI–WP

FAMILY: Sillaginidae
SCIENTIFIC NAME: *Sillago ciliata*
COMMON NAME: Sand Whiting
DISTRIBUTION: TI–WP; WT/S
HABITAT: Sand; rubble flats
GENERAL WATER DEPTH: 220 mm to 20 m (9 in–66 ft)

Sillago ciliata

Sillago robusta

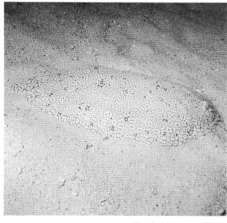

Pandachirus pavoninus

FOOD HABIT: Carnivorous: worms; crustaceans; molluscs
SIZE: 500 mm (20 in)
DESCRIPTION: Whiting generally swim in schools, grubbing in the soft bottom of estuaries, sandflats and lagoons on the coast and around offshore islands. However, when feeding, individuals often separate and work along the outer fringes of the school's feeding perimeter. The sand whiting has no prominent markings except a dark smudge at the base of the pectoral fin. Though larger specimens are referred to as 'bluenose whiting', very few are seen underwater.

Sillago maculata

FAMILY: Sillaginidae
SCIENTIFIC NAME: *Sillago maculata*
COMMON NAME: Trumpeter Whiting
DISTRIBUTION: WT/S
HABITAT: Sand; mud
GENERAL WATER DEPTH: 2–20 m (6–66 ft)
FOOD HABIT: Carnivorous: molluscs; crustaceans
SIZE: 300 mm (12 in)
DESCRIPTION: Well-known to many estuary anglers, the trumpeter whiting is taken by hand line, rod and beach seine and also trawled. Its main identifying features are a number of dark blotches along the side and back as well as a prominent dark blue or black base to the pectoral fin. It is rarely seen by divers as it inhabits the waters of coastal bays.

FAMILY: Sillaginidae
SCIENTIFIC NAME: *Sillago robusta*
COMMON NAME: Stout Whiting
DISTRIBUTION: WT/S
HABITAT: Sand; mud
GENERAL WATER DEPTH: 10–70 m (33–230 ft)
FOOD HABIT: Carnivorous: worms; crustaceans
SIZE: 270 mm (11 in)
DESCRIPTION: Inhabiting bays and estuaries in coastal waters, the stout whiting is also found in deeper offshore waters where it is mainly brought up by prawn and fish trawlers. Owing to its small size it is not usually considered a commercial species but some are taken for food. The first dorsal fin is not so high as it is in other whiting and there is no blotch at the base of the pectoral fin. Its yellow back and silvery belly are bisected by a bright silver stripe running midway along the body.

Pardachirus hedleyi

FAMILY: Soleidae
SCIENTIFIC NAME: *Pardachirus hedleyi*
COMMON NAME: Hedley's Peacock Sole
DISTRIBUTION: WT/S
HABITAT: Sand

GENERAL WATER DEPTH: 5–30 m (16–98 ft)
FOOD HABIT: Carnivorous: crustaceans; worms
SIZE: 150 mm (6 in)
DESCRIPTION: Hedley's peacock sole has a fairly distinctive pattern, though depending on the surrounding terrain or mood of the fish, the overall colour may vary from a pinkish to a white background. Sometimes a number of darker smudges may be present on the dorsal surface and these may cause it to be confused with other species unless careful observations are made. It is trawled and sometimes line caught and, though small, is an excellent food fish.

FAMILY: Soleidae
SCIENTIFIC NAME: *Pandachirus pavoninus*
COMMON NAME: Peacock Sole
DISTRIBUTION: TI-WP
HABITAT: Sand
GENERAL WATER DEPTH: 4–20 m (13–66 ft)
FOOD HABIT: Carnivorous: crustaceans
SIZE: 230 mm (9 in)
DESCRIPTION: A beautifully marked fish, the peacock sole spends most of its time under a layer of sand, ambushing prey and hiding from predators; only its eyes betray its presence. All related soles have tails separate from the side fins. The eyes are on the right side of the head and there are open pores at the base of each fin ray. These pores release a predator-inhibiting secretion that has been tested as a shark repellent. However, as it is not collected in large numbers, a closely related species, Hedley's peacock sole, was chosen for the tests.

FAMILY: Sparidae
SCIENTIFIC NAME: *Acanthopagrus australis*
COMMON NAME: Yellowfin Bream
DISTRIBUTION: TI-WP; WT/S
HABITAT: Rocky and coral reefs; sand; seagrass; rubble

Acanthopagrus australis

GENERAL WATER DEPTH: 1–25 m (3–82 ft)
FOOD HABIT: Carnivorous: molluscs;
crustaceans; worms; fishes; ascidians
SIZE: 580 mm (23 in)
DESCRIPTION: The yellowfin bream is found almost everywhere, from far up tidal estuaries to ocean beaches and offshore rocky reefs; it may also enter and live in fresh water. Depending on location, season, the state of the tide and moon, and the condition of the sea, it can be caught on many different rigs and baits. Underwater, its shy nature and shiny silver scales make it difficult to photograph. The yellowfin bream is usually gregarious but sometimes when feeding, a particular fish (not always the biggest) may continually drive others away from the feeding area. Strangely, such a bream will allow juveniles and fish of other species to feed close to it.

Chrysophrys auratus

FAMILY: Sparidae
SCIENTIFIC NAME: *Chrysophrys auratus*
COMMON NAME: Snapper
DISTRIBUTION: TI–WP; WT/S
HABITAT: Rocky reefs; sand; mud; rubble
GENERAL WATER DEPTH: 5–100 m
(16–328 ft)

FOOD HABIT: Carnivorous: molluscs;
crustaceans; fishes
SIZE: 1.2 m (4 ft)
DESCRIPTION: Cockneys, red bream, squire and snapper (the name depends on the stage of growth) are all one species. Taken by hand line, rods, traps, gill nets and by trawling, snapper is an extremely popular food fish and commands a good price at any market. The larger adult (snapper) tends to inhabit deeper water than the other three recognised stages and is caught by line near offshore and coastal reefs, wrecks, in deep holes on soft bottom, on scallop beds or around low reef and rubble areas in bays and inlets. The older fish often has large bumps on its forehead.

Rhabdosargus sarba

FAMILY: Sparidae
SCIENTIFIC NAME: *Rhabdosargus sarba*
COMMON NAME: Tarwhine
DISTRIBUTION: TWP; WT/S
HABITAT: Sand; mud; rubble
GENERAL WATER DEPTH: 1–25 m (3–82 ft)
FOOD HABIT: Carnivorous: invertebrates
SIZE: 300 mm (12 in)
DESCRIPTION: To the uninitiated, bream and tarwhine probably look alike, yet the differences are easily discernible once compared. The tarwhine has a much rounder forehead, larger eyes and definite golden-red stripes along the body, lacking the black spot at the base of the pectoral fin. The tarwhine swims in schools and often inhabits the same terrain as bream, mixing freely with them, though generally swimming behind. An excellent food fish, tarwhine is caught by lines and nets and in traps.

FAMILY: Sphyraenidae
SCIENTIFIC NAME: *Sphyraena barracuda*
COMMON NAME: Barracuda
DISTRIBUTION: TI–WP

Sphyraena barracuda

HABITAT: Coral reefs; rocky reefs
GENERAL WATER DEPTH: Surface to 40 m
(131 ft)
FOOD HABIT: Carnivorous:
fishes
SIZE: 2 m (6 ft)
DESCRIPTION: In many parts of the world the barracuda has a reputation as a fearsome predator and is thought to be of considerable danger to humans. There is no doubt good reason for the fear because a large adult grows to over 2 m (6 ft) and has teeth that command instant respect. Although it is very common in most tropical waters, unprovoked attacks on humans have mostly been due to human ignorance or a genuine mistake by the barracuda (for example, miscalculation during hand feeding by a diver). Barracuda up to a metre (3 ft) long are usually seen in large schools and provide a stimulating experience for any diver surrounded at close quarters by such inquisitive marauders.

FAMILY: Syngnathidae
SCIENTIFIC NAME: *Hippocampus breviceps*
COMMON NAME: Short-headed Seahorse
DISTRIBUTION: WT/S
HABITAT: Rocky reefs; jetty piles
GENERAL WATER DEPTH: 5 m (16 ft)
FOOD HABIT: Carnivorous: crustaceans
SIZE: 70 mm (3 in)
DESCRIPTION: Although the short-headed seahorse appears to be a very common species, underwater it is often remarkably difficult to find. Owing to its brilliant colours, it also makes a worthwhile addition to an aquarium. Depending on age and location, specimens may have filaments issuing from the points of the body ridges, usually only on the back. This species is endemic to the waters of southern Australia.

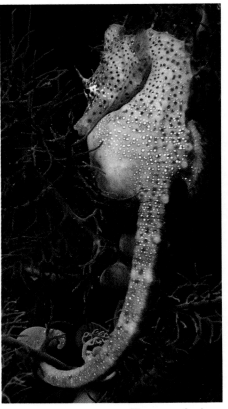

Hippocampus breviceps

Synodus dermatogenys

FAMILY: Synodontidae
SCIENTIFIC NAME: *Synodus dermatogenys*
COMMON NAME: Variegated Lizardfish
DISTRIBUTION: TI–WP
HABITAT: Coral and rocky reefs; seagrass
meadows
GENERAL WATER DEPTH: 5–60 m
(16–197 ft)
FOOD HABIT: Carnivorous: fishes;
crustaceans
SIZE: 260 mm (10 in)
DESCRIPTION: As its common name sug-
gests, the variegated lizardfish is patterned.
Its base colour is white or silver with black,
green, brown or red patterns. The darker
stripe running lengthwise to the tail is

crossed by five dorsal blotches. All the fins
are spotted. Like all lizardfish, this species is
a bottom-dwelling diurnal fish that inhabits
reefs, rubble, sand and seagrass meadows,
although it is mostly seen in the open on
high-rising terrain. It will take a moving bait
but normally waits to ambush its prey.

Synodus houlti

FAMILY: Synodontidae
SCIENTIFIC NAME: *Synodus houlti*
COMMON NAME: Hoult's Lizardfish
DISTRIBUTION: TI–WP
HABITAT: Sand
GENERAL WATER DEPTH: 3–10 m
(10–33 ft)
FOOD HABIT: Carnivorous: fishes
SIZE: 170 mm (7 in)
DESCRIPTION: Owing to their cryptic colouration and secretive habits, many lizardfish
remain unnoticed by most divers. Some rest
on the corals propped up on their pelvic fins
and others bury themselves in the sand and
rubble, waiting to ambush small fish as they
swim within range. Some species of
lizardfish occur in several types of habitats
and some are restricted to one. Hoult's
lizardfish appears to be found in areas of
sand, or sandy rubble, where it partly buries
its body in the substrate. It inhabits inshore
areas, continental islands and offshore locations throughout its range and is a solitary,
diurnal species.

FAMILY: Synodontidae
SCIENTIFIC NAME: *Synodus variegatus*
COMMON NAME: Engelman's Lizardfish
DISTRIBUTION: TI–WP
HABITAT: Coral and rocky reefs
GENERAL WATER DEPTH: 3–20 m
(10–66 ft)
FOOD HABIT: Carnivorous: fishes
SIZE: 250 mm (10 in)
DESCRIPTION: Engelman's lizardfish is a
very attractive little fish with a blotched grey
and red back and line of ten red elongated,

Synodus variegatus

rectangular blocks just above the lateral line
running from the head down to the caudal
peduncle. The dorsal fin has red and white
spots on the rays. It is a bottom-dwelling
reef fish that blends well with its habitat and
deploys a wait-and-watch hunting style,
depending on immobility and camouflage.
Any small fish or crustaceans straying close
are immediately snapped up in a swift
charge. The wide gape of the mouth lined
with a multitude of fine sharp teeth make it
a very capable hunter.

Arothron hispidus

FAMILY: Tetraodontidae
SCIENTIFIC NAME: *Arothron hispidus*
COMMON NAME: Broad-barred Pufferfish
DISTRIBUTION: TI–WP
HABITAT: Rocky and coral reefs
GENERAL WATER DEPTH: 3–25 m
(10–82 ft)
FOOD HABIT: Carnivorous: sessile
organisms; echinoderms; molluscs
SIZE: 500 mm (20 in)
DESCRIPTION: A large, conspicuously mark-
ed species, the broad-barred pufferfish can
be recognised by white lines and spots that
extend onto the tail, as well as a black patch

with a bright yellow circle around the pectoral fins. Base colours vary from brown through to grey, black and dark green and, depending on age, size, and location of the fish, the stripes on the belly and spots on the back may also vary. Line caught, netted or trawled, this fish should never be eaten as it is fatally poisonous.

Canthigaster callisterna

FAMILY: Tetraodontidae
SCIENTIFIC NAME: *Canthigaster callisterna*
COMMON NAME: Clown Toby
DISTRIBUTION: TWP; WTS
HABITAT: Rocky and coral reefs
GENERAL WATER DEPTH: 1–30 m (3–98 ft)
FOOD HABIT: Omnivorous: algae;
  invertebrates
SIZE: 140 mm (6 in)
DESCRIPTION: The colours and markings of the clown toby are very distinctive and a mistake is unlikely to be made with living or recently dead specimens. I doubt if this little fish is ever caught on a line but it is regularly seen by divers. It is poisonous and must never be eaten.

Canthigaster coronata

FAMILY: Tetraodontidae
SCIENTIFIC NAME: *Canthigaster coronata*
COMMON NAME: Banded Sharpnose
  Pufferfish
DISTRIBUTION: TI–WP
HABITAT: Coral reefs
GENERAL WATER DEPTH: 3–20 m
  (10–66 ft)
FOOD HABIT: Omnivorous: algae;
  crustaceans
SIZE: 100 mm (4 in)
DESCRIPTION: The banded sharpnose pufferfish has wide distribution throughout tropical lagoons, on offshore barrier reefs, and in isolated sand pockets of fringing reefs. It prefers sheltered conditions and feeds on a variety of organisms, including algae, crustaceans, worms, sponges and molluscs. It makes an ideal aquarium fish but care must be taken when handling it. It is extremely poisonous if eaten.

Canthigaster solandri

FAMILY: Tetraodontidae
SCIENTIFIC NAME: *Canthigaster solandri*
COMMON NAME: Solandri's Sharpnose
  Pufferfish
DISTRIBUTION: TI–WP
HABITAT: Coral and rocky reefs
GENERAL WATER DEPTH: 5–20 m
  (16–66 ft)
FOOD HABIT: Omnivorous: coralline algae;
  ascidians; molluscs
SIZE: 120 mm (5 in)
DESCRIPTION: Most sharpnose pufferfish inhabit shallow sheltered waters and each species has a definite colour pattern. Solandri's sharpnose pufferfish normally has very prominent light blue lines and specks but in some specimens they are less conspicuous and appear much darker. The red ring around the eye and the black ocellus directly under the dorsal fin are characteristic features. It is an interesting and unusual aquarium fish that is easily maintained. Deadly poisonous if eaten.

Canthigaster valentini

FAMILY: Tetraodontidae
SCIENTIFIC NAME: *Canthigaster valentini*
COMMON NAME: Valentin's Sharpnose
  Pufferfish
DISTRIBUTION: TI–WP
HABITAT: Coral and rocky reefs
GENERAL WATER DEPTH: 1–30 m (3–98 ft)
FOOD HABIT: Omnivorous: invertebrates;
  algae
SIZE: 70 mm (3 in) average length
DESCRIPTION: A rather small species rarely exceeding 100 mm (4 in), Valentin's sharpnose pufferfish is commonly observed inhabiting reef flats, reef slopes and coral heads on mainland reefs, and around continental islands and offshore reefs. Valentin's pufferfish is diurnal and sleeps on its stomach in a curve-tailed position close to, or among, short green algae. Its nocturnal colours are a mixture of mottled greens and blacks, emulating its surroundings. It is mimicked by the small leatherjacket *Paraluteres prionurus* which has almost identical colouration and swims in a similar way. They are easily distinguished as Valentin's sharpnose pufferfish has no dorsal spine, no thorn-like spines on the caudal peduncle (tail junction) and fewer dorsal and anal rays. Both have a shy and retiring behaviour but the pufferfish is far more common than its mimic.

FAMILY: Tetraodontidae
SCIENTIFIC NAME: *Omegophora
  cyanopunctata*
COMMON NAME: Blue-spotted Pufferfish
DISTRIBUTION: TI–WP
HABITAT: Sand; mud; rubble; rocky reefs;
  seagrass
GENERAL WATER DEPTH: 2–100 m
  (6–328 ft)
FOOD HABIT: Carnivorous
SIZE: 250 mm (10 in)
DESCRIPTION: Photographed first by the author in 1970 it has only recently been

Omegophora cyanopunctata

described. The blue-spotted pufferfish lives in areas ranging from sheltered inshore waters to offshore trawling grounds. Its colours are fairly stable, one of the main distinguishing features being blue spots giving the fish its common name. It is a solitary, home-ranging species caught by line, in beach seines and trawled. It should not be eaten as it is deadly poisonous.

Paratrachichthys trailli

FAMILY: Trachichthyidae
SCIENTIFIC NAME: *Paratrachichthys trailli*
COMMON NAME: Sandpaper Fish
DISTRIBUTION: WT/S; CT/S
HABITAT: Rocky reefs; mud
GENERAL WATER DEPTH: 70–170 m
 (230–558 ft)
FOOD HABIT: Carnivorous: fishes
SIZE: 250 mm (10 in)
DESCRIPTION: When the colouration of the sandpaper fish is shown beside that of the slender roughy, it is easy to compare their opposite counter-shading characteristics. The slender roughy has a reverse counter-shading attuned to daylight; the sandpaper fish, living in much darker depths, displays the more accepted counter-shading of a dark-coloured back and light-coloured or silvery sides and belly, as displayed by many open water pelagics to blend with their sur-

roundings. The sandpaper fish can be readily identified by its shape, the three spines on its gill cover and the position of the anus which is flanked on either side by the ventral fins.

Trachichthys australis

FAMILY: Trachichthyidae
SCIENTIFIC NAME: *Trachichthys australis*
COMMON NAME: Southern Roughy
DISTRIBUTION: WT/S; CT/S
HABITAT: Rocky and coral reefs
GENERAL WATER DEPTH: 3–30 m
 (10–98 ft)
FOOD HABIT: Carnivorous: crustaceans
SIZE: 150 mm (6 in)
DESCRIPTION: Unlikely to be confused with any other species, the southern roughy is a small reef-dwelling fish that during the day is mostly confined to its particular hole or ledge. At times it may be seen under one ledge, sometimes solitary and sometimes in a group. Although caught on hook and line during the day, the roughy is mostly nocturnal; venturing out after dusk it hangs almost motionless just above the bottom, waiting for prey.

Chelidonichthys kumu

FAMILY: Triglidae
SCIENTIFIC NAME: *Chelidonichthys kumu*
COMMON NAME: Red Gurnard
DISTRIBUTION: WT/S
HABITAT: Mud; sand; low profile reef
GENERAL WATER DEPTH: 3–100 m
 (10–328 ft)
FOOD HABIT: Carnivorous: fishes; crabs; molluscs
SIZE: 530 mm (21 in)
DESCRIPTION: The largest and most commercial gurnard in the South-West Pacific, the red gurnard may be caught by line near offshore coastal reefs on sand, or trawled on mud bottom. When caught it turns brilliant red and the pectoral fins change from mottled brown to brilliant green with blue spots and edging. The characteristic black patch has white or light blue spots over it. By comparison, the photograph taken underwater shows its natural colouration on the bottom.

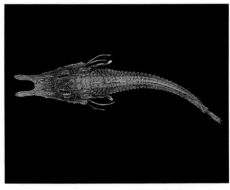

Peristedion liorhynchus

FAMILY: Triglidae
SCIENTIFIC NAME: *Peristedion liorhynchus*
COMMON NAME: Armoured Gurnard
DISTRIBUTION: TI–WP; WT/N; WT/S
HABITAT: Mud
GENERAL WATER DEPTH: 120–300 m
 (394–984 ft)
FOOD HABIT: Carnivorous: worms
SIZE: 300 mm (12 in)
DESCRIPTION: Taken only by commercial trawlers and research vessels, the armoured gurnard with its body encased in an armour-like profusion of spiny scales looks like a prehistoric animal. Its two long, flattened, head spines, combined with its characteristic shape, allow simple identification. Because of its bony exterior it is very easily preserved; some enterprising trawlermen sell preserved specimens as curios to the tourist trade. Colour varies between brown and pink.

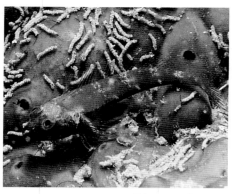

Helcogramma decurrens

FAMILY: Tripterygiidae
SCIENTIFIC NAME: *Helcogramma decurrens*
COMMON NAME: Southern Triplefin
DISTRIBUTION: WT/S; CT/S
HABITAT: Rocky reefs
GENERAL WATER DEPTH: 1–10 m (3–33 ft)
FOOD HABIT: Carnivorous
SIZE: 60 mm (2 in)
DESCRIPTION: The southern triplefin is a small, rock-dwelling fish that occurs intertidally down to 30 m (98 ft) and sometimes beyond. The common name derives from the fish having three dorsal fins. The southern triplefin is territorial and pair relationships are known but their duration is not. The male and female are sexually dimorphic in colour and in the shape of the first dorsal fin; the male usually has a dark face below the level of the eye.

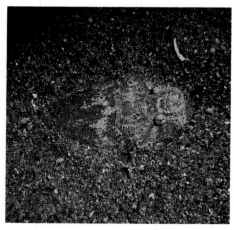

Kathetostoma laeve

FAMILY: Uranoscopidae
SCIENTIFIC NAME: *Kathetostoma laeve*
COMMON NAME: Stargazer
DISTRIBUTION: WT/S; CT/S
HABITAT: Sand; mud
GENERAL WATER DEPTH: 8–150 m
  (26–492 ft)
FOOD HABIT: Carnivorous: fishes;
  crustaceans
SIZE: 660 mm (26 in)

DESCRIPTION: Concealed as it always is under a layer of shell grit or sand, the stargazer has been seen by relatively few divers. It is line caught or netted by trawlers. It can be recognised by its blotchy colour pattern, the wide gap between the eyes and the almost straight posterior margin of the head sculpture. South-West Pacific stargazers are not venomous (though they have spines) and are excellent food fish.

Zanclus cornutus

FAMILY: Zanclidae
SCIENTIFIC NAME: *Zanclus cornutus*
COMMON NAME: Moorish Idol
DISTRIBUTION: TI–WP
HABITAT: Coral and rocky reefs
GENERAL WATER DEPTH: 2–25 m (6–82 ft)
FOOD HABIT: Carnivorous: encrusting
  sessile invertebrates; algae
SIZE: 220 mm (9 in)
DESCRIPTION: The Moorish idol is related to the surgeonfish but lacks the blades on the caudal peduncle. It is a common shallow-water species usually seen in pairs or small groups. In the mating season it often congregates in large schools. Little is known about the purpose of this behaviour but perhaps a higher rate of egg fertilisation is achieved during mass spawning. The Moorish idol is the only representative of its family and owing to its high dorsal fin and unique shape is easy to identify. Underwater it can be approached without difficulty as it swims slowly around searching for the small sponges it feeds on.

FAMILY: Zeidae
SCIENTIFIC NAME: *Zeus faber*
COMMON NAME: John Dory
DISTRIBUTION: WT/S
HABITAT: Rocky reefs; rubble;
  mud; sand

GENERAL WATER DEPTH: 3–100 m
  (10–328 ft)
FOOD HABIT: Carnivorous: fishes
SIZE: 610 mm (2 ft)
DESCRIPTION: Numbers of John Dory appear in the shallow waters of bays and harbours in late winter and early summer and in certain localities up to five or six may be seen on a single dive. The species is caught by hand line as well as being speared and trawled in large numbers. It has firm, white, tasty flesh. Those caught on lines are taken mostly on live bait as the John Dory is an extremely efficient sling-jawed predator, drifting up to small fish and swallowing them whole. A large ocellus (eyelike marking) is found on the side of this species.

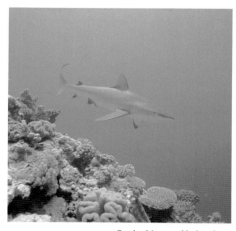

Carcharhinus amblyrhynchos

■ CLASS: Elasmobranchii

FAMILY: Carcharhinidae
SCIENTIFIC NAME: *Carcharhinus
  amblyrhynchos*
COMMON NAME: Graceful Whaler Shark
DISTRIBUTION: TI–WP
HABITAT: Coral and rocky reefs
GENERAL WATER DEPTH: 8–40 m
  (26–131 ft)

Zeus faber

FOOD HABIT: Carnivorous: fishes; turtles; crustaceans

SIZE: 2 m (6 ft)

DESCRIPTION: A sleek, inquisitive species, the graceful whaler shark is a swift, efficient predator that inhabits mostly offshore reefs. Although at some locations it may be sighted only occasionally and does not appear to give divers much trouble, in other areas it is quite pugnacious and when there are 20 or 30 in a group, the fact that they are only 'little ones' does not engender much confidence. It is a thick-bodied shark with a somewhat depressed head, a grey back, white belly and black margins to the pelvic and caudal fins; the ventral tips of the pectorals are also black. It gives birth to living young.

Carcharhinus galapagensis

FAMILY: Carcharhinidae
SCIENTIFIC NAME: *Carcharhinus galapagensis*
COMMON NAME: Galapagos Shark
DISTRIBUTION: TI–WP; EP
HABITAT: Coral and rocky reefs; open ocean
GENERAL WATER DEPTH: 5–60 m (16–197 ft)
FOOD HABIT: Carnivorous: fishes
SIZE: 3 m (10 ft)

DESCRIPTION: Although the Galapagos shark is similar in many ways to the grey reef shark *C. amblyrhynchos*, it can be distinguished by its rounder head and fuller body towards the tail. The grey reef shark is far more sturdy in the front half of the body and is rather steeply angled up to the base of the dorsal fin with a slimmer profile towards the tail. The Galapagos shark has no keels on the caudal peduncle (tail junction), though a dermal ridge is present on the back between the fins. It upper teeth are broadly triangular and serrated and the lower ones are narrower. In the water it usually swims in schools. It is extremely cheeky and not easily scared. Although there are no reported fatalities in Australian seas, I know a few divers who admit to being bluffed out of the water by these fast, sleek beauties. It is found at oceanic islands, not mainland Australia.

Carcharhinus obscurus

FAMILY: Carcharhinidae
SCIENTIFIC NAME: *Carcharhinus obscurus*
COMMON NAME: Black Whaler Shark
DISTRIBUTION: TI–WP; WT/S
HABITAT: Rocky reefs; open sea; coral reefs
GENERAL WATER DEPTH: 3–70 m (10–230 ft)
FOOD HABIT: Carnivorous: fishes; turtles
SIZE: 3 m (10 ft)

DESCRIPTION: The black whaler is a swift, curious, undaunted marauder that inhabits open seas, onshore and offshore reefs and will enter harbours, bays and estuaries. As an individual it can be quite frightening in the water because of its habit of zooming in at full speed straight at a diver, only to turn away at the last moment. The black whaler usually makes a couple of passes and then loses interest; if it does not, a diver should get out of the water quickly. The skin ridge between the two dorsal fins is a distinctive feature.

Galeocerdo cuvier

FAMILY: Carcharhinidae
SCIENTIFIC NAME: *Galeocerdo cuvier*
COMMON NAME: Tiger Shark
DISTRIBUTION: TI–WP; WT/S; WT/N

HABITAT: Open sea; coral and rocky reefs
GENERAL WATER DEPTH: Surface to 40 m (131 ft)
FOOD HABIT: Carnivorous: fish; mammals; birds; reptiles
SIZE: 6 m (20 ft)

DESCRIPTION: A large, thick-bodied shark, the tiger shark has a blunt head, a dark greyish brown back and is off-white on the belly. The younger shark has distinct dark stripes on the back which are faded on specimens over 4 m (13 ft). The teeth are very characteristic and are coarsely serrated, curved to the side, and identical in both jaws. Known worldwide as a proven maneater, the tiger shark is a cosmopolitan species that inhabits the world's major tropical and some temperate seas. Having had fairly close contact and a little time to watch it in action on several occasions, my impression is always of a big, slow-moving vacuum cleaner that just moves in, quite casually, and takes its food in massive gulps. Under normal conditions the tiger shark never seems to move fast, unless it has been frightened, or otherwise triggered into an attack pattern by some action. Even a tiger shark's feeding frenzy is at what seems a much slower pace than that of smaller sharks. More than anything else its sheer size and destructive dentition are enough to make it one of the oceans' greatest scavenging predators. Its young are born alive.

Triaenodon obesus

FAMILY: Carcharhinidae
SCIENTIFIC NAME: *Triaenodon obesus*
COMMON NAME: White-tipped Reef Shark
DISTRIBUTION: TI–WP; WT/N; IWP
HABITAT: Coral and rocky reefs
GENERAL WATER DEPTH: 1–40 m (3–131 ft)
FOOD HABIT: Carnivorous: fishes; crustaceans; reptiles
SIZE: 2.3 m (7.6 ft)

DESCRIPTION: Commonly found on inshore and offshore reefs, the white-tipped reef shark is slender bodied and inquisitive. Although it has formidable teeth and may be a little pugnacious during feeding frenzies or in the presence of speared fish, it is usually fairly placid, staying in the background and causing little concern to divers. It will take hooked fish from lines but is not quite so much trouble as the grey reef shark *Carcharhinus amblyrhynchos*. Unlike many pelagic sharks, the white-tipped reef shark does not need to swim continuously to keep water flowing over its gills; instead, it uses a muscular gill movement for breathing. It bears living young.

Himantura granulata

FAMILY: Dasyatidae
SCIENTIFIC NAME: *Himantura granulata*
COMMON NAME: Mangrove Stingray
DISTRIBUTION: TI–WP
HABITAT: Mangroves; coral reefs; mud; sand
GENERAL WATER DEPTH: 1–25 m (3–82 ft)
FOOD HABIT: Carnivorous: molluscs; fishes
SIZE: 1.5 m (5 ft)
DESCRIPTION: The mangrove stingray has one of the longest tails in relation to its body; this tail may be twice the length of the disc. It occurs on mainland reefs and in estuaries and may also be found in upper river systems where it can be caught on hand lines and in nets. It is common around offshore islands and reefs. It has been seen in groups numbering from four to ten specimens. When approached underwater it is a bit skittish and generally moves away if disturbed. Like most smaller stingrays, the skinned flaps of this species are edible. The tail is also an interesting curiosity as it has a row of spiny nodules running along its full length.

FAMILY: Dasyatidae
SCIENTIFIC NAME: *Himantura uarnak*
COMMON NAME: Long-tailed Ray
DISTRIBUTION: TI–WP

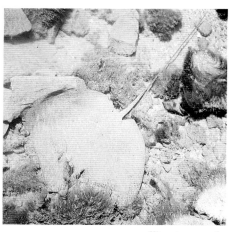

Himantura uarnak

HABITAT: Mud; muddy reefs; sand
GENERAL WATER DEPTH: Low tide to 20 m (66 ft)
FOOD HABIT: Carnivorous: molluscs; crustaceans
SIZE: 1.75 m (6 ft)
DESCRIPTION: One of the larger tropical stingrays, the long-tailed ray is commonly encountered at mainland and offshore locations, and is often seen in large groups. In many estuaries throughout its range and in particular in sheltered sandy or muddy bays it comes into the shallows to sleep, rest, or sun. It may reach 1.75 m (6 ft) across the disc and it has a continuous mesh-like pattern on the back. The tail has around 35 bands and a single venomous spine. At the centre of the back, along the dorsal ridge, there are two prominent white tubercles. It is sometimes caught on hand lines and in trawls.

Taeniura lymna

FAMILY: Dasyatidae
SCIENTIFIC NAME: *Taeniura lymna*
COMMON NAME: Blue-spotted Fantail Ray
DISTRIBUTION: TI–WP
HABITAT: Sand; mud; coral reefs; rubble
GENERAL WATER DEPTH: Low tide to 20 m (66 ft)

FOOD HABIT: Carnivorous: molluscs; worms; crustaceans
SIZE: 2.5 m (8 ft)
DESCRIPTION: Although this stingray is recorded to reach some 2.5 m (8 ft) very few people would ever have encountered such a large specimen. On late afternoons the blue-spotted fantail ray is very commonly seen on lagoon floors and tidal flats where it follows the rising tide, searching for molluscs which are crushed by its powerful teeth and jaws. During the middle of the day it can be found under ledges and coral slabs and in caves. It is not easily approached underwater and seems to be extremely nervous, always seeking a speedy escape. It is fairly simple to identify as its oval body shape and brilliant blue spots are unlike those of any other ray. The tail has one or two venomous spines towards the blue tip.

Taeniura melanospilos

FAMILY: Dasyatidae
SCIENTIFIC NAME: *Taeniura melanospilos*
COMMON NAME: Black-spotted Stingray
DISTRIBUTION: TI–WP
HABITAT: Coral reefs; rocky reefs; muddy reefs; sand
GENERAL WATER DEPTH: 5–120 m (16–394 ft)
FOOD HABIT: Carnivorous: molluscs; crustaceans; fishes
SIZE: 3 m (10 ft)
DESCRIPTION: Looking rather like an interplanetary spaceship, this giant stingray glides along in the depths, and when swimming beside it there is an overpowering sense of wonder at being so close to such a large sea creature. Seeing such a powerful, majestic animal wild and free in its environment, we must pity the so-called 'hunter' who kills it just for the sake of doing so. The black-spotted stingray seems to be more common around offshore islands and cays and is often followed by schools of yellowtail kingfish. It is also used as transport by suckerfish. Its spine is venomous.

Heterodontus galeatus

FAMILY: Heterodontidae
SCIENTIFIC NAME: *Heterodontus galeatus*
COMMON NAME: Crested Port Jackson
  Shark
DISTRIBUTION: WT/S
HABITAT: Rocky reefs; sand; mud;
  seagrass
GENERAL WATER DEPTH: 8–100 m
  (26–328 ft)
FOOD HABIT: Carnivorous: sea urchins;
  molluscs; crustaceans; fishes
SIZE: 1.3 m (4 ft)
DESCRIPTION: Although heterodontid sharks
are relatively harmless, both species have a
strong, sharp spine in front of each dorsal
fin. They tend to struggle violently when
handled and even small specimens can cause
an unpleasant wound that swells and throbs
for some time. The crested Port Jackson
shark can be distinguished from the common
Port Jackson shark by the larger head crests
which end abruptly and angle down sharply
at the rear of the head. The egg cases of the
crested Port Jackson shark are not so
coarsely spiralled as those of its relative and
they have two long curly tendrils at their
base to anchor the egg among bottom
growths.

Heterodontus portusjacksoni

FAMILY: Heterodontidae
SCIENTIFIC NAME: *Heterodontus
  portusjacksoni*
COMMON NAME: Port Jackson Shark
DISTRIBUTION: WT/S
HABITAT: Rocky reefs; sand; mud;
  seagrass
GENERAL WATER DEPTH: 8–200 m
  (26–656 ft)
FOOD HABIT: Carnivorous: sea urchins;
  molluscs; crustaceans; fishes
SIZE: 1.4 m (4.5 ft)
DESCRIPTION: The Port Jackson shark is by
far the more commonly encountered of the
two heterodontid sharks found in South-
West Pacific waters, especially during late
winter when it comes into shallow waters to
breed. Mating usually occurs at night; the
female later lays up to 18 tapered, spirally
flanged egg cases, each containing one egg.
To protect and stabilise the egg during the
development of the young shark, the female
actually screws the egg case into a crack in
the reef under a ledge, or between bottom
growths. After storms, displaced egg cases
are often found washed up on beaches.

Hypnos monopterygium

FAMILY: Hypnidae
SCIENTIFIC NAME: *Hypnos monopterygium*
COMMON NAME: Short-tailed Electric Ray;
  Numbfish
DISTRIBUTION: TI–WP; WT/S
HABITAT: Sand; mud; rocky reefs
GENERAL WATER DEPTH: 1–240 m
  (3–787 ft)
FOOD HABIT: Carnivorous: fishes;
  crustaceans; worms
SIZE: 690 mm (27 in)
DESCRIPTION: Soft, flabby and difficult to
pick up, the short-tailed electric ray is not a
popular fish. Many anglers, trawlermen and
spearfishermen have at some time had contact with it. The initial experience of handling, or being earthed to the short-tailed
electric ray, usually results in the trans-
mission of an electric shock of up to 200

volts. This bottom-dwelling ray is very hardy
and will live out of water for some time; even
when speared it will flutter deep into the
sand or mud and a large effort is required to
remove it. Like this species, the other kinds
of electric rays are all readily identified by
their shape or colouration.

Manta birostris

FAMILY: Mobulidae
SCIENTIFIC NAME: *Manta birostris*
COMMON NAME: Manta Ray
DISTRIBUTION: TI–WP
HABITAT: Oceanic; mid-water column
GENERAL WATER DEPTH: Surface to 20 m
  (66 ft)
FOOD HABIT: Carnivorous: zooplankton
SIZE: 5.75 m (19 ft)
DESCRIPTION: A harmless giant which, in
many regions, is still referred to as devilfish,
the manta ray is really a gentle creature that
will often endure the clumsy approaches of
underwater humans and allow itself to be
touched or ridden. Manta rays are usually
encountered in pairs or small groups but I
have swum with up to a dozen of these
giants in the Indian Ocean some 10 km (6
miles) off North West Cape in Western Australia just on dusk — an extremely exhilarat-
ing experience. Food is sieved directly from
the water and consists of all manner of
planktonic organisms. The young are born
alive and emerge from the mother's body
wrapped in their wingflaps. These soon
unfold and may have a 1 m (3 ft) spread;
young mantas are called pups.

FAMILY: Odontaspidae
SCIENTIFIC NAME: *Carcharias taurus*
COMMON NAME: Grey Nurse Shark
DISTRIBUTION: TI–WP; WT/S
HABITAT: Rocky reefs
GENERAL WATER DEPTH: 5–70 m
  (16–230 ft)
FOOD HABIT: Carnivorous: fishes

Carcharias taurus

SIZE: 5 m (16 ft)

DESCRIPTION: Owing to the ignorance about the sea and its creatures demonstrated in the past, the grey nurse shark is wrongly accused of being a ferocious man-eater. Ruthlessly slaughtered by divers, this ragged-toothed denizen of the deep is really not as harmful to humans as once thought and is now a protected species in many areas, allowing divers to approach quite close to it. The grey nurse shark is a fish eater and has long pointed teeth specially adapted to catching and holding fast-swimming school fish.

Euchrossorhinus dasypogon

FAMILY: Orectolobidae
SCIENTIFIC NAME: *Euchrossorhinus dasypogon*
COMMON NAME: Tasselled Wobbegong
DISTRIBUTION: TI–WP
HABITAT: Coral reefs
GENERAL WATER DEPTH: 2–40 m (6–131 ft)
FOOD HABIT: Carnivorous: fishes; crustaceans
SIZE: 1.8 m (6 ft)
DESCRIPTION: With its thick, squat body, short tail, extensively branched appendages

around the mouth and its characteristic patterning, the tasselled wobbegong is fairly easy to identify. Although there is some variation in colour throughout its range, the whitish-yellow ones seem to be in deep water and the dark browner ones in shallow water. They are often found lying under coral ledges during the day. The tasselled wobbegong is not aggressive but as it has sharp teeth and a tenacious bite, it should not be interfered with as it can turn very quickly and bite its own tail.

Hemiscyllium ocellatum

FAMILY: Orectolobidae
SCIENTIFIC NAME: *Hemiscyllium ocellatum*
COMMON NAME: Epaulette Shark
DISTRIBUTION: TI–WP
HABITAT: Coral reefs; lagoons
GENERAL WATER DEPTH: Low tide to 10 m (33 ft)
FOOD HABIT: Carnivorous: molluscs; worms; crustaceans
SIZE: 1 m (3 ft)
DESCRIPTION: A very common inhabitant of the reef flats, this docile little shark is often noticed by fossickers wading in the shallows. During the heat of the day it stays under coral slabs and among micro-atolls. When disturbed it will blindly poke around until it finds suitable concealment. The epaulette shark is a nocturnal hunter consuming quantities of molluscs, worms and crustaceans which are detected by small sensory papillae under the snout. It reaches a size of 1 m (3 ft) and is harmless, having only grinding plates for teeth.

FAMILY: Orectolobidae
SCIENTIFIC NAME: *Orectolobus ornatus*
COMMON NAME: Ornate Wobbegong
DISTRIBUTION: WT/S
HABITAT: Rocky reefs
GENERAL WATER DEPTH: 5–30 m (16–98 ft)

Orectolobus ornatus

FOOD HABIT: Carnivorous: fishes; crustaceans
SIZE: 2.5 m (8 ft)
DESCRIPTION: A nocturnal bottom-dwelling shark, the ornate wobbegong is found throughout the day in a rather sleepy state, reposing under caves and ledges or in the open on clifftops, rocks and terraces. Though more active at night, it has been seen to take fish during the day. Almost indistinguishable from its surroundings, it may bite if disturbed and tends to hold on tenaciously. Like all large wobbegongs it should be treated with caution.

Orectolobus sp.

FAMILY: Orectolobidae
SCIENTIFIC NAME: *Orectolobus* sp.
COMMON NAME: Western Wobbegong
DISTRIBUTION: WT/S
HABITAT: Rocky reefs; seagrass; sand
GENERAL WATER DEPTH: 3–50 m (10–164 ft)
FOOD HABIT: Carnivorous: fishes; octopus; crustaceans
SIZE: 2 m (6 ft)
DESCRIPTION: An Indian Ocean species, the western wobbegong seems to be more docile

in its natural habitat than the ornate wobbegong *O. ornatus*. Wobbegongs are cryptic carnivores that adopt a 'wait and watch' style of hunting prey. Immobile and camouflaged, they lie in ambush near a cleaning station or schooling reef fish and whenever anything approaches within range, they strike. The needle-sharp, auger-like teeth are designed to hold prey, not for cutting. Small animals are swallowed in a single gulp while larger species may be held until subdued, and then swallowed. Wobbegongs are known to be cannibalistic.

Parascyllium multimaculatum

FAMILY: Orectolobidae
SCIENTIFIC NAME: *Parascyllium multimaculatum*
COMMON NAME: Tasmanian Spotted Catshark
DISTRIBUTION: CT/S
HABITAT: Rocky reefs; algae beds
GENERAL WATER DEPTH: 5–40 m (16–131 ft)
FOOD HABIT: Carnivorous: molluscs; crustaceans
SIZE: 1.3 m (4 ft)
DESCRIPTION: The spotted catshark is easily identified, as the first dorsal fin is behind the middle of the fish's length. The species lays flat, ribbed, yellow egg capsules during early summer. These capsules have anchoring tendrils that the female shark entwines around high bottom growths. There are some three other catsharks in the genus *Parascyllium* and of these at least two are known to occur in the waters around southern Australia. All are spotted or banded, or both, in varying degrees and all are easily recognised by distinctive patterns.

FAMILY: Orectolobidae
SCIENTIFIC NAME: *Stegostoma fasciatum*
COMMON NAME: Leopard Shark
DISTRIBUTION: TI–WP; WT/S

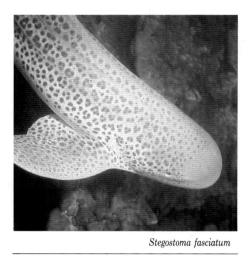

Stegostoma fasciatum

HABITAT: Coral and rocky reefs; seagrass; sand
GENERAL WATER DEPTH: 2–25 m (6–82 ft)
FOOD HABIT: Carnivorous: molluscs; crustaceans; fishes
SIZE: 2.5 m (8 ft)
DESCRIPTION: Although the leopard shark is migratory in some places (only visiting shallow inshore water at breeding times) it does inhabit many coral reef areas. Its blunt head, dorsal keels and long caudal fin, together with its large paddle-like pectorals and colour pattern are characteristic of this harmless species. It has been referred to as the zebra shark but this name applies only to small juveniles which are black or dark purple, with white stripes. Although faint stripes do show on the body of some semi-adults they fade with age. Leopard sharks are slow and awkward swimmers and during the day they lie asleep on the bottom. They usually feed at night.

FAMILY: Pristiophoridae
SCIENTIFIC NAME: *Pristiophorus nudipinnis*
COMMON NAME: Southern Sawshark

Pristiophorus nudipinnis

DISTRIBUTION: WT/S
HABITAT: Sand; mud
GENERAL WATER DEPTH: 20–200 m (66–656 ft)
FOOD HABIT: Carnivorous: fishes; crustaceans
SIZE: 1.2 m (4 ft)
DESCRIPTION: Mostly taken by trawlers, the southern sawshark is rarely caught on a line. Although it has flesh of fair eating quality it is rarely seen in fish shops or other retail outlets. Like so many other good edible species that are not acceptable unprocessed, it is sold as 'flake'. The large live adult has blotched brown patterns and brown spots on the dorsal surface and sides. The southern sawshark is only found in southern Australian waters.

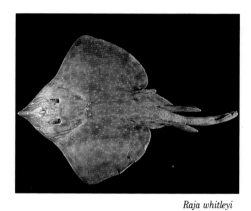

Raja whitleyi

FAMILY: Rajidae
SCIENTIFIC NAME: *Raja whitleyi*
COMMON NAME: Whitley's Skate
DISTRIBUTION: WT/S
HABITAT: Sand; mud
GENERAL WATER DEPTH: 30–100 m (98–328 ft)
FOOD HABIT: Carnivorous: fishes; crustaceans
SIZE: 1.5 m (5 ft)
DESCRIPTION: Not often observed by divers, most skates are generally caught on lines or brought up in trawls. The species are mostly small — 300 mm–1 m (1–3 ft) in length. However Whitley's skate grows to 1.5 m (5 ft) and is thus the largest of the South-West Pacific skates. The entire body is covered with sharp prickles of varying sizes; the largest seem to be those bordering the median line of thorns on the tail. Skates differ from rays in shape, having no venomous barbs on the tail; they have shorter, almost cut-off-looking tails with small dorsal fins at the end.

Aptychotrema vincentiana

FAMILY: Rhinobatidae
SCIENTIFIC NAME: *Aptychotrema vincentiana*
COMMON NAME: Southern Shovelnose Ray
DISTRIBUTION: WT/S
HABITAT: Sand; seagrass
GENERAL WATER DEPTH: 1–25 m (3–82 ft)
FOOD HABIT: Carnivorous: molluscs; worms; crustaceans; fish
SIZE: 1.2 m (4 ft)
DESCRIPTION: Often referred to as a shovel-nose 'shark', this species and the two other species belonging to the genus *Aptychotrema* should be called shovelnose rays, not sharks. They invariably inhabit soft bottom country, living on mud or sand in both offshore areas and protected bays and inlets. They are caught in trawls and also take a baited hook on lines rigged for flathead. The male and female grow to about the same length, the mature male being easily distinguished by its long claspers.

Rhynchobatus djiddensis

FAMILY: Rhynchobatidae
SCIENTIFIC NAME: *Rhynchobatus djiddensis*
COMMON NAME: White-spotted Shovelnose Ray

DISTRIBUTION: TI–WP
HABITAT: Sandy lagoons
GENERAL WATER DEPTH: 1–30 m (3–98 ft)
FOOD HABIT: Carnivorous: fishes; molluscs; crustaceans
SIZE: 3 m (10 ft)
DESCRIPTION: Although smaller specimens may be light brown with prominent white spots along the sides, large adults tend to be black on the back with a white undersurface. The two dorsals and caudal fin are light grey on the leading edges and darker on the trailing edges. A very prominently noduled dermal ridge occurs on the back between the fins and also around the eyes. This ridge is white, as are the edges of all the fins and body. Found in the Pacific and Indian oceans, it is caught by hand lines, in set nets, trawled and speared and has flesh quite acceptable for eating.

Cephaloscyllium laticeps

FAMILY: Scyliorhinidae
SCIENTIFIC NAME: *Cephaloscyllium laticeps*
COMMON NAME: Isabell's Swell Shark
DISTRIBUTION: WT/S
HABITAT: Rocky reefs; sand; mud
GENERAL WATER DEPTH: 25–80 m (82–263 ft)
FOOD HABIT: Carnivorous: molluscs; crustaceans; sea urchins; fishes
SIZE: 1 m (3 ft)
DESCRIPTION: Isabell's swell shark is encountered in trawl nets more often than caught on fishing lines or seen by scuba divers. Its mouth is quite large compared to that of other catsharks and the horny-ridged jaws are armed with small, sharp, needle-like teeth. The male has rather large claspers (sex organs) in relation to its overall length. Mating occurs from spring through summer, after which the female lays eggs.

Squalus megalops

FAMILY: Squalidae
SCIENTIFIC NAME: *Squalus megalops*
COMMON NAME: Piked Dogfish
DISTRIBUTION: WT/S; CT/S
HABITAT: Sand; mud
GENERAL WATER DEPTH: 60–120 m (197–394 ft)
FOOD HABIT: Carnivorous: crustaceans; fishes
SIZE: 1 m (3 ft)
DESCRIPTION: Taken mainly by trawlers working on soft bottom, this little shark is extremely common, often making up 25 per cent of a haul. Most piked dogfish are small specimens of about 450 mm (18 in) and are therefore not commercial. The strong, sharp spines at the front of both dorsal fins can cause injury and care must be taken when extracting entangled specimens from nets. The young are born head first and are much larger than one would expect in such small fish.

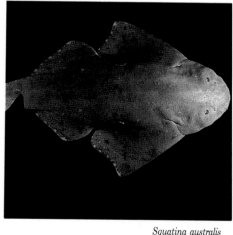

Squatina australis

FAMILY: Squatinidae
SCIENTIFIC NAME: *Squatina australis*
COMMON NAME: Angel Shark
DISTRIBUTION: WT/S

HABITAT: Sand; mud; low profile rocky reefs
GENERAL WATER DEPTH: 10–280 m (33–919 ft)
FOOD HABIT: Carnivorous: fishes; molluscs; crustaceans
SIZE: 1.5 m (5 ft)
DESCRIPTION: Easily distinguished from the ornate angel shark, *S. torgocellata*, by its lack of large brown eye spots and ocelli, the angel shark is by far the more commonly encountered of the two species. It lives offshore as well as in shallow sheltered bays around reef areas, where it generally hides during the day under a layer of sand. At night it hunts crabs, octopus and crayfish and is just as much at home scouting reefs as it is on sand. It rarely takes a baited line but is brought up quite regularly in trawls. The teeth are small but very sharp. It does not permit an observer to approach too closely before it moves away. This ray-like species has an incomplete join between the head and pectoral fins.

Callorhinchus milii

divers, caught on hand lines and trawled. Some forms may lack the bars but seem to retain the large black blotches on the sides and black patches at the rear of the spiracles (breathing vents).

Urolophus cruciatus

FAMILY: Urolophidae
SCIENTIFIC NAME: *Urolophus cruciatus*
COMMON NAME: Cross-backed Stingaree; Banded Stingaree
DISTRIBUTION: WT/S; CT/S
HABITAT: Sand; mud; potholes in reefs
GENERAL WATER DEPTH: 1–200 m (3–656 ft)
FOOD HABIT: Carnivorous: molluscs; crustaceans
SIZE: 360 mm (14 in)
DESCRIPTION: A small but easily identified stingaree, this species has a series of black, cross-like markings, together with a very short tail armed with a single venomous barb. What it lacks in size it certainly makes up for in the toxicity of the one serrated tail spine. As with all stingarees, the young are born alive. It is commonly encountered by

Urolophus mucosus

FAMILY: Urolophidae
SCIENTIFIC NAME: *Urolophus mucosus*
COMMON NAME: Western Stingaree
DISTRIBUTION: WT/S
HABITAT: Sand; seagrass meadows
GENERAL WATER DEPTH: 2–30 m (6–98 ft)
FOOD HABIT: Carnivorous: molluscs; crustaceans; fishes
SIZE: 355 mm (14 in)
DESCRIPTION: Relatively common on sandy bottom and among seagrass meadows in the Indian Ocean off south-west Australia, this small stingaree is an active daytime forager, digging holes in the substrate in search of prey. Parasitic crustaceans of an as yet unidentified species have been taken from the nostrils of the western stingaree. The tail is armed with two venomous spines, the posterior one growing past the commencement of the upper caudal fin.

■ CLASS: Holocephali

FAMILY: Callorhinchidae
SCIENTIFIC NAME: *Callorhinchus milii*
COMMON NAME: Elephant Fish
DISTRIBUTION: WT/S; CT/S
HABITAT: Sand; mud
GENERAL WATER DEPTH: 10–100 m (33–328 ft)
FOOD HABIT: Carnivorous
SIZE: 1.5 m (5 ft)
DESCRIPTION: As the only representative of its family, this uniquely shaped, shark-like fish could hardly be mistaken for any other. It is a wide-ranging species, known to inhabit shallow estuaries. Specimens are caught by fishermen but they are far more common on the deeper trawling grounds offshore. The elephant fish is so named for its rather strange, trunk-like snout. The mouth is small and the skin has a silvery velvet texture with no scales. Despite its strange appearance it is good to eat.

REPTILES

PHYLUM: Chordata
CLASS: Reptilia
ORDER: Crododilia (Crocodiles and alligators), Chelonia (Turtles), Squamata (Snakes)

In the reptiles the four-legged vertebrate plan (tetrapod) is well developed. The head carries eyes, nose, auditory canals and jaws and the brain is enclosed in a stout skull, or cranium. In the snakes the limbs have been lost and in the turtles and tortoises the body is housed in the shell, or carapace. While the terrestrial tortoises are cumbersome and slow walkers, their counterparts, the marine turtles, are swift and graceful swimmers.

Present-day reptiles are cold blooded, air breathing and for the most part land animals that have no internal mechanisms to control their body heat independently of their surroundings. Although land-based reptiles have scaly skins that allow little or no loss of water from the body (sweating) and can conserve body fluids by reabsorption of moisture from urea and faeces, aquatic reptiles excrete fluid urine. Terrestrial reptiles control their body temperature by behaviour: movement towards or away from heat and cold.

Most land reptiles lay shelled eggs, which are buried. This link with terrestrial ancestry is also followed in most marine reptiles, though the majority of sea snakes bear live young. Turtles are well known for their shore nesting. Marine reptiles are affected greatly by sea temperature.

The four major groups of living reptiles are the crocodiles (Order Crocodilia), the turtles and tortoises (Order Chelonia), the snakes and lizards (Order Squamata), and the lizard-like Tuatara, endemic to New Zealand (Order Rhynchocephalia). The first three are represented in the seas.

Chelonia mydas

There are thought to be around 6300 species of reptiles in the world.

CROCODILES (Order Crocodilia)

All crocodiles are found in the world's tropical regions in similar habitats. Their appearance is similar enough for alligators and crocodiles to be often confused. Most can be determined to species level by head shape or tooth location.

Giant aquatic lizards dating from prehistoric times they are ruthless predators and excellent hunters, able to detect prey fishes in muddy water as well as having exceptionally good eyesight in air. Depending on the species, most narrow-snouted freshwater species feed on fish and the larger saltwater forms with wide snouts eat birds, reptiles, fish and mammals and are feared eaters of humans.

Crocodiles grow very large (up to eight metres/26 feet), have extremely good body armour and thick skin, strong jaws and a powerful tail. In many parts of the world they have been hunted for their skins which can be processed into fine leather.

Despite their attacks on humans they are protected in some countries (for example, Australia) and populations have certainly recovered from early exploitation.

TURTLES AND TORTOISES (Order Chelonia)

Turtles have an extremely wide ocean range and although their distribution is centred in the tropics, some may be found in higher latitudes.

Most turtles have strong bony shells covered by large, overlapping plates (the carapace). The limbs are well developed, heavy and paddle-shaped with one or more claws on the anterior edge.

All breeding occurs in the tropics, all eggs are laid on land, and often females may lay several times in one season. However, in many species there appear to be breeding lapses and females may only mate and lay eggs every three to six years.

SEA SNAKES (Order Squamata)

Sea snakes belong to the family Hydrophiidae and most species have valvular nostrils and a vertically compressed, paddle-like tail.

Most give birth to live young, though members of the genus *Laticauda* lay eggs on land. When sea snakes are mating they often appear to be aggressive and divers believe they are being chased to be bitten. Although many Indo-Pacific fishermen have been bitten and killed by sea snakes when pulling nets, or when catching them underwater for their skins, no sport divers are known to have been killed in Southern Hemisphere waters.

Some of the so-called 'attacks' are due to the sea snake's very poor eyesight and curious nature. In their habitat they feed on fish eggs and small fish that live in holes (for example, gobies, blennies), on sleeping day-time fishes that they catch at night, or on sleeping night-time fishes that they catch during the day. All sea snakes should be treated with caution as they have extremely strong venom—some of the deadliest known.

Chelonia depressa

The head of a sea snake, *Astrotia stokesii*

Sea snakes courting, Coral Sea

Chelonia mydas

Caretta caretta

Eretmochelys imbricata

■ CLASS: Reptilia

FAMILY: Cheloniidae
SCIENTIFIC NAME: *Caretta caretta*
COMMON NAME: Loggerhead Turtle
DISTRIBUTION: TI–WP; WT/N; WT/S; TEP
HABITAT: Open ocean; coral reefs
GENERAL WATER DEPTH: Surface waters
FOOD HABIT: Carnivorous: molluscs; crustaceans; fishes; ascidians; sea jellies
SIZE: 1.5 m (5 ft)
DESCRIPTION: Found throughout most of the tropical waters of the world, the loggerhead turtle has a dark brown shell that sometimes has darker markings, if it can be seen through the weed covered surface. The underside is yellow or cream and the jaws have heavy expanded sheaths for crushing prey. The female lays eggs (50 at a time) on continental island beaches and coral cays during summer. The males have long tails and the females have very short ones (as in all sea turtles). Mating occurs at sea, either on the surface or underwater.

FAMILY: Cheloniidae
SCIENTIFIC NAME: *Chelonia mydas*
COMMON NAME: Green Turtle
DISTRIBUTION: TI–WP; WT/S; WT/N; TEP
HABITAT: Open ocean; coral reefs; coastal waters
GENERAL WATER DEPTH: Surface waters
FOOD HABIT: Herbivorous: algae
SIZE: 1.5 m (5 ft)
DESCRIPTION: In the past the green turtle has been hunted ruthlessly for its shell and flesh by both professional and amateur fishermen. Even newly hatched juveniles have been collected, preserved and sold in curiosity shops. Although Australian legislation has given the green turtle some measure of protection, a great deal of destruction still occurs in many areas. It is imperative for the survival of the turtles that their main nesting sites become established fauna reserves. The females come ashore at night on the high tides from October through to March. They lay their eggs in pits dug in the sand above the high-tide mark. Hatching takes place some eight weeks later, generally at night. The sex of a baby turtle is determined by the temperature of the nest. Turtles at Heron Island (on the Great Barrier Reef) mostly hatch as males, owing to nest temperatures being below 28.7°C. At higher temperatures they hatch as females.

Chelonia mydas

FAMILY: Cheloniidae
SCIENTIFIC NAME: *Eretmochelys imbricata*
COMMON NAME: Hawksbill Turtle
DISTRIBUTION: TI–WP; TEP
HABITAT: Open oceans; coral reefs
GENERAL WATER DEPTH: Surface waters
FOOD HABIT: Carnivorous: fishes, reptiles
SIZE: 1 m (3 ft)
DESCRIPTION: Young hawksbill turtles have exceedingly beautiful shells of golden brown, streaked with green, yellow and orange and all patterned with a most impressive design. It was the shell known as 'tortoiseshell' that almost led to its demise due to heavy exploitation by humans for centuries. In older turtles the shell is covered with algae and often has many barnacles growing on and in it. Adult hawksbill turtles somewhat resemble older green turtles (*Chelonia mydas*), though at close range they can be separated by the scales behind the eyes, the hawksbill having three postocular scales and the green turtle having four or more.

Unlike the green turtle, which is a herbivore during its adult life, the hawksbill is a carnivore and can capture and eat other smaller sea creatures with the aid of its parrot-like beak. There is very little published information on its nesting habits, though the author has observed females coming ashore and laying eggs on the upper beach areas of islands in the Dampier Archipelago off Western Australia.

Crocodylus porosus

Pelamis platurus

FAMILY: Crocodylidae
SCIENTIFIC NAME: *Crocodylus porosus*
COMMON NAME: Saltwater Crocodile
DISTRIBUTION: TI–WP
HABITAT: Coastal swamps; rivers; mangrove swamps
GENERAL WATER DEPTH: Surface waters
FOOD HABIT: Carnivorous: fishes; reptiles; crustaceans; birds; mammals
SIZE: 7 m (23 ft)
DESCRIPTION: Throughout its range the saltwater crocodile has been responsible for hundreds of attacks on humans. Though mostly nocturnal, this stealthy, cunning opportunist is bold and fearless when hunting prey, often venturing quite close to human habitation. Most sightings occur in swamps and rivers, though some of the larger adults are regularly seen in open ocean waters and even on the Great Barrier Reef. After mating, females lay their eggs in a self-built humus mound or below the sand onshore and guard them until they hatch. Up to 60 young crocodiles may hatch from one nest.

FAMILY: Hydrophiidae
SCIENTIFIC NAME: *Aipysurus laevis*
COMMON NAME: Olive Sea Snake
DISTRIBUTION: TI–WP
HABITAT: Coral reefs; rocky reefs
GENERAL WATER DEPTH: Surface to 25 m (82 ft)
FOOD HABIT: Carnivorous: fishes
SIZE: 1.5 m (5 ft)
DESCRIPTION: Common to both the Indian and Pacific oceans the olive sea snake is without doubt the most common of sea snakes encountered in the waters of the tropics. It is active day and night and moves on the bottom investigating crannies beneath coral and rocks searching for food, which mainly comprises small demersal (bottom dwelling) fishes. Throughout its range colour varies from brown to yellow. The olive sea snake generally surfaces to breathe at intervals of 10 to 20 minutes. It sleeps on the bottom, curled beneath rock or coral. Owing to the slowing down of its body mechanisms it may maintain this position for many hours without need to surface and breathe. Mainly solitary, it often becomes gregarious during the mating season. The female produces up to five live young.

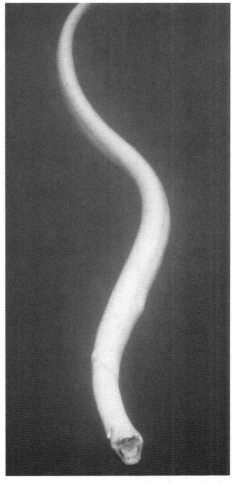

Aipysurus laevis

FAMILY: Hydrophiidae
SCIENTIFIC NAME: *Pelamis platurus*
COMMON NAME: Yellow-bellied Sea Snake
DISTRIBUTION: TI–WP; WT/S; WT/N; TEP
HABITAT: Open ocean
GENERAL WATER DEPTH: Surface
FOOD HABIT: Carnivorous: fishes
SIZE: 530 mm (21 in)
DESCRIPTION: Often seen washed ashore after rough seas or storms, the yellow-bellied sea snake is easily identified owing to its unique colour pattern, which is particularly noticeable on the flattened tail. This species is pelagic and found over a wide area throughout the world. Although venomous, the small mouth and teeth, together with its non-aggressive nature, do not make it a specific danger. It could perhaps be picked up alive by children, although most beached snakes are usually very lethargic, exhausted and near death. Even when in good condition the species is not very agile on dry land. However it is wise to be cautious in any handling of potentially dangerous marine creatures. The yellow-bellied sea snake feeds on open ocean fishes.

Tursiops truncatus

MAMMALS

PHYLUM: Chordata
CLASS: Mammalia (Mammals)
ORDER: Cetacea (Whales, dolphins), Pinnipedia (Sea lions, fur seals and true seals)

 The word mammal refers to the female's mammary glands which provide milk for the young and are among the main distinguishing features of a mammal. Other features include hair, the birth of fully formed live young, ability to regulate body temperature and hold it constant, and a brain of greater complexity than that of most other animals. There are about 4070 species of mammals, many verging on extinction.

ORDER: Cetacea (Whales, dolphins)

Ancestors of marine mammals are thought to have once lived on land. Returning to the sea, they have evolved to be the largest living creatures ever to exist on earth. Even so, by ignorance and over-exploitation humans have reduced many species almost to extinction in a mere 150 years. In some species only a few hundred individuals remain from original stocks often in the vicinity of 100,000. Small isolated populations were decimated by hunting and many specialised forms are now extinct.

Even though most marine mammals are now protected to varying degrees throughout the world seas, and reaction to their plight has been one of the greatest success stories in world co-operation, many are classed as endangered species and will continue to be so for decades. One significant fact remains: that for all the millions of individuals slaughtered over the past century the amount of natural history information obtained was remarkably small, so small that nations are still killing protected species in the name of science. So little is known about some that the entire specimen collection of a species may be represented only by a skull.

Although a number of Northern Hemisphere species have been studied quite extensively, knowledge of many of the Southern Hemisphere forms and such endangered species as river dolphins is almost non-existent. Few Southern Hemisphere species have been photographed underwater and those that have been, only in the last ten years. Many cetaceans are open ocean dwellers. The immense size of the oceans and the inclement conditions there are factors that have maintained the secrecy.

There are about 76 recognised species of cetaceans including all the whales, dolphins and porpoises. Of these, 66 have teeth (feeding on an array of prey ranging from fish to squid and, in the case of killer whales, other mammals) and ten (great whales) have a system of hairy 'plates' called baleen that is used to strain planktonic organisms (krill) and fish from the sea. All cetaceans are excellent swimmers, using both body flex and powerful tail flukes for their main propulsion. Special physiological adaptations allow them to dive to great depths.

Most use echo location to detect prey and even those toothed whales and dolphins which are totally blind do not appear to be at a disadvantage in feeding. The ears may be of pinhole size or completely closed by a membrane. They breathe through one or two blowholes on top of the head and in some species the blowhole is a noise-producing mechanism. Some of the baleen whales (humpbacks etc.) produce unique and complex songs. These are repeated according to identifiable patterns and some have been detected by hydrophones 185 kilometres (100 nautical miles) from their source. In a way similar to bird songs, the sounds consist of an ordered sequence of motifs and themes. Set songs follow set sequences with a beginning and end and each song may last from six to 35 minutes. Each animal may have its own version of a song, which the entire whale population in one region may sing over one season. Songs are thought to have a role in sexual attraction.

All cetaceans have very strong social ties and ocean dwelling forms swim in family pods or combinations of social units forming schools. Although the strongest bonds are between cows and calves, each pod protects, assists and co-operates for the good of individuals within the pod. The strong assist the weak, calving mothers, etc. and there are even instances where deformed individuals incapable of feeding have been looked after and fed by the pod for over 16 years.

Mass strandings are now known to be due to entire herds going to the help of another cetacean in trouble. The pod picks up the distress calls of a sick, injured or confused individual and responds to help, in turn stranding its members. While one live animal remains on a beach (even if all the others have been successfully returned to the sea), its distress signals will call them back to their deaths.

Like all mammals, cetaceans have mammary glands. The mammae (teats) and male sex organs do not protrude from the body, but are instead hidden within slits in the body wall. Very often there are long migrations from the winter feeding grounds to the summer breeding grounds. Set migratory patterns exist with old males, young males and females living in separate groups at certain times of the year. Cetaceans breed seasonally and bear one (rarely two) young at a time and have gestation periods of nine to 16 months. Newborn calves are often covered by a sparse stubble. In natural circumstances they may live at least 60 years.

ORDER: Pinnipedia (Sea lions, fur seals and true seals)

To most people visual similarities (especially in the water) between eared seals, which are distantly related to dogs and bears, and true seals, which evolved separately some ten million years later, are more striking than their differences.

Eared seals (which include the fur seals and sea lions) have a visible ear flap, whereas true seals do not. Eared seals are much more agile on land, taking their weight on their out-turned fore-flippers and being able to rotate their hind limbs forward, whereas true seals are very clumsy on land, 'humping' their way around on their bellies and alternately flexing weight from chest to pelvis.

Even though both groups are extremely agile in the water, each has its own peculiarities. Although eared seals are known to dive to 73 metres (240 feet), most species tend to hunt their food in much shallower water. True seals are the deep diving specialists: Weddell seals regularly dive to 400 metres (1300 feet) and have been recorded at 600 metres (2000 feet).

Modes of swimming also differ. Eared seals are much more manoeuvrable underwater—making long simultaneous sweeps with the fore-flippers they literally 'fly' through the water. On the other hand the true seals use alternate strokes of their hind-flippers accompanied by lateral undulations of the body; the fore-flippers play little part in underwater locomotion and are generally kept close to the body.

Both groups have excellent senses of sight, touch and hearing and in the sensory functions of the whiskers, which play an important part in food location. As opportunistic predators their prey is variable and ranges from krill (in the case of the crabeater seal) to warm-blooded mammals (the leopard seal).

Breeding is generally in spring and summer and all species arrive at traditional land-based breeding sites (eared seals) or, in some cases, pack ice (true seals). Males arrive earlier than females and set up territories. Females mated and conceived the previous season come ashore, give birth, and while still suckling are mated by the terri-tory bull, a week or so after giving birth. Pups often remain with the mother up to six months after birth and are then weaned.

Although some species remain close to their breeding grounds all year, others migrate thousands of kilometres to feeding grounds.

Arctocephalus pusillus doriferus

Tursiops truncatus

Tursiops truncatus

■ CLASS: Mammalia

FAMILY: Balaenidae
SCIENTIFIC NAME: *Eubalaena australis*
COMMON NAME: Southern Right Whale
DISTRIBUTION: WT/S; CT/S
HABITAT: Open ocean
GENERAL WATER DEPTH: Surface dwelling
FOOD HABIT: Carnivorous: krill; copepods (crustaceans)
SIZE: 18 m (59 ft)
DESCRIPTION: There are three species of right whales living in world seas but only one inhabits southern hemisphere waters. The southern right whale was heavily exploited in the whaling heydays and populations were drastically reduced. Numbers appear to be slowly increasing with more sightings each year and the discovery of shallow water calving areas along the southern coast of Australia. This is significant as southern right whales only breed once in three years, the calf staying with the mother for up to 14 months. Southern right whales are fully protected in Australian waters and even close approach by boat or a swimmer can attract heavy fines.

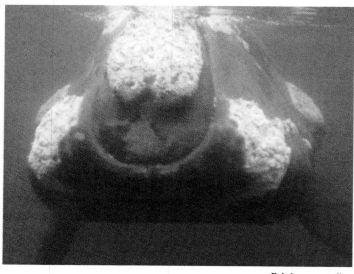
Eubalaena australis

FAMILY: Balaenopteridae
SCIENTIFIC NAME: *Balaenoptera physalus*
COMMON NAME: Fin Whale
DISTRIBUTION: TI-WP; WT/S; CT/S; WT/N; CT/N
HABITAT: Open ocean
GENERAL WATER DEPTH: Surface dwelling
FOOD HABIT: Carnivorous: krill; copepods; fishes
SIZE: 25 m (82 ft)
DESCRIPTION: Although most of the baleen whales have triangular heads, the fin whale is the most pronounced of the larger species. Whaling led to a drastic reduction in numbers of fin whales, but since the 1930s female

Balaenoptera physalus

whales have doubled their percentages of pregnancies, thereby halving the average interval between births. This strategy has obviously been successful, with fin whale sightings increasing throughout the world.

FAMILY: Balaenopteridae
SCIENTIFIC NAME: *Megaptera novaeangliae*
COMMON NAME: Humpback Whale
DISTRIBUTION: TI-WP; WT/S; CT/S; WT/N; CT/N
HABITAT: Open ocean; inshore waters
GENERAL WATER DEPTH: Surface dwelling
FOOD HABIT: Carnivorous: fishes (Northern Hemisphere); krill, small fish and other crustacea (Southern Hemisphere)
SIZE: 16 m (52 ft)
DESCRIPTION: Various stocks of humpback whales are divided throughout world oceans and in most cases there appears to be no interbreeding. In general, these whales cover large areas of ocean during their seasonal migrations and in fact they migrate each year from Antarctica to warm tropical waters to give birth to live young. Humpbacks are one of the few rorqual whales (filter feeders) to favour coastal areas and it was this habit that made them easy prey to shore-based whaling fleets. Owing to a pattern of mating and birthing in the low-latitude, warmer waters during the winter (generally in areas close to shore), this species is the centre of a multi-million dollar whale watching industry. Studies have shown that Southern Hemisphere stocks are increasing.

Megaptera novaeangliae

FAMILY: Delphinidae
SCIENTIFIC NAME: *Cephalorhynchus hectori*
COMMON NAME: Hector's Dolphin
DISTRIBUTION: WT/S; CT/S
HABITAT: Coastal waters; estuaries
GENERAL WATER DEPTH: Surface
FOOD HABIT: Carnivorous: fishes; crustaceans
SIZE: 1.4 m (4.6 ft)
DESCRIPTION: Endemic to the waters of New Zealand, this little dolphin is unlikely to be confused with any other species owing to its rounded dorsal fin and flippers. Total numbers are estimated at around 3000 animals and owing to their inshore lifestyle they are known to accumulate high levels of DDT and heavy metals in their blubber. Research shows that they are seen mostly together in pairs or groups of up to 12 individuals and in some areas these groups may be resident for several years.

Cephalorhynchus hectori

FAMILY: Delphinidae
SCIENTIFIC NAME: *Delphinus delphis*
COMMON NAME: Common Dolphin
DISTRIBUTION: TI-WP; WT/S; WT/N
HABITAT: Open ocean; inshore
GENERAL WATER DEPTH: Surface waters
FOOD HABIT: Carnivorous: fishes

Delphinus delphis

SIZE: 2.2 m (7 ft)
DESCRIPTION: This species is often referred to as the saddleback dolphin owing to the markings on the dorsal surface being similar to a saddle. The species is distributed throughout world seas and can be common in coastal areas as well as open ocean. Groups generally contain around 5 to 20 individuals and a marked dominance hierarchy is maintained. Occasionally groups come together and form huge aggregations numbering thousands. When seen this is certainly a most awe-inspiring sight, especially at sunset on a flat, calm ocean. Even though they are hunted in certain areas, and recent pollution of Northern Hemisphere waters including the Mediterranean has caused widespread losses, they remain the most abundant dolphin in the oceans.

Lagenorhynchus obscurus

FAMILY: Delphinidae
SCIENTIFIC NAME: *Lagenorhynchus obscurus*
COMMON NAME: Dusky Dolphin
DISTRIBUTION: CT/S; WT/S
HABITAT: Inshore waters; open ocean
GENERAL WATER DEPTH: Surface waters
FOOD HABIT: Carnivorous: fishes
SIZE: 2 m (6 ft)

DESCRIPTION: Easily identified by its lack of a beak, the dusky dolphin is among the most visually entertaining animals with high leaps and splash-downs a part of its everyday behaviour. Although colour pattern may be confused with the common dolphin, even at a distance the shape of the head is characteristic. They certainly have a good time in the bow waves of boats and, when encountered for the first time at sea, are quite unnerving. Although mating is shown to be a promiscuous affair with little pair bonding, there are, however, many accounts of dusky dolphins helping other dolphins in trouble, even other species, and going to the aid of humans. This dolphin feeds on squid, fishes and shrimps and mates in spring and summer.

FAMILY: Delphinidae
SCIENTIFIC NAME: *Orcinus orca*
COMMON NAME: Orca (Killer Whale)
DISTRIBUTION: TI–WP; WT/S; CT/S; WT/N; CT/N; TEP
HABITAT: Open ocean; inshore waters
GENERAL WATER DEPTH: Surface waters
FOOD HABIT: Carnivorous: fishes; mammals; squid; birds
SIZE: 10 m (33 ft)
DESCRIPTION: Still bearing the stigma of a killer whale (a hand-down of beliefs from the whaling days), the orca as we know it today is a 'gentle' predator of the oceans, one that has a close knit family or pod behaviour and has proved many times its affinity to humans. Orcas are the largest of the dolphin family and are easily recognised by their black and white markings and high dorsal fin. Pods range between 6 and 40 individuals and pod members remain together for life. Ties even exist from one generation to another and group co-ordination during hunting is highly advanced and implemented by close social cohesion.

FAMILY: Delphinidae
SCIENTIFIC NAME: *Stenella lonigirostris*
COMMON NAME: Spinner Dolphin
DISTRIBUTION: TI–WP; WT/N
HABITAT: Open ocean
GENERAL WATER DEPTH: Surface
FOOD HABIT: Carnivorous: fishes
SIZE: 2–3 m (6–10 ft)

Orcinus orca

Stenella lonigirostris

DESCRIPTION: Occurring in small pods in both temperate and tropical seas, the spinner dolphin is a much slimmer species than the bottlenose dolphin and its dorsal fin is smaller and more curved. It has well-defined markings and is easily distinguished from the bottlenose dolphin. Its name comes from the habit of spinning as it jumps out of the water. Spinner dolphins are very playful and appear in dolphinaria throughout the world. They will come close to boats to ride the bow wave but will move away if divers enter the water.

FAMILY: Delphinidae
SCIENTIFIC NAME: *Tursiops truncatus*
COMMON NAME: Bottlenose Dolphin
DISTRIBUTION: TI–WP; WT/N; WT/S; CT/S; TEP
HABITAT: Open sea; inshore waters
GENERAL WATER DEPTH: Surface
FOOD HABIT: Carnivorous: fishes; squid
SIZE: 4.5 m (15 ft)
DESCRIPTION: The bottlenose dolphin is an inhabitant of the open ocean and may also be seen in bays, harbours and estuaries throughout world oceans. It may be various

Tursiops truncatus

which feed close to surface waters, the gray whale feeds primarily along the bottom, straining small crustaceans and molluscs from the top layers of sediment on the ocean floor. By swimming on their sides along the bottom the grays can scoop up huge mouthfuls of sediment and prey. They then rise to the surface and strain the sediments through their baleen. Food present inside the mouth is swallowed. Before commercial whaling began in the 1850s, the estimated stock of Californian gray whales was 30,000. Whaling ceased in 1946, and the increasing stocks are now around 16,000 animals. A successful whale watching programme has been under way for many years in the lagoons off Baja California in Mexico.

shades of grey on the back and may be white on the belly. The short, stout beak has 23 to 25 pairs of teeth in the jaws, and the lower jaw tends to jut out further than the upper jaw. Dolphins are social mammals and are generally seen in large herds or in pods. Being mammals they must breathe air, and therefore swim close to the surface. However, when feeding they can dive to great depths. Their food is mainly schooling pelagic fishes which are found by echo-location.

Eschrichtius robustus

FAMILY: Eschrichlidae
SCIENTIFIC NAME: *Eschrichtius robustus*
COMMON NAME: Gray Whale
DISTRIBUTION: WT/N; CT/N
HABITAT: Open ocean; inshore waters
GENERAL WATER DEPTH: Surface dwelling
FOOD HABIT: Carnivorous: bottom-dwelling amphipods; invertebrates
SIZE: 15 m (49 ft)
DESCRIPTION: With one of the longest known mammal migration paths reaching from the Arctic icepack to the subtropic of Baja California and back, the gray whale may cover some 20,400 km (12,500 miles) in a single year. Unlike other baleen whales,

Archtocephalus pusillus doriferus (female)

FAMILY: Otariidae
SCIENTIFIC NAME: *Arctocephalus pusillus doriferus*
COMMON NAME: Australian Fur Seal
DISTRIBUTION: WT/S; CT/S
HABITAT: Continental islands; open sea
GENERAL WATER DEPTH: Surface waters
FOOD HABIT: Carnivorous: fishes; squid; rock lobsters
SIZE: 2 m (6 ft)
DESCRIPTION: The range of the Australian fur seal is restricted to a few isolated rock outcrops off the south/south-eastern coastline of Australia. In some of the breeding colonies there may be up to 10,000 fur seals, while others may only support a score or so non-breeding animals. Though totally protected by law these animals are still being shot by people whose nets are occasionally robbed by fur seals. They are separated into species by teeth structure, so it is difficult for the casual observer to separate them in the field. Forster's fur seal (*Arctocephalus forsteri*) is generally found in the Indian Ocean.

Archtocephalus pusillus doriferus (female)

FAMILY: Otariidae
SCIENTIFIC NAME: *Neophoca cinera*
COMMON NAME: Australian Sea Lion
DISTRIBUTION: WT/S
HABITAT: Rocky reefs; sandy beaches; offshore islands
GENERAL WATER DEPTH: Surface
FOOD HABIT: Carnivorous: fishes; squid
SIZE: 2 m (6 ft)
DESCRIPTION: Although numbers of the Australian sea lion were decimated by sealers in the early days of Australia's history, it may still be seen on the beaches and islands along south/south-western coastlines.

During the mating season the breeding males (those that are strong enough to hold territories) may have from six to eight females in a harem. They may mate on the beach, though on some islands the females move to rocky area to give birth. Where there is little competition one big male may have the entire beach area as his territory and will chase off any intruder. Recent research shows that the population fluctuates between 3000 and 5000 animals over its present distribution.

FAMILY: Otariidae
SCIENTIFIC NAME: *Zalophus californianus*
COMMON NAME: California Sea Lion
DISTRIBUTION: WT/N; TEP
HABITAT: Offshore islands
GENERAL WATER DEPTH: Surface waters
FOOD HABIT: Carnivorous: fishes
SIZE: 2.2 m (7 ft)
DESCRIPTION: Unlike the Australian sea lion, the California bull sea lion has territories in the water, whose boundaries are patrolled with vigour. Once a snorkel diver establishes the boundary of a big male California sea lion it can be quite interesting to see how close one can get before the bull barks and asserts authority. It is quite exciting being within a metre of such a fantastic animal and knowing that it will not attack so

Zalophus californianus (male)

Mirounga leonina (female)

long as the territory perimeters are not invaded. On the offshore island rookeries in the Sea of Cortez, Baja California, Mexico, it is easier to get close to the males underwater than it is to the females. This is in direct contrast to the Australian sea lion, where females and juveniles will spend hours cavorting with scuba divers. During breeding season (May to August), each dominant territory-holding male mates with as many females as possible.

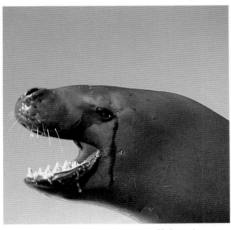

Hydruga leptonyx

FAMILY: Phocidae
SCIENTIFIC NAME: *Hydruga leptonyx*
COMMON NAME: Leopard Seal
DISTRIBUTION: CT/S; WT/S
HABITAT: Sub-Antarctic islands
GENERAL WATER DEPTH: Surface waters
FOOD HABIT: Carnivorous: seals; penguins; fishes
SIZE: 2.8 m (9 ft)
DESCRIPTION: Confined to the Southern Hemisphere, the leopard seal is the only one that is known to hunt, kill and eat warm-blooded mammals. It is an efficient predator of crabeater seals, of which it appears to eat only the skin and attached blubber. While

younger leopard seals have characteristic spotting, older specimens may be quite black. The species is mainly solitary, with some individuals ranging over a wide area of open sea. Although their large size and ferocious nature makes them very formidable in the water, by comparison they are clumsy on land. However, owing to their elongated foreflippers they are much more manoeuvrable on land than other true seals.

FAMILY: Phocidae
SCIENTIFIC NAME: *Mirounga leonina* (female)
COMMON NAME: Elephant Seal (Northern and Southern)
DISTRIBUTION: WT/N–CT/S; CT/N
HABITAT: Coastal waters; offshore islands; isolated coastlines
GENERAL WATER DEPTH: Surface waters
FOOD HABIT: Carnivorous: fishes; squid
SIZE: 4.2 m (13 ft)
DESCRIPTION: Two species of elephant seals are recognised throughout world seas: the northern elephant seal (*Mirounga leonina*) occurs on islands around central California and Baja California in the eastern Pacific; the southern elephant seal is found on offshore islands across the Antarctic convergence from South Africa to South America. In both species the males are much larger (up to three times) than females and have developed large, fleshy, nasal protuberances for sexual display. So different are males and females that each could be seen as another species. Dominant bulls maintain harems and monopolise mating, sometimes up to 100 females per season. The bulls have no maternal instinct and may crush nursing young in their eagerness to mate the mother. Over 10 per cent of all pups born are killed by mating or fighting bulls.

Physeter macrocephalus

FAMILY: Physeteridae
SCIENTIFIC NAME: *Physeter macrocephalus*
COMMON NAME: Sperm Whale
DISTRIBUTION: TI–WP; WT/S; CT/S; WT/N; CT/N
HABITAT: Open ocean
GENERAL WATER DEPTH: Surface dwelling
FOOD HABIT: Carnivorous: squid; fishes
SIZE: 20 m (60 ft)
DESCRIPTION: The largest of the toothed whales roaming world seas, sperm whales are known to dive to depths of 3200 m (10,500 ft), though most records show averages around 1200 m (4000 ft) are more common. They feed mostly on bottom-dwelling giant squid up to 12 m (39 ft) in length and very often their heads are covered with circular scars and scratches made by the suckers of the squid. In this species there is a very strong bond between individuals of specific pods or schools, with members combining to help sick or injured individuals. In the South-West Pacific, divers have observed pods of whales in circular formation tailstanding with heads close to the surface, all moulting huge amounts of skin.

Sea-fan gardens on Stina's Reef, Provinciales.

BIBLIOGRAPHY

R. T. Abbott, *Seashells of the World*, Golden Press, New York 1962.

Joyce Allen, *Australian Shells,* Georgian House, Melbourne 1950.

Dr G. R. Allen and R. C. Steene, *Reef Fishes of the Indian Ocean,* TFH Neptune City 1987.

Robert D. Barnes, *Invertebrate Zoology,* Saunders, Philadelphia 1963.
Invertebrate Zoology (2nd edn), Saunders, Philadelphia 1969.

Isobel Bennett, *The Great Barrier Reef,* Lansdowne, Melbourne 1971.
The Fringe of the Sea, Rigby, Adelaide 1966.

J. C. Briggs, *Marine Zoogeography,* McGraw-Hill, New York 1974.

R. Buchsbaum and L. J. Milne, *Living Invertebrates of the World,* Hamish Hamilton, London 1960.

Dr C. M. Burgess, *Cowries of the World,* Seacomber Publications, Cape Town 1985.

A. M. Clark, *Starfish and Related Echinoderms,* British Museum (Natural History & TFH), London 1977.

A. M. Clark and R. W. E. Rowe, *Monograph of Shallow-water Indo-West Pacific Echinoderms,* British Museum (Natural History), London 1971.

Hubert L. Clark, *The Echinoderm Fauna of Australia,* Carnegie Institution, Washington 1946.

Dr H. G. Cogger, *Reptiles and Amphibians of Australia,* A.H. & A.W. Reed, Sydney 1975.

Neville Coleman, *The Nature of Norfolk Island,* SARC, Brisbane 1991.
Australia's Great Barrier Reef, Child & Associates, Sydney 1990.
Nudibranchs of the South Pacific, SARC, Brisbane 1989.
Tropical Sea Fishes of the South Pacific SARC, Brisbane 1989.
Discover Heron Island, SARC, Brisbane 1988.
Beginner's Guide to Underwater Marine Biology, AMPI, Sydney 1985.

What Shell is That? Lansdowne, Sydney 1985.
Shells Alive! Rigby, Adelaide 1981.
Australian Sea Fishes North of 30°S, Doubleday, Sydney 1981.
Australian Sea Fishes South of 30°S, Doubleday, Sydney 1980.

W. J. Dakin, *Australian Seashores,* Angus & Robertson, Sydney 1953 (revised edition 1987).

Alan Dartnall, *Tasmanian Echinoderms,* University of Tasmania, Hobart 1980.

S. Dawson, *The New Zealand Whale and Dolphin Digest,* Brick Rowe, Auckland 1985.

J. H. Day, *A Guide to Marine Life on South African Shores,* Balkema, Cape Town 1969.

W. Doak, *Beneath New Zealand Seas,* Reed, Wellington 1971.

H. Barraclough Fell, *Native Sea Stars of New Zealand,* A.H. & A.W. Reed, Auckland 1962.

M. Francis, *Coastal Fishes of New Zealand,* Heinemann Reed, Auckland 1988.

David and Jennifer George, *Marine Life,* Rigby, Sydney 1979.

K. Gillett and F. McNeill, *The Great Barrier Reef and Adjacent Isles,* Coral Press, Sydney 1959.

T. Gloerfelt-Tarp and P. J. Kailola, *Trawled Fishes of Southern Indonesia and North-western Australia,* Australian Development Assistance Bureau 1986.

D. W. Gotshall, *Marine Animals of Baja California,* Sea Challengers, Lososos 1982.
Pacific Coast Inshore Fishes, Sea Challengers, Lososos 1981.

D. W. Gotshall and L. L. Laurent, *Pacific Coast Subtidal Marine Invertebrates,* Sea Challengers, Lososos 1979.

J. and I. Greenberg, *The Living Reef,* Sea Hawk Press, Miami 1972.

J., I. and M. Greenberg, *The Fishes Beneath Tropic Seas,* Sea Hawk Press, Miami 1987.

Robert M. Hale, *The Crustaceans of South Australia Parts I &*

II, SA Government Printer, Adelaide 1927.

W. A. Haswell, *Australian Stalk-Eyed and Sessile-Eyed Crustacea,* Australian Museum, Sydney 1982.

Anthony Healy and John Yaldwyn, *Australian Crustaceans,* A.H. & A.W. Reed, Sydney 1970.

E. Heath and R. K. Dell, *Seashore Life of New Zealand,* Reed, Wellington 1971.

L. H. Hyman, *The Invertebrates,* McGraw-Hill, New York 1940–67.

G. D. Kaufman and P. H. Forestell, *Hawaii's Humpback Whales,* Pacific Whale Foundation, Hawaii 1986.

Dr P. Kott, *The Australian Ascidacea,* Memoirs, Queensland Museum Vol. 23 1985.

L. R. Leonardo and M. E. Cowan, *Shallow-water Holothurians,* Filipinas Foundation, Philippines 1984.

C. J. Lerwill, *An Introduction to the Classification of Animals,* Constable, London 1971.

MacPherson and Gabriel, *Marine Molluscs of Victoria,* Melbourne University Press, Melbourne 1962.

H. Masuda, K. Amaoka, C. Araga, T. Uyeno and T. Yoshino, *Fishes of the Japanese Archipelago,* Tokai University Press.

J. L. May and J. G. H. Maxwell, *Trawl Fish from Temperate Waters of Australia,* CSIRO, Sydney 1986.

John Morton and Michael Miller, *The New Zealand Sea Shore,* Collins, Auckland 1968.

J. E. Randall, G. R. Allen and R. C. Steene, *Fishes of the Great Barrier Reef and Coral Sea,* Crawford House, Orange 1990.

E. F. Ricketts and J. Calvin, *Between Pacific Tides,* Stanford University Press 1962.

J. S. Ryland, *Physiology and Ecology of Bryozoans,* 1976. *Bryozoans,* Hutchinson, London 1970.

Waldo L. Schmitt, *Crustaceans,* David and Charles, Newton Abbot 1965.

S. A. Shepherd and I. M. Thomas, *Marine Invertebrates of South Australia Part I,* SA Government Printer, Adelaide 1982.

J. Steinbeck and E. F. Ricketts, *Sea of Cortez,* Viking Press, New York 1941.

Tasmanian Underwater Photographic Society, *Coastal Fishes of Tasmania & Bass Strait,* Cat & Fiddle Press, Hobart 1982.

D. A. Thompson, L. T. Findley and A. N. Kerstich, *Reef Fishes of the Sea of Cortez,* John Wiley & Sons, New York 1979.

T. E. Thompson, *Biology of Opisthobranch Molluscs,* Ray Society, London 1976.

T. E. Thompson and G. H. Brown, *British Opisthobranch Molluscs,* 1976.

Spencer Wilkie Tinker, *Fishes of Hawaii,* Hawaiian Service Inc, Honolulu 1978. *Pacific Crustacea,* Tuttle, Tokyo 1965.

J. E. N. Vernon, *Corals of Australia and the Indo-Pacific,* Angus & Robertson, Sydney 1986.

J. G. Walls, *Cone Shells,* T. F. H. Neptune City 1978.

Richard Willan and Neville Coleman, *Nudibranchs of Australasia,* AMPI, Sydney 1984.

B. R. Wilson and K. Gillett, *Australian Shells,* A.H. & A.W. Reed, Sydney 1971.

Zoological Catalogue of Australia, 7 pisces — Petromiyzonthidae to Carangidae.

INDEX OF COMMON NAMES

INDEX OF SCIENTIFIC NAMES

INDEX OF FAMILY NAMES

PICTURE CREDITS

(l = left, r = right, c = centre, t = top, b = below)

Heather Angel: pages 64 tr, 67 r, 68 br, 69 tc, 115 l, 124 bc.

Kathie Atkinson: pages 64 tl, 141 l.

Daniel W. Gotshall: pages 42 l, 162 tl, 221 br.

A. Kersitch: pages 31 r, 107 r.

Eugene N. Kozloff: pages 47 r, 183 bc, 184 c, 185 bl, 187 tc, 187 r.

Oxford Scientific Films/G. I. Bernard: pages 76 c, 84 tl, 84 br, 102 tl, 123 br, 154 bc.

Oxford Scientific Films/Fredrik Ehrenstrom: pages 57 l, 167 tr.

Oxford Scientific Films/London Scientific Films: page 122 tr.

Oxford Scientific Films/Colin Milkins: pages 92 tr, 97 bc.

Oxford Scientific Films/Peter Parks: pages 93 tc, 173 cc.

Oxford Scientific Films/Kjell B. Sandved: pages 167 bc, 167 br.

Klaus Paysan: page 137 tc.

Doug Perrine: page 231 l.

Bernard Picton: pages 28 tl, 28 bl, 29 l, 30 tr, 37 r, 40 c, 44 r, 45 bl, 76 bl, 116 tc, 137 bl, 150 l, 152 c, 153 tc, 156 r, 162 bl, 166 c, 170 bl, 182 t, 183 l, 185 tl, 186 l, 206 br, 258 tr.

Planet Earth Pictures: page 28 tr.

Planet Earth Pictures/Richard Chesher: page 152 bl.

Planet Earth Pictures/Ivor Edmonds: page 227 bc.

Planet Earth Pictures/David George: pages 64 br, 90 tl, 94 tc, 106 bl, 126 bc, 136 r.

Planet Earth Pictures/D. Gotshall: page 68 c.

Planet Earth Pictures/Jim Greenfield: page 87 r.

Planet Earth Pictures/Bill Howes: page 63 br.

Planet Earth Pictures/Ken Lucas: pages 40 r, 121 tr, 131 bl, 153 r, 155 c, 162 c, 166 tr, 168 bc.

Planet Earth Pictures/Christian Petron: pages 121 br, 164 r.

Planet Earth Pictures/Nicholas Tapp: page 137 tl.

Kjell Sandved: pages 41 bl, 90 r, 115 r.

D.P. Wilson/Eric and David Hosking: pages 28 br, 116 tl, 126 tc, 129 tc, 129 bc, 131 br, 137 r.

Additional photography by Barbara Todd, Gary Bell, Jim Tobin, Malcolm Wells, Bill Rossiter and Steve Dawson.

The majority of the photographs in this book were taken on Nikon cameras with 55 mm Micro-Nikkor and 105 mm Micro-Nikkor lenses in Ikelite on oceanic 35 mm housings as well as Nikonos amphibious camera systems. Film: Ectachrome 64 ISO; Kodachrome 64 ISO; Fuji 50 ISO and 100 ISO.